THE PU

MW00489149

Paul Block:
A Life of Friendship, Power and Politics

Frank Brady

University Press of America,® Inc.
Lanham · New York · Oxford

Copyright © 2001 by
University Press of America,® Inc.
4720 Boston Way
Lanham, Maryland 20706

12 Hid's Copse Rd.
Cumnor Hill, Oxford OX2 9JJ

Library of Congress Cataloging-in-Publication Data

Brady, Frank.
The publisher : Paul Block, a life of friendship, power,
and politics / Frank Brady.
p.   cm
Includes bibliographical references and index.
l. Block, Paul, 1875-1941. 2. Publishers and publishing—
United States--Biography. 3. Newspaper publishing—
United States--History—20th century. 4. Press and politics—
United States—History—20th century. I. Title.
PN4874.B566 B73   2000   070.5'092—dc21   [B]   00-048862 CIP

ISBN 0-7618-1888-X (cloth : alk. ppr.)
ISBN 0-7618-1889-8 (paperback : alk. paper)

This book is dedicated to William Block, Sr., who has sustained his father's dream for over sixty years, and like his father, has truly mastered the art of friendship.

Contents

Illustrations

Unless otherwise noted, all illustrations are courtesy of the Block family, Blade Communications, Inc., the *Toledo Blade* or the *Pittsburgh Post-Gazette.*

Preface

In his day, Paul Block was one of the leading newspaper publishers, advertising representatives, and political apologists in this country, an advisor to Mayors, Governors and Presidents. He was the publisher, owner or part-owner of 14 major daily newspapers, just behind Scripps, Hearst, Gannett, and Knight-Ridder as founder of one of the leading newspaper chains. He was the mastermind behind what became the largest circulation magazine in the United States, *Pictorial Review*. He also helped start one of the first Sunday magazine supplements in America, the now-forgotten *Illustrated Sunday Magazine*, a precursor to *Parade*, which had a circulation of millions. At the time that national advertising was just beginning in this country, Block played a major role in developing the policies and appearance of print ads, which still affect national advertisements in newspapers and magazines today. He made millions in advertising before he even began his own personal publishing empire.

The record of Paul Block's life is the story of a man who loved people. Block considered his friendships his most valuable assets, and this is all the more surprising because he lived in the world of commerce, communications and politics, and succeeded in all of them while remaining surprisingly true to his philosophy. Friendships meant everything to him, and he worked hard to build and maintain them. As a result, he not only developed deep, lasting relationships with his friends, but was also liked by his colleagues, co-workers, and even his competitors. His employees were unusually loyal. His family loved him.

The relatively arduous life he experienced as a child, first in Germany and later when his impoverished family immigrated to the United States, had given Block a sympathetic nature. The trials of his professional journey, as he searched to find his niche, also gentled his personality and produced in him an unusual amount of kindness and empathy.

There is a curious paradox surrounding Paul Block's life, however. He could be open, candid and truly friendly, and at the same time secretive, evasive and aloof. Any attempt at understanding the man must take his two selves into account. Block's son, William, remembers his father as kindly, somewhat impatient, an inveterate gambler in his business ventures, short-tempered at times, honest and fair, proud, never known to swear or tell an off-color joke, and extremely alert and intelligent. Although not formally religious, he would often pray at night with his sons.

He was at home in the plush atmosphere of Delmonico's, or sipping a chocolate ice cream soda at Schrafft's, dining with Presidents, or chatting with printers and typesetters amidst the ink of the pressroom. In the late 1920s, he was named, with William Randolph Hearst and Roy W. Howard, as one of the leaders of the development of modern journalism. Yet today, his name is obscure, virtually unknown.

Block's determination was extraordinary. With no inherited financial resources – in fact, raised in extreme poverty – he relentlessly chipped his way to immense wealth, confident that what he had made, he had earned. This odds-on struggle is one of the most essential and dramatic aspects of his life story.

Block was, indeed, a consummate publisher. But in addition to buying, shaping, and running his own newspapers, he had a business relationship with William Randolph Hearst that was relatively undisclosed until now. Block was responsible for helping Hearst make hundreds of millions of dollars, yet neither his partnerships, nor his dealings, nor his social relationship with Hearst has ever been chronicled. Block is barely mentioned in W. A. Swanberg's *Citizen Hearst*, although Hearst and he jointly owned several newspapers, and constantly socialized and traveled together. Indeed, Paul Block was one of Hearst's only true friends. They laughed over shared amorous adventures, often with the dancers of the Ziegfeld Follies. Hearst so trusted Block that he named him Executor of his will, which covered his vast San Simeon estate and his extensive publishing holdings.

Yet Block and Hearst had a totally different, sometimes totally opposite vision of the place and responsibility of a newspaper. No dime-novel news could ever appear in any Block newspaper, which makes it particularly curious that he and William Randolph Hearst, the P.T. Barnum of publishing, got along as well as they did.

Block had an influence on, and a deep friendship with Presidents Herbert Hoover and Calvin Coolidge, Governors Alfred E. Smith and Herbert Lehman, and the irrepressible Mayor Jimmy Walker. The fact that these political leaders sought Block out as a friend and advisor is indicative of his impact as a man and a publisher. Block esteemed friendship more than anything else in his life: finding friends, making friends, keeping friends.

His relationship with Franklin Delano Roosevelt was more complex and less constant. If it hadn't been for Block, Roosevelt would probably never have become President. Yet once he was in office, FDR lost Block's esteem. He had committed what, to Block, were unpardonable sins. He increased Federal control over business, which Block thought would harm capitalist entrepreneurship. And Block felt that Roosevelt was not pulling the country out of the Depression fast enough, which was not only causing people to suffer, but creating a spirit of pessimism. To Block, optimism was akin to patriotism, and a depressed citizenry maintained and even created a depressed economy. So Block conspired with Hearst, as comrades in arms, to try to defeat Franklin D. Roosevelt, and Block almost single-handedly succeeded.

He was a fearless publisher. He exposed Supreme Court Justice Hugo L. Black's membership in the KKK (which won a Pulitzer Prize for his newspaper); he found that Vice-President Henry Wallace was a member of a secret cult, and almost brought down FDR's Presidency; during a private luncheon with FDR, Block discovered that the President had intentions of "packing" the Supreme Court. When Roosevelt retaliated against Block, his own White House staff urged the President to refrain, and to regain Block's good will and the persuasive backing of his newspapers. Yet in April of 1941, near the end of Block's life, he made yet another turnabout regarding FDR. Like much of the country, Block had been a political isolationist. But he came to realize, even before most people in the government did, that moral and ethical considerations at that point made it mandatory for the United States to support England. In urging the government to ship Britain the provisions it so desperately needed, Block understood that the United States might well become involved in the war, which had until then seemed far overseas. But he argued that we could no longer stand back and watch our allies be destroyed.

No other American newspaper had urged the United States to put its money or materials behind the Allied nations, and none had editorialized in favor of joining the war. Roosevelt fully understood that Block's editorial was not just an ethical statement, but a public backing of his administration. When Secretary of the Navy Franklin Knox addressed the American Newspaper Publishers Association a week later, he was obviously expressing FDR's acknowledgement of Block's editorial by urging the influential audience that the war was "plainly *our* war." And Block's next editorial was his final ratification that he was once again in agreement with Roosevelt. Those two editorials significantly affected public opinion, helped persuade Congress to change the course of the United States, and led the country into World War II.

Block's editorials, which numbered over one thousand, explored a myriad of ideas and exposed his readers to local, national and international themes and issues. Because he himself was so well informed, many of his pieces provided significant data and insights, as well as sound reasoning.

Politically, Block thought of himself as a Republican. He was, in fact, an old-fashioned conservative with progressive ideas. The mix seemed to work for him. It is interesting to note that he never sought political office. He limited his political ambition to influencing the electorate by backing and supporting candidates of his choice, and by acting as an advisor to elected officials. Sometimes he tilted at too many windmills, and backed candidates who really had no chance for success: Hoover in 1932; Landon in 1936; Willkie in 1940. Whatever the result, however, Block was nothing if not sincere about his beliefs...most of the time. When he made compromises with his political convictions, they were almost always dictated by economic factors.

In whatever city he published, he insisted that his newspapers become involved in the cultural and political life of that metropolis, and he therefore exercised a powerful influence on city life in America, from Milwaukee to Los Angeles, from Pittsburgh to Toledo...and beyond. His friendships and relationships were thus sometimes affected by his ability to influence thought and action, and by people's awareness of his power.

The infamous Gentleman Jimmy Walker, the "Night Mayor" of New York City, was an integral part of Paul Block's life. Block had made Walker a rich man, as he had others. But there are few people who give substantial amounts of cash or stocks as unrestricted gifts, so his beneficence almost caused Walker's downfall. It was implied that Block had bribed the Mayor, though no charges were ever brought against Block because it could never be demonstrated that he benefited from their relationship. Nonetheless, Block, as Jimmy Walker's closest friend, suffered public humiliation as a reluctant witness at the trial that eventually led to Walker's resignation and his expatriation to Europe.

There is more to the life of Paul Block than just his notoriety and his obvious impact on American publishing, politics and advertising, however. He was a complex and passionate man, capable of a wide range of emotions, ambivalent about his motivations, loyal to his friends and family, capable of great generosity, yet not without an indignant self-righteousness when provoked. It's important to note that not all of Block's life was noble, upright, chaste or triumphant. It was a life that was filled with a number of considerably poignant detours. Yet despite any lapses in his personality, and some serious financial blunders, he rose to become one of the most influential publishers in American history. His extraordinary business prowess, and his impact on newspaper publishing was, and has remained, galvanic.

Unlike each of the Hearst and Scripps-Howard papers, which were substantially identical to the others in their respective chains, each of Block's newspapers had its own personality and idiosyncrasies, and none of them were ever smug, venal or filled with blather. He was not a rubber-stamp publisher when he had the authority to make decisions over the content and appearance of a newspaper. This was not the case, however, when he was running papers for Hearst; then, Block acceded to Hearst's mandates. One wonders how much distress that cost him.

There are darker sides of Block's life, some apparent and some less clear. Why did he deny for so many years that he had been born in Germany, and claim instead that his birthplace was Elmira, New York? Can we conclude that he was so enthusiastic about being an American that he just deleted his native country from his own self-image? Or was he intimidated by the anti-German prejudice that erupted in this country before and during World War I, and was this his way to protect himself and his family against the wrath and stigma? Even his birth date was listed incorrectly in a number of sources; he always gave it as 1877, when in fact it was 1875. Vanity? Some other aspect of self-protection? Although such details are not particularly significant in the coherent interpretation of the man's accomplishments, the knowledge that certain portions of his life story were manipulated makes one wonder what else was omitted, re-arranged or added to in Block's own private record of himself.

He had a strange business relationship with a secret agent of the Imperial German Government during the first World War. Did that have as-yet-undiscovered political implications, or was it essentially an economic venture; and if the latter, how much does it say about Block's willingness to suppress his political considerations in favor of financial profit? We know that he came away from his 1934 meeting with Benito Mussolini convinced that Italy's leader "was the greatest personality of the present century." Yet a few years later, he came to reject fascism along with nazism and communism, and urged the United States to enter the war to preserve democracy.

He made several serious business mistakes. He was intransigent about

buying the *Brooklyn Standard-Union*, a newspaper that seemed doomed
from the start. He followed the dubious investment advice of his broker,
Sailing Baruch (brother of financier Bernard Baruch), and passed that
advice on to his good friend Florenz Ziegfeld, thus bringing them both
into economic ruin during the 1929 stock market crash. His near-bank-
ruptcy led to a nervous breakdown that he only emerged from with the
warm support of his friends and colleagues.

He was ambivalent about his Judaism, fully aware that it was the reason he was banned from joining the business and social clubs that would
otherwise have welcomed a successful publisher, or the country clubs
near his home in Greenwich, Connecticut. Yet he donated generously to
Jewish charities – as well as Christian charities. Was Block as totally
ecumenical as he appeared? Or was this, too, a business decision, calculated to enable him to move among the Christian business community
with greater ease?

The renowned *New York Herald-Tribune* newspaper columnist of the
1930s, O. O. McIntyre, once described Paul Block as looking somewhat
like the Scottish playwright Sir James Barrie, author of *Peter Pan*, and
although there were great physical similarities between the two men, Block
was certainly not "the boy who would not grow up." His maturity, even
as a young child, astounded all of the adults with whom he came in contact. McIntyre also observed that Block was quick, fluent and moody,
and that description seems accurate. Overall a rather shy man at first
meeting, Block was of medium height and had a resonant and pleasing
voice. He dressed with a studied elegance, and had robin-bright brown
eyes.

Block's life in New York spanned five incredible and sometimes dispir-
iting decades, from the Victorian Age through the Gaslight Era, the Roaring Twenties to the Great Depression, and on to the beginning of World
War II. He grew up with the century, beginning in poverty and ultimately
living in his own opulent suite at the Waldorf Towers, and in his fabulous
mansion and estate in Greenwich.

Block succeeded in overcoming great obstacles to make his fortune,
yet he never achieved the heights of some more renowned newspaper
publishers. It is not difficult to determine what kept him slightly behind
the major publishing barons: they each had "old" money to fall back on.
Block did not. When compared to the life of the silver-spooned William
Randolph Hearst, Block's is a story of perhaps even greater accomplishment: an unschooled son of a ragpicker who was able to become the

friend and associate of Presidents and tycoons, movie stars and famous authors, who dined and worked with Charles Lindbergh and Admiral Byrd, Will Rogers and Irving Berlin, H.G. Wells and Lord Beaverbrook, and who was close to being one of the most powerful newspaper publishers in the country. He has left a dynasty where the presses are still rolling, and a corporation that is still prospering more than 50 years after his death.

Introduction

In the writing of this book, I must admit to difficulties at the outset – based on the paucity of research materials available – that I initially had in reaching a coherent interpretation of Paul Block's life. Block did not keep a diary, and was generally reserved about talking about himself personally; there were few interviews or feature articles about him in the public or trade press, certainly no in-depth accounts of his life. His correspondence was scant, and other than his son William's memoir, there were just a few recollections by some relatives who knew Paul Block when they were children. Even basic facts about his life took an arduous unearthing. Until now, the chronicle of the life of Paul Block has been little more than a footnote in publishing history. How, then, to draw a true portrait of a man I never met, and whose life has been one of relative obscurity, if not actual mystery? Biographers are by nature and definition detectives and archeologists, and ultimately as I worked in musty library basements and drafty newspaper towers, looking carefully through crumbling papers in file cabinets that had not been opened for over a half century, I found the components I was looking for, and I was able to piece together the fragments of Paul Block's singular life. Answers from my queries to such far-flung places as Russia and Lithuania produced some facts on Paul Block's origins. One research library was so strict in allowing me access and use of what they had on Paul Block, that I had to promise *not* to acknowledge them in this book, because of their fear that other researchers would inundate them with similar requests.

Equipped with this primary source material, I decided that my assignment and challenge was to cast light on whatever aspects of Paul Block's exceptional life I came to grasp and ascertain, primarily those accomplishments and detours that were the most significant; the rest I have, by necessity and design, left in shadow. Despite the maddening handicap of not being able to sift through as much research as I would have liked to have culled, I am nevertheless satisfied that I have done my utmost to tell Block's story as fully and completely as possible.

Seldom can an accurate biography be researched and written in haste. The time that I spent learning about Paul Block, and in effect living with him through three years of study, was a great learning experience for me, especially as I am a university professor of the history of journalism. Mark Twain once wrote that there was never an uninteresting life, that inside of everyone existed a drama, a comedy, and a tragedy. I searched for those elements in Paul Block and I discovered and then comprehended theatricality, humor and pathos. The remarkable aspect of his life was how full it was with achievements, disappointments, surprises and crises, the stuff of a true American myth.

As I hunted for elusive evidence about Paul Block and I encountered certain forgotten documents or accounts, I came to learn about the man and I became involved in the ferment of his life through many jolting discoveries: his vacillating relationship with Franklin D. Roosevelt, his secret business partnerships with William Randolph Hearst, his alleged affair with Marion Davies, his interview of Mussolini, his testimony at the trial of Mayor Jimmy Walker, his political wager with H.G. Wells.

It was with the story of the growth of his national advertising representation business, however, and then his role as publisher of first one and finally a chain of newspapers, that the forward movement of his life came most alive for me. The importance and inherent significance of his career and the absolute genius he showed in gaining control of some 14 newspapers, cannot be overlooked, and the record of his contribution to publishing will be found in the following pages.

One of the most valuable resources for this book was Paul Block's editorials – more than a thousand – which stated his views on politics, culture and the social conditions of his day. Reading these ideas and opinions, many of which were published on the front pages of his – and other – newspapers, reveal the true value of the man, and give voice to his passions, his greatness, and his human foibles. In many ways, the editorials are the true testament to who and what Paul Block was really all about; his writings comprise a compelling saga, an elemental force of his personal growth and conviction, and represent a concentrated and impressive view of American life and history in the first half of the twentieth century. Studying Block's newspapers themselves, a backward newsreel in time, also offered me insight into what he was attempting to do, set in the context of his era.

In writing this biography, I attempted neither apology nor eulogy, certainly not hagiography, but *understanding*, and to explain simply, how Paul Block's life came and went, and what it all meant. Throughout the work, I attempted to produce not only the story of a man's life, but an instructional treatise on the world of newspaper publishing, and to a lesser extent, a narrative of how Paul Block built and operated his advertising business.

One day, as I pored through the Block family archives, I found some random jottings written years ago by John Robinson Block, grandson of Paul Block and currently editor of both the *Pittsburgh Post-Gazette* and the *Toledo Blade*; the young John Block had composed the notes for a paper or a book he wanted to write when he was a history major at Yale. He asks two essential questions of himself that, in essence, are perfect themes for a biography of his grandfather: 1) Was Paul Block a man with a message? In addition, 2) Was he considered by any of his contemporaries and associates to be an extraordinary human being?

I believe that in this biography I have answered John Block's rhetorical questions. In short, 1) Yes, Paul Block was a man with both a premise and a mission: in essence it was all about friendships, loyalties, and progressive conservatism. 2) Yes, most of the people who knew him (from American presidents to fellow newspaper publishers to his employees) felt that Block was a rare and remarkable person. That Herbert Hoover begged Block to visit him and stay at the White House so that they could discuss "the fate of the world" might be proof enough of Block's exceptional character and personality.

Dr. Frank Brady

New York City

Acknowledgments

The kindness, courtesy and generosity shown to me by the Block family, primarily William Block, Sr. – Paul's son – and Block's three grandsons, William Block, Jr., John Robinson Block and Allan Block, was overwhelming, and quite out of the ordinary. Without their help and encouragement, I simply could not have completed the book, and I am indebted to, and will never forget, their elegance and support.

I would also like to thank the following for their invaluable assistance: Peter and Barbara Liveright, Alan Gage, John Grigsby, Otto Franco, Michael Packer, Virginia Otis, Peter Rock, Kevin Marsh, Dr. Joy Holland, Herbert Moloney III, Prof. Ben Procter, Daniel W. Bates, Prof. Thom McCarthy, Dr. Roger Wetherington, Cindy Thurston, J. Arthur Kieffer, Tom Byrne, George Irish, Scott Donaton, Paul McCarthy, the archivists at the presidential libraries of Warren G. Harding, Calvin Coolidge, Herbert Hoover and Franklin D. Roosevelt, and of the archivists of the libraries of the *Pittsburgh Post-Gazette*, the *Toledo Blade,* the periodicals division of the New York Public Library, the Lincoln Center Library of the Performing Arts, the rare books division and inter-library loan department of the Butler Library of Columbia University, Mike Hart, Bethany McHugh, Jeff Montross, Suzanne Silva, Russ Sprinkle, Brian Tipping, Jeffrey Zawodny, the Chemung County Historical Society, and Gallagher's Vintage Magazine store: I can honestly say that without the help of the above, I could not have fully researched and adequately written this book.

A final thank you from the bottom of my heart: to my wife, Maxine Brady, writer and editor, who read and copy-edited this manuscript, made suggestions as to structure, tone and point of view, read essential documents, books and articles, and who always distinguished between the weeds and the flowers of my writing. She is the ultimate colleague, friend and professional: I can never pay her enough in gratitude for her contribution.

Prologue

Paul Block was born on November 2, 1875 in Königsberg, East Prussia, and lived there until he was nine years old. His parents, Jonas Hirsch Bloch and Chana Mera Bialostotzki, had emigrated to Königsberg in 1871 from the Lithuanian *shtetl* called Šakiai.

Although most of the records of the life of Jonas and Hannah Marie (as she came to be known) in Šakiai no longer exist, certain facts and details have been drawn from sporadic birth, death and marriage documents. Along with contemporary accounts of life in the town – most translated from Russian, Yiddish, German or Hebrew – these provide a basis to draw a portrait of Paul Block's family roots.

The existence of Šakiai, one of Lithuania's oldest towns, was documented in the 14th century. It was larger than a village but could hardly be called a city by today's standards. It was situated near the Sietarsis River, and not far from the Nieman River, Lithuania's largest and most picturesque waterway which originated in White Russia and emptied into the Baltic Sea. At one time, Šakiai belonged to Poland, and then to Prussia. After the defeat of Napoleon, Russia held the town, as it did during the time that the Blochs were residents. In the 1860s there were close to 2,000 Jews living in Šakiai; they made up the vast majority of the town's inhabitants. Jonas's mother and father, Kalman Bloch and Sheina-Mera Shimberg, also lived in the *shtetl*, as did his two brothers Lieb-Shmerel Bloch and Isher Bloch, his sister Chana-Sora, and their respective families. Hannah Marie's family came from Germany, where she was born, although it is not known whether her parents, too, lived in Šakiai.

Šakiai had all of the essential characteristics, by Jewish standards, of being a *shtetl*. It had *mestechko* – legal permission to be a community; *minyans* – at least three groups of ten men each who supported a rabbi and a synagogue; a *cheder* – a Jewish elementary school; and a *merchatz*, or a *mikva* – a community bath where wives, according to Rabbinical law, were required to bathe on the seventh day after their menstruation.

Although it has been written that the *shtetl* was the hearth of Jewish culture in Eastern Europe, and in many ways it *was* the center of Jewish communal life, Šakiai for the Blochs was far from a picturesque version of *Yentl*; there was no fiddler on the roof bowing melodic folk tunes, or townspeople happily dancing to the *klezmer* far into the night. People tried to make a life despite their impoverishment, but with all of the restrictions and embargoes, it was not a pleasant existence. There were dark, tall pine forests in the region that would have been perfect for play and picnics, but most of the land outlying the town was for farming, and the people of the *shtetl*, even the children, had little time for recreation.

Life for Jonah and Hannah Marie, as for most Jews in their virtually feudal ghetto – a warren of shacks and twisted streets – was at best uncomfortable and insecure, and at times unbearable. Šakiai was located in the province of Kovno, within the region of Lithuania then known as the Pale of Settlement, territory within the borders of czarist Russia wherein the residence of Jews was legally authorized. In the mid-1860s, when the Blochs married and tried to raise a family in Šakiai, almost all Jews throughout eastern Europe were regarded as an eccentric and undesirable part of the population and were confined to primitive communities known as *shtetlach*, of which Šakiai was one. The czarist government viewed the Jews through a prism of superstitious apprehension and Judaeophobia, believing that they inherently possessed what they called "Shylock traits" of avarice and dishonesty. To most of their Russian enslavers, Jews were considered vile and unprincipled, and anti-Semitism was rife in Šakiai.

What was known as Poland and Lithuania had been conquered and partitioned by Russia, Germany and Austria to the point where some of the native languages ceased to be spoken, or were forbidden to exist, to be replaced by Russian or German. Attempts were made to suppress the Jewish culture in Šakiai, but the Jews continued speaking Yiddish and reading Hebrew texts. Local and territorial officials frowned upon the practice but they seemed not to be able to stop it. Their language and rituals were almost all that the Jews possessed.

The non-Jewish elders of Šakiai (as well as of all the other towns and villages of the 336,000-square-mile Pale that stretched from the Baltic to the Black Sea) had many prohibitions against "their" Jews: no owning of land, no building of synagogues close to Orthodox churches, no permission to travel outside the Pale, or even to other towns and villages within it, and no use of Hebrew in public documents. The curriculum of all Jewish schools was modified to include Russian studies and other approved subjects, and to de-emphasize Hebrew scholarship. There was even an edict that Jews were forbidden to wear their traditional garb, a law that was flagrantly ignored. In the largest synagogue in Šakiai, it was customary to conclude the service with a dutiful and obligatory blessing for the Czar; members of the congregation often lowered their eyes during the blessing to avoid noticing an irreverent smirk on the face of a fellow congregant. Although the population of Šakiai at that time was 80 percent Jewish, Jews could not hold office, but they did have committees with minimal power that dealt with such matters as taxes, burials, housing, welfare, education, and the Torah. No Jew, however, was eligible to the post of burgomaster. Many businesses that had been owned by Jews for generations were simply confiscated by the czarists.

These restrictions were difficult enough, but the continual *pogroms* against the Jews made living in Šakiai insufferable. All those in the Jewish community were used as scapegoats to mask the government's inefficiency. Privately, it was held by the czarists that the non-Jewish population was no match, competitively, for the superior Jewish traders, and that therefore everything should be done to keep the Šakiai Jews under control and unprosperous. Although not recorded as law, the understood policy of the Russian government was to exterminate one-third of the Jewish population, keep one-third confined to their respective *shtetls,* and to force conversion to Christianity of the remaining third.

Frequently, a feral mob, laced with alcohol and indoctrinated by the government with anti-Semitic hatred, would throng into the Jewish section of Šakiai and create a riot – what became known as a *pogrom* – inflicting widespread destruction and violence. They would break into houses, loot the shops, desecrate the synagogues, beat, rape, and sometimes kill the Jewish inhabitants of the town. The Jews had no arms with which to protect themselves, no organized plan to resist. The only protest that the Jewish townsmen could resort to was to assemble on certain days in the synagogues, abstain from food and drink, and to intone *selihoth,* old medieval penitential prayers. The Blochs mourned the deaths of their friends and loved ones, and the burning of their Torah scrolls, while the local police did nothing to stop the carnage. In some other *shtetls* in the Pale, uprisings and insurrections were attempted, and each of them were defeated, always followed by more repression and executions. Some of the Šakiai Jews would quietly sing the song about the *pogramchik* rampages: *"Shikker iz a goy vayl er iz a goy"* ("As long as a man is a non-Jew, he's a drunken man") as their only means of secret revenge or retaliation.

Apparently the Bloch family escaped any direct brutality during the years they lived in Šakiai. How they accomplished this is not clear, but it was just a matter of time and chance when their home would be assaulted by a gang of anti-Jewish hoodlums in the ongoing waves of repression and punishment. As were all Jewish families in Šakiai, the Blochs were oppressed materially, culturally, and spiritually and the pall under which they lived promised no hope of respite. The basic test of the Blochs' freedom was, perhaps, not what they were *able* to do in the *shtetl*, but what they were *unable* to do.

In addition to living through and witnessing the *pogroms,* and the daily hardships that became an inescapable part of their lives, the Blochs underwent several extremely sad and depressing personal experiences, and they were worried that there were more to come. They lived with several other families in a cramped wooden house of just a few small rooms, and sanitary conditions simply could not be maintained. The floors were plastered with fresh clay and fortified with manure, and the roofs were tufted with sod. When the rains came, weeds and morning glories sprouted from the rooftops, often along with contagion. Four of the Blochs' children had died in infancy, all from the outbreak of diphtheria that had spread throughout the household. Jonas and Hannah Marie watched helplessly as each child was wracked with a deadly fever, and some asphyxiated from the yellow mucus and croup that prevented their breathing. Their second son, Isher Leib, died before he reached ten months. Then Josel-Ber succumbed within weeks of his birth. Two other children died in infancy. Health conditions in Šakiai were so poor that the average life expectancy of an adult was barely 30 years; 75 percent of the children born in the region died within their first year. The Jews in Šakiai had no doctor, very little medicine except their own home remedies, and virtually no medical assistance of any kind. Typhoid fever and epidemics of cholera, spread from contaminated food and unsanitary conditions, afflicted both children and adults and caused extremely high mortality rates.

Unemployment was endemic, and although Šakiai had many farms, ownership was forbidden to Jews, and employment of a Jew on a farm, although not impossible, was rare. Jonas worked as a peddler whenever he could accumulate a few kopecks to build a small supply of products to sell. Hannah Marie chopped wood for the oven, tended to the children, made several visits each day for water at the communal well, and washed the family's laundry in the nearby river; in the winter she had to chop a hole in the ice to plunge her hands in the frozen water in order to clean the clothing. From time to time some young Jews managed, by dark of night, to flee the *shtetl* and make their way to the slums of Vilna and Kosvo, searching for employment. If they did find work, it paid only a few kopecks a day for 16 hours of hard labor. Most of them wound up returning home to their families.

The usual diet of the people of Šakiai consisted for the most part of a few potatoes and, from time to time, some seasonal vegetables. The discomfort of their empty stomachs was aggravated by a general despair, and the years 1867 to 1868 – the time when several of the Bloch children died –were particularly ravaging as all of Lithuania suffered from a lingering famine. Quixotically, grain prices fell during this period, and this greatly affected the economy throughout the region.

The possibility that their eldest son, Samuel, might be conscripted into the Russian army caused yet another fear in the Bloch household. The boy was nearing the age of 12. Although there are no records to prove it, it is probable that Samuel was the son of Jonas – who may have been a widower – and a stepson of Hannah Marie. Nevertheless, as their only surviving child, he was deeply loved by both parents. According to law, Samuel was not only nearing eligibility for the draft, but would be forced to serve up to 16 years in the army – perhaps as many as 25 years – under horrible conditions that were tantamount to a virtual death sentence. Forced conversions to Christianity were also commonplace among the conscripted Jews. Refusal to serve meant either imprisonment or execution. Samuel was a tailor's apprentice and could undoubtedly find employment in a more prosperous locale than Šakiai...if only he could travel to another city, and stay out of the reach of the draft.

Jonas Bloch came to an excruciating decision: he and his wife would eventually attempt to escape from Šakiai, but the most immediate problem was to help Samuel to not only leave the *shtetl*, but to abandon the Pale altogether and emigrate to another country. The main worry about getting Samuel out of Šakiai itself was to avoid the local *khapper*, or "captor," the designated turncoat-Jew in the town who, for a relatively large salary, functioned to identify young boys to the military police as *nakbutman* (recruit, in Yiddish), so that they could be conscripted. There were also conscription gangs, groups of toughs paid by the government to enter a town and seize virtually every young man who was of draft age. Somehow, Samuel eluded the *khapper* and the draft packs, and left Šakiai, alone. Acting in effect as a scout for the rest of his family, he found his way to Königsberg, some 120 miles from his hometown. From there, he wrote letters to his parents, informing them of his whereabouts and discussing life and conditions in East Prussia.

Šakiai was 30 miles to the border of the Pale and East Prussia, a considerable distance to walk. The Blochs could not afford to travel by train or stagecoach. Wagons were expensive and difficult to procure. Leaving the country was an incredibly difficult feat, physically and emotionally, and the journey may have been one of the first that the Blochs ever made out of the environs of Šakiai. It is probable that they had never even been permitted to visit Vilnius, Lithuania's capital, which was less than 90 miles away. Vilnius was a beautiful city, referred to as the "Jerusalem of Lithuania" because so many Jews lived there. But Jews from *shtetls* rarely gained permission to travel outside their immediate environs.

Even relatively successful Jews who tried to gain legal permission to leave their homes wound up spending years in bureaucratic wrangling, paper work and administrative entanglements that usually resulted in an unsuccessful effort. Judah Bloch, a distant relative and political organizer in Šakiai, could not help Jonas and Hannah Marie to escape. Jonas's father Kalman Bloch, a trader who had made contributions to the synagogue and to other *shuls* in Lithuania, was unable to exert any leverage in assisting Jonas' attempt to exit Šakiai without compromising himself.

However, if the Blochs could raise enough money to bribe the border guards, police and other officials to allow the family to pass into East Prussia, they could leave the Pale illegally and perhaps start a new life under the protection of the German government. Since, obviously, no records were kept of such transactions, it can only be speculated as to how the Blochs left Šakiai. It seems likely that they managed to accumulate enough cash (most probably with the help of Kalman Bloch) to leave Lithuania, possibly journeying by boat along the Niemen during the night and arriving at the border late the next day. Since so many of Jonas's relatives still remained in Šakiai, and he did not want any repercussions to fall upon them, he undoubtedly cleared all of his debts and paid whatever taxes he owed before he left. How much money the Blochs used to bribe the border guards with, and whether such an offer was a difficult and dangerous negotiation, and not just a customary transaction or arrangement, is not known.

After entering East Prussia, the Blochs made their way to Königsberg, through such towns as Gumbinnen, Insterburg and Wehlau, probably by a combination of walking, wagon rides, and passage in a rowboat along the Siesartes and Pregel rivers.

There has been retrospective speculation that many of the Jews who left the Pale did so with a sense of shame, that somehow they were giving up as Jews and leaving their true homes, almost abandoning their families, religion or nationalities. Yet they had suffered years of tragedies and indignities, controlled by a ruthless and tyrannical government. It is probable that Moshe Lurie, the Chief Rabbi of Šakiai, did not discourage emigration by members of his congregation, whatever the motivation and however it could be arranged. Jonas and Hannah Marie may have felt a pang of regret – it is never easy to leave one's home, no matter how lamentable it is to live there – but any patriotic or nostalgic feeling on their part was surely an ephemeral impetus. Their relationship to their country, and to those non-Jews who assaulted the *shtetl,* strangled their Judaism, in effect killed their children and starved their family, filled them with depression and outrage. Because of the political persecution, economic despair and religious intolerance they experienced, they yearned to live in a country that permitted them a freer and more respected life. Even the practice of their Jewish faith could not flourish until, if ever, it was favored or cherished in a land they had yet to discover. The incessant anti-Jewish decrees, the *pogroms*, and the deaths, were simply overwhelming to Jonas, and foreseeing no future other than poverty for himself and Hannah Marie, he had little choice other than to emigrate. Despite their growing aversion to Šakiai, for the Blochs to leave their home was a moment of moral heroism, the beginning of a life-changing adventure which would eventually lead them to America.

•••

Settling in Königsberg in 1871 was not particularly easy for the Blochs. Jonas was 29; Hanna Marie was 22. They dressed differently and spoke a different dialect of Yiddish than the Prussian Jews. Königsberg was on the Pregolya River, near the mouth of the Vislinski Zalev, which empties into the Baltic Sea. It was the capital of the Duchy of Prussia, in a section that was known as northwest Bohemia. Founded in 1255 as a fortress for the Teutonic Knights, Königsberg was the city where philosopher Immanuel Kant was born, lived and taught.

The major difficulty for the Blochs as aliens, was that by law, only a limited number of Jews were permitted to live within the Jewish community in Königsberg. A list, the *Matrikel*, kept track of all legally-permitted Jewish families. It limited Jews not only by the size of their population but according to their occupations, and no Jews not on the *Matrikel* were given authority to live in the community. At the time that the Blochs arrived in Königsberg, there were less than 5,000 Jews, though the city had a population of about 200,000. Jews who had immigrated from the Pale did not enjoy the same standing or acceptance as those German Jews who had been born in Prussia.

Somehow the Blochs secured residence in the Jewish section of the city, and moved into an eight-family gray brick tenement house at 61 *Knockenstrasse*, on the same street where two distant relatives, Levin Bloch and Abraham Bloch, also lived. The city directory of Königsberg lists Jonas Bloch as a *"kaufman"* – a salesman – and his occupation might be the reason that he was given entry to his flat at *Knockenstrasse*. Each of the tenants had different occupations, including the widow E. Braun geb. Vogel, the owner of the property: Rohrer, a baker; Jaspir, a flax-worker; Bierfrund, a railway-shunting stationmaster; Malbin, a Rabbi's widow; Mawitz, a floorworker; and Thurau, a porter. The fact that Hannah Marie had been born in Germany may have also afforded the Blochs a certain cachet of legal acceptance in gaining them housing.

Although there was partial emancipation of the Jews in Prussia, leading to full citizenship through naturalization, Jews were not permitted to change residence within the State, just as it was in the Pale. Eventually, the law was overturned and Jews were granted *Freizügigkeit*, freedom of movement, but for whatever reason, out of choice, necessity or fear, the Blochs remained in the same home in Königsberg for eleven years.

It should not be assumed that the Blochs' escape from Šakiai and their setting up house in Königsberg was the solution to all of their problems, but it was a marked improvement over what they had experienced in Lithuania. If nothing else, there were no *pogroms*, the city had physicians and hospitals, and the Blochs had enough to eat. Jonas found work. Eventually his father and other relatives also came to Königsberg, and Hannah Marie had four children there, all of whom lived: Max, Malvine, Paul and Elfreida, in that order. In a possible attempt to assimilate or in an exercise of politics or reason, the Blochs named their children with popular Prussian names rather than usual Jewish names such as Judah, Esther, Abraham and Rachel.

Prejudice against Jews by the citizens of Königsberg, although much more subdued than the intolerance in Šakiai, existed nonetheless. A huge wooden synagogue, beautifully decorated with historic murals, had been built on the highest hill of the city, and it served as a symbol of shame and annoyance to the gentile Prussians. In retribution, laws were passed that not only restricted the Jews, but oppressed them. A Prussian ordinance forbade sermons to be given in Yiddish; use of the vernacular in public, in any way, was condemned. Further, all prayers had to be not in Hebrew but in German. Eventually most Jews, including the Blochs, began speak-

ing German rather than Yiddish, more because of the economic and social demands of city life, than in obedience to the law. Jewish graduates
of law schools were not admitted to the bar as public or private attorneys.
Jewish scholars were not permitted to be professors at the University of
Königsberg. Other restrictions were applied to the Jews, such as the arbitrary prohibition against wearing shrouds on Yom Kippur.

Paul went to a Prussian elementary school, as did his brother Max and
his sister Malvine, because a revered *yeshiva*, the Jewish *Winkelschulen*,
had closed many years before the Blochs arrived in Königsberg. As Paul
grew, his boyhood experiences caused him to become more Germanized
and Prussianized than he was Jewish. Still, the Blochs attempted to cling
to their Jewishness. Eliezer Lipman Silberman had founded the first Hebrew weekly newspaper in Königsberg, *Ha-Maggid*, and it was surrepti-
tiously read by most Jews in the city, including the Blochs.

Samuel did not escape the pressures of conscription. The Prussian army
also had a draft, and as Jews became more emancipated, they had to serve.
Although the Prussian treatment of military personnel was not as devastating as the Russian army, Samuel had no intention of ruining his life
fighting for a government which was essentially anti-Semitic. In 1883,
with money saved from his work as a tailor, the 20-year old Samuel emigrated to the United States and eventually to Elmira, New York, a city
known to be accepting of Jews, and where some friends and relatives had
already moved. Buffalo and Syracuse, New York; Pittsburgh, Pennsylvania; and Macon and Atlanta, Georgia were other American cities that
not only welcomed Jews but also helped emigrants upon arrival.

Some two years later, in 1885, as European anti-Semitism worsened,
Jonas and Hannah Marie also decided to move to the United States. A
pamphlet which received wide circulation, titled *Hilchot Yemot
Hamashian,* published in Hebrew, praised America as a land of promise,
"a Zion close to Abraham's bosom" for the Jews. Samuel confirmed the
fact that America, and particularly Elmira, New York, were the destinations that his parents should consider: the West cried out for enterprising
workers, there were many employment opportunities, and there was religious freedom. Further, Jonas learned that a prominent American Jew,
Mordecai Noah, had a plan to create a refuge, a *goldenah medina,* a golden
land, for all Jews in upstate New York. Elmira was being considered as
the center of that sanctuary. Jonas had learned that the wretched tenements of New York's Lower East Side were unbearable; he had spent the
better part of the first 30 years of his life in a country town, and although

they had been filled with strife, he wanted to duplicate some of the positive feelings that he had known when he lived close to nature.

Although it was still somewhat difficult for Jews to change residence
within the Duchy of Prussia, there were no restrictions at all for them to
leave the country, except for those who had obligations to serve in the
army. It is not known how Samuel secured a berth on the S.S. Selisian
out of Hamburg in 1883, but it may have been through bribes and gifts.
The anti-Semitic phrase *"Pattern ist Gelt Wert!"* was often heard in the
streets and beer parlors of Königsberg: vaguely translated, it meant "It's
worth money to have them go." The Prussian reactionary mentality would
often offer an anti-Semitic argument called *Masseneinwanderung*: a protest against the mass immigration of unwanted Eastern European Jews
(such as the Blochs) into their country; they were insultingly called
Ostjuden, or "Jewish outsiders." The Blochs knew that they would never
be accepted as bona fide German or Prussian Jews, who enjoyed more
status and respect from the gentiles, as long as they lived in Königsberg;
the acids of nationalism in non-Catholic and non-Jewish Königsberg
seeped into their spirits and they did not choose to tolerate it any longer.

In some ways it was easier for the Blochs to emigrate to America than
it had been to leave Šakiai for Königsberg, although the former was thousands of miles away, and the latter barely more than a hundred. Samuel
was firmly ensconced in Elmira – and he may even have sent his parents
some money for the passage – and the Blochs had saved additional money
for the sea voyage and to get started in the New World. They knew that
Samuel would prepare for their arrival and help them to get settled, and
emigration seemed to be a reasonable alternative to their Königsberg
lifestyle.

And as the prototypical wandering Jews, the Blochs knew they were
adaptable; if Jonas could sell things in Šakiai and in Königsberg, he could
do likewise in Elmira, New York. Perhaps he had even developed this
portable skill in the knowledge that he would eventually, by tradition and
necessity, move from country to country and continent to continent, although it would mean an overwhelming transformation of their lives.

Jonas and Hannah Marie and their four children, which included the
11-month old Elfrieda, left Königsberg en route to America in mid-Au-
gust of 1885, by steamer ferry to the port of Hamburg. They chose to
leave Europe in the summer so that they would not have to endure a frigid
Atlantic crossing, nor the rigors of a winter in their new land.

Upon arriving in Hamburg, their passports were carefully examined, and they were given vaccinations and a complete physical examination to ensure that they had no contagious disease before berthing on ship. They purchased steerage tickets on the S.S. Rugia from the Hamburg-American Line, the largest steamship company in the world, for the equivalent of $23 each for Jonas and Hannah Marie, and $12 each for the nine-year-old Paul, thirteen-year-old Max, and eleven-year-old Malvine. Nothing was charged for the infant Elfreida, who was carried in her mother's arms.

Hamburg was crowded with those waiting for ships to England, America and other destinations. Contemporary accounts reported that hundreds of potential émigrés slept in the streets, parks and doorways of Hamburg while waiting for passage out of Germany. It is possible that the Blochs also camped out for a day or two in a local park while making preparations for departure, such as making straw mattresses, and waiting for the Rugia to sail.

On August 26, the Rugia raised anchor and the Blochs were on their way. In a few days, sailing through the English Channel, they could see both England and France, visible for several hours, before they entered the deep and dark blue Atlantic. The story of how immigrants suffered in the cramped and airless confines of below-deck steerage compartments, vomiting from seasickness, and attempting to sleep on narrow, 18-inch bunks in stifling quarters, has been told many times. It was no different for the Blochs. Jonas, Max and Paul slept in one huge holding pen, actually a cargo hold, along with all the other men. Hannah Marie, Malvine and Elfreida were separated in another area with the rest of the women. The family met each day in clement weather on the steerage deck, where attempts were made to talk, read, or just take advantage of the bracing sea breeze and to escape the fetid air of the chambers below deck.

The food was not Kosher but relatively plentiful: tea for breakfast, beef broth, boiled beef and potatoes for dinner, sour soup, herring (which was said to combat seasickness) and brown bread for supper.

On Monday, September 7, 1885, with virtually all passengers who were well standing on the highest deck that they could reach, silent with wonder and somewhat frightened, the Rugia steamed through the Narrows into New York Bay and docked at the Battery. The Statue of Liberty had not as yet been erected, but the emerging skyline of Lower New York, with some buildings that were fifteen stories high, was an incredible sight for the emigrants.

Within minutes of debarking, all of the steerage passengers were marched, in a state of confusion and under guard, to nearby Castle Garden – *"Kestel Gartel,"* as they kept referring to it – where they would be examined and processed. That first step on American soil had to be an auspicious moment for the Blochs; filled with the pride and pathos of transplantation, they instinctively knew that from then on, life would be changed forever.

New York City was the first port to open an immigration depot to handle the mammoth influx of émigrés. Within the walls of Castle Garden were a myriad of Italians, Irishmen, Poles, Austrians, Germans, Danes and Russians, all speaking their own languages in a cacophony of bedlam.

Castle Garden was a massive stone structure built in 1808 as a fort. It later served as an opera house until 1855, when New York State authorities transformed it into a landing station. Between that time and 1890, when Ellis Island became the official port of immigration entry, Castle Garden received a tidal wave of over eight million immigrants. An avalanche of more than 5,000 immigrants sailing *from Hamburg alone* arrived at Castle Garden in the weeks just prior to the Blochs' entry to America.

Castle Garden's primary purpose was not to inspect as much as it was to protect the hapless newcomers from the crooked swindlers prowling the piers looking for an easy score, ready to sell the non-English speaking foreigners bogus train tickets, or to haul away their baggage never to be seen again.

There were thousands of upholstered seats in the huge rotunda of Castle Garden, and immigrants were invited to sit there until such time as they were met by relatives, or made plans for their journeys to prospective jobs or homes. Many stayed for days before they got adjusted enough to move on to the next step in their new home. Free sandwiches were provided by the Hebrew Immigration Aid Society.

But for many, the Castle Garden experience was a depressing introduction to their new country, a place of chaos and brutality, of sadness and bewilderment, and for some, loneliness and doubts about having left their homes and families. Abraham Cahan, founder and longtime editor of the *Jewish Daily Forward*, described the scene at Castle Garden in *A Providential March*:

> Leaning against the railing or sitting on their baggage, there
> were bevies of unkempt men and women in shabby dress of
> every cut and color, holding on to ragged, bulging parcels,

baskets, or sacks, and staring at space with a look of forlorn, stupefied, and cowed resignation. The cry of children in their mothers' arms, blending in jarring discord with the gruff yells of the uniformed officers, jostling their way through the crowd, and with the general hum and buzz inside and outside the inclosure, made the scene as painful to the ear as it was to the eye and nostrils, and completed the impression of misery and desolation.

The Blochs were perhaps better off than most of the other immigrants. They were a family, and all of the older children were capable of minding Elfreida when their parents had to go off to attend to whatever paperwork or meeting with officials had to be done. The three older children spoke some English, and the Blochs not only had a specific destination – Elmira, New York – but an exact address of their son Samuel, to which they could refer. The majority of the newly-arrived Jewish immigrants had neither relatives nor friendly old-country townsmen whom they could contact upon arrival.

Within 24 hours after their physical examinations, the Blochs were released from Castle Garden. After buying tickets from John N. Abbott, the authorized agent stationed at the port of entry, they walked uptown to the Chambers Street depot of the New York, Erie and Western Railroad and boarded an 8 PM train for Elmira. Snaking along the Hudson and stopping briefly at Binghamton, the train arrived at Elmira early the next morning.

Paul Bloch and his family, like most other immigrants, eventually made the transition to their new lives in the New World. The vitality and independence of America was theirs. But few immigrants have ever attained such success. This is the story of how the child of impoverished, uneducated immigrants moved up the economic and social ladder to achieve not only great wealth and distinction, but considerable influence over American politics, advertising and newspaper publishing, and indeed, over many of the American people.

Chapter 1
A Prodigal Childhood

A New Life in Elmira

By the time the Bloch family reached the city of Elmira, shortly after arriving in America and suffering the indignities of Castle Garden, the autumn trees of the nearby hills were just beginning to be splashed with various shades of yellow, orange and gold. Looking out the train windows at the surrounding countryside, Elmira must have seemed a pleasant-enough town, almost pastoral in appearance. It is situated in a valley between two ranges of stately hills, interwoven by a twisting but placid river, the Chemung; it was also much smaller in size than what the Blochs were accustomed to in the seaport city of Königsberg. Elmira did, however, have a bustling downtown section, with horse-drawn trolleys, hundreds of small and large shops, dozens of hotels and rooming houses, and a thriving industry and business community, which the Blochs would eventually discover. Elmira had an opera house, called the Lyceum, which not only produced highly-elaborate musical presentations and plays, but was also the site at which lectures, often accompanied by stereoptican slides, were presented by some of the most famous actors and speakers of the day. During a typical season, productions included oratorios by Mendelssohn, stagings of Shakespeare's *The Merry Wives of Windsor*, readings from Dickens's incomplete novel *The Mystery of Edwin Drood*, and a lecture by David Ross Locke (known as "Nasby"), the nationally-famous editor of the *Toledo Blade*, who spoke on "The Search After the Man of Original Sin."[1]

Equally important to the stature of the city was the fact that David B. Hill, a native Elmiran who was the former publisher of the *Elmira Gazette,* had just been elected Democratic Governor of the State of New York, affording Elmira a certain chauvinistic cachet. Moreover, Samuel L. Clemens was perhaps the town's best-known summer resident. Using the pseudonym of Mark Twain, he had recently completed *The Adven-*

tures of Huckleberry Finn, to international acclaim, writing most of it at
Quarry Farm, two-and-a-half miles from downtown.[2] Clemens' white-
suited figure could be seen strolling the streets of Elmira almost on a
daily basis; he would invariably stop off at Augustus Klapproth's wood
and marble tavern ("Pure liquors and choice cigars," Klapproth's advertising promised) for a game of billiards, a black cigar – which often came
close to igniting his flowing mustache – and a tankard of ale.[3] After the
Blochs were settled in Elmira for awhile, Paul and his siblings would
often walk to Quarry Farm to see the house in which Mark Twain lived.
Whether they ever talked to the great man himself, is not known, but it is
altogether possible.

Ever since the end of the Civil War, Elmira had become known as a
center of upstate culture, good breeding, and gracious living. Referred to
as the Queen City, it served as a railway and light-industrial center, and as
an interim oasis for vacationers enroute to the Finger Lakes.[4] It was also
a small metropolis that truly welcomed the tides of immigrants that came:
first the Irish who worked on the Chemung Canal, which connected to
the Erie Canal, and then Italians, Poles and Ukrainians who labored on
the railroads. German Jews began coming to Elmira in the 1860s.[5] By
the time the Blochs arrived, there were 25 churches and three synagogues
in Elmira, which gave its inhabitants an enormous variety of religious
possibilities for a city of that size. Church Street was appropriately named,
with places of worship of many kinds stretched along this boulevard across
the breadth of the city.[6] In most temples and churches, services were
performed – on alternate weeks – in English and German. Perhaps because there were religions of every difference in Elmira, it emerged as a
city of great tolerance, and the Blochs, as Jews, would never feel the sting
of discrimination there.

On that September day in 1885, the Blochs must have been filled with
a combination of excitement, awe and trepidation as they alighted from
the train to enter the small city that would be their new home. The newly-
built Delaware, Lackawanna and Western Railroad stopped at the Erie
Depot, and received as many as 70 or more freight and passenger trains
on any given day. The stationhouse was a large, ivy-covered, two-storied
structure with green-striped awnings and a forty-foot high tower that gave
it the impressive appearance of a municipal building, much grander than
one might see at a railroad station in a European town of comparable
population.[7] A life-size statue of an American Indian, with carved head-
dress, perhaps of the Chemung tribe, gave the station platform a true feel-

ing of Americana. Lined up only ten feet from the tracks and circling around almost the entire circumference of the building were dozens of carriages, carryalls, broughams, and even a *carromata* – a long, narrow, two-wheeled vehicle – all with their drivers and horses patiently waiting to take the disembarking passengers to wherever they wished to be driven in the Elmira environs. Most of the coaches had only one horse, but there were a few two-horse carriages. The drivers of the larger coaches eagerly searched the crowds of detraining passengers for large families or traveling parties who might have considerable amounts of bulky luggage or heavy trunks. Many baggageless passengers came to Elmira just for the day, however, either for an excursion to the newly-built recreation and picnic grounds, called Eldridge Park, or to witness the public executions on the square in front of the county jail.

The Blochs quickly learned that, fortunately for them, there was no need to secure public transportation on their first day in Elmira. They were carrying just two pieces of luggage, and the Jewish section of Elmira, their destination, was located only a short walking distance from the depot. Communication in English was not a major problem, even though the family was now in a new city within a new country. All of the Bloch children knew some English, which they had studied in Europe, and Jonas and Hanna Bloch would soon learn the language ("speaks, reads and writes English," according to the census report of 1890). The Bloch children also had made it a priority to become more adept with English when it had been determined that the family was going to go to America.

Elmira itself made it relatively easy for new immigrants to assimilate. Most residents who dealt with the public were multi-lingual, so it is altogether likely that the stationmaster understood requests in German for directions. Not only did a large percentage of the population speak German, but some also used the same East Prussian accent found in Königsberg. Should Jonas Bloch want to buy a newspaper at the station, the newsstand contained literally dozens of German-language periodicals, such as *The New Yorker Staatszeitung*.[8] Thousands of immigrants from Germany and other countries had settled in Elmira and nearby towns in New York State and Pennsylvania in the few years before 1885.[9] The popular image of most German immigrants to the United States becoming farmers was somewhat of a myth; most newly-arrived Germans were disproportionately urban in their chosen destinations, as the huge populations of New York's Lower East Side and other cities across the United States can testify.[10]

As the Blochs walked through the East End of Elmira, they passed modest homes, most well-tended with lovely lawns, some fragrant with flowers and apple trees, partially shaded with mature maples and elms.[11] Hitching posts and horseblocks stood proudly in front of the larger houses.[12] Although there were no paved sidewalks, as there had been in Europe, Elmira had just begun a massive project of installing 150,000 feet of hemlock planking on many of the walkways and paths throughout the city.[13] Houses and other buildings were being constructed on virtually every block.

In the years before Jonas Bloch and his family arrived, several relatives and friends from Königsberg had immigrated to the United States, including his son Samuel, and had settled in Elmira. It was to these compatriots that Jonas and his family went, to determine what lodgings might be available. The question of housing was quickly settled. A man by the name of Moses Bloch lived on John Street, right near Water Street fringing the river. There were a number of boarding houses nearby that had rooms available at a reasonable cost.[14] An entire house could be rented in Elmira for less than $8.00 per month, inexpensive even at that time, and more modest lodgings could be secured for $1.00 per week or even less. Within hours of arriving in Elmira, Jonas Bloch and his family were ensconced in two rooms at 506 John Street. From the windows, they could see the Chemung River, dotted with canoes, snaking through the city.[15] Also visible from their new home was a huge wooden waterwheel at the Arnot Feed Mill, at nearby Newtown Creek. Farmers would bring in their grain to be processed, and they would pay for the service with grain for the miller. Travelling just a short distance down the Chemung, one could find the best bass fishing anywhere in the East. Only two blocks away from the Bloch's new home, at the intersection of Madison Avenue and Market Street, were the circus grounds and a theater where the dramas of the day were performed, such as *Uncle Tom's Cabin, The Last Round-up,* and *Ben-Hur.*[16] Not long after their arrival, at twilight, the Blochs would watch the city's chariot-driven Lamplighter, Carl Bulgey, ignite the gas lamps that not only lined their street but were all over the city.[17]

The Bloch's new home was relatively picturesque and comfortable, and it was probably the first time since leaving Königsburg, and the grueling trip that followed, that the family felt relaxed. More than that, for Jonas, finding a place to live on *John* Street, as his first home in America, must have been a good omen. As he soon learned, the name "John" was often used as the Americanized version of "Jonas" or "Johannes." From that moment on, Jonas Bloch, American citizen-to-be, called himself John Bloch. Later, he changed the family name to "Block," replacing the "h" with a "k" and therefore making it seem less Yiddish, perhaps even more American than the guttural-sounding "h" sound that accompanied the pronunciation of Bloch. Hanna Marie then also Americanized her persona by changing her name to Mary. It is probable that Block changed the family name primarily in order to protect his children from what he thought might be an anti-Semitic reaction by their eventual schoolmates.

Although John had every intention of retaining his family's Jewish and European characteristics, he realized that his aspirations to succeed in this new land of opportunity would require certain transitions. He and Mary wanted their personal family culture to retain Old World values, yet it was clear that they would have to incorporate experiences and even some of the culture of the New World. Yes, for the most part they would change radically, but they would retain their ethnic identities. Like many other immigrants, they would not entirely "melt" into the so-called melting pot; they would not blindly accept any thoughts or manners of their new country that were contrary to their own cherished beliefs.

As soon as the family settled in, John Block attempted to find some work. Most of the Blochs who lived in Elmira – Abraham, Carl, Louis, and Moses – were peddlers, as were some 200 other Jewish residents, more than half the Jews who lived in the city.[18] Since he really didn't have a trade or profession he could use – he worked as a peddler or salesman in both Šakiai and Königsberg – John explored the possibilities of becoming a peddler like everyone else.[19] He wanted to strike out on his own, work for himself in true entrepreneurial spirit, and begin his life in America as his fellow countrymen had done: peddling wares or notions, clothing, other dry goods, or whatever else he could sell.

His savings were virtually non-existent and he needed some income immediately. Often the peddlers began their businesses with borrowed funds, and since their stock was sparse, they needed little if any initial inventory. For ten dollars or much less, and the cost of a sturdy pack, one could be in business as a peddler. The merchandise was, for the most part, stored on their backs or in the peddlers' own homes.

There was a certain romance to open-road, house-to-house retailing in those days. With a pack or two on his back, sometimes weighing 150 or more pounds, the peddler would go through the streets of Elmira, and then trudge all throughout the area to visit isolated farms, mills, small towns, mines, and forest homes, in such sections as Horseheads, Watkins Glen, Waverly, Big Flats, and East Corning, and as far away as Ithaca and Hammondsport, often being away from his family for days or weeks, sleeping in barns, under wagons, or just on the side of the road. Then, these merchants of the road would return to Elmira just for a day or two to see their families, share their adventures, and replenish their stock. New inventory was usually purchased from the firm of T.C. Cowen, who supplied merchants and peddlers with what was known as "Yankee notions," consisting of clothing, utensils, inexpensive jewelry, cooking ware, and other miscellaneous items.[20] Cowen advertised that his "goods could be purchased cheaper than in New York City," and Elmira soon became known as a center for dry goods and supplies for road peddlers all throughout New York State and northern Pennsylvania.

Newly re-stocked and somewhat refreshed, the peddler would go on the road again almost immediately. To succeed, it took a strong back, rugged individualism, and the ability to know what products would sell and how much to take on each journey. Although profits were usually low, and the work generally fatiguing, peddling was a way of avoiding the oppressive and maddening discipline of factory work; many Jews also chose the life of a peddler in order to avoid breaking the prohibition against working on the Sabbath. From Friday at sundown to sundown on Saturday, the peddler would either rest, pray at home, visit his synagogue, or sometimes do all three. Furthermore, although pushcart and on-the-road selling was extremely difficult and insecure, the Jewish peddler of Elmira, as elsewhere, was willing to make short-term sacrifices in order to possibly build a more substantial business in the long run. These itinerant merchants filled a real need, and the vocation was looked upon as quite dignified.[21]

Irving Howe eloquently described the life in *How We Lived: A Documentary History of Immigrant Jews in America – 1880-1930:*

> The Jew peddler became a fixture of the American scene, trudging through distant parts of the country. Penetrating small towns where he was regarded as an exotic, making friends with Baptists who enjoyed his biblical knowledge, bringing words of respect to black families. Some of these peddlers settled in one or another town, becoming the nucleus for a small Jewish community; others remained wanderers, on foot or with horse and wagon – pioneers, too, in bringing to isolated, native Americans some sense of cultural difference.

Some peddlers did extremely well, established a territory and a reputation for fair dealing and honesty, and then would eventually buy a cart and then a horse and wagon so that even more merchandise could be carried, and the territorial parameters could be increased. Before too long, the peddler could earn enough money to open a general merchandise store, or even a peddler-supply depot, or serve as a jobber in Elmira or elsewhere, as many did, and then be close to his family and go on to enjoy a certain prosperity. This peddler-baron sequence was not atypical, and in different parts of the country such wagon-merchants as Adam Gimbel, Benjamin Bloomingdale, Julius Rosenwald, and Edward Filene, would eventually become a part of Jewish mercantile history.[22]

For John Block, however, peddling was not going to be as simple a procedure as it first appeared, and the possible dream of making a rapid fortune, or even an easy living in America, was quickly shattered. Most of the peddlers' sales territories in and around Elmira were already claimed, if not by legal writ, then by informal agreement and tradition. If the silk and scarf merchant, or the pots and pans peddler, for example, had been selling to certain areas and neighborhoods for years, it was expected that no one would encroach on his territory. In any event, should such an infringer attempt to invade an established territory, he would probably not have been successful selling to the loyal customers of the original peddler. The physical strain of long, arduous trips away from home was also a daunting prospect for John Block. He was strong, lean and vigorous for his 45 years but he knew that the weight and bulk of a large backpack, carried over many a dusty and muddy road, was a task that could end up disabling him. Furthermore, he was above all a man who truly loved his family, and the idea of being separated from them several or more days a week, was simply not acceptable to him. Money – or the lack of it – was also an issue. To get started with an inventory, Block could have secured a loan of up to $100 without interest from the Hebrew Free Loan Association of Elmira, but that would have required him to pay it back in small sums every month. He needed whatever money he could borrow for food and lodging. For all of these reasons, and also a lifelong aversion to borrowing – a philosophy that he tried to instill in his children – it was essential, therefore, for John Block to start a peddling business that required virtually no investment, did not compete with the established merchants, and kept him within a reasonable distance of his home.[23]

The Ragpicker

The wagonless John Block became a ragpicker and junk peddler, virtually his only alternative at that time. As it developed, he really would not be a competitor to the only other ragpicking business in Elmira, that of the S.H. Laney & Co., which had several horses and wagons and over a dozen ragpickers to scour the city and its environs.[24] Block went his own way and found streets, customers and businesses that were not being serviced by Laney. By scavenging ash and trash heaps and garbage dumps, and by walking through the streets of Elmira and nearby sections looking for discarded refuse, with a long-handled poker to fathom the mysteries of garbage sacks and ash barrels, Block began to accumulate burlap bags filled with old rags, consisting of discarded stockings, torn and worn shirts and other clothing beyond repair, worn sail cloth, threadbare curtains, rope, hemp, and cotton waste. Occasionally, the more prosperous people in town would give him a soiled and tattered collection of cast-offs no longer needed; on rare occasions he would purchase, for a penny a bag, a fairly large supply of a family's or factory's waste rags. As he scavenged, items other than rags would often come to light, such as scrap metal, legless furniture, bits of iron hoops and nails, broken horseshoes, smashed lanterns, bottles and broken glass, lumps of coal, twisted candelabras, discarded books and knick-knacks, splintered barrels, and all manners and forms of the town's dross and detritus. Discarded shoes were sold to the local cobbler, who would repair them to sell to the poor. Shoes that were unsalvageable went into Block's own woodpile, since old leather burned well and gave a steady heat. John Burnham's biography, *The Ragpicker or Bound and Free*, published in 1855, described the life, similar to John Block's, as follows:

> There is a variety in these little trades and industries, which derive their chief means of life from the wants and luxuries of the Boulevards. You will see an individual moving about, at all hours of the night, silent and active, and seeing the smallest bit of paper in the dark, where you could see nothing, picking it up and pitching it, with amazing dexterity, into a basket tied to his shoulder; with a cat-like walk, being everywhere and nowhere at the same time; stirring up the rubbish of every nook and gutter of the street, under your very nose. This is the Rag-picker. He is a very important individual. He stands at the head of the 'little trades' and is looked to with envy by all the others.[25]

John Block, the ragpicker, seemed somewhat out of place, however. He did not resemble either in appearance or personality, the imagined portrait of someone on one of the lowest rungs of the city's social and employment ladders. He was trim, always neatly dressed, and with his distinguished goatee, balding pate, and benign countenance, he appeared professorial and kindly in demeanor. His Old World courtesy and his amiable eyes stood him in good avail in dealing with the Elmira townspeople. Despite his poverty, Block was held in certain regard; he enjoyed a subdued respect of some of the community because he reused things that others would destroy, and because he did with dignity what others might consider distasteful work.

Mary also seemed to be more than just a cut above that of a ragpicker's housewife. Wearing her dark-brown hair pulled back by a sedate comb in an ornamental bun, short and somewhat stocky, she was a handsome woman with an open face, sparkling eyes, and a nurturing, although stubborn nature.

Within short order, starting in the early morning and sharing the roads with the ubiquitous milk-wagon, John Block was prowling the streets of Elmira with a pushcart, and making a living by selling back his newly-acquired rags to whoever would buy. Later in the day, he would make a second round. The ragman's call, a familiar refrain in Elmira as elsewhere, went something like this:

> Rags to give, old rags to give,
> Rags to give, old rags to give,
> Any old clothes, any old clothes!

At first, his sons Paul and Max would help him on Saturdays, the best day for scavenging; this Saturday work prevented all three, however, from observing the Sabbath, and no record can be found of the Blocks being particularly active in any of Elmira's Jewish temples, of which there were three at that time: B'nai Israel, Shomer Hadoth, and the Talmud Torah.[26] Additionally, there is no record of either Max or Paul becoming *bar mitzvah* boys, a traditional rite that most young men of the Jewish faith undergo upon reaching puberty. Paul never became formally religious but he was nominally a Jew and did believe that everyone needed the solace and comfort of faith in whatever way it was received or experienced.

John Block's customers consisted of women who made rag rugs; factories and businesses that needed wipers and clean-up rags; and poor people

who would wash and bleach the blemished and fragmented rags. With
the magic of needle and thread, these poor people would turn the worn
material into underwear and shirts, and curtains and sheets for the home.
Printers and newspaper companies would re-sell the rags, especially if
they were made of calico, to manufacturers and mills in order to make
rag-content paper. Paper itself, since it was partially made of rag, would
also be thrust into Block's bag and sold, to be converted into new paper.
Other retrieved items were salable, too. Scrap iron was sold to blacksmiths; damaged furniture was bartered or sold to carpenters or to anyone
else who believed it could be cleaned up, repaired, and perhaps painted to
be used or sold again. Soon the Blocks had to move in order to store all
of the junk and bric-a-brac – the brass, copper and lead items – that John
was accumulating. The family then lived in a variety of Elmira houses, –
always staying within the Jewish section in the east end of the city – from
Orchard Street to Madison Avenue, to Water Street, each house larger
than the previous one, and each with its backyard crammed with barrels
of rusted nails, broken beds, and damaged china. The Block family was
not destitute, but life was a struggle and money was always scarce. They
were among the poorest families in Elmira, and John Block worked as
hard as he could to give his children the opportunities that he felt were
denied to him.

As John Block attempted to worry out a living with a growing family
to support, Mary attended to the home, and Paul, Mollie and eventually
Frieda were enrolled in a one-room schoolhouse, Number Eight, only a
few minutes walk from their home. The school consisted of about 30
students, with the schoolmarm teaching all of the subjects. The demands
were rigorous, and the students received a near-superlative education.
Those students who lagged in attention were greeted with a snap on the
head by the teacher's thimble. As everything was taught in English,
the Block children soon began to lose any trace of a German or Yiddish
accent.

Paul had had some good grounding in English when he went to school
in Königsberg, but once he was in the United States, using the language
every day as well as studying it in school, he gained command of English
quickly, and to an unusual degree of proficiency. Intensely curious about
his new country, he read as many books as he could find, and soon discovered that in some ways he could discover things that were more pertinent to him by reading the newspapers. That early interest turned into a
lifetime habit. Paul became the child his parents most depended on to

translate for them.

His rush to master English was partially due to his incentive to communicate with his schoolmates and other children in Elmira. Although there were many immigrants who spoke German, Paul's outgoing manner led him to make acquaintanceships, and later friendships, with people beyond his specific neighborhood. To communicate with them, he *had* to speak English, and he wanted to learn it as quickly as possible because he wanted to *be* like them.

He learned the language so expertly that only a few years after arriving in America he was writing rhyming poetry, in English, which was published in the *Elmira Telegram*. Gifted with an "ear" for language, he could speak perfect, accentless English by his early teens, a remarkable accomplishment. Both of these achievements are also clearly testament to his resolve, and indicate a powerful will to succeed, without which he might not have accomplished what he was eventually able to do in his career.

The less-ostentatious Palmer method of penmanship had just replaced the traditional and ornate Spenserian script that had been taught in school for years. Paul learned to write the new, more efficient way, including the key to correct pen-holding ("1. Put the forefinger flat upon the barrel of the pen-holder; 2. Put the second finger nail under the pen holder.") and from that time on and all through his life, he displayed a careful, bold, easy-to-read style in his handwriting. He studied from McGuffey's *Third Eclectic Reader*, poured over Swinton's *A Complete Course in Geography*, followed the pictorial alphabets in a spelling book, and even learned the elements of elocution. He and his sisters shared everything they learned with 13-year-old Max, who, having already attended a year of *gymnasium* in Königsberg, secured a full-time job as an office boy, and was then made a clerk, at Merchant's Bank on West Water Street.[27]

The *Elmira Telegram:*
Paul's First Job

Exactly how Paul Block secured his first job (other than helping his father), which was in the newspaper business, is not known, but at the age of 10, within just two years of arriving in Elmira, he was working for the *Elmira Sunday Telegram,* although in one interview later on in life, Block thought he remembered starting to work there at age "8 or 9." It is possible that John Block, while selling rags to the *Telegram*, learned that the newspaper was looking for a youngster to come aboard, and then told

Paul about the opportunity; it is also possible that the conscientious Paul Block ferreted out and visited a host of businesses and factories requesting after-school and weekend employment until he found an opening. It is interesting to speculate whether he was attracted to newspaper work as his first career destination to begin with, or whether he took whatever job was available. One wonders, for example, whether if Paul Block had wandered into the Erie Railroad offices, instead of the *Elmira Sunday Telegram*, he would have become a transportation tycoon rather than a newspaper publisher? If he had been employed at Flinsbach's Bakery on East Church Street, or Abramsky's Sweets on John and Washington, even nearer to his home, would he eventually have owned a national baking or foods company such as General Mills?

It is not particularly difficult to understand, however, why a young boy such as Paul Block would become instantly interested in the workings of a newspaper office and printing plant. In addition to giving him a small salary (he actually started the job with no salary, just to receive the experience and wait for an opening) so that he could contribute to the family's coffers, the *Telegram* was an intriguing, often exciting, and usually a cerebral center of activity. The newspaper also had a great deal of status compared to other pursuits in the city of Elmira. As a ragpicker's son, Paul needed as much self-esteem as he could establish on his own, and for a young man who would go on to become a prominent publisher, the *Telegram* was as good an introduction to the world of newspapers as any.

The editor, Harry S. Brooks, sat at a large oak desk in the center of the *Telegram's* newsroom, bathed in gaslight, and barked out commands for more copy, more illustrations, and more advertisements. There was constant discussion among the reporters and editors of the events of the day, not just about brush fires and local runaway horses, but about such news events as why Benjamin Harrison was elected president of the United States, the Great Blizzard of 1888 which centered on New York City, the ravages of the Johnstown flood, London's "Jack the Ripper" murdering six women, the last bare-knuckled title fight of John L. Sullivan, and the significance of Idaho and Wyoming becoming, respectively, the 43rd and 44th states of the Union.

In 1892-1893, Brooks wrote many editorials proclaiming the innocence of Lizzie Borden, of Fall River, Massachusetts, who was accused of murdering her parents. Brooks also did extensive coverage of the 1893 World's Fair in Chicago with articles provided by his friend, the poet-journalist Eugene Field.

As the copy appeared, often precariously close to deadline, the editors sat with their cuff protectors and green eye shades, quietly studying or revising stories before sending them to the composing room. Occasionally the silence would be punctuated by an annoyed curse or a frustrated grunt as an indignant editor damned a reporter for his illegible handwriting. (So undecipherable was some of the handwritten copy that the compositors would often demand double their pay to set the offending stories in type.) But the editing portion of the newspaper publishing process was for the most part surprisingly quiet. A dozen or more editors bent over their desks, dipping their pens into their ink pots, changing a "that" to a "which," correcting a misspelled word or a factual inaccuracy, and dropping soiled pieces of blotter paper, which fluttered to the floor. The scratching of pens on paper was intermittently punctuated with a ping as a wad of tobacco juice hit the communal brass spittoon, in concert with the hissing of the inevitable tea kettle.

As a messenger boy, Paul Block carried drafts of news stories back and forth between reporters and editors, and finally, downstairs to the print shop itself. When he stood in the printing room later on, watching the finished newspaper come off the press and be loaded on the wagons, it must have been irresistibly romantic to Paul to know how the stories came to be written just hours or sometimes barely minutes before. He was, in effect, a part of the action and history of his day, and the musty smell of the ink, the clang of the presses, and the stomping and snorting of the horses ready to take the newspaper to waiting readers all must have contributed to the exhilaration of the impressionable boy.

However he secured his position, or whatever his motivations, he certainly could have found less auspicious environs for the development of his ultimate talents. As journalism historian Frank L. Mott has written: "Many a hustling boy found his first interest in business or journalism, or both, through selling newspapers and magazines after school."[28] *The Elmira Telegram* was among the most prosperous businesses in the city at that time, (ranked eighth in 1892), employing over 60 workers, and boasting a circulation of 180,000, more than five times that of the population of the city itself.[29] The fact that the average circulation for all daily newspapers in the United States in 1890 was barely 5,000, and thousands of weeklies had circulations of less than 1,000, indicates the considerable reach of the *Telegram*.[30] So interesting and well produced was the *Telegram*, it could be purchased all over the northeastern seaboard, as well as overseas on the streets of London. It had the largest circulation of any newspaper in New York State outside of those papers published in New York City,[31] and it also claimed that it had the largest circulation of any provincial newspaper in the United States.[32]

Founded in 1879 by Harry S. Brooks, a tall, thin 27-year-old journalist with a handlebar mustache, the *Telegram* was a well-managed and brilliantly edited newspaper that captured the imagination and readership of Elmirans and others almost as soon as its first issue was off the press. Brooks had had years of experience before he attempted to launch his own newspaper.[33] He had worked for the *Elmira Gazette,* starting as a printer's apprentice at the age of 17. It was a fortuitous time to become involved in the newspaper industry. Publishing was beginning to swell in the United States as a result of increased literacy (illiteracy had declined from 20% in 1870, to 13.3% in 1890[34]) brought about by the proliferation of free schools, advanced printing technology, decreased paper costs, and the need for an advertising medium to market the many products that were flooding and transforming the American economy.[35] Sunday newspapers doubled in number and circulation from the time of the Civil War, and there were more than 200 in the country by the time Brooks founded the *Telegram* in 1879. Retail stores began finding Sunday newspapers an especially valuable newspaper medium, and increased their space to publicize their bargain attractions of the coming week. [36]

Brooks's capital investment to publish the first issue was less than $100, most of it borrowed, and it was an extremely shrewd financial coup even in those days, since the great editor Charles A. Dana, writing in the *New York Tribune* back in 1850, claimed that it should take no less than $100,000 to start a major, albeit daily, metropolitan newspaper.[37] Within less than three months, Brooks had his small investment paid back to him, and as the business developed, it would be the only cash capital ever advanced by him.[38]

Brooks had worked in virtually every department of the *Gazette*: printing, typesetting, money counting, editorial, advertising, and news, and distinguished himself in all the fields that the newspaper had to offer, often becoming superintendent or manager before moving on to the next department.[39] After mastering all disciplines of the newspaper business, he had the confidence that he could edit and publish his own periodical successfully, and that he could compete against the five other newspapers being published in Elmira at that time.

The *Telegram* would be the first Sunday newspaper in Elmira. From one revenue perspective this was a sound business idea, since a Sunday paper would have less advertising competition from the dailies, which had cornered the market for retail businesses that wanted to announce sales or events each and every day. But the *Telegram* would have to develop a new circulation among readers not accustomed to buying a Sunday paper. It would also risk a certain ire among some of the pious, who believed that a Sunday newspaper was at worst irreverent, and at the very least presented competition with their ministers who wanted to maintain the attendance of their congregations at religious services. These people believed that newsboys profaned the Sabbath with their incessant cries of "Extra!" The Elmirans of that time even objected to the delivery of milk by horse cart on Sunday; so when newspapers began to be sold on the Sabbath there was a public outcry.[40] As late as 1896, in Albany, New York, a group of Methodist ministers denounced the existence of Sunday newspapers and called for the use of "all honorable and proper means" to oppose them. In Pittsburgh in 1893, and in Philadelphia in 1903, under the old Pennsylvania "Blue Laws," clergymen went to the courts in order to stop the publication of Sunday newspapers.[41] Some Elmira denizens, but not most, were no less vocal in their condemnation of Sunday papers. Brooks countered that his *Telegram* reached more parishioners than most of the churches, and since he aimed for a moral, if not ecclesiastical tone in his editorial approach, he felt he had every right to publish on Sunday, First Amendment implications and strident moralists notwithstanding. In the Sunday, April 30, 1893 issue of the *Elmira Telegram,* next to the column declaring that the newspaper is *"Published for the People,"* Brooks wrote:

> The attacks upon Sunday newspapers have come more through a lack of knowledge of their real contents, and an unreasonable prejudice, than from any other motive. The people of today, with broad views and independence of spirit, are not inclined to be dictated to by bigoted persons and every attack upon Sunday newspapers, which the masses want and which they will have, only serves to strengthen its cause among the people, and make more readers for it. The Sunday newspaper has established for itself a position from which prejudice, or demagoguery, or cant, can never oust it.

Brooks attempted to trumpet the *Telegram*'s political stance as an independent newspaper, uninfluenced by political parties or partisan control. It was the only such publishing entity in Elmira. Of the major newspapers in the city, the *Gazette* and *The Free Press* were rabidly Democratic, whereas the *Advertiser* had Republican leanings,[42] and the *Evening Star* favored the Greenback Party, a political entity that ceased to exist after 1884. In 1885, a weekly named the *Sentinel* appeared in Elmira, backed by the Prohibition Party, but it could not raise its circulation above 2,000 and quickly went out of business. That left the *Telegram* standing alone in upholding its Independent viewpoint.[43] "The *Telegram* is non-partisan and defies man, woman or child to put a finger on a letter that commits it to any party or a line that advocates the claims of any politician," wrote Brooks.[44]

Initially, Brooks retained his job at the *Gazette*, and with two partners, all working virtually around-the-clock at the *Telegram* on Friday evenings, Saturdays and Sundays, managed to produce a newspaper, struggling to create and finance it issue by issue, using advertising and circulation funds coming in from sales of each previous paper to pay for the next. They established their first office in a small one-story building on Carroll Street. Within three weeks, Brooks left the *Gazette* and became the full-time publisher of the *Telegram*.

The circulation of the *Telegram* grew quickly, because of several additional factors. The first was Brooks's ability and national reputation as a paragrapher – the process of creating short, well-written capsules of news that he would prominently display on the front page. A history of Chemung County describes Brooks's style: "His little paragraphs, brief though they may have been, were short, sharp, and quick, like a Chinese powder cracker. They gave great pleasure to the reader, attracted attention and were frequently quoted." For example, under the headline "Cruelty to Animals," Brooks succinctly wrote the following crime story in all of 40 words: "Clarence Seymour was arrested by Officer Keavin, Wednesday. He was charged with cruelty to animals. He was caught hammering a sickly and sore pair of horses who were stuck with a load of pump logs on Main street bridge."[45]

Also, Brooks refused, for the most part, to accept and to publish what was then known as "boilerplate" news stories. These were general interest or feature stories that were written by a news agency and could be purchased by newspapers throughout the region or the country. The stories were put directly onto printing plates, or on mats, which were shipped to newspapers who bought the service on a daily or weekly basis. Each plate or mat was ready to be slapped on the press, and to be published without change.[46] Although some of the boilerplate stories were extremely well-crafted, and most small-town newspapers had for decades used at least some boilerplate as filler, these stories always lacked a local angle, since the same articles were shipped to hundreds of papers all over the country. *Collier's Magazine* referred to boilerplate as "tainted news" since there was often political propaganda inserted in many of the stories. Boilerplate also lacked originality and it could have no stamp of the editor's personality, let alone his political or philosophical beliefs. Some publishers who consistently used boilerplate for the large percentage of their news and editorial content were actually close to illiterate. All they needed to do in order to publish was to have some typesetters who could compose local ads, and perhaps one journalist to handle a large local story. The rest of the contents of their newspaper would consist of boilerplate: unproofed by them, and lacking local concern, angle or passion.

Harry S. Brooks would tolerate no such unprofessionalism in the *Telegram*. "Railroading" was the term that Brooks used when he referred to those editors who sent their newspapers to press without fully correcting the stories, or, worse yet, perhaps meaning that the newspapers were "railroaded" to other cities without care and accuracy. Editors argued with him that it was better to speed the news to the reader, imperfections, typographical errors, lapses of logic, and grammatical breakdowns be damned.[47] Not so, answered Brooks. He believed that the *Telegram* was more than a business; he saw his newspaper as a social service fundamental to the life of Elmira, and one that could exert profound influence on the city and its citizens.

In November of 1884, with the establishment of the first news syndicate by Samuel S. McClure, Brooks began to take some "packaged" news reports and features, but in all cases he insisted on the heavy use of the editor's blue pencil, adding, changing and deleting whatever parts of the copy that he would eventually publish in the *Telegram*.

Recognizing the social nature of his enterprise, Brooks emphasized to his employees, and even to the novice Paul Block, the ethical, legal and moral implications of everything that impacted upon, or influenced, the editorial direction of the paper. The subtext to the business of publishing, in Brooks's philosophy, was the worth of the newspaper as a service to the individual and the community. On the editorial page of the *Telegram*, under a rough pen and ink sketch of a newspaper carrier (who looks suspiciously like the young Paul Block) with high hat, delivering the news in a flurry of snow or rain, Brooks ran the following notice in every issue:

The Law

> Any person who willfully states, delivers or transmits by
> any means whatever to any manager, editor, publisher or other
> employee of a publisher of any newspaper, magazine publi-
> cation, periodical or serial, any statement concerning any
> person or corporation, which if published therein would be a
> libel, is guilty of a misdemeanor. – _Section 254A of the Pe-_
> _nal Code._[48]

Should there be any further question of Brooks's ethical intentions, his
letterhead bore the following credo: "A STRICTLY HIGH GRADE UP-
TO-DATE FAMILY PAPER." This doctrine may have been inspired by
the slogan emblazoned on the front page of _The Illustrated London News:_
"The Family's Newspaper."[49] Like many Americans, Brooks looked to
Europe for the proper keys to status.

Brooks's vivid to-the-point prose style, as displayed in his paragraphing
and his original reporting and editing, not only pleased his existing readership, it led to increased circulation. Within a short time after founding
the _Telegram_, buoyed by its acceptance, and following his own formula,
Brooks also established two other newspapers, both in their respective
state capitols: in Albany, New York and Harrisburg, Pennsylvania. Since
the _Telegram_ was the only Sunday newspaper published in Elmira, its
sole competition was a few Sunday papers that were shipped up from
New York City, to be sold to the Elmira citizenry. Selling for three cents
a copy, as opposed to the five cents a copy price for New York City Sunday papers, the _Telegram_ would always outsell its downstate counter-
parts. When the out-of-town papers raised their price to seven cents, the
Telegram kept to its old price, and circulation and advertising revenue
soared even higher.[50] There was no other publication in Elmira whose
circulation came anywhere near that of the _Telegram._ When issues of
The World, the Sunday newspaper that Joseph Pulitzer published in New
York, reached a size of 100 pages on May 7, 1893, Brooks was worried
that the increased size might hurt the _Telegram's_ circulation. But the
Elmirans remained loyal and his circulation held.[51] Another competitor,
however, crept up quickly starting in 1881: the _Utica Saturday Globe_, a
weekly paper that was published each Saturday, would eventually sell
nearly 1,000 copies each week in Elmira. Nonetheless, it gained a re-
gional and national reputation, which enabled it to outsell the _Telegram_
as a weekly in such cities as Schenectady, Syracuse, Rochester, and even

faraway Pittsburgh, Pennsylvania.[52] *The Elmira Daily Gazette*, perhaps as a left-handed criticism of its local rival, the *Telegram*, publicly discussed the competition of the *Globe*:

> The *Utica Saturday Globe* is increasing its circulation in Elmira at a rapid rate. Each week's sales improved over those of the week preceding and the paper, already excellent, is growing better all the time. The *Globe* is one of the very best weekly newspapers sold in this vicinity and is increasing its hold right along. It is a well-edited, clean paper that no one hesitates to take in his family and its news is always reliable.[53]

Two incidents, both in 1881 – when the *Telegram* had been published for a little over a year – helped it to propel its circulation to even greater heights. On a Saturday evening in January, an axle broke on the engine of an Erie train, causing a derailment, and a fire spread rapidly throughout the cars. Four postal clerks and an express messenger – two of whom were from Elmira and were well known – were burned to death, and the disaster shocked the community. The *Telegram* was in production for Sunday delivery when the event occurred; Brooks literally stopped the presses, remade his front page, and published a harrowing story with every possible detail. Elmirans and others had the full story the next day, and since the *Telegram* was the only Sunday newspaper in Elmira, there was little that the daily papers could add on Monday, when they published, that was not either redundant or old news. It was the *Telegram's* most significant early scoop.

Another Saturday instance occurred when President James Garfield was shot by Charles J. Guiteau in Buffalo on July 2, 1881. Although word of mouth reports about the tragic incident filtered through the community almost immediately, the *Telegram* had the field all to itself and told the whole story 24 hours later on its front page for the next day's Sunday morning delivery. Such newspapers as the *Gazette*, the *Advertiser,* and the *Evening Star* did carry coverage on Monday and in the days following, until Sept. 19th, when the President died. It was to the *Telegram*, however, that the populace of Elmira and other cities went to get the story first, making it the most conspicuous and widely-read newspaper in the city.[54]

Editors throughout Elmira and elsewhere began to complain that all of the great or exciting events that took place in the city seemed always to happen on a Saturday, the one day that they were not publishing, thus enabling the *Telegram* to reap the benefits of an early scoop, and publish on Sunday, leaving the competition only to rake over the stubble of whatever details, or news crumbs, remained. It wasn't only the great events that occurred on Saturday, however: more crimes were committed on the weekend, social events were more numerous, distinguished visitors to the city seemed to come often on Saturdays. All of this activity produced interesting and meaningful news, week in and week out, and helped add to the *Telegram's* coffers through added circulation and readership.

As compared to its true news value, the *Telegram* was not entirely without its florid side, especially in reporting social events. Brides were invariably described as popular, beautiful, charming and universally beloved. Of one, it reported: "Her sweet disposition and womanly manner has won her a legion of friends."[55]

Editorial appeal itself, however strong in the *Telegram*, was not the only reason for its prosperity. Part of Brooks's success also came through the effort of one of his partners, James H. Hill, who had come to the *Telegram* with a great amount of experience in newspaper distribution, having worked for the Union News Company. Although he was not technically called the Circulation Director – that title didn't really come into use in the newspaper business until years later – Hill was nevertheless responsible for securing distribution and subscriptions not only in Elmira but in other cities as well. His function grew rapidly, due to the impetus of decreased postal rates (from twenty-five cents a pound in the 1870s, to one cent a pound in 1885), free delivery of second-class mail matter, and the extension of rural free delivery to all towns with populations of 10,000 or more.[56]

The influence of shipping newspapers by railway also greatly increased the circulation of the *Telegram*. Since Elmira was a railroad center, and Hill was totally familiar with the schedules of the night trains and specifically which freighthandlers could be trusted to speed the papers to their properly appointed destinations to arrive in outlying cities by Sunday afternoon, soon the *Telegram* could be found in virtually every town, hamlet and city of New York State and northern Pennsylvania.[57]

In concert with Brooks's mandates, Hill concentrated on all aspects of the *Telegram's* circulation: selling copies on newsstands in Elmira and other cities, supervising newsboy sales, home delivery, subscriptions paid in advance, and copies being delivered by mail. The pursuit of advertising was the rationale behind the scramble for a larger circulation, and the

Telegram's claim to have such large numbers of readers was an important incentive in gaining an advertiser's business.[58]

It was at this juncture of the *Telegram's* pursuit of higher circulation and advertising, that Paul Block began his career in the newspaper business. When he was ten years old, Paul Block was hired as a part-time messenger, and one of the newsboy carriers. (He did use the soon-to-be clichéd, "Read all about it!") The other carriers were printer's apprentices for the *Telegram*. Working after school, usually all day on Saturday, and then again on Sunday, Paul's job was to scurry around Elmira, to and from offices and retail establishments, picking up and dropping off advertising copy, news reports, court records, and all other manner of editorial and business material pertinent to the *Telegram*. He also swept down the newsroom and tended the fire in the potbelly stove. On Sunday mornings, in weather fair or foul, he would deliver the paper to homes on a scheduled route; in the afternoons, he would cover the downtown streets of Elmira, especially in the courthouse section, selling copies of the *Telegram* to people out for a stroll. Nimble-footed and alert, within a short while Paul seemed to know virtually everyone in the city of Elmira and began to understand the normal rhythms of small-town life. After a few years, when he was presented with a safety bicycle to speed up his appointed rounds, he enjoyed a bit of fame by becoming known to the townspeople as one of the swiftest cyclists in Elmira.[59] So adept was he at engaging in acrobatics on his two-wheeler, that in the summer of 1890 he brashly challenged the county's coroner, Herman J. Jacobs, also a bicycle expert, to an exhibition of "speed, style and artistic tumbling" that took place on the Inter-State fairgrounds. It is not known who won the contest, but Paul was noted in the local press as being a "lightning bicycle manipulator."[60] Bicycling became such a rage in Elmira that a license was required (it cost fifty cents for a one-time purchase), and laws were established that recognized bicycles as "common vehicles." Thus they had the right-of-way to half the road, the same as a wagon. Should a bike and an animal clash, the new law arbitrarily claimed that the animal owner was legally responsible. [61]

Brooks and Hill noted Paul's precociousness and enthusiasm, and gave the boy more attention than the other young newspaper carriers and apprentices.[62] The boy was eager to learn, was extremely observant, had a great memory, and possessed a natural charm that belied his years. Brooks continually influenced the boy, and assumed the role of mentor, almost that of a surrogate parent or father figure. He was impressed that Paul was so loving and solicitous toward his mother, Mary Block. Brooks wrote to his charge: "No use telling you to be good to your mother. You always have been. And never cease to be as long as you draw the breath of life…and see to it that she at least has enough to live peacefully on until the end of her days."[63]

Paul and the Colonel

When an executive of a firm by the name of A. Frank Richardson and Co. (who were not only the advertising representatives of the *Telegram*, but also investors, and therefore part-owners) came up with an idea that would involve Paul Block, both Brooks and Hill seized upon it and enlisted the boy's participation.

The Richardson people had come into possession of a show dog from Switzerland, a huge St. Bernard, who they claimed was the third largest dog in America. Nearly three feet high, and weighing 175 pounds, the dog was considered to be a magnificent specimen of the breed, a lineal descendant of Barry I, who had become famous by saving the lives of seven mountain climbers who were stranded in the Alps. Named "Colonel" after one of the managers of the A. Frank Richardson Co., Col. P.A.J. Russell, the dog was bought by Hill for the unprecedented sum of $500, to be used for *Telegram* circulation promotions. So unique-looking and gentle was the dog, it was thought by both Brooks and Hill that crowds of people would take notice of it wherever it went, and if Colonel could be identified in the public's mind with the *Telegram*, it would be an excellent promotion for the newspaper. Paul Block, in addition to his other duties, became Colonel's "master."[64]

The *Telegram* constantly searched for ways that the dog could be used for promotions, and eventually had an attractive studio photograph made of Colonel and little Paul. Thousands of the photographs were mailed out in a gilt frame to subscribers and advertisers all over the county and the state. As the photograph of Paul and Colonel hung in hundreds of houses, the boy soon became an Elmira celebrity of sorts. Brooks also mailed copies of the photograph and a lovely pen-and-ink line drawing of the dog to other publications, and Colonel's likeness began to appear in newspapers and magazines throughout the adjoining states. Colonel became known as one of the most famous and beloved dogs in America: "The finest St. Bernard dog on earth," as touted by the *Telegram*. [65]

Paul's main responsibility for Colonel, in addition to directing the construction of his mammoth doghouse at the back of the *Telegram* building, and seeing to it that the dog was well-fed and groomed, was to appear with him at virtually every public function that arose in the city of Elmira, and often in other New York State cities, as well. Paul and Colonel would make appearances at such festivities as circuses, parades, street fairs, exhibitions and political rallies, and usually wherever and whenever they went the crowds would assemble. He went on tour with Colonel to Syracuse, Corning and Binghamton, where under the auspices of city officials, the two visited hospitals and schools to amuse groups of children. On their return to Elmira, their hometown was so proud of the renown that Paul and Colonel had achieved that they were escorted as prodigal son and dog from the railroad station to the *Telegram* office by Prof. Miller's School of Commerce marching band in a parade on Church Street.[66]

Paul quickly learned how to field questions about Colonel from the public: How old is he? What do you feed him? Where was he born? Does he bite? Does the cask around his neck really have brandy in it? (It did!) How do you bathe him? All of this contact with crowds of curious people taught the boy a crucial lesson, one that he would continually apply for the rest of his life: good manners and friendliness were among the most important personality traits one could have. Also, Brooks so believed in courtesy and friendship that he instructed Paul over and over again by example. Emblazoned on the masthead of the front page of every copy of the *Telegram* was the following credo: "Friendship has a power to sooth affliction in her darkest hour." Paul quietly and respectfully took notice.

One of the highlights of Paul's relationship with Colonel occurred when the Richardson Agency invited them both to New York City, put them up in the Waldorf Hotel, which was then located near Herald Square, and had the dog "hold court" in the hotel lobby, almost as if he were something of a royal canine. While keeping an eye on the famed mascot, Paul answered questions and had the opportunity of meeting many of the city's citizens, always holding forth himself, and constantly showing an unfailing courtesy and the ability to carry out an interesting conversation with strangers as old as his grandparents. Reporters and other publishing personnel from the *World*, the *Herald*, and *The New York Times* would invariably stop by to see the wonder dog and talk to its master. Not only did Paul's superb social skills impress the Manhattanites, but all the people from the Richardson agency also noted his grace and charm. These mainly self-taught lessons of unaffected esprit would become one of Paul Block's principal trademarks throughout the rest of his life.

In addition to working with Colonel, Paul also did some sightseeing in Manhattan. One of the things he most wanted to see when in New York City was the Statue of Liberty, which he had only read about. The statue had not been completed when Paul and his family sailed into New York Harbor in 1885.

By the time he reached his early teens, when he attended the Elmira Free Academy High School, Paul Block was given even more responsibilities at the *Telegram*. Whenever a group of visitors or an individual requested a tour of the newspaper, Paul was called upon to conduct it. Occasionally he would allow one of his sisters to go on the tour, too, so that he could arrange introductions for her with the out-of-towners.[67] He spoke well, seemed to know as much about the newspaper as if he were its proprietor, and would invariably conclude the tour with a special visit with his famous canine friend, Colonel. When subscribers came to the office to pay their quarterly or semi-annual subscription fees, Paul treated them courteously, running to Brooks' office to retrieve a special box of cigars, and then back again to the visitors to offer them a complimentary smoke.

A handsome boy with black hair and dark eyes, slender-faced features, thin and small for his age, and looking younger than he really was, Paul usually startled and delighted people when they first met him, because of his cleverness, wit and conversational ability. Brooks quickly realized that his original promotional strategy had resulted in an unexpected double benefit. Not only did the public appearances of Colonel bring positive attention for the paper, but young Paul's agreeable and amusing personality could be a strong benefit to the *Telegram*, as well. Brooks not only wanted to use the boy in the best sense of the word, but also tutor and influence him in all the ways of the newspaper business. As publisher of the *Telegram*, promotion of the newspaper was one of Brooks's main concerns. To create an impressive effect, he devised a dramatic costume for Paul's public appearances. The boy was dressed in a long, black MacFarlane cloak with brass buttons, an attached shoulder cape with yellow piping, black knickerbockers and shiny hightop boots, topped off with a stiff high hat with gold buckle, similar to the head dress worn by gentlemen in the 1830s. The result was that Paul looked not unlike a young prince of the German royal house of Hapsburg, and he effortlessly assumed the role.

Brooks then purchased a black Shetland pony – "Telegram Tom," as he became known – and a Newport pony cart, and had Paul deliver the newspaper every Sunday to the Elmira subscribers, speeding around town with the latest news. Paul, accompanied by a "footman," a younger black child dressed identically in formal garb and high hat, with the unfortunate nickname of Sambo, would start out every Sunday morning at the stables of Charles Cross at the corner of Gray and State streets, lead the pony from his tiny stall, arrange his harness, hitch him up to his cart and head for the *Telegram's* building to collect the day's newspapers for delivery. The sight of the two boys, Paul manipulating the reigns of the 39-inch Tom, and Sambo flicking the whip to give the pony occasional encouragement, was a tableau that often caused excitement, curiosity and even the rollicking humor of the town's residents. The parade of pony and boys was usually accompanied by the loyal and affable Colonel – virtually as large as the pony itself – at the rear. No other newspaper in Elmira delivered its product with such pomp and procession, and part of the reward of subscribing to the *Telegram* became the process of how it was delivered by Paul Block and his associates every Sunday.

On days when the snowdrifts were too high for the tiny pony to negotiate, the *Telegram's* large and impressive wagon would do the job. Pulled by two golden-plumed black geldings, the effect was in its own way as spectacular as the pony cart delivery. For those trips, of course, an adult would take the reigns, with Paul sitting alongside as whipman. The coach was huge, and the *Telegram* claimed it was the only wagon in the world illuminated by electric light; its brass lanterns were needed whenever it made nighttime deliveries to the Erie Depot. Sometimes Colonel would sit between Paul and the driver, and at others the dog would frolic in the snow and run alongside the coach, perhaps evocative of the dog's early life in the mountains of Switzerland.

By delivering the papers and by being exposed to the ideas of reporters and editors, Paul began to assiduously read the *Telegram* and he became interested in and stimulated by the world of journalism and publishing. He felt that he was fit for newspaper work, and became excited at the prospect of moving ahead in the field in whatever capacity he could.

Paul as Newspaper Acolyte
Just as Brooks had learned all aspects of the newspaper business, he began to train the ever-eager Paul Block in every department, and Paul continually asked to try out for virtually whatever position became available. Brooks had become a printer's apprentice at the age of 17, after

graduating from the Elmira Free Academy. Paul was barely 14 and still attending the Academy, but Brooks felt the time had come to begin treating Paul in a more professional way. The processes used in the printing room of a newspaper in the 1880s had not evolved very much since Johann Gutenberg's invention of movable type four centuries earlier. The printer's "uniform" was much the same, too. Paul's outfit was not very glamorous. Instead of a cape, he wore an ink-stained apron. And instead of a high hat, he wore a printer's "dicer" – a square paper hat constructed of two sheets of the previous day's discarded newspaper. These hats had been used in publishing houses since 1784; printers and typesetters wore them to keep ink, grease, oil and paper lint out of their hair and it was considered a badge of honor, or at least an acceptance into the newspaper fraternity, to learn how to fold one of the hats, neatly creased and properly squared.

Paul Block began to learn how to set type by hand. He used a composing stick to gather the little metal letters, one by one: capitals from the Upper Case, and small letters from the Lower Case, and the slender spacing bars, called "ems" or "ens," that indicated the size of the dashes and spaces in between letters and words (and also used as a measurement – the square of the body of any size of type – in computing the cost of composition). He was paid the impecunious sum of ten cents per thousand ems. Then, after each page had been printed, Paul distributed those same letters back to their appropriate cubbyholes, so they could be used to form new words for the next story. It was a painstaking process, and Paul was impatient with himself. Compared to the dozen or so experienced typesetters of the *Telegram*, he felt that it was taking him much too long to set a complete sentence – sometimes as long as ten minutes – let alone a paragraph or a whole story. Brooks didn't necessarily agree with Block's own appraisal of himself. He wasn't surprised that Paul was setting type slowly; the process required skill and patience. He expected that the boy would pick up speed as he gained experience; Brooks had ultimate faith that Paul Block could learn anything.

But Paul's greatest strength clearly consisted of his conversational ability and his winsome personality. Stuck in the bowels of the typesetting room, not talking to anyone, concentrating on taking a story or advertisement from its handwritten script, and setting every word, sentence, and punctuation mark in type, hour after hour, was not Brooks's idea of the best use of the young man's time and abilities. (Paul was not consulted, but would certainly have agreed.) In addition, there were always special projects evolving, Colonel to look after and put on display, tours of the plant to conduct, and the flamboyant distribution, by pony cart, of Sunday's newspaper. Very well, Brooks reasoned, if Paul was not suited for production work, he nonetheless wanted his protégé to learn all of the other aspects of the business of publishing. So Paul was made a novice or cub reporter, and started on a regimen of learning the art of journalism.

Brooks wanted to instill in young Block not just the rudiments of journalism, such as what kind of facts should be written into every story, or the elements of what makes a news story – such as timeliness, celebrity, and conflict – but also how to define and develop news judgment. It was the reporter's job to select from a vast variety of facts, he explained. If done properly, the end result would be a communication with the newspaper's audience, so that after reading the story they would be either more entertained, or informed, or educated...or possibly all three. Entertainment was an extremely important function of a Sunday newspaper, and Brooks wanted the *Telegram* to become known as a vehicle that would stimulate conversation among its readers, rather than necessarily chronicle more cerebral issues.

One of the first general assignments that Paul was given was to visit stores and businesses, government offices, and religious and social groups, attempting to seek out personal items about Elmira's citizenry, and craft the news about them into short sentences or paragraphs, such as:

- Chase, Hibbard & Co., millers, have started laying foundations for a city fire department engine house just east of their mill on West Water Street.
- The annual supper served by the gentlemen of the First Baptist Church was well attended. Dr. William Henry was voted the handsomest man. The program ended with a quartet singing *Silver Threads Among the Gold.*
- Thomas F. Fennell, a Cornell law student and football star, has been named coach of the Cincinnati University football team.

Paul would stay at the *Telegram* late at night, especially on Fridays and Saturdays, and after his and Brooks's work was complete, the older man would often open a bottle of ale, unwrap a sandwich, offer half of it to Paul together with a few Fig Newtons, and hold forth in a fairly structured but informal regimen of news sense education. When it grew extremely late, Brooks would finally accompany Paul home, walking along the misty banks of the Chemung, and continuing his tutelage all the way.[68]

Brooks had a daughter of his own, but he looked upon Paul as a member of the family, perhaps as the son that he never had. Paul reminded Brooks of himself as he remembered his past: a teenager struggling to succeed without the benefits of being born wealthy. (Brooks's father had owned a small general store.) Paul wanted to be everything that Brooks was, and the identification went beyond the newsroom and the publishing business.

Brooks had started a baseball team, the Elmira Babies, within months of the first issue of the *Telegram,* and eventually it became one of the strongest amateur teams in Chemung County. Elmira became baseball crazed in 1880 when one of Brooks's pitchers, Danny Richardson, was bought by the New York Giants and went on to star in the major leagues as a second baseman. In 1888, professional baseball came to Elmira with the formation of the Central League, and the Elmira Babies placed sixth in their first year of competition. Paul was a constant spectator at the games, especially those of the *Telegram*'s team – again, always accompanied by Colonel – and began to learn from Brooks the strategies of the game, in addition to the arcane terminology that accompanied it, such as a "fungo," a "portsider," a "Baltimore chop," and an "apple." Before long, Paul was named manager of his high school baseball team, the Elmira Free Academy, and he attended every game all over the county for several years. His love of baseball was genuine, but it was as much as a result of his respect and admiration for Brooks, as it was for his intrinsic attraction toward the dynamic of the game. This affection for baseball would remain with him for the rest of his life and eventually even permeate his business career.

When it came to specific coverage of a particular news event, Brooks was a bit more formal, and put his instructions in writing. For example, for an investigative article on a check forger who went by the names of Frank Jarvis and L.B. Osman, and who signed checks with the name of C.S. Northrop, Brooks sent the following memorandum (rare for editors even to this day) to Paul Block:

Elmira, N.Y. Aug. 23, 1894

Paul:

> Here is a story that I want you to work up. A fellow by the name of Frank Jarvis turned up in New York with a check made payable to his order signed by C. S. Northrop, commis-

sion merchant of Cochection, N.Y. This check was cashed
and deposited in New York Bank and sent on for collection.
This is only one of a hundred other checks that Jarvis succeeded in cashing in New York. New York banks forwarded
them to Binghamton Owego and Elmira banks...

Here are some things you want to work up: Find out whether
Jarvis or Osman or anybody else was registered at the hotel,
if there happens to be one in Cochection. If so, what day?
Find out from the landlord when he came, how long he stayed,
what kind of a looking rooster he was, what he said and how
he acted.

Look up Northrop if there is any such man there and ask
him what he knows about the matter and what he wants to
say on the subject.

See the postmaster [as to] whether any mail came for such
a fellow named Osman, [and] if so, why he gave it to a
stranger, when it was addressed to Osman, a banker of
Cochection. If he knew that there was any such a man there,
find out what kind of a looking duck came after the mail,
when it was, and what the fellow said, how he looked and
how many letters did he get? Also, whether he has heard
anything since or anything else in connection with the case
that you can get hold of.

H.S.B.[69]

Unfortunately for historical analysis, there is not one example of a by-
lined story written by Paul Block extant in the *Elmira Telegram*, since the
paper's policy and tradition, as was that of most newspapers in this country, was to publish stories anonymously, or at best with italicized initials
placed discreetly at the end of the story. Even the great Theodore Dreiser
never had a by-line during his newspaper career, which lasted from 1892
to 1895.[70] And Emile Zola, addressing the London Institute of Journalists in 1893, warned against the use of by-lines, indicating that journalists
should be anonymous so as to lessen their power and influence in society.

What *is* known is that Paul wrote a number of stories that were published in the *Telegram,* and even contributed poetry to the paper's editorial page. *A Child's Prayer At Christmas* was written in 1890, when he
was 15:

> Christmas is here and with it the joys
> Which usually come then to girls and boys.

There's one little lad I know very well
Awoke this morning with loud joyous yell.
For there b'side his bed, so neatly arrayed
Were each and all things for which he prayed.
His father was rich and that was the cause
He was not forgotten by Santa Claus.

Another I know: a poor little boy
Who also desired some present, some toy
"Oh, dear Santa Claus," prayed this little mite
"You came not last year so please come tonight.
My wants are but few, in fact I agree
Whatever you bring will satisfy me."

Next morn he awoke and quick with one bound
He jumped for his toys but not one be found.
He stood slightly awed, his face flushed to red
But soon he knelt down and silently said:

"Oh, dear Santa Claus, forgive me, I pray
For thinking that you should have come here today.
The people are many, the world is not small,
I ought to have known you can't think of all.
In fact, dear Santy, please don't think me bold
For saying I like you even more than of old.
For p'rhaps some sick girl, or crippled young lad
Received the presents that I should have had.
And maybe next year you'll have something for me."[71]

Three years later, when he was 18, the *Telegram* published the following poem, *Contentment:*

First of all, I beg Thee, Sire,
Give me health, my main desire,
Next, just make my conscience clear,
So not even Thee I'll fear.
Lend me strength, so I may give
To the humbler if they live.
If a fortune be in sight
On the road of wrong, not right –
Give me courage, then, I pray,
From the right path not to stray;
If success or fame be mine,

Let me feel the hand was Thine.
With these thoughts 'tis hard to see
How one can unhappy be.[72]

Both of these poems, although florid and overly sentimental in true nineteenth century, Victorian style, indicate a spiritual and compassionate Paul Block as a teenager. Subsequently, this humanitarian and philanthropic view of the world would permeate Block's later life and be the focus of a great many causes that he backed, and the genesis of most of the personal, business, and political relationships that he established.

As an acolyte journalist, Block had both strengths and weaknesses. He had no difficulty as a wordsmith; by the time he began writing for the *Telegram* virtually all traces of his German usage and syntax had been erased. His memory for names, places, dates and faces was practically eidetic. To prove his memory's strength, he often performed a parlor trick at parties, and sometimes even in the newsroom of the *Telegram*, in which several people would name up to ten items selected at random, such as "chair," "pencil," "window," etc. Someone would write down the name of the objects and number them. Paul would then recite the list, forward and backward, recall any item if given the number, and recite the number of any item called at random.[73]

His strong memory was an important adjunct to his growing journalistic skills, and this quality, combined with his familiarity of the Elmira citizenry, would seemingly have enabled him to report on municipal activities with great accuracy and aplomb. Yet he was not, at first, an excellent reporter. The difficulties he had as a journalist had nothing to do with ability but were because of his youth and his diminutive size. Brooks was reluctant to send Block on assignments to interview city officials, for example; he worried that this faircheeked boy, who was then in his mid-teens, didn't look more than 11 or 12. Although Brooks also acted paternally when he refused to send Paul on any assignments that involved crime or criminals, he was less concerned that the boy would not know how to handle himself than that he would be in actual jeopardy associating with unsavory characters.

The journalistic assignments that fell mostly to Paul Block, therefore, were those relatively safe events where he could put Colonel on display, and therefore be able to do double duty for the *Telegram*: promote the newspaper with an appearance of America's finest St. Bernard dog, and gather facts for a story that would eventually make its way onto the pages of the paper: for example, P.T. Barnum's Circus ("The Most Remarkable and Greatest of all Earthly Display!"); or coverage of the Chemung County Fair, which included not only horse races, foot races, balloon ascensions and parachute descents, but also the extraordinary display of "The Mountain of Human Flesh," Big John Lawes, Elmira's blacksmith, who weighed 640 pounds, and whose waist was said to be 7 feet, 5 inches in circumference.[74]

Stories about horses also seemed to be perfect Paul Block articles, perhaps because of his experience with leading and holding the reigns of Telegram Tom, and also because of his familiarity with Elmira's stables. Such untoward equine events made their way into the *Telegram's* pages: an arc light fell from its bracket and fatally shocked a horse pulling a Dr. Williamson's buggy;[75] a runaway horse pulling a sleigh ran onto the walkway of the Chemung Canal and injured a passerby;[76] another horse was killed when it fell through the planking of the Main Street bridge.[77]

One of the strangest horse stories that appeared in the *Telegram*, was typically un-bylined, although it may well have been written by Paul Block. It seems that one rainy night, a livery stable owner named Thomas Delant was driving a group of young ladies back to Elmira from a party at Strathmont. The coachman's umbrella accidentally fell on the horses, frightening them, and they dashed madly down Hoffman Street, swerving from side to side, with the coach almost overturning. Eventually, Delant gained control of the frightened animals and began dropping the young ladies off at their homes one by one. With only one passenger still in the carriage, it began careening again from one side of the street to the other, but this time without as much velocity or sideways motion as before. Eventually the coach stopped directly opposite Delant's house. The remaining young lady alighted, quite ruffled but unhurt, and began speaking to Delant. It was to no avail. Delant was dead, his body still erect on the driver's seat, the reigns still in his hands. It was believed that he had suffered a heart attack or a stroke at the time that the horses initially ran wild, and he had died shortly afterward.

In the same way that Paul Block approached his budding career at the *Telegram*, through as much hard work as he could tolerate, friendliness to as many people as possible, and loyalty to his employers, so did he follow the same pattern in his social life. He attended the birthday parties and other activities of his friends, traveled to Corning with his schoolmates to attend the theater, and went to dinners hosted by the Elks (Harry S. Brooks was the president of the local chapter) and other civic organizations. Paul was always on hand at the town bonfire on John Street every Independence Day, and he took part in his own family's rituals of anniversaries, religious holidays and occasional songfests. When his parents gave permission, he would attend the political parades often held in the evenings, with flaming torches and vivifying speeches a part of every campaign. He went on sleigh rides, partook of basket suppers, and ice skated on the Chemung or in frozen backyards. A contemporary profile of Paul Block would have portrayed him as an extremely bright, highly conscientious young man trying to simultaneously work his way up on the business and social ladders.

Compared to other immigrant children, Paul Block's early life was relatively secure. He was, after all, raised in a smallish town, away from the possibility of an impoverished and tortured existence in New York's Lower East Side ghetto. But although the Block family was not starving, they were certainly poor. John managed to earn enough to put food on the table, and as he expanded his ragpicking business to also sell junk and rubble and eventually feed for the town's horses and livestock, life became a bit more comfortable. All of the Block children *had* to work, however, and contribute to the expenses of the household. Max, who was older, made the most money and was the main contributor, and Molly, who worked in an office, also gave as much as she could. At first, Paul made a small salary and proudly gave virtually every cent to his parents. That he suffered pain, sorrow, or humiliation while growing up cannot be documented, but we can assume that as a Jew, an immigrant, and as the son of a ragpicker, he was probably looked down on by at least some of his more fortunate classmates and other citizens of Elmira.

Despite whatever hardships he knew, Paul seemed always to have been invigorated by a sense of possibility for achievement, stimulated perhaps by the immigrant's wish to achieve distinction in the New World, and tempered by the stark reality that his father was a ragpicker. No doubt he was also influenced by Harry Brooks, his mentor, who had prospered because of his talent and his hard work, and had overcome his own impoverished if not wholly modest beginnings. It is interesting to note that in the Elmira City Directory for the years 1884 to 1895, Paul's name is rarely mentioned as part of the Block clan, although all of the other children *are* listed. Was this an inadvertent omission, or does it perhaps indicate that he was living apart from his family by choice? Although he demonstrated throughout his later years that he dearly loved his parents, and he displayed a fierce affection toward his siblings, he began to somehow establish a life apart from them, perhaps only symbolically, while he was still in his teens.

Paul Block seemed to crave entrée into Elmira's society. Even as a boy, he actively sought acceptance by the more affluent people he came in contact with, first through his tenure as Colonel's collaborator, and later as a reporter. Paul's vigorous personality notwithstanding, it is altogether possible that one of the reasons he received so many invitations to social occasions was because of his association with Elmira's most glamorous business, the *Telegram*. Partygivers may have had the hope that their event would make its way into the society columns, especially if a staff reporter for the newspaper was on hand. Their hopes were not without justification. For example, after attending the 17th birthday party for his friend George Wyckoff, Paul wrote of the event in the *Telegram* in the sort of florid, grandiose language usually reserved for press releases:

> Mrs. Wyckoff and her son spared nothing to make this occasion a memorable and supremely happy one. The greetings of Mr. Wyckoff's young gentlemen friends were like the dews of heaven, thick in blessings, and the roses of friendship bloomed in the good wishes for a long life and many happy anniversaries in the future.[78]

Introduction to Advertising

Soon after a short apprenticeship in reporting, Paul Block, then only 16 years old, was made an advertising solicitor for the *Telegram*. Brooks felt that the young man's alertness and concentration, together with his natural friendliness ("Always on time, and anxious to work," said Brooks of his young ward. "Optimistic and enthusiastic. A true soldier – not a slacker.")[79] was what he needed on the *Telegram*. He reasoned that Paul's ability to initiate and sustain a pleasant conversation would make him a natural salesman, and that Paul would be particularly successful with prospective *local* advertisers. At that time, what was then called "foreign" advertising was handled for the *Telegram* by the A. Frank Richardson Co. in New York City. (The term "foreign" had no reference, actually, to ads originating in a foreign country. It referred to ads from areas other than Elmira, such as national advertisements which were placed in many newspapers throughout the United States.) At that time, no one on the *Telegram* staff needed to do very much with the foreign accounts except to accept the ads that arrived by mail or were brought by messenger or freight every day from New York City and other towns, and place them in the appropriate position in the newspaper. And classified advertising came in "over the transom," meaning that no sales effort or solicitation was needed on the part of the newspaper: people either walked into the offices of the *Telegram* with their classified ads in hand, or else mailed them in with the accompanying cash or check.

Only local advertising required sustained effort by *Telegram* staffers to acquire and service. The striking difference to the *Telegram* as to how the three basic forms of advertising were garnered and secured, was that local advertisers had to be visited, the competition addressed, and the potential clients *sold* on their decision and convinced to spend money by placing an ad in the newspaper. Who better than Paul Block, thought Brooks, to perform this function? Since Paul was well-known throughout the town because of his bicycle exploits and his flamboyant delivery of the *Telegram* by animal convoy (and his reflective renown through the courtesy of Colonel), his entry to and acceptance by the business folk of Elmira would be, if not guaranteed, at least eminently possible.

Paul's first task for the *Telegram* was to visit virtually every store and business in Elmira and to seek what was known as "Personals," small ads, sometimes consisting of only one sentence, that were announcements of life in the city, needed in the days before telephones, such as "Because of a death in the family, J.H. Hofstedder's will be closed this week," or "Mr. A.K. Smythe will be visiting Elmira on Wednesday, and remaining at Klaproth's until the weekend." Not only was he successful in selling many of these little advertisements, it helped him in establishing further contacts with business people who might be potential clients for further, larger advertisements.

Paul seemed to be born to the trade, possessing a remarkable aptitude for selling. Upon first meeting or talking to the potential client, he was sincerely friendly; he had a gift for putting people at ease, and was not afraid to make small talk to build instant rapport. He truly listened to the contingent advertiser, was realistic and positive in his dealings, and asked enough questions to determine what was really needed: The announcement of a sale? The need to move inventory? A desire to keep the store's or service's name in the mind of the newspaper buyer? He empathized with the customer's problems and attempted to alleviate them, whether it was lack of cash, loyalty to another publication, or the disbelief in the power of advertising itself. His success in securing new advertisers, and retaining previous advertisers for the *Telegram*, was almost instantaneous. In an editorial written some 25 years later, Brooks talked about why some young men succeed, and wove his story around his former errand boy

Paul Block, about whom he said he had always been personally and pro-
fessionally proud: "He had no rich relatives to back him and no financial
friends to aid him. He hadn't any 'pull' anywhere. But he possessed an
over-supply of the most valuable asset any man could possibly have:
'push.'"[80]

Although advertising solicitors are usually held responsible for certain
accounts, as each reporter must answer for specified news beats, in Paul's
case he seemed to infiltrate a variety of the businesses and areas of the
city, bringing in new accounts such as the Silsbee Furniture store on Lake
Street, and talking a clothing and housewares store about to go out of
business to take an ad. They bought a full-page advertisement announcing a storewide sale of everything from men's socks for three cents a pair
to large gray blankets for forty-nine cents each.[81]

Paul's strong memory, his ability to store a wide array of facts and
figures in his mind, came into practical use at this point in his life. He
remembered the names of all of his clients – as well as those of their
secretaries and assistants – could recite how many inches of advertising
space they had taken the week or month or year before, offered the up-to-
the-minute circulation of the *Telegram*, and could compare the advertising prices, lineage and circulation figures of all of his competitors.

As the turn of the century approached, the country entered a period of
nationwide financial readjustment and consumerism. Newspapers saw a
tremendous increase in the amount of advertising, and Paul Block seemed
to have entered a field filled with promise at precisely the most propitious
time. Some stores which had been inserting a half a column of advertising in the *Telegram* just a few years before Paul Block became involved
in advertising, suddenly began to use half-page or full-page advertisements. Individual manufacturers of patent medicines, some with preposterous claims of curative powers, were spending tens of thousands of
dollars in newspapers to market their nostrums. This patent medicine
craze was emerging from its infancy when Paul Block first became an
advertising salesman, and since most of it was placed on a national basis,
eventually running in newspapers all over the country, at first he really
didn't have anything to do with the trend, although it would directly affect his life some years later.

More and more companies began to experiment with advertising, in
attempts to sell everything from breakfast foods to laundry soaps, and
from baking powder to fancy cigarettes. The more advertisements appeared in the *Telegram*, the more they enticed other companies to try to

sell *their* products or services in the same way.[82] In general, business in Elmira was enhanced by the increasing amount of advertising in the *Telegram,* and the more businesses prospered, the more they would advertise. Approximately 50% of the *Telegram's* income came from advertising by the time that Paul Block joined the advertising staff.

From an editorial point of view, the great increase in the size and frequency of advertising often had an adverse effect on the more noble purposes of the American newspaper. Some publishers, as a result of greed or necessity, and sometimes both, did not increase the ratio of editorial or news matter to advertising if the amount of their advertising lineage grew. If a full-page advertisement came in to be published at the last minute, for example, it just simply replaced a full-page of news, thus diminishing the value of the paper to the community and to the public, but increasing the coffers of the publisher. Most newspapers opened their columns to any company that could pay the going rate, often disregarding the content and moral tone of the ad in order to make more profits.

Whitelaw Reid, editor of the *New York Tribune*, and successor of the great literary and political editor Horace Greeley, expressed at that time the viewpoint that newspapers should actually limit their advertising space:

> True policy, it seems to me, would dictate that advertisements should occupy as limited space as possible. If they become too numerous, instead of enlarging the paper, and thus weary the reader with a dreary mass of unattractive printed matter, the price of advertising should be increased, so that where an advertisement before took a stickful, it may now be reduced to half the space and pay the same money.[83]

Although the *Telegram* did have a policy of increasing the amount of its editorial and news columns in proportion to the amount of advertising in any given issue of the newspaper, Brooks was not adverse to accepting what was known as "reading notices," in its most dignified form of usage, and called "puffery" by those who worked for the newspaper. These were paid advertisements, disguised as news accounts but charged for at a premium price, set in the same type and headline style that genuine news stories were in the *Telegram*. Sometimes they even appeared on the front page, with the company's product name buried deep within the text of the column so that readers might peruse the entire "story" before they determined that they had just been given a sales pitch. The story might go something like this: some man met with a terrible accident – perhaps he was thrown from his horse – and was about to die, when someone in the crowd thought of a remarkable remedy, ran to the local pharmacy and returned with a bottle of an elixer, administered a dose, and the injured victim was cured in a few moments – and so on. Almost all of these reading notices were lurid and florid, but they generated sales; the patent medicine manufacturers began to amass fortunes.

Occasionally, these paid reading notices were distinguished by a typo-graphical signal of some sort, usually a rule, star or dagger at the top or bottom of the column, but more frequently there was no sign to indicate to the reader that the account had been bought and paid for and was not a regular news item. Thus readers thought they were reading actual news accounts that told, along with a news story, how wonderful a given prod-uct had been for the person or people in the story. In response, large numbers of readers went out and purchased the product. Reading notices were so effective in stimulating sales that Brooks began to use them as a means to increasing the *Telegram's* advertising revenue. If a client pur-chased a large amount of regular advertising space, the *Telegram* threw in a reading notice for free.

Whether Brooks's editorial and news columns in the *Telegram* were influenced by the dictates of advertisers, other than the acceptance of reading notices, is not now known, but since he was a moral man with a deep sense of ethics, he probably refused to sacrifice the freedom of his press and remained fairly independent in not allowing the whims and desires of his advertisers to reach his editorial pages.

Paul Block's conscientiousness assumed many forms. He voraciously read all of the competing Elmira newspapers so that he could confront their strengths and weaknesses, and be able to point out the disadvan-tages of placing advertising with rival publications. His brief stint at typesetting helped him in discussing the possible layout and design of the ads with potential clients; his experience with words and his command of the language, reflected in the poems that he had written and had pub-lished, also helped him as an "adsmith" in roughing out the text of a possible advertisement.

Paul would razor-out ads from competing Elmira newspapers and bring them to potential advertisers with the suggestion that the *Telegram* could make up a more attractive ad and publish it at competitive rates.

Early on in the history of the *Telegram*, from about 1890, Brooks es-tablished a sales policy that forbade any kind of secret negotiations, re-bates or special discounts to be passed on to the advertiser. All of the

Telegram's advertising rates were clearly printed on the newspaper's rate card, and advertising salesmen such as Paul Block were warned not to promise the potential advertiser anything other than the published rates. Each advertiser, Brooks advised, was entitled to know what circulation he was to receive for his money, and whether he was going to receive as low a rate as any other advertiser in the newspaper. In Brooks's philosophy of publishing, newspapers were common carriers for the community's good, and advertising should be sold for a uniform price to everyone who wanted to avail themselves of the service. But his beneficient concept was not always easy for his salesmen to implement.

The difficulty for a newspaper advertising solicitor in maintaining a strict adherence to the published advertising rates, is that in a competitive market, the potential advertiser may simply refuse to buy space in a particular newspaper unless he is given a discount or a special deal of some sort. Since Brooks would not entertain giving an advertiser a discount on the rates, Paul Block was forced to produce or suggest other incentives in order to sell advertising space, and eventually he did convince Brooks to allow him to "sell" preferred placement, i.e., if a potential advertiser was reluctant to buy space, Paul would offer him the front page, back page or editorial page for his advertisement, for example, at no extra charge. Paul also helped to create a policy that enabled him to actually offer a cash discount for any advertisement that was paid for in advance.

Some of the stories about Paul Block's cleverness in selling advertising cannot be confirmed and are apocryphal but they sound consistent with his style and personality and are worth the telling. One story has him in the office of the manager of an Elmira variety store, together with the advertising solicitors of three other newspapers. The manager was trying to determine in what paper he would advertise. He asked Paul first to give him the circulation of the *Telegram*. "One hundred eighty thousand," Paul answered proudly. The second solicitor then gave the circulation of his newspaper as 200,000. The third mentioned 210,000, and the final ad salesman claimed that his newspaper had a circulation of 225,000. "What do you think of those figures?" the manager asked Paul. "Well," he replied, "If I had been asked *last*, my circulation would have been 250,000!" The *Telegram* received the contract for the advertising because of Paul's cynical honesty.

Another anecdote has Paul trying to sell a tavern owner on taking an ad in the *Telegram*; the man had been advertising in another Elmira publication for years and was satisfied with his results. Trying to come up with an idea that would reach his potential client, Paul noticed that the rival newspaper contained many more obituaries and death notices than the *Telegram.* "Don't you want to stay in business?" asked Paul of the tavern owner. When told that of course he wanted his business to prosper, Paul responded, "Well, you'll go out of business if you continue advertising where you are." Handing the man a copy of the rival newspaper, he pointed: "Look at all of these death notices. Their readers are dying! Our readers are alive and well!" As the story goes, Paul made another sale.

In the spring of 1892, Colonel began to act sluggish, ate very little, and seemed not to be interested in being taken anywhere by Paul. A noted veterinarian was called in to look after the dog, and he was taken to Gloversville for care in the vet's kennels. Colonel grew more and more sickly, and eventually died on June 2nd. He was only six years old. The *Telegram* ran an obituary on the dog, "Farewell Colonel," and mentioned that although all of the children of Elmira would remember patting his shaggy and friendly head, no one would miss him more than his "Chaperone...Paul Block."[84]

Colonel's death marked the end of Paul's childhood at the *Telegram.* His entire focus was now on the advertising department of the paper. In an attempt to be as creative as possible in his position of advertising so-licitor, Paul convinced Brooks to advertise the *Telegram's* own printing and engraving service. Most newspaper publishers were also open for private printing jobs at that time, and Paul came up with a three-inch-by-one-inch column advertisement that displayed some of the possible type styles that could be used by businesses interested in having their printing done by the *Telegram.*

Paul also initiated another idea for the Telegram's self-promotion. He made use of his flair for poetry and came up with the following "house" advertisement, which Brooks ran in the *Telegram* again and again:

PAUL'S POETIC POINTERS

Perhaps you don't know where to buy
Fresh meats, good Cigars or fine Pie?
Pray don't bother your head at all,
Our BUSINESS DIRECTORY shows it all.

If you wish some nice Custom shirts,
Good liquors or Drugs, that cure hurts,

Barbers, perhaps, to cut your hair?
Our BUSINESS DIRECTORY shows you where.

Or pictures to hang on the wall,
Architects to enlarge your hall;
Or books to teach your children dear,
Our BUSINESS DIRECTORY has them here.

When after candy, pure and sweet,
Hotels or Cafes where to eat;
Or a place to shoe your horse quite well,
Our BUSINESS DIRECTORY sure will tell.

If for Real Estate or Money,
Stereopticon lectures funny,
Livery or Doctor to call.
Our BUSINESS DIRECTORY prints them all.

If children grown more knowledge
Send them to the Business College;
When your goods you must Express,
Our BUSINESS DIRECTORY gives address.

When plumbing in your home you want,
Locksmith or Harnessmaker hunt,
Or Hardware store you're looking for,
Our BUSINESS DIRECTORY shows the door.

When for a Milliner you must call,
Or hack to take you to the ball,
Don't look for them until you're lame,
Our BUSINESS DIRECTORY has the name.

When your Saw you would like to file,
Or pictures get of latest style,
Or piano you'd like to buy,
Our BUSINESS DIRECTORY won't be shy.

Last, yet not least, if one should die,
Coffins and tombstones you must buy;
Don't bother about where to go,
Our BUSINESS DIRECTORY it will show.[85]

Though Paul Block was clearly Brooks's protégé, the publisher also took an interest in another intelligent young employee of the *Telegram*. He began to tutor Herman G. Halsted, a bright young man who had become a close friend of Paul's. At first, Halsted had little interest in the business side of publishing, wanting to learn the intricacies of journalism. Halsted was three years older than Paul Block, and looked more mature for his age, so Brooks first tried him out as a cub reporter. The boy did well, and was always reliable in getting the story in on time, but Brooks believed that he really would do better in the sales department. One day Brooks called Halsted into his office and said, "Herman, if you stay in this game long enough you may [someday] earn $25 a week as a city editor. You had better get into the business end of the game."[86] After working as a *Telegram* journalist for several years, and then being promoted to City Editor, nevertheless, Halsted was eventually transferred to the Sales Department to work alongside the more experienced, albeit younger, Paul Block. The two young men became true colleagues – they had always been friends – and when Paul was eventually named Advertising Director of the *Telegram*, Herman showed no resentment at all and enjoyed working with his new boss.

Under the directorship of Paul Block, advertising lineage in the *Telegram* flourished. As part of the *Telegram's* promotion, it began to advertise itself as, "The best advertising medium between the ocean and the Great Lakes." Although the newspaper still continued to sell relatively small ads, for everything from wedding rings to playing cards, it was Paul and his staff who convinced Elmira businesses to begin placing their advertisements more frequently, and to buy space for larger, more impressive ads. He convinced one client, a clothing and shoe establishment called The Five Normile Brothers, that repeat advertising would have a cumulative effect on their customers. As a result, the merchant took a 1/3 page ad (with illustrations of each brother) almost every Sunday; and Paul persuaded McLaren Brown & Co., a dry-goods store, that even though they were about to go out of business, they would minimize their losses if they took out full-page ads that announced the closing of their store.

Paul was also the first advertising salesman on the *Telegram* to secure what became known as "co-op" money for some of his advertisers. He would go to a manufacturer or a distributor and get them to pay one of their retailers a portion of the money that the retailer was going to spend for an advertisement, with the agreement that the manufacturer's product was prominently displayed in the ad. For example, he interested the manufacturer of a rubber boot to pay for part of the 2/3rd page ad placed by the Five Brothers Shoe Store. Although the advertisement was intended to draw customers into the store, it showed an illustration of the boot, thereby benefiting both the retailer and the manufacturer. Other advertising money became available as Paul established this type of two-pronged strategy wherever possible: to the retailer who wanted to increase traffic in his store, and to the manufacturer who wanted more exposure, and more sales, of his product.

Paul developed a few personal rules that he felt were mandatory for good salesmanship – indeed, for the successful conduct of any business. He urged his salesmen to memorize the first names of every potential client, and to address those people accordingly. That habit came naturally to him because he felt it was an important adjunct to salesmanship. He had a penchant for impeccable dress, a characteristic learned from the immaculate Harry S. Brooks. Paul's hair was always carefully combed and parted, and his shoes were perfectly shined. (These were attributes he maintained throughout his life.) But Paul's sales ability went far beyond a cosmetic approach to ingratiation. Through Brooks's constant mentorship, and Paul's attentiveness, study, research, and the business relationships that he was making almost daily, Paul was fast becoming an expert in the professional technique of retailing and selling. He analyzed the operation and merchandising methods of each business upon which he called. In relatively short order, businesses were asking Paul what products, and at what prices, should be advertised.

In 1888 and 1889 two events occurred that greatly propelled the *Telegram's* advertising lineage forward. The first was a huge fire that destroyed the *Elmira Daily Advertiser* building at Lake and Market Streets. The newspaper, which was one of the *Telegram's* most rabid competitors, moved into temporary quarters (ironically the former building of the *Telegram,* which had moved to larger quarters) and after a short hiatus began publishing again, but not before losing several important retail advertisers to the *Telegram.* Shortly after that, the worst flood ever to descend upon Elmira occurred when the banks of the Chemung swelled and the waters inundated the downtown area. The Elmira *Advertiser* was forced to stop publishing altogether since their presses, which were in the cellar of their new building, were submerged under water. The second cessation of publishing by the *Advertiser,* although it lasted barely more than a month, was all that the *Telegram* needed to make even greater advertising advances since many of the retailers who were loyal to the *Advertiser* now began placing their ads regularly in the *Telegram* and remained with them for years to come.[87] A further bitter pill for the *Advertiser* was that until they could dry out and repair their printing presses, they were forced to rent the *Telegram's* presses, adding to their rival's coffers and incurring substantial printing bills.

All of the successful advertising activity and diligence by Paul Block did not go unnoticed by Harry S. Brooks or by others. As the advertising lineage of the *Telegram* grew month by month under Paul's leadership, Brooks realized that his ward's earning power and potential income was limited if he remained with the *Telegram* for any substantial period of time. The executives of the Richardson Company had always been impressed with the young man, and one day when A. Frank Richardson was visiting Elmira, Brooks and he discussed the possibility of Paul moving to Manhattan to work as a publisher's representative for Richardson. Although Brooks realized it would be a great loss for the *Telegram*, he did not want to discourage Paul's possibility for much greater personal success if he moved to New York City. The Stock Market crash of 1893, followed by the worst depression in the history of the country until that time, began to erode the *Telegram's* advertising lineage and although the economy recovered, Brooks felt that Paul's chances of financial security in a larger market such as New York should be seized.

By 1895 national newspaper advertising was coming into its own, and many newspapers established branch offices or worked through a special type of company which represented them for the purpose of selling space to advertisers. These special representatives, located almost invariably in fairly large cities, would contact advertising agency space buyers, account executives and advertisers directly in an attempt to interest them in buying advertising for the newspapers they represented. Richardson believed that Paul Block could become an excellent special representative for this relatively new kind of selling and representation, and with Brooks's blessing, Paul was offered the job.

Although Paul Block was just 20 (at that time the life expectancy for American males was only 43), this was a key point in his career. He already had almost ten years experience with the *Telegram,* and had gained extensive knowledge and direct practical application of newspaper advertising sales. He also had been to New York a number of times for special promotions with Colonel and on other occasions as well, and had developed a love for the rapidly growing, ever rushing city. It was not farfetched for Richardson and Brooks to assume that Paul stood an excellent chance for success working for a national representation company located in New York City.

Every family has prize kin, and Paul was the favored of all of the Blocks: although he would be missed once he was living several hours away by rail from the family, it was John and Mary's belief that he should not be stopped if he wanted to make a move. Paul knew he would miss his family and friends, but the call to industry was clarion. He had had enough of the provincialism of Elmira and a feeling of shame attached to his father's work, and sensed that the town could not provide the success and prestige that his growing ambition demanded. He could barely wait to escape. New York City would become his new home, not only because he would live there, but because it is where he could transform himself and it would be where he felt he would be understood.

Chapter 2
The Birth of
National Advertising

Confronting New York City

When Paul Block moved to New York City in September of 1895, he was like many young men of any time, of any era: filled with purpose and aspirations, wanting to make his mark. Without such ambitions, his ultimate success would have been much less probable. But luck helps, too, as does good timing. Paul's early manhood, and the outset of his career, occurred at an exceedingly fortuitous time. He entered the field of national advertising sales near its outset, when brand names were just beginning to be recognized, and thus sold nationwide, and when retailers and business people were coming to recognize the power of advertising to help them market their products and services. He also brought with him the conviction that someday he would own a newspaper, perhaps one as large and as prosperous as the *Elmira Telegram*, and he believed that New York was the most logical place to begin his assault on achieving that goal. It was an auspicious time and an unparalleled place to commence a career in advertising and publishing.

New York City in 1895 was already the locus of the same types of dreams and aspirations that the city engenders a century later. As a talented, highly ambitious, perhaps even driven young man, Paul Block gravitated to New York as the cosmopolitan Mecca, only to find that he was not alone in his conceit. What Block found in Manhattan were immigrants streaming into the city by the hundreds of thousands, their belongings often limited to the contents of a suitcase or a cardboard box. In contrast, the marble and limestone mansions along Fifth Avenue were populated by New York's opulent class, where a new word, "millionaire," was beginning to be used to describe the inhabitants who were born to, or who had recently arrived at the pinnacle of business-generated wealth. New York City was said to have over a thousand such million-aires alone.[1] These merchant princes were America's royalty, amassing fortunes that heretofore were the province of kings. People began to refer to Manhattan as the Empire City, because of its splash and glitter, its literal silk-stockinged extravagance; the lure for wealth must have been if not overwhelming to Paul, at least stimulating and galvanic.

This was the period that would be aptly called the Gay Nineties, due to the wealth and merriment that the city found itself in after the reconstruc-tion following the Civil War. The second Madison Square Garden, de-signed by Stanford White, had just opened and the mightiest of New York business and society, the elite "400" – exactly the capacity of Mrs. Astor's ballroom, with the implication that only 400 people were worth knowing – came to be seen in its beautiful roof garden, and to cluck over Saint Gaudens' scandalous gold Diana, topping the tower, naked to the waist, ready to shoot an arrow into every young man's imagination. Vaudeville flourished on Broadway and on the Bowery; burlesque and melodrama were at their apogee, and images of the shapely Gibson Girl, drawn by famed illustrator Charles Dana Gibson, seemed to be on billboards and in newspapers and magazines everywhere, personifying the fashionable world and the gaiety of extravagance and vitality of 1890's New York City.

The gaslight pleasures of a would-be aristocracy were in extreme con-trast to the poverty that engulfed the multitude. Immigrants and others worked 72-hours a week, sleeping beneath their sewing machines in in-human sweatshops, often with their families at their sides. New York had developed a netherworld of slum existence, where more than a million people lived in the suffocating warren of some 43,000 tenement houses, crowded, airless, and befouled structures that more than anything else became the icon of big city America at the turn of the century. Thousands of homeless children roamed the streets. There were not, as yet, any public high schools in New York City. Many people not only recalled the horrible Draft Riots of 1863, but some had participated in or observed them and would recount the pillage of those dispirited days.

The sheer numbers of people on the streets of New York was awesome; it was a city of crowds. The clack, clatter and clopping on the cobble-stone streets of horse-drawn hackney-coaches, broughams, and victorias with steel-rimmed wheels added to the cacophony. There were already, it was said, over one million foreigners living in New York, hundreds of thousands of Irishmen – twice as many as in all of Dublin – and more Italians than there were in Rome.[2] One section of the city, from the East River to Third Avenue and from 14th Street south to Catherine Street, was then the most densely populated area on earth.[3] The island of Manhattan was a true metropolis, or quickly becoming one, despite the fact that there was not yet one traffic cop in all of New York, although there were 4,000 patrolmen who protected the two million inhabitants. There were still more than 2,000 farms spread throughout the city. Compared to Elmira, it was a town of immense speed. The rattle of the coaches, and the din of the populace never seemed to quiet down. The smell of the horses and their leavings, and the pungent odor of soap, leather, and axle grease from the carriages constantly penetrated the air of the city.

Paul had planned for his move to New York with as much care as was practical. Once he made the decision to leave the *Telegram*, he began focusing on his life in New York. Elmira, despite its comparatively small size, nonetheless contained different neighborhoods defined by the wealth of its residents. The dichotomy of New York's neighborhoods was even greater. During previous visits to the city, Paul had seen some of the tenements and slums, mainly on the Lower East Side and in midtown near the East River. Despite the fact that that midtown neighborhood would be much closer to his place of employment, he knew he didn't want to live there. Ironically, tenements on the Lower East Side were relatively expensive (a three-room apartment there cost between $8 to $12 a month), but worse, they were degrading, and Paul sought to improve his status, not lower it.

The best area to find an affordable, yet bearable place to live, he learned, was in the relatively northwest section of the city. Since Manhattan's first settlements had been on the southern tip of the island, near Wall Street, every successive wave of population had expanded the city northward. Lord and Taylor had opened the city's first department store in 1867, on Sixth Avenue and 21st Street. Now businesses and shops filled much of the West Side up through the 30s.

Many German immigrants, disillusioned by the brawling residents and dilapidated conditions of the Lower East Side, moved due north to the Yorkville section of the city or to Harlem.[4] Others chose the less expensive Upper West Side. The West Side was not as affluent as the East Side but it was vibrant and, along most of its length, it contained many if not most of the city's private schools, libraries, colleges, department stores, boarding houses and museums.

Paul rented a modest furnished room on West 70th Street, between Columbus Avenue and Broadway, but he found it difficult to sleep at first because of all of the noise, especially the shrieks of the locomotive whistle of the nearby Columbus Avenue El train, and the grinding rattling as it rumbled along its trestle. Ironically, the newsboys in the streets added to the clamor with their evocative cries of "Uxtry! Uxtry!" a familiar refrain for Block. Not so far in the future, he would hire thousands of similar boys to deliver the newspapers he would eventually own.

Paul realized quickly that the Upper West Side was far more than just an economic convenience. Here, he could take a stroll in the evenings, quite late, and find restaurants and hotels and woman-less saloons still open and doing a thriving business. The wide and extended avenue, Upper Broadway, then called the Boulevard, with huge apartment houses and hotels going up seemingly on every corner, and with its center mall of flowers and shrubbery, took on something of an American version of the Champs Elysées. Here, women in their finery strolled with their male companions in straw boaters, as they deftly stepped aside of the speeding horse-drawn phaetons and bicycles sailing past them in the streets.

Developers changed the name of 11th Avenue to that of West End Avenue (north of 72nd Street), hoping to make the street and the whole Upper West Side seem more like London's then-posh West End.[5] As Paul walked in the evenings, the streets were newly illuminated by Edison's incandescent lamps, of which Block would write years later "outranked in importance such wonders as the phonograph, the motion picture, the multiple telegraph, and others of his inventions which have changed the whole course of civilization."[6] Music drifted out of saloons or hotels or restaurants: they were sweet and lively tunes, such as "Sweet Rosie O'Grady," "There'll Be a Hot Time in the Old Town Tonight," "A Bird in a Gilded Cage," and "Ta-Ra-Ra-Boomderee!" Sometimes a pianist played the easily singable songs. At other times, they were produced by the increasingly popular player pianos. Children organized games in the streets: Ringalevio, Kick-the-Wicket, Blind Man's Buff and I-Spy-the-Wolf were played until late at night. Adolescents, playing incessant games of stickball in the streets and alleys, used stationary moorings – hitching posts, poles, porches – to represent the pitcher's mound, the bases, and home plate. Their games were intermittently stopped whenever a horse-drawn wagon drove across the playing field, or a pedestrian innocently wandered through.

The Upper West Side was highly populated with German Jews, and there were German and Jewish restaurants, coffee shops, bakeries, ice cream parlors, and synagogues every few blocks. Little German oom-pah-bah bands, dominated by tuba, trombone and trumpet players, would roam the streets and stand on corners bleating out music from the Old Country. Beer gardens with long open-air tables and benches were scattered all over the area; between steins, customers would join in unison and sing German drinking songs. The number of Jews in Manhattan in 1898 was estimated at 250,000, making it the largest center of Judaism in the world.[7] There was virtually only one foreign language (other than the Latin and Hebrew offered in parochial schools) that was taught in New York City high schools: German. Although Paul did not engage in a deeply religious or nationalistic life, nevertheless, living near people who shared a similar background made him feel comfortable and accepted, despite the fact that he was all too eager to renounce the ways of the Old World and all of its pieties. E. Idell Zeisloft, an Upper West Side author, wrote at the time:

> The dwellers here are not as a rule of the old and historic New York families, or very wealthy as a class, but all are people exceedingly well to do. A fair proportion of them are Hebrews and many are former residents of other cities who have found here the best value for their money.[8]

Paul considered himself fortunate in having a job that engendered a certain amount of respect and afforded him the potential to make a considerable amount of money. Many German Jews at that time, who had been lawyers, teachers and professional people in Europe, were forced to accept work as bartenders, house painters and common laborers.

People all over the city began traveling to their jobs as early as 4 AM.[9] They had to. Fourteen and sixteen-hour days were not uncommon at that time. New York City policemen worked unbearable 18-hour shifts, seven days a week, and unfortunately would end up doing quite an amount of sleeping on the job. Newspaper carriers reported to their offices as early as 4 AM and were on the streets shortly after that, expected to sell or deliver upwards of 500 newspapers each morning.[10] Because of all of this activity, Paul rarely went to sleep before three in the morning, a habit he would never be able to break, and never wanted to. A writer at that time tried to capture the Dickensian flavor of Little Old New York, and it's not unlikely that Paul Block would have agreed with the sentiment:

> New York. It's the great metropolis to all Americans, the
> abiding place of all the marvels that made the fame of ancient
> Baghdad, the Superb. For the stranger, at least, romance lurks
> in every doorway and vice, horrible yet fascinating, stalks in
> all the byways. Life is freer, wickeder, bolder here than any-
> where else. Crowds, the rapid pace, and the everlasting
> struggle, whether for supremacy or mere existence seem to
> create a different sort of being from those who amble through
> life in the smaller town. For the outlander there is always the
> thrill of excitement in the very atmosphere of the Colossus.[11]

Like just about every other Upper West Sider who could afford to own,
rent or borrow a bicycle on Sunday afternoons, Paul would often ride a
"silent steed," as they were called, along the pathways of Riverside Park.
"Bikes" even then cost about $100, beyond Block's reach, and ten per-
cent of all national advertising was for bicycles. Bicycling had become
one of the most popular pastimes in New York, partially because there
was not much else to do on Sundays since the Blue Laws had not only
shut down the saloons, but the museums, racetracks, vaudeville houses
and ballparks, as well. Also, as more streets and park paths became paved
with a smooth macadam, it was easier to glide along on a bike at a fairly
speedy pace. As Paul was becoming more and more interested in women,
he would smile at those ladies in bloomers and those who were forced to
raise their skirts – normally held down by small lead weights sewn into
the hems – several inches above the ankle, to insure that the fabric would
not become entangled in the chain or spokes. In those days, just that little
flash of exposed ankle was enough to stimulate a young man's fancy.
Some of the public were outraged that the bloomer girls did not sport
what they considered proper feminine cycling attire.

Working on Park Row

Building and construction was profuse in the New York of 1895 and
the term "skyscraper" – a word that had been used to describe the exceedingly tall masts of some ships – was just coming into its own. Streets
seemed always to be ripped up with one or another construction project.
The Richardson Co. was located downtown on Park Row, on the corner
of Nassau and Spruce Street, in the Tribune Building, one of the first so-
called skyscrapers. A large eight-story edifice that was past its days of
glory, it had been built in 1873, and was at that time the tallest office
building in New York City, its Florentine campanile tower exceeded in

height by only one other structure in the city, that of Trinity Church with its soaring spire. At 260 feet, built of red brick and gray stone, with a patinae copper roof, it had an impressive entrance staircase and an imposing clock tower that did not quite dominate the skyline, that accolade going to a massive skyscraper with a golden dome that was owned by *The World*.

The Tribune Building, at 154 Nassau Street, housed the *New York Tribune*, one of the city's most prestigious newspapers and the nation's leading organ of Republican opinion. Just behind the building was the famed Mergenthaler Linotype Company; its front windows faced Printing House Square, which was noted, fittingly and symbolically, for Ernst Plassman's bronze statue of Benjamin Franklin holding a copy of his Pennsylvania Gazette in hand as a moral beacon to all of the publishers along Newspaper Row. All of the important daily newspapers in New York – 17 of them, some now forgotten – were in the Park Row area at that time. In addition to the *Tribune* were the *Sun*, *The Times*, *The World*, the *Star*, the *Mail & Express*, the *Commercial Advertiser*, the *Daily News*, the *Evening Telegram*, the *Press*, the *Recorder*, and the *Journal*. Of the major New York City papers, only James Gordon Bennett's *Herald*, located in what had been Dodge Square and recently named Herald Square, had moved from the area.

Also on Park Row, just one block away from the large metropolitan dailies and nearer to Chatham Square, was the center of the foreign language press, dominated by many German-language newspapers, a few Chinese publications and even a Swedish daily. But for Paul Block, Park Row was more than just a location, more than New York's rendition of Fleet Street. It was almost hallowed ground for newspapermen, the locale where such legends as Horace Greeley and William Cullen Bryant and Joseph Pulitzer had distinguished themselves in the publishing industry, the place where journalists from many parts of the country, such as the renowned Richard Harding Davis, David Graham Phillips, Theodore Dreiser and Stephen Crane gravitated to because talent was quickly discovered and rewarded there. Fortunes and reputations could be made...and demolished just as quickly. It was said that if a journalist wished to gather experience and knowledge of the world, in addition to developing expertise in writing, one year on Park Row was more than equivalent to four years in college.[12] Block found his university, his new place of business, and his new home in Park Row.

Park Row had seen the Tribune Building nearly destroyed during the

Draft Riots of 1863, when twenty-two of the rioters, who were calling for
Horace Greeley's head because of his abolitionist sentiments, were killed;
and where *The New York Times* put in a revolving cannon and laid in a
store of rifles in the editorial office for their journalists to ward off any
invasion of the mob.[13] So dominant in the consciousness of New Yorkers
was the world of Park Row newspapers that when the circulation of *The
New York World* reached an unprecedented 100,000 copies in 1885, a
celebration was held in nearby City Hall Park: thousands of spectators
gathered to watch while a cannon was fired one hundred times, once each
for every thousand copies.[14] In honor of the event, each employee of *The
World* was given a tall silk hat. By the time Paul Block arrived in New
York, the circulation of *The New York World* had risen to more than
500,000, a readership so great at the time that it was over 100,000 more
than the combined circulations of the *Herald*, the *Telegram*, the *Sun*, *The
Times*, the *Tribune*, the *Evening Post*, the *Mail & Express*, the *Commercial Advertiser*, and the *Morning Journal*. [15]

Horace Greeley had been dead for more than twenty years, having left
the *Tribune* to the management of Whitelaw Reid, the tall, suave and
cultured Ohioan, by the time Paul first went to work at the Tribune Building. But Greeley's presence was visible: Each morning, Paul would give
silent obeisance to a large bronze statue of Horace Greeley, seated in a
characteristic pose, as if he were engaged in a heated, or perhaps enlightened conversation, perched at the front entrance of the Tribune Building.

Virtually all of the support services that were needed to help the vibrant
newspaper industry at that time were located near Park Row, and added
to the neighborhood's color: stables and blacksmiths for the horses and
delivery wagons, and wooden shacks for the bicycle outriders who sped
in front of the horses shouting to make way; paper distributors, legions of
newsboys and assorted urchins, most of whom slept for five cents a night
at the Newsboy's Lodging House at 49 Park Place atop the old *Sun* building; advertising agencies just coming into their own; typesetting and printing machinery equipment companies, and as in the case of the Richardson
Co., virtually all – some seventy-five – of the publisher's representatives
of newspapers from around the country. A vaporous odor of printing ink,
beer and whiskey from the saloons that bordered the newspaper offices,
and the droppings of the delivery horses, was overpowering. There was a
beer saloon in the basement of the Tribune Building, where it was rumored, more stories were hatched and written than in the newsroom upstairs.

It was to this nucleus of journalism, the heart and history of the newspaper business, that Paul Block would travel each day by the newly-opened elevated line on Columbus Avenue, with cars propelled by a steam engine which rained sparks down on the horses and pedestrians below. When he could afford the time, he would occasionally opt to journey downtown by horse-drawn streetcar or trolley along Broadway. Upon arriving at the Tribune Building, he would bypass the caged elevator and simply go the first floor offices of A. Frank Richardson and plunge into the business of being a special publisher's representative. The female secretaries of the company were permitted to keep their skirts no higher than three inches off the floor, since it was not carpeted.

Although the telephone had been invented some twenty years before, there were few such instruments at the *Elmira Telegram*, so Paul was a bit surprised to find telephones – although they were difficult to hear through, or to be heard – to be in such widespread use in many of the offices in Manhattan. The first long-distance call in this country had been made just two years before. Telephone wires, not yet hidden underground, were stretched and crisscrossed, like intrusive black webs, from building to building all throughout lower Manhattan. The reporters, editors and people who worked in Block's office who used the telephone were unsure as to what to say when they received an incoming call and picked up the receiver. Some said, "Go ahead." Others used such phrases as "I'm ready," or "Can you hear me?" Finally the simple word "Hello" – although it seemed too abrupt for some – seemed to be the most efficient way to answer. Eventually Block would learn to master the instrument to help knit together the Richardson Company with the newspapers and advertisers they represented. The mimeograph machine, the Dictaphone, the addressograph, and other mechanical devices were coming in to common use. Unfamiliar to him at first, they ultimately made office work easier. Typewriters so revolutionized the newspaper and related industries that they changed the ways people worked, and they brought about a change in hiring practices. Considered "gender-neutral," typewriters became acceptable for women to operate; thus women began to be hired to assume clerical jobs that had previously been held by men. The women were not called secretaries; they were known as "type-writers." A few typewriter machines then began to appear in the newsrooms. They were used by reporters and business staff alike. But although typewriters – Remingtons for the most part – were beginning to be used more and more frequently in the newsrooms, and were saving composition costs because the copy was easier for the typesetter to read, there were some editors and reporters who objected to them, claiming that a journalist who used a typewriter would sacrifice a certain freedom of style, because he would begin to lean on what would become a mechanical or rote habit.[16] Mechanical advances did make major inroads into the industry, however. The large printing presses that were in use by most of the newspapers could print and fold 90,000 4-page papers in an hour, and metal printing type that Paul as a boy used to set by hand was now set by the linotype machine (first used in the same building that Block then worked, as far back as 1886) though still character by character.[17]

The Richardson Company was a relatively large corporation. It represented more than 1600 newspapers throughout the United States, from North and South Dakota to St. Louis and Des Moines. Some of these newspapers were small in circulation, but represented the only contact with the public in their area that national advertisers could use to reach potential buyers of their products or services; other newspapers that Richardson represented, such as the *Seattle Post-Intelligencer*, the *Louisville-Courier Journal*, the *Kansas City Star* and the *Memphis Commercial Appeal*, dominated the circulation and readership in their respective medium-sized cities.[18] Paul Block not only had to become quickly schooled in the advertising rates and requirements of these publications, but he had to learn their political preferences, their editorial positions and their geographical predilections, so that he could intelligently discuss the client's needs and wants, without insulting their partisanships. He had to understand every point regarding make-up and design of ads, circulation, and specific policies of the newspapers that he would represent so that he could successfully combat any argument that may be brought forward by a prospective advertiser. He was instructed by Richardson never to make a second call on an advertiser without having a new idea, something of interest to present to his prospect.[19] Additionally, someone in the office would collect dozens of rival newspapers every morning, and any new advertisements that might have appeared were clipped and given to Paul if they applied to his territory, so that he might follow them up as leads and solicit those advertisers.

Richardson was at his height of advertising celebrity in 1896. *Newspaperdom*, a trade journal for the industry, published in its pages the first and only full-page photograph in its history, that of Richardson, looking proud and prosperous, with the caption reading: "A Man True to Newspapers, True to Advertisers."[20]

Richardson employed close to one hundred people in his office at the Tribune Building and his location was wisely chosen: virtually all of the other special representatives also had offices in the same building, so that it was convenient for a visiting publisher or an advertiser to do business in one central place. Additionally, many newspapers had small offices for their own employee representatives located in the Tribune Building, and if there was need for additional advertising or the desire to discuss the placement of or negotiate the price of an advertisement, all one would have to do was to walk down the hall to another office and start doing business. The *Toledo Blade's* loyal employee, Frank T. Lane, for example, was located on the same floor as the Richardson Company, which also represented the *Blade*, and so there was constant interaction between representatives of the two companies.

Lane was a man in his early 50s when Paul met him, known for his quaint, dry humor, and he was somewhat of a legend because he had worked closely with the famed David Ross Locke, (known as "Nasby"), editor of the *Toledo Blade*. Lane virtually held the *Blade* together when Locke traveled the nation and Europe giving speeches. A tall, thin blonde-bearded man, Lane was also one of the country's most outspoken proponents of the publication of the weekly newspaper. The *Blade's* weekly edition was one of the most prosperous in the nation at that time, mainly because of his efforts. Lane wrote an article for *Newspaperdom* on local, state and national weeklies in which he said:

> More than half of the people in the United States live in the country and since they do not get to the post-office more than once a week, they prefer a well-edited weekly, for general news, to anything else.[21]

Paul Block and
William Randolph Hearst

In addition to Lane and other advertising and newspaper people, it would be interesting to know whether Paul Block became aware of, or actually even met at the time that he first arrived in New York, another young newspaperman who had just come to New York within days of Block's arrival, and who had also started working in the Tribune Building. The man was the sphinx-faced William Randolph Hearst, who at the age of 32 had just purchased the *New York Journal*, which had been founded by Joseph Pulitzer's self-indulgent younger brother, Albert, and was one of the least distinguished newspapers in the city (known to be read only by "washer women" and factory workers), and its sister-paper the German-language edition, *Das Morgen Journal*, both for $180,000. Hearst was said to have actually celebrated the purchase by doing a jig and clicking his heels together. We know that Paul Block and William Randolph Hearst would eventually become close friends and business associates, and their lives paralleled each other's in numerous ways, but unfortunately we can only speculate about precisely how and when the two men actually met.

Although they worked in the same building for several years and both were dedicated to the newspaper business, at first the differences between Hearst and Block were vast: Hearst arrived in New York with a fortune of some $7,500,000 to spend on his ambition to build up the *Journal* so that it would have "the biggest circulation of the world."[22] According to how Park Row newspaper people saw him at the time, "William Randolph Hearst broke into New York with all the discreet secrecy of a wooden-legged burglar having a fit on a tin roof."[23] In contrast, Block arrived quite quietly and unassumingly in New York with little more than the suit on his back, $25 dollars to hold him over until he received his first pay envelope, and the desire to someday own his own newspaper. Hearst came from one of the richest families in America; Block came from one of the poorest. Hearst was a Harvard-educated socialite and aristocrat, the son of a multi-millionaire U.S. Senator, who entered New York having been immensely successful as the publisher of the *San Francisco Examiner*, and as an instant celebrity who brought all of his circulation schemes with him to the big city. He was ostentatious in dress, often sporting beribboned hats and brightly-colored suits, which seemed to be in great contrast and character contradiction to his often shy and somewhat diffident behavior. He was 32 years old, upward of six feet two and somehow appeared taller. Block, who was five-feet-six and described as "short," was a European immigrant, barely out of his teens, who had never been to college, had worked on a small-town newspaper, was known in New York only by few people other than those he worked for at Richardson, brought with him only his charm and a certain breathless ambition to succeed, and was extremely conservative in dress, which seemed to be in contrast to his outgoing and friendly personality. But if their backgrounds, styles and present stations in life were greatly dissimilar, their publishing philosophy, which they would eventually share, was perfectly in tune: both men believed that friendship and cooperation were the most far-reaching concepts that they could use in business and that circulation had to be increased through relentless promotion. Hearst's roaring vendettas, his political propaganda, his brash headlines and his personal, headstrong journalism would instantly propel him to the forefront of newspaper publishing, and although Block would never become anywhere near the sensationalist that was Hearst, he respected the older man's business and promotional acumen and eventually would look up to him as a mentor. "There Is No Substitute For Circulation," was the *Morning Journal's* slogan, and Block heartily agreed with the sentiment.

Unlike many publishers, both men also had knowledge of how printing a newspaper actually was done: they were comfortable in the pressrooms of newspapers, often visited and talked with the pressmen and the compositors, and could discuss the intricacies of the printing process. It was said of William Randolph Hearst that no publisher of his day knew more of the printing process; he even designed a new typeface. Not surprisingly, it was a bombastic style that was called "The Hearst" by typographical sales companies; and he brought to newspaper publishing such innovations as better use of readable typography throughout the paper, and such mechanical improvements as electrical drive for presses, the four-color rotary printing process, and two-color front-page illustrations.[24] Hearst and Block were not alone as potential newspaper publishers with detailed knowledge of the complex printing process. Adolph S. Ochs, publisher of *The New York Times* at that time, who had risen from being a printer's devil, may actually have been a close third to Hearst and Block in his knowledge of printing.

Hearst bought his way into the ownership of a newspaper by way of an inheritance, but he firmly believed that anyone in the newspaper business, no matter how minor the position, could rise to the highest editorial or corporate position.[25] Little did he know, of course, that six floors away from his new office was a young man, Paul Block, who was then on a fairly low rung of the publishing ladder, yet who had every intention of making the ascent to the levels that Hearst was suggesting.

It seems possible that Paul Block became aware of Hearst just by working in the same building as the flamboyant publisher and reading and following the sensational rise in circulation of the *New York Journal*. It is not likely that at that time they socialized or even dined at the same eateries: Hearst often ate in the private *Journal* dining room (he loved hot dogs, liberally coated with mustard), or as ironic contrast, in New York's best and most expensive restaurant, Delmonico's. He also belonged to two of New York's most elite gathering places, the Union Club and the Metropolitan Club. Conversely, when downtown at the office, Paul was more likely to eat in the beer saloon in the basement of the Tribune Building, or when the saloon was transferred to the top of the building, he took the rattling open-cage elevator to the appropriate floor. Often he would take advantage of the enormous free lunch at Andy Horn's. This traditional watering and dining spot for the newspaper fraternity had a fairly elaborate buffet table which consisted of assorted breads and rolls, hard-boiled eggs, cold cuts, potato and beet salads, baked beans, pickled herring, and pretzels, and was open to all for a five-cent schooner of beer. On occasion, Block would simply cross the street from the Tribune Building, and for a few cents purchase a lunch consisting of fruit and sugar-roasted peanuts from one of the many pushcarts lining the edge of the park, and top it off with a glass of free ice-water. If he chose to have something a little more substantial, he could purchase a variety of sandwiches for three cents ("two for five") and a cup of coffee, chocolate or tea for two cents, from a nearby food stand As a Jew, even if Paul had had the money to join one of the city's exclusive men's clubs – funds that he didn't have at the time – he would have been barred from entry.

There were various other opportunities for the two men to meet, however. During the momentous Yale-Princeton game on November 28, 1895, a special "bulletin stand" was set up in Printing House Square to provide constant updates on the game's progress. Half of the publishing and advertising fraternity in the nearby buildings came out that day, and people were there as much for the social possibilities as for the opportunity to follow the contest as a sporting event. One can imagine the gregarious Paul Block, new in town, introducing himself to the already-famous William Randolph Hearst.

Within relatively short order, Paul Block plunged himself into learning the business of being a publisher's special representative, applying what he already knew about advertising space sales to this new form of selling. Since he certainly was not a complete novice, he knew the special language of publishing and this was extremely valuable as he started out: what an agate line was, for example (a column-wide line $1/14^{th}$ of an inch deep used as a standard measurement in selling advertising space), and a cutline (the text that accompanies an illustration), and what a T.D.R. was (the traffic department representative of a newspaper who was in charge of all the mechanical details of communication). What he didn't know he learned rapidly, and by the end of his first year in New York he had become one of the leading salesmen for Richardson. And whatever he did and wherever he went, he attempted to make and maintain friendships.

This approach to business, which he invariably infused with a certain ceremony and civility whenever he called on a prospective advertiser or on a publisher, gained him entry where others might have been barred. Special representatives were much more than just mere salesmen. They, as Paul did, served as guides, philosophers and friends of the publishers, and they made themselves available for consultations about competitive rates, newspaper conditions around the country, circulations and other matters of importance. In this capacity as adviser, Paul's sense of responsibility grew.

Although there were a variety of financial arrangements between newspapers and special representatives, as they were called, publishers basically paid the representative's firm a fee of 15% commission (some reps accepted 10% if they were eager to secure the account) on whatever advertising was originated by the representative. Therefore, if the special representative convinced an advertiser to place an advertisement that cost, for example, $100 in the particular newspaper that he represented, the rep firm would receive $15 each time that same ad was placed. Out of that 15%, a small commission would be paid to the salesman. Repeat business was the conduit to success in the special representative field. If an advertisement proved to produce results, the advertiser would run it again and again – perhaps for years – and the special representative would receive his commission without doing very much further work after the initial sale other than to monitor the position of the ad, the frequency of the insertion, and to handle the billing.

The first special representative in the United States was L.H. Crall who, twenty years before Paul Block began his work with Richardson, had rented an office in the summer of 1875 in the Bennett Building on the corner of Nassau and Fulton Streets. Crall hung a makeshift sign on the door, indicating that he represented the *Cincinnati Times*, the *St. Louis Globe-Democrat*, the *Chicago Inter-Ocean*, the *Milwaukee Sentinel* and the *Cincinnati Enquirer*. Eventually, as he secured more newspapers to represent, Crall moved into the Tribune Building as its first tenant, and still occupied offices there with a thriving business when Paul Block began to work for Richardson.[26]

It is believed that when he first started at the Richardson Co., Paul Block received a salary of much less than $15 a week, although it was a raise over what he had earned from his last salary at the *Elmira Telegram*. Most beginning reporters at that time were earning $12 to $15 a week, not much more than Block, so if he had any temptation to move from the business side of publishing to that of a journalist, he remembered Brooks's admonition that the only way to make substantial money in the newspaper business was to be involved in sales and publishing. After being at Richardson for close to a year, he began to also receive a small amount of money each week in commissions. Out of the money he made, Paul sent a large portion of it – $8 to $10 – home each week to help his parents and siblings. His funds were scarce and he was forced to live a relatively abstemious life during this period. But if he could not afford extravagances, he was as a result given the gift of time, and much of it was spent at the office working on his accounts.

Because he had knowledge of publishing and was in need of additional income, he also began to work at various Park Row newspapers in the evenings after he left Richardson's offices at 6 PM.[27] He worked mostly doing clerical work in the advertising departments of the respective newspapers, gathering the galleys of the ads ready to print, and keeping track of what advertisements were to appear in what positions and where in the newspaper. The only difficulty he had with the moonlighting arrangement was an inconsistency of the days and hours that he was available to work, since he was being constantly called out of town to service his Richardson's accounts. Eventually, although he enjoyed the extra income, the demands of his work at Richardson became so intensive that he had to give up working anywhere other than at his principal job.

The special representative firms were concentrated primarily in New York because it was the focal point of most national advertisers and advertising agencies and the strategic center of investment capital. If an out-of-town newspaper was to prosper, it needed advertising, and not just that of the local variety – which was the principal source of income for most publications. For many newspapers outside of New York City, it was impossible to approach all of the potential advertisers scattered throughout the country, and just too expensive to open up an office in Manhattan and staff it with sales personnel. The special representative business came into existence, therefore, as a result of newspapers needing to increase their net profits from advertising other than what they were able to solicit with their local sales force. If the *Denver Post*, for example, could not maintain its own representative in New York, then a firm such as Richardson would see to the paper's needs. Such an arrangement with a representation company would cost the newspaper nothing except for the commission it would pay for each insertion that the surrogate company acquired.

Some newspaper publishers objected to paying what they called double commission: they were upset at paying one percentage to the special representative and one to the advertising agency that might actually write and place the advertisement. When the billing procedure was explained to the publisher, however, it was understood that the newspapers were receiving the same net amount of money, even if the advertisement was processed through both an advertising agency and a special representative company. Block would explain it like this: as special representative he would accept the advertisement from the advertiser and forward it on to the advertising agency (which, in some cases, might be responsible for writing and designing the ad), billing the advertiser 15% over and above the stated net rate card rate. The advertising agency would then deduct its 10% commission from the regular rate card rate before sending the advertisement on to the newspaper, therefore charging it only that 10% for services rendered, and the special rep company gained its fee over the top of the original rate.[28]

For many advertisers, just before the turn of the century and then beyond, they began to see how advertising dramatically increased their annual sales, and as newspaper circulation grew, bringing more readers in contact with the advertiser's product or service, their sales would sometimes produce astounding results. As circulation of newspapers increased, publishers raised their advertising rates, and the amount of advertising placed actually went up as advertisers were making more and more money as a result of their ads. Block began to prosper.

Retail businesses were convinced that the traditional way of advertising with billboards and circulars was paling in comparison with the ads that they were starting to place in newspapers, and they demanded even higher circulations to reach more potential customers. Accordingly, to the extent that the newspapers could raise their circulations, they could charge more to advertise.

In this attempt to grasp wider readership, newspapers introduced such features as serialized novels, lurid tales of horror, extensive sports news, and political commentary, and they used such techniques as livelier language and banner headlines – sometimes four or five inches high – that screamed the news; often these were teamed with large, crudely drawn illustrations. Block would sometimes have to explain, excuse or apologize for the excesses of some of the newspapers he represented. Eventually pages of cartoon strips and extensive sporting news were incorporated into most newspapers as a further inducement for the reader to buy the newspaper, which were fast becoming not just vehicles of information but diversions of entertainment in their own right. Hearst published the first full-page photograph ever to appear in an American newspaper, and the circulation of his *Morning Journal* soared. "Illustrations embellish a page and stimulate the imagination of the masses," he said.[29] There was a revolution in content, design and approach going on in American newspapers, and Paul Block was on the periphery, wanting more involvement. It would not take him long to join the inner circle.

Yellow Journalism

The circulation wars that ushered in the so-called Yellow Journalism years between Hearst's *New York Journal* and Pulitzer's *New York World* had begun to rage soon after Block arrived in the city, and these two newspapers created their own contemporary mythos, with such extravagances as chartering special trains, at great expense, to speed their respective newspapers to outlying cities such as Syracuse, before the competing paper arrived by way of a train on the regular railroad schedule.[30]

Hearst gleefully hired away many of the more outstanding reporters, editors and illustrators who had contributed to, and were largely responsible for, the success of *The World*, and it was rumored that he paid these journalistic stars virtually any salary they demanded.[31] He also imitated *The World* in design and content. Although Block did not particularly approve of the *Journal's* many fabrications, which were unparalleled in newspaper history, he could not help but take notice.

War was particularly potent circulation-building material for newspapers. Hearst and Pulitzer seemed to do everything possible to plunge the country into a war, not necessarily for moral or political purposes, but simply to create larger circulations in their respective newspapers. For months before the Spanish-American War of 1898, Hearst's *Morning Journal* and Pulitzer's *World* stirred the country to a frenzied war psychosis by not only reporting the events in Cuba but by actually making up much of the news that they published.[32] Hearst went further than Pulitzer: his paper described the nonexistent "rescue" of the niece of a Cuban revolutionary president; it published a stolen letter from the Spanish Ambassador to Washington which denigrated President William McKinley's handling of the situation; it offered a $50,000 reward for information on who was responsible for sinking the U.S.S. Maine. Hearst even sent his own ships to Havana to investigate the cause of the sinking.[33]

The term "yellow journalism" in describing the work of Hearst and

Pulitzer is not totally synonymous with mere sensationalism, a technique which both men went beyond. They used huge banner headlines that screamed tension and unrest across the breadth of their respective front pages; increased the size of photographs and illustrations; faked interviews; and offered sympathy to the underdog...all in order to enjoy gains in circulation.[34]

Block followed the race between Hearst and Pulitzer with spirited and some professional interest. Like virtually everyone else in New York, he too read the daily reports of the Spanish-American War – but he read them not only for their twisted and exaggerated content, but also to see how effective the stories were in producing reader interest, and ultimately what effect the articles were having on circulation. Eventually he would convince the rich publisher to allow him to represent the advertising in some of Hearst's papers.

Paul was worried. A friend of his, who would be one of the 4,000 Americans who either died or were killed in the war, went to fight with Col. Theodore Roosevelt's Rough Riders, and Paul took to writing his poetry as a response, composing "A Rough Diamond." Here is a part of the poem:

> 'Tis true he's serving time Sir –
> But God knows who it's for
> It's for our dear old blessed flag-
> For Jim is off to war.
>
> When President McKinley
> Called for our men to fight –
> He was among the first to go –
> He left that very night.

Hearst insisted that every story in the *Journal* must contain some element of love, power, hate or sympathy and his reporters and editors had to militantly follow the dictum. Pulitzer was close to giving the same orders to his personnel. It seemed that virtually everyone in New York City, including Paul Block, was reading two or three newspapers each day. As their business increased as a result, newspaper advertisers were ecstatic over the leaps, bounds and eddies of circulation and readership which was translating itself into additional sales of their product or service.

As the system of special representatives grew – eventually almost ev-

ery major daily newspaper in the country outside of Manhattan had a
special representative in New York – the advertising agencies began to
concentrate on the more creative aspects of advertising, on providing service to the advertiser, on the preparation and writing of copy, and on
overall campaign strategy. Block, as the publishers' representative, was
left to the task of convincing the potential publisher on the idea of issuing
a new rate card to raise the advertising rates; this would enable the special representative to earn a satisfactory margin, and allow the newspaper
to realize a somewhat larger profit and volume of advertising than it had
received before the arrangement was made.

Paul Block's job of selling was two-fold: he was asked to try to open
new accounts with newspaper publishers so that Richardson could serve
as their representative, and he was also directed to convince advertisers
and advertising agencies to buy space in the publications that Richardson
represented.

Part of the job might have seemed relatively effortless for Block, consisting of virtually nothing more than order-taking or collecting advertising copy to be sent to the newspaper, but it really was a much more complex procedure and operation than it first appeared. If an advertiser had
already decided, perhaps, to advertise in a specific newspaper, and if that
newspaper happened to be represented by Richardson, Block would have
to negotiate the price, determine the amount of space required and the
date of the insertion, the number of insertions required, and the position
of the advertisement as to what page it would appear on; and then he
would forward the copy to the selected newspaper, and follow up by sending proof copies of the advertisement, after it appeared, to the advertiser.

As his relationship with certain advertisers grew, his job took on marketing and public relations aspects, in addition to the handling of the traffic of the insertion. Block would help the agency plan a successful advertising campaign, gather statistics of his newspaper's territory to impress
the potential advertiser with the value of the publication he was selling,
and even assist in the writing of copy if so requested. Paul would often
prepare a presentation, based on discussions with other sales representatives of the Richardson Co., and his own knowledge and intuition, that
would demonstrate where the publication he was representing would fit
into an advertiser's campaign. With the help of others at Richardson, he
would sometimes actually write an advertisement on speculation, trying
to come up with an approach that he believed would benefit the advertiser, and then have the ad designed and set in type, to be then presented

to the prospective advertiser for approval. This strategy worked often when he was faced with a struggle attempting to get his publication included in an already existing advertising schedule. Delivery to an advertiser of a proof copy of an ad that Paul had created, and a reliance on his knowledge of local conditions and competing businesses, combined with a comparison of the rates and circulations of the other local newspapers, often enabled him to finally make the sale.

Occasionally the publishers that he represented became irritated if they were not receiving the amount of advertising that they believed they deserved, and an attempt would have to be made to assuage them by generating additional advertising lineage. Where the job became really difficult, however, was when Paul attempted to open up new publishers to take Richardson as their representative, and also to convince advertisers to place their ads in one of Richardson's publications when they were already entrenched in a business relationship with another publication, and were steadfastly loyal in placing their advertising in those other papers. Here Paul relied upon his background in selling for the *Elmira Telegram*, using a combination of his personal traits: charm, conversational ability, and sincerity.

The business of advertising in newspapers, coinciding with the growth of business in general, was rapidly expanding in 1895. "A revolution in advertising," was how the *New York Sun* described the change in an editorial early in 1896:

> The development of the art of advertising during the last four or five years have been remarkable. The newspaper advertisement has changed radically both in form and character. It is no longer a bold and dry announcement of a private business, to which a great part of the newspaper readers gave no particular attention, but has become a feature of the journal that compels everybody's attention.

By the mid-1890's, at the very time that Paul Block had entered the field of national advertising, corporations were beginning to place advertisements on a large and frequent scale, and the entire future of American business was intertwined with how much it believed in advertising. Such giant corporations as Eastman Kodak, Sears Roebuck & Co., the Quaker Oats Company, and many others owe their growth to the success of the newspaper and magazine advertising that they placed starting in the mid-1890s. Advertisers appeared in newspapers for the first time and began to sell everything from breakfast foods to baking powders and from bicycles to church organs. As more and more machines made mass production possible, a means of quantity distribution had to be found, and advertising created mass demand for the profusion of newly-made products. It had been the custom of European manufacturers to determine what customers wanted and then to exert effort to give it to them. The new American way consisted of producing something consumers ought to have, and then convincing them and teaching them, through advertising, to want it.[35] The age of consumerism was born:

> In the penny papers, advertising, as well as sales, took on a more democratic cast. Advertising in the established journals, which heretofore had addressed the reader only insofar as he was a businessman interested in shipping and public sales, or a lawyer interested in legal notices, increasingly addressed the newspaper reader as a human being with mortal needs.[36]

Paul Block could not only sense but could see how the industry was exploding within a short while of starting his new position. No single industry in the United States showed such a continued and remarkable growth in the 40 years up to the time that Paul Block moved to Manhattan; on the aggregate, by the turn of the century some 100 million copies of newspapers were being distributed daily throughout the country, more than one for every person, since the population at that time was 76,212,168.[37] National newspaper advertising, as opposed to local ads, eventually began to account for 25% of all of the advertising placed in newspapers.[38] With just a few exceptions, this multi-million dollar expenditure was all placed through special representatives such as Richardson.

No sooner had he arrived in New York, however, did Paul Block find himself constantly leaving the city on business trips. A great amount of the selling and work of the special representative took place not in the main office in New York City, but wherever the publisher had his newsroom and plant, or the advertiser had his main headquarters. It was the newspapers that were published outside of New York City that needed representation, and many newspapers looked toward national advertising as their major source of income, especially if their local advertising was thin due to competing newspapers, or because of a lack of department stores (which were becoming prolific advertisers), manufacturing plants or other services in their specific area.

Block's approach to the advertiser or agency was nothing if not forthright: he did not try to wheedle an advertisement just for the sake of another sale, but used a certain proportion of discrimination in advising just how much advertising the potential advertiser should use and how often it should be placed. The newspaper that he was representing could only thrive in the long run, if the advertiser also prospered, and Paul felt that it was up to him personally to see that the campaign in the pages that he represented would be a positive success. He also tried never to disparage the competition, and this noblesse oblige impressed potential advertisers wherever he traveled. His theory was that with the proper advertising copy, and with a judicious amount of space apportioned, and placed in the right publication at the right time, any product or service could be made to benefit from advertising copy.

A. Frank Richardson personally gave Block the benefit of the knowledge and experience that he had accumulated over many years in the advertising business. Advertising was somewhat of a game, he contended, but not a game of chance. Though neither of the men was good at playing baseball, both loved the game, and he counseled Block – much to the young man's delight – with baseball-related platitudes that nevertheless made sense. Richardson later outlined these ideas in an advertisement he placed in *N.W. Ayer & Son's Newspaper Annual*. He likened the advertising business to the art and science of baseball, claiming that, in a sense, neither was a game:

> A man with a trusty right arm in the pitcher's box, a catcher with nerve, quick and sure, three alert and safe basemen, and a lightning athlete for short-stop - these supported by wily and errorless sprinters in the field, playing together, safe batters too, and in practice, will snatch victory from all the boasting duffers the world can put against them. It's a case where the race is to the swift...and the sure. All depends on the players. So in advertising: everything depends on the newspapers; they are the advertiser's players. A sagacious selection and proper placing of these and his team will win the game every time.[39]

Richardson was well-known in the field of advertising because of his incredible knowledge of the true circulation rates of newspapers all over the country. Publishers were infamous for their inflation of circulation figures in order to draw in more advertising, because the higher their circulation appeared, the more they could charge for advertising. Despite all kinds of sworn statements and accountant's tallies, it was difficult to know exactly how many copies a particular paper was printing and distributing.

Richardson accumulated circulation information in a variety of ways, but his favorite ploy was to travel to a city of a paper that he was representing, or was considering representing, check into a hotel and leave instructions to be called at 3 o'clock in the morning. Upon arising, he would dress in more leisurely garb than his traditional three-piece bespoke suit, then go the newspaper in question and relaxedly walk into the pressroom and strike up a conversation with the printers who would be working on the morning edition of that day's newspaper. Because of his knowledge of printing, he often was thought to be a visiting pressman himself, and the printers would gladly pass the time of day talking about their equipment and their newspaper. Eventually the question of the amount of the print run would arise, and in relatively short order, Richardson would be able to determine the true circulation of the newspaper. In one instance, Richardson discovered that a newspaper that he represented, which was touting its circulation at 30,000 copies a day, really was printing only 10,000.[40] He demanded that Paul also attempt to discover the true circulation of any newspaper that he was representing if it appeared in any way suspect.

Talking about the newspapers that he represented, in an interview that he gave to *Fowler's Publicity*, a reference volume on the advertising business, Richardson said:

> All of these papers have a definite and Known Circulation, and they afford advertisers every opportunity to investigate for themselves. Advertisers in them buy space as they buy merchandise, by measure and by count, and not by statement and claim. Years ago I established the principle of "Known Circulation," and I have done business along this line, and will always continue to.[41]

He instructed Paul: known circulation carries weight, makes money and earns money ... for everybody involved, including the newspaper, the advertiser and the special agent. On the other hand, he made it clear that the value of any specific newspaper could not be estimated on the strength of circulation alone. If a product or service could only be sold to a particular audience, often it would not matter whether the circulation was small or not. There was a great deal of difference between the readership of a newspaper in North Dakota, for example, who might be comprised mainly of ranchers and farmers, than an audience of New York readers who might be office and factory workers. On the one hand, the market for grain might be a natural advertisement; on the other, an advertisement for a Broadway show might be more appropriate. In order for the advertisement to be successful, Paul had to know the wants, needs, traditions and buying habits of the readership of the newspaper in which the ad would appear.

The consideration of season was also an important factor in determining what products to sell at what time of the year. Amazingly, some manufacturers were unsure of their own product's suitability for an advertisement at a particular time of the year. As simplistic as it may seem, it became Paul's job to point out that advertisers should not sell straw hats at Christmas time or woolen underwear during the summer. If one of his advertisers did poorly with a particular advertisement, the blame would often be placed on Block: "You should have advised me to wait," was a common criticism offered with contempt by advertisers toward special representatives if their ad had failed to produce the anticipated result. Block found it more difficult to accept the contempt than the potential loss of an account.[42] However, although there is only anecdotal evidence to support it, once Paul Block obtained a client, he kept him on his roster, and it has been said that he never lost an account for any failure on his part during his half-century in business.

The insistence on the accuracy of circulation figures of those newspapers he represented gave Richardson, and all who worked for him, a reputation of being scrupulously honest and reliable, and his business continued on the ascent. Yet despite the fact that Paul worked for a company that was held in great esteem by newspaper publishers, at first the pursuit of advertising sales was not an easy task. Many buildings bore signs that stated: "Beggars, peddlers and advertising men not permitted here." Businessmen had good reason for disliking and distrusting advertising special reps. Some advertisers (and newspapers) had been cheated in the following way: a dishonest special representative would convince an advertiser to place an advertisement at the rate of say 30 cents per line, based on the publication's circulation, when the actual rate for the newspaper might only be twelve cents per line. The advertiser was unaware of the real circulation and the real rate and would pay the representative the money requested to place the ad. The dishonest representative would pocket the difference between what was paid by the advertiser and what was owed to the newspaper. There was a second way some special representatives cheated their clients. Many of them knew the accurate circulations of the newspapers that they represented (which might have been perilously low), but they were in collusion with the publishers, so they simply lied to the advertiser as to the true figures. This skullduggery, which was fairly common, gave special representatives a bad name. Some publications actually stopped paying commissions to special representatives, refusing to entertain any new business with them and opting to work directly with the national advertisers that had been brought in previously.[43]   Threats and lawsuits invariably followed.

There is no record of Paul Block experiencing any of those specific difficulties. He was even able to gain entry to some very problematic accounts, which sometimes required him to use the greatest of finesse and courtesy, and eventually he made his sales with these companies. He soon learned that when he visited a national advertiser, he had to concentrate on the territory or region that the advertiser was attempting to reach, in addition to promoting the circulation or other demographic advantages of the newspaper being represented. And he began to use the phrase, "The territory I represent," rather than "The newspaper I represent."[44]

When calling upon newspapers, either that he represented or those he was attempting to secure as clients, Paul attempted to influence the advertising manager or publisher to alter the information found on the newspaper's rate card. Other than just the rates, the circulation, the size of the columns and pages, and the closing dates, these cards were often barren of any other helpful information for the potential advertiser.[45]   Paul asked for more information about the readership of the newspaper: their income, class, occupation and interests, so that when presenting the newspaper to a potential advertiser, perhaps to be included in an advertising campaign, the demographics of the territory would be quite clear. Other questions of the newspaper would be asked, such as: "What is the average cost of homes in your locality? What is the average rent paid, the average wage earned? How many nationally-advertised products are advertised in your city? What lines are neglected by manufacturers, and what lines are pushed through your advertising columns? How many homes in your community are wired for electric lighting? What is the chemical character of your water supply? Is there a marked demand for some lines of products in your community?"[46]

When presenting a specific newspaper to a potential advertiser, Paul was questioned about such things as: Is the circulation guaranteed? Is the circulation regularly audited? How large is the gross press run? Are unsold copies returnable? How much of the circulation is urban? How much suburban? Rural? How many copies are sold on the streets? On newsstands? How many are home delivered? What percentage of your readers are women? What percentage are men? Perhaps most importantly to some buyers were such factors as how much advertising, and what categories, had been placed with the newspaper the previous year, and so far how much had been placed in the then-present year compared with the corresponding period the previous year. An exhaustive examination by the experienced space buyer would invariably take place and Paul had to be prepared with the right answers, or be able to telephone or telegraph with dispatch either Richardson or the home newspaper to secure the information that he needed. Space buyers also considered the influence of the newspaper on its readers, the impact of its news, the appearance of its contents, what other advertisers in similar lines, products or services have been using the paper, and what its political and business policy was.[47] Since Paul had often visited and stayed in contact with the newspapers he represented, gaining as much information about them as possible, he could offer the potential advertiser much more than the stereotypical tales of widening circulation, and great gains in local, classified and national advertising. He was able to discuss a much more significant topic: how the sale of a given product or service may be effectively promoted in a given territory. He quickly became known in the advertising industry for being able to answer that question honestly and effectively.

Paul had two very difficult problems to face in his negotiations with some of the newspapers that he represented. One was their policy of wanting to charge higher rates for national advertisers than they did for their local advertisers, claiming that since the local advertising comprised most of the income realized by a newspaper, that they should be given special status. And the other problem was the newspaper's occasional insistence that if a national advertiser placed the name of a local retailer (such as "Buy our Goodyear tires at Acme Garage," for example) in their advertisements, then the special representative should be denied a commission.[48]

The argument that Paul used for the first problem was an attempt to convince the newspaper to standardize their rates for both local and national advertisers and to point out that money that came into the community from national advertising stayed there in full, as opposed to money from a local merchant, who might for example buy some chairs, and only the profit of the chairs would remain. For the second issue, as a matter of ethics, he advised the newspaper to pay the special representative his commission, because if the rep had not brought in the national advertiser in the first place, the newspaper would not have had any advertisement, nor made the profit – local or national – to account for.

Aside from the skepticism concerning special representatives, space buyers in advertising agencies and for newspapers were as sophisticated then as they are today, and they bargained for the lowest rates (and looked for the highest circulations) that they could achieve. The buyers also always insisted on gaining the best possible position in a newspaper: often the back page, page three, page two or center spread. Some small but consistent advertisers asked, for example, for their ads to be surrounded by news or other reading matter ("island" position, it was called)[49] – not by other ads – or to be on the top of the editorial page. Often as not, the space buyers would demand that their special positions be not charged special rates but "run-of-paper" rates, usually the lowest rate offered by a newspaper. If Block could not deliver the position or rate demanded, he simply would not accept the insertion order.[50]

When dealing with advertisers, Paul also had to remain au courant as to what were the editorial positions, and even stylistic innovations, of the newspapers that he represented. For example, as early as 1895, there was a movement afoot to reform spelling in newspapers, such as dropping the "ue" when the preceding vowel is short, or a diphthong: this resulted in new spellings such as "catalog," "epilog," and "synagog;" or to drop the final "e" from words ending in "ite" when the "i" is short, e.g., as in "hypocrit" or "requisit," or to change "ph" to "f" when so sounded, as in "fantom" instead of "phantom," and "telegraf" not "telegraph."[51] Some of these changes eventually worked their way into our language but there were advertisers who steadfastly opposed them and did not want the new spelling changes to appear in their advertisements. It was up to Paul to negotiate this trivial but sometimes emotionally charged conflict that arose between the advertiser and the newspaper.

Traveling Ad Representative

In the 1890s, most business travel, except for the very rich, did not have the comfort or cachet that it does today. Unless one owned a private car or could avail oneself of what was considered first-class accommodations, transportation by railroad was arduous at best; in the winter the railroad cars were unheated, and in the summer it was necessary to keep the windows open to avoid near-suffocation, but the unwanted side effect of open windows was that virtually every passenger would arrive at his or her destination covered by soot and slightly singed from the sparks and cinders that flew into the car from the train's engine. Food, if it was available in transit, was usually consumed in smoking cars, reeking with cigarette and cigar smoke, and torpid trains seemed to take forever before they arrived, wheezing and chugging, at their destinations. When he had to journey between relatively close cities, Paul would travel by horse and buggy – and in winter often by sleigh through the snow-laden back roads of New York State. He was forced to endure the difficulties of outrageously bumpy roads, sweltering and dusty coaches, cramped seats, foul-smelling fellow-passengers, and other difficulties of that kind of travel.

One of the first accounts that Paul was given to service was the *Elmira Telegram*; it was a natural choice on Richardson's part since Paul had been the advertising manager of the newspaper and knew all of the advertisers, the space rates, special discounts, circulation figures and demographics. He corresponded with the new advertising manager and with Harry Brooks, and made occasional visits to Elmira to see his "Old Boss," as he would invariably describe Brooks. In concert with the business he conducted at the *Telegram*, he would invariably visit his family and friends, and remain in Elmira as long as possible before moving on to another city and another sales call.

Before long, Block convinced two other Elmira newspapers into being represented by the Richardson Co.: the *Elmira Advertiser* and the *Elmira Evening Star*. Since these newspapers were dailies, and the *Telegram* was a weekly, and since their circulations were relatively small (both less than 9,000) compared to the *Telegram*, which had begun to slip from its circulation height of 186,000 but was still well above 100,000, there really was no competitive factor, and so there was no conflict of interest on Paul's part. If an advertiser wanted to reach the Elmira population, Block would often sell advertising space in the three newspapers for one packaged price.[52] Richardson bought ads himself in trade publications advertising the *Elmira Telegram* as a "Good...honest...family...paper," which was "Clean, bright and entertaining,"[53] and this also helped Paul's efforts in selling advertising on a national basis for the *Telegram*. Eventually, Block was given the responsibility of representing all other New York

State newspapers that Richardson had contracts with, and soon Paul became known as a trustworthy and efficient special representative not only
throughout New York, but in Northern Pennsylvania and in New England,
as well.

In New York State, in addition to the Elmira newspapers, Paul represented the hugely successful *Saturday Globe* (with a circulation of 294,000
at its height)[54] published in Utica, the *Albany Telegram*, the *Rochester
Democrat and Chronicle* and the *Syracuse Post-Standard*. In Pennsylvania, he represented the *Harrisburg Telegram*, and an illustrated, 16-page
family weekly out of Williamsport called *Grit* which, when Paul started
working with it, had a highly respectable circulation of over 62,000, and
finally grew to over 100,000. [55]

On one of the occasions that he visited Elmira, late in 1898, Paul convinced his oldest friend Herman Halsted, who was still employed as an
advertising salesman for the *Elmira Telegram*, to join him in New York,
so that the two friends could become business colleagues again, this time
working for Richardson. Harry S. Brooks was sorry to see Halsted leave,
especially since he had become the beau of Brooks's daughter, but actually encouraged him to begin a new venture, and reiterating his belief that
Halsted would never make any money if he stayed in the editorial side of
publishing. He was making $10 a week at the *Telegram* that time. Al-
though Halsted was older than Paul Block, he looked up to the younger
man and was influenced by him, an interdependence that would ultimately
last for both their lives.

Halsted arrived in New York on January 1, 1899, moved into the Old
Empire Hotel on the Upper West Side and stayed in the same room where
Paul had then moved, the two men sharing the same double-bed for nearly
a year. He was paid $12 per week by Richardson, and gave Paul half of
that, $6 per week, to help defray the cost of the room. Could Halsted
make the successful transition from being a journalist to that of being an
advertising man? Newspaper reporting teaches a man to dig up the facts,
but it doesn't necessarily teach him how to sell with that information. In
terms of copywriting, however, Halsted was already highly-schooled in
the use of the language and he proved to be a superb composer of ads.

With his colleague Paul Block at his side, within a relatively short while
Halsted proved to be just as good a salesman as his friend, and just as
reliable and trustworthy. When an opening occurred for a manager of
Richardson's Chicago office, Halsted was appointed and he went off to
manage the sales force in the Windy City,[56] and Paul was temporarily

separated from his friend, business associate and roommate for close to two years.

On the few evenings in any month where he had some time for recreation, Paul occasionally attended what was considered a novelty at the time: "movies," or "flickers," as they were called, projected at Bial's Music Hall, Keith's Union Square Theater, and the American Biograph. Offerings consisted of such programs as a brief story of Rip Van Winkle, a screening of the famed Fitzsimmons-Corbett fight for the world heavyweight championship, or just a film of waves breaking on a pier so realistically that spectators in the front rows feared they would get wet. Frequently, the films served as interludes in vaudeville programs. Paul enjoyed the films, and the businessman side of him was intrigued by the commercial potential of the new invention. He would eventually become involved, albeit briefly, in the motion picture business.

Concurrently with the advent of movies came another invention that was not so quietly sweeping New York City and the nation: the horseless carriage. Just at the turn of the century, as the last horse-drawn carriages were being seen on the streets of New York, the first motor cars – single engine Winton's – were making their debuts. By 1899, some 4,000 motorcars were in use (compared to 10 million bicycles and 18 million horses and mules, nationwide), most of them using steam or electricity. *The New York Times* clucked at what it called, "The noisy, odorous contraptions," and enigmatically deplored the "near indecent" French word, "automobile." However, despite the protestation of the eminent Grey Lady of news publishing, the word caught on and a popular song, "Love in an Automobile," became the hit of the city.[57]

Block was not yet close to being able to afford one of the new automobiles, but he became interested in everything about them: riding in them, eventually owning one, and ultimately understanding what effect their manufacture and sale would have on the world of advertising and his future income. He was one of about 8,000 people who gawked at the models of 32 horseless carriage makers at the New York Auto Show on November 3, 1900. On occasion, for the relatively expensive fare of five cents, he would ride the city's first autostage, or autobus, propelled by electricity along Fifth Avenue.

As more and more companies began to advertise nationally and the advertising revenues continued to rise, profits rose for this aspect of advertising. Some of the ads, such as the one for men's shoes manufactured by W.L. Douglas ("This is the Best $3 Shoe in the World," stated the headline in the ad) performed double-duty: they sold shoes directly to the public, and they also reached wholesale buyers.[58] Yet, as often happens when a new product or concept upsets the status quo, there was a back-lash – a problem with the new source of advertising that Paul Block had to address wherever he went. Not all retailers were favorably disposed toward any product that was nationally advertised which they, in turn, could sell. By all rules of business logic, it should follow that if Lifebuoy Soap took and paid for a page of advertising in a local newspaper, for example, and a drugstore sold that brand of soap, the store would make a handsome profit on each sale of a cake of Lifebuoy soap because it did not have to pay for the advertising itself.

But the retailers, in a display of Yankee independence, had arguments against that logic. They believed it to be to their advantage to sell their own brands and lines, products that they controlled, rather than become distributors for other people's products at certain set prices. Many rural and city stores at that time carried only one or two "brand" name products; almost everything else, from soda crackers to yellow soap, was displayed in barrels, boxes and jars, and was bought or bartered for in bulk from the manufacturer. Cheese came only in wheels and bricks; vinegar was bottled by the store owner or his family; there were tubs of salt mackerel, and kegs of sour, dill and sweet pickles; large cloth bags of granulated, powdered, white, brown and dark brown sugars lined virtually every general store: unprocessed, unpackaged, and tended by the hands of the proprietor, not a national company.

Newspapers began to complain that they were losing a certain amount of local advertising because of the proliferation of all the national advertising. There was an additional argument: if the retailer advertised and did not have enough products to satisfy his customers, it would build enmity among their loyal following of regular purchasers. Paul heard that the buyers at Macy's Department Store in the 1890s once refused a magazine's bid for advertising because, "The nature of our business is such that goods will in most instances be closed out before we are able to announce through you that we have them for sale."[59]

What Paul had to do was to educate the newspaper's advertising managers so that they could inform the retailers that turnover is where the most money is made in retailing. National advertising did help the retailer by taking from him a large part of the selling burden, and the advertising space salesmen had to convince the retailer that his normal selling expense was so high, and his margin of profit so small, that he really could not afford to devote to non-advertised items the extra selling expense and effort that would be necessary to move those products off the shelves.

Block emphasized the importance of informing the retailer of the huge advantage he had when he featured nationally-advertised goods. Before long, retailers began to understand the strength of national advertising and everyone was made happy: the newspapers, the retailers, and Paul Block. One druggist even went to the extent of eliminating from his stock every item that was not nationally advertised if he could find an advertised substitute, claiming that he could not afford the extra selling expense of non-advertised items.[60]

Paul became involved in every area of advertising in newspapers: he developed business for both the advertiser and the newspaper; rendered one-on-one service to both parties; insisted that advertisers pay their bills promptly; convinced newspapers to improve and extend their credit line; and helped to weed out frauds.[61]

Advertising in newspapers grew rapidly, and Richardson's company grew along with it. In approximately 1897 he opened an office in London, at 12 Red Lion Court in the Fleet Street section, so that he could service British companies that wanted to advertise in American newspapers. Shortly after that, sometime in 1898, Richardson had to expand his New York offices, and he moved his entire operation three blocks west from Park Row to Temple Court.[62] Richardson's success reflected the health of the American economy. The Dow Jones Industrial Index, which in 1896 initially monitored stock price movements of twelve companies, was now publishing continuously with figures on hundreds of companies. The picture of the economy represented by Dow Jones was strong and growing.[63]

The commentators of the day were well-aware of the power and influence of advertising. A story in *Harper's Weekly* in 1897 mentioned the possible lasting impact of the burgeoning field:

> Advertisements are now part of the humanities, a true mirror of life, a sort of fossil history from which the future chronicler, if all other historical monuments were to be lost, might fully and graphically rewrite the history of our time.[64]

Patent Medicine Advertising
Another publication that Paul represented was the *Worcester Telegram-*

Gazette in Massachusetts, and he would travel to Worcester constantly to service them and to visit the nearby patent medicine manufacturers, many of which were located in the New England area. These companies were enormous national advertisers.

The patent medicine business, which started in the early 1870s, was not quite past its height in popularity in 1895. Most promoters of these instant "cure-alls" presented their products as derivatives of America's popular folk-cure tradition, and behind every bottle of snake oil, the bottlers implied that they were themselves simple folk who just happened on a cure of whatever ailed the public. Incurable paralysis could be cured, claimed the makers of Dr. Chase's Blood and Nerve Food; Oxydonor was said to cure such maladies as Bright's Disease, rheumatism, neuralgia, insomnia, sciatica, fever, dyspepsia and virtually "all forms of disease in men, women and children." Although these nostrums would prove to be bogus, consisting for the most part of a high alcohol content, somehow the public took to them blissfully unaware that the contents relied mainly on alcohol and a variety of opiates. There was virtually no magazine or newspaper in the country that was not running advertising for patent medicines.

> As for patent medicines, it is questionable if any good beyond wealth for the purveyors and security for new periodicals came out of advertising for the vast number of fake nostrums that promised to grow hair or cure any and all of the ills known to humankind. The claims went unchallenged until federal government agencies were empowered to demand truth in advertising. A few newspapers acted independently to ban the worst of the medical quackery. A major effort at proscribing such advertising followed a decision by the *Ladies Home Journal* in 1892 to print no more medical advertising of any kind. The *Journal's* editor, Edward W. Bok, took to printing chemical analyses of some of the more widely advertised preparations. A shocked public learned that many of the cures were laced with alcohol, cocaine, or morphine. Hundreds of thousands of mothers had been quieting their teething babies with a widely advertised soothing syrup containing morphine.[65]

Despite the growing suspicion that patent medicines were at best fraudulent and possibly harmful, Richardson continued to accept that kind of advertising and placed it in those newspapers that he represented; he also became intensely interested in just how much money the patent medicine manufacturers were making. Some of the advertisements that Richardson placed, often with Paul Block handling the insertion order, were for "cures" for such maladies as consumption, epilepsy, impotence, rupture, hair loss, obesity, nervous disorders, syphilis and premature ejaculation.[66]

Richardson would also have delivered to his newspaper accounts complete stories – with pen and ink illustrations – of the "cures" that some of his advertisers claimed to have produced, with the request that these articles should be published as "feature news." Many newspapers were happy to receive these reading notices because they charged a premium price of almost double the regular advertising rate to publish them. They also published them to insure future advertising placements from Richardson.

By 1899, Richardson himself was making a substantial amount of money in the newspaper representation business, but his interest in patent medicines as a way of making even more money continued to grow.[67] The nephew of Jenness J. Richardson, publisher and traveling special representative of his own newspaper – one of the first special reps in the country – of the Davenport, *Iowa Democrat*, A. Frank Richardson had been practically weaned on newspapers all of his life, and apparently sought a change in his business career.[68]

Richardson was a stout man, given to an incipient double chin, who sported the traditional handlebar mustache; he dressed impeccably and parted his hair in the middle. He was somewhat stodgy in his approach to business, and when he had an idea he approached it carefully but relentlessly. He went at the patent medicine business with a conscious endeavor that almost bordered on obsession.

Although the patent medicine manufacturers comprised, at that time, the largest single user of advertising space in newspapers in this country, Richardson apparently believed he could make more money selling the nostrums directly.[69] Between 1899 and 1904, the gross sales income of patent medicines in this country increased a staggering 128%.[70]

Richardson was not unique in his interest in acquiring patent medicine companies. Four of the largest advertising agencies in the country, Pettengill, Rowell, Lord & Thomas, and N.W. Ayer, maintained direct interests in patent medicine firms.[71] Richardson, and eventually Paul Block, had a close working relationship with the Pettengill Agency, and then Lord & Thomas, and were placing advertising of the patent medicine firms that Pettengill represented and owned.

After selling tens of thousands of dollars of advertising for patent medicines for such products as Swamp Root and Kranitonic, Richardson eventually invested a large amount of money in companies owned by a Dr.
T.A. Slocum and a Prof. Peake and took over their operations as president, leaving Slocum and Peake to concern themselves with manufacture
and distribution.[72] The major product being sold by Slocum was something called Ozomulsion, or "Slocum's Consumption Cure," which, it
was claimed in its advertising, cured consumption, the word that was
then used for the disease we now call tuberculosis.

Richardson became so involved in the patent medicine business that
from almost the first day of Paul Block's arrival in New York, he could be
found more often in the offices of Slocum and Peake at 183 Pearl Street,
than in his newspaper representatives' office in the Tribune Building. With
the offices located within walking distance of each other, Richardson attempted to run both businesses in transit, almost always favoring his new
interest of patent medicines, however.

Although Paul Block was no stranger to the advertising of patent medicines – as indicated, the *Elmira Telegram* was not adverse to carrying
such ads – he was a bit surprised and somewhat disillusioned when he
arrived in New York to find A. Frank Richardson involved in what was
slowly becoming known in the publishing world as a bunco game upon
the sick and the suffering.

For $5, Dr. Slocum also offered the following products that he claimed
would effect a "cure":

1 large bottle of Psychine
1 large bottle of Ozomulsion
1 large bottle of Coltsfoote expectorant
1 large tube of Ozojell
3 boxes of Lazy Liver Pills
3 Hot X-Ray Porous Plasters

This "cure" was touted as giving great relief for consumption. For
$10, one received twice the above amount of drugs, and a written "guar-
antee" that the consumption would be "permanently and infallibly" cured.
An investigative reporter, Samuel Hopkins Adams, had a laboratory test
conducted for *Collier's Magazine* on the medicine called Psychine and
found that it contained mostly water, about 16% alcohol, and a dash of
strychnine, all adding up to a bottle of shameless quackery, a fraud that
was as heartless as it was, eventually, illegal.[73]

There is nothing to indicate that Paul Block approved of Richardson's new-found patent medicine business, but on the other hand he did have to service the patent medicine accounts that Richardson handled, especially those that appeared in the *Elmira Telegram*. Richardson was adamant that the remedies that he handled were above reproach and pointed to the editorial approval of the respected industry magazine, *Printers' Ink*, as to his rationale:

> There may be proprietary medicines that possess little value; yet the majority of them have been thoroughly tested and proved before they were exploited in newspapers. That so many of them have been in the market for years and are stand-bys in respectable families is highest proof of their merit.[74]

It was several years before the public knew that Richardson was behind the scheme that supposedly provided a cure for consumption, and despite the fact that New York State passed a law in 1898 against misleading advertising, the patent medicine business still continued unabated. The census of 1900 placed the net income of the patent medicine business in the United States at $59,611,355. In terms of how much the public was paying for patent medicines at that time, it was probably more than $100 million a year.

In 1906, when Richardson was confronted by Adams about the genuineness of the medicine, the following exchange took place and appeared in an article in *Collier's* called "The Great American Fraud":

> Question: "Mr. Richardson, will Ozomulsion cure
>   consumption?"
> Answer: "Sure, we have testimonials to prove it."
> Question: "Have you ever investigated any of these
>   testimonials?"
> Answer: "No."[75]

After studying the relationship of the newspaper industry to the field of patent medicines, one might easily conclude that at the turn of the century there was a conspiracy between both groups to defraud the public. The nostrum makers actually forbade the newspapers that carried their advertising from printing negative news about the patent medicine business, and the newspapers went along with the embargo. For example, when a patent medicine company placed an insertion order for advertising space, stipulating the price of the ad, the amount of space to be used each issue, and the position it was to occupy, it also included a caveat that went something like this:

> First – It is agreed in case any law or laws are enacted, either State or national, that are harmful to the interests of (insert name of company that is advertising) that this contract may be canceled by them from date of such enactment, and the insertions made paid for pro-rata with the contract price.
>
> Second – It is agreed that (insert name of company) may cancel this contract, pro rata, in case advertisements are published in this newspaper in which their products are offered, with a view to substitution or other harmful motive, also in case any matter otherwise detrimental to the company's interests is permitted to appear in the reading columns or elsewhere in the newspaper.[76]

Invariably, the newspapers were happy to sign such contracts, and for years thousands of them were put into effect in both dailies and weeklies all across the country. This embargo prevented the papers from running news stories and any other articles deemed detrimental to the nostrum companies about people dying from drinking, for example, Perona, Liquizone and other "cures," or accounts of local health boards trying to prevent the sale of the bogus cure-alls.

The articles in *Collier's* by Samuel Hopkins Adams, exposing the nostrum makers' grip on a large section of the newspaper industry, incensed the public and finally led to the enactment of the Pure Food and Drug laws, and eventually to the end, for the most part, of patent medicine manufacture and advertising.[77]

By the fall of 1900, after five years of working with Richardson, Paul Block apparently could no longer cope with his disillusionment of the continued chicanery being foisted on the public by the patent medicine business. Additionally, Richardson announced that he was personally going to become even less involved in his special representative business, although not giving up the ownership of the company, and he was going to appoint his nephew, Wallace C. Richardson, who was a relative newcomer in the business, to become chief operating officer. What Richardson didn't seem to understand was that the newspapers themselves were making more money from advertising the patent medicines than were the proprietors of the medicines themselves, who were spending on the average of one-third to half of their entire receipts on advertising.[78]

It took Hearst a number of years to share Block's distaste for patent medicine advertising. It wasn't until February of 1912 that Hearst announced that his *New York American*, the *Evening Journal* and *Das Morgen Journal*, would no longer accept objectionable medical advertising.[79]

Paul was incensed that he was not the one who was chosen to run Richardson's business, especially since he was now bringing in the largest amount of income to the company through his sales, and was actually serving, de facto if not in name, as office manager. He was respected by people in the industry, and by the other special representatives, and he could see no reason why Richardson was passing him over. Many years later, Dina Block, Paul's wife, conjectured that he might have been rejected because he was Jewish and that, despite Paul's obvious contributions to the company, Richardson had a touch of anti-Semitism and did not want to reward Paul with a promotion because of his religion.[80]

Whatever the real reason, Paul Block gloomed for a short while and then resigned from Richardson. It was a bittersweet denouement. The years he had worked on Newspaper Row had been times of growth and development. He had made many contacts in the publishing and advertising industries, polished his own distinctive brand of sales presentation, saved some money, and most importantly, he came into contact with the world of national advertising and newspaper publishing in virtually every possible way.

Block's Political Emergence

Parallel to his personal development and the sharpening of his business experience, Paul Block was attempting to understand his own growing political sensibility. He was attracted to Police Commissioner Theodore Roosevelt's progressive attempt to reduce corruption and to clean up the city, but wavered on how strictly the future President enforced the Sunday liquor laws and the closing of saloons. Although Block was a near teetotaler, and did not approve of feral saloon society, many of his German friends were not and they were outraged that their favorite beer parlors and gardens, where they spent quiet afternoons with their friends and families, had been closed on Sundays by Roosevelt.[81] Block felt that the question was not so much a contest between those who wanted to drink on Sundays and those who did not, but an argument that promulgated

"...a statute which restricts [their] personal liberty," as he wrote later.[82]

On September 25, 1895, only weeks after Paul arrived in New York, there was a protest parade where angry Sunday drinkers carried a coffin labeled "Teddyism" through the streets, but despite the antagonism displayed toward Roosevelt, who seemed to have as much, if not more power than the Mayor, Block felt the Reform Movement was trying to do the right things for his new home town.[83] Block was probably further conflicted when in November 1897, the Tammany candidate for Mayor, Robert A. Van Wyck, was elected in a landslide, defeating his Reform Party candidate; and when Theodore Roosevelt defeated Van Wyck's brother at the polls for Governor, his confusion about over which party to follow and support probably also grew.[84]

In New York City in those days, Jewish immigrants often voted for Tammany Hall-picked candidates; but unlike the Irish of the city, the Jews were less committed to the patronage that Tammany provided. In 1894, and again in 1901, the Democrats lost control of the mayoralty, mainly because of the swing vote of the Jewish population.[85] In any event, Paul Block did not consider himself a Jewish voter. Unlike many of the Jews in New York, he was not in the garment or tailoring business, and he had no need of patronage or welfare benefits that Tammany Hall could have provided. He was achieving a certain commercial success and social status on his own, and did not rely on help from or for people of his religious or national origins. He voted as his conscience dictated, and this, for the most part, meant a ballot for the Republicans.

By the time Mayor Van Wyck was sworn in to office on January 1, 1898, Block, as a New Yorker, found himself in the world's second-largest city (second only to London), with 3.4 million inhabitants.[86] The cities of Brooklyn, Queens and Richmond had joined with the Bronx and Manhattan to form one vast municipality, sharing the police, fire and health departments, but still retaining some local governance. This consolidation did not appear, at first, to have a direct effect on Paul Block's life, but it did afford him a cachet in that New York City became even larger in population and reputation, and when he visited other cities and states on his endless sales trips, it was with more weight of prestige since he was coming from the undisputed cultural, population and business capital of the country.

Being tutored by Harry S. Brooks, who had run an independent, non-political newspaper, Block's sensibilities were more liberal than conservative as a young man, although his business dealings seemed to create continued conflicts in his beliefs. In the newspaper business at that time, both in the editorial and business offices, often one's party affiliation affected the acceptance, hiring, sales potential and promotions of any individual: having a political affiliation that was in concert with the editor or publisher meant success; having the "incorrect" affiliation often led to failure.

When Paul visited his various newspaper accounts, the subject of politics and politicians, local and state governments, laws and repeals, would inevitably arise. Often, because he now lived in New York City and was thought of as something of a sophisticated or knowledgeable cosmopolitan, he would be asked his opinions about all manner of things, but especially as they devolved upon politics. His political philosophy had to coincide, he felt, with the prevailing winds.

Richardson was a staunch Republican and he may have secured many of the newspapers that he represented, such as the *Toledo Blade*, through his political advocacy. How strict Richardson was with making his salesmen pay obeisance to, and mouth, the party line is not known but it is altogether possible that Paul kept his liberal sentiments to himself while he worked there. When Paul visited the *Elmira Telegram*, he had no trouble talking with Brooks about politics since they were of basically the same mind (although Brooks was a declared Republican), but when he went across town to visit the *Elmira Gazette*, he had to remember that they leaned toward the Democratic Party, and then when he finished up with his day's sales calls at the *Elmira Advertiser*, he had to adjust his thinking once again back to the Republicans.

Despite its name, the *Rochester Democrat and Chronicle* was a Republican newspaper, as was the *Syracuse Post-Standard*, both of which were Block's accounts. Block's flirtation with conservatism actually would come later in his career when it seemed to be consistent with his wealth and stature, but for many years he would assume a posture of political expediency and fence-sitting that he used opportunistically to advance his business. This is not to imply that he did not have fervent convictions, but he simply could not synthesize more beliefs than he could digest; he was willing, however, eventually to take the time, and pay the price of learning the intricacies of what makes the American government operate.

During his time on Park Row he began to demonstrate his maturity, not only in his personal and political life but as a businessman. He had absorbed most of the beneficial pieces of advice Richardson had offered, and all of the deeply important and many favorable interactions that he experienced with the older man ever since he was a child. The maturing Paul was astute enough, however, to discard any of the untoward or unethical asides that seemed to be infecting Richardson's operation by the time the latter had become totally involved in patent medicines.

Their schism, the alienation that divided Block from Richardson in December of 1900, was not unexpected. Paul had been planning a possible move for many months before he actually left Richardson's employ, and he had begun collecting references and recommendations from his various accounts. As early as October 31, 1900, Block received the following letter from George Batten, a Park Row advertising agent who went on to become one of the principal partners of BBD&O:

> This is to certify that we have known Mr. Paul Block for the past five or six years, which is during his business career here in the City.
>
> We regard him as one of the ablest solicitors that it is has been our pleasure to meet. Our entire business with the office he represents has been transacted with him personally.
>
> We have found him gentlemanly, intelligent, energetic, and best of all, reliable.
>
> George Batten [87]

Stephen Smith, a special representative of the *Minneapolis Tribune*, who worked on the same floor as Paul Block at the Tribune Building, and who was something of a competitor, nevertheless sent Paul the following:

> November 10, 1900
>
> Dear Mr. Block:
>
> I have the pleasure of stating that I have known you for the past five or six years and have had personal knowledge of your work in connection with the A.F. Richardson Agency.
>
> For several years prior to February 1st, 1898, as junior partner of Dauchy & Co., I had the pleasure of meeting you in connection with your soliciting advertising, and for the past three years as a Special Agent I have known a great deal about your work.
>
> I have noticed your special ability as an advertising solicitor, and several Advertising Managers have spoken to me in

the highest terms of your work, and that commendation was brought about by my meeting you in their offices, which led up to the conversation. From what I know, and also from what such managers have told me, you have been very successful, unusually so in soliciting advertising for your agency. Wishing you the best of success, I am,

Very truly yours,
S.B. Smith[88]

F.A. Allen, the director of Pettingill & Company, then the oldest newspaper advertising agency in the country (established in 1849), wrote the following:

December 1, 1900

Dear Mr. Block:

I understand that you terminate your connection with Mr. Richardson today and I am also given an inkling as to the reason. I certainly think you did valiant service for your employer in this office and your efforts deserved to be recognized. I want to say that I will gladly do anything I can for you – It simply is for you to say what. I sincerely hope that you will get located and when you do, let me know.

Very truly yours,
F.A. Allen[89]

Block's idea was to go into business for himself, but he wasn't sure that he really had enough capital to even sustain himself personally, let alone launch an independent operation until funds began coming in. He really did not have the money it would take to initiate a new venture. The letters of reference above that vouch for his general character, situating him in place and time, verified that people of substance knew him, but they hardly sound as though they are written to someone who intends to start a new business. It is probable that he collected these letters and others to show to prospective employers should he be unable to initiate his own new business, and had to gain another sales position.

As it developed, he was fully prepared to take an entrepreneurial chance, feeling that there was virtually nothing he didn't know about the special representative business, and that his connections and his friendships would sustain him. His reaching out to and connecting with people over the years in Elmira and New York City had not been either opportunistic or disingenuous. He made every effort over the years to make friends with whomever he came in contact. Copies of letters of thanks, encouragement, condolences, or just courteous missives of bonhomie, found in the Block family archives and others, were sent by him almost daily to a retinue of friends, associates and admirers, often as not with a gift of flowers or candy.

At about this time, Paul Block became interested in the life of Napoleon Bonaparte, perhaps because he observed that Hearst had a portrait of the emperor over his desk, and read everything he could find concerning the famous general. Later in life he also viewed Abel Gance's epic of the screen, *Napoleon*, mainly about the young life of the emperor, and was influenced by what he saw. His employees bought him a bust of Napoleon (which took a prominent position in his office) and Block bought himself a pair of dueling pistols that supposedly belonged to Napoleon. It was not necessarily the glamour of Napoleon's life that attracted Block, but his philosophy of achievement. This interest by Block may have resulted in an unconscious patterning of Hearst. "Circumstances!" exclaimed Napoleon. "I make circumstances." Block believed that in business, as in war – as Napoleon demonstrated – the ability to take advantage of conditions that help, and to overcome conditions that hinder, keeping always alert to the circumstances of the times, was the key to success. Napoleon also achieved seemingly impossible victories because of his mastery of details. The half-hidden opportunity, the whispered rumor, a countless mass of little things leading to an accumulation of small advantages, was the foundation of victory. Block approached his business in the same way that Napoleon planned his battles: a great general – or businessman – overlooks nothing. It was also Napoleon who said that one must change one's tactics every ten years if one wishes to maintain one's superiority. By 1900, selling advertising for the *Elmira Telegram* and the A. Frank Richardson Co., working for others for a total of ten years, Paul believed that the time had come to make a change.

Further, the theory of his approach to his new business would rest in copying virtually every detail of Richardson's operation and refining the weaknesses; but if his job at Richardson proved anything to him, it was to help him define his ethical standards. He hoped that in establishing his own business he would not repeat any of Richardson's mistakes.

Chapter 3
The Entrepreneur

Starting His Business

It took Paul Block barely a few months, at the end of 1900, to situate and organize himself to begin his own special representative business. At first he could not afford an office, so he worked and operated out of his own lodgings, a comfortable but relatively inauspicious gas-lit room of dark oak furniture in the newly-built Hotel Lucerne on West 79th Street, between Amsterdam Avenue and Broadway, not far from where he had been living. The actor James O'Neill, father of playwright Eugene, also kept an apartment at the Lucerne at that time.[1]

Block had maintained his preference for the Upper West Side, and he found that for many reasons it was advantageous to live in a hotel: it afforded him the opportunity to easily retrieve telephone messages, a place to receive mail and packages, and the use of a lobby that was tastefully decorated with fringed shades, deep carpeting and large stuffed leather chairs, where he could meet business associates. He also chose the Lucerne because of its wood-paneled, ground-floor saloon, which had the best free lunch – including a memorable lobster salad – in town. It is possible that some of his hotel expenses were paid through "due-bills;" he gave the hotel advertising space in one of the newspapers he represented for a free or reduced-price room.

Although Block had saved several hundred dollars from his years at Richardson, money was tight. He borrowed $3,000 from Herman Halsted, and in the fall of 1901 he used that money to open his first office as "Paul Block, Incorporated," at the 311 Vanderbilt Building on the corner of Beekman and Nassau, within the shadow of his old office on Park Row. Initially he hired a 15-year-old secretary and an office and errand boy, but his first major employee was his sole investor, the ever-loyal Herman Halsted.

Block's first client was the *Worcester Telegram-Gazette*, which he had been representing for the five years he had been at Richardson. The publisher of the newspaper, George F. Booth, respected Block and had no difficulty in switching loyalties when the young man contacted him and told him that he was going into business for himself. Often, the only foreign or national advertising person that a newspaper dealt with was the special agent himself, not the firm for which the agent worked, and close ties between publisher and the individual representative would sometimes result.[2] Equally important, Booth felt that it was less cumbersome and more efficient to allow his accounts to remain with Block, rather than risk taking on a different representative suggested by Richardson as Block's replacement. Booth knew how Block thought and how he worked. The young Block had brought substantial advertising into the newspaper, improving its profit margin. Booth saw no reason to change representatives.

The *Worcester Telegram-Gazette* was owned by the Stoddards, a publishing family who had been the proprietors of newspapers in upper New York State and in New England since the 1700s.[3] Henry L. Stoddard, who was the biographer of Horace Greeley and who had been on close terms with every President since Lincoln (with the exception of Garfield), was highly impressed with Block as a result of a few brief meetings.[4] Stoddard had just purchased a controlling interest in his first New York City newspaper, the *New York Evening Mail*, and although he did not as yet appoint Block as his special representative for that newspaper, he sought the young man's advice to help him increase his advertising lineage on the *Mail*,[5] which Block was already attempting to do for the *Worcester Telegram*. Eventually the two men would become business partners.

Despite the fact that Worcester was much smaller than Boston in population, the *Worcester Telegram* had a reputation for being one of the finest newspapers in all of New England. Slowly, with perseverance, finesse and relentless promotion of the *Telegram* and his own reputation as a special representative, Block elevated the *Worcester Telegram's* advertising lineage higher than any other paper in Worcester; it carried more advertising than either the *Boston Post* or the *Boston Herald and Traveler*. Most of the largest advertising agencies in the country, such as J. Walter Thompson and the H. K. McCann Company, began doing business with Block, and such national advertisers as the Postum Cereal Company, Armour, Lever Brothers, and the AutoStrop Safety Razor Co. bought multiple insertions in the *Worcester Telegram*.[6] Eventually, even the strong advertising performance of New York City newspapers began to pale in comparison to what Block was experiencing with the *Telegram*. Only *The New York Times* and *The New York World* at that time had a greater annual lineage than the *Worcester Telegram* under Block's stewardship.[7]

Subsequently securing the *Washington Post* to become its special representative was another important step forward for Block's business. In 1900, when Block approached the *Post* to become its special representative, it was owned by two distinguished Americans: Frank Hatton, former Postmaster General, and Beriah Wilkins, member of Congress from Ohio. Hatton and Wilkins had molded the newspaper to become independent in politics – it had been Democratic in its leanings, but it had also absorbed the *National Republican* – and it was a critical success: its influence among its readers was hardly surpassed by any other publication in the country. "If you want a careful analysis or survey of Washington – ask the *Post*," Block proclaimed in a promotional ad.[8]

The publishers of the *Post* believed that they could increase the newspaper's national advertising profits by bringing in a more dynamic representative, and chose Block because of his knowledge of and contacts in, the advertising field. The *Post* had been the first daily newspaper in Washington to emerge with a Sunday edition and publish seven days a week, sounding a death knell for many of the old Sunday-only weeklies.[9] (The *Sunday Elmira Telegram's* circulation began to slip at that time, and continued to decrease as more dailies also began to publish on Sundays.) Block was enlisted especially to try to increase advertising in the Sunday edition of the *Washington Post*. With such full coverage and front-page stories as the death of President William McKinley, followed by the succession of Theodore Roosevelt, and the January, 1901 death of Queen Victoria, ending her 64-year reign, circulation figures for the *Washington Post* increased markedly, and made Block's job of selling national advertising in the newspaper that much more practicable.

He could not yet quite escape accepting advertising for patent medicines, however. Since the *Washington Post* was primarily interested in increasing advertising revenues, it was reluctant to decline ads from any source. So it encouraged Block's efforts to engage as many advertisements as possible, including ads for patent medicine. One such ad, which appeared in the October 14, 1901 issue, promised to cure rheumatism or neuralgia if one consumed one to five bottles of Mexican Eureka.[10] If no cure ensued, the ad promised, the money paid would be refunded. This ad ran at least once each week – sometimes more often – in the *Post* and was financially successful for the nostrum maker. Governmental and public opinion pressure was mounting against such spurious products, however, and not long after Block began working for the *Washington Post,* the paper changed its advertising acceptance policy. Like many other newspapers in the country, because of governmental pressure as well as ethical and legal grounds, the *Post* began to refuse patent medicine advertising.

Ideally, Block would have preferred that all of the newspapers that he had represented for Richardson would become his own clients. That was not to be. His beloved *Elmira Telegram,* for example, was under a strict, enforceable contract with Richardson (who was also part-owner) and Block therefore could not acquire that newspaper's business. As a result, he had to cease his many business trips to his old home town of Elmira, most of which had invariably led to convenient social asides with his family.

Despite his early successes in gaining a few newspapers, Block's business venture was financially precarious. The first year was a constant struggle. Paying the loan back to Halsted in small installments, sending money to his parents, keeping up with his overhead, and trying to retain a few dollars for personal expenses left no profit for the company. Paul Block, Inc. lost $3,600 at the end of its first year.[11] One by one, however, over the next few years, many of those newspapers that were not committed to – or who were dissatisfied with – other special representatives began to agree to allow Block to represent them. Gaining this new business was often more difficult than it appeared, however.

Very early on in his new venture, Block instinctively thought he had an opportunity to secure the *Memphis News Scimitar* as its representative. He had been to Memphis on several occasions for Richardson, who had previously represented the rival newspaper, the *Memphis Commercial Appeal.* Before resigning from Richardson, in a seed-sowing visit of his own, Block had met the *News Scimitar* people, including the president and publisher, Bernard L. Cohn, and had received a cordial welcome. Cohn was a New Yorker by birth, a graduate of Columbia University, and had risen through the ranks of the newspaper business, first as a reporter, then as an advertising solicitor. Block and Cohn felt that they had much in common and both men respected one another.

The two leading Memphis newspapers were combatants in every way: the political realm, news scoops, circulation numbers, and advertising lineage. It was a competition not only for the readership of the 150,000 residents of the city of Memphis but also for its suburbs and nearby rural areas, as well as potential newspaper buyers and advertisers in relatively nearby Arkansas and Mississippi. The blood feud was so incendiary between the two publications that lawsuits were common and even a pistol duel was being noised about (as late as 1906) between the two Editors, West J. Crawford for the *Appeal*, and Gilbert D. Raine for the *Scimitar*. Raine eventually lost a $500,000 libel suit against Crawford, for calling him a "Confessed common, cowardly, cur, and admitted infamous liar," as well as other unkind and insulting slanders, in a *Commercial Appeal* editorial. [12]

It was into this abyss of bickering that Paul Block entered in 1901 after traveling for two days by train to Tennessee. In his previous visit, it seemed to Block that Cohn had implied that he was favorably disposed to giving him the position of special representative for the *Scimitar*, should he ever go into business for himself, but that his Editor and Advertising Manager would also have to approve such an arrangement.

Perhaps because of the ongoing lawsuit with the *Commercial Appeal*, however, and other distractions that the executives of the *Scimitar* were experiencing, Block did not receive a particularly positive response when he made his formal presentation to the three newspapermen in Memphis. To impress them, he had arrived in the city with some national advertising orders in his briefcase, ready to be placed in their newspaper as soon as a contract was signed. He was also prepared with as much of the demographic material concerning the city of Memphis that he could research, and with other pieces of information about the kinds of advertisers he believed he could secure for the *Scimitar*. The city was known for its active shipping trade since the Mississippi River at Memphis was at its deepest and could accommodate large vessels. Most of the city's population worked in its foundries, carriage and wagon factories, saw and planing mills and a number of small manufacturers; in addition to being an industrial center, Memphis, as the South's wealthiest section, had become a financial nucleus for an enormous cotton and hardwood market. The newspaper that succeeded in Memphis had to speak to both a hard-working blue-collar constituency, and an upper-middle class, gentle but dynamic Southern aristocracy. Block believed he could produce national advertisers who wanted to reach both groups in the Memphis area market.

Since he felt and hoped that the business agreement between the *Scimitar* was a certainty, he had taken the gamble of arriving in Memphis with very little money in his pocket; his strategy was to hand over the insertion orders as the first business between him and the newspaper, and collect partial payment immediately, before returning to New York. Cohn introduced Block to the two executives and they all sat down to hear what he had to say. Block explained his strategy and showed them the figures to support his reasoning. Although Cohn was supportive and wanted to begin a working relationship right away, the other two men sat stone-faced and unresponsive. They would have to think it over, they said. There were other special representative companies that they were considering. Paul Block, Incorporated was a brand new venture, and to them, untested and without reputation; by way of contrast, the *Memphis Commercial Appeal* had just recently contracted to be represented by the long established C. S. Beckwith Company, one of the largest and most successful special representative firms in the country.

Block was devastated at not being accepted, and felt that he would be thought of as not rising to the challenge; furthermore, he was somewhat worried about returning to New York without virtually a penny in his pocket for meals enroute, although he did have a return ticket for the train. His face flushed, but he did not want to show the concern and anger that he was feeling. Somehow he maintained a courteous and respectful mien. As formally as he could, and with a smile on his face, he thanked everyone in the meeting for their time and the opportunity that they had given him to present his business plan. He was particularly deferential and grateful to Cohn; "Thank you for the faith that you have shown toward me," he said sincerely to the older man. He asked if he might be able to present another proposal to the *Scimitar* sometime in the future, concerning his potential representation of the newspaper.

Cohn, feeling badly that the arrangement could not be secured, promised that Block would be given that chance, just at the moment that the other two men, observing the deep affability and affection evinced by Block, began reconsidering their position. And then Block was asked to momentarily step out of the room and not to leave the building. Within minutes he was called back in. Now everyone was smiling. Because he was so impressive and gracious in the moment of defeat, he was told, the triumvirate had decided to acquire his services as their special representative. His gentility and amiability were so pronounced, and his presence so agreeable, that all of those involved in making the decision whether to do business with him felt that they simply could not do otherwise but to sign a contract.[13] To the *Appeal* people present, Block's cordiality had a touch of the famous Southern courtesy about it. He was not the brash New Yorker that they had expected him to be, but someone who it would appear would maintain the dignity of their newspaper whenever he represented them.

Being contracted by the *Memphis News Scimitar* as their special representative turned out to be much more than a momentary triumph: thereafter, Block dealt with the *Scimitar* for many years, and as an object lesson, he liked to tell the story to the new salesmen who he ultimately employed in his own firm, of how he landed the *Scimitar* account. True salesmanship, he would teach somewhat humorously, is the art of letting someone else have your own way. Primarily, one must think twice before saying nothing, but to say nothing, except to be friendly and courteous, is half the strategy of selling. No one, with the possible exception of Paul Block himself, could have guessed at that time that before long he would be the owner of the *Memphis News Scimitar*, and some of the very people who had judged him that day would then be in his employ.

Years later, Bernard Cohn wrote a heartfelt letter to Block expressing his thanks over the prosperity of the *News Scimitar* and virtually begging him for his editorial input on some of the changes that Cohn was introducing:

Dear P.B.:

Once again I want to say that I have you to thank for what has been to me and mine a splendid year and a happy one. The conditions under which I am working with you, the understanding and the encouragement you have given me, have given me happiness and the will to accomplish what we most desire as to *The News Scimitar*.

I am herewith enclosing a copy of today's paper. We have started the Ledger service as you will note from page two. You will also please note the Woman's Page on page fifteen and the Magazine and Comic Page on page sixteen. Please note the copious use of pictures; also I believe there is plenty of news space. Please look it over carefully and let me have your criticism. To my mind this is the best all around paper we have ever gotten out from a regular news and feature standpoint and far overshadows anything in this section. Of course it is a lot looser in news than we have been printing in the last few months and practically double that of last year. I hope to use today as a standard for space requirements and see if we can do it and make money. Under the new paper price I think we can.

Will you let me have your criticism of it as a whole – and also any particular things which you think can be improved. I hope to hear you say "This is a pretty good paper." If I don't get you to say it this time, I am going to keep at it until you do.

> With kindest regards,
> Cordially yours,
> Bernard

In general, the amount of national advertising in newspapers continued to increase since many new papers throughout the country were making their debuts. Local advertising was also expanding rapidly, in large part because dry goods stores were constructing multistory buildings, called department stores, which were absorbing other retailers in a form of retail Darwinism. These dynamic marketers invariably placed many large advertisements, often full-page ads, to sell their wares. *The Dry Goods Economist* correctly observed that: "The newspaper of today is largely the creation of the department store."[14] This profusion of advertising dollars into their newspapers made the publishers want even higher circulations (which would justify charging higher space rates), and caused them to then look toward other venues for still more possible advertisers. These were key reasons that Block's operation grew quite quickly, but his future prosperity rested on the advent of brand name products which sought national exposure. By 1904, there were 13,513 weeklies and close to 3,000 dailies, all of them eager for national advertising of name-brand products and mass-produced goods.

Unwilling to merely reap the accidental good fortune of doing business in such an opportune time, Block did virtually everything possible to take advantage of the great advertising boom. Each social gathering, sporting event or trip to the theater became a business opportunity, during which he sought out and garnered new accounts. Little by little, Block used these occasions to find new business and to build his own personnel base.

A case in point occurred at a Dartmouth football game. Block was introduced to Charles Boyle, a former star for the team, who had become advertising manager for the New England territory of *The Delineator,* a woman's magazine that consisted mainly of sewing patterns. Block was so impressed with this large and genial man that during half-time, he offered him a job.[15] Boyle went on to play an important role in the Block organization, especially when Block eventually became involved in women's magazines himself.

Every day Block scoured all of the New York City newspapers, and many of the out-of-town publications as well, for potential leads for new advertisers. He worked far into the night, virtually every evening, composing letters to existing clients, checking out circulation data, and analyzing competitive advertising rates.[16] *Editor & Publisher* magazine in 1903 referred to Block's spirit in always giving the newspapers he represented the credit for his gains in business: "It will be seen that Mr. Block is as modest as he is successful," they wrote, to which Block also thanked the "good hard work" of Herman Halsted, and a new assistant, William M. Messiter.[17]

He also deepened his understanding of what kinds of advertising worked best in terms of copy, design and overall content, and what was the dramatic message inherent in every product, so that he could guide his advertisers into producing a successful advertisement. These new kinds of ads appealed to the underlying emotional motivations of the consumer, and such products as Palmolive soap, which heretofore had been sold simply and purely as soap to clean your hands, now were being touted as a way of "achieving that schoolgirl complexion."[18] Decades later, Madison Avenue became devoted to the concept of using emotional or psychological factors to beguile consumers to buy, but Paul Block was one of the earliest proponents of this technique. His ads *succeeded* in selling products, so advertisers continued to place more ads in the papers he represented.

The nature of the consumer was changing. While from 1880 to 1910 the population of the United States had doubled, the ability of the consumer to choose the sources of his purchases increased by a much greater percentage. This was for the most part influenced by significant commercial and communications advances. The aggregate circulation per issue of publications in the U.S. had multiplied by five, the length of the street railway lines had multiplied by eight, and the length of the telephone lines increased by twenty. Changes in retailing were also related to the expansion of the use of the automobile as autos extended the trading area, and as a result of the spread of affluence. The American population was shifting, too. In 1880 a little over one-third of the population of the United States lived in cities of more than 25,000; within a few years after the turn of the century nearly one-half of the American population was living in cities of that size. The country was speeding up and crowding up, and the ways that products and services were advertised became markedly different after 1900. These changes impacted upon the lifestyles of the average American consumer, and were reflected in people's reactions to the stimuli exerted by national advertising.[19]

Concomitant to these changes was a certain growing consciousness and ethical standard that the consumer began applying to the advertising policies of newspapers. With the realization that patent medicines were not what they purported to be, for example, the public was demanding a higher moral standard in advertising than had been present just 10 or 20 years previously. Paul Block became aware of this growing unrest and began discussing the issue with the advertisers and newspapers with which he worked. It was a delicate and crucial point for the publishers. On one hand, newspapers made the greatest bulk of their profits by running advertisements, and it seemed incongruous to tell purveyors of patent medicine that their advertising dollars were not acceptable. Yet on the other hand, readers wanted their newspapers to be ethical and honest in everything they published, news stories *and* advertisements. In addition to the moral issue there was the very real business danger that irate readers might stop buying a newspaper that offended them, and might switch to a competitor. Block held numerous conversations with his clients, gently using a combination of logical analysis and illustrative anecdote in an attempt to dissuade them from carrying these often spurious ads. Although he succeeded in convincing some newspapers, there were still many publications that continued to accept patent medicine advertising, and they looked to Block to supply those ads and fill their pages.

•••

Block's representation of the *Topeka State Journal* continued for decades and only abated when the newspaper ceased to publish. As the capital of Kansas, the city was alive with packing houses, foundries, creameries, railroad and machine shops, printing plants and flour mills. The *Journal* had a hold on the readership not only of Topeka but all of Kansas, as well. The editor, Frank P. McLennon, oversaw and approved every photo, advertisement, article and comma before it was inserted into the paper. "That is enough to guarantee a newspaper's quality," Block once quipped, hinting at his admiration of a truly hand's-on editor. The two men considered themselves more than just business associates, but close friends.[20]

As well as becoming involved in the city of Topeka, Block also became the representative of a newspaper in Ohio, the *Cleveland News-Leader*. Strangely, even though Cleveland was then, in 1914, the fifth largest city in the United States, it had only three daily newspapers, while other cities of comparable or even smaller size, boasted seven or eight papers. When Block secured the representation of the *News-Leader*, it already had the highest circulation and the largest advertising lineage of any other paper in the city. It had entered publishing history as one of the first newspapers in the country to have an attached automatic folding device when the papers came off the press: until then, the carrier boys folded the newspapers themselves.[21] Block helped the paper increase its foreign, or national, advertising by over 35 percent in his first years of representing the *Cleveland News-Leader*.

Block continued to maintain contact with some of the other publications that he had been representing for Richardson, through personal visits, correspondence and the telephone. In time, he started to win some of them over. Within barely a year he had secured the *Rochester Democrat and Chronicle*, the *Syracuse Post-Standard*, the *Milwaukee News*, the *Jamestown Post*, and, as noted, the *Washington Post* and the *Topeka State Journal*. A trade publication of the day, *Advertising News*, noted and lauded his exploits in a story featuring the young man's new company:

> The special representative of today combines personality, adaptability, thorough knowledge of the advertising field, locally as well as generally, and thoroughness of detail. The specials are a wide-awake and aggressive set of men, capable of producing results for the publications they represent, and none are more so than Paul Block.[22]

Although the records of the earliest days of Paul Block, Inc. no longer exist, it is possible through an examination of the advertising rates of the day and an inspection of the ads that Paul Block had sold, to make an extremely rough estimate as to how much money his new business began to gross. By the time he had secured the advertising representation of the six newspapers named above, he could have brought in some $50,000 to $60,000 of billings per month, per paper. Out of that gross amount, he deducted his 15% commission, which may have netted his new-found business close to $270,000 a year, well over several million dollars in comparison to today's currency. Not all of that money went into Block's pocket, however. He had a large overhead: his office space, staff salaries, the advertising and promotion of his own company, and the loan repayment to Halsted. Paul Block was not quite an overnight success in his new entrepreneurial venture, but nevertheless he reached a certain ascendancy fairly early on. By 1903, *Editor & Publisher* referred to him as, "One of the best-known newspaper representatives in the country," and if there was any doubt to that fact in the reader's mind, the magazine published Paul Block's photograph on its front cover.[23] He was still in his twenties.

Two weeks after the publicity and commendation he received from *Editor & Publisher*, the first narrative film produced in the United States, *The Great Train Robbery*, was shown in New York: Paul Block attended a performance because of his growing interest in the medium.

The financial success that Paul Block was beginning to experience, which he continued to undergo for the next three decades, not only gave him personal satisfaction, but it enabled him to help friends and relatives. Desiring attainment for himself, he helped others to find a foothold for themselves. He sent his two sisters, Blanche and Frieda, to Elmira Female College and paid their tuition; he helped his father to give up the junk business and move into a slightly more respectable field, that of selling grain and feed, and he bought his mother Mary an electric automobile (which she refused to drive herself, and made her children act as chauffeurs). Mary Block's electric automobile was picked up every evening by its manufacturer, the owner of the local bicycle shop, John Willys, who took it back to his garage, literally plugged in the car for a battery re-charging every night and brought it back to her in the morning. Willys went on to form the Willys-Overland Automobile Company and become one of the great auto tycoons.[24]

As soon as Block's two sisters graduated from college, Paul invested in a jewelry business that his brother Max had started in Buffalo, and he helped to buy a large, comfortable house for his parents in that same city. All of the Blocks, with the exception of Paul, then lived in Buffalo until his mother's death in 1910. Block also began at that time a consistent tradition of philanthropy, which started modestly with small donations to worthwhile groups and charities, but gradually increased in amount and frequency, and would continue all of his life. No records or figures were kept as to exactly how much of his own money Block gave away, but it was most probably in the millions in pre-World War II dollar value.

By the end of 1903, Block had six full-time salesmen working for him, and had sent Halsted off to Chicago to open an office there to handle all mid-western (and western) advertising. Block's secretary, Miss Healy, eventually married Herman Halsted when he returned to New York in 1905, and since he was needed more by Block in the New York office, he was persuaded to return to Manhattan. Paul Block, Inc. also moved to larger quarters at 132 Nassau Street, but as the business began to prosper, he gave up his downtown office and moved to the newly-opened Fuller Building, which quickly became referred to – as it is to this day – as The Flatiron Building because of its implausible wedge-like shape; the name is actually an unimaginative metaphor for a richly-decorated French Renaissance ornamental masterpiece of architecture. It was the tallest skyscraper in New York at that time, and as it was being constructed, skeptics stood at what they considered a safe distance to watch it crumble at the first high wind. Almost 100 years later it is still proudly standing.

The move to the 21-story Flatiron Building was a significant symbol of the progress of Paul Block's business, and placed him in the social, political and business center of the city. A showplace and prestige address of its time, one of the first office buildings in the United States to have an elevator, it quickly became an icon not only of the city but of the age of opulence; the building bisected Fifth Avenue and Broadway at 23rd Street, and from its plush rooftop restaurant, and from many of the windows, office workers could see all the way to New Jersey to the west and Brooklyn and Queens to the east, in addition to a sweeping and commanding view of virtually the entire uptown and downtown areas of Manhattan. Rents were high and Block was one of the first major tenants of what became, and remained for years, one of the most luxurious office buildings in New York City.

The building was clearly denotative of Manhattan, and a subject of seemingly endless interest for photographers and artists. Edward Steichen and Alfred Stiegletz, among others, saw the Flatiron as a mystical tower, rising softly out of the haze, almost a part of the natural landscape."[25] The Flatiron also served as one of the first sightseeing depots in the city, from where open-air buses would leave every hour on an excursion to what the tour company promised to be an authentic look at the city's neighborhoods, including "the Bowery – with its endless procession of human wrecks."[26]

Across the street stood the great political and fashion center, the Fifth Avenue Hotel, famed for its "Amen Corner" where political notables, office seekers, and partisans met to discuss and influence the politics of the city, and sometimes of the country. Block immediately began to frequent the hotel's restaurant, where he conducted his non-stop combination of business and social activity. For years, the Fifth Avenue Hotel remained the largest hotel in the world, dominating the Madison Square section of New York, in concert with the Flatiron Building, as the hub of city life.

Shortly before Block moved into his new offices, a short film was made and distributed, entitled *The Flatiron Building on a Windy Day*. It demonstrated how the building acted as an unwitting wind tunnel, generating great updrafts as the airy blasts from both the East and Hudson rivers swept down 23rd Street to converge upon it. Because of its pie-like prow, the building's corner quickly became known as the windiest in the city, and young boys would often dawdle in front of it in order to catch a glimpse of the hosiery and lingerie of the women walking by as they valiantly, but often in vain, tried to hold down their long skirts. Loitering to watch the ladies became a punishable offense. Nonetheless, the voyeuristic practice became so prevalent that policemen patrolled the area to chase the young men away. The officers' gruff command became a catch phrase that entered our language.[27] In shooing the loungers away from 23rd Street, the cops shouted: "23 Skidoo!"

The fact that Block could move his business into what was New York's most lavish office building was testament to the success that he was experiencing. It seemed that each new newspaper that Paul Block secured would result in him gaining another paper, in a parlaying effect, as his reputation grew. He was making money, in some cases considerable sums, for the newspapers that he represented, and he was increasingly a topic of conversation within newspaper and advertising circles. *The Fourth Estate*, a journal for the newspaper industry, published an article in 1906 on Block and his associates, which said in part: "Among the special newspaper representatives of the country, probably there is none better known or more liked and respected than Paul Block."[28] In addition to the papers he was already working for, such as the *Washington Post*, he eventually secured the *Chicago Inter-Ocean*, the *St. Louis Times*, the *Toledo Blade*, and with the help of his friend Henry L. Stoddard, the controversial *New York Evening Mail*.

Love and Friendship

1906 turned out to be an auspicious year for Paul Block. In addition to seeing his business expand propitiously, he met a young woman named Dina Wallach, and fell in love. Block was 32 when he met the 18-year-old Dina, and at first it had seemed that there would be no possibility of marriage. He was always traveling, and when he was home in New York he was usually working, often far into the night and on weekends. So the opportunity of establishing a serious or, ultimately, a permanent relationship with a woman was, if not impossible, certainly difficult. But by 1906 he had realized that if he didn't marry soon, he might remain a bachelor. Most of his friends and business associates were long married, including Halsted and even some who were much younger than Block. Many of them already had small families.

Block met Dina Wallach through the efforts of his new salesman, Harry M. Lasker, the 25-year-old younger brother of the advertising innovator Albert Lasker. Lasker the elder, who had made the Chicago advertising agency Lord & Thomas into one of the most prestigious in the world, had asked Block through a letter of introduction whether he could possibly find a place in his company for Lasker's brother Harry, who was moving to New York. Albert Lasker knew Block as a result of having placed advertising through him for such products as soaps, cigarettes, household wares and Campbell Soup; in about 1905, Lasker had also bought space in Block's newspapers for John N. Willys, the bicycle salesman coincidentally from Elmira, New York, who was the inventor of Mary Block's electric automobile.[29] The fact that Block and Willys knew each other from their early Elmira days helped to smooth the way in negotiating where and how much advertising on a national basis should be considered for the Willys-Overland.

Block took Harry Lasker into his company more as a favor to Albert, rather than because he believed that the young man was going to be a particularly important asset to his business. But if he was anything, Harry Lasker was cordial and a bit of a social butterfly, having been raised by an aristocratic and wealthy Texas family and then living in the North Shore section of Chicago. Harry was continually invited to parties or other social engagements in New York, and he made certain that his new employer, Paul Block, would receive an invitation as well.

The three Lasker sisters, Florina, Henrietta and Loula, all went to college, lived in New York and became friends with Dina Wallach. They might well have met at an Upper East Side Synagogue they attended, near where they all lived. When Dina invited the Lasker girls for an afternoon lunch at her home on East 79th Street, they asked whether their brother, new to the city, could be invited as well. Harry, in turn, gently inquired of Dina whether he could also invite his friend Paul Block, but the 64-year-old Karl Wallach, Dina's father, and her step-mother Blanche, refused the request, feeling that she already had too many beaus, and saying that she could only have one young man at a time to lunch. Dina's sisters closest to her age, Esther, Clara and Belle, and her brother Sidney, an affable young man, were also present that day. The younger Wallach children, Harry, Martha and seven-year-old James, were shepherded off somewhere to not disturb their older brother and sisters when they were entertaining.

The lunch, on a Sunday afternoon, was a festive affair. Afterward, the group retired to the front parlor where Dina played the piano and all joined in for a series of popular songs. The Wallachs were wealthy Upper East Siders; Karl had been a schoolteacher when he emigrated from Germany, and had quickly become involved in real estate, buying up tenements and other low rental apartments first on the Lower East Side, and then in the Yorkville section of Manhattan, from Third Avenue to the East River. Dina had attended a finishing school, The Misses Moses' Boarding and Day School, and studied French, music, dancing, etiquette and other subjects befitting a Jewish upper class *demoiselle* of post-Victorian New York; the moral standards, attitudes and conduct of the Age of Innocence, permeated with a certain stuffiness and hypocrisy, somehow melded with the Judaism that was practiced in the Wallach household.

Karl Wallach looked and acted the part of a prominent *burgomeister*: rotund, with a prominent belly, often thoughtfully smoking a long clay pipe and sporting a wardrobe of loden clothing in the style that he had become accustomed to in his native Germany. With a perennial feather in his cap, he lorded over his properties and his family of eight children with a paradox of qualities as though he was nothing less than a mayor of a medieval fiefdom: he was all at once formal, severe, kindly and with a sense of fair play and impartiality.

German was the official language of the Wallach household, although English was spoken to American-born visitors. The family was proud of their accent, which was somewhat Hannoverian. They understood Yiddish but considered it somewhat of a vulgar dialect, an East European "ghetto vernacular," low-class in origin, and felt that if they used it freely it would hamper their assimilation into the upper classes of Jewish New York. On Friday evenings, at a candle-lit dining room table decorated with lace and silver, Karl would read from the Talmud in Hebrew, a language he studied formally all his life through weekly lessons with a Rabbi. All of the servants, those who lived with the Wallachs and those who came to service on a daily basis, spoke a fairly high German.[30]

In the middle of the afternoon that the Laskers came to lunch with Dina and the Wallachs, the telephone rang in Karl's upstairs study. Dina ran hurriedly up to the second floor, and discovered that the call was from Paul Block, inquiring for Harry Lasker. Perhaps it was a pre-arranged signal so that Block could become involved in the festivities, after all. Whatever its intended purpose, the call seems to have had an immediate effect on Dina. "He has such a pleasant voice," she said to Lasker coyly, "filled with heart...and so soft," and then handed him the telephone receiver. Block asked if he could come over to the Wallach's home to pick Harry up, and Dina told Harry that that would be acceptable, and further instructed him that when Paul arrived he should be invited in to meet everyone. She was intrigued by the voice she had heard on the telephone.

It was hours later, in the late afternoon, when Paul finally arrived at the Wallach's home. It had been snowing heavily and he had secured a hansom cab to take him across Central Park. It was slow going. The streets were unplowed and many horses and some cabs were sliding, toppling and falling dangerously. There was such a heavy accumulation of snow on the sidewalks and in the alleys that when Block arrived at East 79th Street, the driver was forced to park his horse and cab in the gutter rather than the driveway. This caused disruption and undoubtedly annoyed other drivers because it made it difficult for cabs and horses to get through the street, but it was the only space that had been at least partially cleared by the ongoing traffic.

Although Block had expected to stay for just a few moments after being introduced, he spent the rest of the afternoon with the group, playing piano duets with Dina, trotting out the various memory tricks that he had learned in Elmira, and generally captivating the entire party: his repertoire included stories of growing up in Europe, his adventures in cities all over the country, and his opinion of the young, self-confident and outspoken President of the United States that he and most everyone else admired so much, Theodore Roosevelt.

But if Paul had captured the attention and affection of everyone that afternoon, he in turn, was smitten by Dina Wallach. Although not traditionally beautiful, she had a refreshing, youthful refinement about her and she seemed to hang on his every word. For Paul, it was love at first afternoon. "If that girl doesn't have a steady beau, I'm going to marry her," he proclaimed to Harry Lasker just minutes after they eventually left the party.

A few days later, Paul had a five-pound box of candy delivered to Dina, with a decidedly unromantic note: "Thank the man for the candy," meaning that she shouldn't forget to tip the delivery man. The accompanying missive was somehow altogether frank, charming and paternal, and it bespoke a familiarity that Paul really had not earned from the few hours that he had spent with Dina, but she was taken by its sincerity and practicality.

Shortly after that, Paul went to Chicago and other midwest cities, visiting his existing clients, and stopping by prospective newspapers and advertisers. He was gone from New York for close to two months, but almost daily he penned a letter to his new-found *inamorata*. From the very beginning, he assumed that Dina was the woman he was going to marry, and his early correspondence, which often went unanswered by Dina, indicates his resolve and interest. As the following excerpts show, these mostly undated notes were fresh, rough-hewn, presumptuous and totally heartfelt:

> Dear Dina - Need I tell you that your little note made me happy? Need I tell you that your voice, even though faintly heard over the phone, gave me joy? No, for my Dina knows that my life needs these pleasures which, only thinking of her, gives me and so she knows that no matter how busy – no matter what section of the country I'm in, my heart is where *she* is and my thought with *her*.

•••

> Hello there Dina – You see I'm writing to you even though I haven't heard from you – but I'm sure you haven't forgotten me...

•••

April 11, 1907

> Dear Dina – I'm not trying to start a correspondence with you – I'll leave that for...the Harry Lasker's, but I must be frank and tell you that I am grateful for your messages. But you don't like people to compliment you, so again I'm in a fix...Some day, when my ship comes in, and my business needs no more study, I may call over to 79th Street and ask

> Miss Dina the method to pursue to study the New York girl.
> But she may not be there.

When Paul returned to New York, he began his pursuit of Dina in person and in earnest. Elaborate boxes and baskets of candy wrapped in gold foil, costing as much as $25 – an absolute fortune in those days – were sent on a regular basis. Flowers arrived for Dina routinely at the Wallach's house. Paul received permission from her father to take Dina to the theater (accompanied by Harry Lasker and his sister Loula) to see the farcical romance, *His Excellency the Governor*, with Ethel Barrymore and her brother John ("Beyond description" Dina wrote in her souvenir program); and five nights later, on April 30, 1907, he took Dina to the Shubert musical, *The Orchid*, with Eddie Foy.

Karl Wallach was not at first impressed with the young man who was courting his daughter. He expressed his concern to Dina, who was not so slowly falling in love with the suitor. A protective father, Wallach wanted his daughter to marry well. But for him, that meant not only future wealth, but breeding and family background and an adherence to the Jewish traditions that he valued. Yes, Paul was Jewish and he could speak German. Yes, he seemed charming and attentive. But what were his real prospects? Wasn't he merely a salesman whose father was a junkman? Wasn't he 14 years older than Dina? Didn't he live in a hotel? Neither did he know Hebrew, nor did he belong to a Temple. "Where love is thick, faults are thin," Wallach said, quoting an old Jewish proverb, implying that Dina was overlooking some of Paul's failings because she was attracted to him.

Paul persisted, and eventually, when visiting Dina in the summer of 1907, at the Wallach family's country place at Westwood, New Jersey, he proposed while she was swinging in a hammock on the lawn. He nonchalantly asked, "When are you going to marry me?" Dina was immediate with her response: "When you ask my father." Paul, who was a bit fearful of the imposing Karl Wallach, and knowing Wallach's somewhat less than confident feeling toward him, assumed an indignant pose. "I would never ask *anybody* for permission to marry his daughter!" he said, at which point Dina, knowing that out of respect, tradition and intimidation, she simply could not, and would not, marry without her father's permission, replied, "Then let's forget about it."

Paul would not forget about it, however, nor did Dina really want him to. When the family returned to the city at summer's end, Paul paid a

Sunday afternoon visit to the East 79th Street house, and respectfully approached Karl Wallach for his daughter's hand. "My most important concern is whether you can support her," Karl said. "I wouldn't have asked her to marry me if I couldn't support her," Paul replied somewhat flippantly. Wallach told Block that he would think it over and he would give his answer in a few days.

The very next day, Wallach dressed formally, and announced to the household that after breakfast he was traveling downtown to The Flatiron Building, unannounced, just to see what kind of an operation Paul Block was running – and how prosperous it was. Dina sneaked upstairs and called Paul on her father's telephone: "My father is going to see your office! I just wanted to warn you!" Immediately, Block went into action. All of his salesmen were on the road and only his secretary and office boy were present. All three scrambled to clean up the office, neatly stacking papers, sweeping the floor, hastily wiping the wooden desks, emptying wastepaper baskets, and straightening the chairs.

By the time Karl Wallach arrived, the office was humming, bright and shining from its instant sprucing. Paul had copies of newspapers from throughout the country, and he could point out ads that had been placed there by Paul Block, Incorporated. His carefully organized accounts ledgers delineated all of the income, expenses, and other pertinent material essential to the special representative business. Then, by pure serendipity, an out-of-town newspaper executive paid a visit to the office at that very moment to discuss the possibility of having Paul Block represent his newspaper. Karl Wallach was a businessman; he could see that the company, though relatively new, was doing quite well. Apparently he was sufficiently impressed and at long last satisfied with Block's prospects, because he agreed to have a luncheon with Paul in the posh restaurant atop the Flatiron Building.

"It looks like he is a smart boy," Wallach told his relieved daughter upon his return home. Just a few weeks later, on December 18, 1907, Dina Wallach and Paul Block were married. Because Paul's mother was seriously ill, the couple only had a small ceremony at the Wallach's elegant home. At 5 PM that Wednesday afternoon, Rev. Dr. Schulman of Temple Beth-El in Manhattan officiated at Paul and Dina's marriage, standing under the traditional Jewish *chuppa*, a canopy of white silk in honor of the "royal" couple being joined together. Paul, wearing a *yarmulke*, stepped on and broke a glass, a symbol of the destruction of the Temple and a reminder that Jews should never forget the sufferings of Israel.

Although only immediate relatives were present, Dina wore a traditional white satin and lace gown, with orange blossoms fastened to her veil. Afterward, the couple left for a brief honeymoon at the Chalfonte Hotel in Atlantic City, New Jersey. When Paul returned to New York with his new wife, they settled down in a Manhattan apartment, and Paul went at his work even more zealously.

Most families have enduring myths – stories passed down from generation to generation, told and retold around dinner tables, at weddings and graduations, whenever family members gather together. The Block family legend, which is accepted by most of Paul Block's descendants, supposedly explains how Paul became so successful, first in advertising and then in the publishing business. According to the family narrative, Paul was struggling desperately until he married Dina Wallach. The wedding gift of $15,000 ($10,000 in West Shore bonds, and $5,000 in cash) that the newly-married couple received from Karl Wallach was what really enabled him to expand his business and to compete financially. So goes the legend. In reality, this was not entirely the case. As indicated previously, even before Paul met Dina Wallach, he had been noticed and lauded as one of the most well-known, respected and successful special newspaper agents in the country. He recognized instantly that the wedding gift from Karl Wallach was really addressed to Dina, and for implied use in their home rather than his business. Block's pride would not allow him to take the money under any other condition. Seven days after the marriage, while still in Atlantic City, Paul wrote to his father-in-law, and it is interesting to note how quickly and tenderly he ingratiated himself into the Wallach clan, now his *machetunim*, or relatives-by-marriage:

> My dear Father –
>
> In our happiness, on this, our first little trip, I have overlooked numberless things, including the letter which I wanted to write you.
>
> May I therefore take this time in thanking you, for both Dina and myself, for the beautiful gift you gave her in the shape of ten thousand dollars worth of West Shore bonds and the check for five thousand dollars.
>
> They will be kept for Dina and if my ambition is fulfilled, it won't be long before I will save enough more, so that Dina will own double the amount which she has now.
>
> I don't think I have to tell you again what I think of your gift. Fifteen thousand dollars is not a small sum and it isn't

every father who is willing, or able, to give this sum to each of his children. Sometimes, when I think of how hard you worked and how you saved and toiled without thinking of yourself, I really feel sorry for you, but I am reminded that it is all for the love of your children and that this makes you happy. I know, of course, that all you ask in return, is to see your children provided for and happy and I believe, dear Father, that I am able to do this for Dina now and always.

I believe Dina will tell you how very happy we are and I know this will gladden your heart.

> Devotedly, your son
> Paul
> December 26, 1907

That some of the wedding gift money was used for joint expenses is fairly certain, but Paul Block was on his way to financial independence, and it wasn't until almost 25 years later that he came close to having any major reverses. At the time of his marriage, though, his life was exemplary in many ways, beginning to be prosperous. It was time to branch out, and he began to explore other mediums. His first new venture was in magazines.

Illustrated Sunday Magazine

Just months before Paul Block met Dina, a new periodical, the *Illustrated Sunday Magazine*, opened its offices in The Flatiron Building. It was a supplement to Sunday newspapers. Almost instantly Paul Block became their first special representative for national advertising. The rationale for an attractively designed and beautifully printed supplement rested on the fact that several activities, notably the proliferation of automobiles and increased numbers of sporting events, were consuming the public's interest; the owners of Sunday newspapers felt they had to compete for their readers' attention to keep circulation and advertising on an upward path. Some daily newspapers had begun producing their own special Sunday supplements, but found it difficult to do so with their existing editorial staff; they needed new personnel who were trained to think as magazine writers and editors, to be able to assign and acquire feature articles – with a more literary bent – a chore that hardboiled newspaper journalists and editors were unqualified or unwilling to do. *The New York Times* had started an *Illustrated Magazine* in 1896 but suspended it in 1899, because of the difficulty of staffing it adequately and the lack of facilities for printing the increasing number of copies needed. William Randolph Hearst also started the *Sunday American Magazine*, with tales of sex abnormalities, horror, romance, gossip about the ultra-wealthy social "400," and other assorted oddities. Eventually this was turned into the *American Weekly* and grew into a supplement for all Hearst newspapers and many non-competing papers who used it to boost their own circulations.

There had been other illustrated newspapers and magazines in the past, going back to the *Illustrated London News* in the mid-nineteenth century, as well as other periodicals such as *Gleason's Pictorial*, *The Weekly Herald*, the *Police Gazette*, and even *Harper's Weekly* and *Harper's Bazaar*.[31] *Frank Leslie's Illustrated Newspaper*, which started in 1855, featured hairbreadth thrills and sensational crusades, and contained line-cut engravings, superbly executed but often romanticized and exaggerated, on half of its 14 pages. The goal of the *Illustrated Sunday Magazine*, however, was to be illustrated throughout, with photographs and drawings, engravings and paintings on *all* of its pages.

The *Illustrated Sunday Magazine* may have been the first Sunday supplement that was produced by an independent staff. Its reporters, artists, and all personnel were not employees of a newspaper. They worked solely for the *Illustrated Sunday Magazine*. And the magazine was published solely as a cooperative adjunct to any newspaper that wanted to buy it for its own readers, to have it included along with their regular Sunday paper, similar to the way *Parade* is produced and distributed today. Perhaps because it was considered a *supplement*, no contemporary history of journalism even footnotes the *Illustrated Sunday Magazine*, nor is there virtually any archival coverage of its existence, and deep research into its origins, operation and ownership could net very little information. This is a strange lapse, since in 1907, barely a year after its inception, it boasted a circulation of close to two million and advertising revenues of over $500,000 annually.

The *Illustrated Sunday Magazine* became one of the most popular periodicals in the country, and such prestigious newspapers as the following made it their official Sunday supplement:

Pittsburgh Gazette-Times	*Boston Herald*
Washington Post	*New Orleans Picayune*
Cleveland Leader	*Detroit Free Press*

Milwaukee Sentinel	*Philadelphia Record*
Providence Tribune	*Omaha News*
Louisville Courier-Journal	*Memphis Commercial Appeal*
Baltimore American	*Minneapolis Tribune*
Des Moines Register and Leader	*Columbus Dispatch*
Rochester Democrat and Chronicle	*Denver Republican*
Hartford Courant	*Richmond Times-Dispatch*
Kansas City Journal	... and others

Block's position with the supplement was much more than being its special representative: many of the newspapers that became part of the cooperative were secured by Block, and shortly after he began working with the publication, he was named Advertising Manager, with a salary in addition to commission, in charge of *all* advertising that came in. It is estimated that he personally made well over one million dollars from the *Illustrated Sunday Magazine* alone in the years that he was associated with it.

Each issue was shipped in stereotype mats to the subscribing newspaper, with the top of the front page containing the logo and with a space underneath left blank so that the newspaper could then insert its own name when it printed the supplement. The result personalized the magazine, making it appear that it was published by that newspaper's editors; for example:

Illustrated Sunday Magazine
of the
Detroit Free Press

Promoting itself as a literary periodical, the *Illustrated Sunday Magazine* was as impressive to look at as it was to read. Published in four colors on glossy paper stock, it generally consisted of about 20 pages, though some newspapers included an additional 4 to 8 pages of local-oriented features of their own. Lavishly illustrated by such great artists as James Montgomery Flagg and Howard Chandler Christy, the *Illustrated Sunday Magazine* also contained some of the most famous and popular writers of the day. A typical issue might include a travel story from the *Rue de la Paix* or from Japan written by Richard Harding Davis, a tale of northern adventure by Jack London, an article on the state of the theater by Lee Shubert, a novella – in series – by George Randolph Chester, a mystery by Mary Roberts Rinehart, a western saga – in installments – by Rex Beech, and an article on how millionaires made their fortunes.

Because of the high circulation figures, and the quality and reputation of the newspapers that carried it, the advertising for the *Illustrated Sunday Magazine* was plentiful. Block brought to its pages such renowned national names as The Cream of Wheat Company, Nestle's Food, Coca-Cola, Pond's, Quaker Oats, Bon Ami and Carter's Ink. Additionally, literally thousands of other less known advertisers who bought small ads kept coming back because their expenditure was cost effective and they made money after each insertion. Block accepted advertisements that touted everything from Gulf Coast acreage, hair brushes, and typewriters, to ladies' shoes, desk lamps, and instruction on how to write motion picture plays (even well before the onset of sound movies).

Pictorial Review

With large amounts of money coming in from the commissions he was earning from the *Illustrated Sunday Magazine* and his other regular newspaper accounts, Block ventured into another enormous money-maker: the woman's magazine called *Pictorial Review*. He became the Director of Advertising for *Pictorial Review* in 1907, sharing the same title and arrangement that he held for the *Illustrated Sunday Magazine*.[32]

It is interesting to note how Paul Block's business would increase cumulatively and geometrically each time he secured the rights to represent a new publication. If potential advertisers didn't want to advertise their products in a daily newspaper, for example, Block would suggest that they try placing an ad in the Sunday supplement or the magazine, or vice versa. If one particular newspaper was not attractive to the advertiser for whatever reason, Block had others that could be tested. What this meant is that the more publications that Block came to represent, the greater opportunity he created for himself to sell the prospective client on buying *some* space in at least one of his periodicals. And all the while, part of what the advertiser was buying was not just circulation or position or exposure, but the honest character of Paul Block, his true politeness and his charm, which he lived up to and played upon; it was the very core of his personality.

Pictorial Review was a women's magazine that emerged from the dress pattern business created by William Ahnelt, a German immigrant who used to live in Elmira, New York. It is possible that the Ahnelt and Block families knew each other since they both lived in Elmira in the early

1890s. Ahnelt's firm, The American Fashion Company, published a number of dress pattern catalogs. In addition to *Pictorial Review*, Ahnelt also produced small-circulation fashion publications for the women's garment industry, the women's tailoring trade, and the retail fur trade.

In 1899, *Pictorial Review* was born in order to give the patterns even more exposure and promotion; pictures of the American Fashion Company's patterns ran throughout the magazine. Although there were other pattern catalogs in the U.S., from a competitive standpoint Ahnelt's were superior: His drawings were accurate, his fashions were *au courant,* his instructions were concise and simple to follow. And the illustrations let a woman see what the finished piece of clothing would look like on her. Conventional pattern drawings just showed a piece of clothing: a blouse, a dress, a jacket. Such a drawing would show what the collar looked like, but not how high it came on the wearer's neck. Ahnelt engaged artists to make complete illustrations, drawings of a woman *wearing* the garment. Consequently, women could select clothing that would be flattering as well as stylish. As artists such as John Held, Jr. and Warren Davis were drawing covers in other magazines of highly stylized interpretations of the women of the age, *Pictorial Review* rejected the stylized lady and used figures of ordinary women, or of realistic looking chubby babies, to whom the reader could more easily relate.[33]

Ahnelt's patterns became famous among women who sewed; for those who could afford it, they would tear out a pattern they liked from the magazine and bring it to a tailor or dressmaker so that the garment could be made by them. *Pictorial Review* expanded The American Fashion Company's base, and those customers in turn became faithful readers of the magazine.

Pictorial Review entered the industry slightly later than its competition (*McCall's* and *Delineator*). Each of them evolved in the same way. At first these magazines published only patterns, and then had to expand to include feature material. For example, the editor of the *Delineator,* the famed novelist Theodore Dreiser, ultimately published distinguished fiction and took on such causes as women's suffrage and the maltreatment of children in orphanages.[34]

In its first year, *Pictorial Review* contained merely fashion, but then Ahnelt realized he had to expand the scope of the magazine beyond just a vehicle for his patterns. As his competitors had done, by including a combination of feature material and patterns, Ahnelt believed that each element would sell the other. By its second year, *Pictorial Review* included serials, stories, reviews of plays and books, as well as articles on fashion, health, beauty and entertainment. Its subtitle described its contents more accurately: "An Illustrated Monthly Devoted to Fashion, Society, the Stage, the Arts, and the Home." A different four-color cover appeared every month. Each cover was actually suitable for framing, and covers of *Pictorial Review* started to be seen in homes all over the country.[35]

In the beginning, *Pictorial Review* was a lavish and extravagant publication that catered to the lifestyles of the *nouveau riche* and upper middle class, and to those who were striving to arrive at similar status. Home dressmaking became less of a dreary chore and more of a pleasant (though necessary) pastime because of the easy-to-follow guides and patterns found in the magazine. Subscribers would be shown the latest Paris fashions as well as practical everyday street dresses. William Ahnelt's pattern business had become the largest and most successful in the world, and he started a school where many future American fashion designers received their first training. His easy step-by-step method of design-it-yourself clothing was so popular that *Pictorial Review* started to become competitive with the huge circulation fashion magazines such as *Vogue* and *McCall's*.[36]

In 1904, subscriptions were $1.00 per year and single copies were 15¢. In order to boost circulation, *Pictorial Review* offered subscribers incentives to get free merchandise. In one Christmas give-away, a subscriber who induced ten friends to subscribe to the magazine would receive, absolutely free, "a magnificent fur scarf." There were choices of black Manchurian lynx, mink, Persian lamb, and Australian sable; many women subscribers were eager to own such fashionable and valuable items and began signing up their friends. Subsequently, *Pictorial Review's* subscriptions escalated.[37]

The demand for the patterns also increased to such an extent that new retail outlets were opened all over the country, giving *Pictorial Review* subscribers an alternate way to shop for patterns. All a subscriber had to do was write to the magazine's headquarters in New York and they would tell her where the closest outlet was located, so she could obtain the patterns she needed quickly, without much travel or waiting for the mail. After finding a style in the magazine in the morning, the subscriber could go to the outlet, pick up the pattern she wanted, and be making the garment that afternoon or evening.[38] The retail stores also drew in passersby and women who lived nearby. They looked through the large books of the American Fashion Company's patterns, and could purchase their selections on the spot. They could also buy a copy of the latest issue of *Pictorial Review*. Many did.

Feature stories of a helpful and utilitarian nature permeated the pages of the magazine. Articles such as "What the Kindergarten Does for Children," by Florence K. Geer, was an extremely informative and important article, and young mothers especially took interest in it. "Cooking Lessons Made Simple," by Margaret Hall, was also a highly practical article for the newlywed or busy woman of the day.[39]

Photographs of society favorites produced such interest that portraits of women in high social position, not just in New York and Newport, but from all over the country, were published. It became a *coup*, if not a status symbol, to have one's picture published and displayed in *Pictorial Review,* and the magazine had no dearth of applicants wanting photographic publicity or who were willing to pose. The magazine also published travel guides for excursions abroad to Europe. There were helpful hints on how to pack, what to bring and where to stay. Travel to Europe was by steamship, and the guide would inform the reader of the best ship accommodations. It offered suggestions to enable the reader to receive the most benefit from a cruise: for example, spend as much time as possible in the open air, and do try to sit at the captain's table. The travel guides were especially helpful for the inexperienced traveler on a first trip in one of the luxury floating hotels. Seeing an illustration of the ship in print and reading about a possible voyage gave the armchair traveler a sense of vicarious adventure, and a serious traveler a comfortable feeling of security of an impending trip.[40]

Pictorial Review may have focused on the rich and famous, but that did not stop some of the riffraff from sneaking onto its pages, continuing to haunt Paul Block. Like practically every other publication in America, *Pictorial Review* still carried advertisements for all sorts of patent medicines. There were headache and neuralgia cures, cures for alcoholism, deafness, and even crossed eyes. There were advertisements directed especially at women – how to lose weight, hair growing tonics, and hair removers. Eventually Block refused to accept all patent medicine advertising and placed a product guarantee notice in the magazine promising to reimburse readers for any losses suffered by purchasing a product or a service advertised in *Pictorial Review.*[41]

Most of the advertisers that Block brought into the magazine were distinguished, legitimate and helpful. Quaker Puffed Rice cereal, which was sold by grocers everywhere in the United States, Old Dutch Cleanser, Mennen's toilet products, Dodge touring cars, Carnation Milk, Fels-Naptha soap, Domino's Sugar, and Heinz's 57 Varieties were all popular items that were advertised in *Pictorial Review*. Del Monte canned peaches advertised with full-page, four-color ads, as did Palmolive Soap ("Cleopatra washed her face this way. She kept her youth for a lifetime.") and Ford's "Closed Cars," which promoted a spanking new Tudor sedan for $590. *Pictorial Review* was to go on to great success as a mass circulation women's journal, and the quality of its advertisements had almost editorial appeal among the readers, some claiming that they bought the magazine more for the ads than the feature content.[42]

Early mass-market magazine publishers often sold their publications at a low rate to gain subscribers and to capture a substantial part of the market. Advertising dollars closed the revenue gap. Mass market women's journals, however, did not compete in price in those years. They all stayed within close range of each other. Women's journals could be found for sale in a new type of retail establishment: department stores, and some publishers sold their patterns there, too.

Paul Block revolutionized *Pictorial Review,* and he changed American advertising in the process. When Block first became associated with the magazine, William Ahnelt paid slight attention to the editorial or business aspects of *Pictorial Review*, allowing others to make all the decisions as to what was to be included. He was interested in his pattern business. Block wanted to make changes, and Ahnelt, perhaps not understanding their significance, gave him the authority to do so.

In 1907, the editorial offices of *Pictorial Review* were located at 14th Street and Broadway in New York City. Block operated out of his office in the Flatiron Building, renting additional space to accommodate new representatives that he had hired, not just for *Pictorial Review* but for his other publications as well. Back at Union Square, just a few rooms housed the entire *Pictorial Review* plant. There were 100 people employed at the tiny headquarters. *Pictorial Review*'s circulation was about 150,000 copies per issue; there were seven other women's magazines with a larger circulation. Yet *Pictorial Review* was immensely profitable: advertising revenue was consistently increasing, and at that time, a few hundred dollars paid for all of the literary features and articles for one issue. Sometimes Ahnelt would not pay the bills promptly, and Paul Block wanted to change the unprofessional tactics of the magazine as they progressed further into the twentieth century.

In examining the growth of *Pictorial Review*, there seems to be no secret formula that accounts for its success. The staff was diligent and hard-working. Deadlines were met. Gains in advertising and circulation did not happen easily, and time was needed to achieve ascent. The magazine had to increase its volume of advertising. Paul Block instilled confidence in his staff and convinced them that they would one day top their competitors.[43] He looked to the women of America for support, and saw that their needs for information, guidance and entertainment could be supplied by a well-edited and attractive magazine. At that time, women were wearing long flowing skirts and virtually every woman wore a hat. Clothing, rather than appliances or other products and services, had a greater place in women's interest. Women wanted to know more about the latest fashions, and how to decorate and clean their homes. Additionally, movies and plays were attracting more of women's attention, and they wanted to know what was going on in the entertainment world. Block commissioned movie producer Samuel Goldwyn to pen a series of articles, "Behind the Screen," which provided an intimate look at the burgeoning motion picture industry, lavishly illustrated, and with stories of such Hollywood stars as Charlie Chaplin, Mary Pickford, Douglas Fairbanks, Theda Bara, Mae Marsh and Geraldine Farrar. It was an exciting moment for women. The turn of the century was really the time to experience the *new*, a time of fascination and affluence as the nation was experiencing progress.

As circulation increased and higher revenues from advertisers were streaming in, it enabled the magazine to offer higher fees to writers of stature, as an enticement for them to submit their work for publication. An important asset to the circulation and stature of the magazine occurred when Edith Wharton, who had just written *The House of Mirth,* began a series for *Pictorial Review*, with a working title of *Old New York*, that would eventually be called *The Age of Innocence*, an elegant minor-masterpiece that would garner her a Pulitzer Prize. Block paid her the unprecedented sum of $18,000 for the serial, and when the publishing house of Appleton and Co. came up with a $15,000 advance against royalties for the future hardcover book, Wharton instantly became one of the leading money-making writers in America. The distinguished critic of the *New York Evening Post*, Henry Seidel Canby, said of *The Age of Innocence* that it was like the work of Jane Austen and Guy de Maupassant in its articulate study of human nature rather than its broad-ranging manifestations. *Innocence* was followed by a short story, *Miss Mary Pask*, that Wharton had dashed off at home one day while recovering from the grippe, and for which Block paid her $1,800.[44] Further precedent was set when Block paid Wharton $40,000 for the serial rights of *The Children*.

Pictorial Review also published in serial form Booth Tarkington's *Alice Adams*, as well as the works of Joseph Conrad, Kathleen Norris, Carl Sandburg, Alexander Woollcott, and other celebrated writers. The magazine conducted a fiction contest and awarded the whopping prize of $13,500 to the 25-year-old Norwegian-American author Martha Ostenso for her gripping first novel of a troubled immigrant family in Minnesota, *Wild Geese*, which ran for eight installments.[45] The readers' appetite for fiction seemed insatiable and eventually no issue of *Pictorial Review* went to press without installments of at least five or six long short stories or novellas.

Fiction was not the only category in which *Pictorial Review* distinguished itself. In a departure from what most magazines of that day and age published, *Pictorial Review* bravely discussed such controversial topics as birth control and sex education, the former topic in the form of a contest to solicit from subscribers their opinion as to birth control's pros and cons. The feature produced thousands of letters from readers, and the magazine published many of the ideas. Paul Block knew that *Pictorial Review* had to stay with the times to insure its success, and he constantly searched for ways to influence the content, distribution and advertising direction of the magazine.[46]

As noted, *Pictorial Review* was hardly successful when Paul Block first became associated with it: single issues were bringing in barely $5,000 a month in total advertising; by the time Block molded the magazine into what he thought was its true potential, some single issues were realizing over $10,000 per page and over one million dollars in advertising.

He began advertising in trade publications across the country. All of the ads that he ran in these journals promoted the strengths of *Pictorial Review* to space buyers, potential advertisers and advertising agencies who eventually became convinced that magazines were more than just a conveyor of messages but commercial products in themselves which could serve as instruments to sell their products or services. The ads that promoted *Pictorial Review* were always signed in script on the bottom with his distinctively bold signature, *"Paul Block,"* as if to tell the world that he personally endorsed what the ad proposed, that he stood behind all circulation and lineage claims, and that he was primarily responsible for all of the positive aspects of the features and qualities being discussed. Block's ads talked of the glories of the magazine in such a convincing way that the editors of *Pictorial Review* felt that they had to improve the magazine to live up to the advertisements. *Pictorial Review* started spending enormous amounts of money letting the American public know more about... *Pictorial Review*.

In 1910, *Pictorial Review's* circulation was up to 625,000 copies per month and the magazine had truly become a force in magazine publishing.[47] The parent company's patterns were growing in popularity and the advertising volume showed great increases. By early 1912, *Pictorial Review's* circulation was over 700,000 copies per month and by November 13 of that year, it had reached a milestone with a circulation of one million. Helpful and entertaining articles, literature of renown, and fine illustrations continued to grace its pages. It contained new household departments to fill a woman's almost every need for practical information, entertainment purposes, and household knowledge; there were human interest stories illustrated by Howard Chandler Christy, more artistic covers and above all, the famous *Pictorial Review* patterns, which were a feature no other magazine could quite duplicate.[48]

Pictorial Review used the most advanced printing presses, and beautifully printed copies became – and still are – collector's items. The most important factor in the growth of *Pictorial Review*, according to Block, was to keep the magazine unique in content, and highly attractive, while maintaining a close relationship with the readers and the advertisers to keep them both coming back month after month.[49] They did.

In the history of contemporary magazine publishing, no major circulation journal succeeded without advertising. But then again, magazines with their attractive presentational possibilities – glossy paper stock and startlingly beautiful four-color ads – together with their huge circulations, and vast financial resources, were becoming important mediums in the advertising business. Paul Block offered national manufacturers the opportunity to publicize their goods to wide-ranging markets and to build brand and trademark recognition with handsome and attention-grabbing graphics. Advertisers willingly paid high rates for space in *Pictorial Review*. In turn, *Pictorial Review* relied heavily on Paul Block and the bountiful revenues from the advertisers. In 1912, almost one-third of the ads in *Pictorial Review* featured clothing and fabric; additionally, major advertisers such as Heinz Baked Beans, Kellogg's Corn Flakes, Coca-Cola, and Welch's Grape Juice were featured on the front cover, back cover and the second and third covers (the inner front and inner back) of the magazine.

Advertisements formed an integral part of the design of the magazine. Initially, the ads had been spotty and irregular. Paul Block influenced the advertising agencies and art directors to address their ads to general home audiences, but to make them elegant, and many of these ads became frameable. The ads were not only attractive but contained useful information about the products. Block narrowed the focus of the ads directly to women and began to employ a persuasive style of advertising. Soap was no longer praised for cleaning but was used as a "beauty aid." Women were told that they needed to cultivate and enhance their attractiveness. Appeal shifted from emphasizing health and time-saving, to themes that emphasized that buying the right products would produce a certain happiness and a feeling of satisfaction. More ads for cosmetics, creams, and perfumes began to appear in the magazine.

Many traditional ideas and stereotypes about the female sex came into play. Utilizing concepts that are decidedly not politically correct today, advertisers felt that women followed commands and directions more easily than men, and therefore believed that appeals would be most effective if they were directed to women's *feelings* and not their intellects. Women did begin to pay more attention to the advertisements as well as the articles, and more and more women became the principal buyers of products in their households. Receiving the monthly issue of *Pictorial Review* was similar in a way to a visit from a good friend, or a letter from a family member where information would be shared, ideas explored and conversation of a sort conducted. It was as if the subscribers had joined a social club, rather than just merely purchasing or subscribing to a magazine.

When World War I commenced in 1914, the cost of paper escalated but that did not seem to affect *Pictorial Review*'s print runs at first. Paul Block was making a great deal of money for the magazine...and for himself. By that time *Pictorial Review* ranked third in total paid advertising space carried among the leading women's magazines. It also ranked second to *Ladies Home Journal* among the 15¢ women's publications.[50]

The United States had not entered the war as yet and American manufacturers were taking advantage of America's neutral position by shipping all over the world. The economy was spiraling upward. Paul Block was highly optimistic and enthusiastic about the future. From March, 1913 to September, 1914, *Pictorial Review* showed advertising gains in all but three of its issues.

Eventually, the war did have a profound effect on *Pictorial Review*. Women's contributions to the war effort forced Americans to re-assess their ideas about a woman's proper role. Wartime also revealed the importance of women's magazines. The government drew on the staff of *Pictorial Review* and Paul Block for assistance in its public information efforts. The magazine went on to supply significant information to millions of Americans about food and energy conservation as well as news of the war and its victims.[51]

After the United States joined the war, *Pictorial Review* focused on ways women could aid the war effort. Various volunteer opportunities were described. Columns provided practical information about the military and how it touched the lives of wives and mothers. *Pictorial Review* carried pledge slips for women to sign, on which they vowed to remain meatless and wheatless for a prescribed number of meals, confirming their commitment and contribution to our soldier's needs. *Pictorial Review* published editorials in support of these programs which carried an endorsement by Herbert Hoover, who was then the head of the U.S. Food Administration. As a result, Block established a close working relationship with Hoover which continued into Hoover's Presidency, and would ultimately last all of his life.

Pictorial Review unequivocally supported female suffrage, taking up the position for women's rights very early on in 1913. By the next year, the magazine was urging its readers to work for the constitutional amendment to gain female suffrage. *Pictorial Review* claimed in its editorials that it was just a matter of simple justice that women have as much a right to a voice in government as men.[52]

It is not an overstatement to say that by 1915, *Pictorial Review* was one of the most profitable magazines in the country. The business had grown to an enterprise that occupied a 12-story building covering half the block on Thirty-ninth Street between 7th and 8th Avenues, in the very heart of the garment district. Everyone connected with the magazine – advertisers, agencies, special reps, and executive employees – was making money, and especially Paul Block and William Ahnelt, and they were spending it, too. In the 1915 Christmas issue, *Pictorial Review* had an eight-page, four-color editorial section that, from an artistic standpoint, was the most beautiful work ever offered in a woman's magazine. The editorial and art cost of the section was close to $25,000. There was also a story by Sir

Gilbert Parker which cost another $25,000, the largest amount ever paid for one story by a magazine – a record that would hold for decades to come. The circulation had escalated to two million copies per month.[53]

The Philanthropy of Paul Block

As soon as he began to accumulate what might be considered minor wealth, Block became a prodigious contributor to various charities. He not only contributed to Jewish organizations and causes, but donated thousands of dollars to Catholic and Protestant charities as well. Although no specific record or accounting of Block's contributions was ever kept, it appears from archival references that during his lifetime, he donated millions of dollars to a variety of charities. In today's dollar value, such contributions could easily be equal to ten or more millions of dollars. Undoubtedly some of Block's contributions had political and business overtones; some might have been done to ingratiate himself; but the majority of his donations were motivated out of kindness and generosity, and perhaps a personal philosophy that urged him to give back to the world some of the wealth it had given to him. He recognized and empathized with the invisibility of the poor, and would not forget his origins. He drew up a will that called for a trust to be established upon his death, so that his corporation would continue to support numerous causes and charities.[54]

One of the first recipients of his donations, not surprisingly, were two organizations in his home town of Elmira. He made repeated, generous contributions to the YMCA and YWCA organizations there. Halsey Sawles, who was on the board of the YWCA of Elmira, sent him more than one letter of appreciation over the course of the many years that Block supported that organization. "For Elmira girls, I personally appreciate very much your generosity and your interest in the old town," Sawles wrote.

It seems totally unlikely that Block supported these organizations consistently, over a span of two decades, because he was seeking some kind of personal gain. As a successful adult he felt an obligation to help the city's youth. Undoubtedly it also gave him both satisfaction and pleasure to do so.

As his business world expanded, Block extended the locations of his charitable interests. Wherever he did a significant amount of business, particularly if he owned or was doing business for a newspaper in a certain city, he began to support key charities there, often supporting their community funds and other significant organizations. One of his major concerns was children. In addition to annual donations for community centers, Block set up numerous scholarships to enable deserving students to go to college.

His philanthropy continued throughout his life, interwoven with his businesses and his social activities.

The baronial-looking Ahnelt – Block's son William described him as looking like a Prussian officer, with white hair and an imposing moustache – and the spiffy-looking Block, became more than just business associates. They developed a friendship based on mutual respect and a shared camaraderie.

At Block's request, Ahnelt also became an investor and director in the *New York Evening Mail*, a newspaper for which Block would eventually serve as part-owner and publisher.

Ahnelt built a huge mansion on the seacoast in Deal, New Jersey, that resembled a medieval castle, and called it Ahnelt Hall. *The New York Times* referred to it as "one of the show places of the coast."[55] During the summers, Block would take his family to nearby Elberon, rent a large house by the beach, and constantly visit Ahnelt for dinners, picnics, games of croquet, and especially leisurely contests of billiards after meals, complete with the requisite cigars, coffee and brandy.[56]

Pictorial Review continued to contribute to the war effort. The magazine employed a group of young girls who devoted their spare time to making clothing for the little children of France who had been made orphans during the war. Hundreds of garments made by the American girls were sent abroad by the National League for Women's Services. Every one of the girls had also become a member of the American Red Cross, for which they sewed many more garments to be distributed by the Belgian Relief Committee, including 2,000 hospital gowns for injured soldiers. Subsequently, the magazine made arrangements with the American Red Cross authorities to design a special line of *Pictorial Review* patterns for Red Cross purposes which were then donated to the government.[57]

1917 was a banner year for *Pictorial Review*. In an advertisement in the December issue of *Printer's Ink*, Paul Block stated: "This was the greatest year in the history of the magazine. The magazine had gained in total advertising volume by over 46,000 lines. This was not only the greatest gain in our history but the largest gain made by any other women's publication with one exception, *Ladies Home Journal*."[58]

Paul Block also noted a substantial increase in *Pictorial Review's* newsstand growth. It was estimated that each month, half a million women

approached newsstands and selected *Pictorial Review* over the other magazines. In spite of war conditions, the magazine was still flourishing, but
because of the war and the increase in paper costs, *Pictorial Review* had
to raise its price to 20¢ an issue. *Pictorial Review* continued receiving
high praise for its distinctive stories and editorials, putting it in a class by
itself. Paul Block wrote in a promotional ad:

> Is it any wonder that *Pictorial Review* is the women's maga-
> zine of today? That it has the most remarkable 'natural' growth
> ever recorded in the field? That, combining with such un-
> usual literary merit, the best and most authoritative practical
> features, it serves advertisers and readers better and better all
> of the time.

Actual demands for the February, 1917 issue were greater than could
be supplied; every issue sold out at the newsstands or was mailed to subscribers. Among women's magazines, *Pictorial Review* had moved from
last place to second in ten years.[59]

In May 1918, *Pictorial Review* broke two additional records. It carried
more advertising than any issue published in its history, and the advertisers had spent more money than ever before. By 1919, Paul Block declared *Pictorial Review* as America's first women's magazine with the
largest circulation of any 20¢ magazine in the world. On account of this
great growth, he announced that executives from rival magazines including Harry W. Brown of *Ladies Home Journal*, Stacy Bender of *Woman's
Home Companion* and F.C. Coleman of *Delineator* would be joining the
advertising staff of *Pictorial Review*. Paul Block said of the magazine:
"The growth of *Pictorial Review* represents the greatest tidal wave of
success there has ever been in the women's magazine field. It is a circulation that has not yet attained its peak." Block's hiring of these pre-
eminent names in the industry was insurance that *Pictorial Review* would
not just be on top, but remain there. Block went on to say, "The progressive American woman, whether in industry or in the home, has come to
depend on *Pictorial Review* for the news, thoughts, and leadership she
demands." In many ways, Paul Block contributed to that leadership.[60]

When World War I came to an end, the world changed its perspectives
as well as it preoccupations. There was suddenly money available to
spend on luxuries, not merely necessities. There was also an influx of
new products, some newly available after the hiatus, and some which had
just entered the marketplace. *Pictorial Review* increased its revenues
considerably because of a resultant spurt in both advertising and circula-

tion. It added an additional 12-story plant to its original location on 14th Street and Broadway in New York City. It also established additional offices on Seventh Avenue and 39th Street. By Christmas of 1919, *Pictorial Review* had passed the 2 million mark of sales for each monthly issue. It had become the largest circulation of any monthly magazine in America.[61]

Paul Block was proud of these accomplishments and, in a special segment of the magazine, he wanted to thank his staff. He published their pictures and wrote a few words about each of them, showing his appreciation and how much he valued his association with them; but his associates would not let him publish just *their* pictures unless he ran a photo of himself first. At first he demurred and then finally complied. He was honored that he was held in such high esteem by his co-workers.[62]

The circulation of *Pictorial Review* continued to increase despite a raise in price to 25¢ an issue. By 1923, it was no longer perceived as a magazine for women only. Its readership included men as well as women, the rich *and* those who aspired to be, homemakers *and* dressmakers, newlyweds *and* couples who had been married for years. As part of its ongoing self-promotion, the magazine offered scholarships for young men: During the summer months, *Pictorial Review* gave these men the opportunity to work for the magazine with their salaries going for tuition to the college of their choice. *Pictorial Review* paid expenses such as transportation to and from the office and the men received bonuses for exceptional work. Block inserted large advertisements in the magazine that announced: "We reward the public." But this was not just a publicity stunt. The scholarship program made college possible for hundreds of young Americans.[63]

In 1924, with its circulation then well over the two million mark, William Ahnelt congratulated Paul Block in a somewhat formal letter. It was Block's 25th anniversary of inaugurating his own business. Ahnelt wrote:

> Dear Mr. Block,
> On part of the staff of The Pictorial Review Company, please accept our congratulations.
> You have every reason to be proud of your achievement but you must be proud of the fact that everybody who knows you points to you as a shining example of what can be accomplished by hard work and brains. Success and good luck to you in the next 25 years.
>
> Yours very cordially,
> William Ahnelt[64]

A speech to the Associated Dress Industries of America shortly after the stock market crash in 1929, is given here since it presents an absorbing example of Block's voice and philosophy, a growing interest in, and knowledge of, the economic prospects and perspective of the country, and his not quite-so-subtle promotion of national advertising. Although it is not a paradigm of oratory, it indicates how astute Block was in both examining the larger picture of the country's dilemma and maintaining the balance of concern of his own specific business. It is a business call to arms that predates Franklin D. Roosevelt's 1933 Inaugural Address in which he intoned the famous line: "The only thing we have to fear is fear itself." Block said, in part:

> Mr. Chairman and Gentlemen:
>
> I have been in the newspaper and magazine business so long and have seen so many concerns become successful through advertising that I honestly believe that I would not go into any business which could not be advertised.
>
> There are two reasons for this: First, because I believe I could build a bigger business with advertising; and secondly, and this second reason seems much more important to me than the first, I would wish to be in a position to leave to my heirs an article which had a trademark, which itself might bring to them an independent income.
>
> I know a little concern whose factory burned down one night and everything in that factory was destroyed, except one thing, the most important thing, their "trademark." The business was not a large business, but that trademark was worth at least a half million dollars. It took quite some time to build a new plant and new machinery, but in the meantime they had the goods made up elsewhere and the sale of these goods just kept on just the same, and while on this subject it may interest some of you, Gentlemen, to know what values certain advertisers have placed on their trademark: The Goodrich Tire Co. has a good will valuation of over fifty-seven million dollars and most of this good will is for their trademarked articles. For 1918 the American Tobacco Co. had a good will valuation of over fifty-four million dollars. Nearly all of this is for the value of a half a dozen trademarked articles, which this company manufactures and advertises. The Liggett & Meyers Tobacco Co. placed a valuation of forty million dollars on their trademarked articles and good will.

I am interested in a magazine. At one time it was but a small publication. To-day it is the largest monthly magazine in this country. It is the "Pictorial Review." I hope most of you, Gentlemen, are acquainted with it. I don't want to advertise my publication to you; in fact, I feel rather embarrassed to speak of it at all, but I want to tell you a few words about it, merely to emphasize what I tried to impress a few moments ago about an advertised article selling better, and at the same time giving the Consumer more for his money. When we started to advertise our magazine, we sold a million copies per month. To-day we sell 2,100,000 each month. When we started to advertise, we thought we had a pretty good publication, but our advertising agents who prepare our copy, spoke about our magazine in such a wonderful way we just simply had to improve the magazine to live up to what our advertisements said about us. Instead of paying $5,000 for a serial story, we began to buy stories that cost us $25,000 and upwards. Instead of paying a few hundred dollars for one of our short stories, we paid $2,000, and in some instances close to $5,000 for just such a short story. We increased the size of our magazine. We added a number of colored pages. We added a rotogravure section; in fact, we made our publication so much better that our readers got twice as much for their money as they had received before we started to advertise. It is true, we have been spending $500,000 per year just to tell the American public about "Pictorial Review," but the results we have received convince us that we have made no mistake.

Advertising brings consumers a better article, because you have got to make good with the Consumer, and it brings the price down, because a large volume of sales permits you to make a small net profit on each article.

Paul Block had brought *Pictorial Review* to the pinnacle of its field. The story ends, however, not without blemish. Through his efforts, Block made himself a substantial fortune, certainly millions, from the magazine. William Ahnelt also made vast sums of money, but he resented Block's ultimate control of the magazine and he became jealous of Block's fame (more people had grown to know the name Block than Ahnelt in connection with *Pictorial Review*). Greed also came into play: Ahnelt irrationally resented the fact that Block was becoming rich, ignoring the reality that the more money Block made, the more that he – Ahnelt – also made, and Ahnelt earned a much larger percentage. Ahnelt convinced himself that the magazine could and would continue to receive as much advertising as he had in the past, without Block. They argued, bickered and defended their respective positions.

The denouement of their business relationship occurred when Ahnelt and Block disagreed over the cover and subscription price of *Pictorial Review*. 1931 was the most dispirited year of the Depression, and although there was a devoted loyalty by its readers to the magazine, a slight dip in the circulation, both on the newsstands and through the mails, was occurring. In addition to his problems with *Pictorial Review*, Block was also having financial difficulties with some of his newspapers, and was in no mood to quibble over what he believed had to be done to spur sales. *Pictorial Review's* cover price was lower than *Good Housekeeping*, but higher than its three other major competitors, *Ladies' Home Journal*, *McCall's*, and *Woman's Home Companion*. When Block learned that the *Ladies' Home Journal* was going to reduce both its cover and subscription price even more, he insisted that *Pictorial Review* reduce its price to keep it more in line with the other three magazines, or else suffer a hemorrhaging of circulation, with an obvious reduction of advertising sales. Ahnelt contended that price was not the most important factor in maintaining *Pictorial Review's* circulation. As it developed, he was drastically wrong.[65]

After failing to come to any kind of compromise, Block left *Pictorial Review* in 1931. It was rumored that shortly after Block's exit, the stubborn Ahnelt realized that his circulation and advertising were slipping away, and he begged Block to return to the magazine two years later. Block refused. Ahnelt actually owed Block some $100,000 in commissions which were never paid to him despite *Pictorial Review's* continued, but then eventually fading, success. Over the years that followed, Paul Block tried in vain to retrieve the debt but it was never paid. Fortunately, he had many other sources of income and dreams of how to make even more, and his life at that time was more than financially secure. He was deeply disheartened by the dishonesty and obstinacy of Ahnelt's act, however, because he had assumed that his business relationship was about trust, friendship and respect; and the betrayal was not only of him but of Ahnelt's own conscience. The bond between the two men was broken irrevocably.

The question of what Block was going to do with the relatively large staff of salesmen who had worked exclusively on *Pictorial Review* was quickly solved, primarily through the help of William Randolph Hearst.

It was at this juncture that Block convinced Hearst to allow him to provide the representation of national advertising for some of Hearst's papers in cities where Hearst owned two or more newspapers, while Hearst's own company represented his other papers. The arrangement was not mere beneficence on Hearst's part. Block had inroads into certain national advertisers that Hearst wanted but couldn't service. Appointing Block to represent him added to Hearst's coffers, while also aiding Block. For example, in San Francisco, the *Examiner* (owned by Hearst) was represented by his own firm, the Hearst Advertising Service, while the advertising for Hearst's other papers, such as the *Call Bulletin*, went to Paul Block. In New York, where Hearst owned three newspapers, *The Journal*, the *Sunday American*, and the *Daily Mirror*, Hearst gave Block the representative business of the *American*. Similar arrangements were made in Milwaukee and Chicago.[66]

Pictorial Review began to decline in the early '30s, immediately after Block's exit. In retrospect, it is difficult to determine whether a connection between both events can be established, although it may well have been likely. Block had been the mooring for *Pictorial Review,* the steady influence that was the catalyst of the magazine's success. The Hearst Corporation took over *Pictorial Review* in 1935 in an attempt to revive the publication. Seeking a circulation boost, it also acquired the ailing *Delineator* and then merged it with *Pictorial Review*. The merger temporarily increased *Pictorial Review-Delineator's* circulation, vaulting it back into first place. But the increased circulation did not improve the financial condition of the magazine. Advertising continued to decrease. There was no longer a Paul Block to bring in, and retain the blue-chip advertising that the magazine had experienced for years. In 1939, The Hearst Company announced that the March issue would be the last. The combined publication died a victim of the economic depression and its failed advertising market, and perhaps because of Ahnelt's betrayal of Paul Block.[67]

When Ahnelt died in 1943, his widow wrote the likewise recently widowed Mrs. Paul Block to ask her to forgive the debt of $100,000 incurred by her husband. Dina Block replied, "No, I can't. Paul wouldn't have wanted it that way. That was not the way he did business. Paul's business was based on friendship and a handshake. I'm sorry, I just can't."[68]

Block never entered into the magazine business again: whether it was because of his bittersweet experience with Ahnelt or not, is not known. As it developed, he had become more interested in the speed and impact of his daily newspapers, not just to represent them for advertising, but also to own them, and to use the platform they afforded him to express his growing political and social philosophy.

Chapter 4
A Newspaper Empire Begins

New York Evening Mail

In the 19th century, Americans were almost entirely dependent on newspapers for their information, their entertainment, and perhaps for some, their education. It is not surprising that their appetite for news and information outgrew what could be supplied with one morning paper. A spate of evening newspapers began to emerge just prior to the turn of the century, although a few such papers had been in existence since 1783. It was not until the late 1880's that evening editions really begin to flourish, however, and New York City alone witnessed the birth of three new evening papers at that time. One of the most successful upstarts was the *New York Daily News*.

> This cheap Tammany paper, which flourished among the tenements and was notable for its reports of the lottery and policy drawings, sold from 100,000 to 175,000 one cent copies daily through the [18] seventies and eighties. After the Daily News came the Evening Sun, in March of 1887. It was an inexpensive, colorful and modern evening newspaper. Seven months after the Evening Sun came the Evening World, another one cent publication which soon outstripped its rival in circulation, gaining 182,000 by the end of the period only 10,000 behind the morning World. [1]

Aside from these New York evening papers, there also existed the *Evening Post, Evening Telegram, Evening Express* and *Evening Mail*. Initial reaction to the evening papers among existing newspaper publishers was negative, mainly due to the fact that evening papers didn't attain the same high circulation numbers of morning dailies but did compete for basically the same advertising dollars.

The newspaper world continued to grow and innovate after the turn of the century. This was Paul Block's milieu. Like many astute business-men, he watched carefully as the newspaper industry absorbed the changes wrought by the evening papers and assumed a new role in the conscious-ness of the American public. The evening paper phenomenon would have caught his attention simply because of its eventual success with advertis-ers. At that time in his life, Block was primarily an advertising man, but he was soon to become a consummate publisher, first of evening papers and then of morning dailies.

Though initially maligned as extraneous, evening papers eventually found a niche as the primary reading material for women and children – the people who were at home when the paper was delivered. Advertisers, realizing these papers reached a large number of consumers, tailored their ads to that market and the evening papers adapted themselves after the ads.

> Daily beauty hints, the bedtime story for the "kiddies", the comic "colyum", the woman's page, etc. ...crowded the space devoted to the news. Even the editorial page was "popular-ized" in form. Enlarged size came when department stores and other advertisers learned that the evening paper went to the home and was read by women. [2]

Thus a pattern established itself in the early years of the 1900's: morn-ing editions carried largely political news, evening editions contained entertainment and family stories, and the newly created Sunday editions contained a combination of everything, along eventually with brightly colored cartoons for the children, to satisfy every member of the family.

Block analyzed these emerging trends with great interest. Because his advertising company was inextricably linked with the newspaper indus-try, he already knew a great deal about that business, and soon had an opportunity to put his knowledge to good use. When he became pub-lisher of the *Newark Star-Eagle* in 1916, he spent the next two years learning more about the executive administration of a newspaper. Until that time he had accumulated vast experience in the sales, marketing and production aspects of publishing; now he was also beginning to master the editorial, circulation and distribution elements of the business. He was in a prime position to start a new phase of his business career; all he needed was an opportunity. Another evening paper, with its heavy reli-ance on advertising and light editorial tone, was a perfect vehicle in which to hone his skills. The fascination of owning a New York City paper would not abate, and though the possibility always seemed to loom just beyond Paul Block's grasp, it remained a primary goal.

In 1900, the highly reputable journalist Henry L. Stoddard, who had known Block from the *Worcester Telegram,* had made the leap from editorial supervisor to controlling stockholder of the New York *Evening Mail,* formerly the *Mail and Express.* The *Evening Mail,* which was founded in 1867 as a Republican paper, had survived into the 1900's, although it was not then a particularly successful evening sheet, with circulation running less than 50,000 copies a day, five days a week. (The Saturday edition had half the circulation of the regular daily paper). Competitively, the *Evening Mail* was far behind the *Evening Journal* with 700,000 copies daily, the *Evening Sun* sold 150,000 daily, the *Evening Telegram* had a circulation of 158,000 each day. Only the *Evening Post* with 25,758 daily copies, had a smaller circulation than the *Mail.*[3]

Stoddard, a skilled editor, tried to bring the paper to a higher prominence within the city of New York, and then signed a contract with Block to help him do it. At first, Block would represent the *Mail's* national advertising; later on, he would also be in charge of local advertising, as well. The two men began an excellent working relationship, with open communication, that would develop into more than just a good friendship. Paul looked upon Stoddard as a father-figure and mentor, as he had done with Harry S. Brooks in Elmira, and readily accepted Stoddard's counsel. Block had found his ideal colleague – and his opportunity.

In 1908, Paul Block's association with the *Evening Mail* changed radically. No longer limiting his concerns exclusively to advertising, he assumed the position of Vice-President of the newspaper at a time when its circulation had dipped so perilously that its managers didn't even list it in national directories of periodicals, for fear that they would receive no advertising if a potential advertiser knew the paper's true figures. Block, of course, became totally in charge of the *Mail's* advertising department, and he immediately began to work on bringing more advertisers into the paper, while simultaneously trying to influence Stoddard to run more attractive and newsworthy features so that the circulation figures would rise. It took years to achieve, but with Block's encouragement and thrust, the circulation would eventually advance to 200,000.

Although it took Stoddard more time than Block would have liked, eventually he introduced new features such as a column called "In and Out of the Film Studios," which reported news about upcoming productions, sprinkled with gossip and inside information of the burgeoning industry; H.L. Mencken's syndicated column of criticism, satire and observations of the national scene; and strong, hard-hitting editorials concerning such matters of interest as the mayoralties of George McClellan, William Jay Gaynor and John Hylan, wastage of coal in city agencies, and the plight of Federal Land Banks. The public noticed and responded, and the *Evening Mail* circulation and readership loyalty toward continued to rise.

Block traveled from offices of his advertising company, in the Flatiron Building, down to the *Evening Mail* at 25 City Hall Place in the Park Row section of the city, whenever he was needed. He worked closely with Stoddard, who was the President of the corporation and Editor of the paper, while still maintaining control of his special representative firm, and continuing his involvement in the *Newark Star-Eagle*. From what can be gleaned from the history of the *Evening Mail*, Stoddard and Block were a gifted and outstanding team, with an admirable blending of skills. Stoddard was a writer and political analyst of great ability – he attended, wrote about and was an influence at virtually every political convention of his day – and Paul was becoming an exceptional businessman and organizer. Throughout their entire fifteen years of business association they never had a serious breach of trust or friendship.

Advertising revenues throughout the country were improving by 1911, and by that time Block began experiencing some small prosperity for the *Mail*.[4] Before long he began touting the *Evening Mail* as "New York's fastest growing newspaper," and although that might have been exaggerating the point, the paper was beginning to make substantive strides in circulation and advertising.[5]

On his trips out of town to garner national advertising for the growing number of newspapers that he was representing, as well as for the *Newark Star-Eagle* and the *Evening Mail*, Block was relentless in his approach to those advertisers and agencies that he believed he could ultimately sell. During one call he made, a stenographer was present who transcribed in shorthand Block's presentation of the *Evening Mail* and the advertiser's responses. The unnamed company had rejected Block the previous year, and really had no intention of going into the *Evening Mail* any time in the future. The resulting dialogue was published in a trade journal of the day as an exemplary model of salesmanship and Block's indefatigable technique: "A bundle of nerves that radiates activity, alertness, get-thereness in typical American style, and that never stops fighting until after the battle has been won." It is possible that the following transcript was edited for publication and is not exactly verbatim, but it is nevertheless intriguing to look into how Block danced with the potential advertiser, how he limited his own talking when necessary, how he asked relevant questions, and how he tailored the conversation to the buyer's needs. It provides us with a fascinating glimpse into the masterful way that Paul Block sold:

> BLOCK: "I told you a year ago to keep your eye on *The Evening Mail* – that it was growing faster than any other New York newspaper. Then you said that business was not good enough to take on another medium in New York and I agreed with you, but I said I would see you for this year's business and here I am, and I expect to be able to convince you that *The Mail* should have your advertising this year, that is, if you care to let me tell my story."
>
> ADVERTISER: "Go ahead, Mr. Block. You are always interesting in what you say. If *The Mail* is going ahead as you intimate it is, then it is my business to get as much information about it as possible because all advertisers are looking for good mediums. I am after home circulation."
>
> BLOCK: "Glad to hear you say that. Home circulation! Why, that is *The Mail's* stronghold! You know, our motto is, 'One paper in the home is worth a thousand on the highway.' We are reaching out for a home circulation, and we are getting it, too. How much have we got? We are just crossing 100,000 and increasing every day. Every paper gets into the hands of a buyer who takes it home where there are other buyers. It goes into the homes presided over by successful men – good family men, who are able to indulge their families to every reasonable desire."
>
> ADVERTISER: "Aren't your people too high class to pay any attention to my advertising? You know that the article that I sell is not high-priced. It is for use in the home, to be sure, but will the wife who is absorbed in social matters direct its purchase?"
>
> BLOCK: "How did you make your money? You didn't get it in a hurry, did you? A hard, long struggle wasn't it? Do you throw any of it away? Doesn't *your* wife use judgment in buying? Don't you impress upon your children the importance of getting their money's worth when they make purchases? I'll warrant that in your own family, sur-

rounded as you are by every luxury, you read advertisements carefully, and I will leave it to you if most of the
articles bought are not advertised articles."

ADVERTISER: "That's true."

BLOCK: "I thought you knew all about that. Nothing can
get in the columns of the paper that the management doesn't
think will be acceptable to the readers. All advertisements
printed are carefully scrutinized. That's the reason that advertising is so valuable in *The Evening Mail*."

ADVERTISER: "But your circulation is really small by comparison with all of the other New York papers."

BLOCK: "That's true, but wouldn't you prefer to pay a base
rate of 25 or 30 cents a line, against a 40 or a 50 cent rate,
if *The Evening Mail* takes your advertisement into homes
where the mere appearance of your advertisement means
that your article is properly introduced – received with faith?
Isn't it worth any price we ask to guarantee that you are
not hemmed in on all sides by fake or unclean or preposterous advertisements? An advertiser, like the man, is
known by the company he keeps. I'll tell you that it is
worth while to be represented in a newspaper that will print
only clean news and clean advertisements."

ADVERTISER: "Does *The Mail* maintain its rates?"

BLOCK: "Absolutely. You can do business with us upon the
specific guarantee that your rate will be the same as that of
any other advertiser making a similar contract. I will write
this guarantee in the contract if you wish me to. What sort
of contract shall I draw up for you?"

ADVERTISER: (interrupting)"I didn't say I wanted to make
a contract, did I?"

BLOCK: "No, but you wouldn't be asking me questions if
you were not interested. You would not take up your own
time or mine. We are both pretty busy, you know."

ADVERTISER: "Well, I *am* interested, I must admit. But I
want to think it over. How long will you remain in town?"

BLOCK: "Going to return to New York this afternoon. Had
you not better decide now? Our rates are to be increased
the first of May, and a contract signed now will protect
your present rate."

ADVERTISER: "Well, what can you do for me in the matter
of position? Will you give me page 2 or 3 at the run-of-
paper rate?"

BLOCK: "Cannot do it. The rate on those pages is 30 cents,

and if you want position you will have to pay 5 cents a line extra for it. If you want top position it will cost you 6 cents a line more."

ADVERTISER: "Well, what *will* you do for me?"

BLOCK: "You use very conspicuous copy. Why not take the run-of-paper rate – 25 cents a line – and take your chances of being treated well? *The Mail* does not carry very much, very big, copy, and it uses judgment in its make-up. No newspaper is more painstaking in its efforts to please advertisers – to treat them fairly."

ADVERTISER: "What will 20,000 lines cost me at the run-of-paper rate?"

BLOCK: "$3,750 – 18 3/4 cents a line."

ADVERTISER: "That's the best you can do? The very best?

BLOCK: "Yes, sir."

ADVERTISER: "All right. I'll telephone my agency to give you a contract. Go and get it before your start East."

BLOCK: "Thank you, sir."

As the twentieth century entered its teen years, events conspired once again to change the pace of the newspaper industry. Tensions in Europe exploded into what eventually became known as the Great War, and while the government of the United States at first officially remained neutral, many newspapers declared themselves either pro-British or pro-German. Some Americans agreed with the isolationist stand of the *New York World*: "If Europe insists on committing suicide, Europe must furnish the corpse for Europe's funeral." Paul Block never fully declared himself on either side in the years before the United States entered the war, possibly because he was attempting to remain unaligned and impartial for political and business reasons. Years before, when he had gone from paper to paper in Elmira selling space, first to Democrats and then to Republicans, Block had learned not to let his political and emotional feelings get in the way of a business deal. He maintained the same professional neutrality now. Stoddard and Block, while entertaining their private opinions, remained editorially silent as to which side they favored, but as the war progressed it became impossible for the *Evening Mail* to maintain objectivity or unalignment. Readers demanded increasingly more news coverage and bulletins in the nightly editions. Newspapers found it impossible to print both the war news and the other routine news without increasing the size of the regular issues, to such an extent that financial returns would not pay for the growing cost of production.[6] Given the public's expectation that evening newspapers would carry the most current war news, it became incumbent on the publishers to drop space reserved for advertisers and local news.

> After the outbreak of the war the evening papers assumed a position never before held in the history of American journalism. Many of the papers of this class consisted of features which had no more value than last year's almanac and an editorial page of the human interest type. The war made a decided change by putting more news into the pages of the evening papers. The difference in time between America and Europe often gave the late papers a monopoly on war news: the late editions had not yet gone to press when the European armies bivouacked for the night. [7]

Because of all the additional expenses, it became increasingly difficult to keep the *Mail* solvent. Despite the growth of many evening papers and an unprecedented dip in newsprint prices, in 1915 Stoddard decided to sell the waning *Evening Mail*. Block left the operation of the paper at that time, although both men still retained a large number of shares of stock. Their decision to part with the *Evening Mail* just when evening papers were garnering some respect as vital and viable newscarrying entities in this country was due partly to their desire to distance themselves from the partisan world of publishing, which was polarizing over the war, and partly due to finances: the *Mail* had begun to lose almost $1,000 daily. [8] It is possible that the *Evening Mail* was financially within Block's grasp in 1915, should he have wanted to become sole owner at that time, but for the reasons cited he let the opportunity pass.

The following year, Block became publisher of the *Newark Star-Eagle*, a story that will be presented later on in this chapter. But his relationship with the *New York Evening Mail* continued and took a wholly unexpected turn.

Block may have had a difficult time synthesizing his loyalties in the years before America joined the war, because many of his close friends and business colleagues were German, and he had a certain attachment to his own roots. He knew how to keep partisanship from spoiling a deal, but many of his business associates found it impossible to separate the two. Both he and Stoddard felt the weight of the public's opinions pressing in on them. They were relieved when, in 1915, the paper was sold to Dr. Edward A. Rumely, an American-born physician who had been educated in Germany at Heidleberg, and also had a degree from Oxford.

When the *Evening Mail* was sold, neither Stoddard nor Block knew that they were embroiling themselves even more deeply into a political nightmare. While they were aware that Dr. Rumely was an acknowledged German sympathizer, this was not particularly rare in the immigrant city of New York, or a country that had 2,000,000 German-born residents. America was strictly neutral and it was not a crime to support German policies, as many German-American businessmen did. Many believed that the European conflict was purely a struggle for economic domination between Germany and the United Kingdom, and that there were no real ethical issues involved. Henry Stoddard *did* stipulate to Dr. Rumely that he was unwilling to have the *Evening Mail* pass into the possession of anyone planning to further German purposes, and received Dr. Rumely's word of honor that everyone who was to be involved in *The Mail* was a good American.[9] Thus it was that Dr. Rumely, in spite of his German connections, assumed control of the paper in June of 1915, barely a month after the sinking of the *Lusitania,* which had inched the United States closer to war.

Immediately upon assuming control of the *Evening Mail*, Dr. Rumely had begun publishing editorials sympathetic in tone to the Germans. His basic desire in owning a newspaper was to promote certain tenets of the United States Progressive Party, to balance what he considered the excessive coverage given to the allied armies by the American press and to elicit support from important German-Austrian businesses in New York against the British blockade, which he regarded as unwarranted and illegal.[10] The *Evening Mail* trod a very fine editorial line prior to April of 1917, when the United States declared war against Germany. The newspaper was publishing articles that promoted German values and the German lifestyle, while not declaring outright full support for the Germans in the war. One series in particular, entitled *"How German Women are Trying to Help Germany Win the War,"* written by an American woman, described the intense frugality the Germans were practicing while under the British blockade.[11] The piece did not overtly criticize the British but instead led the reader to this conclusion by praising the German fortitude and dedication. Another piece published in the *Evening Mail,* entitled *"The Kaiser's Strange Adventure,"* spoke of a "chemical" weapon the Kaiser developed to eradicate the world, possibly as a scare tactic to suggest Germany's superiority. Articles written by Dr. Rumely, even when criticizing Germany's war behavior, contained references to the "skilled

technical abilities of the German people" and their "excellent work ethic."
Dr. Rumely might have considered these relatively benign endorsements
harmless enough, but as America approached direct intervention in the
war, his pro-German writing began to attract U. S. Government attention.

And, as if writing pro-German editorials wasn't dangerous enough for
Dr. Rumely, he made no effort to hide his long involvement with German
politics and politicians. During his eventual trial, several embarrassing
letters and notes surfaced. They were written sometime in the year 1914
to Dr. Heinz Bernhard, a chief German propagandist in the U.S. In these
letters Dr. Rumely exhorted Bernhard to purchase an Irish newspaper,
with the idea of turning the Irish against the English with German propaganda. More damaging still was Rumely's written assertion that "I myself invested several thousand dollars into this paper about a year ago in
the hope that I might influence it along the lines of effort that I am making toward creating a more favorable sentiment in this country for Germany."[12] Dr. Rumely claimed that he felt it incumbent upon himself to,
if not defend, at least present Germany fairly in the increasingly pro-ally
American press. But to the public, Dr. Rumely was merely a puppet
dancing to the Kaiser's tune. By the year 1916 it was widely acknowledged that the *Evening Mail* was a propaganda tool for the German government, right at the time that Germany was warned that the U.S. would
break off diplomatic relations unless it discontinued its U-boat attacks
against unarmed vessels. So infamous was the *Evening Mail*'s reputation
that when S. S. McClure, the handsome Irishman who was Editor-in-
Chief of the newspaper from early 1915 to early 1916, tried to disembark
in Liverpool, England, a year after having left the employ of the *Mail,* he
was detained and then deported by British authorities for being a German
agent.[13] Even Henry Stoddard admitted that rumors of the true [German]
ownership reached him in 1917, just as the U.S. was to fully engage in
the war. When his stock options matured, he considered regaining control of the *Evening Mail*, but upon the advice of his friend Col. Theodore
Roosevelt, he decided to wait for further developments. Block took
Stoddard's cue and bided time until he could better discern the *Mail's*
direction.

1917 was a pivotal year for Dr. Rumely and the *Evening Mail*. The
newspaper was losing money, heavily. As the war progressed and anti-
German sentiment fomented in the streets, Dr. Rumely's *Evening Mail*
grew less and less popular. The situation became so difficult that Rumely
resorted to some public relations of his own, finessing a brief biographi-

cal piece on himself in *Editor & Publisher,* wherein he is described as "a newspaper maker who reduces all questions to a practical basis, eliminates the useless and retains the vital."[14] Despite his best efforts, Rumely could not improve his circulation or advertising revenue. His original seed money was being used up in plant improvements and other technical changes, so he somehow borrowed another $626,000 to see him through 1917. Exactly who was supplying Rumely this money is what the U.S. Government wanted to know, and every time Rumely borrowed more he brought them closer to the answer.

During this time, from 1915 to 1917, Paul Block adroitly avoided becoming too closely associated with Dr. Rumely, although it does not appear he severed all ties completely. Based on a statement by Stoddard in 1921, both he and Block retired from active participation in the *Evening Mail* when Rumely bought it in 1915, but it is known that Paul Block had communication with Rumely about advertising and other matters at various times throughout Rumely's three-year tenure at the paper. Block, astute as he was becoming about politics and public opinion as a result of Stoddard's tutelage, managed to avoid implicating himself in the eyes of the public and the Government, despite dealing with a known propagandist for the Germans. Just prior to Rumely's arrest there was a strong anti-foreigner feeling emerging in the country, almost a mass hysteria, spurred on by Col. Teddy Roosevelt and his "anti-hyphenism" campaign. Tales of conspiring with the enemy were everywhere, and it was increasingly common for people to be arrested and charged with acts of treason or espionage against the United States. Many Americans with German names were fired from their jobs. At some war bond rallies, German-Americans were forced to parade as objects of ridicule and humiliation. Symphony conductors even began to avoid performing the works of Bach, Mozart and Beethoven.

As the end of the War neared, in the summer of 1918, Dr. Rumely was arrested by the U.S. Government, first on a perjury charge and then for treason. The United States Postal Act of August 24, 1912 obligated the editor, publisher, business manager, or owner of every publication entered as second-class matter (except religious, fraternal, temperance, scientific, or other similar publications), to file no later than April 1 and October 1 of each year, and publish a statement of ownership and management.[15] Dr. Rumely duly listed himself as the owner, but in 1918 he was arrested for failing to disclose to a U.S. Alien Property Agent that the true owner of the *Evening Mail* was the German Imperial Government.

Amidst the upheaval, the *Evening Mail* was almost shut down. It was able to keep publishing because of a clause Stoddard had inserted into the original deed of sale, which stipulated that in the event the property should ever become jeopardized, the bond holders would enter, take possession and conduct it for their own interest. The government approved what might be called a political receivership, and the *Evening Mail* returned to the experienced hands of Paul Block and Henry Stoddard as the two largest shareholders. Paul Block now had co-ownership of his second newspaper (the *Mail* and *The Newark Star Eagle*). His consummate skill in business politics had not only allowed him to remain a majority shareholder in the *Evening Mail*, but enabled him to navigate through the intricacies of Dr. Rumely's tenure to emerge unscathed in public opinion.

When viewed in retrospect, this period of American history lends itself to charges of paranoia, especially toward people whose background might not be 100% American. There was, however, justifiable cause to be suspicious; the German government worked hard to establish a network of propaganda in the United States. Paul Block, maneuvering through this political minefield, had to contend with being a Jewish immigrant who spoke German, and who had strong ties to the German business community. Not only was it a risk for him to know Dr. Rumely, but a far more famous associate of Paul Block's, William Randolph Hearst, was called in before a special Senate Judiciary Committee that was investigating Germany's efforts to control newspapers. Block was not yet a business partner of Hearst's, but had recently been signed on as a special representative for some of Hearst's newspapers, and was even referenced in regard to propaganda publishing in the judiciary hearings. Hearst, an outspoken supporter of Germany and staunchly anti-British, insisted on publishing German rhetoric in all of his papers. Many peers criticized him stridently, but he continued to print German war bulletins and the Potsdam view of the war until the U.S. officially joined the Allied Forces. Americans demanded action against Hearst under the sedition laws, and his newspapers were barred from many homes and clubs. He was burned in effigy.

Bruce Bielaski, a U.S. Secret Service Agent, gave testimony for one solid week to the United States Senate on the various activities of the German Imperial Government in attempting to buy the *Washington Times* and the *Washington Post*, reading mostly from files supplied by the British and American Secret Service.[16] Bielaski cited cables from a former German diplomat, Count Johann Von Bernstorff, to Dr. Bernhard Dernburg, one-time chief of the German Propaganda Services, which stated that, "The *Washington Post* had been offered to him for $2,000,000 with an option to buy it back again after the war for $1,500,000, or to put the paper at their disposal for two months for $100,000."[17]

Later, Bielaski testified that Von Bernstoff had deplored the death of John R. McLean, publisher of the *Washington Post*; Von Bernstorf wrote that: "The elder McLean had given his newspaper an entirely anti-English character," and that "the paper will be lost to us if it cannot – as is very desirable – be put in the hands of Mr. Hearst," the implication and assumption being that if Hearst bought the paper, which he wanted to do, with his rampant pro-German sympathies, he would be in Germany's pocket. Von Bernstorf went on, according to Bielaski, to protest an alleged change in attitude toward Germany by the *Washington Post*, and blamed Edward B. McLean – John McLean's son – who took control of the *Post* upon his father's death, for the pro-British, anti-German editorials that had begun to appear in the paper. The Bielaski testimony was vigorously disputed by Edward McLean, who denied that his father ever offered the *Washington Post* for sale to the German Government, and he proclaimed that the statement was an example of "another Von Bernstorf lie."[18]

While Hearst was never accused of offering to sell his papers to the Germans, the depth of his pro-German sentiment also came to light in a series of communiqués known as the "Palm Beach Telegrams," read aloud by Bielaski to the Senate. According to one message, it was sent in response to a query Hearst had received from the newspaper *Vossische Zeitung*, in Berlin, asking for opinions from leading American circles on the American-German rupture.[19] Hearst stated his belief that "The American people did not want war with Germany, as Americans from childhood have been taught to regard both Germany and France as their proven friends." Although the statement in retrospect seems wrongheaded now, it was harmless enough on face value, but with the irrational climate sweeping the country, Hearst received enormous criticism as a result. Even more seriously, Hearst was implicated in what became known as the notorious "Zimmerman Telegram."

> In his message relating to the Zimmerman note, which showed the hand of Germany in an effort to involve the United States in trouble with Mexico and Japan, Mr. Hearst was alleged to have attacked the President, the Attorney-General, the Postmaster-General and Col. Edward M. House.[20]

The Zimmerman Telegram was written by the German Foreign Minister, Arthur Zimmerman, to the governments of Mexico and Japan, urging
both countries to fight on Germany's side against the United States. In
return for Mexico's allegiance, Germany offered to help it to "reconquer
the lost territory in Texas, Arizona and New Mexico." The telegram also
instructed Mexico to seek assistance from Japan in its war with the U.S.
The communiqué so enraged Wilson that the note constituted one of the
most important factors in leading the President to declare war on Germany.

It was Hearst's shockingly cruel response to the 1915 sinking of the
Lusitania, though, that crystallized the public's feelings about him. He
commented that the sinking, with the loss of 114 American lives, was due
to the incompetence of the crew. When Hearst's statement became known,
he resoundingly earned the epithet of the most hated man in America.[21]

Interestingly, many of the key German players mentioned in the Senate
hearings (and in connection with Hearst), Dr. Dernburg, Von Bernstorff,
Samuel Untermeyer and Dr. Heinrich Albert – the number one German
agent in the United States – would surface again when Rumely's case
finally came to trial. On July 24, 1915, a U.S. Secret Service Agent had
managed to snatch a briefcase of Dr. Albert's, the contents of which revealed that he had received $28 million dollars to finance a variety of
disruptive acts and gain control of whatever newspapers he could. Dr.
Rumely was then mentioned in passing in the hearings, as "so attached to
Dr. Dernburg as to be his shadow," and "the drawer of propaganda money
that Louis A. Hammerling was to use for German propaganda advertising."[22] With both Hearst and Rumely so thoroughly enmeshed in the
German propaganda web, Paul Block did not want to highlight his association with them. Unfortunately, though, his name also came up at
Bielaski's Senate hearing as being associated with the two men.

Block was cited for another reason, too. A freelance magazine writer,
Edward Lyell Fox, was accused at the hearing of inciting anti-Japanese
feelings along the Pacific Coast through articles he wrote for the *Illustrated Sunday Magazine*, which was distributed as a supplementary part
of the *Los Angeles Herald* and other newspapers.[23] The belligerent foreign policy stories by Fox also proclaimed that England and Japan were
more menacing to the neutrality of the United States than Germany, and
that Americans would be dupes if they permitted a single drop of American blood to be shed on foreign soil. Although unpatriotic and jingoistic,
the comments did not seem all that *outré* to a fairly large section of the

American public. One of the popular songs of the day echoed those sentiments: "*I Didn't Raise My Boy to Be a Soldier.*"

Paul Block had increased his involvement in the *Illustrated Sunday Magazine* and had become co-publisher with Norman E. Mack, but it is not known how much influence he had on the editorial policy of the publication. Certainly, it can be assumed that he would have been aware of the direction of the content and, if he had wanted to, he could probably have prevented the publication of the articles.

Eventually charges were brought against Fox, but for reasons that are not clear, no formal legal complaints were lodged against the *Illustrated Sunday Magazine*. For an astute observer, however, it seemed suspicious that Block's name kept appearing in hearings of the Department of Justice in relation to propaganda charges. Shortly after the naming, but not the accusing, of the *Illustrated Sunday Magazine* in the propaganda trial, circulation plunged from 1,200,000 to 675,000 in one year. It cannot be proven whether this decline was as a result of the scandal, but there was a precipitous drop in advertising that accompanied the loss of readers. The outcome was that Block severed all ties with the *Illustrated Sunday Magazine* as it fell from its esteemed position in the pantheon of periodicals, and it soon ceased publishing altogether, seemingly to be forgotten entirely, even to this day, by journalism historians.

During this period of time, a charge surfaced about yet one more possible connection between the German Government and the *Evening Mail*. One of the directors of the newspaper, Hugo Reisinger, was the grandson of the then-late beer magnate Adolphus Busch. It was alleged that Reisinger received money from his grandmother to try to wrest control of the *Mail*. Justice Department investigators claimed that a large part of the cash that was raised in this country for German propaganda was furnished by Mr. Busch's widow, and that she was directly interested in the editorial manipulation of the *Mail*. Upon further questioning by Federal authorities, Mrs. Busch denied any culpability, and the matter, unable to be proven, was reluctantly dropped by the government.

Block survived this period without permanent damage to his reputation, but it is probable he underwent some non-public government questioning regarding his relations with Rumely. The arrest of Dr. Rumely took place on April 8, 1918, virtually a year after America officially entered the war. Before his arrest, Rumely was questioned by an Alien Property Agent in Washington, D.C. and asked specifically if he was the sole owner of the *Evening Mail*, to which he replied "Yes." The U.S. Govern-

ment, believing themselves to possess evidence to the contrary, charged
Rumely with perjury, and shortly thereafter, treason. Also arrested with
Rumely were S. Walter Kauffman and Norvin R. Lindheim. The three
men composed the financial committee of the S.S. McClure Newspaper
Syndicate (the oldest newspaper syndicate in the United States), one of
the businesses allegedly used to fund Rumely's purchase of the *Mail*.
Initially, the trial was to be held in Washington and much time was lost
while defense lawyers sought a change of venue to move it back to New
York. After numerous delays, the trial was relocated to New York City,
only to be delayed again due to illness of Samuel Untermeyer, who was
representing Kauffman and Lindheim. The trial of Rumely, Kauffman
and Lindheim did not officially begin until November 8, 1920, more than
two years after the initial arrest, and less than a week after the first regular
radio broadcasting service, KDKA, began in Pittsburgh, Pennsylvania;
details of Rumely's trial were not, however, broadcast over the air. In
answer to the charges against him, Dr. Rumely maintained that he never
lied about the *Evening Mail* ownership, and all money used to buy the
paper was from American citizens, not the German government.

   With the question of ownership central to the trial, the prosecuting office was intent on establishing a link between Rumely and German Imperial funding of the *Evening Mail*. Their first round of evidence focused
on the convoluted chain of check dispersals that Rumely underwent every time he needed cash for the newspaper. It was pointed out that Rumely
purchased the *Evening Mail* for $735,000 in 1915, using money drawn
from various banks in the United States that had German accounts.[24]
The accounts were in the names of Von Bernstorff and Dr. Heinrich Albert.
Dr. Albert had instructed various banks to issue cashiers' checks in the
name of Walter Lyon, then a member of the Wall Street firm of Renskorf,
Lyon & Company. Lyon deposited the cashiers' checks into that firm's
account, only to have a single check re-issued to him for the entire amount,
that he would then turn over to Rumely. As a result, the prosecution was
able to establish clearly that Rumely was drawing his money from German government accounts, although they were unable to say definitively
that the German government directed the allocation of the funds. Prosecution called in clerks from all the various banks to testify about the
origins of the money. One of them was Frank H. Sickles, from the Central Union Trust Company, who claimed the German government had
over $9,000,000 in its account from the sale of German bonds. This would
have been counted as a governmental source had the prosecution been

able to prove irrefutably that Rumely's money was drawn from that specific account.[25]   There were several "dummy" accounts spread around the world, with one named "Perez" moving large amounts of cash through Dr. Albert's and Von Bernstorff's accounts most frequently.

In the course of defining the payment's paper trail, Dr. Rumely's past was exhumed and poured over and examined with excruciating detail. The prosecution easily established a strong sympathetic link to Germany, but, as Rumely's lawyers were quick to point out, as soon as the United States joined the war, Rumely published only patriotic editorials. As for his actions prior to war, unpopular though they might have been, they were not illegal. Rumley's copious notes and letters were read aloud to the jury, in which he actively wrote of buying a newspaper to support German interests, but an irrefutable link between Rumely, the *Evening Mail*, and the German government was missing.

The prosecution still had a very strong case against Rumely. The most awkward and sensitive point was the source of the cash. They could trace the flow from the United States to Rumely, but proving the distribution of monies from Germany to the U.S. was much more difficult. By stressing the defendant's strong ties to Germany and obvious intimacy with German officials and propagandists, the prosecution did all they could to insinuate, detail and construct the connection. They did have evidence of telegrams and wires arriving to Rumely from Germany on government cables, and so hoped, in the face of these facts, to make their case. Quite wisely, Rumely made no effort to hide his background, sympathies or attempts to buy into the newspaper publishing business to promote Germany's causes, though these were the very reasons he wanted to gain control of the *Evening Mail*. While admitting everything frankly, Rumely's lawyers stressed repeatedly that it wasn't a crime to hold anti-British sentiments, or to know Germans or to want to support them prior to 1918. Rumely's main concern was to convince the jury that the source of his cash was not the German government, although, in light of what the prosecution had displayed, it was going to be difficult for him to prove. He needed to find a plausible person who was American, wealthy, living in Germany and with access to government wires, to name as a source of cash. Bizarrely enough, there was such a person who died right before Dr. Rumely's arrest: Hermann Siecklen, the German born Coffee-King.

Hermann Siecklen was a member of the new wealthy immigrant class of America. He was a citizen of the United States, having immigrated at age fourteen. As he grew older, he spent more and more time in Germany with his family and new German wife, at his Bavarian castle, which is where he was ensconced when the war broke out. Because of his infirmities and the danger of traveling by boat, he did not return to the United States, and he died in Germany in 1918. As far as cover stories go, he was a perfect alibi for Rumely. It is possible that Rumely was telling the truth about Hermann Siecklen's involvement with the *Evening Mail* since it was difficult for the court to discern the truth. History may never know, as neither Siecklen's widow nor his business manager could effectively prove or disprove the connection between Rumely and Siecklen.

> The defense proposed that Siecklen had himself purchased the *Evening Mail*, he being an American citizen in Germany at the outbreak of the war and finding it a losing venture was anxious to get rid of it on pretty much any terms. In his negotiations, according to this account, he had of necessity used the wireless, which was under control of the German government, because the British Navy had seized all cables connecting with Germany but that it was his own money that he had employed in purchasing the *Evening Mail*. On this theory Dr. Rumely, a native-born American, bought the paper from Siecklen, an American citizen and it was not money advanced by the German government at all that paid for it. If that contention should be established, the charge that the Trading with the Enemy Act (treason) was violated would fall to the ground.[26]

Naturally, the defense could not insist that Siecklen bought the *Mail* outright, since Henry Stoddard, its previous owner, had never met or had any communication with Siecklen. Therefore, Rumely and his lawyers constructed an elaborate theory of how Siecklen intended to buy the *Evening Mail* but was prevented from doing so as the war intervened.

Mr. Kauffman, a well known attorney in New York, testified that Dr. Albert approached him asking for help in purchasing a paper for an American citizen then in Germany who did not want the British to know he was planning to buy such a newspaper. Dr. Albert also told Kauffman that he (Albert) was spied upon and shadowed and wished to conceal his part in the transaction.[27] Having reached an agreement with Kauffman, Dr. Albert then approached his good friend Dr. Rumely about "buying" the *Evening Mail*. Most important in Kauffman's testimony was his recounting of how he approached Siecklen himself in 1916 with the aim of convincing him to supply more money for the paper, which was suffering heavy financial losses. Kauffman stated that Siecklen, reluctant to lose the newspaper entirely, made an initial loan of $75,000 and then another $150,000 in January. These extra loans would account for almost all the money Rumely mysteriously received in the early part of 1916 and 1917.

Rumely's story about Siecklen seemed somewhat credible, but was far from perfect. Rumely himself had no record of payments made to Siecklen, or any way to prove the coffee magnate's part in the ownership of the *Evening Mail*. He swore that he signed a note to Siecklen agreeing to "share" the ownership of the paper, but no note was ever found among Mr. Siecklen's documents. Additionally, there was no reason for Siecklen to hide his ownership of the *Evening Mail*, even if he was living in Germany at the time. Rumely's defense maintained that Siecklen did not want the British in particular to discover his ownership because he planned to heavily criticize their oppressive naval blockades, and yet, dependent as he was on water travel to ship his coffee from South America, he couldn't risk their retaliation. So, it was argued, Rumely was to be the owner, while Siecklen stayed in the background.

In the end, Rumely was convicted of two counts, both in failing to report having received money from the German Imperial Government, but was found not guilty of counts three, four and five, which related to his knowingly hiding the German Imperial Government's ownership of the *Evening Mail* and parts of the company, the S. S. McClure Newspaper Syndicate. Rumley's sentence of a year and a day in Federal prison (which would have caused him to lose his citizenship) was commuted to one month by Paul Block's friend, President Calvin Coolidge. Nothing could be found in the research of this book to indicate that Block influenced Coolidge's decision, but it is altogether likely that Block's leverage on, and connection with the President, was the deciding factor.

An interesting part of Dr. Rumely's trial is how he managed to salvage the *Evening Mail* and keep it from being dissolved, as was the usual practice of the U.S. Government when seizing non-profitable businesses. Rumely was evidently already trying to get out of the newspaper business, because he made an arrangement with Paul Block and Henry Stoddard several months prior to his arrest that brought them into prime position to run the *Evening Mail* once he was ousted. As early as 1917, Rumely was approaching friends and business associates, offering shares of S. S. McClure stock, *Evening Mail* stock, or notes in exchange for cash. Paul Block is listed as one of the people who gave him money,

although the record does not indicate exactly what Block received in return. In all likelihood it was additional stock in the newspaper, since he
emerged as the second largest shareholder of the *Evening Mail*. At some
point in the beginning of 1918, Rumely made a private deal with Stoddard
and Block, and the two assumed President and Vice-President roles on
the paper's masthead, although Rumely still held the title of Publisher.
Just exactly what the arrangement was between Rumely, Block and
Stoddard is unclear, but it probably relates back to the clause Stoddard
inserted into the initial deed of sale reverting the newspaper to the primary stockholders in the event of an emergency. Contrary to usual policy,
the U.S. Government permitted Block and Stoddard to keep publishing
the *Mail* even during Rumely's trial, and even though the law stated that
property could not be sold or allotted until the owner undergoes a conviction.

   Adolph S. Ochs, owner of *The New York Times*, and Donald Seitz, publisher of the *New York World*, were asked by representatives of the Justice
Department to become involved in the *Evening Mail* matter, and appraise
its value should the paper be eventually taken over. It was the policy of
the Government not to conduct a business taken from alien enemies if
that business showed a loss, and so plans were being made, upon Rumely's
conviction, to sell it.

   Block and Stoddard announced that the real reason they had taken over
the management of the *Mail* was to conserve the heavy financial interests
that they both had in the paper, and that if a price for the property sufficient to protect their individual investments could be secured, they would
sell it. For whatever reason, no interested buyers came to the fore, and
the two men continued the operation. Stoddard and Block knew at least
eight months before Rumely's arrest that he was being investigated, and
were able to maneuver themselves into the best position to pick up control of the paper. When Rumely went to prison, Stoddard continued his
role as Editor, and Block assumed the official title of Publisher, although
he had unofficially been performing that role for three years.

   In avoiding the publicity surrounding the Rumely trial, Paul Block demonstrated his political adroitness and determination to let nothing get in
the way of business or friendship. As a salesman, he depended upon the
strength of his reputation to succeed. He could not afford to become
overly associated with any one doctrine or philosophy. In the highly emotional atmosphere of the war, nationality counted for almost everything
in the eyes of the world. That Block, with all of his German connections

– not the least of which was his association with the infamous Mr. Hearst – survived the *Evening Mail* scandal without any great stigma attached to either his personal or business name, is an incredible accomplishment of controlling and minimizing his losses. That he also emerged with co-ownership of the paper bespeaks his intense commitment to realizing his dreams, no matter what the circumstances. For Block, there was no *Evening Mail* scandal or problem, there existed only the *Evening Mail* opportunity.

In the summer of 1919, in order to defray the mounting costs of the mortgage on the *Evening Mail* building, Block and Stoddard leased a floor and some additional space to a fledgling publication called the *Illustrated Daily News* which later changed its name to the *Daily News* – "New York's Picture Newspaper" and became the newspaper with America's largest circulation. The *Mail* also leased the use of its printing presses to the *News*, and that fee was substantial.[28] The two newspapers also began to share some expenses, such as the cost of delivery by trucks, a communal lunchroom, and a wire-service teletype machine. Each paper had exclusive hours apportioned to it on the wire machine; the *News* used it for the evening hours for news to be published in its morning paper the next day, and the *Mail* used the wire service copy during the mornings and afternoons for release in its evening paper. The understanding was that whatever news came in during the exclusionary time "belonged" to the respective paper on duty, and would not be used by the other newspaper.

Within a short while of the new sharing operation, the *Evening Mail* editors began to suspect that the *Illustrated Daily News* was publishing some of the news that "belonged" to them, having arrived during the *Mail's* designated time slot. It was believed that someone on the staff of the *News* was appropriating some of the stories that rightfully belonged to the *Mail*. To test their theory, an editor of the *Mail* typed the following one-sentence bogus alert (a synopsis of a story to come, but which could also run as filler) on teletype paper, and placed it in the basket where all wire service stories were put for the *Mail*:

> Ekafasti, Greece – Burglars today broke into the village
> bank and stole one million drachmas, about $7.38.

In the next morning's edition of the *News*, the filler was published word-for-word. In a move to retaliate and embarrass the *News*, that afternoon's edition of the *Evening Mail* carried the following notice, prominently published on the front page:

> Our esteemed contemporary, the Daily News, has printed
> a news item with a date-line, "Ekafasti." It's astounding that
> when this word is spelled backwards, it says, "It's a fake."[29]

Shortly after that, as a circulation promotion, the *News* began running a contest for readers – one of the first in the newspaper industry – with huge cash prizes. As the circulation began to soar and ever-growing numbers of subway-traveling New Yorkers became regular readers of the *Daily News*, the paper could no longer find the time-slot demands that it needed in leasing the *Mail's* presses. It acquired its own. That ended the agreement with the *Mail*, and almost before he had started the arrangement with the *News*, Block was searching for other means of income.[30]

National advertising did not cascade onto the pages of the *Evening Mail* even under the new management, even though the talented Paul Block was out there trying to convince advertisers to give the newspaper a test. The large circulations of the competing evening papers, in addition to the morning dailies, dwarfed the *Mail's* readership, and the paper was often passed over whenever an advertiser or an agency was planning a campaign. Nevertheless, Block did what he could, and brought in three important department stores, Gimbel Brothers, Wanamaker's, and Bloomingdale's, all of which took large-scale space almost on a daily basis. Block greatly increased the entertainment advertising section with small but consistent ads for theater, movie and vaudeville performances, which were combined on the same page with restaurant ads for places to eat in the theater district. He brought in ads for furniture outlets, clothing, and food stores, and small space advertisements for a multitude of mail-order products and services. On some occasions he convinced a national advertiser such as Coca-Cola to place an advertisement in the *Newark Star-Eagle* or one of the other publications that he represented, and he would offer them an ad for the *Evening Mail* at a greatly reduced combined price.

By 1920, however, Block realized to his own surprise that he was not happy publishing *The Evening Mail*. Despite certain successes in advertising and circulation, the paper never seemed to be a perfect match for Paul Block's potential, or to take best advantage of his resources. He was more interested in creating chances for large gains than in profiting from the small, though secure, amounts that *The Mail* provided. The business and economic picture provided their own stresses. In the autumn of 1919, there had been 18 major strikes in the New York area, and virtually the entire business community of the Atlantic Coast was shut down; following that came the recession of 1920, and advertisers hastened to cancel their contracts not only in the *Mail* but in all publications throughout the city. The circulation had dropped to barely over 100,000, half of what it had been just six years before.[31] The winter of 1920 was brutal in New York City: the rivers were frozen, the subways short of coal, influenza and pneumonia killed thousands. Stores, offices and factories closed at an unprecedented 4:30 PM every day. Business virtually stopped. The *Mail's* advertising dried up. Although Block had personally escaped the Rumely stigma, he felt that the *Mail* itself had not. Combined with the paper's weakening financial condition, late in 1920 Block began telling friends and associates about the possibility of divesting himself of his interest in *The Evening Mail.*

On February 16, 1921, Stoddard made the following announcement on the editorial page:

> "It is with regret that I announce the withdrawal of Mr. Paul Block as publisher of the *Evening Mail.* Mr. Block has been my associate and friend for over 15 years. When I sold the *Evening Mail* in the winter of 1915, he retired with me from its control, but in July, 1918, he joined with me in its repurchase.
>
> "In the upbuilding of the *Evening Mail* to its present strong and prosperous position, Mr. Block as publisher has done his full share; his spirit, vision and energies, always unbounded, have been an inspiring influence in all that has been accomplished.
>
> "Mr. Block's many other interests are constantly requiring more of his time; they make impossible that active participation in the company's affairs which the position of publisher obviously demands.
>
> "Only recently, he added the Duluth (Minn.) Herald to the list of publications with which he is associated in major cities. It was on the announcement of this latest acquisition that Governor Miller telegraphed Mr. Block. "I hope your many successes in the East will be duplicated in the West,' a sentiment that I warmly endorse.
>
> "Mr. Block remains a member of the board of directors."

Shortly after Block sold out his part of the *Evening Mail*, Stoddard realized that he really couldn't operate the paper without him. A rumor that lasted no more than 24 hours circulated to the effect that the *Mail* had been bought by Henry Ford. Stoddard only wished it was true.[32] *The Evening Mail* eventually became one of the many papers that was merged into *The New York Sun*.

Block had now divested himself of his one holding in a New York City newspaper, and it exasperated him. Although *The Newark-Star Eagle*, was somewhat successful, he still wanted his presence known in the great metropolis.[33] He had learned, though, to pick his properties carefully. At the moment, New York did not seem to offer him the opportunity he wanted. One day, he still had hopes of owning another New York City newspaper, but for the nonce, he had other responsibilities, and other possibilities.

Newark Star-Eagle –
The first years: 1916-1920

By the time he was 40, Paul Block had spent well over 30 years in or connected with the newspaper business in one capacity or another. Not only had he worked for the *Elmira Telegram* directly in a variety of positions, and in a freelance situation for other New York newspapers while working for Richardson, but he learned all aspects of the business of newspaper publishing as he traveled around the country talking to, servicing, and learning from publishers, editors, advertising managers, and other newspaper executives.

In 1916, the newly-renamed Paul Block and Associates was realizing substantial profits from the *Illustrated Sunday Magazine*, the *Pictorial Review*, and the commissions he was receiving from advertising his company placed in more than a dozen major newspapers. The business was operating smoothly, and he had surrounded himself with honest and competent sales representatives and office personnel. His brother Max would join the company shortly and become its Treasurer. Paul and Dina were relatively happy, they had two little sons, Paul Jr. and William, and Block was feeling secure about his family and business life. He decided that this was the time to expand his business onto a different level. He would try to purchase some newspapers of his own. Unlike William Randolph Hearst or Frank Munsey or James Gordon Bennett, however, he decided to do this conservatively, since he did not have unlimited reserves of cash or access to credit. To protect his family and his existing business, he began his apprenticeship as a press baron without investing any personal savings of his own, or depleting funds from his company.

At first, he approached his long-time client, the *Syracuse Post-Standard*, and suggested that a portion of the money that was owed to him as a special representative be used, instead, to issue him stock in the newspaper. The publishers of the *Standard* were agreeable to this arrangement, as were the owners of the *Memphis News-Scimitar*, especially since both newspapers were seeking additional investment and had already realized sizable profits from Block's advertising clients. They also thought that once Paul Block became a part-owner of their respective publications, he just might exert even more effort and imagination in securing additional advertising for them, since he would have more to gain under such an arrangement. Eventually, buying additional shares to combine with the stock that was issued to him as payment, Block accumulated enough to become the sole owner of the *Memphis News-Scimitar.*[34]

His dreams of ownership went beyond Syracuse, New York or Memphis, Tennessee, however. Block desperately wanted and needed, for his own personal satisfaction and potential business growth, a New York City newspaper. To him, ownership of a daily newspaper in Manhattan implied many things: status among the great publishers such as Adolph S. Ochs, William Randolph Hearst and Joseph Pulitzer; a possible huge circulation with concomitant high advertising rates; political influence through endorsements and news coverage; and entree into the glamorous life of the most vital and magical city in the country. Although he had sixteen major newspaper accounts in 1916, Block's pocketbook did not match his ambition. Even if a New York City newspaper had been for sale – and there weren't any available at that precise time – he probably would not have been able to raise enough capital to buy one. If ownership in New York City was not an immediate possibility for Paul Block, then a daily newspaper nine miles west on the Passaic River, in another major metropolitan area, would have to do. He set his sights on acquiring *The Newark Star-Eagle*.

In 1916, the population of Newark, located in Essex County, New Jersey, was close to 400,000, with a surrounding greater metropolitan population of nearly 600,000, making it the 16th largest city in the country. Newark sat in the long shadow of Manhattan, but it was its own town with its own combination of grittiness and wealth, and as many private homes as any other major metropolitan area in the United States. An important trade and manufacturing center, there were also quarries of brown stone scattered throughout the Newark vicinity. One of the largest cotton thread factories in the country was located there, and manufacturers of jewelry, iron, steel, leather, clothing and many other products employed tens of thousands of workers.[35] It had a bustling downtown that boasted an avenue of newspaper offices on Broad Street, Newark's own version of Park Row or Fleet Street, where many of its 27 newspapers were edited and published.[36]

Block had been representing the *Newark Star and Advertiser*, an evening paper, for years (from about 1910) and became concerned when its owner, ex-Senator James Smith, Jr., who had bought the *Star* in 1906 and had been struggling with it for over a decade, was filing for bankruptcy and putting the paper up for receivership.[37] In terms of reach, the *Star*, at 44,949 average daily circulation, was considerably behind the other leading evening paper, the *Newark Evening News*, which had an average daily circulation of 74,444, and which claimed to reach every home in the city of Newark.[38] Smith could not compete in advertising with the stronger *News*, and decided to leave publishing altogether.[39] Smith also owned the weekly edition of the *Star*, called *The Sentinel of Freedom*, which had been published since 1796. It had ceased publication the year before. In addition to the waning *Star*, Smith announced that he was also abandoning his morning paper, *The Newark Eagle*, whose circulation had dwindled to 20,677.

Block saw the demise of the *Star* as a crucial blow to his income. It had been a reliable source for placing advertising, and he and his advertisers had made money from the paper over the years. When the announcement was made that there would be a public auction of the two newspapers, Block, who was out of town, dispatched his trusted ex-football star employee Charles J. Boyle to Newark to make an offer for the *Star* on his behalf.

The bidding, held in the Board of Director's room of the Fidelity Trust Company on January 17, 1916, was both formal and dramatic. Louis Hood, general counsel for the trust company, which had been acting as a receiver for the two newspapers, took charge of the proceedings. About a dozen people filled the tension-permeated room, all seemingly interested in the property. Hood explained the conditions under which the assets of the company were being sold and announced that he had one bid of $150,000 which would be the starting upset price. Upon hearing the call for bids, Andrew M. Lawrence, a former Chicago newspaper man, offered $155,000, which was immediately topped by Boyle, in behalf of

Block, for $160,000. Although Boyle wanted to continue the bidding, he would and could go no higher on Block's instructions. Businessman J.S. Rippel then bid $165,000, quickly answered by William Wallace Chapin, former publisher of the *Seattle Post-Intelligencer*, the *San Francisco Call*, and the *Chicago Herald.* A bidding war ensued, with the price rising in $5,000 increments until Lawrence made the top bid: $235,000. When the auctioneer failed to hear a further increase, he slammed down his gavel and sold both newspapers to Lawrence. But the auction was not over. Under the terms of the sale, which had been widely published in the newspapers, the purchaser was required to deposit a minimum of 10 percent of the purchase price, or its equivalent, to the receiver. Lawrence drew his check on a Western bank for $23,500, but Hood asked for either cash or a certified check, and refused to accept Lawrence's offer unless that stipulation was met. Lawrence reached for a phone and after a delay of some twenty minutes, admitted that he could not comply with the request of cash or certified check at that very moment in time.[40]

Hood re-started the bidding; and for a brief moment, Boyle believed he might have a chance to secure the paper, but the bidding commenced at $230,000, which was the next-highest bid before Lawrence's. Chapin offered $235,000, the bid was accepted without challenge, and after a number of phone calls, Chapin was able to arrange for his bank in New York to immediately transfer the down payment deposit to the Fidelity Trust Corporation.[41]

Block's failure to acquire the *Star* as his first newspaper disappointed him, but it is likely that even if he had been able to buy the paper for $160,000, he might have found it difficult to manage it alone financially. As it developed, he was soon given a second opportunity to buy the *Star*. Very soon. It seemed that Chapin really had no intention of publishing or owning the newspapers himself. In less than a week's time, he announced that he wished to re-sell both papers, asking for a slight profit in the transaction, which was what he had had in mind all along.

Block moved quickly. Days later, while visiting the *Toledo Blade*, for which he had served as special advertising representative since 1908, he discussed a possible joint ownership arrangement of the Newark papers with the lessees of the *Blade*, Nathaniel C. Wright and Harry S. Thalheimer (who later changed his name to Talmadge, because he didn't want to be thought of as pro-German). They were both publishing entrepreneurs who had earlier evinced interest in the Jersey papers. The three men formed a business consortium, as equal partners, to attempt to buy the

Newark papers and perhaps other properties. Their immediate plan was to make an offer to Chapin as soon as possible. Block could not return east immediately, and Boyle was also out of town, so Block asked Herman Halsted, who he had recently named Vice-President of Paul Block Associates, to negotiate on his behalf.

Again, the newspapers went to auction, but this time there was no Lawrence or Chapin to bid against, and with three partners – Wright, Thalheimer and Block – there was more cash with which to speculate. On January 25, 1916, Paul Block finally won and became a part-owner of his first major metropolitan daily newspaper. $235,000 in full was paid to the receiver but the final purchase price of the newspapers, which included Chapin's profit, was never disclosed. It was believed to be around $300,000, each partner putting in roughly $100,000.[42]

Then a startling announcement was made to the citizens of Newark: commencing Monday, January 31, 1916, the *Eagle* and the *Newark Evening Star* were going to consolidate under the new ownership, and would thereafter be published only in the evenings under the single title of the *Newark Star-Eagle*.[43] The new newspaper's "Declaration of Principles," perhaps influenced or written by Paul Block, was optimistic and sincere:

> Under this consolidation, one of the most important in the history of New Jersey journalism, the new *Star-Eagle* will be enabled to give to the people of Newark and the State a newspaper of the highest type of efficiency. With the combined newsgathering and mechanical facilities of the two papers, the full telegraph and cable service of the great Associated Press, the complete leased wire reports of the United Press and the augmented staff of trained editors, reporters and state and staff correspondents, the *Star-Eagle* hopes and intends to give its readers a clean, fair, accurate daily newspaper, complete in every detail.
>
> In its editorial and news policies the *Star-Eagle* will be absolutely independent. It will bear the label or wear the collar of no man or interest or party. It will, to the limit of its ability, serve the interest of the people of the city and the state as fairly and honestly and effectively as its light can lead, <u>and it will serve no other interest</u>.[44]

No sooner had the purchase been made than Arthur Brisbane, the brilliant editor of Hearst's *New York Journal,* offered to buy the *Star-Eagle* from Block either with his own money, or with Hearst's.[45]   Block was flattered by the proposal, and realized that he could turn a quick profit, but his long-range plans did not really include becoming a newspaper broker. He wanted to be an owner, a publisher of newspapers in every sense of the word. There would be, he sensed, future negotiations with Hearst and Brisbane on other newspapers, but for then Block held to his conviction that he could become a successful publisher, and he refused to sell.

The Newark Star-Eagle was true to its word in remaining Independent for several years after Block and his two partners bought the combined paper, but by 1919 it listed itself as "Independent-Republican," which is what Block then considered his own political persuasion to be, and as a result, the newspaper's endorsements for political office or appointments became, if not overtly Republican, then at least predominantly sympathetic to the GOP on most issues and platforms.[46]

The arrangement that was agreed upon by the three new owners was that as soon as he could divest himself of other responsibilities, Paul Block would become publisher of the newspaper. Eventually he did assume control as a hands-on publisher, a position he retained for almost a quarter of a century. Herman Halsted was named Treasurer of the organization, and Grove Patterson, the legendary editor of the *Toledo Blade*, would be called upon to do double duty and serve as Editor of the *Newark Star-Eagle*, traveling back and forth from Ohio to New Jersey as the need arose.

As the population and literacy of the city increased, the circulation of the *Newark Star-Eagle* also ascended under the stewardship of the new triumvirate, but it did so slowly, with rarely more than about 1,000 new subscribers per year, until it reached its height of about 50,000 in daily sales. It remained there until the boom years of the mid-1920's when it climbed to 85,000. During the same period, however, the readership of the competitor, the *Evening News*, swelled to 100,000 copies each night.[47] Both papers made money and had established a satisfied constituency; although they were theoretically competitors for each advertising dollar spent and each copy bought, they eventually lapsed into the role of friendly rivals – an unusual arrangement for newspapers in the same city – rarely encroaching upon each other's established accounts or readers. Ironically, the major competition for Block and his *Newark Star-Eagle* turned out to be the daily newspapers from New York City that were shipped to Newark by ferry every day. In order to compete with them, Block issued a special shopper's guide supplement, with no news or features – just ads – and charged advertisers, most of them local retailers, only 60% of the full rate that they would have had to pay if they'd taken space in the regular *Star-Eagle*.

With the new ownership, the *Star-Eagle* turned into a spunky and somewhat idiosyncratic effort, billing itself as "Jersey's Most Interesting Newspaper," which it probably developed into. It established and maintained a grip on its readers with such departments as a daily feature page that included favored recipes sent in by readers for such delights as sweet potato pudding or butter cakes,[48] a daily wrap-up of the crisis in Europe; a column of unusual news stories (e.g. an account of a man who used his wooden leg as a weapon,[49] or a couple that gave a formal party to announce their legal separation).[50] Every Friday it included a magazine section, mostly directed toward the female readership (who Paul Block understood better than many publishers because of his experience with the *Pictorial Review*); it contained such features as a lovelorn column, a romance – in serial form – by British novelist Ruby Ayers, and a style column ("The chemise dress – is it doomed?").[51]

Editor Grove Patterson's front page column, "The Way of the World," filled with sage advice and observations of faith, tolerance, influence and culture, from the moral value of philanthropy to how friendship matures with age over the years, was also a highly popular feature. The working relationship between Grove Patterson and Paul Block, which began at the *Newark Star-Eagle* and eventually continued at the *Toledo Blade*, was one of mutual admiration and would survive some 25 years in an era of turbulence in the country and in the newspaper industry.

The editorial position of the *Newark Star-Eagle* remained relatively independent, although basically Republican, always leaning toward the right, and thoroughly humanitarian. A plea for funds for Palestine, for example, to help the Jews and to provide emergency support for the destitute of Europe, was a lead editorial that may have met with opposition from a reactionary public.[52] A denunciation of prejudice against blacks in the North ("There are said to be more members of the Ku Klux Klan above the Mason-Dixon line than below it.")[53] displayed a certain courage in demanding that blacks be given the right to vote.

More than occasionally, the *Newark Star-Eagle* would comment on New York, its big sister slightly to the East. It often backed Alfred E. Smith, the Governor of New York, supporting his stance against Prohibition,[54] his proposition to build new hospitals and prisons,[55] and other policies. The fact that Smith, a Democrat, and Block, a Republican, had developed a friendship over the years, had *everything* to do with the more than friendly coverage and support that Smith received in the *Star-Eagle*; it also demonstrates a certain political or opportunistic expediency on Block's part. Friendship was of paramount importance to him. Issues of politics, religion, race, class, and nationality paled when it came to relationships with his friends.

Eventually, Block would begin a series of front-page editorials written and signed by him that he would run in the *Newark Star-Eagle*, and later in other newspapers that he came to acquire. He used the editorials to praise, to condemn, to exhort and to entreat. And the editorials were influential. Because of his successful backing of a movement to increase the salaries of the Newark police force, he was unanimously rated as an honorary member of the Patrolmen's Benevolent Association of Newark, New Jersey.[56]

Clearly, Block's title of Publisher was in no way a hollow or token symbol. There was virtually no aspect of the business that escaped his notice, attention and involvement, from the editorial page to the news carriers, and from the printing presses to the sports coverage. He continually brought in national advertisers that greatly bolstered the finances of the newspaper. Such frequent and large-space advertisers as Chesterfield and Camel cigarettes, Cliquot Club sodas, Michelin and Goodrich tires, Post Toasties cereal, Ford and Chrysler automobiles, Wrigley's Chewing Gum, Standard Oil, Coca-Cola, Bayer's Aspirin, and General Electric, came back to the *Newark Star-Eagle* time and again, and these advertisements, combined with a huge increase of local Newark advertisers from such traditional retailers as Bamberger's Department Store (which eventually ran a whopping 1,400,000 lines of advertising in the *Star-Eagle*), McGregor's Clothes, Kresge's, Bond's, and Ohrbach's greatly heightened the profits that the newspaper began to enjoy.

Now that Block, as publisher of his own newspaper, had the responsibility of filling as many of the pages as possible with advertising, he experienced a different type of tension than he had undergone as a special advertising representative. With the salaries of hundreds of employees to worry about and a mounting overhead, he was forced to pay even more diligent attention to the ledger books, and somehow approach the gathering of income more creatively. If he discerned, for example, that any particular day or week was "thin" – there was less advertising than normal, for whatever reason: the season, the economy, a salesman failing to fulfill his quota, national or international events that might pre-occupy the mind of the advertiser – Block would place "house" ads of his own in the space that normally would have been paid for by a regular advertiser.

He tried everything that he thought might turn a profit in bringing in enough returns to justify the space used. Through the pages of the *Newark Star-Eagle*, he sold travel, accident and life insurance;[57] attractive leatherette shopping bags; a 96-page self-published book, *World's Favorite Songs*, especially arranged for the newspaper by his friend Irving Berlin;[58] and a leather-bound, gold-stamped Bible, suggested as a meaningful Christmas gift.[59]   As another promotion, Block offered his readers free copies of a booklet that contained the "Three greatest documents of American history": The Declaration of Independence, the Articles of Confederation, and the Constitution of the United States. Thousands of readers responded.[60]

Some promotions were successfully launched for different purposes. Although they didn't bring in any direct profits to the newspaper, they did promote the name of the *Newark Star-Eagle* in an institutional way, and perhaps solidified the paper's image with the citizens of Newark. Block ordered the construction of a huge board that was mounted to the side of the newspaper's garage, on the corner of Halsey Street and Bradford Place; on it were posted sporting results of events as they were taking place: round by round for boxing, inning by inning for baseball, and touchdown by touchdown for football. Block had learned how much people enjoyed being informed about sporting events when he first came to New York City at the turn of the century. His notices were even more extensive than the ones he remembered at Park Row. Box scores and other pertinent details were posted as the action of the game or the bout progressed, and loudspeakers were placed on both sides of the mechanical board. When an event was being carried on the radio, the play-by-play news would be broadcast to the crowds below; when it was not, Block hired Bob McHugh, a popular Newark radio personality, to re-create the game or fight by reading the wire service reports directly from the Polo Grounds or wherever the event took place. As the scores and details of the game would be posted, hundreds, sometimes thousands of sports fans would congregate in the newspaper's parking lot and follow the action, and they roared, cheered and sometimes booed in true bleacher style.[61] Fans "watched" the World Series (including the famous struggle between the Yankees and the Giants in 1923), the Dempsey-Firpo championship bout, and the classic struggles of college football games such as Harvard-

Princeton, or Princeton-Yale.

Detroit Journal

In the early months of 1917, when German U-Boats were menacing and sinking ships in the Atlantic waters, the Kaiser was attempting to starve Britain, and President Woodrow Wilson was doing everything he could to head-off a full-fledged war, Paul Block became involved in the purchase of his second newspaper, the *Detroit Journal.*

Agreeing with his partners, the co-owners of the *Newark Star-Eagle,* Harry S. Talmadge (formerly Thalheimer), N.C. Wright and C.C. Vernon, Block believed that the time was right for many reasons to acquire the *Detroit Journal.* He had been trying, unsuccessfully, to convince the newspaper to let him be its special representative, but could not dislodge their commitment to the company that they had been doing business with for years, Verree & Conklin, Inc., of New York. If he were to buy the *Journal,* not only would he gain its special representative business, but he'd be purchasing a paper that he was sure was about to grow in readership and in advertising. Block believed that Detroit, the country's fifth largest city with a population of one million, already the automobile capital of the world, was booming and would continue to grow. Although there were other competing newspapers in the city, he was certain that he could sell enough advertising to recoup his investment. Scripps's *Detroit News* – the beginning of the Scripps-Howard dynasty of newspapers – had by far the highest circulation in the city. But Scripps was having an ongoing disagreement with Joseph L. Hudson, proprietor of Detroit's largest and first real department store, about the rapid transit system. Although Hudson's was a frequent advertiser in the *News,* the store was continually canceling its traditional "Page Three" advertising whenever the debate about the transit system heated up. Block realized that Hudson's, by definition, had to advertise somewhere, since quick sales – the very strategy and rationale of department stores – bespoke lavish advertising. He intended to make the *Journal* the preferable venue for Hudson's, thereby guaranteeing the paper almost a daily full-page of advertising and sometimes more. This hoped-for promise, combined with potential advertising from automobile, truck, tire and accessory companies headquartered in Detroit, suggested that the *Journal* was an assured investment.

The *Journal* had been established in 1883. By 1917 it had a circulation in excess of 100,000, was respected by the citizens of Detroit, and enjoyed a reputation of being heavily religion-oriented.[62] The *News,* because it fought for lower utility rates and greater independence from the State legislature, was often denounced as being a socialist newspaper. The *Journal*, in complete contrast, was considered to be the most conservative newspaper in the city, and appealed more to Detroit's growing moneyed class.

When Block learned of the death of the editor of the *Journal*, Harry C. Hetherington, and the ill-health of the general manager W. B. Lowe, he assumed, correctly as it developed, that the publisher and principal stockholder, E. D. Stair, who was also owner of the morning *Detroit Free Press,* would be amenable – because of his loss of reliable and key personnel – to an offer to sell out. After a formal appraisal and accounting was conducted, Block and his associates offered Stair $700,000. Stair wanted and demanded more but quickly accepted their next bid, $800,000; and on January 30, 1917, the ownership of the *Detroit Journal*, including the building at the corner of Fort and Wayne Streets, became the property of Paul Block and his partners.

Two side-by-side editorials – one farewell word from Stair and the other an introduction from the new owners – greeted the *Journal's* readers on the first evening of the takeover. Stair's comments were warm and reassuring: "Parting with *Journal* men brings pangs of regret, softened only by the knowledge that each one is to remain with the paper at his own pleasure. If *Journal* readers pronounce that the paper has been honest and endowed with proper courage under our stewardship we will rest content." Block attempted to ingratiate, or at least connect, the new ownership with the readers, and to explain what the operative philosophy or approach of the paper would be: "The new owners of *The Journal* enter upon the management of this newspaper with a deep sense of their obligation and responsibility to the imperial city that they will seek to serve...*The Journal* will be, in the broadest sense, a free newspaper. With its political principles basically Republican it will hold itself completely independent of partisan control...with the Associated Press and supplemental cable and telegraph services, with an increased corps of state and domestic correspondents and an augmented staff of skilled editors and news gatherers, it will be the constant effort of the management to give to the people day by day and every day a metropolitan newspaper dependable and complete."

Unlike the arrangement he had with his partners at the *Newark Star-Eagle*, Block did not operate as publisher, in fact or in shadow, of the *Detroit Journal*. He did not take the title of Publisher – that went to

Talmadge – but he protected his investment by visiting the offices and news-room as often as possible, and by receiving monthly balance sheets chart-ing the profit or loss of the advertising lineage, and the rise and dips of the circulation. There was very little loss of readership, even during the sensi-tive transition time. Block made contact with the Hudson department store people and established a rapport with them to assure continued advertising. He helped to promote, through publicity in the paper, the Italian coloratura Amelita Galli-Curci, a favorite of the Hudson family, and that also aided him in cementing his relationship with the store.[63] Hudson's responded by becoming the paper's leading and most consistent advertiser.

Block also insisted, much to the consternation of his partners, that the *Journal* publish a large photograph and a story about Marion Davies, the 20-year-old actress and Ziegfeld Girl, when she appeared at the Garrick Theater in Detroit.[64] Davies was Block's alleged former mistress, and ru-mors were being spread that they were still engaged in an affair – though actually she had since taken up with William Randolph Hearst. But not even a whisper appeared in print about Block and Davies or Hearst and Davies.

Block was relentless in gaining automotive advertising for the *Journal.* Large, lavishly illustrated ads for the Stutz touring car, the Apperson Rodaplane, the 7-passenger Oldsmobile, the 12-cylinder Packard, Scripps-Booth's roadsters and coupes, the Hupmobile, Goodrich Tires, and The Electric Auto-Lite Company appeared frequently.

In the years following the new ownership, the *Journal* covered key stories that gained new readers: the ongoing drama of the Great War (referred to simply as the War), the Sacco-Vanzetti case of the two immi-grants and anarchists charged with murder; the death of the automotive engineering Dodge brothers, the 19th Amendment granting women the right to vote, the campaign and election of Warren G. Harding as Presi-dent; and the brutality, flying spikes, and mean-spirited temper tantrums of baseball's Ty Cobb, "The Georgia Peach," of the Detroit Tigers. It all helped to increase the circulation and, by association, the advertising of the paper. Ty Cobb's antics epitomized the determination and defiance of Detroit itself, and helped push the city into the national limelight. Although the *Journal's* circulation did not reach the level of the *News*, it exceeded its competitors in automobile advertising: the *Journal* far sur-passed both the *News* and the *Detroit Free Press* combined, by many tens of thousands of lines.[65] The *News*, however, boasted that it carried more advertising of all kinds than any other newspaper not only in the city of

Detroit or in the state of Michigan, but in the entire country.

Grove Patterson operated as Editor of the *Detroit Journal*, the *Toledo Blade* and the *Newark Star-Eagle,* simultaneously. (Despite the fact that Detroit and Toledo are only hours apart, one wonders how he managed that in the days before fax machines, the internet and frequent, reliable transportation). Patterson enthusiastically described how the *Journal*, under his watch, approached the process of newsgathering:

> The staff was probably not more than half the size of that of the *Detroit News* but it was as fast and hard-hitting a company of men and women as I have ever seen put together in a city room. They were young, they were Detroiters, and they knew that rapidly growing, sprawling, industrial city up one side and down the other. Rex Glasson, our city editor, even had a close personal relationship with Henry Ford, and was one of the few newspapermen I have known who did. Time after time the *Journal* beat the *News* on a Ford interview or a Ford story.[66]

Patterson was so talented a writer and editor that Stair offered him the job of Editor of the *Detroit Free Press*. He turned it down, wanting to remain with Paul Block. Glasson's relationship with Henry Ford was so pronounced that even Ford's own newspaper, the *Dearborn Independent*, much to its embarrassment, was often out-scooped by the *Journal*.

Since the *Journal* was experiencing such prosperity and editorial excellence, it would seem that the Block partnership would want to hold on to the paper to maintain its good fortune. However, in July of 1922 the group made an announcement that was one of the most remarkable transactions in newspaper history. Despite the fact that circulation was up to 146,000, and advertising sales had tripled under the new ownership, Block and his partners were discontinuing publication immediately, and selling the paper's good-will and subscription lists to the *Detroit News* for $1,700,000.[67] The sale did not increase the number of the 20-some papers in the Scripps-Howard chain, but as a result of eliminating the *Journal,* it would afford them, thereafter, little competition in the Detroit market.

The uniqueness of the transaction was that it furnished striking evidence of the value of good-will and circulation, expressed in tangible figures. Block and his partners were not selling the machinery, the presses, the type, or the office furniture, but simply the *idea* of the newspaper, *and* the abandonment of its title, along with the loyalty of its readers who, presumably, would then switch over to the *Detroit News*. Since the tangible assets were appraised at $300,000 and the equipment and furnishings would be, for the most part, shipped for use at the *Newark Star-Eagle,* Block had tripled his and his partners' investment in less than six years.

To the public, Messrs. Block, Talmadge, Vernon and Wright announced that they sold the *Journal* for two basic reasons: their other "large business interests," which were taking too much of their time, and also because they felt that they should withdraw from the Detroit area as a result of the intense competition of the two other evening papers.[68]   The fact that William Randolph Hearst, with all of his promotional and financial resources, had recently bought the *Detroit Times* the previous fall, would also have an effect on the *Journal's* publishing rivalry. When the final contracts of sale were signed, at 8 o'clock in the morning on July 21st, with William E. Scripps representing the *News* and Talmadge signing for the *Journal*, Block was back in New York, feeling ambivalent. He was elated at making such a fine profit, but dispirited and somewhat mournful in seeing a great old newspaper go under, and sorry to have lost control of such a successful venture.

Talmadge walked back to the *Journal* office, called a meeting of all the employees and informed them that the issue that they were working on would be the very last in the newspaper's forty-year history. Each employee was given four week's salary. Block gave Grove Patterson a bonus check for $35,000, an enormous sum in those days. That evening, on the front page of the *Journal*, the denouement, with just a hint of posed regret, was elaborated upon and reported to its readers:

> With this issue, the *Detroit Journal* ceases publication, its title and good-will have been purchased by the *Detroit News...The Journal* on this, the last day of its publication, has the largest and strongest circulation of its entire history. Only the present overcrowded condition of the evening newspaper field and the necessity for some merger in the interest of decent American journalism, could have persuaded the *Journal* to sell, or the *News* to buy.[69]

As it developed, there *were* a few tangible properties that went along with the sale: the *Journal* mailing list galleys, all advertising contracts, 600 tons of newsprint, the newspaper's photo and research "morgue," and its Associated Press membership. Many of the *Journal's* printers, reporters and office personnel were absorbed by the *News*.[70]

What was the *real* reason that Paul Block sold the *Detroit Journal*? Despite the protestations of the partners to the contrary, since the publication was doing so well, and had proven that it could compete among the other evening papers – in addition to Detroit's morning newspapers – the explanation had to lie elsewhere. The truth of the matter is that all of the partners had begun to grow weary of each other's styles. Block believed that Talmadge, Wright and Vernon were too reckless and self-indulgent, as was a new partner brought in by Talmadge, Frederick S. Buggie. In an atypical attitude, Block took an instant dislike to Buggie, who he felt was little more than a street thug, and he even refused to shake Buggie's hand upon meeting him. Block's partners believed that he was too politically conservative and autocratic, and that he had become a lobbyist for his own special proclivities and agendas, political and social.

Block's main interest did lie in the *Newark Star-Eagle* and in the other newspapers he owned by then: the *Memphis News-Scimitar* and the *Duluth Herald*. He felt that in order for the *Journal* to continue to realize greater net profits, he would have to be in Detroit constantly to keep checking on Talmadge and the others. He did not believe that the worst reconciliation was better than the best divorce; he could no longer tolerate his partners, and although it took him longer than he would have liked, he began to investigate how a business schism could be effected.

Memphis News-Scimitar

Block had been the advertising representative and a major stockowner of the *Memphis News-Scimitar* for 13 years, but in 1921, buoyed by some cash that he received from selling out his interest in *The New York Evening Mail*, he became tempted by the offer proffered by his longtime colleague Bernard L. Cohn to purchase the controlling interest in the newspaper.[71] For an undisclosed sum, Block bought all of the shares owned by Sam E. Ragland, the *Scimitar's* majority stockholder, and formed a new corporation with John H. Hertel and S.C. Dobbs, who had been stockholders. Now the two men became directors. Block named Cohn as the president of the corporation and insisted that his friend maintain his title of publisher. At the moment of purchase, Block could not be reached for comment to the press, but a spokesman in his New York office, perhaps under Block's instructions, claimed that there would be no change in his relationship with the paper – Block would still remain as special advertising representative – and that the management of the editorial and publishing departments of the paper would continue as it always had.[72]   But the assumption of the responsibility of ownership, however, produced a feeling of anxiety on Block's part, and he knew from the moment he became "The Owner" that he would be held responsible for actions performed in response to circumstances over which he had no control, especially living in New York. He therefore became publisher *de facto*, although not in name, and inserted his authority wherever and whenever possible.

The arrangement turned out to be perfectly agreeable to Cohn. He needed all the help he could get, he respected Block's experience and analytical ability, and he acknowledged that if it hadn't been for Block's bringing in a quantity of national advertisers in the previous few years, the *Memphis News-Scimitar* would have ceased to exist. Block had acquired such prestigious advertisers as Ford, Chevrolet and Oldsmobile, together with Bayer Aspirin, Pepsodent Toothpaste, Coca-Cola, American Tobacco Company, Vicks VapoRub and Wrigley's Chewing Gum. The local advertising in Memphis by such department stores as J.C. Gerber's, Bry's, and B. Lowenstein had been adequate, but not enough to sustain the paper. Because Block was, in effect, supporting the newspaper through his efforts with hundreds of thousands of dollars of advertising each year, his influence on everything that the *Scimitar* did or wanted to do was of consequence even before he became the owner. Now, as owner, he stepped up his active participation even more in all areas of the paper, from newsstand promotion to editorial philosophy, and from subscriptions to special circulation builders.

Memphis was a prosperous city at that time, the fourth largest in population in the South, behind New Orleans and with almost the same number of people as Atlanta and Louisville; its population was greater than that of Nashville or Richmond. It was a rip-roaring river town, filled with steamboat captains, gamblers, and assorted salts, rascals and scamps, and as a result had no scarcity of crime, scandal and other sensational news. Because of the nearby plantations and cotton mills, and its location on the Mississippi, the city's businesses were thriving and Block intended to try to have each and every one of them as advertisers. In order to do this, he knew that he had to raise circulation.

Learning from some of his experiences with *The New York Evening Mail* and the *Newark Star-Eagle*, he began a relentless promotion that included conducting tennis tournaments, and convincing his readers to engage in a series of contests, the winners of which would receive cash prizes.[73] One contest asked: "What is a pessimist?" Mrs. W.P. Moore won a prize with this answer: "One who looks for bacteria in the milk of human kindness."[74] Another asked readers, "What did you see today?" Maud M. Gross came up with this observation: "I saw a woman swat a fly on her husband's bald head. The husband kissed his wife and said: 'Thank you darling, that fly has been bothering me for half an hour.'"[75] To the question, "What is the greatest love?" Mrs. Virginia Cashen won with a mini-essay that said, in part: "The greatest love is that which is least tinged with selfishness. It expresses itself in service."[76]

Within his first year as owner, Block initiated the unparalleled – for that time – airplane delivery of editions of the *News-Scimitar,* printed at 12 noon in Memphis, and arriving in Helena, Arkansas, a distance of about 100 miles, by one o'clock that same afternoon. Although he was proud of the accomplishment, Block felt that newspaper distribution by air was just in its infancy. "Air transportation has scarcely reached the stage of its beginning," he wrote. "Within the next few years afternoon papers will be available 100 to 200 miles from the place of publication within an hour or an hour-and-a-half after they leave the press. It will not be many years before newspapers will be delivered to their out-of-town readers by airplane in the ordinary routine of affairs."[77]

Block's most dramatic promotion for the *News-Scimitar* was offering his readers an opportunity to star in a motion picture.[78] As a front-page promotion and support for the Memphis Loew's State motion picture theater, which was a daily advertiser in the *News-Scimitar*, Block secured actor-writer-director Edwin August to come to the city to conduct screen tests for all those who cared to audition for a future part in a yet-to-be-decided film. The scouting expedition on August's part was genuine. He explained his rationale: "Who would take the responsibility of stating that there is not an unknown screen star is this city? There is talent here, perhaps of greater value than you find on Broadway. Screen beauty contests have their advantages but in the screen tests I make, I hope not only to secure beauty but an example of any talent they may have."[79]

Edwin August, well known at the time, had starred in more than seventy silent films, including several directed by D.W. Griffith, and he had also written and directed over a dozen other motion pictures. August's association with Griffith brought him a great deal of reflected glory and Memphis moviegoers remembered the connection. Griffith's *The Love Flower* was a big hit when it arrived in Memphis that year.[80]

Block's promotion wasn't just for those who wanted to audition. Notices in the newspaper invited the general public to the theater to watch the screen tests being conducted, and then back again a week later to see the results. August set up the stage of the Loew's State to look just like a studio movie set with lights, cameras, scenery and props. He sat in a director's chair, and gave direction to the would-be thespians, such as: "You have just learned that your mother died, and now you have to tell the sad news to your father." "You are furious that your husband has forgotten your birthday and you lash into him when he comes home from work." "You are afraid to ask the young lady sitting next to you for her hand in marriage."

All day long, hundreds of applicants – drama students from high schools and colleges, amateur actors, summer stock players, fading professionals, and just those who hoped to be noticed – came and went for August's auditions. The pages of the *Memphis News-Scimitar* published as much news copy as possible extracted from the event: interviews with Edwin August, the names and addresses of all of the auditioners, and photographs of a selected number of Memphis belles. At the screening of the unedited rushes, some of which were unintentionally hilarious but others quite professional, people in the audience were eager to know whether anyone would be brought to Hollywood. August said he was impressed with the results, made note of the names of several men and women who he thought had possibilities, and headed back to California. It is not known whether any Mary Pickfords, Rudolph Valentinos or John Barrymores were discovered in Memphis as the result of the auditions but Block's promotion made the requisite splash that he wanted: it convinced the Loew's people that he was giving their advertising the editorial support that they wanted, since as a result of the attention given to August and his screen tests, attendance at the Loew's State rose considerably.

To build readership of the newspaper, Block gave permission to the editors of the *News-Scimitar* to purchase certain syndicated writers and columns, and to assign others of note. Famous names began to grace the pages of the paper, such as L. Frank Baum and "The Wonderful Stories of Oz;"[81] George McManus's cartoon strip, "Bringing Up Father;" the advice column of Dorothy Dix, who Block proclaimed as "the world's highest paid woman writer;" a series by actress Pola Negri: "My Secrets of Beauty;" stories about how his friend Florenz Ziegfeld selected the beauties that appeared in the Follies; and the revealing memoirs of Germany's Crown Prince Wilhelm.

One of the best journalists on the *News-Scimitar* was Null Adams, a student at the University of Tennessee, who worked first as a sportswriter for the newspaper and then as a crime reporter, all while he was finishing college. Adams was assigned all manner of stories (his first for the newspaper was about a couple who leaped from the Mississippi Bridge in a murder suicide pact) and his articles were considered a major factor in building circulation. The *News-Scimitar*'s major competitor was the *Commercial Appeal*, but most people considered Block's paper to be the most reliable. Traditionally known as the city's leading paper, the *News-Scimitar* had early on encouraged the city park system, its artesian water system, and it had "sold" Memphis not only to its own citizens but to many people from around the country who thought that the city was a disease-breeding swamp because of its devastating yellow fever epidemic at the turn of the century.[82]

Block's political position with the *News-Scimitar* was consistent with his past and then-present conservative views; the paper promoted itself as independent but it was certainly Republican in backing the Grand Old Party for virtually all elections and issues. He opposed, but diplomatically, many of the programs suggested by the tall, red-headed "Boss of Memphis," the former Mayor Edward H. Crump, as being unable to solve the enormous racial and low-income problems that infested the city.

During Block's first two years with the *Memphis News-Scimitar,* from 1921 to 1923, Warren G. Harding was President of the United States. Block had some correspondence with Harding at that time, but it was more of a salutary than political nature; they exchanged letters of holiday felicitations, and other cordialities. Block believed, however, that Harding and he were "very intimate" and he considered Harding a "friend."[83] Calvin Coolidge, who had a much deeper and more long-lasting relationship with Block, succeeded to the Presidency upon Harding's death that August. He acknowledged Block's and Harding's friendship in a letter he sent to Block at the end of 1923.[84]

Actually, Block had wanted the relationship between himself and Harding to be stronger, since the President had been the owner and editor of the *Marion* [Ohio] *Star,* and therefore until that time the only Chief Executive in the history of the country ever to have been a real newspaperman. (Herbert Hoover's ownership of the *Washington Herald* would come later.) The long talks between them about the newspaper business and the affairs of the country that Block envisioned might occur when Harding arrived at the White House, never did take place. Nevertheless, Block backed Harding editorially when the President was criticized for trying to inspire the support of the American people for additional military expenditures. ("I bid you make ours an efficient, conscientious and effective navy, " Harding said in a speech, "and I pledge you in return the conscience and confidence of 110,000,000 Americans.")[85]

Block also sympathized with Harding's predicament with his own cabinet, which seemed more interested in the concerns of big business and other financial interests than with the plight of the common man,[86] but there was one area where Block and Harding vehemently disagreed: Harding had supported the 18th Amendment and the Volstead Act, and Block kept fighting for repeal of Prohibition. It is possible that this disagreement in fundamental political philosophy on this one issue was why the two men were not as close as perhaps both of them would have liked to have been. As it developed, because of the corruption of Teapot Dome and other administration scandals that besmirched Harding's name, the distance that had grown between Block and him probably served Block's reputation in the long run.

Block's political relationship with the city of Memphis itself was affable and staunchly loyal and he spoke to such issues as the local stadium not having enough lower-priced, good seats for the Memphis baseball team;[87] backing a resolution to retain married women school teachers;[88] demanding that the city council give Memphis firms – not outsiders – the contract to re-construct the water system;[89] and asking readers to support the financially-sagging Memphis Symphony Orchestra.[90]

There was one issue, however, over which most of the citizens of the city of Memphis and Paul Block disagreed: improved conditions for blacks and the change of the social and moral code in all areas of their lives. In the early 1920s millions of Southerners opposed any advancement for blacks, and the Ku Klux Klan were recruiting by the tens of thousands. Prejudiced treatment of blacks was commonplace in the segregated cities of the South, and beatings and lynchings were not uncommon. Memphis was no exception. Highly attended lectures talked of the dangers to the white race should blacks be afforded any more liberty than they already had.[91] The more involved Block became in Memphis the more uneasy he became. As a result, he spoke out through editorials and news coverage not only for white Memphians to embrace and help their black citizens, but to the whole Republican Party to do so as well.[92] It was not a popular stand with the people of Memphis and it even displeased some of Block's own editors on the *Memphis News-Scimitar*.

Block also made sure the issues of concern to Jews were amply covered in the paper. Although he did not editorialize about their problems, coverage of such stories as Henry Ford's alleged anti-Semitism,[93] and the joint statement of Woodrow Wilson, William Howard Taft, and Cardinal O'Connell challenging the American public to aid in the fight of anti-Semitism, were plentiful.[94]

In May of 1925, a 39-year-old black man by the name of Tom Lee figured closely in Paul Block's future with the *Memphis News-Scimitar*. Lee had taken his employer (a contractor who repaired levees) to Helena, Arkansas in a small 28-foot wooden skiff, named the *Zev*. Alone on the return trip home, Lee was the sole witness to the capsizing of the *Norman*, a sidewinder that was carrying 150 passengers returning from an excursion. Although he could not swim, Lee quickly went into action, pulling people from the water, bringing them to safety on a sandbar, and going back for more. Miraculously, he saved 32 passengers, (18 passengers and five crew members drowned) including the captain of the *Norman*, who otherwise would have been swept away by the raging Mississippi. Tom Lee was acclaimed a hero. Still dressed in his wet and rumpled clothes from the river, he was given a gold watch and received a citation by the Mayor of Memphis. Resolutions were made that cited and recognized his bravery. Nonetheless, not all white Memphians cared to join in his praises, even though all of his 32 survivors were white.[95]

Not only did Block have the *Memphis News-Scimitar* do extensive news coverage of the event on the front page, but he also wrote an editorial indicating how proud the city was of Tom Lee's heroism. Despite some grumbling from some of his editors, Block contacted the White House to see whether President Coolidge would receive Tom Lee for a special commendation. That contact grew into a series of letters and phone calls Block made, to clarify the idea and set up all of the arrangements. Coolidge was receptive to the visit, and that summer Block, Lee and George Morris, editor of the *News-Scimitar*, traveled to Washington where Lee, as one of the few blacks ever to be invited to the White House, met the President and received an award. It was a proud moment for Tom Lee, for all of the blacks in this country, and for Paul Block. Photographs of the President in the White House garden, with a beaming Paul Block, thumbs locked in his jacket pockets in a stance of dignity and self-esteem, and a subdued and unassuming Tom Lee shaking hands with the Chief Executive, appeared in newspapers all over the country. Lee was taken on a tour of Washington and given a reception by the Colored Tennessee Society. He just did what anyone would have done, Lee said, discounting his valiant contribution with humility and a touch of humor. "They were the sensiblist drowning folks I ever saw."[96]

The photograph of Tom Lee and Paul Block with President Coolidge, which appeared on the front page of the *Memphis News-Scimitar* the day after they were at the White House, seemed to incense more Memphians than it pleased. What Tom Lee did was not that extraordinary, some of the bigots contended. He didn't even swim to save them, others hissed. They just couldn't bear the idea that a black man had been invited to the White House and that he had been elevated as the city's most famous citizen. Block began to receive a large volume of hate mail filled with stupid and cruel remarks; leaders of the Ku Klux Klan, which had infiltrated the Memphis city government, were furious with what they considered Block's overly-appreciative acknowledgement of Tom Lee.[97]

Block was disgusted with the reaction that some of the Memphians had to Tom Lee's heroic act, and he also felt that the interconnectedness that he had with his editors, and his influence upon them, was deteriorating. Most of the editors of the *News-Scimitar* felt that in order to compete successfully in Memphis, the paper had to swing to the left, to the Democratic Party, and Block's intransigent Republicanism was becoming less welcome. Almost immediately he felt that he had to rid himself of his involvement with the ownership of the *News-Scimitar.* Because of his long-standing relationship with the paper it was not an easy decision to make. The financial coffers of the paper weren't booming, but it wasn't doing all that badly in terms of advertising and circulation income. It would have been a good investment for the right person. Nonetheless, he knew that finding a suitable buyer for the paper, and one that would pay his price, would not be easy.

Charles Mooney, president of *The Commercial Appeal*, considered buying the *News-Scimitar* and going into the evening news business along with his morning paper, but he couldn't come to terms with Block as to a price. Mooney began making plans to start his own night paper, the *Evening Appeal*, but died of a heart attack before the paper could publish its first issue.[98]

During the beginning months of 1926, Block entertained bids for the *Memphis News-Scimitar*, and was approached by representatives of the Scripps-Howard chain with an interest to buy. Because of the booming economy of the 1920s, Scripps-Howard had temporarily become, with 26 papers, the largest newspaper chain in the country, just slightly ahead of Hearst's newspapers. The Scripps-Howard people owned such evening papers as the *New York Telegram,* the *Baltimore Post,* the *Toledo News-Bee,* and the *San Francisco News.* They had begun to made inroads into the South by starting the *Knoxville News-Sentinel,* the *Covington Kentucky Post,* and the *Birmingham Post,* and they also owned the *Memphis Press,* a weak competitor to Block's *News-Scimitar,* which had been started in 1906 by the Scripps-McRae League, the forerunner of the Scripps-Howard organization. They were searching for additional, larger properties to add to their holdings.[99]

The Scripps-Howard management was infamous for almost ruthlessly establishing a personally-controlled chain of newspapers. E.W. Scripps would often lend money to a young and enthusiastic publisher to start a new newspaper in an area that he felt could support a competitive paper, and he would supervise the editorial and publishing aspects of the paper with an iron hand. If the paper succeeded, he would – by previous agreement – take 51% of the stock of the business, and if it failed, he would take the loss.[100]   Up until just six years before he came to buy the *Memphis News-Scimitar,* Scripps had personally started and financed twenty-six of the thirty-two papers that he owned.[101]   In the case of the *Memphis News-Scimitar,* because it was so highly regarded, he felt it would be better to take it over rather than to start another newspaper in the city. Scripps's business philosophy of newspapers was similar to many of the other chain owners: great economies could be realized with centralized accounting systems, national advertising sales agencies, combined purchasing offices – especially for the buying of paper in bulk – and complete feature and newsgathering arrangements for all the members of the chain. Block, in a less ambitious way, was attempting to effect the same strategy in buying up as many newspapers as he could. Scripps-Howard bought the *News-Scimitar* from Block and immediately combined it with the *Press,* to create a new entity, the *Memphis Press-Scimitar.*

Throughout 1926, even as Block was committed to removing himself from the *Memphis News-Scimitar,* he turned his primary concerns and interests toward the state of Ohio. He had decided to purchase the *Toledo Blade.* This project would become the centerpiece of his professional attention and business. At the same time, though, his personal life was undergoing a wrenching interlude.

Chapter 5

The Jazz Age

The fabulous era that became known as the Roaring Twenties, which ushered in what also became known as the Jazz Age, was for the most part a period of great ebullience and social activity for Paul Block. New York City seemed to be in the center of that madcap time, and Block, as the wealthy publisher of eleven newspapers at one time or another during the 1920s, which provided him entry to a vast network of parties, events and performances, was an integral part of the very nucleus of this frolicsome and history-making period. He conducted his personal life in society around several discreet areas, and although they often intersected and linked up in some ways, for the most part one social province was distinctly separate from the other.

His membership in the Criterion Club, the only New York organization of its kind that catered to prosperous Jews (who were barred from joining other gentlemen's clubs) enabled him to meet and interact with many of the mercantile and financial princes of the city, such as Maurice Wertheim, Simon Guggenheim, Jacob Schiff, even some of the Rothschilds. Founded by wealthy German Jews before the Civil War, the Criterion Club's minutes were kept in German, and until America's entry into the Great War, an oil portrait of Kaiser Wilhelm II hung in the lobby. Although Paul Block, the ragpicker's son, may have come from humbler beginnings than most of his fellow club members, Block's growing wealth and publishing influence, combined with his geniality, and his fluency in German, instantly ingratiated him into the inner circles and cliques of the Club. Block was a poor bridge player but he loved the game, and was known to engage in long, tedious, nerve-racking and high-stakes games, which he often lost. Even Dina criticized him for talking too much, or humming out loud, while he was playing. Some of the improprieties of contract bridge, such as mis-calling "six spades" as "little slam," or unnecessary hesitations to deceive opponents, were by tradition apparently overlooked by all the players. It is not known whether Block engaged in any of these gaffes, but he took the game as seriously as anyone in the Club.

Within a short time of becoming a member of the Criterion Club, because of his popularity, he was named President and served in that capacity for several years. Later, the Criteron changed its name to the Harmonie Club, and still operates today.

If the Criterion Club was established by Jews as a counter-measure to not being allowed into elite gathering places such as the Union Club or the Metropolitan Club, they showed no tolerance toward another minority: women. Like most clubs of that day, women were rarely permitted inside the doors. On occasion, they could enter if accompanied by a male member, but could only be entertained in certain unrestricted rooms. Not only did the "no-women-allowed" policy supposedly enable the men to speak more freely, which was the stated reason for the feminine embargo, but it also served as a perfect alibi for those who were engaged in philandering or other secret revelry revolving around Café Society games. "I'm sorry I won't be home this evening, dear," said the husband to his wife. "I'm going to the Club tonight." And of course the husband in question would go off, wifeless for the evening, to his carousing and merrymaking, all the while the wife believing her husband was at a membership club, chatting or discussing issues with friends or playing harmless games of cards or billiards.

Paul Block may or may not have engaged in this kind of disingenuous hi-jinks, but it is altogether possible since he loved the night-life of Café Society, with its music halls and restaurants, its flappers and its movie stars; there were over 100,000 speakeasies in New York City during Prohibition, and the possibilities of mischievous amusement were plentiful.

He began to frequent Manhattan's well-known night spots with William Randolph Hearst; they were a pair of dashing rakes of a sort. What cemented their friendship was their shared interest in newspapers, their attraction to the night-life of Tin Pan Alley, and an equal obsession to acquire great wealth and all of its trappings. Hearst could sense that Block was an ambitious, self-made man on the make, not only for women but for fame, power and prosperity. To Block, Hearst was a mentor; to Hearst, Block symbolized all of the energy and rags-to-riches glamour that he wished that he had had, instead of the silver-spooned background that he incongruously resented.

Night after night, the two men sat in the second row of the orchestra of the New Amsterdam Theater watching a performance of Florenz Ziegfeld's

Stop! Look! Listen!, each man fantasizing about which one of the gloriously almost-unclad chorus girls they would meet backstage after the performance. Not so curiously, they were the only two men (other than cast and crew) in all of New York City who were permitted entrée backstage by Ziegfeld, and they attended most of the opening night post-performance parties. "Oh, I remember Paul Block!" said a former Ziegfeld Girl almost 70 years later. "He was always at every party that Flo Ziegfeld gave."[1] The showman favored the two newspaper magnates for obvious reasons: Hearst because he was a constant promoter of the Follies and also an investor in Ziegfeld's theater, and Block because he was the publisher and owner of a New York area newspaper and was also prone to publicize Ziegfeld's extravaganzas.

Hearst and Block would often take turns wooing the beautiful Ziegfeld "girls." One night in 1916 the flamboyant Florenz Ziegfeld, master of both the revue and of his famous Follies, the nation's arbiter of feminine beauty, introduced Paul Block to the beautiful Marion Davies, one of his Ziegfeld Girls. Because of that meeting, Paul Block inadvertently became the impetus for the love story that became the basis for one of the greatest movies ever made: *Citizen Kane.* The parallels between the life of William Randolph Hearst and that of the protagonist in *Citizen Kane* are unmistakable: Both Hearst and Kane were born in 1863 and went to Harvard; both went on to amass newspaper empires; each man took up with a much younger woman, and each became the most hated man in America.

William Randolph Hearst
and Marion Davies

What is not generally known is how Hearst met Marion Davies in the first place. Paul Block began to date the young dancer from the Ziegfeld Follies. She was a bright and fetching teenager from Brooklyn, with a slight, charming stutter. Although there was a two-decade difference in ages – Marion was 17 and Block was in his 40s – and he was married, it didn't stop him from pursuing and winning the attention and heart of the young woman. He accompanied her to glittering parties, plied her with gifts, took her to dinner at Delmonico's, and entertained her in his private suite at the Ritz-Carlton. Somehow he kept mention of his love affair with her out of the headlines and gossip columns.

Block referred to Marion as being "dainty," in the days when that term meant something choice or pleasing, rather than in today's parlance in which it indicates a beauty of delicate proportions or diminutive size. She loved being in the company of and in the center of men, could talk to them on their terms – from how the Yankees were doing to the state of the Bull Market, and from the Machiavellian politics of Tammany to the bitter-sweet joys of Prohibition – and she always drank her Scotch straight up. Nevertheless, she was alluring and coquettish and, as it developed, irresistible to Block. At first, for whatever reason, Hearst didn't seem to even notice her.

Block thought she was exquisite, and had acting talent that could be used in the mushrooming new business of motion pictures, a field he was interested in exploring. Although he was already becoming rich, he did not have anywhere near the resources of Hearst, and so when Block wanted to produce a film that would star Davies in her first role for the screen, he tried to interest his older, more affluent friend in investing some of the money to finance it. There were not enough stars to go around in the burgeoning film industry, Block argued, and Marion's attractiveness and charm suggested that she had all the earmarks of stardom. Mary Pickford and Rudolph Valentino were earning huge salaries, (Pickford made $350,000 a picture in 1919, a higher amount equivalently, than many superstars were making in the 1990s)[2] and Block felt that introducing Marion to a film career would not only make vast sums for her, but would prove lucrative for the people who backed her, too.

Hearst had begun a limited involvement with motion pictures, but they were for the most part all shorts or newsreels. He was not ready, he said, to go into feature film production. In fact, he had just learned that Charlie Chaplin had signed a deal with First National to make eight features at a salary of over a million dollars, and the thought of the mounting costs of making a film drove even the Croesus-like Hearst to act more like Ebeneezer Scrooge.

Since Hearst was intransigent about not investing and could not be persuaded, Block – who was always a bit of a gambler with his own money – generated the cash himself: $23,000. In those days that was a great deal of money to speculate on a film.

Marion had an idea that she would like to play a gypsy girl so she would be able to dance, and Block knew that for her first film, it would be best to exploit her dancing ability, rather than concentrate on her acting talents, so they were both in agreement as to a general approach. Since it would be a silent film, her stuttering would not be an issue. Live piano music would accompany her on-screen sashaying.

Fred Guiles, Marion Davies's biographer, has indicated that Block walked into a reporter's hangout on the West Side of Manhattan and offered "$25 to anyone in the room who could come up with a story idea about a white gypsy, which would not be offensive to a general audience." That version of how the film came to be written is almost accurate. The detailed truth was that Block asked several of his *own* reporters from the *Newark Star-Eagle*, which he had just acquired as publisher, to cross the Hudson and to arrive at the Ritz-Carlton on a Sunday afternoon. For $25 each, with beer and sandwiches provided, they were to come up with a screenplay. By 10 o'clock that evening (remember: in the days of silent film, there were only small bits of dialogue, which were printed on occasional inter-title cards), they had sketched out the basic action of the film.

Block and his neophyte screenwriters created a story of how a rich man's daughter, named Romany, has been kidnapped by gypsies, and after various adventures, complicated by the appearance of an imposter who tries to take her place, she is finally reunited with her family. Block hired Marion's ex-brother-in-law, George Lederer, to direct the film. Its interior scenes were primarily shot at the Pathé studios in New York, and the cast and crew went to the woods of Westchester and New Jersey for the outdoor scenes. Block was on the set and location throughout the entire production, mainly to protect his investment, but also to keep an eye on his flirtatious inamorata. To lend authenticity to the film, Block hired dozens of "real" local gypsies to act as extras.

For over a year, Block was relentless in promoting *Runaway, Romany,* which had a Christmastime release in 1917. It was competing against such films as John Ford's first effort, *Straight Shooters,* and *Wild and Wooly* with Douglas Fairbanks. Block bought huge ads in most of New York's papers, listing all of the theaters where the film could be seen, a convention of advertising that was rarely practiced in movie ads at that time. He also made a deal with dozens of the newspapers for which he acted as special representative. If they ran a large ad for *Runaway, Romany*, and also agreed to publish a condensed story with stills of the film as advanced promotion, he would forgive some of the commissions that were owed him, so that no money would change hands. Some 40 newspapers agreed to the exchange.

Block's friend, the diminutive tycoon Adolph Zukor, who had just merged his Famous Players Company with 12 other companies in order to dominate film distribution in this country, took *Runaway, Romany* under his wing and had it block-booked, as it was then called, in as many cities as possible. But even the enterprising Zukor could not make any money with the film.

Despite the promotional efforts on everyone's part, *Runaway, Romany* was simply a failure, critically and at the box-office. Marion looked lovely, almost luminescent, on the screen, but she appeared wooden and unsympathetic some of the time, and fidgety and histrionic at others. The storyline was trite, and the cinematography unexceptional. Block ended up losing virtually all the money he had put into the film, which had paid for almost the entire production and promotion budget.

Instead of chiding him, however, Hearst was supportive and enthusiastic, a certain knavery on his part notwithstanding. At Block's urging, he saw an advanced screening of the film, and when Hearst walked out of the darkness 63 minutes later, he insisted that Block introduce him to Davies. Sitting in that darkened screening room, watching the flickering images, William Randolph Hearst, one of the wealthiest and most powerful men in the country, had fallen in love with Marion Davies. They began a relationship that scandalized the country – since Hearst was married and living in "sin" with Marion – and would last for nearly 35 years. Although it sounds like a cliché from a B-film, Hearst actually said to Marion after he first saw *Runaway, Romany*: "Marion, I'm going to make you a star." He spent the rest of his life trying to do just that. She did go on to make a score of well-received comedies, but like Susan Alexander in *Citizen Kane*, she never achieved the stardom that Hearst promised her…or the celebrity and acclaim that the filmic Charles Foster Kane assured Susan that she would have some day.

Block would eventually lose his mistress to Hearst, but he never lost his affection for, or his attraction toward her. In some ways, there was some relief to their separation: He didn't want the situation with Marion to jeopardize his marriage, and he had a growing family. But the three – Paul Block, Marion Davies and William Randolph Hearst – would remain friends for the rest of their lives. They traveled together and Block would become a constant visitor at Hearst's castle, San Simeon. Hearst named Block the executor of the will of his estate, his entire property and fortune. The two men went on to become business associates in advertising and publishing, and Block became an important consultant for Hearst's newspapers, visiting them, and writing long, detailed and substantive memos as to how they could be improved. Hearst once said that he knew no other man in America that he could trust as much as Paul Block.

Block never made another film, but used his vast talents in friendliness and bonhomie toward a wide variety of people, and to acquire newspapers throughout the country. Not ashamed to be excluded from Marion's bed but satisfied to be included in her social sphere, for the rest of his life Block continued to promote her in his own newspapers with feature stories and photo spreads, gossip column items and large advertisements, championing her great beauty, comic talent, and exuberance. He signed personal letters to her with the complimentary closing of, "Your Eastern Press Agent," and in a humorous vein, he would remind her that there were only two people in the country who could get her picture on page one of any number of newspapers: William Randolph Hearst and Paul Block.

•••

Block made many friends who were well-known or famous during the years he was generating and accumulating his own great wealth. His capacity for friendships, and the broad range of people he cultivated, was remarkable. He believed that the closeness he could achieve with people was his most important talent and possession, and during the Roaring Twenties, and all throughout the Thirties, he was the quintessential "man about town," who clicked with a colorful and glamorous procession of show business stars, athletes, politicians, songwriters, theatrical producers and successful businessmen. Block lived, worked and played in the vortex of wide-open speakeasies, multi-million dollar gates, a mansion in Greenwich, Connecticut, explosive political scandals, limousines with plum-colored upholstery driven by a liveried chauffeur (he had one of the first Rolls Royces imported from England to the United States after World War I), and a posh private railroad car all his own.

Paul Block became one of the most gregarious playboys in New York City, with strong ties to the town's leading gliterati: the silk-hatted Mayor Jimmy Walker; Governor Al Smith, the man from the streets known as the "Happy Warrior" (among other gestures, Block supported and contributed to Smith's campaign for President); and virtually all of Café Society and the New York elite, with such notables as George Gershwin, Irving Berlin, Babe Ruth, Fanny Brice, Bernard Baruch, Eddie Cantor and Will Rogers counted among his acquaintances.

Because he was friends with many entertainers and celebrities, Block started supporting the arts, in small ways at first, buying tickets to fund

raisers and attending shows and concerts. In time, he increased his donations significantly. Here, as in other aspects of his altruism, he divided
his support among different groups.

He started donating money to the Jewish Theatrical Guild of America
when he was still a young man. Singer Eddie Cantor, comedian George
Jessel, and composer Irving Berlin were all members of the Guild, and
the four men eventually became quite friendly.[3] Block realized that he
could raise even more money for his favorite charities by getting these
and other famous friends to help. In gratitude for his work, singer Sophie
Tucker sometimes sent him personal invitations to her performances.[4]

Eddie Cantor and Paul Block went on to become very close. Once,
when Cantor sent a $100 donation to a cause that Block backed and was
directly involved in, Block returned the money to Cantor, replacing it
with his own donation. Cantor said to Block, "With the fine things that
you do, if there is a law of compensation, I would like to be around to
celebrate your 100th birthday. God bless you."[5] Block and Cantor supported one another's favorite charities. The singer had established the
Eddie Cantor's Camp Committee, to enable impoverished children to go
to camp in upstate New York; Block regularly sent contributions. And as
a favor to Block, Cantor would give free performances to help raise money
for community chest drives in Toledo, Ohio. The two men would get
together beforehand and have a good time planning what songs and jokes
Cantor would perform.

Block also endorsed the Episcopal Actors Guild, "The Little Church
Around the Corner," at One East 29th Street in New York City. Play-
wrights Henry Miller and Edward Albee, and actress Mary Pickford, were
active members of the Guild's Advisory Board.

The Pet Popularity Fundraiser was held to raise money for charity, and
celebrities sometimes participated to help increase the levels of contributions. Impresario Florenz Ziegfeld took his daughter Patricia to the event,
along with her pet black bear, which was named Jack Dempsey. Block, a
good friend of Ziegfeld, cast his "vote," in the form of a donation to the
Women's League for Animals, to help elect Patricia's bear as the most
popular pet.

•••

Block enjoyed New York theater, especially light musicals or comedies.
He was often critical of what he called "problem plays" or heavy dramas:

"I have enough worries in my life. I'm not going to the theater to become depressed." But the theater to him was more than its dramatic content and its effect on his emotions. Movies, although enjoyable, were the medium of the masses. Broadway theater was the status symbol of the elite, the rich and famous. To Block, a night at the theater was an opportunity to dress up in his most tasteful clothing, experience an evening of elegant dining, and to be seen by and meet other prominent people.

When he was invited to attend a special performance of Nikita Ballef's *La Chauve-Souris* troop from Moscow to perform Johann Strauss's operetta *Die Fledermaus*, he accepted with delighted anticipation. The evening was to be a benefit for starving Russian artists and their families. Seat prices started at $25, depending on their location, and went up from there, whereas Broadway plays in that era usually cost only $1 for admission. At a time of gala affairs in a city known for its pageants, the *cognescenti* all knew that the performance of *La Chauve-Souris* was going to be one of the most spectacular and exquisite productions ever seen in New York. Block arrived at the theater dressed in a top hat and wearing a white tie and tails, and from the moment he stepped out of his cab, he was captivated by the proceedings. Opening the door for him, acting as a doorman, was comedian Ed Wynn, who expected tips – *big* tips – to be given to him as donations for the benefit. The Russian-born Al Jolson stood in the lobby, as a sort of *maitre d'*, and was also collecting "tips" from the arriving theatergoers.

When Block took his 9th row center seat in the orchestra, he discovered that virtually no one in the audience was less than a well-known celebrity. In Block's row alone sat playwright Eugene O'Neill, Secretary of Commerce Herbert Hoover and financier Jay Gould. Movie stars such as Charlie Chaplin, John Barrymore, Geraldine Farrar, and Dorothy and Lillian Gish were seated throughout the theater, as well as musicians Irving Berlin, Fyodor Chaliapin, John McCormick, Walter Damrosch, George M. Cohan, Jascha Heifitz, and Sergei Rachmaninoff, and there were literally hundreds of writers, publishers, government officials and tycoons. The conversation in the lobby and before the performance seemed almost historic to Block, as he watched Adolph Ochs, publisher of *The New York Times*, talking with the rotund critic Alexander Woollcott, and then with humorist and short-story writer Ring Lardner and film director D. W. Griffith. Also in Block's row, five seats to his right, was the Russian mystic Nicholas Roerich, a man who would figure importantly in Block's life almost twenty years later in an odd confluence that almost brought down the re-election of Franklin Delano Roosevelt to the presidency.

Two comedians, the bald-pated Leon Errol, and the bespectacled Walter Catlett, walked up and down the aisles selling cups of "water" – actually Russian gin – for a hefty price.

Before the music began, a Russian doll was auctioned off; the bidding was spirited and rose to $700, and the top offer was placed by the theatrical producer Morris Gest.

Block was delighted with the magical evening. The operetta was a farcical story of misbehaving upper-classes, love affairs and tax evasion, with much champagne, a costume ball, and switched identities; in effect a situation comedy with epic proportions and great lilting music. In all, $11,000 was raised at the benefit, enough to feed hundreds of Russian families for months.[6]

Although he had met many famous people through his business contacts, never before had Block been surrounded by such a quantity of august and resplendent people. To Block, somehow he had become one of them, and on that evening the mythology of success had become real.

Gentleman Jimmy Walker

Mayor Jimmy Walker was probably Block's closest friend during the 1920s, and Walker's reputation as one of the raciest and most debonair officials the city ever knew was well-deserved. He wrote lyrics for Tin Pan Alley, never started work before noon – nor did Block, since the two men were often out so late the night before – kept show girls on the side (usually at Block's suite at the Ritz-Carlton Hotel), entertained Betty Compton at the publisher's mansion, "Friendship," in Greenwich, Connecticut, and took seven long vacations during his first two years in office. Walker personified the devil-may-care spirit of the 1920s. He once said of his late-night revelries that "A man should never go to sleep on the same day that he got up," and although the comment was humorous, he was serious. His *elan vital*, combined with an irreverent spark, was undoubtedly at least partly why Walker was greatly loved by the public.

For the entire time that Walker was in office, Paul Block was at the Mayor's side, advising him, dining with him, attending baseball games and other events with him, socializing with women – usually not their wives – and thoroughly engaged in a whirlwind of celebratory activities and escapades. If there was a certain amount of status or reflected prominence in Block's association with Gentleman Jim, as the mayor was called affectionately, in all ways it was reciprocated. *The New York Times* referred to Block as "a close personal friend of Mayor Walker."[7]   Block's reputation as a man of wealth, philanthropy and political influence was on the rise, and almost at its apogee.

Because Paul Block spent a great deal of time with Jimmy Walker, they were thrown together in numerous charity situations. They were both the guests of honor at the Century Theater in New York City on behalf of the Grand Street Boys Association because of their support.[8] At one of the Mayor's receptions in City Hall, Captain George Fried of the S.S. America of the United States (U.S. Merchant Marines) thanked Block for his large contribution, and assured him that "The Captain's cabin is yours."[9]

Walker's association also gave Block entrée to the political scene. The two went down to Atlanta, Georgia in March 1928 for the unveiling of a Memorial for General Robert E. Lee. President Calvin Coolidge and his cabinet had been invited, as were Governors, Senators and Congressmen from every state, and other noteworthy invitees from across the country. Block paid a $1,000 fee (actually a donation) to become a member of the Stone Mountain Conferee Monumental Association, and he was included in the Founders Roll of the Stone Mountain's Memorial, which was a statue of Robert E. Lee and his horse, Traveler. Part of Mayor Walker's role at the fund-raising event was to induce people to buy commemorative Stone Mountain Memorial half-dollars. Block helped both the memorial association and his friend's efforts by making a liberal purchase of the coins.[10]

Walker wanted to spend time with Block as much as Block did with him. During the 1920s, Block was also on friendly terms with a host of other celebrities and achievers: Governor Alfred E. Smith, Governor Franklin D. Roosevelt, President Calvin Coolidge, future President Herbert Hoover, publishing magnate William Randolph Hearst, and any number of Senators, Congressmen, business tycoons, and government officials, as well as a bevy of entertainers, playboys and entrepreneurs. Because of his wide reach as a publisher he was invited to many events, to which he often encouraged the Mayor to accompany him. He also constantly provided all manner of tickets to the Mayor for his personal use and pleasure: six box seats for all New York games at Yankee Stadium; performances of Broadway plays such as *Macon, Three Cheers, New Moon, Kingdom of God*, and front-row seating at the 1,000-performer Freiburg Passion Players that was held at the Hippodrome.[11] How did Block secure these tickets? Sometimes they were complimentary passes given to him by the producer, occasionally it was a trade-out of a due-bill (he gave advertising in his newspapers in exchange for a specified number of tickets), but mostly he just purchased the tickets to be given to business associates for promotional purposes, and to friends as a courtesy. At a later date, Block's generosity toward Mayor Walker would cause them both great embarrassment.

Their loyalty as friends was well-known, and sometimes they jointly made headlines in New York City newspapers, as happened in January 1928, when Block was unanimously elected president of the New York Press Club.[12] A date was set for his inauguration the following week at a gala affair to be held at the Pythias Temple. Both men were eager to be there since Walker had agreed to induct Block into the new office, and Block was bemused and pleased that he was going to receive such an honor from the other publishers, editors and reporters of the city. Ironically, the affair was to be held at a renowned building that was located on West 70th Street, just across the street from the building in which Block had lived in a furnished room when he first came to New York almost penniless, thirty-five years before.

Just days before the event, which was to include speeches and a vaudeville show, followed by a dance, one of Walker's aides brought his attention to the fact that an invitation had been sent out to the newspaper fraternity all over the city by the Press Club's Vice-President, George F. Dobson, soliciting $5 for a ticket of admission to the inaugural. Mayor Walker became irritated when he learned that the invitation bore his name and Block's, as if *they* were asking people to pay for an event that, by tradition, had always been free. In his private reception room at City Hall, Walker raised his voice angrily about the invitation, stating that he was mortified on his own and Block's behalf, and that the newspaper community would think that both of them were less than generous. He said he refused to attend the inaugural under the circumstances, and Block, as a good friend who often disliked the same issues as his compatriot, immediately left town on the guise that he had important business in Cincinnati that could not be postponed. The trouble with Walker's ire at City Hall was that it was displayed in front of eight to ten reporters and members of his official staff. The next day he read about his irritation in *The New York Times*, and other papers, and that solidified his sulking position.

Four hundred people showed up at the gala but it was all fairly pointless since the guest of honor and his celebrity-inductor were not present. A month later, Walker *did* induct Block as President of the New York

Press Club, but this time with less fanfare and without charging a fee to attend. Whatever the shadings and substance of their friendship, the dynamics of that relationship would soon be tested, and they would experience troubles that were more difficult to solve than an embarrassing gala.

Walker earned the nickname "Night Mayor of New York" for his late evening prowls around town, usually with an entourage in tow, often with Paul Block included. The lifestyle suited Block since he rarely went to bed before dawn in any event. But whereas Block maintained his family life, and he did love Dina and the children, Walker constantly strayed from his wife Allie. His philandering centered on chorus girls, starting with Ziegfeld girl Yvonne "Vonnie" Shelton in 1917.[13] By 1924, Walker's wife Allie was brought out only occasionally for the odd publicity photo with her husband the Mayor. In some ways, Block and Walker traveled widely divergent paths in their personal lives but in others they mutually benefited from each other's company. They continued to exchange favors the way friends do; Block was often included in city events and official welcoming committees, and was seen in the pages of New York newspapers probably more than he would have liked, usually standing next to the Mayor as he inspected a traffic light, talked to a policeman, or greeted a crown prince. Walker was as much involved in the concept of friendship as Block. This loyalty to friends was inherited by Walker from his father, and like his father, he disliked hearing criticism of his friends, justified or not.[14]

If Walker was free any evening, Block would invariably invite the Mayor to dine with him. Other guests at the table were often leading entertainers from Block's circle of friends: Irving Berlin, Arthur Hammerstein, George Gershwin.[15] Block and Walker did enjoy musicals, and may well have had an ear for musical talent, but it is clear that they also enjoyed being part of the entertainment world.

Walker often sent Block letters of introduction for young men he knew who were in need of a job, always with a casual note asking if he could "perhaps do something for Mr. So and So."[16] The mayor respected Block's keen business mind, and he would involve Block in government programs to improve housing in the city, one of Walker's constant concerns. In 1927, Block, along with August Heckscher, a wealthy philanthropist, both pledged to erect two blocks of low income housing units on land that the city government had purchased specifically for that purpose.[17] Without Paul Block's financing, Walker's solution to New York's chronic low income housing problem would never have been realized. Gifts, requests, suggestions and kind deeds flowed naturally between one and the other.

While the two men were on a trip together to Havana, the mayor was notified that a heroic New York fireman named Captain John Roberts had died in the course of duty. Walker was upset. When Block found out what had happened, he told Walker that he would send financial assistance to the fireman's widow. Walker telegraphed the fire commissioner, John J. Doorman, to notify Mrs. Roberts of the donation to come.

On the way back from Cuba, Block and Walker spent several days in Palm Beach at the Breakers Hotel. When they arrived in New York City, Block found that the community of fire fighters and their families all felt gratitude that their efforts were appreciated, and surprise that a private citizen would offer financial assistance to one of their own. Block was formally commended for his effort.[18]

Such donations became a pattern. Whenever Block learned that a policeman or fireman had been killed in the line of duty in New York City, he arranged payments to their widows. City officials began to work with him in these charitable ventures. Block had checks sent to the police commissioner or the fire commissioner, whose offices distributed them to the widows of men who had died defending the safety of the community. Block tried whenever possible to avoid letting the press know of his contributions; they were rarely known outside the police or fire departments.

In 1926, the height of the hedonistic Jazz Age, Jimmy Walker fell in love again, this time with Betty Compton, a chorus girl with bobbed, jet black hair who "...walked right out of an F. Scott Fitzgerald novel."[19] Block, being intimately acquainted with Walker's love life, generously lent his apartment at the Ritz Hotel for the Mayor's assignations with Ms. Compton, although due to the destructive quality of their fights he often wished he hadn't.[20]   Against advice from Tammany Hall, Walker also took a vacation cruise to Cuba, as the guest of Paul Block. The two men were wined, dined and feted all over the island, meeting scores of government officials and dignitaries, visiting the racetrack, and generally having a grand old time. Their exploits, mainly social engagements, made almost daily fodder for newspapers around the United States.

Though Block had been raised as a Jew, religion played a relatively minor role in his life. In the advertising and newspaper worlds where Block made his mark, there were many businessmen who were also Jewish. But a number of the people he worked with, socialized with, or did business with were Christians. Perhaps because of his years as a sales-man, perhaps because it was so important to him to establish and main-tain friendships, he incorporated an ecumenical attitude into his philoso-phy and this applied not only to his relationships, but to his numerous charitable donations.

He did make major, ongoing contributions to the Federation for the Support of Jewish Philanthropic Societies of New York City. By 1928, he was donating about $10,000 annually, and in 1931 Block was named chairman of the Emergency Appeal of the Federation for the Support of Jewish Philanthropic Societies of New York City. Later that year, Gover-nor Franklin D. Roosevelt wrote Block a letter commending the work the Federation was doing during the Depression and stressing the importance of charities during that devastating business crisis. That same year, Block increased his subscription to $25,000 annually, an extraordinary amount of money during the Depression.[21]

The United Jewish Appeal of Newark, New Jersey became an inad-vertent beneficiary of Block's generosity because, at that time in 1936, he owned *The Newark Star-Eagle*. But not all of his donations were made in expectation of return favors. Block made substantial contributions that were earmarked for overseas charities. He donated funds to the New York Campaign for Relief of Jews in Europe, and to the American Pales-tine Campaign.

Keeping his contributions impartial, Block also helped build New York City's magnificent Cathedral of St. John the Divine, giving so generously to the church's building fund that his name was inscribed in the Book of Remembrance, preserved in perpetuity in the Cathedral. Interestingly, one contribution was earmarked for the Cathedral's Press Bay Project. It was to be a memorial to the press.

During Christmastime of 1926, Block's name appeared in the head-lines of *The New York Times* because of his large donation to the City's Neediest Fund. He instructed that the money was to be distributed one-third to Jewish charities, one-third to Protestant charities, and the other one-third to Catholic charities. By that time, Paul Block was becoming known for his philanthropy,[22] not in the same class as a Rockefeller or a Carnegie, but effective and appreciated, nonetheless.

Jimmy Walker was now firmly ensconced in Paul Block's family, and frequently went for drives with him and his boys on Sunday afternoons.[23] Sometime after their return from Cuba, Paul stood outside his Park Av-enue apartment house with his son William – who he called Billy – wait-

ing for the Mayor to arrive for a quick afternoon drive around town, and
eventually into the country. Billy, a naturally inquisitive child, began
asking questions about Walker, who was one of his favorite visitors.

> "How much salary does the Mayor get?" queried the boy.
> "$25,000," Paul responded.
> Billy considered this and asked, "Does the city give him
> a home?"
> Block answered "No, but they give him an automobile."[24]

Billy went on to ask some questions about entertainment and how Walker
could afford to do all of the things he did. "I really don't know," responded his father. Those innocuous questions led Block into a legal
entanglement that almost wrecked his emotional life. The Mayor drove
up, they went off in his chauffeur-driven touring car and Billy thought no
more about his questions, but Block mulled them over considerably during the next few days. Sometime after that exchange, Paul Block opened
a joint stock account through his broker, Sailing Baruch (brother of financier Bernard Baruch). The new account was in both Block's name and
the Mayor's, although he didn't ask the Mayor to contribute to it. His
intention, he later explained, was simply to make the Mayor a little money
to help defray his high cost of living. Block had provided this philanthropic token of friendship for other people: He had opened an account
for his chauffeur, Daniel Handley, and for a number of associates, and
perhaps some relatives, often without any of them knowing about it. Once
the accounts made any kind of substantial profit, he would send an unexpected check to the beneficiary.[25] If the accounts lost money, then he
would just assume that loss and no one knew about it. Block didn't monitor the joint Block-Walker account; he deposited some initial seed money
and then let the healthy stock market do the rest. By the time he closed
the account, almost two years later, it had made him and Mayor Walker
almost $250,000 each.[26]

Block Granted a Knighthood

Perhaps as a result of his struggles as an immigrant, Block was interested in helping the poor of New York City (and other cities, as well).
Partially because of his association with Mayor Jimmy Walker, he had a
special concern for the city's Italian community. Walker was born and
bred in Greenwich Village (bordering the section called Little Italy), a

neighborhood of Manhattan where many Italian immigrants lived, and most of his friends and neighbors had been first or second generation Italian Americans. By the time Walker ran for the mayoralty, there were over 1 million Italians in New York City – one out of every five New Yorkers – and they were beginning to exert influence on the Democratic party and the elections, being the third strongest voting block, along with blacks and Jews. Walker, who was already friendly toward the Italian community, also wanted to curry their votes, and while so doing, he often invited Block to fund-raisers, campaign dinners, ribbon-cuttings, and other benefits. Many of these events concerned themselves with the Italian poor.

By the late 1920s, Block was donating directly to causes that helped the Italians, and one of his most active allotments was the Italian Hospital, located on 83rd Street and the East River, in the shadow of Carl Schurz park. Block became a member of the Campaign Committee that was formed to raise enough money to expand the capacity of the hospital from 94 to 225 beds, and to modernize the emergency room and maternity ward. He contributed fairly large amounts of money to the fund, and sought out his friends and business associates to contribute as well. He found that his fellow members of the Criterion Club were a fruitful source for bequests. Over a period of a year, Block helped the Committee raise close to 2 million dollars from such people as Adolph Lewisohn, Charles H. Sabin, Felix Warburg, William K. Vanderbilt, William F. Morgan and Mortimer L. Schiff.[27]

Most of the nurses and other personnel in the hospital were Missionary Sisters of the Sacred Heart – a religious order founded by Mother Cabrini, the first U.S. citizen to be canonized as a saint – and although they all spoke Italian, the new direction of the hospital was to make it non-sectarian and open to anyone regardless of their race, religion or nationality. This openhearted and charitable approach was an additional impetus for Block to try to help the Italian Hospital.

A short film was produced about the work and goals of the hospital, and Block used his contacts in the motion picture industry to insure that the film would have wide distribution in theaters in the New York area. It seemed like the whole city got behind the fundraising campaign, people donating pennies in some cases, and others giving up a week's salary to help out.

In the spring of 1928, Block had the opportunity of showing the hospital to Prince Potenziani, the governor of Rome, who was in New York for a brief visit to meet with members of the Italian-American community. The Prince talked with children who were ill, and he remarked at how pleased he was with the quality of care and treatment that the poor of the city were receiving. When he told Block about the crippled and ill children of Rome, Block made an instant contribution and continued his largess for years to come.

Block was taken with the humility and gentleness of the Prince. He wrote in one of his editorials: "He has shown us how really democratic and how human a man can be, whether brought up among the aristocracy or the sidewalks of New York."[28]

At the beginning of 1929, Block received notification that His Majesty Vittorio Emmanuel III, the King of Italy, was going to bestow upon him the title of Knight, as a Cavalier of the Order of the Crown of Italy, one of the greatest royal orders in all of Europe. In medieval times, Knights were either members of the nobility or were holders of non-hereditary dignities conferred by a sovereign in recognition of personal merit or service rendered to the country. Block was specifically cited for his help and contributions to the Italian community of New York, his pledges to the Italian Hospital and his offerings to the children of Rome.[29] In addition to the accolade, the reward of the title conferred upon Block the right to use the impressive coat of arms of the Order, and entitlement to prefix *Cavaliere*, or *Cav.*, to his name. The decree granted to Block was signed and sealed by the King, and countersigned by the Premier of Italy, Benito Mussolini. [30]

Funding Byrd's Expedition to Antarctica

The handsome and nationally-popular Admiral Richard E. Byrd had made a memorable flight over the North Pole in 1926. Shortly afterward, he announced that he wanted to take a crew on a considerably more risky adventure: the first overland excursion to the opposite side of the world, the South Pole. Many people doubted that the venture could be accomplished. Although Byrd was a Navy hero, this was to be a private venture, and funding became his first challenge.

On August 31, 1927, Paul Block handed Byrd a check for $5,000 toward his "Antarctica Expedition to the South Pole." The next day, Byrd sent a letter thanking him for his contribution. His letter was enthusiastically grateful, but nevertheless remained politely formal:

September 1, 1927

My Dear Mr. Block:

The very first thing I am doing upon my return here is to reiterate my appreciation of what you did for me last night when you surprised me so pleasantly by handing me that check for $5,000.

Of course, what you subscribed to the expedition will be a big help but the way in which you did it will be just as big a help to me, and so you see, I am doubly grateful to you. You must not mind my thanking you.

You showed trust in me which I shall try to be worthy of. I will, of course, consider it my duty to administer the affairs of the expedition as economically as possible. I am going to make a periodic report of expenses to all subscribers as I did on the North Pole expedition.

With high esteem and regard,
Very sincerely yours,
Richard E. Byrd

It took Byrd more than a year to make all the arrangements for the expedition. Block's continued and very public support had assisted him in raising the considerable amount of money needed to hire the men, purchase the supplies, and mount his expensive excursion. Shortly after that, Block gave Byrd an additional $5,000. On October 9, 1928, Byrd wrote to Block again, just before he took off for the South Pole. This letter, on Byrd's Antarctica Expedition stationery, indicates that by then their relationship was not just one of donor and recipient, but of two friends:

My Dear Paul,

So long old fellow. I shall never forget the way you have stood by us during this very critical time. You have my ever-lasting gratitude old fellow. With devoted good wishes to you and the family from all of us.

Your friend,
Dick B.[31]

At another point, Byrd referred to himself as "having no better friend" than Paul Block, and counting himself as "proud to be one of his friends." [32]

When Byrd reached Antarctica on August 20, 1929, he named the site of his headquarters Little America. Each of the buildings and snow houses he and his crew erected, which provided shelter for the men, their provisions, and their scientific equipment, was named in honor of Byrd's friends. One of the houses in Little America was called the Block House, named after Paul Jr. and Billy Block, the sons of Paul Block.[33] And as Byrd explored the frozen reaches of the South Pole, he named some of its features for the family of his friend and benefactor. Hence, there are now two huge snow-covered mountains, each higher than 10,000 feet: Mt. Paul Block Jr., and Mt. William Block, and a Paul Block Bay. Byrd had previously sent Billy, who was at Hotchkiss at the time, an American flag that he carried with him on his flight across the North Pole in 1926. Billy presented the flag to his school.

Duluth Herald and
Duluth News-Tribune

Paul Block was incredibly busy managing his various businesses, but he thrived on the work and the pressure. Although he complained about all the work and traveling he was forced to do, he also claimed that he just could not move any more slowly. When Block was approached in 1921 by one of the veterans of journalism, Michael F. Hanson of the *Philadelphia Record*, to see whether he would be willing to discuss a partnership to purchase a Minnesota newspaper, Block was more than amenable for such a discussion, despite being over-burdened by his burgeoning empire. He nodded in assent when he learned that the *Duluth Herald* was up for sale, and that two of the key people from the *Herald* had announced their desire to retire: the 90-year-old editor Theodore White, and the aging publisher Anton C. Weiss. The owners were seeking a buyer and the rumor was that the paper could be purchased for a relatively small amount of money. The circulation and advertising revenue were static, and although the *Herald* boasted offices throughout the United States and even in London, Paris, Berlin and Peking, there was little news or advertising revenue emanating from those sources.[34]

Hanson, who was general manager of the *Philadelphia Record*, wanted to operate his own newspaper after a lifetime of working for other people, but he didn't quite have enough money to become a sole owner of his own business. Block thought that he and Hanson would make a compatible business team, since they had known each other for years as a result of Block's handling the *Record's* foreign advertising. Like Block, Hanson did not have a formal college education, but had experienced decades of working his way up in the newspaper field from the positions of book-keeper, salesman, and advertising manager to that of general manager and *de facto* publisher. He had become a sort of business overlord of the Wanamaker newspaper properties, which included the *Philadelphia Press*, when it was then owned by the distinguished Philadelphia department store family, and Hanson was widely known in financial and social circles in the City of Brotherly Love. Despite his status and entrenchment in Philadelphia, Hanson was willing to move himself, his wife and nine children to Duluth, should an arrangement be made to buy the paper.[35] Block, as always, would remain based in New York and function as an absentee, although thoroughly involved, partner.

In January of 1921, Paul Block and M.F. Hanson followed Horace Greeley's suggestion, went west, and bought the *Duluth Herald* for a sum that was kept confidential but was rumored to be less than $500,000. With Block supplying virtually the entire investment, both men assumed new titles and responsibilities: Hanson became president and publisher, and Block named himself vice-president and treasurer. They began issu-ing the newspaper, which averaged 24 to 48 pages depending on the in-tensity and profusion of the news and the amount of advertising, six eve-nings a week.[36]

Duluth was situated on the western end of Lake Superior, and as one of the leading shipping points in the United States, there was a fair amount of industry in the city to make it relatively prosperous. In the year after Block and Hanson took over the *Herald*, the city experienced steady growth: iron ore shipments doubled; a briquette plant, an automotive truck factory and a butter-producing operation came into existence; and new stores and retail shops sprouted up all over Duluth.[37] With a population of barely 100,000 (larger than its population today), however, there was little opportunity to expand circulation in the city of Duluth itself, and so Block began to concentrate on distribution of the paper across Lake Su-perior throughout Michigan's copper country, and upward to northwest-ern Minnesota, and even over the Canadian border to Winnipeg.[38] Work-ing with his Editor, the formal but astute journalist Stillman H. Bingham, Block instituted a column, "News of the Northwest," which carried im-portant sections that covered not only news about Minnesota, but Michi-gan, Wisconsin and the Dakotas, as well. These measures resulted in an increase in circulation and advertising, and the paper's profits began to increase fairly rapidly. Within two years of assuming control, Block had increased the circulation of the *Herald* to that of the largest in the state of Minnesota, with the exception of the newspapers published in the Twin Cities.[39]

Publishing the *Duluth Herald* was not without its difficulties, however. The so-called infamous "Gag Law" of Minnesota came into effect while Block was publishing the newspaper; it provided that "malicious, scandalous and defamatory" newspapers and periodicals could be suppressed by injunction as public nuisances. In addition, as one of the most restrictive censorship laws in the country, it permitted the courts to regard resumption of publication, if an injunction had been imposed, as a contempt of court and to subject the publishers to fine or imprisonment.[40] Just a year before Block bought the paper, the city of Duluth, alias Zenith in Sinclair Lewis's novel *Babbitt,* had been declared hopelessly small-minded and provincial, and the gag law seemed to exemplify the personality of the city. Eventually, in 1931, the law would be struck down as unconstitutional by the U.S. Supreme Court, which found that censorship by injunction is contrary to the Bill of Rights. But for six years Block was under the stress of what an arbitrary Minnesota court *might* find objectionable in his newspaper; by prior or post restraint, it could effectively put him out of business, and perhaps even send him to prison, should he or his editors not be careful. There are very few soft benches along the road to success, he said somewhat bitterly at that time.[41]

Block had no intention of sensationalizing or libeling anyone in the *Herald,* but the worry of censorship because of the "Gag Law" always haunted him. As a result it's possible that the paper was not as fearless as it might have been, at least for the years that the censorious law was in effect. Perhaps to indicate his sincerity in publishing a law-abiding paper, and to head off the censors who seemed to be just waiting for Minnesota newspapers to make a mistake, Block had the following proclamation appear on his editorial page every day:

> The Herald will be glad to have its attention called to any
> misleading or untrue statements that may appear in its news,
> editorial or advertising columns.

Most of Block's editorials for the *Duluth Herald,* which were unsigned, concerned local or Minnesota matters such as a call for the opening of the Great Lakes-St. Lawrence waterway, the elimination of the state personal property tax, the reforestation of 172,000 acres near Duluth, better passenger service to and from the West, farm prospects and opportunities in the area, a new union passenger train station, and an intelligent city plan. He would also take on international concerns from time to time, such as settling the German reparations debt in a realistic way, the reduction of the size of European armies, the recognition of Russia and the restoration of trade relations between it and the United States. He was steadfastly against Prohibition and not only wrote editorials condemning it, but covered breaking news from around the country, publishing stories that were in any way sympathetic to repeal by striking down the Volstead Act.

In addition to the editorializing that he did in Duluth, Block became thoroughly involved, behind the scenes, in the political life of Minnesota. The following note indicates how much he cared to influence the electorate, how much he still related to the German-American community and how he was attempting to put words into the mouth, and ideas into the head, of the President. Block wrote to C. Bascom Slemp, secretary to Pres. Calvin Coolidge, the following (in part) on Sept. 29, 1924:

> I hope that you do not think I am troubling you too much about the Minnesota situation, but I am so anxious to see the State go Republican, that I have my mind on it all the time.
>
> My anxiety is not only to see it go Republican, in order to insure President Coolidge's election (as I think the President will easily be elected without Minnesota), but I think it would be a great victory for conservative, decent, clean government, if the State of Minnesota would come back to the Republican Party, not only for the President, but also for the United States Senatorship and Governorship, and I understand that all this can be accomplished, especially if something like the following would be done: —
>
> "If some German Americans for whom the Germans out there have respect, would come and tell them that the war is over, that the Dawes plan is a good thing for Germany and the whole world, and that they must not risk their homes, their farms and their business by deadlocking the electoral college, and unsettling things by the threat of constitutional disturbances and Government ownership of railroads, etc."[42]

After Slemp showed him Block's letter, the President responded (in part) a week later:

> You are always among my most cheerful and reassuring correspondents.

> Regarding the phases of the Minnesota situation to which
> you refer, I am glad to have your views about these, and shall
> bring them to the attention of the campaign managers as soon
> as possible.[43]

Much as he was interested in dabbling in politics, Block nonetheless had a newspaper to run, and he went about increasing the local advertising that appeared in the pages of the *Herald*. He convinced such retailers as Siewert's Haberdashers, the Duluth Pioneer Auto Company, Hockin, Brace and Paleer House Furnishings, The Glass Block (Duluth's largest department store), and the Minnesota National Bank of Duluth, to take out larger and more frequent ads than they had done previously. It was with national advertising, however, that Block really helped the *Herald's* advertising lineage to surge forward. Such blue-chip advertisers as The Twentieth Century Limited, Chesterfield, Old Gold and Raleigh cigarettes; Standard Oil; Eastman Kodak; and Lever Brothers, all entered the pages of the *Herald* with full or half-page ads. The Lucky Strike ads bore an endorsement and photograph of his friend, actress Betty Compton, Mayor Jimmy Walker's inamorata: "To maintain a slender figure, no one can deny the truth of the advice: 'Reach for a Lucky instead of a sweet.'"

Block enjoyed visiting Duluth, was invigorated by its cool, dry weather, and often brought Dina with him whenever he had business in the city.[44] They usually went during the warmer months and always stayed for a week or two at the mammoth Hotel Duluth, a part of the Schroeder chain, which was known as one of the safest and most fireproof hotels in the nation. It boasted the most opulent lodgings in the city, and Block took a lavish suite for his stay there. All of the hotels in the Schroeder chain proudly carried the slogan "Sleep in Safety." The residents of the Hotel Duluth, including Paul and Dina Block, were therefore shocked and terrified when in August of 1929 a 350-pound black bear from the nearby woods outlying the city, driven by hunger and thirst, crashed through the plate-glass window of the coffee shop of the hotel at 6 o'clock in the morning. Not finding what it wanted in the closed restaurant, the bear proceeded to scale a flight of stairs to the second floor, where it was shot dead by Police Sergeant Henry LeBeau before it could climb higher. The incident highlighted the fact that Duluth was still a rustic, mid-western city that was located within a short distance of wild animals. At that time, Duluthians could hunt deer, ducks and partridges within the city limits. Two other bears were shot and killed the same week of the hotel incident, their invasion of the city attributable to the unusual scarcity of berries brought about by protracted dry spells that summer in the woods of their natural habitat.[45] It is not known whether Paul and Dina Block ever stayed at the Hotel Duluth after that, and if so, one wonders if they ever again ate in the coffee shop or checked into a room on a lower floor.

•••

Later that month, the Blocks were guests of Florenz Ziegfeld at his island in the Laurentian Lakes, five miles west of Quebec. Ziegfeld's island, which he dubbed Camp Patricia (it was named after his daughter), consisted of luxurious log cabins, a dormitory for the help (including a cook from Dinty Moore's restaurant in New York City) and a special house for his wife, the actress and singer Billie Burke.

On the day that the Blocks were to arrive, a gambler's hunch prompted Ziegfeld to write out a telegram to his stockbroker at Lehman Brothers, instructing him to sell all of his holdings. When the mail boat arrived at the island, Ziegfeld had the postman agree to send the telegram when he arrived back at the mainland. Minutes later, Block and Dina arrived at Camp Patricia, and the first thing that Ziegfeld told Block was that he was divesting his entire portfolio.

"It's a mistake," Block countered immediately, because he had been making a fortune in the market. "Well, it's too late," said Ziegfeld, pointing to the mail boat still visible in the distance. "I just sent a telegram to my broker to sell everything."

Block became excited. "Stop the boat! Bernard Baruch is holding on to his stock. Don't sell!" Block explained that Sailing Baruch, his stock broker (who was Bernard Baruch's brother), had told him that the financier was not going to sell his investments, and Sailing had recommended that Block hold fast to his. The two men jumped into Ziegfeld's motor boat, and soon overtook the mail boat, retrieving the unsent telegram.

On October 29th, Ziegfeld woke up to learn that he had lost more than a million dollars. Sailing Baruch had lied in order to keep Block's account. Bernard Baruch *had* divested. It is reported that Ziegfeld fell sobbing into Billie Burke's arms when he told her of his loss. "I'm through," he cried.[46]

When the Stock Market crashed, and the great Bull market that had fueled the American economy came to an end, Block did not consider the Ziegfeld incident a premonition of the Bear market that arrived so resoundingly. In fact, despite the Stock Market crash, Block was still in an acquisitive mode, and when the opportunity emerged to purchase the competitive morning and Sunday paper, the *Duluth News-Tribune*, Block and partner Hanson made an instant bid of $750,000 for it. Once again, Block was to provide virtually all of the purchase price. The offer was accepted and for a short while the two men operated both papers, each publication at its respective location.[47] Block and Hanson assumed the titles of co-publishers, and Block was made President of the holding corporations called the Herald Company and the Paul Corporation. The advertising representatives of the *News-Tribune* had been Burke, Kuipers & Moloney, and when Block assumed ownership of the paper, his advertising company, Paul Block & Associates, took control of the space sales. All three of the partners of Burke, Kuipers & Moloney were offered positions with Paul Block & Associates; Herbert Moloney accepted, and wound up working for Block for many years.

In the midst of his negotiation for the purchase of the *Duluth News-Tribune*, Block received an unsought and unexpected bid for the *Duluth Herald*. A local businessman named R.D. Handy had a political agenda that he wanted to exercise by owning one of the city's papers. He offered Block $1,550,000 for the *Herald*. Block refused the bid.

Block made sure that people he backed politically, and those he knew socially, were continually covered in the pages of the *Duluth News-Tribune* and the *Herald*, even when on occasion such coverage wasn't journalistically warranted. When former New York Governor Al Smith bought a hurdy-gurdy organ so that he could play tunes on it such as *East Side, West Side*, also known as *The Sidewalks of New York* – his campaign song – Block insisted that it make headlines in the *Duluth News-Tribune*. Praise for Mayor Walker's decision to run again in New York was editorialized by Block, despite the fact that Duluthians had little interest in the political future of the best-dressed mayor in the country.

But inevitably, as the results of the Depression swept across the country by the early 1930s, there was an extreme turn-around in the prosperity of Duluth newspapers. Circulation dropped. Block trimmed staff salaries. In order to gain and secure advertising, both local and national, the sales staff had to become more diligent and aggressive. It was a scramble. Eventually, to cut costs even further, Block brought the two newspapers under one roof on West Front Street, and combined many of the departments in an attempt to consolidate.[48] Because of the reduced advertising sales that he was experiencing, Block allowed more local news to be expanded and published in order to keep the paper's size to a respectable amount of pages. As a result, women's groups, civic organizations and sports all received more space than usual: that in turn helped to build circulation somewhat, but advertising was still thin.

R. D. Handy, perhaps sensing or learning that the newspaper was in trouble, and thinking that he might be able to purchase it at a bargain price, came back to Block and asked if he would now consider selling it "at a reasonable price," withdrawing his offer of $1,550,000 of three years before. Block responded in writing to his assistant: "This is no time to sell newspapers, any more than it is real estate, unless someone had a lot of money and is willing to buy for the future. For this reason, I do not think it would pay Mr. Handy to come and see me because I value my Duluth newspapers just the same now as I did two or three years ago."[49]

As he would do with many of his other newspapers over the years, Block tried everything he could, promotionally, to maintain a profit for the *Duluth News-Tribune,* while also keeping the *Duluth Herald* prospering. He introduced a magazine supplement to the Sunday paper; it was filled with photographs, fashion articles, short stories and non-fiction exposés. He started a column called "Minute Biographies," in which basic facts about a famous person's life would be presented – but not in prose form, just phrases and words, separated by ellipsis. The piece on Ben Hecht, for example, read: "... he used to be a newspaper man himself...he used to be a lot of things...he's a lot of things now...columnist...novelist...playwright...scenarist...short-story-writer...man-about-town..."

As a circulation booster, Block offered prizes for the best last line of the following limerick:

> "There was a young man of Superior
> Who suffered a complex inferior,
> But with a glad shout.
> He said, "That's all out –

The winner was Duluthian H.N. Veak, who finished with:

> Tonight when I call I will query her!"[50]

Block promoted the classified section of both papers by running full-page illustrated ads indicating how businesses, home-sellers and buyers, pet owners and used automobile sellers could best use the section. He sponsored a bowling championship, asked his readers to vote for America's favorite poem (they chose *In Flanders Field* and *I Have a Rendezvous With Death*), sold insurance policies to his readers, placed ads for booklets that explained seemingly everything – how to make tasty meals with canned foods, how to fix plugged-up pipes and simple leaks, how to swim, how to start and tend a small vegetable garden, and how to properly apply mascara – all for four cents each. He offered a free screening of George M. Cohan's film production of *The Home Towners* to members of the local historical society. For a short time he ran an ad every week called "Marvel-Tuesday," which offered large discounts on special items sold by all of the advertisers listed in the ad, such as the Kinney Shoe Store, the Duluth Fur Company, and Economy Dry Cleaners.

As hard he tried to maintain his spirits, Block began to understand the ravages of the Depression and began thinking that maybe he should have sold the *Herald* to Handy after all, when the price was right. He attempted to not only keep his own natural optimism alive, but that of his readers, as well. He wrote at that time: "The country has been through a serious economic depression, the effects of which have been more than economic. Unemployment brought a whole train of hardships – hunger, undernourishment, illness and worry…there is no place in the scheme for pessimism, discouragement or despair. They will accomplish nothing. They are worse than useless. They will retard recovery."[51]

Despite his optimism, by June of 1936 Block could no longer maintain his financial interests in either of the Duluth newspapers. The Ridder brothers – Victor, Bernard and Joseph – of nearby St. Paul, owners of the *Dispatch* and the *Pioneer Press* of that city, long building their own newspaper dynasty, made Block an offer to buy both of his entities. Their idea was that they would cease publication of the *Herald* and continue only with the *Duluth News-Tribune*, believing that even though one was a morning paper, and the other an evening, they canceled each other out on occasion as far as some advertising was concerned.

Still retaining the *Newark Star-Eagle*, the *Toledo Blade* (purchased in 1926), the *Milwaukee Sentinel* (purchased in 1929, the same year he bought the *Duluth News-Tribune*), and the *Pittsburgh Post-Gazette* (acquired in 1927), Block agreed to sell the Duluth papers to the Ridder brothers. A purchase price of $1,500,000 was agreed upon for both newspapers, and Block, because of the sinking national economy, was happy that he received nearly the same amount that Handy had offered him six years before.[52]   He had made a handsome profit from the sale of the newspapers at a time when many businesses were closing down.

Block had inserted into the Agreement of Sale the caveat that he would continue to act as the sole representative for the two papers to "solicit and procure foreign advertising [today known as national advertising]...for the term and period of three years."[53]   Both Block and the Ridders were delighted over the new arrangement. They knew, as did just about everyone else in the country, that there was no one better than Paul Block and his company in securing national advertising, and by engaging Block in an exclusive arrangement ("...that during the term of this agreement, it [he] will not act as the advertising representative of any other newspaper in Duluth, Minnesota"[54]) they would be relieving themselves of a certain amount of damaging competition, should Block have any thought of becoming the representative for one or more of the other Duluth papers.

Two weeks after the Agreement was signed and the money changed hands, and Block was no longer owner of the two Duluth newspapers, the Ridders became skeptical and somewhat alarmed that the three-year exclusivity contract with Block as their special representative might not be enough time in terms of the protection of their advertising interests. They proposed: would he consider an amendment to the Agreement that advanced the time from three years to five years? Block was agreeable, and in July of 1936 he signed a revised five-year contract with the Ridders to continue to represent their Duluth newspapers.[55]

Chapter 6
The Trappings of Wealth

Lancaster New Era

During all of the time that he was trying to build the circulation and profits of the *Duluth Herald* and his other newspapers, in the space of five years Block also bought, operated, and eventually sold the small-scale but thriving *Lancaster New Era*, an evening paper deep among the Amish and Mennonite people in Pennsylvania Dutch country. Buying the *New Era* was a curious choice for Block, since Lancaster was such a relatively small city; the only consistent pattern to his decision was that it was a Republican newspaper in a primarily Republican stronghold, it came out in the evenings, and the price was right.

Steeped in history, the city of Lancaster had been the nation's capital for one day (Sept. 27, 1777), and served as Pennsylvania's capital from 1799 to 1812. Located in a fertile tobacco and grain region, Lancaster had few industries other than cigar manufacturers and boiler and engine works, when Block took over the *New Era* in 1923, but the 1920s were a time of prosperity and the paper was entrenched not only in the city itself but throughout Lancaster County and even to Lackawanna County as far north as Scranton.[1] Some homes and restaurants in the town dated back to the time of the Revolution (Valley Forge lies only 30 miles away). The population of the sleepy city was barely 60,000, and the *New Era* had a circulation of just above 20,000. There were two competing newspapers: the *Lancaster News-Journal* and the *Lancaster Intelligencer*, both owned and operated by the Steinman family of prominent Lancaster lineage. Neither of the Steinman's papers, however, were as well subscribed or possessed the fairly broad advertising sales of the *New Era*.

In order to buy the *Lancaster New Era*, Block went into partnership, reprising his business relationship with Michael F. Hanson of the *Duluth Herald*, with Block as president and publisher, Hanson as vice-president and treasurer. His partners thereafter included Arthur D. Marks, who was then business manager of the *Washington Post*, as secretary of the newly-formed *New Era* company. All three would be absentee owners, Hanson remaining in Duluth, Marks in Washington, and Paul Block in New York, but they all planned to be in constant touch with the editorial and business management and to go to Lancaster on a routine basis and whenever else it was necessary.[2] Part of the charm of ownership, thought Block, was the ability and excuse to travel to Lancaster by his private railroad car, since the town was situated on the Pennsylvania and Reading railroad lines. Should he prefer to be driven to Lancaster, it was only a day's relatively-easy drive from Manhattan through the rolling hills and picturesque and fertile farms of Pennsylvania, through a series of quaint towns with such whimsical names as Bird-in-Hand, Paradise, Smoketown and Dutch Apple.

Once the ownership papers were signed in late February of 1923 giving over control of the *New Era* to Block and his associates, Block went to Palm Beach, Florida to spend two weeks at the Breakers Hotel, a posh resort for the wealthy, to take a respite against the cold of winter.[3] He decided to invest as much as he could in trying to make the *New Era* the most important and profitable paper in the small city. Its offices and newly-modernized printing presses were located on Queen Street in the first building off the town square, near the Central Market that dated back to Colonial times, and within a short walk to the Fulton Opera House. From the windows of the *New Era*, Block could see the Civil War monument dedicated to those men from Lancaster who died fighting for the Union.

Block wanted the *New Era* to be not only geographically in the center of the life of Lancaster, but also financially and politically at its core. The slogan for the *New Era* had been "Lancaster County's Home Newspaper," and Block had every intention of keeping it that way, with just a sprinkle of crowd-pleasing thrown in. "We want to help make the *New Era* a better and bigger newspaper than ever before," he wrote in an editorial on the front page on his first day of control.[4]

Within days of taking over the paper, Block included all kinds of new features, such as a four-page color comic supplement: it provided a major boost to circulation since his competition only ran a few comic strips – as did most newspapers in the United States at that time – not a separate supplement, and those were in black and white. In the *New Era*, Lancasterians began reading and chuckling over a newly-introduced (by the *Chicago Tribune*) character, "Moon Mullins;" they loved the Hearst-originated "Katzenjammer Kids;" followed the adventures of the madcap characters in "Gasoline Alley;" and eventually became thoroughly involved in a little blank-eyed and feisty curly-head named "Little Orphan Annie." Most of the comics came from the Hearst-owned King Features Syndicate.

Following the principles of his friend and associate William Randolph Hearst, Block suggested to the editors that they look for stories about entertainment. "Readers want only so much information," he said. "They want to have a good time when they read the paper. Let them." *All* stories, he demanded – news and feature – had to be livelier and more galvanizing.

Block also insisted of his editors that they re-vamp their design sense and give the paper a facelift. The *New Era* had to not only read well and entertainingly, it had to look good and he asked, in true Hearstian fashion, that headlines be made larger, and that more photographs be used.

As genuinely important as the comic supplement and entertainment aspects were, however, Block realized that the heart of the *New Era* was in its news coverage and he was hardly miserly when it came to hiring the best reporters and editors he could find to insure the quality of coverage he sought. He suggested that the existing editors search among the recent college graduates of nearby Franklin and Marshall College to recruit cub reporters, with the hope that a college education would add depth and dimension to a young journalist's perceptions. Oliver Keller, a graduate of William College, and only in his mid-twenties, was the distinguished Editor of the *New Era* when Block bought it, and he remained in that post until Block divested himself of the paper.

As he was helping to find the editorial center of the *New Era*, Block traveled to Lancaster constantly, usually by train but sometimes by automobile. On at least one occasion, bringing his car to Lancaster produced some untoward results. At the end of one motor trip to the city with his son Billy, Block had his liveried chauffeur park his huge, powder-blue, convertible Rolls Royce limousine in front of the *New Era's* offices. While Block met with his editors and business people for several hours in the upstairs' newsroom, a crowd slowly began to gather around his car. At first George, the chauffeur, stood near the car with his goggles perched over the brim of his cap, having a cigarette. He assumed that the townspeople were simply interested in the splendor of the automobile, and were showing their curiosity. But then he observed them studying and whispering about the New York license plate with Paul Block's initials prominently displayed: "P.B."

Supposing that the onlookers thought that Paul Block was a celebrity – and in some ways he was – and that they had made the leap of connection from the initials to Block's name, George thought nothing further until the crowds began to increase to several hundred people. Dashing upstairs, he told Block what was happening, and when Block left the building later on to be driven home, he finally learned why there was so much interest in his automobile.

Just days before, newspapers all over the country, including the *Lancaster New Era*, were running a story on their front pages about "Peaches" (Frances Heenan) and "Daddy" (Edward) Browning, the incongruous May-December marriage of a 15-year-old girl and a 51-year-old millionaire realtor, wedded in 1926 after a three-month courtship. During their honeymoon, the always-dubious *New York Evening Graphic* reported that the infamous Daddy dressed up as a sheik, brought his pet goose to the bedroom, barked at his bride, and subjected her to any number of perversions. As their marriage progressed, and as he chased her around his various palatial homes and apartments – with talk, or at least whispers, reaching the press of whips, chains and other sexual paraphernalia – Browning outraged the public by reporting to the newspapers virtually every detail of their relationship: the color of Peaches's nighties, what she did and didn't wear, and the size of their bed. She claimed to have convulsions as the result of his bizarre treatment. Both Peaches and Daddy seemed always interested in speaking to the press, and he was not averse to calling an actual press conference to outline the details of their latest contretemps. The day-by-day misadventures of the couple captured the attention of the public and boosted the circulation of many newspapers, including that of the *Lancaster New Era*. Everyone seemed to have an opinion on the factual or fictional romps of Peaches and Daddy.

When the Lancasterians saw the initials on Paul Block's automobile, and it had been previously reported that Daddy Browning's car was also a powder-blue Rolls Royce, they assumed that the "P.B." stood for "Peaches Browning" and that she had come to the newspaper to be interviewed as America's most talked about celebrity of the moment. Although Block thought the whole event was amusing, the townspeople felt let down when they discovered who the real "P.B" was that afternoon. [5]

In a history of the Steinman family and their involvement in Lancaster newspapers, J. Hale Steinman was quoted as saying that upon buying the *Lancaster New Era*, "Paul Block immediately started to try to put the

Steinmans out of business by adding many new expensive features to his newspapers." This was not the case at all. Block had no desire or strategy to put anyone out of business, but he did have to protect his and his partners' investments in trying to publish a competitive newspaper. Block thought that competition among newspapers in the same city was not only healthy but essential to each publication's development. The Steinmans resented the infusion of outside money, and of new publishers from New York and other bustling cities coming into Lancaster, and chauvinistically feared that Block, perhaps with the aid of his associate Hearst's financing, would so out-promote and out-circulate their own publications that they might be forced out of business. Hearst's empire had grown to 31,000 employees who published 28 newspapers and 13 magazines. His annual payroll alone topped 57 million dollars. Despite Block's protestations to the contrary, the Steinmans believed that if Hearst and Block were partners in other newspapers, they must also be in partnership in the *New Era*. With this newspaper, it just wasn't so.

The Steinmans didn't take long to retaliate. Within six months of Block's purchase of the *New Era*, they issued the first Sunday newspaper in Lancaster's history, the *Sunday News*, which was delivered free to subscribers of the *Intelligencer Journal*. The idea was to create an editorial and advertising package so attractive that circulation and space sales would have to increase markedly. It did just that and the Steinmans' newspaper prospered even more than the *New Era*, despite the fact that they issued their comic supplement in black and white.

Block continued trying to improve the *New Era*, but compared to all of his other papers before, during or since then, it was – if not insignificant – at least not a major factor in his financial empire. Competition for readers and advertisers, even the hiring and retention of boy newspaper carriers, became so fierce between Block and the Steinmans that in 1927, he offered to buy them out so that there would be only one paper servicing Lancaster. Not only did the family refuse to sell to Block, but in the winter of 1928, with their circulation topping an all-time high of 30,000, they made a counter-offer to buy out Block.

Block agreed to sell the *New Era*, its name, printing presses and equipment, and the building on Queen Street for $925,000. At first the Steinmans could not come up with that amount of cash. Banks held that a newspaper's "good-will," which the family had offered as security for a loan, was worthless, and the equipment, the tangible asset, was worth only $75,000. Eventually, a loan of $250,000 was secured on the building itself, the

Steinmans obtained several other loans from a variety of sources, and the family purchased the *New Era*.

The Steinmans' enmity toward Block over what they considered to be the goading ownership of the *New Era* ceased immediately upon signing the transfer of papers. Just to show that there were no feelings of resentment, and because of their great respect for his ability to gain national advertising, they asked Paul Block to remain with their company as special advertising representative, which he was happy to do, continuing to operate and sell space through Paul Block & Associates out of his New York office.

Newark Star-Eagle – 1926

In 1926, almost ten years to the day after he became a part-owner of the *Newark Star-Eagle*, Paul Block made an offer to his partners to buy them out so that he could become sole owner. He also knew he would ultimately divest himself of the *Lancaster New Era*, and he wanted more time to spend on continuing to build the *Newark Star-Eagle*. It wasn't that he had been running the *Star-Eagle* all by himself – his partners were hardly silent – but Block had other not-so-secret reasons for wanting to run the operation on his own. He had had difficulties with Talmadge and his follower, Buggie, at the *Detroit Journal* and the *Toledo Blade*, and he really wanted to dissolve the partnership. From a business point of view, it was an excellent time to take a financial gamble: the circulation of the *Newark Star-Eagle* had risen to 90,000 copies a day, and the advertising had gained over one million lines in the previous year alone.

Newspaper appraisers, bankers and other consultants were asked their opinions as to the value of the newspaper at that time, and the consensus was that it was then worth ten times its 1916 purchase price: in other words $2,300,000 dollars in 1926. The multimillion dollar appraisal seemed reasonable to Block since he believed in the future of the paper and he believed in himself. Block stated that there were other factors to be considered in determining the value of a newspaper:

> If a city has too many newspapers the competition is very intense. If there are two or three newspapers of greater importance or have larger circulations than the one in question, then it naturally reduces the value of that paper. On the other hand, if the field is a good one, say like the field in Newark – where there is only one evening newspaper other than the *Star-Eagle*, and that Newark was, and is, a growing town, it

naturally makes a second evening paper have greater value than if it was the third, fourth or fifth.[6]

Additionally, the *Newark Star-Eagle* had earned and was enjoying the respect and goodwill of the people of Newark and its suburbs.[7] He knew this from letters that came into the paper, from the large turnouts at the various promotions offered, and from the climbing circulation.

The partners with whom Block had bought the *Newark Star-Eagle* in 1916 had changed during the interim. When Nathaniel C. Wright died in 1923, his partnership had been replaced by Fred S. Buggie. Clarence C. Vernam of the Street and Smith Publishing Company in New York, also became a part owner of the *Newark Star-Eagle* at that time. One of the major reasons that Block didn't like Buggie, was that when Block's contract as special representative of the *Toledo Blade* came up for re-negotiation, Buggie attempted to force Block to take a lesser percentage. Buggie also hinted that he should get a percentage of Block's earnings, "off the top." Buggie threatened to terminate Block's contract unless he agreed to the demands. Block refused out of strength. As the leading special advertising representative in the country at that time, Block knew that it would be absolutely devastating for the *Blade* to dispense with his service, so he surmised that Buggie would back down. Buggie did finally withdraw his demands but Block never forgot or forgave the insult or pressure.

In 1926, Block met with Buggie, Vernam and Talmadge to discuss the possible buyout. Block's interest in making the change was self-serving, but his motivation was not just because he wanted the pride of ownership or desired control. The wounds that he perceived from the *Detroit Journal*, and received from Buggie at the *Toledo Blade*, were still raw although several years had passed. He also believed that Talmadge, and perhaps the others, were cheating him out of a fair amount of profits that he demanded should accrue to him. To make matters worse, Block's accountant informed him that Talmadge had made improper payments to various groups and individuals, amounting to $100,000 over the previous year, while also awarding them automobiles, player pianos and radio sets, all without receiving permission to do so from the other partners. Block was so upset and angry when he learned of the duplicity that he wanted to end the relationship immediately...at any price.

Talmadge, sensing Block's eagerness to become independent, asked if he wanted to buy out the partners and how much he would be willing to offer. Block named a figure of $1,200,000, which was to be divided evenly among the three other partners, so each would receive $400,000. Talmadge requested 48 hours to think it over. The next day, Block received a hand-delivered letter from Talmadge stating that he had conferred with the other partners and they wanted $1,350,000. Block said he would have to check with his lawyers and accountants, but that he thought that he would agree to that figure. By the next morning, Talmadge had raised the price to $1,590,000, and before the day was out had raised the price to $2,300,000. Furious, aware that Talmadge knew how desperately he wanted to sever the partnership, Block said he would agree to the new asking price, but he would not go above it *under any circumstances*. If Talmadge did not accept that figure, and no higher, within 24 hours, Block would then refuse to buy at any price. Block realized that Talmadge really never had any intention to retain the paper himself. His offer to Block had been a ploy to learn what Block would pay...and then to raise the price to whatever he thought Block would spend to consummate the purchase.

During the negotiations for the sale, Block mentioned a possible legal suit against Talmadge as a lever to insure culmination of the contract. Finally, with bitterness on Block's side, all four men agreed to the purchase price of $2,300,000, and Block became sole owner.[8]

On that very day, February 6, 1926, almost as if he wanted to wash the record clean, Block had notices posted all over the *Newark Star-Eagle* plant, newsroom and business offices, announcing the new owner and inviting every employee to a special "get-together" dinner that evening at the *Achtel-Stetter* German restaurant in Newark. Over 300 staff members of the newspaper attended.[9] Block was so proud and excited over purchasing sole ownership that he wrote to President Coolidge to tell him about it. His letter shows why Coolidge so admired and respected Block – partially because of the steadfast loyalty shown to him.

> When I received your recent courteous letter I planned to come to Washington and accept your kind invitation to call on you. However, I have been rather busy in a re-arrangement in the ownership of the *Newark Star-Eagle*, in which for many years I have been interested.
>
> My paper has over 90,000 circulation each evening – is the second largest newspaper in the state, and is the largest Republican newspaper. That it will endorse and fight for the

honorable and consistent policies you represent, I need not state.[10]

Henry Auth, the manager of the *Star-Eagle*, who had witnessed and participated in the various incarnations of the paper for 25 years, acted as toastmaster and introduced Paul Block. It was a proud and captivating moment for Block as he ascended the dais, approached the lectern quietly, and greeted his employees with a smile. He reviewed briefly his thirty-year experience in the advertising and newspaper business, and declared that the friendships he had formed had been the most valuable fruits of his activities. And then he offered the surprise of the evening. "My ambition," said Block, "is to see that the *Star-Eagle* continues its progress. With the cooperation of the employees, I am confident that this will be brought about." In gratitude to his personnel, and as a sign of his respect and appreciation for them, he made an extraordinary announcement: for the first time in the history of the newspaper (as well as the first time for virtually *any* newspaper), all employees would receive a free life insurance policy (the amount of which would be determined by a sliding scale related to length of service), full pay for holidays, and a week's vacation every year – with pay.[11]

People began to cheer, some almost cried. The foreman of the pressroom, Bert Cox, was overwhelmed by the announcement. "It's a foregone conclusion, " he said, "that the men will reciprocate this generosity. Our men often have mourned, rather than enjoyed, a holiday because of their loss of a day's pay each time. This is particularly true of the married men, of whom we have many. These men also could not always afford a vacation, and heretofore they have constantly kept at their grind, fifty-two weeks a year, year in and year out." After that night, the employees of the *Newark Star-Eagle* felt that they were the luckiest workers in the industry, and they weren't far wrong with that appraisal. Circulation was nearing 100,000, making the *Star-Eagle* the healthiest newspaper in Newark, and in New Jersey, as well.

A few months later, Block sued Talmadge in New York Supreme Court on two counts, both over accounting procedures: the first complaint stated that Talmadge wrongfully disbursed funds to himself and others during the time he was Managing Director of the *Newark-Star Eagle*; and the second accusation went back to a contract that Block and Talmadge had secretly signed in 1908 when Talmadge was trying to raise money to become one of the lessees of the *Toledo Blade*. Block had decided to back him and paid Talmadge $25,000, at that time a relatively huge sum, for a one-third interest of all the profits Talmadge might make, less his salary, from the *Blade*. Block estimated that over the years, this amount would be approximately $160,000. Talmadge did not deny the terms of the contract, and claimed that he did pay Block what was due him up to 1919, whereupon the two men signed another contract which released Talmadge from his obligations, and rescinded Block's interest in his earnings. Block could not deny the existence of the second contract since it was produced, with his signature, in court, but claimed that Talmadge had induced him to sign it, along with many other documents, and that he had not been aware of the import of the document.[12]

To complicate matters, Talmadge then sued the *Toledo Blade*, which Block took over just three months later, for breach of contract, stating that he had an agreement with the Locke estate (the previous owners of the *Blade*) from 1924, giving him the right to operate the newspaper until 1934. Both of these cases would stretch out over the years and both were finally settled out of court for an undisclosed sum, but perhaps canceling each other out, with payment going *to* Block from Talmadge and *from* the *Blade* to Talmadge.[13] As a slight retaliation for all the trouble Talmadge was causing him, Block continued to refer to Talmadge as Thalheimer, spitefully refusing to accept his new name in court records, correspondence and other communiqués.

FRIENDSHIP –
Block's Private Railroad Car
By the mid-1920s, with all of the newspapers that were then under Block's control either as owner and/or publisher, in addition to the 16 or more major newspapers that Paul Block & Associates were representing, Block had need to travel constantly and he did so almost always by train. He also enjoyed traveling, looking upon it as a universal metaphor for change and observation, and as a symbol of liberty. He didn't only want to *read* about issues and people, even in his own papers; he wanted to meet and see the people who were involved, and discuss the issues head-on with them.

On some occasions, when he had to transport a number of his associates with him, or he wanted to entertain and travel in comfort, he would lease a private car to be attached to the train. Not only was this a great expense, but it lacked the personal touch he sought. Since he was flush with cash in the mid-1920s, Block decided to buy his own railroad car.

In the late 1920s, perhaps the ultimate luxury available to the very wealthy was owning a private Pullman railroad car. For status reasons, it seemed to be somewhat more prestigious than owning a yacht. Henry Ford had bought one. William Randolph Hearst, E. F. Hutton, the Whitneys and John D. Rockefeller were also members of this exclusive minority. Paul Block was not to be denied entry into this elite community.[14]   In 1928, he purchased a five-room, all steel Pullman "Pioneer" railroad car.

The Pullman was named after its manufacturer, George Mortimer Pullman, who was one of the innovators of "sleepers" – railroad cars that could accommodate long distance travelers. He built his first "Pioneer" model in 1864, and it was the most splendid of the line. The Pullman Pioneer was fitted out with a brand new design: hinged upper berths. During the day, they were folded up into the wall, hiding bed, pillows, and all bed linens, and turning the car into the equivalent of a plush sitting room on wheels. At night, the train's porters opened and made up the beds, and the wealthy travelers slid between expensive sheets, falling asleep amidst a feeling of luxury as the train clicked off the miles.

To provide extra comfort for its very privileged owners, the Pioneer had several special features. It rested on a specially cushioned four-wheel base, providing a less bumpy, more comfortable ride. It was also longer, higher, and wider than any other car on the rails. That made it more spacious inside, but as a result it was too big to come alongside some of the platforms of the bigger cities, such as Chicago, or pass beneath their bridges. Some of Pullman's customers had enough influence to have the railroad tracks and station platforms modified to accommodate the larger train. Mary Todd Lincoln knew of the Pioneer car, and after the President's assassination in 1865, she asked to have a Pullman Pioneer added to the funeral train for her own personal use. The railroad, with Pullman's guidance, was left with little choice but to make the construction changes necessary along the funeral route. The same necessity also occurred when General Ulysses S. Grant traveled to his home in Galena, Illinois aboard a Pullman Pioneer. Paul Block had endured years of riding normal trains from one city to the next, visiting newspapers he represented or hoped to represent, or traveling to meetings with the staffs of his own papers. He knew how cold and damp the trains were in the winter, and he remembered how excruciatingly hot it was to ride on a train in the summer. Burning cinders would invariably fly in through the window as the train rolled down the track. His clean clothes would become black from the soot, and sometimes the soot and smoke made it hard to breathe. But still there was something romantic and adventurous about being on a long train ride. With his success, though, Block no longer needed to bear such discomfort. With the purchase of his own railroad car, Paul Block became part of the great American train mystique.

He was now an aristocrat of American society. And like his wealthy colleagues, he had to give his railroad car a name. Henry Ford had called his private car, The Fairlane. C. M. Schwab's car was named The Lorretto. Harry Payne Whitney's was The Wanderer. Joseph E. Widdners owned The Lynnewood, and Hearst rode on The Constitution, but was more often in Block's train than his own. Paul Block's car was named after the way he lived his life. He named his private car Friendship.[15] The name was derived from Block's philosophy: that business was synonymous with friendship.[16]

Friendship took about a year to build and was completed in August, 1929. It measured 83 feet, 6 inches, bumper-to-bumper, and weighed about 42 tons. Furnished with new berths made of exquisite hardwood, it had a sleeping capacity of eight people. The original cost of Friendship was $75,000, but that just paid for the steel car and the Pullman equipment. Block, at first to his wife's pleasure and then to her concern, spent considerably more decorating and furnishing the interior.

Dina enlisted the assistance of the engineer of the Pullman Car and Manufacturing Corporation to supervise the interior decoration of the car. Prints were submitted for her approval, and Dina made the final choices for the draperies, seat covers, and all other appointments. She chose a rich, deep green as the key color for all of the rooms, with specially designed brass lamps, clocks, and other accessories.

Friendship contained four bedrooms, a dining room, observation living room, observation platform, kitchen, pantry, and crew quarters for two. The master bedroom had an adjoining bathroom with a shower, bath and toilet. The other three bedrooms were also equipped with bathrooms.[17]

The dining room on Friendship was spacious and extended the width of the car. Its large table was surrounded by eight chairs, all upholstered in a dark green, and the draperies were lined in Parma (violet) satin. The room was designed to reflect sophistication and elegance, because the Blocks entertained honored and distinguished guests, such as William Randolph Hearst, aboard the Friendship while they were traveling.

The observation room was attractive and practical as it was completely enclosed in shatterproof glass. Decorated in colors to match the dining room, the living room was comfortable, luxurious, and provided an often exciting view.

The kitchen was entirely modern, and the Blocks traveled with their own private chef, a big jolly man named Sims, and a steward-waiter named Green. Meals were served on the finest China, and the silverware was polished and inspected by Dina Block, almost as if she were hosting a State dinner, to ensure that guests would have the ultimate service.

Friendship itself, however, was not the only place to eat when Block traveled across the country. An Englishman named Fred Harvey ran all the restaurants for the Santa Fe Railroad. He owned a hotel in Florence, Kansas, which catered exclusively to railroad patrons. Harvey went on to operate 15 hotels, 47 restaurants and 30 dining cars on the Santa Fe Railroad. The Harvey Houses, as they were called, served good food from varied menus amid furnishings Harvey imported from England.[18] Before a meal stop on the Santa Fe, the conductor would telegraph ahead and tell the restaurant that Paul Block or whoever else would be dining there, and the number of people in the party, so the food would be ready when the train arrived.

Paul Block employed a number of innovative ideas on Friendship to make the car distinctive and personally his, and he had them built at a considerable expense. He installed a Delco battery-charging unit, which was an asset when Friendship was parked in spots where recharging under normal conditions was impossible. He also had a thermostatic heat control system installed, and he added an auxiliary heater as part of the kitchen equipment in case the steam heating plant of the engine became defective. Additional ventilators were added in the private rooms, and there were two working telephones on board, which kept him in constant touch with his enterprises.

Block researched private train travel as thoroughly as he did his businesses; he discovered and inculcated as many modern conveniences he thought would make Friendship pleasant as well as safe. This all came at a price. The final cost of Friendship, after all of the accessories were put in place, was close to $100,000.[19]

Because Block constantly combined his business and social life, he entertained frequently, and used Friendship as a vehicle to entertain many of his guests. Friends and associates from Broadway and Hollywood, politicians he had befriended or was courting, and editors and clients from the newspaper industry were often on board. One of his most frequent passengers, naturally, was William Randolph Hearst, who once wrote in the train's log: "Well, I don't know. I have been on my dear friend Paul's wonderful car so much that I almost think my residence is here." At each stop, both Hearst and Block would send the steward out to the station's newsstand to purchase copies of their own and other newspapers. Usually a long, spirited discussion would then take place as the two men analyzed the content, style, and approach of the components of each daily. Hearst would often lay out copies of his own papers on the floor of the car, remove his shoes, and with a strange prehensile ability move the pages about with his feet, toe-point to certain stories, and conduct a curious newspaper dance as he held forth on the strong and weak points of what was spread before him.

Another frequent guest aboard Friendship was actress Marion Davies, the unpretentious and cheerful movie star who had been Block's inamorata and was by then Hearst's mistress. She, too, enjoyed life aboard Friendship, and commented in the train log that she was grateful for Paul Block's marvelous hospitality.[20] She particularly liked young Billy Block, and became attached to the boy on coast-to-coast trips on the train.

Block not only entertained on Friendship, but also used it for business meetings and matters of importance for his burgeoning empire. Friendship would pick up newspapermen in cities such as Chicago and Kansas City. One of these wrote in the train log: "The greatest joy in life comes from making others happy; a complete and understanding realization of the truth of this philosophy make a friendship with Paul Block a very real asset." Block's hospitality, and especially his generosity, touched many people, even President Calvin Coolidge. Block had offered Coolidge his railroad car, which would be at the President's disposal for a private trip. The President wrote to Block saying that he appreciated the offer but would not need the car, but he was nonetheless grateful for the generous and kind thought.[21] On some occasions, Block would attach Friendship to the campaign train of a favored politician, and spend time with the candidate as he traveled the trail to election. At other times he would offer the exclusive use of Friendship to business associates or friends who he believed could benefit from it.

During the long rides aboard Friendship, Block and his guests developed close-knit relationships. Friendship became their shared home, and the guests became family. He loved the arrangement because all of his fellow passengers were hand-picked and he didn't have to suffer the ennui of sitting next to a travel bore in the public lounge waxing about his trip to Boise, or the importance of his stamp collection. Block's guests rode in luxury, and they were served delicious formal dinners while the landscape of America passed, almost if it had been arranged by Block for their viewing pleasure.

The Friendship's annual maintenance ran from $35,000 to $50,000, close to 1 million dollars in today's equivalent. During the Depression, some people undoubtedly considered such an expenditure decadent, but Block had entered the category of the rich and famous with the likes of the Vanderbilts, Rockefellers and Whitneys, although his wealth was never in the same class as their fortunes. He took great pleasure in owning the train. After a hard day at the office, Block could walk from his apartment on Park Avenue to Grand Central Station and board at 5:30 PM for an overnight trip to Chicago. He would dine with friends, relatives, and associates, catch a well-deserved night's sleep, and awake to a breakfast of fresh strawberries and filet of sole. He would find his newspaper under the door. His trousers and jacket would be neatly pressed. It was an elegant way to travel, and Block was proud of it.

Friendship was usually attached to the 20th Century Limited, which the New York Central Railroad called "the greatest train in the world." By the 1920s, the Century was running regularly in several sections of the country. Trains such as the Century ushered in a feature that made the luxury "limited" trains possible: they had safe vestibules that enabled passengers to cross safely and comfortably from one car to another. Paul Block and his guests could easily stroll the length of the train to the bar, lounge or dining car, if they preferred to eat there. They were no longer confined just to his private car.[22]

The Century had a reputation for always being on time. Paul Block would instruct his office boys to take any Chicago-bound mail over to Grand Central Station and post it in the mailbox of the Century, which was open until a few minutes before its departure. The mail was sorted en route, and it invariably arrived before the Post Office's air mail service.

The Century and The Broadway Limited were intense rivals. They were both on identical schedules, and for several miles just outside of Chicago, they ran on adjoining tracks. When they ran alongside each other, passengers on both trains couldn't help being at least a little nervous, as well as excited: the trains averaged 60 mph for nearly 1,000 miles, and would thunder inches apart as they raced each other. These were the fastest trains in the world, and they reduced the running time to Chicago from 20 hours to 18 hours, then to 16 hours.

But they were not the only great trains running during the 1920s and

'30s. Paul Block had Friendship attached to whichever of the grand trains was traveling to the destination he wanted to visit. He used the Panama Limited, which went right down the middle of the country to New Orleans. The Havana Special went across Florida to Key West, where it made connections to boats steaming to Havana. Block frequently used The Super Chief, run by the Santa Fe Railroad, for trips to California to visit William Randolph Hearst's castle, San Simeon. It took only 39 hours and 40 minutes between Chicago and the West Coast.[23] Once there, Friendship would slide in to Hearst's own railroad siding, which had been built to run from the perimeter of his ranch.

Friendship was Paul Block's dream. He cherished the private railroad car for the luxury and the glamour it brought him. It enabled him to meet and forge strong relationships with business people and with celebrities, and by traveling comfortably it provided him with a new way of looking at things. His guests were from the world of entertainment, such as Maurice Chevalier; great newspaper editors such as Arthur Brisbane and Edmond Coblentz; and people such as Jimmy Walker from the political arena. All of them reveled in the beauty, comfort and splendor of Friendship. And Block reveled in their companionship.[24]

FRIENDSHIP –
Block's Connecticut Estate

Just as Block was always arriving and departing on Friendship, a part of him also wanted to be anchored, and to have a home where he could dream in peace; a mini-San Simeon, where he could also entertain and rejuvenate himself and others.

In 1926, Paul Block bought a 186-acre estate in Greenwich, Connecticut, an exclusive bedroom community north and a bit east of New York City. He had been shown the estate by his friend Bernard Gimbel, who lived quite near in a grand country house of his own, called Chieftains. Gimbel was one of the brothers who owned Gimbel's Department Store (the store that Macy's "wouldn't tell," a line from a longtime advertisement between the rival companies), and the retailer had long done business with Block, placing advertisements in several of the newspapers that Block owned or represented. The men had become good friends, and one weekend, when Block was visiting Gimbel's suburban estate, Gimbel told him that land bordering his was for sale.

They visited it together, and Block was extremely impressed. The large Colonial house was built on a gentle hill, giving it an excellent view of the countryside.[25] Standing on the porch, you could see the surrounding woods and fields all the way down to the Long Island Sound. On days with good visibility the panorama was exceptionally beautiful, with a view that extended five or six miles.

Block had never lived in a suburb; at that time, he and Dina were living in Manhattan at the very elegant Hotel Pierre. His idea was to have a country home for weekends and other times, and to maintain his and Dina's Manhattan apartment. Since they had two young sons, a change in lifestyle seemed like a good idea. Business was extraordinarily profitable, Block's holdings were becoming more substantive and he believed it was an opportune time to make a major real estate investment. He and Dina were shown the house, the extensive grounds, and the rest of the buildings on the property. It was considerably more extensive than what she was sure she wanted, but Block was enthusiastic, and Dina fearfully agreed to the purchase. Because it was not a new house, Block humorously reassured Dina that all of the troubles that a new house might have developed were already solved.

The land extended almost a mile along King Street, then back through wooded land to the Byram River. Block purchased it for $350,000 on May 17, 1926 from Tillie S. Jaretzki, the wife of a wealthy lawyer. In a promissory note, he agreed to pay the balance of the mortgage to Mrs. Jaretzki in five payments, ending January 1, 1929.[26]

Although he took title in 1926, Block was years away from moving in with his family. He began to develop the property and turn it into much, much more than just a gracious home. He wanted to create a showplace and a refuge, a place of quiet and calm which he ranked in importance along with good health. The new residence, a red brick three-story mansion with a slate roof, was inviting and gracious. Its window frames were painted white, as were the balconies outside several of the upper rooms. Four tall white columns graced the front porch. Dina set about coordinating the redecorating and furnishing.

Meanwhile, Block began making profound changes to his property. During the next few years, he spent a million dollars on improvements. When he purchased it, the land had been graded in three levels, with the house at the high point, then sloping gently down to fairly flat ground. The house was surrounded by a series of gardens, beginning with the rose garden; on the next lower level were the formal gardens, arranged in what was for that time an unusually modern style, with walks and convenient resting places.[27]

Block had a tennis court built, adjoining the formal gardens. He commissioned the design and construction of a nine-hole golf course. Near that he installed a swimming pool, with two bathhouses. Then he hired an Olympic swimmer (who had worked for the Zeigfeld Follies) to be the swimming instructor. William Block, Paul Block's younger son, recalls that she taught him how to dive, which he made reluctant attempts at mastering.

Block spent $75,000 putting in a water system, including Artesian wells and four pumping stations. He redid the 12-room farm house, where his newly acquired farmhands lived. There were also two small cottages on the estate, as well as a cattle barn and an ice house.

Dina Block, with the assistance of her interior decorators, turned the main house into an impressive home. It was designed for company, because Block intended to use it to entertain colleagues, business associates, and political acquaintances, as well as his friends. The mansion was imposing. It had four main rooms on the first floor, six bedrooms and six bathrooms on the second, and four rooms and four bathrooms on the third floor. There were also ten servants' rooms.[28]

Dina followed the convention of making the house look something like an English country home, with leather furniture in the library and a large, formal living and dining room. The bright and capacious sun porch, though, was done completely in the opposite vein. With tall glass French doors opening onto the lawn, this high-ceilinged, slate-floored room was airy and spacious, filled with plants that thrived on the light. It was intended for casual meals – usually breakfasts and lunches. Dinners were always held in the very formal dining room. As she had with the train, Dina made the house the reflection of her personality, as much as or even more than Block's.

It wasn't until early 1929 that Block and his family moved completely into their Greenwich home, although they had been visiting it on weekends since 1928. Once again, he selected the name "Friendship," this time as the name for his new house. He didn't originate the name. Block had often visited the home of Ned McLean, owner of the *Washington Post*. (McLean's wife owned the Hope Diamond.) It was a huge mansion on Connecticut Avenue in Washington, D.C., and McLean had named it "Friendship." Block loved the name, and adopted it for his own home. It symbolized his feeling about his relationship with virtually everyone he worked and dealt with.

As soon as the building, renovation and decorating of his estate were finished, Block began to use it as a focal point for entertaining, which he did frequently. There were guests for cocktails, lunch and dinner, and friends were invited to stay for a weekend or longer. Dina Block ran the house, supervised the large staff, and managed the running of the estate. She commented years later that it was an enormous enterprise, and a difficult burden on a woman.[29]

The house was large enough, and busy enough, to require two chambermaids who spent all of their time doing nothing but cleaning it. There was also a laundress, a gardener, and several farmers, since part of the acreage was used as farmland. The greenhouses were used to grow vegetables as well as flowers. But Block was careful to retain a good amount of woodland, where his visitors – and family – could go for leisurely walks. The estate was noted for having a number of valuable, beautiful trees scattered about, including a particularly magnificent copper beech tree.[30]

Paul Block traveled much of the time. When he was home at Friendship, the estate was a place to relax with friends. Mayor Jimmy Walker visited frequently. In short order, he began to use Block's house, clandestinely, to entertain and spend time with his then-mistress Betty Compton, although William Block does not recall this as a fact and disputes it. The Mayor would often arrive late, after the children were in bed, and he'd be gone in the morning before they arose. In case of an emergency, only his closest confidants knew how to reach him. When asked about his whereabouts by the press, Walker would often claim, with a sheepish grin, that he was walking from appointment to appointment and therefore could not be contacted.[31]

On November 4, 1928, just after arriving at Friendship to spend an evening discussing the upcoming national elections with Block, Walker received a call from one of his aides that the gambler-gangster Arnold Rothstein, one of the most prominent criminals in New York, had been shot in the Park Central Hotel in Manhattan, and had been rushed to Polyclinic Hospital. The names of Walker and Rothstein had been linked for years and it was believed that Rothstein was the connection between Tammany Hall politicos and the underworld; further, rumor had it that it was Rothstein who had selected Walker to be the Mayor of New York City and had influenced the Tammany machine to put his name forth as a nominee. In a matter of minutes, Walker had Block's chauffeur drive him back to Manhattan to visit Rothstein. Two days later the gangster was dead, by coincidence just as the national election results came in. Herbert

Hoover – much to Block's delight – was swept into the White House.
Hoover defeated Block's other friend, Al Smith.

In the days that followed Rothstein's murder, there was much talk and
rumor about the fact that Jimmy Walker was doing little to capture the
killer of his friend ... perhaps because he knew the assailant personally.
Will Rogers, who was temporarily off the lecture circuit, on loan from the
Ziegfeld Follies, was starring as King Pompanola in the Caldwell-Burnside
comedy, *Three Cheers*. He adlibbed every night about whatever news
story tickled his fancy ("I only know what I read in the papers.") Rogers
was relentless about the murder, telling his audience that Mayor Walker
was so busy with his "other activities" (read Betty Compton) that he simply did not have time to solve the case.

Walker sent word to Will Rogers at the Globe Theater, through his press
secretary, that the comedian should "lay off" him, which only made Rogers
all that more diligent in mentioning the case every night.

Although Block had not seen the show, he heard of Rogers' diatribe,
and he wrote an editorial that he published in his *Newark Star-Eagle* and
Brooklyn Standard-Union (and in space that he purchased in *The New
York Times*), taking issue with the cowboy philosopher. Block wrote that
it was unfair and distasteful of Will Rogers to jibe at not only Jimmy
Walker but all prominent men and public officials who had their reputations to uphold.

That diverted Rogers' scathing wit from Walker to Block, himself.
During every performance of the day that Block's editorials ran, Rogers
lambasted Block from the stage of the Globe Theater:

> "Mr. Block is mad at me ... He's printing pieces in the
> papers about how awful it is for me to make cracks about our
> prominent men ... Of course, I've never said anything about
> Mr. Block ... not a word until tonight ... But I would if I had
> known how bad he wanted it ... And I promise to say some-
> thing about him the first time he comes to this theater ... That
> ought to put him back in good humor again ... He asks what
> right do I have to make light of the names of the mighty?
> Course he's talking about Jimmy Walker. There ain't no-
> body but me and Jimmy should be slower to get mad at each
> other ... We both make our living by kidding the public."[32]

Block never again went up against Will Rogers, "America's most complete human document," as Damon Runyon called him. Rogers was a

man of words and ideas; he had an x-ray view of the sociology of America and its people. Within a short while, Block insisted that Rogers and he should not allow politics to interfere with their friendship. When Rogers was killed in an airplane accident in 1935, Paul Block was one of the few close friends who were invited to a private memorial for the philosopher cowboy. "Into the tiny church came Will's old friends," remembered Rogers's wife Betty. "Every person in every pew was a comrade, an intimate, an old tried friend."[33]

To a large degree, Block used his estate, Friendship, as an extension of his work. There, he entertained his customers and advertisers, as well as other publishers and their editors, just as he did on his private railroad car. He threw parties for his employees, many of them around the swimming pool, which was dotted with a group of small cabanas. When there were guests for dinner, Paul held forth in the formal dining room. These were mostly adult affairs. If the children were present, they were expected to be quiet and well-mannered – respectfully silent.

Paul Block enrolled his sons into the prestigious Hotchkiss preparatory school in Lakeville, Connecticut. From that point on, he was constant in his support of the school. Block contributed to the building of dormitories, and donated a moving picture machine for the students. He gave $500 to the employees of the school, and told them to dispense it among themselves. Because of his association with Richard Byrd, Block invited the Admiral to speak at commencement exercises; and Byrd donated the flag he had erected at the North Pole. When Block's eldest son, Paul Jr., graduated from Hotchkiss, Block gave the school a $100,000 gift for the building of a new chapel.[34]

Later, the two boys went on to attend Yale, and Block then began to make major contributions to that University. He donated $100,000 in 1930 for a program of studies in the field of journalism, to promote an understanding of the press as a major enterprise and as a powerful factor in human affairs. An important part of the program was the establishment of a series of lectures by men prominent in the newspaper field, such as Colonel Robert C. McCormick, publisher of *The Chicago Tribune*. In addition to giving lectures, they would be available for conferences with the students and for collaboration in courses on the press. Yale University named the program "The Block Foundation," in Paul Block's honor.[35]

Block regretted that he did not spend as much time with his sons as he would have preferred: traveling and business often kept him away. In a study of the correspondence from Block to his two sons, he appears to have been a concerned, overly-solicitous father; whether this affection and interest went beyond the bounds of the written word is difficult to know, although it is altogether likely: William Block remembers that his father was warm, caring and affectionate.

Sometimes Block dined alone with Dina, excluding the boys, perhaps because of his preoccupation with business.[36] "We really never said much," recalled Peter Liveright, Block's nephew and a frequent guest at Friendship. "Uncle Paul would preside at the head of the table and talk about all manner of things and we'd just sit, and sit, and sit...and listen."[37]

But Block cared for his boys, and fostered their interests. He had a darkroom and a chemistry laboratory built for Paul, Jr., to encourage his son's hobbies. Billy, in addition to swimming lessons, was given his own horse, and he learned how to ride quite well. He became so adept that he was entered into a horse show, but the mare was so intransigent that Billy was thrown, although not seriously hurt. The boys also became beneficiaries of their father's early interest in moving pictures. Block had a "Projection Room" built, with two film projectors. A large screen and a loudspeaker were placed in the adjoining Bar Room. On scheduled occasions a professional projectionist would come over from nearby White Plains to screen first-run movies, supplied by Block's friend Adolph Zukor, and Block's contacts with 20th Century Fox and Metro-Goldwyn-Mayer. The family and the ever-present guests watched such films as Chaplin's *City Lights*, *All Quiet on the Western Front*, and *The Front Page*, in addition to scores of Busby Berkeley 1930s musicals and any comedies that starred the Marx Brothers.

In retrospect, William Block theorized that his father bought the large estate and equipped it with the pool, the tennis courts, the golf course and other sporting and entertainment pleasures because, being Jewish, Block knew that neither he nor his children would have been allowed access to any of the exclusive country clubs nearby. With his own estate and his many parties, in effect he created his own country club.[38]

Bernard Gimbel, who had first introduced Block to the Greenwich area, was delighted that they became neighbors. To both their surprise, some time after Block had purchased the property a local real estate agent approached him, claiming that it was his company that had first presented the estate as a property for sale. Block disagreed; he contended that he had first learned from Gimbel of the estate's availability. In fact, Block had signed a sales agreement with the original owner, saying that if there were any real estate commissions involved in his purchase of the estate, she would pay them. The real estate dealer demonstrated that he had written Block a letter, which Block had forgotten about and not acted upon. Not satisfied, the real estate company sued.

Block managed to get the case postponed for seven years. When he asked for yet a further delay, the judge said, "Absolutely not; this has been going on too long already." So in court, Block, who had been representing himself, asked for a two-hour lunch break. That time, the judge approved his request. Block contacted Max Steuer, the brilliant criminal lawyer who had represented the owners in the scandalous Triangle Shirt Factory fire (and succeeded in having them acquitted), and asked the man to represent him. Steuer rushed from Manhattan up to the courthouse in Greenwich, walked in, conferred with Block *en passant*, and asked the judge if all the parties could meet with him in his chambers. Again the judge agreed. Steuer presented Paul Block's compromise suggestion that the fee be split three ways; Block was willing to pay a third, he proposed that the original owner pay a third, and suggested that the real estate company drop its claim by one third. Amazingly, all parties acceded, and the case was amicably resolved that afternoon.

When the amount of commission was tallied by thirds, however, there was an amount of a few hundred-odd dollars left over. "Judge, is it alright if we toss for it?" asked Block brazenly, looking at the real estate agent to see if he would agree. "It's alright with me," stated the judge, probably delighted to a denouement of the case after so many years. The real estate agent flipped the coin, and Block won. Although he had to pay several thousand dollars in commissions, Block was delighted and satisfied with the irony of his small victory.

Paul Block continued to live at his Connecticut estate for the rest of his life, even as his sons grew up and moved away. Returning to Friendship after a day at his office or after a several-week business trip, it was his seat of peace, his place of reflection, and most of all the locus point for the multiple relationships that were intrinsic to his business success, and his happiness.

Newark Star-Eagle – 1929-1934

Over the next seven or eight years, Block made few changes in the personnel policies of the *Newark Star-Eagle*, and his workers universally loved him. But things started getting difficult when the stock market crashed on Black Tuesday, October 29, 1929, a day of unparalleled frenzy that plunged the nation into hopelessness. Almost instantly, the jobless rate in some cities reached over 50 percent; two million Americans wandered the country as vagrants; even Babe Ruth took a $10,000 salary cut.[39] The last thing Block wanted to do was to let people go from the paper, but prospects looked bleak.

By 1934, the *Newark Star-Eagle's* circulation had begun to drop, and advertising revenues were down by 20 percent. Block began searching for answers as to how he could keep the paper going, and readily grasped at whatever straw offered a solution. While on a trip to England in July of that year, he met the famed newspaper mogul Lord Beaverbrook. At first, Block was not impressed with the make-up and layout of Beaverbrook's *London Daily Express*. Each morning, however, Block saw how the London public was eagerly snapping the *Express* off the newsstands, and scanning the front page as they walked to their jobs or rode to work in the Underground or on the double-decker buses. "When I first saw the *Express*," Block said when he returned to the United States, "I thought the British should come over here and learn how to make up a newspaper. After about a week of reading the *Express*, however, I decided that we should go there for the same purpose."[40] One of the major differences between Beaverbrook's *Express* and most American newspapers was that almost every story on the front page was self-contained, condensed to an irreducible minimum of facts so that the stories did not "jump," or continue, to an inside page. This technique is the hallmark of *USA TODAY*; the two newspapers are similar in other ways, as well. In effect, the *Express* was sixty years in advance of its time. The reader could read the whole story, as given, without turning a page, and scan the day's news quickly and easily. There were other differences from contemporary newspapers, as well: the headlines in the *Express* were livelier and often contained alliteration, puns and occasional sensational doggerel. Beaverbrook also ran a minimum of three photographs on his front page, but Block was already doing that with the *Star-Eagle*. Block liked what he saw in the *Express*, and aside from its ribald non-conformity, which he felt went somewhat too far, he decided to adopt some of its techniques for the *Newark Star-Eagle*, hoping that a change of appearance might bolster circulation and advertising. When he learned that William Randolph Hearst had also been impressed with the success that Beaverbrook was achieving through the format, and had decided to change all of his morning papers throughout the United States to conform to a more lively style,

Block felt even more confident in making an appearance change in *his* paper. The changes that he would put into effect at the *Newark Star-Eagle,* he announced, would be permanent, and would also serve as a test as to whether to introduce the format changes to the other publications with which he was involved.[41]

When the new *Newark Star-Eagle* was printed in the early afternoon of October 31, 1934, Paul Block waited impatiently in the pressroom and stood at the foot of the folding machine as the first copies came rippling off the press. He carefully examined what he had wrought. In the history of publishing, it was the most startling alteration and drastic change of a major American newspaper in such a short space of time. The newspaper was barely recognizable from the day before: the traditional logo, *"Newark Star-Eagle,"* which had been emblazoned on the front page for almost two decades, had been re-designed so that the word *"Newark"* was greatly reduced in size and the words *"Star"* and *"Eagle"* were made larger. Only two front-page stories jumped to the inside, one on a labor dispute among chain stores that was being mediated in Washington, and the other on how two Newarkers had won $75,000 in a lottery. Other stories, such as the selection of the Bruno Hauptman jury in the trial of the kidnapping of Charles Lindbergh, Jr., or an editorial criticizing President Roosevelt's welfare reforms, were boxed and stood alone without continuing on to another page. New type faces were used and the paper bought 15 new fonts of type, all in the Century family, for the makeover. Coincident with the drastic innovation in layout was Block's change of paper stock. Instead of the flat white 32-pound weight newsprint that the *Star-Eagle* had been using, Block switched to a heavier and better grade of paper, 35-pound, and had it slightly tinted in pink; the difference in cost was not substantial. According to Block, his decision to use a subdued color instead of white had two rationales: it made the newspaper more noticeable and distinctive on the newsstand, and he had learned of a study that indicated that using a color made reading easier under artificial light.

Block hired several different editors and make-up men to help introduce the change more easily. One problem became evident immediately, however: the clever headline-writers and truncators of stories in the *London Daily Express* had had a lifetime, or at least decades, to learn their craft; it was much more difficult than Block had expected to re-train his staff to write sharp-witted story heads, and to condense articles so that they still made sense, were accurate, contained all the facts, and were entertaining. The whole process of sharpening and shortening stories and their headlines seemed inconsistent with what the *Newark Star-Eagle* editors had been doing for years.

An impromptu survey of readers, conducted at newsstands during the first few days of the changeover, suggested that Block may have blundered. Some readers felt positive about the change but others were sharply opposed to it, claiming that they wanted their "old" *Newark Star-Eagle* back and that the new pink concoction had a certain undignified air about it, almost as though it was a variation of the *Police Gazette*, a sensational periodical which had also been published on colored paper stock. On his desk, Block kept placing back-copies of the old *Star-Eagle* next to the newly-designed paper and comparing them. To him, the new paper looked "more newsy, more sparkling and better in every way."[42] He realized, however, that his readers were disagreeing with him. "Habit is a very difficult thing to overcome," he wrote.[43] Block showed integrity and a respect for those who regularly read the *Star-Eagle* when he decided to publish in a subsequent issue a series of letters from readers *on the front page*, denouncing the change. He then spent the entire weekend working with layout people and editors trying to "calm down the paper considerably."[44]

Not so ironically – since Block was copying him – Beaverbrook felt that the *Star-Eagle*'s new look was a great improvement. He wrote to Block from London:

> A change of that kind requires courage and is inevitably an anxious period for those responsible, as well as an interesting one.
>
> We are watching the *Newark Star-Eagle* very closely. But our interest is not merely parental.
>
> We are learning something from your newspapers. You may have taken our form, but you have modeled it into something that is an improvement on our own use of it.
>
> So now we are modeling ourselves on the *Newark Star-Eagle*.
>
> Your sincerely,
>
> Beaverbrook

In the midst of all the turmoil, Block signed a lease on a new apartment on the second floor of 400 Park Avenue, at the corner of 54th Street, and made plans to move in on Election Day. It was a prestige building and one of the best addresses in New York City, but he had wanted a higher floor. Nothing else was available, however, in his preferred building and he was committed to staying south of 57th Street...so he could walk to and from the office every day.

It took Block only a few days to acknowledge that the *Newark Star-Eagle* experiment was having disastrous results. With circulation hemorrhaging – perhaps because old-time readers didn't recognize the paper, or didn't approve of its new look – Block admitted his mistake and reverted to the original format of the *Newark Star-Eagle* which everyone in the city seemed to know and, if not love, at least prefer.

The Newark Bears –
Block's Baseball Team

Paul Block was in love with the national pastime of baseball. British historians have said that the battle of Waterloo was won on the playing fields of Eton. For Block, the corporate strength of America, and his own executive ability, rose from the dust of back lots and high school baseball stadiums. He had managed the varsity baseball team at the Elmira Free Academy, and helped Harry S. Brooks in the management of the *Elmira Telegram* team. What he had learned in those early years about sportsmanship, camaraderie, and competition became the foundation for much of the success in his adult life. When he moved to New York, Block attended as many major and minor league games as he could, followed the joys and agonies of the progress of New York teams, and used long leisurely afternoons at Yankee Stadium for his own enjoyment, as well as for both his social and business obligations. He would have liked to have owned a New York baseball team but he didn't have the kind of large cash reserves that it would have taken. He discussed his love of baseball and the city of Newark in a lead editorial in the *Star-Eagle* as early as January 2, 1925:

> The Newark baseball club of the International League is supposed to be for sale, and most fans ardently hope that another season will not pass under the conditions that have prevailed for several years.
>
> Just now the club is even without a playing field. It has been weakened by the sale of players, and the uncertainty about grounds combined with the unsatisfactory management makes the outlook very gloomy. All baseball fans like to

> engage in pipe dreams during the baseball months, but there
> is mighty little material for pleasant dreams in the local base-
> ball situation.
>
> In the meantime Walter Johnson, outstanding figure in the
> national sport and one of the biggest drawing cards, is look-
> ing around with the idea of buying a baseball club somewhere.
> Walter has the brains and temperament suitable to the man-
> agement of a big league club, but he lacks enough money to
> swing a deal alone. Several Newark men with money to spare
> have shown indications a time or two that they may be inter-
> ested in acquiring the Newark franchise. Wouldn't Newark
> capital and Walter Johnson make a wonderful combination
> in the management of the Newark ball club?

Johnson made attempts to raise money for a Newark team, but nothing came to fruition. Then, at the height of Block's prosperity at the *Newark Star-Eagle*, Johnson hit a metaphorical home run: he convinced Block himself to take over the team.

On September 8, 1927, Paul Block purchased the Greater Newark Base-ball Club, known as the Newark Bears, at a receiver's auction sale for $360,000. Magnanimously, he also agreed to assume the obligation of paying back $147,040 to the Citizens Committee of Newark, which had contributed the money when the club was involved in financial difficulty. The tie-in with the *Newark Star-Eagle* seemed more than natural. Block would provide a community service, give his newspaper direct access to news and features about the team and be engaged in a pursuit of pleasure that he enjoyed all of his life. The practicality of ownership may also have been a major factor in Block's decision to buy the Bears. He was quoted as saying at the time, "Since baseball profits are a byproduct of the newspapers, a newspaper might as well own the team."[45] Paul Block's son, William Block, Sr., believes that his father's decision to buy the team really had nothing to do with the paper, however: "He was such a great baseball fan and hero worshiper that he loved the idea of owning a base-ball team."[46]

The city of Newark had had an eventful and colorful baseball history. The Eastern League began in 1884 and Newark won the championship flag in 1886, beating Baltimore of the American Association in a minor league World Series. In 1887, Newark found itself in new company with six clubs from the New York State League of 1885. The Bears seemed to be spiraling downward and were last in a curtailed race of 1899; because of lackluster attendance the league was disbanded on June 13, 1900. A new era in Newark baseball began in 1902 with Walter Burham looking after the finance and management of the club. The Bears still finished last but they made some money. Burham controlled the club through 1908 and then he sold out to some businessmen from Illinois, and when they grew weary of a team without profits, some investors from Brooklyn took charge. Brooklyn produced a real club in 1913 and won the International League pennant.

Federal League competition drove the Bears out of Newark in 1915. The Bears were back in 1916, 1917, 1918 and 1919 with different leaders, different owners but not particularly different results. Then they moved to Syracuse, New York in 1920, leaving Newark without any baseball team of their own. In 1921, the Akron, Ohio franchise moved into Syracuse and the Bears found themselves homeless, so they briefly settled in Providence, Rhode Island. In 1926, Charles A. David brought the team back to Newark and built it a new ball field named after himself, David Stadium, and the Bears were finally back in the International League. The team led the league in attendance that year.[47] However, in 1927, everything appeared dark and dismal for the Bears and their fans when Charles David inexplicably decided to sell the team.

A chapter in sports history that was unprecedented in baseball was about to take place when Paul Block bought his own professional baseball team. Not only did he buy the club and save baseball in Newark, but he also reimbursed, with interest, the fans who had contributed to the club when it was owned by Charles A. David. In a statement issued to *The New York Times* at the time of the purchase, Block went back to his roots and his heart: "All my life, I have been interested in baseball. The greatest thrills I ever got out of the game were when I used to go back to my old hometown in Elmira, New York and would go to the ball game and see hundreds of youngsters waiting at the gate, hoping that somehow they would get in. You can bet I saw to it that they got in. To see them run through the gate looked better to me than seeing Ruth or Gehrig hit four home runs in one game."[48]

Owning the Bears became much more than just a financial investment for Paul Block. He was fulfilling a boyhood dream. He had his own baseball team now and it was not going to be just another minor league team. He wanted it to be a team of which he, and the fans of Newark, would be proud. He wanted the best group of players that his money could buy and he would only settle for the best. Like another baseball entrepreneur of contemporary times, George Steinbrenner, Paul Block did things in a big way.

Four months after he bought the Bears, in January, 1928, Block quietly went to Washington, D.C. and signed Walter Johnson as manager/player. Fans, players, and owners of other baseball teams were all shocked. Johnson was one of the greatest pitchers the game has ever known, the player who had more shut-outs than any other pitcher in history (110), a record that stands to this day. In 1907, when playing for the majors, his overpowering fastball accounted for a record-breaking eighty-six consecutive scoreless innings.[49] The seasoned Ty Cobb, one of the great hitters in baseball, once said that the most terrifying experience in baseball was playing Washington on a cloudy day with Johnson pitching: you just couldn't see the ball, it was so lightning swift. Grantland Rice, the distinguished sportswriter, described Johnson's pitching style as "a full, smooth, half side-arm that sent the ball on its way like a bullet."[50] Johnson had wanted the Bears, and now he had the opportunity. The signing of Walter Johnson was of such moment that when President Calvin Coolidge read about it in the papers, he sent Block a letter of congratulations. Then came signings of other players of big league caliber: Jacques Fournier who was regarded as one of the best slugging first basemen, and Hugh McQuilian and Al Mamaux. Block then turned his attention to spring training camp.

That January, Block was also involved in another surprising announcement concerning baseball. He had been approached by a representative of the Brooklyn Robins, one of the best minor league teams in New York, to see whether he would be interested in purchasing the team. As he was known to be acquiring newspapers, it was thought that perhaps he would also start buying up baseball teams. New York Mayor Jimmy Walker, who was being talked about as the next president of the American League, was mentioned as a possible partner of Block in an attempt to buy the team. A reporter of *The New York Times* interviewed Block to confirm the rumor. "It is true," said Block, "that I have been asked whether I would be interested in the purchase of the Robins as an associate with Mayor Walker. To this I answered that I would be very much interested."

As it developed, the two owners of the Robins, Steve McKeever, and the estate of Charles H. Ebbets (of Ebbets Field fame) could not come to an agreement on the price or terms of the sale. The Ebbets estate wanted to sell, but McKeever was intransigent about even considering it. "I will never sell my share. Baseball is my life hobby, and I propose to remain in it as long as I live," he declared.[51]

Block had his heart set on a pennant, so he did everything in his power to land a flag for the city of Newark. Although the Bears were a minor league team, Block ran it on a major league scale. He spent money lavishly for players and sent his team to spring training camp in Florida on cruise ships, then put them up in the best hotels, and bought them the best equipment available. To the players it was like going on vacation. They stayed at the fabulous Ponce de Leon Hotel in St. Augustine and basked in the sun; a trip to the beach was almost mandatory to test the warm Florida waters. The spring training home ball park was small, with a capacity of only 1,000, but it proved to be an elixir for the players who had never been treated as well as they were by Block. For years, this was the training spot of big league teams like the New York Giants and the Cincinnati Reds, and the cachet seemed to inspire the newly re-vitalized Bears. Things were running smoothly and looked more than promising for the reborn team. Then Block began to have difficulties.

Walter Johnson, who was signed as a player/manager, was preparing to lead his first minor league club when he became ill. In February, 1928, he came down with a bad case of the flu. Although not fully recovered, he made the two-hour drive from Daytona Beach, where his family spent the winter, to St. Augustine to open the Bears's training camp. Fighting a fever for the next two weeks, Johnson tried to manage the team and practice. He would work out briefly, throw a few pitches and then grow weary. In an exhibition game with the New York Giants, Johnson grew pale and weak. Block, devastated that he might lose his star attraction, called upon Dr. Harry Kaufman, the Washington Nationals' team physician. Kaufman traveled down to Florida immediately but could not determine the cause of Johnson's illness. He advised that Johnson check into the Riverside Hospital in Jacksonville, Florida where an examination found both kidneys badly infected. His condition deteriorated and Johnson asked Dr. Kaufman if he could go home to Washington, D.C.[52] Dr. Kaufman agreed. Just being home was a tonic in itself and his condition improved dramatically. Johnson had narrowly escaped death. Cheered by a flow of letters and telegrams from his adoring fans, he began to recover but he would have to remain hospitalized for almost two months. Until then, Paul Block had to look to the Bears's coach, George McBride, to replace Johnson while he recuperated. Other than that, the team was healthy and Block was optimistic as they made their way back north to Newark to start the season.

Opening day, April 18, 1928, marked not only the start of the baseball season: it was an important social event for the city of Newark. Block was feeling especially bullish and proud, not only because it was his team but as it happened, just a few weeks previously, the stock market had its busiest day in history (on March 28, 1928) and most of his holdings had experienced gains as blue-chip issues reached an all-time high.

Naturally, he had his *Newark Star Eagle* provide the baseball event unprecedented coverage, and he distributed a 36-page special edition on the Bears; the game also made banner headlines in New York papers, as well. Much like opening games today, it was a day full of celebrities and political dignitaries. Boxer Jack Dempsey was in attendance, as were Block's friends New York Mayor Jimmy Walker and Governor Al Smith, who was campaigning for President against Herbert Hoover. The Mayor of Newark, Thomas L. Raymond was also on hand and all of the dignitaries sat with Block in his private box. Walter Johnson's wife, Hazel, and their 12-year-old son, Walter Jr., represented the recovering manager who was still in the hospital, and she threw out the first ball. Mamaux pitched a splendid three-hitter and Jocko Conlan homered for the Bears.

There were no less than seven bands that paraded all over the ballpark prior to the singing of the "Star Spangled Banner" and the opening pitch. Floral pieces were strewn in the infield near home plate. Block thought of everything to make the contest a memorable day. The afternoon turned out to be one of the major highlights in the history of all minor league baseball. During the seventh inning "stretch," Mayor Walker spoke over the radio – the game was broadcast – and wished Walter Johnson "a speedy recovery."

When the chalk-line dust cleared, the Bears had shut out the Toronto Leafs by a score of 6-0. And, in a matter of hours, by the end of the day, the baseball buzz was back in Newark. Walter Johnson was scheduled to return on April 28. Three hundred fans met him at the railroad station to greet him and his family. Back on the job, wearing a suit, a heavy coat and a hat instead of a uniform, Johnson sat in the dug-out watching the Bears lose to Buffalo, the 1927 league champions. The Bears left the next day on an 18-day road trip but their manager stayed behind to continue his recovery. By May 14, 1928, Johnson was back to normal and took charge of the club when they played in Rochester.[53]

"Walter Johnson Day," the brain child of Paul Block, took place on June 23, 1928, and was a star-studded affair with a motorcade through downtown Newark, ending at the ball park with gifts and tributes. In its first year under the helm of Paul Block, Newark finished seventh with an 81–84 win-loss record, 10 games behind champion Rochester.[54] Though this was an excellent result for a minor league team, Block was disappointed with the record – but not with the attendance: some 300,000 fans, more than for any other team in the International League, came out to support the Newark Bears, regardless of its record and the Bears's place in the standings. Their attendance was profitable for Block, but he rewarded Newark far in excess of their team loyalty. Block's generosity to Newark was enormous. He gave tickets to thousands of school children to come and see the games. The Bears's franchise created revenue for the city, and most of all gave the people longed-for hope and plenty of dreams of games to come. Block had saved baseball for Newark and had become something of a local hero.

The Bears's 1928 season did not go by without further difficulties. Paul Block had tried to buy himself a championship, picking up former major league stars at tremendous salaries for the minor leagues. Unfortunately, in addition to a wealth of proven talent, some of the players that he had purchased came with a certain resentment at having fallen to the minor league level. The two biggest headaches on the team were "Goodtime" Bill Lamar and "Handsome" Hugh McQuilian, who were both out of shape when they arrived in Newark and seemed to have no regard for training rules. They were just plain lazy. Block had invested a great deal of money in these players and their ennui was a major disappointment. Walter Johnson was also unhappy with himself for not getting rid of them before they could affect the team morale. The 1928 season had ended with more bad news. The Washington Nationals wanted Walter Johnson back to manage their team for the 1929 season. Clark Griffith, the Nationals owner, approached Block to secure Johnson's release from Newark. Reluctantly, Block agreed. "It had been my hope that Walter Johnson remain in Newark for many years," he lamented.[55] Tris Speaker, the talented outfielder whose major league career had just ended in Philadelphia, would take the helm. A player who had averaged .344 – one of the highest in baseball – over a 22-year span, he replaced Johnson as the coach for the Newark Bears.

Tris Speaker, like Johnson, was another great player who years later was named to baseball's Hall of Fame. Through his superlative hitting, Speaker had scored an enormous number of runs in his career, just behind Lou Gehrig's record. Hiring him was yet another bold move by Block to give his Bears credibility. Speaker retained Jack Onslow, an excellent baseball coach from the St. Louis Cardinals, to assist him.[56] Unfortunately for Block and the fans of Newark, Speaker could not deliver a championship team and the Bears dropped to seventh place in the standings. Nevertheless the Newark fans kept coming to the games. It was their hometown team and nothing seemed to dampen the Newarkers enthusiasm for the Bears.

Paul Block was a perceptive and effusive owner, but although he was paying high salaries to his star players, they did not display much loyalty. He had given Walter Johnson a great chance to prove his leadership skills and he also supported him during his illness, but all Block received in return was what he considered disloyalty when Johnson went back to Washington. Johnson never really gave Block and the Newark Bears a second thought. Good faith seemed to never enter Johnson's mind. Although Block thought that Johnson himself would win 15-20 games on the mound, he only pitched once. Tris Speaker quit mid-way during the 1930 season and had to give way to Al Mamaux.

Al Mamaux, who had been a pitcher for the Brooklyn Dodgers and the Pittsburgh Pirates, was well-liked by Block and the feeling was mutual. Mamaux was, in fact, a 25-game winner for the Bears in 1927, many of them in seven straight innings in the second game of a double-header. In the 1928 season under Johnson, he was hit by a line drive back to the mound and developed an infection and was out for nine weeks. In spite of this obstacle, he still contributed 15 victories. Mamaux was a gamer, and a true athlete, respected by his teammates and opposing players as well. When he took over as manager on June 28, 1928, the Bears were in seventh place. Mamaux had never managed a team before but he seemed to rise to the opportunity given him by Block. The players started hustling and playing together as a team should. Mamaux showed them the possibilities of winning and fanned their desire to work harder to win. The Bears climbed up the ladder and finished in fifth place. The fans, who had not given up faith, now really started to believe. Paul Block smiled. Baseball, his baseball, was back in Newark.

Minor league teams are usually supported by their local communities, but Newark residents, urged on by Block, were atypically affectionate and demonstrative. Traditionally, major league teams have parades at the end of the season, when they return from the World Series; but the Bears started their season with a parade on opening day. The whole season was one big event, always chronicled with great detail, color and fanfare in Block's *Newark Star-Eagle*. To inspire the fans to become more involved, the *Newark Star-Eagle* held an annual contest. Fans (and readers) cast ballots for their favorite player, who was then crowned and showered with gifts at a game at the end of the season.

The team was the center of the city's community life. On the Fourth of July and other holidays, there was always some kind of celebration at the ball park. People came by the thousands to picnic near the flag-bedecked park before the game. Right after the game, local bands often gave concerts, and the fans remained to listen as cool breezes drifted across the field. Dances were often held on the field after the game. Block's ownership of the Newark Bears was bringing a good deal of appreciation to the *Newark Star-Eagle,* and a good deal of satisfaction to the team's fans.

Al Mamaux was rewarded for his loyalty and his work for the 1930 season. He was re-appointed manager in 1931. From the start of the season, it looked like Paul Block finally had a championship team. William Block remembers the colorful season well, since he attended many of the games sitting in his father's box:

> The year that Mamaux became the player-manager, we had a pretty interesting team. Not only was Mamaux pitching well, but we had in right field a fellow named Ike Boone who could hit the ball a mile. The problem was that he was pitifully weak on defense in right field. Every time he went after a ball you held your breath in the hope that he would catch it. But he was a tremendous hitter, and he drove in a lot of runs, and they had to play him. They had in center field a fellow named Woody Jensen, and Woody was not only covering all of center field, which is a tough assignment, but also half of right field for Boone. And in left field was Jocko Conlan, who later became an umpire. Jocko was a feisty little guy, who one day chased somebody up in the stands, because the man made some insulting remark. Jocko almost missed his time at bat.[57]

Strong pitching was the catalyst of the team, especially with Mamaux's whirling and hurling expertise, and having a manager who could inspire and lead his players added to the Bears' success. The team, in a thrilling season that went down to virtually the last pitch, lost to the Rochester Red Wings by just two games. Rochester was the major league powerhouse, having won the pennant in the three previous years. It seemed as if the Bears and Block would finally win their own pennant the next year, but just when everything appeared strong, Block was damaged by heavy losses in the stock market.

The Depression left Paul Block in financial difficulty and, like many other people, he was forced to sell many of his properties. 1931 was one of the most difficult years of the Depression, and even though the Bears's season was a success, Block realized that he had to give up the team that he had grown to love. But he didn't want his sale of the Bears to hurt its chances. He had traveled far with the team and he still wanted to give the city of Newark a winner.

Block had befriended Colonel Jacob Ruppert, the scion of the founder of one of the biggest breweries in New York City, who was famous for making the smartest baseball deal ever: he was the man who brought Babe Ruth to the Yankees by paying $125,000 to the financially troubled Boston Red Sox, a move the Red Sox would regret for the rest of their baseball lives. Ruppert was also the owner of the New York Yankees, the most fabulous franchise recorded in baseball, and most people agree that the 1927 Yankees, under Ruppert's stewardship, was probably the greatest baseball team in history.[58] He was responsible for the transformation of Ruth from a stellar pitcher to a slugging outfielder, perhaps the strongest hitter of all time.[59]

If Ruppert could get involved in the Bears, Paul Block conjectured, Newark was almost guaranteed a winner. On November 12, 1931, in the *Newark Star-Eagle*, Paul Block humbly announced the sale: "I think the baseball fans of Newark will agree that I tried hard to give them winning baseball during the four years I owned the Bears and, although we were not lucky at first, during last season we came to within two games of first place. Rochester, which has won the pennant in our league for three consecutive years, as everyone knows, is owned by the St. Louis Cardinals and, naturally, this ownership has been very helpful to the Rochester club. I am confident that Colonel Ruppert, who is one of the finest gentlemen and sportsmen in the country, will be, because of his ownership of the New York Yankees, able to do much more for the Bears than I could. After all, I am only a newspaper man."[60]

Colonel Jacob Ruppert bought the team – bats, balls and mitts – and the Bears became the Yankees' first minor league franchise. While talking of the purchase, Colonel Ruppert suddenly stopped and said: "The fans of Newark owe Mr. Block no little credit. He has turned over to me the nucleus of a fine ball club, a modern stadium and thanks to his untiring efforts, our task will be a comparatively easy one. I do hope the fans of Newark appreciate what Mr. Block has done during the past four years. He ran minor league ball on a major league level and it is my hope that I will be equal to the task of continuing where he had left off." Although Block was devastated by the loss of his team, he must have felt somewhat gladdened when he realized what he had done for the city of Newark.

The fans expressed regret at the passing of the club from Paul Block's hands. They had truly lost a friend. But as a true friend, he gave them the biggest gift a friend could give: his personal sacrifice. He knew that by giving up the Bears, the Yankees would be able to provide Newark with the championship team the city deserved.[61] All in all, the fans' support of Block was overwhelming and they thanked him for his hard work and dedication.

Al Mamaux, the Bears's manager, was also sad to see Block sell the team. In a statement he made from his home in Brooklyn, Mamaux said, "Mr. Block was a wonderful boss to work for." Mamaux was an ex-Yankee and he was excited and had high expectations of being re-appointed manager in 1932. Mamaux said, "This is a great time for the city of Newark and I think we can't miss next year." He was right.

Paul Block recognized the disadvantage the Bears had had. The victorious champion, Rochester, protected by its financial connection with the St. Louis Cardinals, was the most highly organized of all the minor league clubs. Block knew this and indicated it in the announcement of the sale of the Bears to the Yankees. This challenge, however, was exactly what stimulated Colonel Ruppert. If there was anything Ruppert enjoyed it was a war of the bank books. Block was aware of this and he knew the Bears were in highly capable hands.

The rehabilitation of the Bears would continue, and Newark fans welcomed Colonel Ruppert and the Yankees. Yet Ruppert was reluctant to discuss the future of Al Mamaux, who had brought the team into second place after a thrilling race in the 1931 season. It seemed most probable that Mamaux would not get the post because he had not had the opportunity to display his skill as a teacher. Paul Block let it be known to Colonel Ruppert and the Yankees that Mamaux had established himself as a leader of the highest order, and every young player pointed out that during the previous season the team showed significant improvement. Nonetheless, other candidates' names started surfacing. Though it appeared Mamaux would not get the job, Paul Block remained loyal to his ex-manager until the bitter end.

The new owner not so modestly named the Newark ballpark Ruppert Stadium. Paul Block soon realized that the Bears were not just a baseball team but had become another acquisition in Ruppert's huge empire. He owned the Ruppert Brewing Company and, in 1918, was elected to Congress from the Fifteenth District and re-elected three times. He built Yankee Stadium. He acquired Babe Ruth in the most controversial trade in baseball history. Block said, "I guess we can stroke his ego a little by having the ball park named after him." Block still had *The Newark Star-Eagle* and his other newspapers, and even through all the turmoil of selling the Bears, he still managed to raise $30,000 for the Newark Community Chest Fund that year. He loved the city of Newark, and its citizens loved him.

Paul Block's dream of seeing a pennant flag flying over the city of Newark came true. The Bears not only won the pennant in 1932, but in 1933 and 1934 as well. In 1937, the Bears fielded what was said to be the best minor league team of all time. They had Charlie "King Kong" Keller, a devastating slugger who had been ignored by other teams because they thought he had no potential. He hit .353 that season and later became famous as a star player for the Yankees. Even though Paul Block was no longer owner of the Bears, he delighted in the team's success. "Give the players a chance to succeed," he would often repeat. When asked what made Charlie Keller such a great slugger, Block said, "I don't know what he's got, but I wish I had it" – a bit of Newark Bear's magic. The 1937 Bears were overwhelming. They went on to win 109 games and lost just 42. They captured the league title by 25 games and they were welcomed home in Newark's biggest parade ever. The city went wild in celebration. Eventually, every single starter and manager went on to play in the major leagues.

Even though he had not personally produced a championship Newark team, Block's shrewd business skills and the friendship he had made with Colonel Jacob Ruppert provided the means necessary to see that the city of Newark won its championship flag. The city's favorite team went on to gain four championships. Block's love of the game and his love for the city of Newark had made all of this possible. He still felt as close and as proud of those glorious '30s teams as he did when he was the owner. If not for him, there would have been no 1937 team – the best team ever in minor league baseball. There might not have been *any* baseball in the city of Newark, and some of the fans thought it was altogether possible that they would never see an enthusiast and supporter like Paul Block

again. He took a team that had been so amateurish that a catcher sometimes substituted as a pitcher, a third baseman fielded in hip boots, and a
Bear hit was a bid for laughter – and he made it into a winner.

Chapter 7

Reshaping the American Newspaper

Toledo Blade

The story of Block's initial involvement as owner of the *Toledo Blade,* which he had bought in the summer of 1926 for $4,500,000, is a drama worthy of a *film noir* classic, complete with forged identities, hard-boiled detectives, underworld thugs, a hotel rendezvous, a mysterious woman, secret meetings, a double-cross, and a nighttime office break-in to photograph secret documents.[1]

To begin with, a young, attractive woman, with a slight air of mystery about her, arrived in Toledo in mid-June of 1927. Driving a Chrysler coupe, she was accompanied by a young man who was about 30 years of age. The woman rented a furnished room for herself in the Blackstone Apartments on Ashland Avenue, where she gave her name as Dorothy Day and said she was from Los Angeles. She had a telephone installed immediately, and made nervous and furtive inquiries of the landlady about the safety of the mailboxes.

Within a few days, she later claimed, she had a prearranged, clandestine meeting in a room at the Commodore Perry Hotel with three people: Frederick S. Buggie, former circulation manager of the *Toledo Blade*, who had been an employee of Block's *Newark Star-Eagle* and *Detroit Journal*; Buggie's attorney, Frank Lewis; and a man only identified as "Benny." Day was there because she had been hired by a private detective by the name of Walter Baker to, as she said, "Do a job that no one else could do." In true cloak and dagger style, all she had been told by Baker was that after she arrived in Toledo she should call either Lewis or Buggie, and that they would fill her in as to her assignment and what was to be done.

She was instructed by the three men that she was to go undercover in an exercise of business espionage. Her first secret task was to apply for a job as a clerk or stenographer at the law firm of Smith, Baker, Effler and Eastman, the attorneys for Paul Block and the *Toledo Blade*, and if she failed to be hired, she should attempt to ingratiate herself and gain the confidence of one of the firm's employees. What the men sought were contracts and documents concerning financial arrangements that Paul Block had made with Buggie and his partner Harry S. Talmadge. They wanted Day to secure the documents, or copies of them, in any way that she could.

According to her later confession and testimony, she claimed that she was told that Buggie and Talmadge wanted copies of the letters of arrangement, and any memos pertaining to it, that both had with Block and with the Locke family – the previous owners of the *Blade* – prior to Block's purchase. Talmadge and Buggie contended that they had several more years to run on a contract to operate the *Blade*, but when Block took it over, their contract had been cancelled and their services terminated. They claimed they were to receive annual salaries of $25,000 and a percentage of the net profits of the *Blade,* which they estimated to be over $600,000. Since both men would undoubtedly have had personal copies of the contracts themselves, it seems unlikely that the covert search would have been for the contracts specifically, but more likely for other documents or letters that might have compromised their positions.

The man known as "Benny" did not say very much, according to Day; later, from a description that she gave of him, he was thought to be any one of three Bennys: Benny Harris, an infamous Toledo gambler; or Benny Hoffman, one of the circulation managers of the rival *Toledo News-Bee*; or another Benny Harris, a newsstand dealer and bookmaker. It was thought by Block, although it was never proven, that to prevent the *Blade's* success, the *News-Bee* – hungry for circulation – was employing underworld toughs to intimidate the newsstands that sold the *Toledo Blade*, and the boys who carried it. Another theory circulating at that time was that gangland forces had infiltrated the *Blade* under the managerial team of Talmadge and Buggie, and indeed, the very reason that the Locke estate sold the paper to Block was to take it away from underworld influence. Block believed that any one of the disreputable Bennys could be linked to, or employed by Buggie and Talmadge to assist in their attempt to undermine the *Blade*.

The next morning, Day – in her role as corporate spy – applied for a job as a clerk or stenographer at the firm of Smith, Baker, Effler and Eastman. She was interviewed by the office manager, who was impressed by her appearance and comportment – as part of her disguise, she was expensively dressed and exquisitely coiffed – and although the firm had no full-time openings at that moment, she was considered for a position as a substitute worker for someone who was soon to go on vacation. During the time that she was at the law firm, Miss Day began talking with a file clerk, Marie Fisher, and in order to insinuate herself, Day invited Fisher out to lunch.

Fisher was a bit overwhelmed by her impressive new acquaintance. She was awed by the attractive outfit that Day wore that day. After Fisher admired it, Day told her that she, too, could have the same kind of clothing, in addition to $1,000 in cash, close to a year's salary (Fisher was making $25 per week at the time) if she would cooperate and secure a key to the law firm's office for just one or two evenings. Fisher was frightened – if she was caught, not only would she be in legal trouble, but she would lose her job. "Don't worry about the loss of your job," said Day, "I guarantee you a full-time position with another law firm, the one Frank Lewis is a partner in [Doyle & Lewis], and of course they'll defend you legally if it ever comes to that."

Fisher said that she would have to think it over but temporarily agreed to the subterfuge. She returned to the office and reported the conversation with Day to her employers, attorneys Effler and Eastman. Told to pretend to collaborate with Day and play into her hands, Fisher met with Day several more times. Meanwhile, Eastman told Block what was going on. The *Blade* hired a private detective agency, which was to report all of the activities directly to Block with detailed, typewritten, single-spaced memos delivered to him at least once or twice each day. On August 7th, with Le Roy Eastman's guidance and permission, Fisher gave Day a key to the office. Eastman immediately called Block and then notified the private detective agency to be on hand the next night, when the purloining of the documents was to take place.

That evening, the two lawyers, Effler and Eastman, seated in a parked car a half-block from their office, waited in darkness. The detective, ensconced in a men's room on the floor of the law offices, patiently marked time, signaling the two lawyers with a flashlight – three quick flashes shined twice – as soon as he spotted Day and an accomplice enter the building. Accompanying Day was a woman photographer who was going to take photographs of the documents in question. The lawyers were in the building in a matter of minutes, and together with the detective, they burst into the file room to catch Day in the act of rifling through Block's and the *Blade's* file marked "Buggie and Talmadge." Caught in the act, the shocked Day was whisked into the conference room, and in relatively short order she "confessed" the whole story: She had worked for Buggie on the *Detroit Journal*, her real name was Dorothy Polk, she had done unlicensed freelance detective work for the previous two years, and she was known for always completing the task for which she was hired. Except this time.

The Toledo police were summoned and within an hour she was behind bars in the local jail. The photographer somehow convinced everyone that she had been hired just that day, and that she never knew Miss Day-Polk before then and had no idea that what she was doing was illegal. She claimed that Day-Polk had told her that she worked for the law firm and just needed a photographer for about one hour to take some pictures of various documents that were needed in a hurry. Day-Polk backed up her story. The photographer was released. All of the Toledo newspapers gave the story front page coverage, and the mysterious Dorothy Day and who she was really working for was content for conversation in Toledo's clubs, speakeasies and restaurants for weeks.

The story does not end with the temporary incarceration of Day-Polk. When the trial came to court, she refused to name anyone who influenced or paid her – especially Buggie and Talmadge – and she was eventually acquitted on what seemed to be a technicality. The judge held that since Effler and Eastwood knew that she had the key, indeed had instructed Fisher to give it to her, and since they were both on the premises before any documents were either photographed or stolen, it was a form of illegal entrapment on the lawyers' part, and therefore Day was legally guilty of nothing. Fisher seemed to have double-crossed everyone: telling the lawyers about the scam but also accepting the money from Day to produce the key to the law firm's offices. In a matter of days, her bank account showed three deposits of $300 each; a week later she bought a new car, making people think that she might have known more than she was willing to reveal, and was paid off with an addition to the originally-promised $1,000 not to say anything to anyone.

Since no case could be brought against Buggie or Talmadge because a connection to Day-Polk could not be proven, the two men did what many think is the best strategy when on the defensive: attack. They sued the *Blade* and Paul Block for breech or cancellation of contracts, asking for over two million dollars in compensation. To add to Block's troubles, Buggie also sued the attorneys Effler and Eastman for slander; and Frank Lewis personally took Block to court in a $100,000 libel complaint. Louis H. Gould, a real estate agent, also sued Barton Smith, executor of the Locke estate, for an alleged breach of contract, claiming that Gould was the one who had originally found Block as the buyer of the paper.

Over 50 years later, the question of how the purchase of the *Toledo Blade* was made by Block, and under what circumstances, was still being noised about. One bizarre theory was that the whole affair was a deep Masonic plot to take over the paper, arranged by Florance Cottrell and Barton Smith, with the cooperation of Paul Block. The fact that Block was not a Mason, although Cottrell and Smith were, fairly discounts the idea of the cabal as pure rumor.[2]

It took years of depositions, briefs, testimony, examinations, counter-suits and appeals, before all the parties agreed to agree, and a settlement of an undisclosed sum was made out of court. No record of how much, if anything, Block paid, or to whom, could be found in the research for the preparation of this book.

Block retaliated against Talmadge several years later. Learning that Talmadge had bought the *Bridgeport Post*, in Connecticut, Block comandeered and organized all his resources into gaining the advertising representative business for the competing *Bridgeport Standard Telegram*, and then went about securing every possible national ad for his new client. In a kind of wild justice, he took the hugely profitable national advertisements away from Talmadge's *Post*. William Block said of his father's Connecticut tactics: "My father was a great believer in friendship and loyalty, but when someone did him wrong, he never forgot. It was sweet revenge."[3]

•••

During the first few years of his ownership of the *Toledo Blade*, Block was optimistic about its potential, but wary and weary of all of the legal troubles in which the paper was ensnared. Fairly early on in his proprietorship, Block wrote: "Through the stresses and the strains of the years, the *Blade* emerges strong, vigorous, true to its original ideals, fit for the changing times, and, as ever, endeavoring to serve the community where it received its birthright."[4]   Somehow, of all of the newspapers that he became involved with, represented, owned, leased or published during his career, the *Toledo Blade*, inexorably intertwined with the city of Toledo, captured his heart and imagination the most.[5] It also invaded his pocketbook: it was the most expensive single purchase of a newspaper he ever made.

Block had been special advertising representative for the *Blade* since 1908, and as his business prospered, and the country grew, so did the paper. In his new relationship with the *Blade,* he came to think of it as a laboratory of sorts, and a field for experimentation, the results of which could be applied to his other papers. He nurtured the *Blade* and cared for it as a favorite child, his flagship, and would never permit anything to harm or debase it. He wanted it to establish a new focus, a new ratio between the news and the reader, the advertiser and the editor.

•••

The history of the city of Toledo and the state of Ohio is engaging and fascinating. Since everybody talks politics in Ohio, perhaps it is not so remarkable that the state is the birthplace of seven Presidents (Grant, Hayes, Garfield, Harrison, McKinley, Taft and Harding), and was the fourth most populous state in the Union when Block took over the *Blade*. Toledo was one of five cities that showed the most growth in private home ownership between 1910 and 1920. It was a great manufacturing area, the iron ores of the Lake Superior district being easily transported to it by way of the other Great Lakes. In 1926, Ohio was and still is, just slightly behind Michigan as the second largest manufacturer of automobiles and related products, and it is first in the union as the maker of all kinds of glass: cut and plain glassware, safety glass, plate glass, and automotive glass. In the mid-1920s, it was ranked seventh in the country in the value of its agricultural products, and third for its industrial production.

Unholy Toledo, situated on the Maumee Bay seven miles west of Lake Erie, in what might be called the heart of the Middle West, was a feisty and somewhat corrupt city in the 1920s, where rum-running gave it an infamous but glamorous reputation. The police seemed not to notice the machinations of the gangland thugs, perhaps because of the bribes they were receiving. All throughout Prohibition, Toledo became infested with gangs who practically ran the local government. The *Blade* chronicled all of the turbulent events centered around speakeasies and brothels, bookmakers and bank robbers.[6]

But the *Toledo Blade* was not all crime coverage. It was neither afraid to upbraid nor too shy to commend the lofty and powerful, either editorially or in its news pages, and as a result it irritated many enemies, and endeared many friends. As one of the first newspapers west of the Alleghenies, the *Blade* covered matters national and local. It single-handedly prodded Toledo's alderman to pass or repeal ordinances. It openly questioned the county prosecutor, but its stated convictions were tempered with fairness. It published a front page story on the opening of the Valentine Theater, one of the handsomest legitimate halls in America, as one of the great social and dramatic evenings of the city's season.[7] It included in-depth stories of the impeachment of Andrew Johnson. It covered the dispirited and crippling railroad strike of 1906. It could be dogmatic and unpredictable at times: as a Republican paper it stood up to the state machine and backed Theodore Roosevelt, the Progressive Party candidate in 1908. It literally had a ringside seat when Jack Dempsey defeated – some say punished – the giant Jess Willard in the third round for the heavyweight championship of the world, in an outdoor arena in Toledo. The Dempsey-Willard contest was the richest sports exhibition ever held until that time, and sportswriters from the *Blade,* using a megaphone, announced the bout blow-by-blow from the paper's balcony to hundreds of sports fans below. The newspaper chronicled the fight in detail in its pages the next day.

Until the Toledo Fire Department was mechanized in 1916, the *Blade* published dramatic photos of galloping horses pulling water-pump trucks to raging fires. The paper ran an interview of General Tom Thumb and his Lilliputian Family, who were on tour in the city as part of the P.T. Barnum show. All of the wars found coverage in the *Toledo Blade*: most of the stories were updates on the battles but often with a local angle that discussed and reported on the movements, victories and defeats of the young Ohio men, officers and units from Toledo who were fighting in the Mexican War, the Civil War, the Spanish American War, and World War I.

There is a tradition, or at least a belief or superstition, that no man could be elected in the city of Toledo, from Mayor to Judge, from Sheriff to Postmaster, without the support of the *Toledo Blade*. The paper had such credibility that its readers believed the accuracy and honesty of its news coverage, endorsements, and editorials. The *Toledo Blade* became more than a newspaper to most Toledoans. Reading it became part of the daily routine, virtually a visit with an extended family, a longstanding habit that they preferred to continue. Block had no intention of damaging the crucial relationship between the *Blade* and its readers.

The *Blade* was also somewhat sweetly self-conscious at times, with stories that took Toledoans behind the scenes, demonstrating to them, through words and pictures, just how the paper, *their* paper, was published, from the editing desk to the composing room, from the stereotype department to the printing presses, showing operators pounding the keys that would eventually make lines of type cast in the linotype machine from molten metal.[8]   One full-page article told how spruce trees from northwestern Canada were felled by lumberjacks, floated down the river to the great mills and were eventually made into the paper on which the *Blade* was printed.[9]   Readers began to paternally refer to the newspaper as "my *Toledo Blade*," rather than "the *Toledo Blade*."

The original *Toledo Blade*, which had served the city through every Presidency since the administration of Andrew Jackson, was a weekly that was founded in 1835; later it became a tri-weekly, and in 1848, prompted partially by the telegraph invented by Samuel F. B. Morse, which provided the latest stock market figures and other news from around the country, it went daily. An editorial at that time proudly announced:

> The magic wires are here and we are in connection. We shall be able henceforth to furnish our readers with the latest news – the daily condition of the eastern market, and all that kind of practical intelligence which is now eagerly sought after by the business world. The expense incident to that employment of the telegraph, we can ill bear, but a conviction that your enterprise in this matter will not go unrewarded induces us to hazard the experiment of a trial.[10]

The *Blade* also issued a weekly edition, published on Thursdays, which was distributed nationally; at its height it had a circulation of over 250,000. Its claim was that it was distributed to and read in every county in the United States.[11]   Even as early as 1897 its circulation was over 125,000, making it at that time ten times larger than any other newspaper, daily or weekly, in the state of Ohio.[12]

David Ross Locke was perhaps the *Blade's* most famous editor. During the Civil War, writing satirical articles under the preposterous pseudonym of Petroleum V. Nasby, the name he had selected to suggest elements of his interest or personality (the "Petroleum" made reference to the petroleum oil excitement in Pennsylvania that was then taking place; the "V" was for the turbulent volcano Vesuvius; and "Nasby' suggested Locke's interest in English history, especially the battle of Nasby, where Cromwell defeated Charles I), he gained not only national attention but his columns were known throughout the world. Written in a kind of backwoods dialect popular at that time among humorists, Locke would philosophize on issues grand and trivial, local and national, even his own column, e.g., "Wut posterity will say I don't know; neither do I care. It's this generalashun I am goin for."[13]   He was a close friend of Mark Twain who greatly appreciated Nasby's humor. He even avoided taking sides with either the Union or the Confederacy; both Presidents, Abraham Lincoln and Ulysses S. Grant, were so impressed with Nasby's homespun writing style (and spellbinding and side-splitting speeches on the Lyceum lecture circuit) that they offered him positions of high responsibility in the government, which he invariably refused. Perhaps apocryphal, there is a story that Abraham Lincoln supposedly had read and was amused by a collection of Nasby columns on the afternoon that he was assassinated, and a cache of Nasby's writings were found in Lincoln's pocket when he was shot in Ford's theater.[14]   Another story has indicated that Lincoln read some excerpts of Nasby's columns to his Cabinet before he presented them with his Emancipation Proclamation.[15]

Succeeding Nasby at the *Toledo Blade* was his son Robinson Locke, who was editor and president of the company from 1888 to 1920, and who had been well-grounded in the newspaper business by his father. The two traveled the world together, and although Robinson was the authentic editor of the *Blade* in every way, his real love and interest was the theater. He wrote all of the theater reviews that appeared in the paper and he began a collection of clippings, photographs, programs and advertisements about the stage and film – and especially anything to do with his idol, Shakespeare – from newspapers and theaters all over the country. It became the largest collection of theater scrapbooks from that period in the world and is now housed in a special room in the research wing of the New York Public Library.

When Block took over the *Blade*, he was interested in the history of the paper and realized that the assignment of having it live up to its past stature was mainly his responsibility. He was buoyed by the fact that it had so many loyal and talented staff members, permeated as it was with capable and knowledgeable people. Astonishingly, Charles W. Pearson, who had been hired by the *Blade* in 1893, was still reporting on activities about the East Side of the city 32 years later; Florance E. Cottrell, who was vice-president and treasurer, had started with the *Blade* before the turn of the century, and was largely instrumental in helping Block become the owner. Other key employees included the two zealous associate editors, Lucas J. Beecher and Frank M. Warwick; Stanley Speer, the *Blade's* business manager and Block's indispensable factotum; the brilliant, legendary and often gruff city editor, Fred Mollenkopf; and a press of printers who had been with the company for over 25 years: Charles Wagner, Clint Egelton, Frank Davis, Ellsworth Sloat and Otto Klinck. But of all his employees, the one he came to rely upon and respect the most was his editor and vice-president, the incessantly curious and globetrotting Grove Patterson, one of the great American newspaper men.[16] Block and Patterson established a forthright and respectful working relationship that flourished for many years.

Patterson had come to the *Blade* in 1910 as News Editor, two years after Block had started as the paper's special advertising representative, and although the two men had known each other for some 15 years, and Patterson had worked for Block on the *Newark Star-Eagle* and the *Detroit Journal*, they really didn't become close until Block assumed the role of publisher of the *Blade*. Patterson had studied at Oberlin College, worked as a reporter on several small Ohio papers, and served as managing editor of the *Toledo Times* before going to the *Blade*. He had received a great amount of experience on the *Toledo Times* since his job was to cover the entire city of Toledo (population at that time of more than 150,000) with only two other editors and four reporters.[17] At the *Blade*, Block and Patterson enjoyed each other's company. Their relationship was similar to Block's association with Hearst: although they came from vastly different backgrounds, they walked on common ground; in their professional abilities, they considered one another equals. They also had a surprising amount of similarities.

Paul Block was a lifelong late riser. So was Grove Patterson. In their thirties, quite late in those days, both men wed their respective wives. Although Patterson was a college graduate, he had little interest in books, with the exception of history; Block read sparsely, but also favored history. He kept *au courant* by reading dozens of newspapers and kept up with business and industry through reading trade magazines. Block and Patterson were virtually the same age. Joseph P. Kennedy, the Ambassador to Britain and father of a future President, was a mutual friend. Block and Patterson had kind hearts, were known as "soft touches" and hated to fire anyone. In signing memos or letters, they each used their initials,

"P.B." and "G.P." respectively, and often referred to each other in that way. They lived for and talked incessantly about the newspaper business. Both were staunch Republicans. Both had famous and powerful friends: Paul Block had, among many others, Admiral Richard Byrd and Mayor Jimmy Walker; Patterson's friendships included Winston Churchill and H.L. Mencken. Their shared philosophy of handling men was identical: "Commend a man when he does well. When he does badly he suffers enough without any criticism."

The differences between Grove Patterson and Paul Block should be noted: Patterson was a truly gifted public speaker, always at the ready and in demand (but only to relatively small groups because he spoke softly, and couldn't project his voice far); Block could speak in front of an audience, and possessed a pleasant, well-modulated voice, but he wasn't a particularly sought-after speaker, nor did he enjoy the process. Patterson was a large man for those days: nearly six feet tall; Block was five feet six inches. Patterson was more deeply religious than Block ("I could not possibly be an atheist," he once wrote), whereas Block, although nominally a Jew, seemed not to express any strong religious convictions: religion in Block's belief was an expression of the spirit which should be translated into one's everyday life, not necessarily in a church or a temple. "Every normal person is religious to some degree," Block once wrote. "Some, who do not go to church often, and some who rarely go, are nevertheless religious at heart, as shown by their many kind acts."

Patterson was more self-assured than Block and less of a worrier. He was somewhat concerned about the security of his job, however, when he heard that Paul Block had bought the *Toledo Blade*, because Block had let it be known that he was going to make personnel changes, especially with the Talmadge-Buggie management of the paper. In his memoir, Patterson described visiting Block's mansion, Friendship, in Greenwich, Connecticut to discuss his future. The dynamic of that moment:

> Getting down to business in a short time, Mr. Block told me that he wanted me to remain with the *Blade* with the title and authority of editor. He assured me of the greatest freedom in the matter of editorial operation, policy and personal independence. Recalling a trivial incident, as one does on personally memorable occasions, I remember that in the course of our conversation I did not hesitate to recount my foibles and my weaknesses. I told him that all my newspaper life I had detested time clocks, that I kept wholly irregular

hours, that my life in Toledo would be, as it had been in the
past, devoted to the *Blade*, but as to just when I would be in
the office or where else I would be, I couldn't say. I told him
that when I went to bed at night, I was never definite about
when I was going to get up.

"That's all right," he said. "When and if you wake up, you
might telephone the office and see what's doing and then go
back to bed."

….as I was getting into the car to take me to the station, he
said very earnestly: "When will you tell me that you are going to stay with me always?"[19]

In a matter of days, Patterson wrote to Block and told him that Toledo
was his home and that he wanted to remain with the *Blade* and with Block.
"I have never had cause to regret the decision," Patterson wrote later.[20]

Patterson's column, "The Way of the World," which appeared on the
editorial page of the *Toledo Blade* every day, was a journalistic achievement that lasted for close to 25 years. So revered were his words that
people pasted the columns into scrapbooks, mailed them to friends and
relatives all over the country, and carried them in their wallets until, yellowed by age, they would fall apart. A brief sampling of his distinctive
prose style:

- An editor's function is to sit at the window of life and to
  look out upon the passing procession. It is his function to
  study the kinds and classes of human beings who make up
  that procession, to interpret their movement and their direction, to write about their actions, and to measure the
  motives of their leaders. Above all, it is an editor's business to understand people and the changing scene.
  Science takes the world apart. Philosophy puts it together
  again. Religion gives it meaning. The editor sees all and
  writes about it all.[21]

- The Maumee Valley, now delicately tinted with fruit trees,
  is an enchanted land. Sometimes the Maumee seems to
  me to be grand, lordly, like some of the far reaches of the
  Mississippi. Again it is a winding stream, bending back
  and begging fishermen to follow.[22]

- I could never be called a crusading editor. The history of
  crusades is that they don't do anything for a newspaper.

There are exceptions, of course, when a newspaper de-
votes itself to some great cause. But the ordinary petty
crusades, the snarling attacks, don't win readers.[23]

• Communism is the movement of second-rate people, terrorized by fear of life and hopeful of some sort of permanent security.[24]

In October of 1933, after returning from a trip to Russia, where he saw
the end of the old order and the beginning of the new, Patterson wrote a
brilliant travelogue/political analysis, "Way of the World in Russia," which
appeared as a series in the *Blade*: "Old men and women, aimlessly bound
for somewhere, downed by Bolshevism."[25]

Perhaps because Block was the new publisher and still finding his way,
however, and beset with the controversy with Buggie and Talmadge, the
circulation of the *Toledo Blade* actually went down a few thousand copies to 124,232 within a short while after he took control.[26] The paper was
also engaged in a bitter circulation war for its Toledoan readers with the
Democratic Scripps-Howard owned newspaper, the *Toledo News-Bee*.
Block claimed that the *Blade* was publishing on the average of 12 pages
more each day than any other Toledo paper, and therefore readers were
getting much more for their money. But at first, this didn't seem to accel-
erate circulation. At every opportunity, the *News-Bee* screamed front-
page banner headlines anytime that Block or the *Blade* seemed to be engaged in a controversy, such as the Talmadge-Buggie affair. This may
also have cut down on circulation by some readers made incredulous, and
it may have reduced advertising sales by some advertisers made
skeptical.

All the declining figures had little impact on Block, however, other
than to strengthen his resolve and sharpen his skills. He insisted on broad-
ening the reach of the paper, invested money in promotion, and stepped
up subscription, newsstand sales and home distribution. He gave gifts
and money incentives to the almost 2,000 boy carriers who had paper
routes, not only in Toledo itself but also in such outlying areas as Columbus Grove, Bluffton, Dundee, Perrysburg, Sylvania, and the larger towns
of Upper Sandusky, Napoleon, Bowling Green, Findlay and Tiffin. Block
then brought in even more national advertising.

Starting in November, 1926, Block formed the "Blade Christmas Club,"
into which he made a sizable contribution, and then asked readers to do-
nate, also, in order to "bring joy and sunshine into thousands of homes

that otherwise would be joyless on Christmas Day."[27]   The Club received
an avalanche of money and, as a result, several thousand children in the
Toledo area were given toys, gifts, and festive Christmas dinners.

By the end of 1926, the *Toledo Blade* had developed the largest circulation of its entire history: 130,000 copies per day, averaging 35 pages
each issue, which was about 10,000 more copies than in the winter of
1925. To be able to publish more suburban and state news, Block put on
many more correspondents to cover the news in outlying areas. By the
end of 1927, after barely a year of ownership of the *Blade* and the struggle
with the *News-Bee*, he could boast of a circulation greater than all other
Toledo newspapers combined, and his paper carried more national advertising, more local advertising and more classified advertising than any
other newspaper in the city.[28]

While Block was trying to build the *Blade*, there was a great industrial
expansion in the city. The Libbey-Owens Sheet Glass Company constructed a $3 million plant for the manufacture of unbreakable glass; some
1,500 additional jobs were added to the company's payroll. Improvements were also made to triple the capacity of the Ohio Central railroad
docks. There were jobs in East Toledo, which meant much more commerce, more jobs, and "a more prosperous Toledo," as Block put it.[29]
When a Toledo businessman, C.O. Miniger, and his associates constructed
Toledo's highest downtown skyscraper, the 30-story building became a
symbol to Block of "the growing prosperity of the people and the growth
of business in the community."[30]

•••

Some biographical portraits of Paul Block, such as the ones included in
George Seldes's *Lords of the Press* and Ferdinand Lundberg's *Imperial
Hearst*, describe him as nothing more than a glorified salesman, merely a
merchant of news and a sham stand-in for Hearst, a physically and intel-
lectually small man who really knew only about advertising, very little
about publishing, and absolutely nothing about editorial matters and journalism itself.[31] In one book, *Gentleman Jimmy Walker,* by George Walsh,
Block is brutally described as an unctuous publicity-seeker who liked to
bask in the glory of famous people.[32]   This is an unfair and distorted
characterization of the man. Apparently those critics of the press were
writing from only superficial information about Block. They knew that
he had made his initial business success from advertising, and they knew

that he had important and famous friends. But they did not know the depth of the man's influence on his newspapers and on the industry itself, or the warmth and counsel he offered people, which led them to seek his advice.

Patterson, writing about his employer after Block's death, claimed that Block was generous in money and thoughtfulness; critical and exacting; gracious to those he liked; different and unusual in his manner of getting things done than other successful men who Patterson had known; had a strong reliance on his own judgment; and was thoroughly dynamic.[33] Giving a balanced view of Block, Patterson also said that he found him to be hard on occasion; unforgiving of disloyalty; driven by impulse to make mistakes; disregarding of advice; and unable to serve as a keen judge of human nature. Nowhere is there a comment or perception of incompetence or sycophancy. Even if some of the criticisms of Block were accurate, and a great deal of his talent *did* lie in the field of advertising, why – some of his colleagues felt – was that objectionable? As Adolph S. Ochs, publisher of *The New York Times* wrote, stressing the importance of advertising to newspapers:

> Advertising is the very lifeblood of a modern newspaper, and enables a newspaper to best serve the public welfare, to be independent, to be courageous, to be enterprising. The better the class of advertising the better the newspaper. You can more readily judge the character of a newspaper by its advertising columns than by any other outward appearance. As good advertising is of prime importance, it calls for the best talent, and that is the same talent the possession of which is essential for a good editor, copyreader, headline artist, and all others engaged in gathering and presenting news and expressing opinion. Advertising, to be effective, must compete with every part of the newspaper. There is no better training for the highest and most lucrative positions of journalism than in the department of advertising.[34]

Indeed, Patterson relied on Block's judgment (and obediently followed his directives) on all matters concerning the newspaper, including editorial issues and concerns, and since Block contributed what became an indelible impression on the editorial side of the *Blade*, it left no question as to who was the newsroom's shadow boss. Patterson even looked to Block for personal advice, although on occasion he already knew the answer, and wished he didn't, to the counsel he sought. When he was approached to run for Congress, for example, Patterson wrote to Block asking him what he should do. Block replied:

> December 19, 1935
> Dear G.P.:
>
> I think the Editor of the Mansfield, Ohio *News Journal* has probably given the greatest reason why you should not run for Congress. In his fine editorial, copy of which he sent to me, he writes:
> "Grove Patterson is a successful newspaper editor; he has traveled much in his own country and abroad; he is a keen observer and sound thinker. He is happy in his work – probably much happier than he would be as President of the United States. And, anyhow, Grove was not cut out to be a politician – he thinks too honestly."
> I think the last sentence of the last paragraph tells the story.
>
> Very sincerely,
> P.B.[35]

Patterson immediately took Block's re-directed advice, and never ran for any office.

The Peach:
Advent of the Feature Section

Here is the genesis and history of how Block influenced and finessed the newspaper's Feature Section, and helped to augment the *Blade's* already-established reputation and increase its circulation to that of the largest in the city of Toledo. With the birth of a self-contained Feature Section, virtually a miniature magazine in itself, (perhaps one of the first in any newspaper in this country), the *Blade* added to its reputation and stature as an excellent entertainment vehicle, as well as a provider of news.[36] A front-page notice in the first edition of the new section proclaimed boldly: "We believe our readers will find this one of the most interesting sections ever issued by a daily newspaper."[37] For over 60 years, long after Block's death, it has attempted to live up to that credo.

Block didn't initially plan to revamp the Feature Section of the *Toledo Blade*. The impetus came in 1936 after he visited England and spent time discussing publishing with Lord Beaverbrook. Block examined Beaverbrook's *London Daily Express*, and came away with ideas concerning two of his own newspapers: the *Newark Star-Eagle* and the *Toledo Blade*. After returning to the United States, he had several discussions with William Randolph Hearst about revamping the make-up, appearance and content of the *Toledo Blade*. Hearst had no financial interest in the *Blade*; he and Block were used to sounding each other out on newspaper publishing issues. Shortly after that, Block had dinner with George Longon, publisher of the *Kansas City Star,* and his editor, Ray Roberts, and they too discussed the ideas Block had begun to inculcate in London. After an examination and analysis of the make-up of the paper, Block said almost angrily: "I can't understand the *Kansas City Star* makeup. It reads and looks almost like a telephone book." Longon's reply was: "You know P.B., we often discuss in board meetings changing the make-up, but then somebody comments that we're doing pretty well and so no change is made."[38] Block became so concerned with the appearance and content of his *own* newspapers that he decided to experiment with Feature Section publishing.[39]

He began with such a section in his *Newark Star-Eagle*, then extended his innovation to the *Blade* on Feb. 3, 1936. In concert with the new section, Block announced an increase in the single copy price of the *Blade* from two cents to three cents. The production costs of the *Blade* had been steadily increasing, and in 1935 the cost of newsprint and delivery was more than $115,000 in excess of the entire revenue received from the newsstand and subscription sale of the paper. Because of the ongoing Depression, the *Blade's* advertising lineage had been dropping as well, from $2,112,757 in 1936 to $1,833,498 in 1938, so Block attempted to raise his circulation revenue. If it couldn't pay for the entire production costs, at least it would cover a larger percentage than it had been doing.[40] In an apologetic editorial, he wrote: "The recent increase in the price of print paper, the additional Social Security Tax and the many other increasing costs that go into the making of a newspaper such as the *Blade* have been so great that it has been found necessary to establish the new price."[41]

Block's experimentation with light feature material, although not in a separate section, had actually begun many years before that when in the early 1920s, he published photographs and line drawings of beautiful women, and occasional cartoon features, on the front page of his *Memphis News-Scimitar*. He had also published many light features and photographs in the *Toledo Sunday Times*, and in the rotogravure section of the *Toledo Blade*, which was started on November 7, 1926.

Before he inaugurated the separate Feature Section in the *Blade*, however, at the beginning of 1936 Block began to publish a special "Blue Streak" edition, the last edition of each day's newspaper to hit the newsstands. This new edition of the *Blade* included the regular content of earlier editions, in addition to late news flashes and local news, complete final markets, and the latest up-to-the-minute sports scores. Sold on newsstands and by street-corner vendors, the Blue Streak edition could easily be identified by a heavy blue line, about a quarter of an inch wide, which ran along the entire right hand margin of the paper. The Blue Streak was published on traditional white newsprint; it replaced the previous last edition of the *Blade*, which had been identified by a front page that was printed on peach-colored paper.[42] Block had ideas and priorities for the use of the color peach in his new feature section.

Other ideas were incorporated into the *Blade* to make the paper look more readable and attractive. In addition to the new section, the *Blade* published its first three-color picture, a religious theme, on Easter Sunday in 1936.[43]

But certainly one of Block's most important innovations was the new feature section. The entire 4-page section was printed on peach-colored newsprint. The word "peach," or the expression "to peach on someone," was a slightly arcane definition for tattling; and for something to be "peachy" meant, of course that it was just fine or dandy. Hence, together with the symbolism of the color of the paper stock, the new feature section projected an attitude, an impression, an innate purpose. Its rationale was that it would be something that is going to inform. Its appearance suggested playfulness. Two days after he began to publish the new feature section, Block hit on the inescapable name for it: "The Peach."

In those bleak years of the Depression, in order to maintain his circulation over that of the *Toledo News-Bee* and his other competitors in the city, Block felt he had to thoroughly change his approach to features in order to gain readership. He included a variety of new features and columns in The Peach, such as "Eli Culbertson on Bridge," Osborne Bond's stamp column, Dr. Wiggam's "Let's Explore Your Mind," and the most renowned columnists of the day: Walter Lippmann, Dorothy Thompson, Westbrook Pegler, Ernie Pyle, Dorothy Kilgallen, Hedda Hopper, Eleanor Roosevelt, Emily Post, and Walter Winchell.

The thought behind the Peach was that the section could be easily identified by the reader, and that it could be pulled out from the rest of the newspaper for a few quiet moments of easy reading, either at home or on a bus or streetcar. It was Paul Block's belief that the Peach could either help the *Blade* substantially or actually ruin it if not done correctly.[44] He gambled.

To begin with, the section contained columns, personality profiles, diversionary articles, a daily short story, puzzles, photographs, and reviews of movies, theater, radio and restaurants, listings of radio programs, a calendar of local events, and entertainment advertising. Although readers of the *Blade* took to the Peach immediately, it was not an immediate success in 1936 in building circulation. Because of the price increase and the general state of the economy, circulation dropped from 130,507 in 1936 to 129,612 in 1937, but by 1938 it had shot up to 132,139. These increases adversely affected the circulation of the *Toledo News-Bee*. A year after the *Blade's* feature section arrived, the *News-Bee* retaliated by starting its own feature section, printed on pink paper. It was too little, too late. The *News Bee's* circulation began to drop, its maintenance and paper costs were rising and in 1938 (despite the fact that it was owned and backed by the enormous financial resources of Scripps-Howard), the *News-Bee* was bought out by Block and printed its last copies. Almost immediately, the circulation of the *Blade* rose to 153,286. The purchase arrangement was unusual: Block paid the *News-Bee* $780,000 for a covenant in which Scripps-Howard agreed not to purchase, invest in or operate another newspaper in Toledo for 10 years, and an additional $100,000 was paid for the paper's good will and reputation. The Peach and Pink Wars of Toledo, as they came to be known, were over.[45]   In a statement issued by the *Blade's* office upon the demise of the *News-Bee*, Paul Block said he sincerely regretted the suspension of his competitor, and that he recognized that the *Blade* had an added responsibility to the people of Toledo in publishing the best newspaper he knew how.[46]   Block discussed the state of publishing at that time:

> Because the cost of producing a newspaper today has become so high, and the volume of national advertising, on account of adverse business conditions, has been so greatly reduced, it has been made difficult for the leading newspaper in cities like Toledo to remain profitable and a situation has been brought about in such cities that it is now doubtful whether there is room for a second evening newspaper.

> In many important cities, where formerly two evening pa-
> pers were published, only one remains today. These include
> St. Paul, Louisville, Memphis, Des Moines, Denver, Omaha,
> Youngstown and others. [47]

Shortly after the inauguration of the Peach in the *Blade*, Block also started a similar section in another of his newspapers, the *Pittsburgh Post-Gazette*. In a comparison with 11 other relatively large daily newspapers throughout the country, such as the *New York Sun,* the *Washington Star*, and the *Detroit News*, only one other newspaper could boast of a daily feature or sports section which preceded Block's, and that was the *Milwaukee Journal*, which had a green-sheeted section wrapped around the final edition each day.[48]

For years, Block agonized over the exact content of the Peach, its kinds of illustrations, number and types of columns, even the specific shade of the peach-color paper that he sought, constantly gathering samples of paper stock from mills and distributors to discern which shade was the best.[49] He discussed the matter with ophthalmologists, showing them samples of the various peach colors to determine which shade would be the most restful for the eyes, and therefore most acceptable to the majority of his readers.[50] For comparison purposes, he secured copies of any newspaper published in the United States that had *any* section published on peach stock or any similar color, such as could be found in the *Des Moines Register* and the *Columbus Evening Dispatch*.[51] In a memorandum to the General Manager of the *Blade*, Florance E. Cottrell, he wrote: "...I cannot stand for this kind of peach color...the present color is terrible...it isn't peach: it is reddish brown."[52] He complained to Grove Patterson that "...the color of our Peach paper seems to have gotten darker, and that makes the printing look worse. We must have a lighter Peach...we must demand of the paper company that they furnish us a satisfactory light Peach paper, or we will have to get our paper elsewhere."[53] A light pinkish-yellow is what he wanted, as in the color of the fruit. He believed that the front page of the Peach had to grab and hold the reader, or else not only would the section fail, but the newspaper as a whole would lose circulation.

On at least one occasion, the entire print run of the *Blade* was deliberately split between a light peach stock and a darker one, so that it could be determined which one the public preferred. (The lighter edition sold slightly better).[54] At Paul Block's insistence, high-level meetings were held regularly with Grove Patterson and some of his reporters and editors, to discuss issues concerning the Peach. Personnel from advertising and circulation also met, to discuss in depth the appearance and focus of twenty or thirty of the past Peach sections.[55]   Each month Block would go through the 20-odd Peach sections and critique them, sending long, agonizing memos to his staff pointing out everything he liked or didn't like, from the point size of the headlines to the features and photographs selected.[56] He continually suggested that his editors study *Life Magazine's* style in telling a picture story, and on one occasion he offered the New York *Daily News* as a possible model of well-done picture story editing. His editors became so perplexed and frustrated as to what Block really wanted with the Peach, regarding its content, color, and layout, that they once made up five sample sections of the same day's Peach, with different photos and different front page features, gave a code number to each sample, and had them delivered to Paul Block for his approval and stated preference. The sample newspapers consisted of:

1. One with a large number of photographs with some features and stories added.
2. Another with a straight combination of photographs, short features, and two additional stories, but laid out differently than No. 1.
3. One that contained a large feature story, two large photographs and some short features.
4. Similar to No. 3 but with a different layout.
5. Similar to No. 3 but with two columns (of Ernie Pyle and Neal O'Hara at the top of the page) and other design differences.[57]

Block immediately replied with a three-page, single-spaced letter as to which sample he preferred: No. 1. It contained, among other things, five photographs, one of a model in a gypsy-inspired hat (perhaps Block was thinking of Marion Davies and her role in *Runaway, Romany*); a shot of a large army cannon – framed by palm trees – being fired by American troops training in Puerto Rico; a model posing with the latest style of playsuit; a millionaire couple enjoying their honeymoon in Palm Beach; and a still-life of a springtime vista of the Alps. Stories on the front page of the section were all self-contained, with no jumps (that is, none of the stories were continued on an inside page). The topics of these stories included how football coach Fielding H. "Hurry-Up" Yost once humorously blundered away a particular play; a short piece on the theft of dogs; a column of tidbits and trivia by Neal O'Hara, called "Pull Up a Chair;" and an article on a study as to where most people propose marriage (6% in those days popped the question by letter or wire). Another attempt at changing the front page of the Peach was made when the editors deleted all of the copy and ran only photographs. Paul Block instantly vetoed this approach.[58]

So irritated did Block become over the editorial approach to the Peach that he reduced the salary of its editor, Lou Schwab, and threatened to fire him unless he markedly improved the section: this from a publisher who prided himself in never firing anyone in forty years in the newspaper business.[59,60] Eventually, after literally hundreds of memos, letters, telegrams and telephone calls over a period of years, a virtual library of editorial opinion and discussion, Block's editors gave him what he wanted.

Paul Block's legacy of the Peach still lives six decades after his death, and is one of the most highly-read sections in the *Toledo Blade*, fulfilling Block's hope to his editors: "We are not trying to control the Peach Section or dictate terms on it. All we are thinking about is to make it such a great section, that no one will ever want to stop reading it."[61]

Washington Herald

As if Block didn't have enough worries about all of his papers in 1926 – at the time he was publishing five newspapers other than the *Toledo Blade*, and representing dozens of others – Hearst suddenly asked him if he would be willing to take over as interim publisher of the *Washington Herald* in the nation's capital.

Block knew and liked Washington, D.C. mainly through his years as the special representative of the *Washington Post*, but he was aware that as a publisher it was extremely difficult to make money with a newspaper in Washington. Papers that emanated from the capital often had prestige and a certain amount of circulation, but it was hardly a prosperous city. Advertisers were more prone to buy space in more upscale cities such as New York or Boston. Stanley Walker, city editor of the *New York Herald-Tribune*, once wrote about the peculiarity of D.C. newspapers: "[A Washington newspaper] may have a voice that demands respect, but the advertising revenue is hard to get. It may be a splendid show window, but a hollow shell as a business proposition."[62] Neither the Scripps-Howard afternoon tabloid *Washington News*, nor Ned McLean's superbly-edited, liberal *Washington Post,* was studded with advertising. The conservative *Washington Star* was one of the few newspapers in the capital that was relatively advertising rich.

Because Block's publishing interests were so intertwined with Hearst's – he was representing many of Hearst's 28 newspapers – and it began to appear that he might become involved quite imminently in other holdings, he felt he couldn't turn down Hearst's request. Shortly before that, Arthur Brisbane had bought the *Washington Times,* an evening paper, and at first he steadfastly claimed that it was his money, not Hearst's, that was invested in it. Hearst then wanted Block to take over the morning *Herald*, with the same promise that he supposedly gave Brisbane: Hearst would buy it back from him if it developed that the paper was a poor investment. Block's friend, Herbert Hoover – before he became President, and while he was Secretary of Commerce – had owned a fairly large interest in the *Washington Herald*, and as a result was an excellent news source during that time. Hoover had sold his portion of the *Washington Herald* to Hearst in 1922.[63] It is possible that because Block felt such a close connection to Hoover and Hearst, he built an anticipated attachment for the *Herald* through projected nostalgia. Block reluctantly agreed to see what he could do with the *Herald*.

As it developed, the whole Washington project proved to be neither profitable nor rewarding for Block. Both the *Times* and the *Herald* were losing large amounts of money before he even began as publisher of the latter, and each were pale copies of the *Washington Star* and the *Washington Post*, lagging far behind them in every way as competitors. There were other problems that beset the *Times* and the *Herald,* as well.

Brisbane was in trouble because he admitted in court that a group of German-American brewers had given him $500,000 to purchase the *Times*, and he was being investigated by the United States Secret Service.[64] Because of this anti-American scandal, Brisbane then sold the paper to Hearst (or did Hearst really own it all along?). That is why Hearst wanted Block to take over the *Herald* – because Brisbane couldn't buy it or assume responsibility for it under the circumstances, and Hearst was trying, oxymoronically, to continue to establish the world's most pretentious and ostentatious low profile.

Block was in and out of control of the *Herald* in less than a year. He rarely visited the paper and was simply holding it for Hearst until the time came when he knew Hearst would buy it back. The owners of the *Washington Post*, knowing that Hearst was having financial difficulties with both papers, made an offer to buy the *Herald* but their bid was not accepted.[65]   Eventually, Hearst sold both the *Times* and the *Herald* to a good friend of his, Eleanor "Cissy" Patterson, the redheaded scion of the renowned newspaper family, who had gone to work for Hearst as the editor of the *Herald* at the lordly salary at that time of $10,000 a year.[66]   She combined both newspapers into one, the *Washington Times-Herald*, and unlike anyone else had been able to do in years, ruled the paper with an iron blue pencil, expanded its feature coverage, and introduced personal journalism to Washington, with somewhat of a disregard for objective reporting. Before long, she managed to make the *Times-Herald* into a highly successful venture, and outstripped all other Washington papers with a circulation that neared 500,000.

Block was so uninvolved with his brief stint at the *Washington Herald* that no biographical reference books, histories of journalism or even articles in the trade press of the time mention the fact that he owned it for a short while. Even though he wasn't hiding the fact, only in his deposition against Buggie in 1927 did his ownership come out publicly:

> Question: Can you tell us some of the properties, or all of them if you can, that you have bought and sold in the past few years?
>
> Answer: [Block] I bought the *Memphis News-Scimitar*, which paper I also sold ten or twelve years after I bought it. I bought a one-half interest in the *New York Mail*, which interest I also sold a number of years later. I bought the *Washington Herald*; I bought the *Duluth Herald*; I bought the *Lancaster New Era*.
>
> Question: That is of Lancaster, Pennsylvania?
>
> Answer: Lancaster, Pennsylvania.
>
> Question: And the *Duluth Herald* was of Duluth, Minnesota?
>
> Answer: Duluth, Minnesota.
>
> Question: And the *Washington Herald* was of Washington, D.C.?
>
> Answer: D.C. And I also bought the *Newark Star-Eagle*.

Block and Charles Lindbergh

In June of 1927, when Charles Lindbergh made his triumphant entry into Manhattan, with the greatest tickertape parade in the history of the city – before or since – Paul Block was on the welcoming committee. Block had met Lindbergh earlier that morning on the *Macom* – the official yacht of the Mayor of the City of New York – which had awaited the aviator's arrival while docked at Staten Island. The adulation and subsequent frenzy that Lindbergh was afforded throughout the world for his solo flight across the Atlantic was small in comparison to the worship he received in New York City. Hundreds of thousands, perhaps millions, of spectators lined the streets for a mere glimpse of him. Block was unruffled, but impressed and honored at being in the company of one of the greatest heroes that this country had ever known.

Block was not in the official car that carried Lindbergh, Jimmy Walker and New York's official greeter, Grover Whalen, up from the Battery through the stately Wall Street canyons in a blizzard of confetti. But he was waiting for Lindbergh on the dais erected on the steps of City Hall. Lindbergh had become an international hero, and Block's friend Walker ceremoniously pinned a medal on him and proclaimed:

> You can hear the heartbeat of six million people, and the story they tell is one of pride and one of admiration. As you went over the ocean, you inscribed on the heavens themselves a beautiful rainbow of hope and courage and confidence in mankind. Colonel Lindbergh, New York City is yours. I don't give it to you. You won it![67]

On "Lindbergh Day" the New York Stock Exchange was closed, as well as all schools and most offices in the city, including Paul Block & Associates. For days afterwards in New York City, Lindy was given medals, bouquets, kisses and honoraria of tens of thousands of dollars, and more felicitations and handshakes than he could tolerate.

Two nights after he burst upon New York after attending literally dozens of tributes and receptions, Lindbergh was given a "private" performance of the extravaganza *Rio Rita*, one of the greatest smash-hit musical comedies ever to be staged on Broadway; it was mounted in Zeigfeld's brand new theater, uniquely shaped like an elliptical eggshell. The theater was packed that night with specially-invited guests, the gliterati of New York, who came more to get a closer look at Lindy – even to shake his hand or give him a peck on the cheek – rather than to enjoy the spinning, stamping and cavorting by the lavishly-costumed performers.

Although the regular cast of singers, dancers and comedians performed that night in their regular roles and routines – including a Central America marimba band, a group of troubadours, and dozens of beautiful dancing girls – three special stars, the most famous in show business, made an impromptu appearance...out of respect to Lindbergh: Will Rogers, Al Jolson and Eddie Cantor. They were all at their most entertaining: Jolson sang three choruses of *Toot-Toot-Tootsie, Goodbye,* a song he would make even more famous a few months later, as the first ever to be recorded on screen, in the film *The Jazz Singer*; Eddie Cantor, in black face, did a rendition of *If You Knew Suzie*; and the laconic Will Rogers drawled off a cascade of one and two-liners, all somewhat irreverent or illuminating that sent the audience rollicking. But when Rogers talked of Lindbergh, although lighthearted, he was thoughtful. "I wish he was twins," he said of the famed flyer. "There is a hundred and twenty million people in America all ready to tell Lindbergh what to do. Well, he might be the means of saving us in the next war. His inspiration will do more for American aviation that anything than has happened since the Wrights invented [airplanes]."[68]

Seated in Lindbergh's box with him was Jimmy Walker and Betty Compton, William Randolph Hearst and Marion Davies, Grover Whalen, and Paul and Dina Block. There was also an army officer whose name has been lost to memory. It was a great moment for the audience just to be in the same theater as Lucky Lindy; it had special significance and distinction for Block to be one of Lindbergh's fellow box-mates.

As the big stars trotted out their favorite songs and monologues, Block was variously transfixed and given to hysterical laughter, but he became annoyed when he noticed that Lindbergh was paying little attention to the show, seemingly uninterested even when his own name was mentioned. Throughout the performance he talked with his army colleague about all manner of aviation technicalities and flying lore such as radial engines and pontoons, wingspans and landing fields. Block felt that since the whole evening was one of respect for Lindbergh, the aviator should have reciprocated with if not rapt attention, at least feigned politeness. Years later, William Block recalled his father's reaction to Lindbergh's affront: "That really infuriated my old man."[69]

As soon as the performance was over, Lindbergh ducked out of the theater, and drove himself to Mitchell Field on Long Island to fly a borrowed army plane to Bolling Field. He was back in New York the next day, this time flying the *Spirit of St. Louis* to Roosevelt Field, the site of the commencement of his historic flight He was then ultimately feted and honored during Charles Lindbergh Day in Brooklyn.[70]

That night, Block was invited to a party in Lindbergh's honor at William Randolph Hearst's cavernous apartment. Jimmy Walker was there, as was Charlie Chaplin, and dozens of the city's most influential and glamorous people. With no mention of the guest of honor, Chaplin let it be known that of all the people he had known in his entire life, it was *Hearst* who was the person who made the deepest impression on him.[71] Block listened, and part of him agreed. Certainly he found it difficult to forgive Lindbergh for his jaded attitude at the special performance of *Rio Rita.*

Brooklyn Standard-Union

Apparently satisfied with the balancing act that he was performing on the tightrope of publishing, in 1928 Block searched for more challenges. He was determined, even intransigent, to buy what everyone was saying was a dangerously risky property, a Brooklyn daily newspaper called the *Standard-Union.*[72] Brooklyn was the third largest city in the United States in 1898 when it merged with New York City to become one of the five boroughs.[73] There was a uniqueness and charm about the borough of Brooklyn that interested Paul Block. In some ways it reminded him of a greatly larger version of Elmira. Brooklyn, in many ways, was superior to its big sister, Manhattan. It was a city of not just houses but homes, a city of churches, and eventually of temples, too, and much later, of mosques. It had the greatest seaport in the world and, of course, it boasted one of the most spirited baseball teams in the history of the game, the Brooklyn Dodgers. It seemed to retain its nineteenth century pastoral ambience well into the twentieth century – a stroll down Montague Street in Brooklyn Heights, with its old street lamps, brownstones and quaint shops, had a Victorian or Edwardian feel to it – but Brooklynites always retained a certain feistiness and pride in who they were and where they lived.

In the year 1800, the population of Brooklyn was less than 5,000 and a quarter of those were black slaves who were forced to live there.[74] But over the next two generations, Brooklyn's population exploded. The *Brooklyn Standard-Union*, originally titled *The Union*, was founded by William Berri in 1863, the year of the great draft riots in New York City.[75] It was a fiercely partisan time and a group of 60 powerful Republicans in Brooklyn, who supported Abraham Lincoln's war policy against the South, considered the Democrats to have clearly enunciated "defeatism" about the war. They wanted a publication that would champion their own point of view. By 1869, there were 400,000 people living in Brooklyn. For many years, the *Brooklyn Standard-Union* was a popular and dependable institution. The Berri Estate owned the paper until 1927.

Brooklyn was a major marketing center for a variety of unusual products such as glass, steel, buggy whips and glue. During the Roaring '20s,
more than 500,000 people moved into Brooklyn. Coney Island literally
had become America's playground. Paul Block saw potential in
Brooklyn.

He had tried to acquire the *Standard-Union* earlier but was outbid at a
public auction on May 4, 1927 by a syndicate headed by Joseph J. Early,
President of the Union Publishing Corporation.[76] Block asked his friend
Governor Alfred E. Smith if he could help him to somehow gain control
of the paper. "Should you think of anything in this matter that might
assist me, I shall deeply appreciate your advice," he wrote. Smith really
did little to aid Block's pursuit of the *Standard-Union* other than to send
him a note of congratulations when Block did succeed in purchasing the
paper.[77] Mayor Walker, on the other hand, did help him by relaying an
anonymous bid for the paper in Block's behalf, which was ultimately
accepted.

About a year later, on August 4, 1928, Paul Block confirmed the purchase of the *Brooklyn Standard-Union*. He would not disclose the amount
he paid for it other than saying it was in the neighborhood of $1 million.
In a statement, Block said, "I wanted a newspaper nearer my home. The
paper is independent in politics and will continue to be so." He added
that "There was no political interest concerned in the transaction," disregarding the fact that the *Standard-Union* had always been a Republican
newspaper, and that Block's own Republican sensibilities were growing
stronger.

Joseph J. Early, who was managing editor of the *Standard-Union* for
many years before he became part owner, would remain under the Block
ownership as associate editor. Block not only respected Early but had
faith in what he could accomplish. Keeping Early on the payroll would
hopefully increase Block's chances for a successful newspaper.

Block also appointed Ik E. Shuman, a young Southern newspaper man,
who resigned from *The New York Times* to take the *Standard-Union's*
executive editor position.[78] Block hoped Shuman's exuberance and vi-
tality would filter down to some of the older newspaper men on the staff.
Shuman had covered a number of important assignments for *The New
York Times*, including a trip to Honduras and Santo Domingo to report
Col. Charles Lindbergh's goodwill flight. He also established a New
York reputation while he was on the staff of *The New York Evening World*

in 1924, when he wrote a series of articles on housing conditions. The stories contained suggestions on what New York City should do to relieve congestion, and how to eliminate the slums. Many of the *Standard's* suggestions were followed and incorporated into law. This was the type of no-nonsense journalism Block admired.

Daily newspapers were quite popular in Brooklyn.[79] There were also many weeklies, and Paul Block had instant competition from both categories of newspapers. The *Brooklyn Eagle*, Brooklyn's greatest and most enduring newspaper, and the *Brooklyn Daily Times* were Block's chief competitors, and if he could not quite match their level of news scoops, he was determined that he could surpass them in advertising lineage. Although the *Standard-Union* was a Brooklyn newspaper, that did not stop Block from publishing articles and editorials about Manhattan in his paper whenever he could. One could conclude after a close examination of the *Standard-Union* under Block's ownership (in the absence of a Manhattan paper, which he always wanted) that he attempted to emulate those papers being published across the river.

The paper also carried advertising from some key Manhattan establishments. Some of Manhattan's luxury hotels of the day, such as the Hotel McAlpin and the Hotel Martinique, would advertise in the *Standard-Union*, and these ads were placed without money actually changing hands. Block had used this technique with the Hotel Lucerne many years before. It worked this way: After negotiation, Block would place an advertisement for a hotel in one of his newspapers on a "trade-out" basis. For each dollar value of the advertisement placed in the *Standard* by the hotel, Block would receive the same amount of value for staying at the hotel. This "due bill" procedure was used for business entertainment purposes, or even for recreation for his friends and relatives. For example, if a hotel accrued several hundreds – or even thousands – of dollars in advertising, Block could put up his visiting friends, relatives, or business associates at that hotel or use its restaurant, with no cash outlay by himself or his company.

Women's rights issues were of major concern. The Nineteenth Amendment, passed in 1920, had given women the right to vote in state and national elections. It also opened up a wellspring of outspoken interest in topics that had been repressed for years. Block understood women's interest in the legal and political issues that concerned them, as well as in business and domestic issues. He suggested relevant articles and news stories to be run in the *Standard*, and solicited advertising for products or services that were of interest to women, such as ads for a women's trade paper, *Woman's World* of Chicago.

In Block's own promotional ads for the *Standard*, which he ran in trade journals across the country, he pointed out that Brooklyn had more than two million people and was as big as Boston, St. Louis, and Cleveland combined into one, and that Brooklynites had many wants that needed to be satisfied.[80] The tobacco companies were one of the biggest advertisers in the *Standard-Union*. An ad for Lucky Strike cigarettes pictured a sultry Jean Harlow, telling the world how she always reaches for a Lucky. Chesterfield Kings, another popular brand of cigarette, also advertised in the *Standard-Union*. For many years, smoking had been frowned upon for women; but along with their new legal rights, women had also gained social "permission" to use cigarettes, which were not considered at that time as a threat to health. In contrast, Block ran several columns that were deliberately focused on helping the paper's readers. There was a Health and Pure Food Page, and a column called Who's Who in Brooklyn's Business World, where companies could advertise their products or themselves. The *Standard-Union's* circulation increased to about 50,000 by 1930, an improvement that implied possible growth, but which was nonetheless way behind at least a dozen of New York's other daily newspapers.

Paul Block was competitive, but his business was built on friendship, and this affected whatever arose in his day-to-day operations.[81] On February 1, 1929, a fire temporarily damaged the *Standard-Union* building. All of Block's competitors, including the *Eagle* and the *Daily Times*, gallantly offered to print the *Standard-Union's* daily issues for him. Fortunately, the damage from the fire was not that extensive and the *Standard-Union* was able to publish using its own equipment. Block realized, however, how unusual it was for competitors to make such an offer, and was grateful for it.[82]

Block met socially with his competitors as they entertained and relaxed at the brownstone headquarters of the then-new Brooklyn Press Club on Livingston Street in Brooklyn. Many a business deal was conceived, negotiated and consummated at the Club, and it didn't seem to matter to the other members that Block was Jewish. Block also had something in common with the *Daily Eagle's* editor. Walter Johnson, Block's former manager of the Newark Bears, was suing the *Daily Eagle* for running a series of articles that he claimed exploited his career. Johnson had asked for an accounting of the profits derived from the publication.

He said "I have contributed the stories and the *Eagle* is still profiting from these articles," estimating the damages at $50,000. Block laughed and let it be known that he had lost more money than that when Johnson managed his team. As noted, the Newark Bears finished second-to-last place in 1928 in the league standings when Johnson was manager.[83]

Prohibition also affected Paul Block and his newspaper.[84] To increase circulation growth, the *Standard-Union* ran some stories about the bootleggers and the mob in the Brooklyn area. Block received a threat that they would get to him through his family, and so he hired a detective, who was on vacation from the New York City Police Department, to protect his family. Still fearful for their safety, Block ceased publishing articles about the mob. The threats diminished and finally disappeared.

•••

On the Saturday before Election Day in 1928, Block was invited to ride in a "pre-Victory Parade" that was organized to help Governor Alfred E. Smith's campaign for the Presidency, and Franklin D. Roosevelt's run as Governor of New York State. It appeared that Block, a life-long Republican, was throwing his support to the Democratic party...at least to the New Yorkers who were running. Because of his charming manner, Block was asked to ride in the second limousine of the motorcade – which paraded through downtown Brooklyn, along Eastern Parkway and Flatbush Avenue – sitting next to Eleanor Roosevelt and the wife of the rich banker, Herbert H. Lehman, who was running for Lieutenant Governor. Mrs. Roosevelt commended Block for a full-page editorial that he had published in the *Brooklyn Standard-Union* just two days before. In it, Block referred to Roosevelt as a statesman, a husband and a father who had sympathy for the needs of the women and children of the State; he lauded Smith's valiance as a fighter and his policies of progressivism and broadly humane administrative actions; and he implored the voters of New York to vote for Roosevelt and Lehman, because they were "two men of such unusual and such outstanding character and competence."[85]

Mrs. Roosevelt wistfully remarked that Block's editorial was so uncompromising, and so reasoned, that if it had appeared in a Manhattan paper, the election would probably be assured. As soon as the after-parade party was over, Block went into action. He called some of Roosevelt's staunchest supporters such as James A. Farley and Henry Morgenthau, Jr., and by the end of the day, using his own money and that of others,

Block bought advertising space for the *Brooklyn Standard-Union* editorial and placed it on page fifteen of *The New York Times* of November 5, 1928, less than 24-hours before the election. In part, Block stated:

> Mr. Roosevelt, as a lawyer, as a financier, as a civic and welfare worker, as a legislator and statesman, and as a man, has shown he possesses the honesty, the courage, the idealism, the ability and the leadership so necessary for the office to which we now have the opportunity to elect him. Colonel Lehman, as a business man and banker, as a philanthropist whose heart and money have gone to all parts of his own country and to all parts of the world, as an officer in the Army, and as a citizen who has given generously of himself and his money to civic affairs, has shown he possesses the qualities of character, heart and mind to serve with distinction with Mr. Roosevelt.[86]

As the election returns came in, it quickly became clear that Al Smith would not only lose resoundingly in the popular vote, but only be able to achieve a scant 87 electoral votes to Herbert Hoover's massive tally of 444. At first, it also appeared that the Roosevelt-Lehman ticket would go down in defeat as a part of the Hoover landslide. However, after the last vote was counted and verified, Roosevelt emerged the victor over his Republican opponent, Albert Ottinger, by a narrow 25,564 votes, a plurality of 0.6 percent, the thinnest margin for the Governor's seat in the modern history of New York State.

Did Block's editorials serve as the deciding factor in easing Roosevelt into the Governor's mansion? Although possibly not the ultimate catalyst, the editorials may well have increased Roosevelt's returns in New York City and thus have been partially responsible for the success of his political future. No direct expression of gratitude about the election by Roosevelt to Block could be found in the preparation of this book, but some five years later, in 1933, when Block brought up the story of the editorials to Roosevelt, the President's secretary, Louis Howe, responded by saying that the President was happy to be reminded of the incident and was further gratified by Block's generous expressions regarding his Presidency; Roosevelt sent his appreciation.[87]

•••

During the time that Block owned the *Standard-Union* – 1928-1932 – the borough of Brooklyn was in some ways enjoying a Golden Age. It referred to itself as "America's Fourth Largest City;" by the end of the 1920s and an unprecedented building boom, its population of 2.5 million was far ahead of Manhattan's 1.8 million. With so many people engaged in all kinds of activities, there certainly was no shortage of news, opportunities and problems for Block's *Standard-Union* to report on and write about.

All during that time the *Standard-Union* came under fire because of its views about Prohibition.[88] Although a majority of Americans disapproved of Prohibition, a sizable minority favored it, and Block championed the former view. Senator Brookhart of Iowa claimed that all of the talk about drinking was just a dodge invented to sell more newspapers. He said that he *knew* there was not any drinking going on. Brookhart's cure for the present condition was a congressional investigation of newspapers, including the *Standard-Union*. Nothing untoward was found, and the investigation withered. Block enjoyed Mayor Walker's comment about the Prohibitionists: "A reformer is a guy who rides through a sewer in glass-bottomed boat."

The *Standard-Union* embarked on a crusade to make the streets of Brooklyn safer for the children; this was one of Paul Block's ongoing pursuits.[89] Being a parent himself, he wanted Brooklyn to be a place where families could raise their children without fear. Coney Island was a dreamland amusement park. It was the playground of the people, and of celebrities. Charles Lindbergh rode the Cyclone roller coaster and Sigmund Freud was a frequent visitor to the famous park. But Coney Island was not without corruption and crime, and the *Standard-Union* would continually publish articles and run feature stories informing picnickers and beachgoers to be aware of criminal activity. As a result, Block and the *Standard-Union* earned a reputation for their honesty and accuracy. The paper's circulation continued to rise. Paul Block's and the *Standard-Union's* crusade against crime did not go unnoticed. A letter from his friend Jimmy J. Walker highly commended Block: "Public sentiment is an added force in compelling the observance of law and without public sentiment, it is difficult to enforce any law." [90]

One of the articles which appeared in the *Standard-Union* had a great impact on Brooklynites. The headline read:

Women Attack Man as Auto Hits Baby

Detectives rescue driver and arrest him, child unhurt. Joseph Codella, the 15-month-old son of Mr. and Mrs. John Codella, slept in his carriage outside the home of his parents late yesterday afternoon. An automobile driven by George Forshay of Brooklyn zigzagged crazily up the street and jumped the curb and knocked the sleeping Joseph out of his carriage into the street. [91]

The article went on to explain that a dozen women rushed out from nearby houses and threatened Forshay.[92] Mrs. Codella picked up her baby and ran with him into her house. The neighborhood women advanced on Forshay and started to drag him from his car. Driving by in another car, Detectives Quinn, Reilley and Cannon of the Ralph Street Station saw the accident. They stopped and arrested Forshay, charging him with intoxication and reckless driving. Baby Joseph was not seriously injured.

"The purpose of the present crusade is to arouse such a public statement and to educate the drivers to live up to the golden rule," Mayor Walker's letter continued. "Parents too have a duty to their children to impress upon them the danger of indifference to traffic regulations. Let everyone, drivers, parents, and children do their share. I hope every motorist and parent will cooperate with their newspaper in reducing the pitiful toll of children's lives in traffic accidents."

Block had a great fondness for children.[93] Partially because of his vigorous support of parks and playgrounds, Block was chosen as guest of honor on Big Brooklyn Day, an event for the children of Brooklyn. Under the auspices of the Brooklyn Department of Parks, the Fourteenth Annual Exercises of the Summer Playgrounds was held in Prospect Park on August 24, 1929. Twelve hundred children participated and more than 10,000 mothers and children were present. It was a spectacular affair, and Block wanted to do something special for Big Brooklyn Day, so he asked President Hoover to write a letter to the children. Hoover complied.

Thousands of men, women, and children came to take part in the celebration to honor not just Brooklyn but Paul Block. When Block was introduced and he told the crowd that he was going to read a greeting by the President of the United States, the people of Brooklyn cheered wildly; their emotion and pride was so astoundingly powerful that it energized Block. He then began to read:

"Through you I send my cordial greetings to the children of Brooklyn who are to participate in the Fourteenth Annual Exercise of the Summer Playgrounds under the auspices of the Brooklyn Department of Parks. They owe much to Brooklyn for its pioneer work and wise foresight in providing cheerful places for children to play. Children have an inalienable right to constructive joy and that is a product of the playground. Yours faithfully, the President of the United States, Herbert Hoover."[94]

The President's letter not only pleased the people of Brooklyn; it was profoundly important to Paul Block. In a very special way, on that day he had made Brooklyn seem more significant than its big sister, Manhattan.

The *Standard-Union's* circulation increased, but Paul Block was soon spending a great deal of money keeping the paper afloat during some of the toughest economic times that America has ever experienced.[95] The stock market crash of 1929 at first took more of a toll of fear than of dollars. The staff of the *Standard-Union* were starting to be concerned that their jobs were in jeopardy. In an effort to restore their confidence, Block published an editorial in the paper informing his employees that their positions were secure and that the paper was still definitely in business. Governor Franklin D. Roosevelt, among many others, commended Block for his initiative. He wrote, in part: "I am heartily glad to hear of your fine action in guaranteeing employment to those under you during the year 1931."[96]

While his employees were worried about their jobs, Block was actually negotiating for some time to try to purchase the *Brooklyn Times,* in the belief that a consolidation of the two newspapers would not only benefit both papers but was a necessity.[97] Unfortunately, his bid to buy the *Brooklyn Times* was too late. Block's paper was near bankruptcy. Fremont C. Peck, publisher of the *Times*, would not budge or consider a sale. Block insisted that the merger of the two papers was a financially sound idea, and if he could not buy the *Times*, he asked if Peck would consider buying the *Standard*. In a matter of days, on March 12, 1932, Peck bought the *Standard* at an almost total loss for Block. Paul Block's statement about the sale said:

I have sold the *Standard-Union* to Fremont C. Peck, owner of the *Brooklyn Daily Times*, and with tomorrow's issue, the two newspapers will be consolidated. I have always believed

> that a combination of the *Standard-Union* and the *Brooklyn Daily Times* would bring about a very successful newspaper property and, for this reason, I tried to purchase Mr. Peck's newspaper and consolidate it with mine. However, Mr. Peck could not be influenced to sell his paper and the negotiations pending for a number of months have ended with his acquisition of the *Standard-Union*.

All of the feature writers, comic strips, and columns were retained in the combined newspaper,[98] as were many of the staff of the *Standard-Union*, estimated at 75-100 people. It was understood that the men in the higher positions would assume their same assignments in the combined merger. Joseph J. Early was named associate editor. Ik Shuman, executive editor of the *Standard-Union*, went on to work with Paul Block & Associates.

Block was concerned that some of the other employees would find themselves out of a job.[99] In a statement from Daniel Nicoll, Block's assistant, he said, "The main concern of the company now is to find jobs for the men thrown out of work because of the merger. Arrangements have been made to give employees one or two weeks extra salary depending on length of service and other conditions." The Depression was taking hold, and Block's heart and pocketbook went out to his former employees. A few who were willing and able to move were given jobs in Newark, Duluth, Milwaukee or Toledo, all cities in which Paul Block owned newspapers.

At that point, Paul Block still retained the *Newark Star Eagle,* which he had owned since 1916, the *Toledo Blade*, and his four other newspapers, but never again would he own a newspaper in New York City. He still, however, called New York City his home and continued to live there in his apartment at the Waldorf Towers.[100]

Block had helped to make the Brooklyn streets safer for children. He had given Brooklynites something to cheer about every time they read the headlines of his newspaper. People said that Brooklyn lost a true hero the day Block sold the *Brooklyn Standard-Union*.

Brooklyn went on to survive the good times and the bad.[101] The *Brooklyn Times-Union* and the *Brooklyn Eagle* continued publishing their newspapers well into the 1950s, but both seemed to lose touch with their readership and were not aware of the growing concerns and problems of the increasing numbers of black and Hispanic members of the community. The beloved Brooklyn Dodgers left town. Coney Island, America's playground, deteriorated. It seemed everyone was giving up on Brooklyn. the *Brooklyn Eagle*, the last daily in Brooklyn, closed its doors in 1955, and to this day Brooklyn remains the only American community of two million people without its own daily newspaper.

Chapter 8
Business in Transition

There was no reasoned or accurate way that anyone could predict the direction of the stock market in 1929. There were many conflicting signals. All through the previous year the economy had been booming. In 1928, Arthur Brisbane, Hearst's editor of the New York *Journal*, had been indignant when the Federal Reserve Board issued a cautious and ambiguous warning that speculation was approaching the danger point: "If buying and selling stocks is wrong, the government should close the Stock Exchange. If not, the Federal Reserve should mind its own business."[1] During visits to the White House, even as late as early 1929, before Hoover took office in March, Block's friend, the usually quiescent President Calvin Coolidge, had made assurances to him – as he did to the nation – that the unprecedented growth in loans that made it easier to buy stocks with less cash (or on margin) was still safe, and that he saw nothing unfavorable about the process. *The Nation*, however, steadfastly disagreed with "Silent Cal" and in an editorial reported that Wall Street was "overflowing with inexperienced suckers attracted by big, easy profits" in the greatest bull market the country had ever seen.[2]

When Herbert Hoover was swept into the White House later that year, defeating New York Governor Alfred E. Smith in a landslide, Block was in a quandary of what to do with his investments and his allegiances: he was eager to protect his holdings but wanted to accumulate more money; he also admired and had a close friendship with both men. He continued his backing of the new President, but continued to keep in touch with the Governor. His primary affiliation, however, was with the President: Block and Hoover became lifelong friends. Hoover had been elected because of his promises of prosperity: all of Block's newspapers had quoted or paraphrased his famous campaign speech: "There will be a chicken in every pot and a car in every garage." This spirit of optimism by the new President of the United States also affected Paul Block's sensibilities, and he therefore took no alarm at the whispers of financial instability that might soon come, even though he had heard that some large traders were quietly unloading their shares.

Block continued to buy more and more stocks on margin and proceeded to speculate by becoming involved in additional newspaper properties. Even shortly after the Crash, where he personally took great losses when his broker sent out a margin call and he was unable to meet the demand, Block seemed if not buoyant about the future, at least sanguine. He pointed to his advanced advertising contracts or the promises that he had received for increased advertising: "Standard Brands, Inc., which owns such food products as Fleischman's Yeast, Royal Baking Powder, Royal Gelatin and Chase & Sanborn Coffee, is planning to spend more money for advertising next year than ever before. The Colgate-Palmolive-Peet Company, manufacturers of soaps, toilet articles and other such preparations, has plans for an even more aggressive advertising and merchandising campaign for next year than this year. Good securities will again improve in value. The earning power has in no way been changed and impaired and, in many instances, has been increased and is being increased over the past and previous years."[3]

Milwaukee Sentinel – 1929

Only three weeks before Black Tuesday, Oct. 29, 1929, Paul Block purchased the *Milwaukee Sentinel*, the city's only morning paper. Before he even arrived in Wisconsin to sign the ownership papers, he was ensnared in controversy. The contention involved Block's association with William Randolph Hearst. Block's business arrangements with Hearst were the same for the *Sentinel* as the dealings he had established with Hearst for the *Pittsburgh Post-Gazette* two years before. Their business relationship was criticized throughout the industry and in the trade press with the implication, and in some cases the accusation, that Block served as a "dummy" or "stooge," helping Hearst to buy newspapers that Hearst was not able to acquire directly, usually because their owners would not sell to him. Now, after more than a half-century has passed, with much archival material inadvertently destroyed, lost or missing, and virtually no one alive who can remember or wishes to reveal the details of the financial arrangements between Hearst and Block, we shall probably never know the exact story concerning the Milwaukee newspapers. But much about their complex relationship can be reconstructed. First, here is a brief history of the *Sentinel* prior to Block's connection with the paper.

The reputation of the *Sentinel* was long and distinguished. A rabidly Republican paper, it was founded in 1837 by Solomon Juneau, Milwaukee's first non-Indian settler and first mayor, and it became a daily in 1844, even before Milwaukee had been incorporated as a city. Passing through various publishers, it was bought in 1901 by Charles F. Pfister, the millionaire owner of Wisconsin's largest meat packing firm, who held it until 1924. The paper had the singular distinction of being the first newsroom in America to own a functioning typewriter, upon which some of the journalists would take turns learning to type their stories. The typewriting machine was developed by C.L. Sholes, who was editor of the *Sentinel* in 1866 and 1867.[4]

By the late 1920s, Milwaukee's population had risen to nearly 600,000. Aside from its famous beer industry, the city had considerable other commerce, aided partly because of its fine harbor on the Western end of Lake Michigan, and its closeness to Chicago. Milwaukee had no less than six daily newspapers, several German language papers, and even a Yiddish weekly, the *Milwaukee Wolhenblat.*

Hearst's past and then-present reputation as a sensationalist, his investigation by the U.S. Attorney General's office for sedition because of his pro-German sentiments during World War I, the attack on him by the Women's Christian Temperance Union and the Anti-Saloon League (ironic since Hearst was a near teetotaler), and even the old charges that he was to blame for the Spanish-American War, produced such a climate of hate that boycotts were organized throughout the country against him and his publications and he was burned in effigy; he was also blamed by his detractors for fanning the flames that led to the assassination of President McKinley. It was reported at the time that when captured, the assassin Leon Czolgosz had a clipping in his pocket of Hearst's *Journal* vilifying McKinley. Mobs seized Hearst newsboys to prevent them from distributing their papers, and readers cancelled their subscriptions to Hearst newspapers. There were many newspaper readers and advertisers who spurned Hearst so intensely that they refused to give him their money or support, whether it be for a three-cent newspaper or a $1,000 full-page advertisement.

In Milwaukee, though, there was a huge German population, and Hearst's pro-Germany stance before the war was not looked upon all that critically by some of its citizens. During the early twenties, he indirectly acquired several newspapers in the city. First, Hearst bought the *Wisconsin News*, an evening paper, the city's oldest newspaper of any kind. But he did not purchase it in his own name. In order to ease his acceptance into Milwaukee, Hearst again used Arthur Brisbane, his editor and oracle of editorials throughout the Hearst chain, as his business partner. Brisbane claimed (just as he had when he "purchased" the *Washington Herald*) that it was *his* money – not Hearst's – which effected the transaction. Hearst also bought the *Milwaukee Telegram*, a Sunday paper. Then, in 1924, in his ongoing attempt to dominate the Milwaukee newspaper business, Hearst had Brisbane buy the *Milwaukee Sentinel*, again claiming that it was not his money but Brisbane's that was used. Although no price was ever announced, a record of promissory notes payable to the Pfister estate in the amount of $750,000 indicates that that may have been the purchase price, a bargain even at pre-Depression rates.[5]

Later that year a secret, undated memorandum was uncovered from Brisbane to his staff at the Hearst-owned *New York Journal* that indicated that it *was* Hearst's money all along:

> Mr. Hearst has just purchased the *Milwaukee Sentinel* from Mr. Charles Pfister and paid a fortune for the exclusive morning and Sunday newspaper Associated Press membership for that city.[6]

Afterward, when Hearst was interviewed about the memo and his ownership of the *Sentinel*, he couldn't deny that it had been his money that had been used to buy the paper, but he claimed that Brisbane had slightly misinterpreted his involvement: he really didn't *own* the newspaper outright but had taken a five-year option on it, and he was not at all sure that he would recommence as publisher in 1929 when the renewal period arose.

True to his five-year-old pronouncement, in September of 1929, barely a month before the stock market crash, Hearst offered Block the ownership of the *Milwaukee Sentinel* for what was reported as "an undisclosed price."[7] Since at that time the sale price of newspapers regularly reached the trade press, and it was customary for the buying and selling parties to reveal, or at least hint for publication what amount of money had been paid to purchase a major metropolitan paper, Block's and Hearst's refusal to discuss the financial arrangement between them immediately caused suspicions not only among journalists in the trade and public press, but many of the citizens of Milwaukee, as well.

The financial arrangement worked as follows: Block set up what one of his associates called a "camouflage" corporation, of which he was sole owner of all of the stock, but the money to buy such stock and all operational funds for the corporation was supplied by Hearst. A separate agreement, co-signed by Block and Hearst, stated in part:

> I [Paul Block] agree to enter into such negotiations subject to and to the extent indicated by such instructions as you may give from time to time and upon your request I will enter into a contract for the acquisition in my own name such stock or properties and/or acquire in my own name such stock or properties, upon such terms as you may approve, agreeing to hold for your sole account and benefit and subject to your direction and control, both as to the operation of such properties and the ultimate disposition of such stock properties...You [William Randolph Hearst] agree to provide such sums as I may be required to pay acquiring such stocks or properties as aforesaid, and to hold me harmless from any loss which I may suffer as the result of action taken by me under this agreement.[8]

In other words, Block agreed to take over certain newspaper properties for Hearst, operate them as publisher, but invest no money of his own; nor would he be legally responsible if any untoward expenses should occur that could not be met out of the operating budget, since Hearst had agreed to indemnify him for any such loss. The arrangement, although legal, was certainly clandestine and unprincipled, since Block had to imply, perhaps even lie, to businesses, banks, even to most of his own employees and associates, that *he* was the owner of the *Sentinel*, not Hearst. In fact, he *was* the owner on paper and became thought of as such to the public, but Hearst was the true proprietor, posing in the background, ready to step in whenever he wanted to and when it was convenient for him financially to do so.

In compensation for establishing the arrangement, Block received up to (but not more than) ten percent of the net profits of the paper's revenue to be paid to him on a quarterly basis. He also received *de facto* assurance that Paul Block & Associates would continue as the advertising representatives for the paper (since as publisher, he had the right to hire whomever he wanted: in this case, his own firm), and this, of course, brought in additional income for Block.

The *Baltimore News* and the
Baltimore American

In July of 1929, just before Block's purchase of the *Milwaukee Senti-nel*, he traveled to Maryland to spend time analyzing Hearst's two news-papers, the evening *Baltimore News* and the Sunday *Baltimore Ameri-can*. The circulation of these two newspapers wasn't particularly low (though they were not as large as what Baltimoreans called the Sunpaper, the competing *Baltimore Sun*), but Hearst was not making money with the papers and wanted to know why. Hearst had purchased both the *Ameri-can* and the *News* from Frank J. Munsey in 1923 (the same year that he also bought the *New York Mirror*) for the above-par price of $4 million dollars, and at that time the *American* had had a larger circulation than the *Sun*.

But almost from the moment he had bought them, his circulation had begun to drop. His lurid and overdrawn headlines, his "pink" edition, fashioned after the racy *Police Gazette,* his profuse use of photographs, especially to accompany crime stories, and his eventual change to tabloid form seemed – if anything – to hurt his newsstand sales, rather than bol-ster them.

The fact that Hearst trusted Block's outsider's judgement more than his own editors and business people in Baltimore is interesting to note, and indicative of their long-time friendship and mutual respect. Hearst asked Block if he would spend some time at his Baltimore newspapers to deter-mine what was wrong and whether there was any friction between de-partments, any mal-performance, any disorder of intent from any sector of the newspaper that might have an impact on expense, profit or circula-tion. Hearst wanted Block to assume the mantel of an efficiency expert and come back with some answers. Block was flattered and a bit self-effacing at being asked to insert himself into a business that was not his own, and immediately wrote to Hearst that he was clear as to what *he* would do if he owned the Baltimore papers (he would have sold them, he said) but modestly pointed out that such a decision clearly marked the distinction between the two men: "The difference between W.R. and P.B. is the difference between great wealth and a lot of ability as compared with a little wealth and modest newspaper knowledge."[9]

Block mounted a Napoleonic campaign for the external review of the internal operations: he arrived in Baltimore with his two assistants, Dan Nicoll and Henry Auth, positioned himself with his headquarters in a hotel across the street from the newspaper (which was within the shadow of the competing *Baltimore Sun*), and began a series of interviews of all the top-level people in Hearst's papers, from the publisher to the advertising manager, and from the editor to the circulation director. He had Nicoll and Auth meet with the printers, the distributors, the department heads of personnel, payroll and accounts payable, even the boy carriers, and report back to him with their appraisals.

In less than a week, Block had formed a clear interpretation of the future of the *Baltimore American* and the *Baltimore News*. He told Hearst that if the methods of publishing the papers were not changed, Hearst would never realize a profit, nor ever break even. One of the problems was that Baltimore, like Washington, D.C., simply did not have a large enough universe of local advertisers to support all of the newspapers in the city. The only way that Hearst's Baltimore papers could yield larger revenues, Block contended, was to drastically cut expenses. While "thinking aloud," as he said, Block advised Hearst to reduce his overhead and then only give the papers six more months to see if a profit could be made. Some of the suggestions that Block made to effect savings were: cutting down the number of mailers in the circulation department (there were 19 workers and Block felt the job could be done by virtually half that amount); eliminating a few of the eight editions of the *News* since there were only slight changes made in each edition, and therefore circulation did not increase greatly with the new editions but the expense to publish them did; abandoning plans for securing an additional printing press, which cost more than $1,000,000 dollars; raising the advertising rates (comparing the *News* with the *Sun*, Block pointed out to Hearst that the competitor carried over 17 million lines of advertising every year as opposed to seven million in the *News*); reducing the number of stereotypers, pressmen, editors, reporters, and clerical workers. "The office seems to run wild with men," Block revealed.

In addition to those suggestions, Block was adamant that Hearst include more local editorials; he felt that the current editorial page was much too national in scope and focus, which resulted in lower circulation because readers couldn't identify with the paper. Have an editorial on a local issue *every day*, pleaded Block, and the editorials should contain more invective and more conviction. He went on to recommend that in order to make money, Hearst would also have to reduce the number of pages in every issue. "The size of the paper must be cut," wrote Block emphatically in his report to Hearst. "One woman's page is enough. Local editorials must be used. One hundred and ten columns of news and features are plenty." (In fact, at that time the competing and more profitable *Sun* was running only 120 columns of news, and Hearst was providing his readers with five pages more news than the *Sun*, some 150 columns, all of which were expensive and difficult to produce.)

In total frankness, Block also chided Hearst, although gently, that if he truly wanted to make a profit in Baltimore he would have to give up his constant last minute increases in the size of the paper: "You must stop sending messages to add two more pages or four more pages of this or that kind of news or features, because what is the use of cutting off people if two weeks later you have to add them again to take care of these additional pages?" He also suggested that Hearst consider buying out the *Baltimore Post* and merging it with the *News*, thereby eliminating another competitor in the advertising-weakened city. Hearst agreed to buy the *Post*, but it took him five years to convince its owners to sell.

Block told Hearst that he wished that he were 10 years younger. If he had been, he implied, he could have jumped into the position of publisher of the *Baltimore News* and *Baltimore American*, and made a profit with both. From Block's understanding of the situation, there was no central guiding force to unify all of the departments of the paper and get them to work together; a true publisher could make the difference so that editorial, news, circulation and advertising would all work symbiotically.

The enigmatic Hearst took all of Block's suggestions under consideration and began putting many of them into effect. Years later he would often say that if he hadn't listened to Block, he might have been out of business in Baltimore much sooner than he eventually was. As he began to change his course in Baltimore, Hearst – together with Block – forged ahead in Milwaukee.

Milwaukee Sentinel – 1937

Journalist Robert W. Wells, in his book *The Milwaukee Journal*, a 100-year chronicle, mentions that owner Harry J. Grant heard a rumor early in 1928 that "Paul Block was to take over the *Sentinel* to take the curse of Hearst ownership away."[10] Some people believed that Hearst began to divest himself of some of his newspapers when he learned that that stock market seemed to be on the brink of a crash; others contended that no money passed between Block and Hearst – which was, in effect, true – just an agreement for Block to be the titular head of the *Sentinel*, simply to relieve some of the pressure on Hearst's controversial stature.

Many years later in the late 1940s, in an attempt to reconstruct the history of Block's business affairs, his trusted assistant publisher Dan Nicoll wrote the following:

> There was never any question in my mind about their [the Milwaukee newspapers] being owned by W.R. Hearst. In all of my discussions with Mr. Block from time to time, over the years, the controlling factor in the handling of matters concerning these newspapers was the knowledge that Mr. Block was the agent for Mr. Hearst and Mr. Hearst the owner....the real ownership was never hidden from me by Mr. Block because, as his top representative, I had to be in possession of the facts in order to properly carry out Mr. Block's wishes covering the operation.[11]

Block had arrived in Milwaukee on September 25th, ensconced himself symbolically in the Pfister Hotel (owned by the family of the original owner of the *Milwaukee Sentinel*, Charles F. Pfister), ate green turtle soup and crawfish dinners at Kalt's Restaurant, and blatantly but politely refused to answer questions targeted at him by the press. Each time he left a meeting held in one of the hotel's conference rooms, he was questioned. The litany went something like this:

> "Can you divulge the financial considerations in the purchase, Mr. Block?"
> *"No I can't and who said there was going to be a purchase?"*
> "Was the transaction arranged directly with Mr. Hearst, or with Mr. Brisbane?"
> *"No comment."*
> "Will Mr. Hearst be coming to Milwaukee to discuss the sale of the Sentinel?"
> *"I haven't the faintest idea."*

By October 1st, Paul Block took control and operational ownership of the *Milwaukee Sentinel* and he made the following announcement in a front-page editorial:

> With today's issue the *Milwaukee Sentinel* passes into my ownership. I am aware of the long and distinguished career of this newspaper, now nearly 100 years old, and of the high character of the many men and women who have been and

are still associated with it. It is my purpose to publish a newspaper that will be fair, just and independent in all its relations
to public questions and to the people, no matter what may be
their political beliefs, their race or religion.[12]

As he did with the *Duluth-Herald* and the *Lancaster New Era*, Block
relied on Michael Hanson to take charge of the day-to-day business details of the *Sentinel*, giving him the title of assistant publisher.

It is not difficult to ascertain in retrospect that Block was a surrogate
for Hearst in the purchase of the *Sentinel*, but Block was also continuing
to build his own empire, which he had started thirteen years before, gaining experience as a publisher, making additional contacts and accumulating revenue so that he could buy more properties.

Perhaps all of the above factors had some bearing on the truth of Block's
involvement in the *Sentinel*. What is certain is that immediately upon
assuming control, Block took his title of publisher seriously. In a matter
of days, he changed the typographical dress and appearance of the *Sentinel* to conform to that of his other papers, the *Newark Star-Eagle, Brooklyn Standard Union, Duluth Herald, Duluth News-Tribune, Toledo Blade*,
and the *Pittsburgh Post-Gazette* (which will be discussed in a future chapter). More and larger photos found their way onto the pages of the *Sentinel*; there was a shift from narrow 8- and 9-column pages to a more modern 6-column page, and white gutters between columns instead of rules
became standard make-up. These changes created a cleaner looking page
that was easier to read. Block increased the quantity of news, brought in
a large amount of national advertising, introduced a second section with
its own "front page" – or "break page" as it came to be called – of more
local news, and retained most of the traditional *Sentinel* features. Arthur
Brisbane's column, "Today," which was gospel to many readers not only
in Hearst papers but syndicated throughout the nation, was slightly de-
flated in status. It still appeared on the first page, but was dropped to the
bottom of column one and not so prominently displayed as it had been.
(Actually, nonchalant Hearst had told Block that it was all right with him
if he dropped Brisbane's column altogether.) In its place was Paul Block's
eponymously-signed editorial, often addressed to local issues but usually
concerning his opinions and judgments on national or international questions, such as his lauding Cabinet Member Andrew Mellon as the "greatest treasury head since Alexander Hamilton;"[13] or his bringing attention
to his philosophy of "friendship personified" by noting President Hoover's

successful attempts at bridging close ties with England's Prime Minister MacDonald ("Friendliness is truly a worker of miracles, and it is as ready to serve nations as individuals.")[14]

In his first issue, Block solicited and published congratulatory letters from many of his friends, most of whom were nationally famous: former-President Calvin Coolidge, ex-Governor Alfred E. Smith, Governor Walter Kohler of Wisconsin, and Mayor Jimmy Walker. Walker wrote, in part: "Your latest acquisition, *The Milwaukee Sentinel*, which I am informed you will take over tomorrow, will undoubtedly constitute an important member of your steadily increasing journalistic family. It is a paper whose fine tradition I know will be rigidly preserved under your guidance."

In a humorous secretarial or clerical mix-up, New York State Governor Franklin Delano Roosevelt, perhaps eager to ingratiate himself with Block's Republican readers since he planned to run for even higher office, wrote Block *two* letters of congratulation. The first, from Warm Springs, Georgia, dated Sept. 29, 1929, the day *before* Block made the announcement that he was the new owner, stated in part: "I congratulate you and I congratulate the citizens of Milwaukee. You have always been associated with clean and independent newspapers. I feel confident that you will continue to devote your papers to that conscientious public service which has been their aim in the past."[15] Exactly a month later, on October 29, 1929, (coincidentally the day of the stock market crash), Roosevelt wrote to Block again: "I do not know whether I have written to congratulate you on the acquisition of *The Milwaukee Sentinel*. It always has been a splendid paper, noted for the courage of its opinions, and I know that under your ownership it will continue its fine influence."[16]

Through his editorials and news coverage in the *Sentinel*, Block attempted to reach the people of Milwaukee by addressing the issues that most concerned them: he fought for the construction of the St. Lawrence Seaway, and he continually criticized and called for the repeal of Prohibition. As a result, in a city that made its reputation and half of its income on beer, ale and lager, the owners of the Schlitz, Pabst, Pilsner and Miller breweries became ardent supporters of Paul Block personally. The people of Milwaukee championed Paul Block for his efforts.

Within the first month of his ownership of the *Sentinel*, Block performed a kind deed that made national headlines. An editorial he wrote saved two orphaned Finnish sisters, both teenaged factory workers, from deportation to their native Finland. Block pleaded that the girls should remain in their foster home in northern Wisconsin (which was not unlike their native land), because they really had no family to go home to. Hundreds of letters of protest in behalf of the girls filed into the *Sentinel*, and Block sent his editorial and a collection of copies of the protest letters to Secretary of Labor John J. Davis, and to President Herbert Hoover. Hoover was touched by the plight, ordered an investigation, and the girls were permitted to remain in the United States.[17]

For half the winter of 1929 it was literally tough sledding for the *Sentinel* in all senses of that phrase. Milwaukee was snowbound and freezing and the streets were not passable because of the deep snow. This prevented the *Sentinel's* delivery trucks from distributing copies to subscribers, especially those in the outlying districts. Block's solution was to have the boy carriers deliver the papers by sled where possible, and to trudge by foot through the higher snowdrifts. As a result, all home subscribers received their copies without fail every day. Each boy was rewarded with either a sled or a wagon to keep.

Block's successes in distribution were not matched in all other areas, however. As the Depression began, it didn't take long for him to realize that despite all of his optimism about the economy, he was in trouble with the *Milwaukee Sentinel*. Four to five million Americans were jobless, 400,000 depositors of the Bank of the United States found the doors of their local banks padlocked, bankruptcies were rampant, many people were not buying virtually anything – including basic necessities – and in a matter of months from the time of the Crash, advertisers had no budget to work with because of the scarcity of cash. In mid-September of 1930, with the ink hardly dry on his ownership papers of the *Sentinel*, Block realized that something had to be done to confront the oncoming economic disaster: either he had to bring in more income, or else he had to reduce costs. If he couldn't do either, he would have to convince Hearst to sell the *Sentinel*. Always in the back of Block's mind was the hope that he would make the *Sentinel* so successful that he himself would want to buy it from Hearst, but he had to be assured that a profitable newspaper was a certainty.[18] The *Sentinel* did not look as though it was going to be a straightforward and effortless ascent.

Block approached Hearst to determine how the evening *Wisconsin News* was faring in terms of lines of advertising and numbers of circulation. Both departments of the *News* were drastically low in revenue and subscriber and newsstand sales. Hearst had tried all kinds of promotion as circulation boosters. For example, he gave away free dishes and silverware to anyone who would take a home subscription to the *Wisconsin*

News; for just a few cents extra, subscribers of the *News* could also have delivered to their homes, on an exclusive basis, Hearst's Sunday *Herald-Examiner* from the nearby windy city of Chicago. Neither of these gestures worked to markedly increase his numbers. The *Milwaukee Journal*, the key competitor of both papers, had a higher circulation and was selling more advertising space, and the struggle to match the *Journal* was diminishing the efforts and energy of both the *Wisconsin News* and the *Milwaukee Sentinel*. The *Journal* was also way ahead of the *News* in coverage of local Milwaukee and Wisconsin news; the only advantage the *News* possessed over the *Journal* was its superior photo section. When Hearst began publishing a tabloid magazine section for the *News*, he printed it on pink paper – a mistake, Block felt at that time – instead of investing the money to publish color photos on white paper: "Which is what I originally had in mind," Block said to Hearst.[19]

Block first suggested that Hearst abandon the *News* so that there would be only one paper to worry about. "I have always felt that the thing to do there [in Milwaukee] is to publish one newspaper, and I am convinced that it should be a morning paper with a Sunday edition," Block wrote to Hearst.[20] When Hearst was negative to that idea ("One shortens sail in a storm, but as the storm passes one spreads more canvas if the desire is to reach one's destination," he said somewhat philosophically),[21] Block proposed that both papers at least pool their resources, and combine their operations in terms of advertising, editorial and production costs and facilities. Consolidation of the circulation departments alone, Block pointed out, could easily save $4,000 a week, perhaps a million or more dollars over several years.[22]

Again, secret negotiations began as the two newspaper publishers paradoxically barred all other newspapermen, especially those from opposing newspapers, from any of the details. Since both men were continually traveling to and from their various holdings and interests, Hearst would often send telegrams to his attorney Geoffrey Konta, in New York, to be forwarded to whatever city Block was working in at that time. These telegraphic missives possessed a somewhat-cryptic air because Hearst never used Block's name for fear that someone in either Konta's office or Block's would recognize it, and then a connection between the two could be firmly established, resulting in the end of Hearst's cover and exposing him as the true owner of the *Sentinel*. The wires also demonstrate how grateful Hearst was for having Block to work with. For example:

> PLEASE TELL OUR FRIEND THAT I AM IN HEARTY
> SYMPATHY WITH EVERYTHING HE HAS DONE IN
> MILWAUKEE AND I WISH THAT OUR PUBLISHERS
> WOULD REALIZE THAT NOTHING PERMANENT CAN
> BE BUILT EXCEPT ON THE FIRM FOUNDATION OF A
> GOOD NEWSPAPER STOP THE IMPROVEMENT OF
> THE SENTINEL AS A NEWSPAPER IS ENORMOUS AND
> UNQUESTIONABLY THE APPRECIATION OF THIS
> FACT BY THE CITIZENS IN MILWAUKEE WILL FOL-
> LOW STOP WRH [23]

And:

> PLEASE TELL OUR FRIEND I WILL WAIT UNTIL I SEE
> HIM BEFORE DISCUSSING NEW YORK MATTER BUT
> STILL WANT TO TALK THE MATTER OVER WITH HIM
> STOP I REALIZE THAT I HAVE IMPOSED A GREAT
> DEAL UPON HIM AND THAT I SHOULD BE CAREFUL
> NOT TO IMPOSE TOO MUCH STOP I APPRECIATE IN
> ANY CASE ALL THAT HE HAS DONE AND ALSO HIS
> KINDLY FEELING AND WILLINGNESS TO HELP STOP
> PLEASE EXPRESS THANKS FOR ALL THIS AND SAY I
> WILL DO AS HE SUGGESTS ABOUT MATTER WE
> HAVE IN MIND WITHOUT ABANDONING IDEA STOP
> WRH [24]

In the last week of October, 1930, Block took his private railroad car, Friendship, from New York to Milwaukee. As he rode, he composed the following notice, writing with his pencil on his special letterhead, crossing out, adding, and deleting until he had it exactly the way that he wanted it. On October 30, 1930, to the surprise of Milwaukee residents, the following startling notice ran on the front page of both newspapers:

ANNOUNCEMENT

Beginning November first, the business of the *Milwaukee Sentinel* and the evening *Wisconsin News* will be amalgamated and both papers published under the direction of Mr. Paul Block.

Under this arrangement it will be our ambition to make both the *Sentinel* and the *News* better newspapers than they have ever been.

The combined circulation is now over 175,000 copies per day, which is larger than any daily in Wisconsin and we expect these figures to be even higher with the improved papers which our combined experience and efforts will make possible.

WILLIAM RANDOLPH HEARST
PAUL BLOCK

Block closed down the printing plant and the editorial and business offices of the *Sentinel*, and moved into the *Wisconsin News* building. A few printers, office workers and reporters were laid off, and the two papers were then issued as a combined daily: the *Sentinel* in the morning, and the *News* in the evening. Block's goal was to reach a circulation of 100,000 circulation for each paper (they were running about 85,000 each at that time). Expenses were reduced but only minimally at first. "If I were permitted to cut down expenses without hurting the paper much, I believe I could make both papers break even," Block informed Hearst, "but until I get such orders I shall continue to work along the lines we are following now, as that is my understanding as to what you desire."[25] This conjoined arrangement for the *Milwaukee Sentinel* and the *Wisconsin News* continued for seven years: Paul Block acting as publisher of both papers, Paul Block acting as advertising representative for both papers, Paul Block acting as strike-mediator for both papers, Paul Block acting as owner for both papers...all, always in the psychic shadow of Hearst.

The Newspaper Guild, which had been formed in 1933, consolidated in 1937 after the Supreme Court upheld the constitutionality of the Wagner Act, assuring the Guild a permanent stronghold in the world of newspaper publishing. Due to the further recession of 1937 to 1939, publishers were closing down newspapers and attempting to cut costs, as was the *Sentinel*. Block found the experience taxing. Eliminating any job, whether clerical or editorial, or even reducing the number of people in a department became a difficult process. The Guild contract demanded minimum wages, paid holidays and vacations, overtime pay, sick leave and other benefits, and a minimum of employees in every department.[26] Block's pruning of the *Sentinel's* expenses became arduous and complicated. Many of Hearst's papers were ensnared with strikes, and Block was trying to comply with the Guild's demands to avoid an outright shutdown or lockout of the *Sentinel*.

He became more than annoyed when he discovered that the militant organizer of the Guild at the *Sentinel* was a young reporter named Perry Hill, who had been a friend and former schoolmate of Paul Block, Jr. (when they were at Hotchkiss). Block had given Hill his first job with a newspaper during the depths of the Depression, which was no minor gift, and he felt that Hill displayed no gratitude.[27] Hill agitated for a strike at the Guild's headquarters at Sabel's Tavern on Third Street, a place that Block thereupon avoided. It rankled Block that Hill, who got his start at the *Sentinel*, went on to become one of Milwaukee's most revered editorial writers (ultimately for the *Milwaukee Journal*, where he worked for over 40 years.)[28]

Although the *Sentinel's* circulation and advertising lineage climbed, there was a decline on all fronts at the *News*. Block then changed course and begged Hearst to allow him to spend some considerable amount of money to promote the *News* and increase its circulation.[29] He also asked permission to lower the advertising rates of both papers, and was even negotiating with the competing *Milwaukee Journal* to lower its rates also, so that more advertisers would come into both papers. Hearst was adamant about not lowering the rates, calling the strategy "ineffective." He wired a night letter to Block directly which, in a few sentences, and in a mentoring tone, clearly indicates his philosophy of publishing :

> I BELIEVE ADVERTISERS USE PAPERS THEY WANT
> TO USE AND ARE NOT INFLUENCED BY LOW RATES
> TO USE PAPERS THEY DO NOT WANT TO USE STOP
> ONLY SENSIBLE PLAN THEN IS TO MAKE ADVER-
> TISERS WANT TO USE THE PAPER, AND THIS CAN
> ONLY BE DONE BY EFFECTIVE PROMOTION AND
> LOTS OF IT, PLUS OF COURSE GOOD PAPER STOP

Eventually, when the economy was at its lowest ebb, Block changed his tactics and felt that the advertising rates should be raised. He went back to the *Milwaukee Journal* to see if they would go along with the new strategy. They wouldn't.

By 1936, plagued with overwork and sagging finances, Block began divesting himself of some of his properties. He complained that it was making him sick, that he was actually suffering from headaches, to see that the *Milwaukee Sentinel* and the *Wisconsin News* were the only newspapers with which he was associated which were costing more to operate every year than the previous year.[30]   Although he was the publisher and titular owner of the two Milwaukee papers, it became obvious to him that with Hearst's resolute rule, he would not be able to run the papers the way he wanted to.   Block believed that the reason he was making very little money as a result of the arrangement was because Hearst was intransigent in not following his advice.   Block had already abandoned his interests in the *Brooklyn Standard-Union* and the two Duluth papers. The *New York Evening Mail*, the *Detroit Journal*, and the *Lancaster New Era* had been divested years before.   His entities in 1936 consisted of the *Toledo Blade*, the *Newark Star-Eagle*, the *Pittsburgh Post-Gazette* and the Milwaukee papers, enough for any man to cope with, especially one that also ran the most successful and one of the largest special representation advertising companies in the country.   The anticipation of change made him happy, and when Hearst proposed to "buy" him out of the *Milwaukee Sentinel*, he welcomed the chance.

This time, Block was not averse to speaking to reporters.   He called a press conference at the Hotel Pfister and made the following statement: "When I took over the *Sentinel* from Mr. Hearst it was understood that within 10 years he reserved the right to buy it back, and proceeding under this arrangement, I am disposing of my interest in the *Sentinel* to Mr. Hearst as he has elected to exercise this privilege."[31]

The fact that no one knew of the 10-year option that Hearst had on the *Sentinel* until Block revealed it, seemed not to confuse or annoy people, although pundits did point out that Hearst had finally achieved what he wanted all along: the best newspaper in Milwaukee, which he now owned openly.   Block continued as special advertising representative of the *Sentinel* – the name of which Hearst retained.   Hearst changed the name of his evening paper, however, from the *Wisconsin News* to the *Milwaukee News*, and he renamed the Sunday edition of the *Sentinel* to the *Milwaukee News-Sentinel*.   Block sadly said goodbye to Milwaukee, the *Sentinel* and the *News*, but not to Hearst.[32]

Los Angeles Express – 1931

During the early 1930's, when Block was still continuing to acquire and become publisher of more newspapers, and his special representative business was at its height, he received a visit from his British friend, the puckish Lord Beaverbrook, who took an opulent suite near Block's at the Ritz-Carlton Hotel while he stayed in New York.   One night in 1931, Block and Beaverbrook dined alone in the hotel suite and talked of publishing, the deteriorating political situation in Europe, and all manner of business and financial matters. Just before the dinner was over, the financier Clarence Dillon, head of the banking house of Dillon, Read & Company, dropped in for a post-prandial night cap. Beaverbrook, not knowing that Block was acquainted with Dillon, introduced him by saying "Clarence, I want you to know Paul Block, who is the publisher of twenty newspapers."

Block was on his feet in a moment, not wanting Dillon to get the wrong impression of exactly what his holdings were. "Just a minute, please," he corrected Beaverbrook, uncomfortably. "I am *not* the publisher of twenty newspapers. You are quite mistaken. I am the publisher of *seven,* and I wish it were one."[33]

Block was being neither modest nor sarcastic, but sharing the privacy of his true thoughts about the newspaper business and his role as a publisher. He had just acquired his most recent newspaper, the *Los Angeles Express*, the city's oldest newspaper which had been founded in 1871, and within the first days of his ownership he seemed to be embroiled in a rationale as to the proprietorship of the *Express*.

The *Express* had been experiencing a circulation drop and decline in advertising for over 10 years, and for that reason its selling price was reasonable. Block had considered buying it at the repeated urgings of William Randolph Hearst. In addition to their backstage socializing, the two men had already been working together for a number of years at that time with Block representing the advertising of many of Hearst's 27 newspapers. Hearst was a man with an abiding suspicious nature but one of the few men he trusted was Block. They trusted each other. Hearst, who owned the *Los Angeles Herald* and the *Examiner* at that time, prevailed upon Block to enter the Los Angeles field when he learned that the *Express* was for sale, because according to Hearst, "As a competitor of mine in other cities, I had learned to admire him and esteem him highly."[34]

When the announcement was made of Block's purchase of the *Express*, many people in the newspaper industry doubted Hearst's and Block's intentions. The prevailing belief was that Block was secretly being used to buy newspapers that were unwilling to sell to Hearst for all kind of reasons: his sensationalism, his politics, and the critical articles he ran about President McKinley. Along with a bereaved nation, Hearst's competitors also did not easily forget the old business wounds that he inflicted upon them. There was a desire to harness Hearst's growing monopoly of newspapers, which were spreading like a cancer throughout the country. As the most vilified publisher in newspaper history, it was exceedingly difficult for Hearst to enter negotiations to buy additional papers. His entry into acquisitions was often clouded: as much as it was tempting to prospective sellers, even Hearst's vast wealth simply could not buy him a newspaper if the owners were philosophically or politically opposed to him. Most American publishers did not appreciate Hearst's journalistic formula, as successful as it was: "Get the news. Get it first. Spare no expense. Make a great and continuous noise to attract readers; denounce crooked wealth and promise better conditions for the poor to keep readers. INCREASE CIRCULATION."[35] It was as if those who opposed him were saying that they would rather see their papers go out of business than to sink to the level of yellow and sophistic journalism that was Hearst's trademark.

Not everyone in the publishing industry was convinced that there was, indeed, a Block-Hearst axis behind the buying of the *Express*. In a story about Block's acquisition, *The New York Times* stated: "The announcement sets at rest that the paper will be merged with the *Evening Herald*, in which William Randolph Hearst is interested."[36]

Other newspapers and reports, however, were not as certain that the matter was settled. Throughout February of 1931, the press was writing stories to the effect that the $2,800,000 that Block had invested in *Express* stock, making him President and Publisher, was really Hearst money;[37] more than 50 years later the contention still continues, and the following account is based on a combination of research and speculation. What is known and can be surmised is as follows:

Hearst was heavily invested in the film industry and was a large stockholder in Metro-Goldwyn-Mayer.[38] He had successfully used his newspapers' editorials to break the strike of Actor's Equity in 1929, and wanted, as future security for his film interests, to control as many of the Los Angeles newspapers as possible. For Hearst, the acquisition of another newspaper was a fairly simple proposition. He had the necessary funds to buy what he wanted. He once wanted to buy the Louvre and had enough money to do so (but the intercession of the French government occurred to keep the country's great museum safe, and safely French). With Hearst's centralized accounting system, national advertising sales agencies, central purchasing offices, and his ownership of King Features Syndicate and the International News Service, one more newspaper to him was just another cog in his immense circuit of advertising and circulation.

Hearst, it was surmised, knew that the owners of the progressive *Ex-*

press, Guy Earl, Jr. and Edward A. Dickson, would not sell to him because of his anti-union political convictions, despite the fact that they needed to divest. Hearst admitted being interested in purchasing the *Express* and, so the story goes, since he was being blocked by the owners, he then loaned Block the money to acquire the newspaper, with the promise that Hearst could buy it back at some future date. Publicly, Block denied such financial manipulation, and just days after he took control he wrote a signed, front-page editorial in the *Express,* in an attempt to dispel the rumors:

> The Los Angeles "Times" this morning published a story in which it was asserted that a rumor names Mr. William Randolph Hearst as the actual owner of the *Evening Express.*
> Whether the "Times" published this to hurt me and the *Evening Express* because of my recent announcement that it would be my policy to operate a dignified, progressive newspaper and because such a policy may eventually affect such prestige and circulation as the "Times" may have, is not quite clear.
> To our readers, however, I repeat that the writer is now both the owner and the publisher of the *Evening Express.*[39]

> *Paul Block*

Although the *Los Angeles Times* was once voted by a group of Washington correspondents as one of the least fair and reliable newspapers in the country, its statement nevertheless angered and pained Block.[40] He claimed that he preferred the friendship of his contemporaries, and would not engage in a prolonged controversy but, however, he would not be swerved by criticism.[41]

One might ask why the liberal publishers of the *Express* would refuse Hearst as the buyer of their newspaper but accept Block, a known conservative, although a progressive. The answer might be embedded in the fact that Block was known to be a friend and a backer of two prominent Democrats, Mayor Jimmy Walker and Governor Alfred E. Smith (who was attempting to run again for President). Hearst had maintained a grudge against Alfred Smith ever since Smith ran for Governor in 1922, when he had refused to have Hearst, then a New Yorker, on the ticket with him in Hearst's bid for United States Senator. In 1931, Hearst was in the process of doing everything he could do to block Smith's nomination.[42] Despite the fact that Hearst had spent millions of his own funds in campaigning and using all of his newspapers to promote himself, the only elected office Hearst had ever managed to win was a brief stint in Congress. That was followed by his loss as Presidential nominee in 1904, the Mayoralty race of New York City in 1905, the Governorship of New York in 1906, and the defeat as independent candidate for the Presidency in 1907. It could, therefore, apparently be believed by the *Express* stockholders that Block was not being used by Hearst, because of the patent closeness of Smith and Block, with the inference that as Hearst and Smith were enemies, then Hearst and Block could not *possibly* be friends. Notwithstanding the stockholders' belief in Block, *did* Hearst front the money for Block to buy the *Express*? No research could be unearthed, either in the Hearst or Block archives, to prove that he did, although an examination of the events that transpired later indicate that that may have been the case all along.

In bidding farewell to the *Express,* the publishers referred to the relinquishment of their control to the "able hands of Mr. Paul Block,"[43] to which Block responded, somewhat ponderously, on the front page: "I have purchased the stock of the Express Publishing Company and am taking over its destinies beginning with today. If a progressive, independent newspaper, dignified in its news policies and appearance, is desired in the homes of Los Angeles, then the new *Evening Express* should become a real successful publication, because nothing will swerve me from publishing a newspaper of this class."

When it was announced that Block had entered the Los Angeles newspaper market, with Hollywood in the midst of its Golden Age and all that implied in terms of coverage of the film world, comments and congratulations poured in to the *Express.* Los Angeles Mayor John C. Porter wrote formally to Block: "Knowing of the sterling achievements you have scored in Eastern cities where you publish newspapers, I am sure your efforts in behalf of Los Angeles and its citizens will be most meritorious."[44] James Rolph, Jr., Governor of California, cabled Block: "The news of your entry into the California newspaper world as publisher of the *Los Angeles Evening Express* has just reached me. It is my pleasure and I am most happy to extend to you a hearty welcome to the Golden State of California."[45] Even New York Governor Franklin D. Roosevelt felt it was an important step forward for Block. He said: "Citizens of Los Angeles are to be congratulated on the coming of the *Los Angeles Evening Express* into such able and vigorous hands as those of Paul Block. The continuance of the honorable record of this old and famous paper is assured."[46]

And from his close friend and supporter, New York Mayor Jimmy Walker, Block received the following:

> Dear Paul:
>
> I congratulate you on the purchase of this newspaper. I know what it will mean to Los Angeles. Your record of honesty, fairness and progressiveness in the conduct of your newspapers in other cities ought to cause the people of Los Angeles to expect a great deal from you, and knowing you as I do, I am sure they will not be disappointed.
>
> Sincerely,
> James J. Walker[47]

If Block was being duplicitous about the purchase of the newspaper, and had actually bought it for Hearst or was running it under Hearst's control, he certainly didn't act as though he was merely a foil. In a matter of days he began to transform the paper. He assumed command as a strong and working publisher, quickly becoming involved with many facets of the newspaper. True to his usual strategies, he had its format redesigned, added more coverage of society and women's issues and activities, increased its Wall Street news, and expanded the sports section. Perhaps he was inspired by the slogan of *The New York Times*, "All The News That's Fit to Print," which had been emblazoned not only on that paper's front page since 1896, but was also in electric lights on the wall of the Cumberland Hotel overlooking Madison Square where Block could have seen when he had his office in the Flatiron Building. Block editorialized in the *Los Angeles Express*: "The main object will be to have the *Evening Express* a clean, dignified newspaper with news that is fit to print so that it may be welcome in every home."[48]

To stem any further criticism that he was working behind the scenes to move the paper over to a more conservative political sway, Block secured the services of columnist Walter Lippmann, one of the great liberal writers of the day. The *Express* would publish Lippmann's four-times a week syndicated column, "Today and Tomorrow." That single act was a signal that the *Express* was not subservient to Block, because Lippmann, whose articles were often quoted on the floors of Congress, belonged to no one; his column was a trenchant and controversial commentary of what went on inside the news, and as soon as his articles began to appear in Los Angeles, they helped build the prestige of the *Express*. Block immodestly but rightfully claimed that his act of signing Lippmann on to the paper was nothing less than "the greatest single journalistic achievement in Los Angeles in years."[49]

The World

Just eight days after taking over the *Los Angeles Express*, Block found himself embroiled in another controversy, one that had its genesis on the other side of the continent, in New York City, the capital of American newspaper publishing. Once again, he was charged with a perceived Hearstean association, similar to the accusations that he had faced in Los Angeles and other cities. This time, Block was said to be attempting to secretly purchase, on Hearst's behalf, what many people then believed to be America's greatest newspaper: *The New York World*.

On the evening of February 20, 1931, a colleague of Block's in New York telephoned him in Los Angeles to inform him that the three editions of the *World* – morning, evening and Sunday – might be up for imminent sale, and that there was a rumor that a court proceeding was likely to take place concerning the fate of the newspaper. Block, like almost every other newspaper entrepreneur in the country, had long been interested in *The World*, and when he had previously heard, back in the summer of 1930, that the three Pulitzer scions – Herbert, Ralph and Joseph, Jr. – owners of the paper, were considering ridding themselves of *The World*, Block's dream of being publisher of a truly New York City newspaper was reinvigorated. For months he had dreamed about the possibility of becoming publisher of *The World*, with or without Hearst's money.

The potential sale itself was controversial. Joseph Pulitzer was acknowledged to be in effect, the real founder of *The New York World*, since he had bought it as a moribund paper and brought it to greatness. For two decades, ever since his death in 1911, a codicil in his legal will enjoined his sons and their descendants from taking any action that would close the paper. Pulitzer's will referred to "…the duty of preserving, perfecting and perpetuating *The World* newspaper as a public institution." As a result, it was believed that the Pulitzer family would not, or could not, legally sell the paper, since the central provision of Joseph Pulitzer's will was that his sons could not sell their stock in the company, "under any circumstances whatsoever."[50] The will also stipulated that one-tenth of the estate belonged to the principal editors of *The World*, so that any potential sale would also have to be approved by the editorial executives of the newspaper. Moreover, the employees of *The World* had stated for years that should the family ever decide to sell, they would be interested in purchasing it as a joint venture. According to James Barrett, editor of the City Desk, it came as no shock to *The World*'s employees that the paper was up for sale. "Everybody knew for a long time [close to two years] that the paper was on the skids," he noted.[51] The situation was troublesome, since the Pulitzers had publicly stated their distrust of their own workers, and never commended any journalistic coup that the paper's staff accomplished. Spitefully, the family had no intention of allowing their editors to purchase control of *The World*.

Thirteen years after Joseph Pulitzer's death, in 1924, Ralph and Joseph Pulitzer had actually confirmed their family's desire to hold on to the newspaper at that time. They wrote a letter that was published in *The Fourth Estate*, to the effect that the rumor circulating that they wanted to sell was "patently ridiculous."[52] However, seven years later, when the brothers became worried and harassed over the money that they were losing on the paper, they reluctantly decided to oppose their father's will.

Ostensibly, Block stated that he wanted to own *The World* because it was known as a newspaperman's newspaper. Not a day had passed since his arrival in New York in 1895 that he did not pore over its pages. As Philip Pearl wrote of it: "*The World* was read in Harlem, in Hell's Kitchen, in the colleges, on the East Side, in Greenwich Village, and especially in all newspaper offices. It appealed alike to the intelligent and the simple because it was imbued with a fundamental sympathy."[53] It was no ordinary newspaper, and had a tradition of journalistic brilliance under the successive helms of three great editors, Charles Chapin, Frank Cobb, and Herbert Bayard Swope. Virtually everyone in the newspaper industry acknowledged that *The World* was simply but effectively written, sharply edited, politically independent (although its soul was liberal and Democratic), unconventional, audacious, courageous, and without counterpart during its heyday, and even among newspapers today. Its pages contained some of the most exciting journalism ever published, and it broke more exclusives and enjoyed more scoops than all of the other New York papers combined. It was also known for its incisive political and social cartoons.

The World was a powerful influence in shaping public opinion; it seemed to fulfill a certain function of involvement necessary for the American consciousness at that time. Despite its past *fin de siècle* twinge of yellow, by the time of World War I and throughout the 1920s, with American journalism in its golden age, much of its glamour, glitter and muckraking was reflected in the pages of *The New York World:* the manhandling of William Jennings Bryan by Clarence Darrow at the Scopes "Monkey Trial;" the Swope crusades against the Ku Klux Klan; a memorable series by William Allen White on the depression of American farms; Alexander Woollcott's historical profile of Noël Coward; an almost bloody debate between Ralph Pulitzer and Heywood Hale Broun on the Sacco-Vanzetti case; the sponsorship of the first air flight from Albany to New York City; a series that broke up legalized gambling in New Jersey; editorials that brought about the erection of the Statue of Liberty; and political support that was largely responsible for the nomination of Woodrow Wilson.

The World maintained a robust circulation of about 300,000 throughout most of the 1920s. In the late 1920s, however, the principal New York tabloids, the *Daily News,* the *Mirror*, and the *Daily Graphic*, had begun to speak to and captivate New York's workers and subway riders, and inched their respective ways into *The World's* circulation. Ralph Pulitzer, who had assumed the position of publisher upon his father's death, made a series of business decisions that virtually brought *The World to* financial ruin. Ralph did not act, think like or even look the part of an editor, journalist or publisher, and that was one of the reasons he wanted to discontinue his relationship with *The World.* Writer Irwin S. Cobb described him as "a bookish, kindly, retiring gentleman, more fitted, I think, for the life of a poet happily scribbling pastoral verses in the proverbial garret, than to be a cog in the racketing, grinding power houses of a great newspaper shop."[54] Nonetheless, Ralph was in charge and, often in disagreement with *The World's* managers, he changed some of the paper's business policies.

When he had the daily *World* raise its price to three cents – a penny more than its direct competitors – its circulation plunged by 100,000 in less than a year. *The Sunday World* also fell upon hard times when, as a result of killing its second news section in January of 1930, circulation spiraled downward. Additionally, to save money, an inferior quality of paper was substituted for the Magazine section, which resulted in seriously blurring and darkening of all the color photographs. Circulation waned, and advertising plunged partially because readers were dissatisfied with the Magazine that they were receiving. The size had also been cut successively from 20 pages to 16, and finally to 12. When the price of *The Sunday World* was then foolishly (as it turned out to be) raised to 10 cents, the circulation – which had been 500,000 – plummeted in about six weeks to a dangerous low of 135,000.

Although it had invented the "op-ed" (opposite editorial) page that is so ubiquitous today, and some of the most illustrious names in journalism were writing for it, the daily *World* failed to keep pace with its competitors as to hard news, and it was forced to reduce its size, because of lack of advertising, to 28 or 32 pages, as compared to the 56 or 64 pages found at that time in *The New York Times* and the *Herald Tribune*.

The Pulitzer sons claimed that *The World* had lost close to $2,000,000 dollars in 1930, and that by February of 1931, they only had $400,000 dollars cash remaining in the business, and under those circumstances they would be forced to cease publication in 90 days. Since the paper employed some 3,000 workers, many people believed that the Pulitzers were heartless in wanting to divest. The nation was already filled with so many unemployed in 1930 – the worst business year in the history of the United States – that any business with a large number of employees that voluntarily closed shop, was considered close to seditious. It wasn't only the employees who were concerned over the demise of *The World*, however. Readers all over New York and throughout the country were alarmed that they would possibly be losing their leading liberal newspaper.

From California that Friday, Block called his attorney Max Steuer, told him to see what he could find out about the impending sale, and informed him that he was interested in making an offer.[55] Steuer called Block the next day and said that as far as he could determine, there were no court proceedings pending involving the sale of the newspaper, but that there was a hearing planned for the following Tuesday that would discuss the "construction" of the will.

On that Monday morning, over breakfast, Steuer was casually reading his copy of *The New York Law Journal* when he spotted a brief legal notice to the effect that the matter of the sale of *The World* was to come before the Surrogate's Court the very next day, Tuesday, February 24, 1931. Upon further inquiry, Steuer determined that Roy W. Howard, the short, dapper chief executive of the Scripps-Howard chain, had already bid $5 million and that the brothers Pulitzer had tacitly accepted the offer, pending approval by the court.

More telephone calls and telegrams between Block and Steuer followed, and Block instructed the lawyer to go to court the next day, and make a counter bid. Should an auction "war" erupt, Block told Steuer that he was to offer $500,000 over and above any bid that Scripps-Howard would make. Strangely, this was going to be the second bid that Block had made for *The World*. He had made an unofficial offer in August of 1930 when he had heard rumors that the Pulitzers might be willing to sell. At that time Block let it be known through intermediaries that he would pay the more-than-considerable amount of $10 million dollars for *The World*; but he reduced that amount the very next day to $8 million, and then withdrew it completely when he learned that only the morning and Sunday editions of the newspaper were being mentioned as properties for sale. It was the evening edition of *The World* that really interested Block, and when he also found out that he would have to discontinue the use of the title *The New York World* after a "reasonable time" [six months], he temporarily withdrew his consideration to become owner of the paper.[56] Even then, critics of Hearst were claiming that Block was acting on Hearst's behalf, and they conjectured that Block did not have $10 million dollars and could not borrow or raise it on his own. Block, affronted, challenged the hearsayers by claiming that should he ever buy *The World*, he would pay for it with a combination of his own money, a series of loans, and the issuing of bonds. Nonetheless, the latest news that the title, reputation and assets of *The World* were for sale – all three editions, including the crucial evening edition – greatly re-invigorated Block's resolve to capture control of the paper.

Block had barely settled in as publisher of the *Los Angeles Express*, and the gold-leaf lettering of his name had barely dried on the door of his office. Nonetheless, he had his private railroad car, Friendship, made ready, and he told Steuer that he would be in New York in a few days, as soon as the train could get him there. (As much as Block believed in the future and convenience of aviation, he rarely chose to travel by plane.) Block continued to confer with Steuer as Friendship steamed eastward. Whenever the train stopped for any appreciable time, Block would alight, whether it was Kansas City, Chicago or Cleveland, and telephone Steuer for the latest news, and give any further instructions that he wanted followed.[57]

Because of a prior commitment (a trial concerning the Bank of the United States), Steuer could not be at the Surrogate's Court precisely at the starting time of 4:15, and so he sent an assistant to see whether the hearing could be temporarily postponed. Judge James A. Foley, glancing out the window of his courtroom from which he could see, ironically, the golden-domed Pulitzer Building, home of *The World*, refused the request, and the hearing commenced. To add to the legal machinations taking place in the courtroom, a wartime atmosphere prevailed: every newspaper in the city had from two to five reporters and one or two photographers covering the hearing, and each succeeding hour brought more whispers and conjectures as to the fate of their colleagues. W. H. Garrison, a reporter for *The World*, described the dramatic atmosphere later: "From the river we heard the shrill long drawn-out siren of a tugboat. It sounded like a banshee's wail, or a dirge."[58]

The story of the sale of *The World* was the lead front page news article in *The New York Times*. Whether *The World* would be sold, merged or shut down was so important to readers in New York City and to newspaper publishing in general, that the *Times* and the *Herald Tribune* (and virtually every other major metropolitan newspaper) had prepared "obituaries" and background material about the colorful and meaningful history of *The World*, ready to insert on an instant's notice as soon as the matter was settled, just as papers do in preparation for the death of a famous person.

On the witness stand, the Pulitzer brothers, one by one, offered evidence to the judge as to their financial plight, and gave arguments as to why they should be permitted to sell the newspaper, despite the fact that they would be countermanding not only their father's legally executed will, but his spirit and intentions. Before the judge had an opportunity to respond, Steuer rushed into the courtroom, somewhat breathless, and asked for another postponement, this one for two days until Thursday, so that he would have an opportunity to discuss the possibility of the purchase with his client more fully. Paul Block was due to arrive in New York on Wednesday. Roy Howard asked the judge whether he could make a statement, in his own interest, about Block's postponement plea. Howard asserted that a delay of even 48 hours would be disastrous to his negotiation for the paper, "because of the disintegration in circulation, advertising and morale of the staff certain to result in the publicity about the sale then being incurred."[59]

Perhaps as a ploy, Howard implied that if the postponement were granted and he was prevented from going through with his current contract, he would drop the negotiation if he was legally able to do so. Howard also pointed out that the reason the *World* was failing was because it was midway between the higher class of newspapers such as the *New York Times,* the *Herald-Tribune,* and the *Sun,* and the tabloids on the other side. If he were permitted to merge the *World* with his *Telegram*, he argued, at least some jobs would be saved, and the new *World-Telegram* would prosper.

Ironically, as Howard spoke of the "morale" of the staff of *The World*, Pulitzer newspaper reporter Joseph Brady, who was seated in the courtroom, was busily engaged in making notes of the story which would be published in what might turn out to be the very last issue of the newspaper he represented.

When Steuer continued to reason with the judge for the postponement, John G. Jackson, the tall, gray-haired and inflexible attorney for the Pulitzers, mumbled – but loud enough so that everyone in the courtroom could hear – three words: "William Randolph Hearst." Steuer, standing at the bar, whirled, his face red, his normally soft voice filled with indignation, and contested Jackson, saying: "If the counselor is implying that my client, Mr. Paul Block, is secretly acting in behalf of Mr. Hearst, then he is grossly mis-informed and inaccurate. Mr. Block's interest in these newspapers is on no one's behalf but his own."[60] Judge Foley refused the postponement, invited Steuer to remain in the court (which he did), and went on with the hearing.

The argument as to whether Block was an independent agent or whether it was Hearst's money all along that propelled Block into the role of potential buyer of *The World* was consequential and highly relevant to the Pulitzers. Throughout their so-called "yellow wars" and beyond, Joseph Pulitzer and William Randolph Hearst had fought like street thugs with a total lack of respect for each other, each striving to gain every reader for his own respective papers. After years of battle and enmity between those two men, Pulitzer's children had come to loathe and distrust Hearst with an almost Shakespearean intensity. No amount of money was large enough to tempt the Pulitzers to sell to Hearst, no matter how financially desperate they were; if Block was to be Hearst's shadow-publisher of *The World*, the Pulitzers would simply not even *consider* a sale to him.

No one knew what Roy Howard or Paul Block would do with *The World* should they be permitted to buy it. Would they keep publishing it? Would they merge it with another paper? Would they simply scrap it to reduce the competition? Rumors, gossip and speculative chitchat circulated – that Roy Howard was already installing new wires in the newsroom of the *Telegram*; that Paul Block was to become publisher of a newly-merged newspaper, the *World-American*, owned by Hearst and edited by Herbert Bayard Swope; that an extra night crew of printers and typographers was ensconced in the *Telegraph's* plant; that a new *World-Telegram* masthead had been designed and was sitting on Roy Howard's desk. Almost all of the rumors, with the exception of the Hearst-Block-Swope

association, proved to be true.[61]   In the smoke-filled 15th floor newsroom of *The World* on Park Row, the staff sat around in a pale of funereal
gloom, in a sort of haunted editorial house, awaiting the results of the
court proceedings.

The next day, on a clear and relatively mild Wednesday morning, Block
was in court with Max Steuer at 11 AM, only to learn that the hearing was
temporarily postponed until 1 o'clock. When the hearing finally began,
Block and his lawyer huddled discretely, whispering conspiratorially as
they earnestly discussed the intricacies of the hearing. Throughout the
afternoon, Block was concerned, but relatively and atypically calm.

The employees of *The World* had made an offer to buy the paper. If
their bid was not accepted, the staff hoped that the judge would at least
refuse Scripps-Howard's offer and allow the Pulitzers to sell to Paul Block,
if not to them, so that the paper would be kept afloat. Block then made a
magnanimous gesture. He told Steuer to tell the representatives of *The
World* that if, indeed, he was allowed to buy the paper, he would sell it
back to *The World* employees, at no profit to himself, if they could raise
the same amount of money that he had paid for the newspaper. Steuer
talked to the representatives of *The World*, and said: "I am authorized by
Mr. Block to say that, if his offer is accepted, he will give the employees
of *The World* not ten days but thirty days in which to take the paper off his
hands at the same price he pays for it. He wants no profit, not even my
fee."[62]   The representatives were ebullient and literally cheered at the
prospect of Block as their personal *deus ex machina;* quite suddenly he
became a hero in the making to the thousands of *World* employees. In
another statement, Block raised the amount of time to be given to the
employees to 45 days.[63]   John T. Gibbs, the former managing editor of
the *Philadelphia Record* and a *World* reporter, who was interested in purchasing *The World* himself, wrote of the tension and relief of the moment:

> Optimism guided the gossip of the groups around *The
> World's* office, who discussed the situation. Paul Block's of-
> fer surely would prevent the sale to Scripps-Howard. The
> appearance of the busy Max Steuer had its significance; po-
> litical factions were interested, it was whispered. Mighty
> names were mentioned as probable backers of Block, or as
> independent bidders.[64]

The other names that were being bandied about as possible purchasers of *The World*, or backers of it to keep the paper operative, were Bernard Baruch, the Ochs family, Whitelaw Reid, Frank Gannett, William Griffin, Herbert Bayard Swope, and J. David Stern, many of them giants of the newspaper industry. All of those mentioned *were* interested, but no arrangement with the Pulitzers could be worked out.

In a dramatic moment, an employee of *The World* rushed into the courtroom with an armload of newspapers and, without asking permission, in a bold strike of independence, began distributing copies. On the first page was a two-column box which showed that the advertising and circulation of *The World* was actually gaining. The brothers Pulitzer almost audibly gasped, since the information was so contradictory to their testimony. Herbert Pulitzer immediately sent an aide to *The World* newsroom, with the instructions that any future editions or printings of *The World* should delete the advertising and circulation statistics box.

Suddenly, as if he had come to a newfound realization, Block approached Roy Howard, and the two went outside the courtroom to confer; and then before the judge had reached his decision, Block made a startling, and inexplicable announcement: he was withdrawing his offer altogether. The cherubic James Barrett of *The World* was particularly confused and incensed at the latest development by Block, and wrote:

> Mr. Block withdrew his offer of purchase, saying he had not understood that the Pulitzers had already entered into a contract to sell to Scripps-Howard. Both these statements had a strange flavor. Before making his offer to the *World* employees, Mr. Block had talked with Mr. Steuer and had a half-hour conference with Mr. Howard. Is it possible that he had not learned in these two long conferences that a contract existed between the Pulitzers and Howard? Or had he not read the morning papers, in which this contract was explained? And, if he knew there was a contract which would cause his withdrawal as a bidder the next day, why did he raise the false hopes of the *World* employees by making his apparently generous offer to them? This is one of the enigmas of the situation.[65]

The wire services issued an advisory about Block's withdrawal. Here is City News's copy:

SURROGATES' COURT – WORLD SALE

PAUL BLOCK, OWNER OF THE BROOKLYN STAN-
DARD UNION AND OTHER NEWSPAPERS THROUGH-
OUT THE COUNTRY, TODAY – THUR. – UNCONDI-
TIONALLY WITHDREW THE OFFER MADE FOR THE
PURCHASE OF THE *Worlds* (Morning, Sunday and
Evening) THROUGH AN ANNOUNCEMENT MADE BY
HIS ATTORNEY, MAX D. STEUER.

MR. BLOCK BASED HIS WITHDRAWAL ON TWO
FACTORS; THAT HE DID NOT WISH TO OPPOSE THE
EFFORTS OF THE EMPLOYEES TO OBTAIN CONTROL
OF THE PAPER AND THAT HE DID NOT WISH TO IN-
TERFERE WITH THE CONCLUDED DEAL ENTERED
INTO BETWEEN THE PULITZER BROTHERS, OWNERS
OF THE *Worlds*, AND ROY HOWARD, OF THE SCRIPPS-
HOWARD NEWSPAPER INTERESTS, PUBLISHERS OF
THE *New York Telegram* AND OTHER PAPERS.

Not revealed at the time was the fact that in withdrawing his competition for the purchase, Block implored Howard to let him have at least one
of the three *Worlds*. Roy Howard, however, was intransigent.

"Why did you want to spoil my party?," he demanded to
know.
"Honestly, Roy, I didn't know that it was you. I thought it
was Herbert Swope," replied Block.
Howard, who should have been relieved that he was getting what he wanted, was caustic in his response: "Well, you
got yourself into it – now get yourself out."[66]

It was close to 11 PM, late Thursday night, when Judge Foley issued
his decree: he said that in order to preserve whatever assets belonged to
the estate, the Pulitzers had the permission of the court to sell the paper,
but he did not have jurisdiction over whom the Pulitzers chose to sell to,
meaning that the Scripps-Howard contract could be accepted. A statement was issued at 2 AM Friday morning that henceforth, the new *World-
Telegram* would be published by Scripps-Howard: "Not the death of *The
World*," said Roy Howard, "but its rebirth." His pronouncement was little
balm to the 2,800 employees who were instantly laid off, because both
the Sunday and morning *Worlds* were immediately discontinued. The

Pulitzers never issued a word of thanks to the staffers of *The World*, some of whom had been working there for over 50 years.[67]

Howard did apportion $500,000, against his $5 million dollar purchase price, to be shared equally among *The World* employees, as their ten percent ownership as indicated in the will. It came to roughly $250 for each employee. The staff was devastated. Reporter Frank Sullivan perhaps best summed up what many were feeling when he wrote: "When I die I want to go wherever *The World* has gone and work on it again."[68]

It is difficult seventy years later to determine what Paul Block was really attempting to do in the maneuverings and vacillations of his negotiations for *The World*. Since he was in a financial quagmire with his *Brooklyn Standard Union* and, as it would eventually become known, he *was* acting as Hearst's secret agent in purchasing newspapers, it is altogether likely that Block was really negotiating for Hearst in his attempt to buy *The World*. There were other operative factors at play, however, and admittedly the following is pure speculation.

The World had been fierce in its anti-Tammany exposés, and one of the major foci of their investigations and editorials was New York Mayor James J. Walker. Just days before the sale of the newspaper was consummated, Walker was making headlines in *The World,* accused of being involved in the cover-up of the police corruption scandal concerning Vivian Gordon, a vice case witness found strangled in Central Park. Block may have conjectured that if he could gain control of *The World*, it would be one less newspaper – and the most respected one in the city – to add fuel to the downfall of his closest friend. As publisher of *The World*, Block's editorials would have lauded Walker, rather than serve as implicating him. When Block learned that Scripps-Howard really had no intention of continuing the political or journalistic efforts of *The World* (Howard cancelled the memoir series of General John J. Pershing, for example, on the first day of the *World-Telegram's* existence), Block may have felt that his rationale for taking over the paper was no longer necessary.

It is also known that the coveted membership in the Associated Press wire service, enjoyed by the morning *World,* was something that Hearst wanted desperately to buy, for use in his *New York Journal*. The A.P. wire service was a membership that was only offered to a maximum number of newspapers within a given area. A newspaper that already "owned" such a membership had the right to sell it to another paper. Roy Howard's newspapers controlled United Press, the major competitor to A.P., and on the day after he bought *The World*, he claimed that he had received six

offers to buy the A.P. membership. Since he was doing away with the
morning *World*, that membership was his to sell or keep; he was going to
retain the A.P. membership from the evening *World* for his new *World-
Telegram*. The sale of the membership was valued at $500,000 in income
to him, so Howard was careful not to dislodge his rights to it. In order to
conform to the technical requirement that an Associated Press membership had to be used only by a morning newspaper, or it would be recalled,
he put on a skeleton staff in the offices of his *World-Telegram*, and instantly invented a new morning newspaper, with a limited circulation of
250 copies; called *The New York Repository,* he published it until such
time as he sold the AP membership. He didn't have to wait long. Within
a week, he sold the membership to...William Randolph Hearst.

The probable scenario of Paul Block and *The World* could then be drawn
as follows: working clandestinely for Hearst, and with Hearst's money to
back him, Block made a genuine offer to buy *The World* for the following
reasons: first, because Hearst wanted *The World* to go under in order to
lift the circulation of his *Journal*; second, because after he was owner of
The World, Hearst could transfer the Associated Press membership to his
own newspaper; third, by eliminating *The World*, Block would be helping his friend Jimmy Walker. The puzzle of why Block offered the employees of *The World* the opportunity of buying back the paper can be
solved by his statement to Roy Howard that he had thought it was Herbert
Bayard Swope who was behind the purchase from the Pulitizers: Swope
was a known Jimmy Walker-hater, and Block felt that if the paper had
been sold to Swope, Walker would not have a chance in the pages of *The
World*. When Howard agreed to sell the AP membership to Hearst, and
also to "go easy" on Walker in the *World-Telegram,* Block agreed to withdraw his competitive bid.

Months later Adolph Ochs, publisher of *The New York Times*, who was
in Honolulu at the time of the hearing, said: "Had I been in New York, I
am sure I could have saved *The World*."[69]   Block mused: "Only in your
imagination can you revise."

Los Angeles Express –
1931-1932

Back in Los Angeles, Block continued to insist on three major ap-
proaches to the news in what he was calling "The New *Los Angeles Express*": brevity, clarity and accuracy, and he made sure that the paper's
reporters and correspondents were trained to write in that way.[70]   He did

not just concentrate on the appearance and editorial improvement of his new newspaper, however; he brought in several of his top salesmen, a group of intelligent and loyal men from New York, to begin a relentless campaign to increase advertising sales. As a result, The May Company, the largest and oldest Los Angeles department store, came in with full-page and double-page spreads announcing a store-wide sale in celebration of its 50th anniversary;[71] and national advertisers such as Chesterfield cigarettes[72] and Wrigley's Juicy Fruit chewing gum[73] greatly increased the size of their advertisements. The amount of advertising escalated markedly because of the increased circulation due to Block's promotional efforts and the new editorial features upon which he insisted. In what became one of the most outstanding accomplishments in newspaper publishing history, in a matter of months Block helped propel the circulation of the *Express* from 90,000 when he took over, to 140,000 copies per day.

The rumors about Hearst being the shadow publisher of the *Express* still persisted, although no one doubted that it was Block's ability that was making such an immediate success of the newspaper. Block went about his business, did not move his residence to Los Angeles, but became thoroughly involved in the life of the city, visiting as often as possible and spending a good deal of time working with his staff in the *Express*'s $1,000,000 building.

Being publisher of the *Los Angeles Express* naturally entailed a constant involvement with the motion picture industry. Block had lunches with Sam Goldwyn, parties with Charlie Chaplin, and constant invitations to Hearst's San Simeon, which was always populated by movie stars. Since he had a longstanding fascination with movies, Block found this serendipitous aspect of his job wonderfully exciting, and he took full advantage of it. When actress Billie Burke came to Los Angeles in June of 1931, accompanied by her daughter Patricia, to star in the theatrical performance of *The Vinegar Tree* (and ultimately to be given a part in the movie, *Bill of Divorcement,* with John Barrymore and a newcomer in her first role, Katherine Hepburn), Block was in town to greet her at the train station and to insure that her arrival would be given extensive coverage in the *Express*.[74] Billie and her husband, Florenz Ziegfeld, had remained close New York friends with Block, and he was always particularly solicitous in trying to give his friends as much publicity as possible.

In a short while, Block began to present his opinions about matters that directly concerned the city of Los Angeles and the state of California, through a series of his signed front-page editorials, most of which reflected his own special interests and agenda. He was unabashed in stating that he understood his role as publisher of the *Express* to be that of a promoter, crusader and protector: "It is my ambition that it [the *Express*] may, in the future, contribute in an even greater measure to the welfare of the city and state."[75]   He commended the California Legislature for enacting limiting assessments for public improvements, and also for reapportioning congressional and legislative representation.[76]   In a somewhat self-serving editorial he urged his readers to "Buy in Los Angeles," because "L.A. has some of the greatest stores in the United States;" in other words, he was suggesting to his *Express* readers that they patronize his advertisers.[77]   He promoted the importance of the Hollywood Bowl and its "Symphonies Under the Stars" series: "Not only have the concerts proved a stimulus to the cultural advance of the community, but they have spread the knowledge that we as a community appreciate the finer things."[78]

Surprisingly, however, one of the major crusades that his editorials took at that time was not directed against the city of Los Angeles or the state of California, but toward Hollywood itself. Without naming specific film studios or producers or directors, Block blasted the burgeoning advent of gangster films, such as *Alibi, Little Caesar, The Secret Six* and *Scarface*, which were coming into their own in the relatively early talkies of the late 1920s and early 1930s. The films, which often told how their protagonists became involved in criminal activities, usually offered little moral resolution. Block was incensed. Though he realized he might alienate members of the film community, he felt that he had an ethical obligation to protest. He wrote:

STOP GANGSTER FILMS

Recently, a number of moving pictures have been shown in public which ought to be stopped. We refer to those which include racketeers and gunmen and make heroes of them, place them in gilded palaces and even though some of them finish up by being shot, others escape and continue to live a life of ease.

A recent picture shows a youth mixed up with gangsters but trying to reform, and is then murdered by his companions.

In another picture, a boy who decides to visit a priest for

help in his desire to reform, is called "yellow" by the gang and is killed by them on the steps of the cathedral.

Instead of teaching the youth of today that gangsters and gunmen are as poisonous as snakes crawling loose on the streets, there are pictures which almost have the contrary effect.

There are enough evils already existing in our midst to make it simple for the youth of America to lose regard for law and order and these gangster films do not make the problem any easier.

Many fine pictures are shown on the screen – they are entertaining and often educational. The gunmen and gangster pictures are disgraceful and are not needed and we urge the Board of Censors to give particular attention to them.

Paul Block
Publisher[79]

Members of the Screen Writers Guild and the Authors' League of America criticized Block's call for a "movie clean-up," expressing resentment at the "intemperance, hysteria, injustice, and in some cases outright falsehood which characterizes certain expressions" against films.[80]

Aside from, or perhaps because of the success that the *Express* was experiencing, the pundits continued to cluck at every opportunity where it appeared that Block and Hearst were in partnership. When it was discovered that the same trucks that delivered Hearst's *Herald* were also delivering Block's *Express*, Block replied: "This was arranged by us to eliminate wasteful distribution, and it is in accordance with established and ethical practices of newspaper distribution in nearly all cities of the country." Although that form of combined newspaper distribution was true then, as it is today in many cities, the very appearance of the Block and Hearst newspapers being dropped off together at newsstands made the skeptics sure they were correct that Block was merely being controlled as a creature orchestrated to aid Hearst's expansion program.

Barely 10 months after he purchased the *Los Angeles Express*, Block did what many people felt was entirely predictable: he suddenly sold his newspaper to...William Randolph Hearst. In a public statement, he offered the following rationalization: "When I purchased the *Express* early this year, I had planned to spend a substantial part of my time in Los Angeles, but because of the present business conditions I find it necessary to give all of my attention to my [other] newspaper interests."[81]

The essence of Block's statement rings true in that he was having difficult financial problems and didn't quite know what to do with the ownership of his *Brooklyn Standard Union.* It doesn't explain, however, or
even allude to why he sold the *Los Angeles Express,* especially since it
was doing banner business and its circulation was way up; nor does it
reveal any clue as to whether Hearst had been the real owner initially. In
the midst of the great slump of 1929-1932, all of Block's newspapers,
with the exception of the *Los Angeles Express* and the *Newark Star-Eagle,*
were either in the red or displaying a lackluster performance in advertising lineage and circulation. It is possible that he simply had to divest
himself of at least some of his holdings in order to maintain others. In
retrospect, however, it appears that Hearst had been the true owner of the
Los Angeles Express all along, and that Block ran the paper as successfully as he knew how, both out of ethical reasons and because of self-
serving interests in gaining its national advertising representation, despite the fact that he knew that he would ultimately sell the paper back to
Hearst.

Hearst's comments at the time of his acquisition were, at best, self-
interested and totally startling to both the newspaper industry and to the
readers of the *Express:* "Mr. Block has made a fine paper of the *Express*
and its circulation growth has been phenomenal. We are therefore proud
to take over this property and combine it with the *Evening Herald,* continuing the news services of both the *Herald* and the *Express* and the best
features and writers now associated with each publication. I believe
through this consolidation that the *Los Angeles Evening Herald and Express* will be one of the greatest evening newspapers of the country."[82]
The fact that two other Los Angeles newspapers, the *Hollywood News*
and the *Citizen,* had merged just weeks before Block's announcement,
indicated that the market in that city, at that time, was strained at best.
Few people took those business problems into consideration, however.
The incident gave them yet another basis to dislike Hearst, and a reason
to begin to doubt Paul Block.

Block continued to make money from Los Angeles, however. He took
over the national representation of the advertising for the newly combined *Los Angeles Herald Express.*

To complicate the sale, just five days before he relinquished control,
Block and the *Express* were sued for $150,000 in damages for libel. The
charge was brought by Helmuth H.J. Haalcke. In a series of articles pub-

lished in November 1931, the *Express* had exposed gambling and vice conditions in Los Angeles and its suburbs. Haalcke's hand laundry, located in San Pedro, was named by the *Express* as being a bootlegging operation and a concealed brewery (the Volstead Act was still in effect). Upon purchase of the *Express* corporation, Hearst assumed all legal debts and contracts for Block, past, present and future, and he settled the Hand Laundry Still case, as it came to be known out of court.

Despite the fact that he had proven otherwise in Los Angeles, however briefly, Block believed that it was extremely difficult to find a way to break even on a second evening newspaper in most communities. The cost of producing a newspaper had risen to such heights, and the economy was in such shambles, that it had become a problem even for the newspaper that had the highest circulation in a city to make a profit, so the *second* newspaper in circulation really had no chance to succeed financially.

Block cited the stories of a number of second evening newspapers that had either been suspended or been consolidated. He named publications in Buffalo, Rochester, Syracuse, St. Paul, Denver, Toledo, Des Moines, Milwaukee, and a number of other cities.[83]

Chapter 9
In the Shadow of Power: Advisor to Presidents

Toledo Times

Almost immediately after divesting himself of the *Milwaukee Sentinel*, Paul Block began a process of trying to solidify the *Blade's* position in Toledo by buying the *Toledo Times*, the only Sunday and morning newspaper in the city. Primarily owned by the Dun family, the *Times* was slowing eroding the *Toledo Blade's* profit base by greatly discounting its own job printing business, which virtually eliminated all of that income from the *Blade*. It was also cutting into the *Blade's* advertising profits by offering certain advertisers drastic reductions in space rates at prices that the *Blade* couldn't profitably match.

On August 11, 1930, Block signed letters of agreement to purchase most of the stock of the *Times* for $874,250. The offer was consummated on August 26th, with the understanding that John Dun, one of the owners of the *Times*, would continue as editor with his own editorial, advertising and circulation staff, which was separate from the *Blade's* staff. Block would represent the *Times* as special advertising representative, however, and as a method of reducing overhead, the *Times* would be printed in the *Blade's* plant. Dan Nicoll, Block's assistant, said: "Our plant in Toledo is big enough to handle a morning, evening and a Sunday proposition."[1]

Block took the then-empty building that had been owned by the *Times* and temporarily turned it into a free employment agency for the thousands of Toledoans unemployed because of the Depression. In true Hooverian fashion, however, Block announced that the service he was going to provide was "not to encourage idlers or to attract the unemployed from other cities but to register and investigate the needy in our own city and provide employment as rapidly as possible."[2] Within a few months, he then turned the building over to the City Welfare Department of Toledo, and gave the department all of the records his agency had obtained on those who sought employment. Mayor William T. Jackson used the old *Times* building as it was intended, for those out-of-work, and also as a clothing exchange for warmer garments as the winter months approached.[3]

The intense news and editorial rivalry that the *Toledo Blade* and the *Toledo Times* had carried on for years did not abate even though they were now owned by the same person.[4] From the time he bought the *Times*, Block showed total impartiality and non-interference, and permitted it its own editorial point of view and direction, limiting his involvement to the *Times's* national advertising, and as its printer; in this case he played the role of a silent owner.

Block's Influence on the *Toledo Blade*

All throughout the mid and late 1920s, the 1930s, and until the early 1940s, Block continued to influence and direct Patterson as to what he wanted accomplished editorially with the *Toledo Blade*. Some thought it was an indefatigable pursuit of an unattainable perfection.

Block's directives were delivered in many ways, but the two men developed an effective and comfortable routine for working together. Every day, no matter where Block was (often but not invariably in his New York office, or at his home in Greenwich), a copy of the *Blade* was delivered to him. He would pore over it, from the front page masthead to the classifieds, and then either telephone Patterson with his comments of adjustments and amendments or, if there was time and the matter serious enough, send a letter or a telegram stating his wishes as to what he wanted added, deleted or changed in future issues. He preferred to put everything in writing, and wanted everyone else to do so, also. To emphasize the formality, he had memo stationery printed (in red) for the *Blade* which carried a warning in large type on the top of the page: **AVOID VERBAL ORDERS**. His employees understood, and complied.

Block insisted that Patterson had free reign to do what he wanted to do as editor of the *Blade*, but in reality Block's requests and requirements always superceded Patterson's, and only infrequently did the two disagree. Patterson has said that Block never questioned any monies spent on editorial improvement as long as they truly made the *Blade* a better newspaper.[5]

Block believed that the publishing of a newspaper was a learning process, and that whatever instructions he gave to Patterson were not just a non-essential reaction on his part or a recitation of trivial *lacunae*, but an explication of his long-range thinking. Ultimately, he hoped, his outlook would somehow arrive at the desks, or in the working styles of the *Blade's* reporters and editors, and gradually become part of their agendas, how they might come to see the operation and philosophy of the paper. A sampling that follows, extracted from a few of the missives that Block addressed to Grove Patterson, will serve to show how he approached some of the editorial concerns of the *Toledo Blade*:

October 29, 1935
Would you be good enough to tell those who write our important headlines to always try their very best not to get too many words in a line. By doing this, it means the headline is crowded and does not look as dignified as I like to see the headlines of the *Blade* appear. I also like to see the second line staggered. In other words, the first line should stop about an inch before the margin and the second line to start about an inch from the left margin. The enclosed from Friday's paper is what I have in mind.

June 27, 1936   (dictated)
My purpose in writing you now is to be sure that you help them [the editors and reporters] to put our paper where it will lead in all classifications, such as society and clubs and society pictures and club pictures. Also, in sporting news and in financial news, in theatrical news and in radio news.
By the way, am I correct in my understanding that each day, Miss Carr, our Society Editress, telephones to find out how much space she needs? It seems to me the way it should be done is for her to tell the Editorial Department just how much she needs on the next day, and for her to run all the important news and pictures, which for reasons she best knows, *must run on that day.*

February 27, 1940
[Writing about the letters to the editor column, "The People Speak."] I also notice the letter in last Friday's paper by J.F. Gibson, in which he calls attention to the historical errors made regarding Boulder Dam. I wonder if there should not

have been an editor's note when the original error was made, in which note we could have told of this error.

August 27, 1940

I have tried pretty hard since the *News-Bee* went out of the field to make our paper independent, so far as the news is concerned, but it is a hard thing to do when our top men are intimate with the Republican leaders and not so intimate with the Democrats. I want the *Blade* to be an Independent paper, not a Republican paper.

I repeat, I don't want to harm anyone – I would like to help people and not hurt them – but I want the paper to be run as a real newspaper should be run. If I can't do this, then I would rather get out of the newspaper business.

Sept. 4, 1940

I have been quite unhappy about a lot of things lately that occur in our editorial department.

I am not happy over what has been going on in the connection of *Blade* reporters writing for political organizations or candidates, and I could not publish a paper that permitted it.

I wrote an editorial which I sent to you, which is to appear on the first page of the paper and signed by me, which distinctly states that these political stories will not be written by the *Blade*, and that the *Blade* will in no way be responsible for them, and now if I were to permit our own people to do political work during the campaign, one of them might be writing a column or some of the contents of it, which, if it were ever found out, would prove that the *Blade* could not be trusted, and that I could not be trusted.

Block's comments not only influenced the editorial focus of the *Blade*, but provided guidance and leadership even though he was often not working in the Toledo office. "I have found P.B. to be a practical idealist. He is the most tolerant man I have ever known," Grove Patterson wrote during Block's first year as owner of the *Blade*.[6]

Block was known for his expertise as a publisher, but his knowledge of journalism, reporting, and the editorial function was vast and impressive. At the beginning of 1934, when he was balancing the publishing of seven newspapers, Block traveled uptown from his office to Columbia University, where he spoke at the Pulitzer School of Journalism to an audience of all its budding reporters and most of the professional faculty. Attributing the success of a newspaper to the abilities of its reporters, Block gave an informative lecture that touched on the logic and ideology of journalism. He insisted that the students continue their education if they wanted to become meaningful journalists, and that a background in politics, economics, sociology, literature, science, business and finance was necessary to enable the reporter to interpret the news, not just to report the facts. In rare form, he went on to capture the imagination of the students:

> I have often thought that any occurrence anywhere in the world could be made of surpassing interest to anybody if a really good reporter covered it. Fundamentally, news is drama. Drama is conflict. If we could make clear to every reader of a newspaper the conflict in the event we are reporting, we could have a publication of such amazing dramatic variety that the reader would receive enlightenment and entertainment to such a degree that he would loath to stop reading... such a newspaper would record not merely the acts, but what motives precluded the acts and what the acts *mean* to the persons involved, whether they be individuals, families or nations.

Switching topics, Block took a swipe at Prohibition, musing: "I often wonder why so many people get excited about the eighteenth amendment, and almost forget the first ten amendments, by virtue of which we have in America the freedom of the press." Block finished by saying that every attempt had to be made to stop even the *smallest* of restrictions by the government to interfere with public expression in newspapers: "In this way, we shall maintain in this country the principles of democracy as against those of communism on the one hand, and capitalistic fascism on the other." Block's talk on journalism was a natural story for newspapers themselves. It made headlines.[7]

The Editorials:
Commentaries on Politics, Economics and Society

Perhaps Block's most profound impact on newspaper publishing, however, was made through the editorials he personally wrote and signed; some 600 in all ran in the *Blade* virtually once a week for some 15 years.

There has been some speculation as to whether Block wrote the editorials himself or whether they were all penned by editors, writers and "ghosts" who worked for him. The answer is complex. In an interview given more than 25 years after Block's death, Herman W. Liebert, who worked for Block and was a boyhood friend of Paul Block, Jr., claimed that he had been Block's editorial writer from 1933 to 1941. Liebert said that he had taken over the writing of the editorials after Ik Shuman, the Managing Editor of the *Star-Eagle*, who supposedly worked directly with Block in that capacity.[8] But what, precisely, were Leibert's and Shuman's roles as "editorial writers"?

It is certain that Liebert began working for Block as a reporter and then as a columnist (for a column mostly of capsule reviews called "New York Day Letter") at the *Newark Star-Eagle* in 1932. After Shuman left the paper, Liebert was given the post of helping out in the preparing of the editorials. Block knew what he wanted to write. By that time he had already penned more than 250 signed editorials, and had written hundreds of them, unsigned, going back to 1916, before he employed Liebert to help him. In order to appraise Block's editorial contribution, and also to know exactly how Liebert and Block worked together, it's essential to understand the importance of editorials to newspapers.

One of the major factors that distinguishes one newspaper from another is not only its content or presentation, but its point of view. Readers desire not only information and entertainment, but they look toward newspapers for interpretation and comment about local, national and international issues. Traditionally, newspapers have published editorials that have lent support to political campaigns, endorsed or opposed civic projects, offered theories on favored projects or people, and commented on important news to the readers, from the death of a princess, to a town ravaged by a tornado, and from a children's baseball team that achieved a surprising victory, to a blind man who climbed a mountain. Block wrote about all of these people and causes, disasters and joys, and as a result, he cast the matrix of the *Toledo Blade's* perspective. As the editorials set the tone of view of the paper, and reporters and editors took note, Block's ideas as reflected in his editorials also affected how the news at the *Blade* was collected and reported, which stories were covered and why, the size and depth of articles, topics of features, and even the approach taken in the obituaries. Without actually designating his editorials as policy to be followed by his staff, Block was making it clear several times a week – whenever the editorials appeared – what kind of paper he wanted the *Blade* to be.

Although Block was not a formally educated man in that he did not attend college, he had spent a lifetime with some of the chieftains of the country, from mayors and governors to Presidents and moguls, and through constant discussions over several decades had learned a great deal about government, politics, civic affairs, and business. He was also brilliant, and what is known in today's parlance as a "quick-read." Liebert confirmed this, and added this judgment of his boss: "PB had very strong ideas about international and national politics, which he did not hesitate to express very, very vehemently."[9]

Two or three times a week in the early afternoon, Liebert would visit Block at his suite at the Ritz-Carlton, and Block – often still in bed (being a late riser) – would begin dictating a given editorial to the young man who, not knowing shorthand, scribbled as fast as he could in a special abbreviated format that he had devised on his own for taking notes.

Block's interests were broad and eclectic: He condemned a speech by Adolf Hitler in 1933 in which the new dictator was asking for frontier revisions of national boundaries while most of Europe wanted pure non-aggression pacts.[10]   Block favored the manufacturer's sales tax as the solution to the problem of how to raise money needed to finance the Depression-ravaged government's reconstruction program.[11] He demanded that the U.S. government recognize the Soviet Union.[12] He made the unusual suggestion that there should be a three-cent coin, simply since "so many things cost that much" (and perhaps because he fondly remembered the 3¢ silver coin from the 1880s).[13] He overreacted against President Roosevelt's brain trust, calling it ludicrous, often communistic.[14] In a piece that was more eyewitness news than editorial, after attending the trial of Bruno Hauptmann in the Lindbergh baby kidnapping case, Block described how the defendant broke under ridicule and manipulation by the prosecution.[15]

> He cringed, lied, faltered, lied again, and was as near a collapse as any witness I have ever seen in a court room.
>
> If there was any sympathy for him before New Jersey's most capable Attorney-General started his cross-examination, it was forgotten during that half-hour before the adjournment of court. Everyone in the court room knew that Hauptmann had been cornered – was trying to find a way out and saw that no way of escape was open.
>
> I watched the jury carefully. For the first time during the entire day their eyes and ears were open and attentive. It seemed to me that they looked at Hauptmann with disgust

and, although I may be wrong, it also appeared to me that his
doom was sealed with the jury during that short half-hour of
cross-examination.[16]

As soon as Block had dictated his daily or weekly editorial, Liebert
would swiftly take his notes back to the newsroom, and type them up,
making any grammatical or syntactical changes as were necessary in the
translation from spoken to written word. "Sometimes," said Liebert, he
would "do research on the facts," checking dates, spellings, complete
names and anything else that he felt was necessary. A messenger would
then take that draft back to Block, who would carefully read it and, if
necessary, phone Liebert to correct any misunderstandings or lapses of
logic that he felt had crept into the piece. Occasionally, Block would
have a second meeting with Liebert on a given editorial. Liebert admitted that he would sometimes take liberties with some of the editorials and
if he had gone too far, "I heard about it in no uncertain terms." Often
Block would ruminate over a single sentence or an idea, which Liebert
had changed for stylistic reasons. Block often disagreed with such changes.
"That's *not* what I told you," Block would say peremptorily, and even if
Liebert could prove that Block had uttered that very sentence based on an
examination of the notes, Block would still not permit it in the editorial.
He would end the matter by simply claiming that the sentence, as recorded by Liebert, was not what he *meant* to say, and it would have to be
changed.

Unlike most editorialists, Block only expressed those views and ideas
that he felt were consistent with his own philosophy and political persuasion. Although editorial writers on most newspapers write what they
please and choose their own topics, they are always open to a possible
veto from a superior. In Block's case, since he was the owner of the
paper, no one could reject his copy and no one dared to interfere with
anything in it. Joseph Pulitzer once said, "I want an editorial writer who
comes to work mad at some injustice every morning."[17] In Block's case
it was inequality in the afternoon, but the result was the same: indignation, often for the underdog, fired by passion. In a letter to Hearst, Block
revealed at least another one of the more pragmatic reasons why he wrote
the editorials for all of his papers: "To link myself up a little to the paper,
especially since I do not live in the cities where the papers are published."[18]

He campaigned for funds for the Toledo YMCA, asking his readers to
send money to expand the facilities.[19] In addition to his crusades for

contributions from his readers, Block also donated his own money to Toledo hospitals. His largest contributions, however, were not in Ohio for the most part but in New York City, where he helped build Manhattan Eye, Ear and Throat Hospital through continuous personal contributions. For the sake of equality, he also contributed substantially to the Mt. Sinai Hospital Building Fund, and donated money to St. Vincent's Hospital and the Sisters of Charity hospital. There were also substantial monies donated overseas to a group of German clinics and hospitals owned by the University of Berlin which provided for charity cases.

At times, Block's charity contributions were interconnected with his social, political or business interests. While he may have had primarily philanthropic reasons to contribute to the United Hospital Campaign Committee, it might not have been a complete coincidence that his friends Fiorello LaGuardia and Alfred E. Smith were on the board of directors.

He commended the city government and Edward D. Libbey for the construction and continued expansion of the Toledo Museum of Art, one of the finest in the country.[20] He sponsored a plan and continually urged the city council to establish safety zones in order to make the streets safer for pedestrians.[21] He begged for contributions to help those Toledo children who were going to school each morning without breakfast or warm enough clothing.[22]

Should any Toledoan fail to read one of his editorials, Block created a mission statement listing what he considered to be the most important goals of the city, and he had the proposals emblazoned on his editorial page:

The Blade's Toledo Program

- **Make Toledo an airport.**
- **Complete intercepting sewers and build disposal plant.**
- **Improve streets.**
- **Abolish most hazardous grade crossings.**
- **Rush development of St. Lawrence Waterway.**

Block's editorials were read by members of Congress, passed around with accompanying memos to the White House staff, debated over by members of city councils, political parties and governmental offices, sometimes criticized by other newspapers, and often tacked up on bulletin boards all over the country. Occasionally, one of his editorials would be placed in the *Congressional Record*, for example when he became critical of his own party after attending the 1932 Republican Convention and wrote a front page editorial, "A Party Without a Program." In sum, Block complained: "It is pathetic to find how few of the professional politicians understand the human mind. Today with unemployment conditions so bad, we are in the worst depression this country has ever seen. The speeches made by the administration leaders would be humorous if they were not so pathetic. Not a single constructive suggestion was made. Every statement referred to the wonderful things that have been done; meanwhile millions of men are out of work and wondering how to get food for their families."[23]

Were all of Block's editorials his ideas and not Liebert's? Was Block fair and just in his appraisals and opinions? Why did he feel that unlike many other editorials in newspapers, his had to be prominently signed? These are questions that beg an answer in an attempt to understand Paul Block and his motivations. First, even Liebert didn't deny that Block *dictated* the editorials to him, that Block had "the great instincts of a newspaper man," and that he would let nothing be published without his total approval. [24] Block never claimed that he "wrote" every word that appeared in the editorials, only that they expressed purely his own ideas, and that they were directly dictated by him to Liebert, who acted as stenographer/editor. In a letter to President Calvin Coolidge, Block wrote: "I would like you to read an editorial I dictated a few days ago to be published in my papers."[25]

Block's first language was German, and he readily admitted that he needed some help in constructing the flawless English that he wanted to appear above his name. His editorials had to be concentrated and pointed, and simply written so that the average reader could understand and relate to them, a task that he hired Liebert to complete. Often, extremely busy men in business, government and entertainment work with a writer to polish their own rhetoric: Washington's Farewell Address and Lincoln's Gettysburg Address were "written" by their assistants but are no less important in their content or the measure of the men who conceived and delivered them.

Although Block was self-reliant in his editorial beliefs and pronouncements, he was willing to discuss the expression of his ideas with certain people. His son Paul Block, Jr., was someone whose judgement he respected. Paul Jr., went to work for his father on the *Toledo Blade*, and was a brilliant wordsmith and scholar, a graduate of Yale, and perhaps the only scientist with a Ph.D. in chemistry who ever became publisher of a major American newspaper. On occasion, in an attempt to strengthen his father's writings, Paul Jr. would suggest changes in Block's editorials – but ever so diplomatically, pointing out that what was said in conversation, or dictated, might be confusing to "other minds when the close scrutiny of the printed word is possible."[26] Sounding something like an English teacher, son lectured to father: "In conversation we do not have to make sure that a modifying clause refers definitely to one word or expression, because our intonation brings out the meaning." For example, Block had written an editorial titled "New Deal Bureaucrats and Dictators," which appeared in his newspapers on April 13, 1936. When Paul, Jr. saw it printed in an early edition, he suggested that his father delete the word "public" before the use of the word "servant," as being more forceful; take out the modifier "almost" as weakening the phrase "If he objects to almost anything that is pro New Deal;" and substitute the phrase "legal authority" as somewhat more precise than "law and order" in the phrase "Private papers are being seized without law and order..." Paul Jr. sent his proposed emendations to his father, with the caveat that after seeing what he had in mind, Block would be "able to improve on them again, and in this way have a really smooth editorial for recopy." Block took those suggestions he liked, ignored those he didn't, and the editorial was changed for the later editions.

On some occasions, when Block was particularly concerned over the importance or influence that one of his editorials might have, he would seek out and confer with others prior to publication as to whether any changes should be made. In November of 1937, Block composed an editorial about what he considered to be the unfortunate state of the Republican Party, and its continued condition of discord, particularly attacking certain Republican leaders who he believed sought to divide the party against itself. In the editorial, Block mentioned fear among some Republicans that then-former President Herbert Hoover was possibly aspiring to capture the 1940 nomination, when in fact he had no intention to run again.

Since millions of Block's readers might be affected by his words, he wanted Hoover to read the editorial first, to make sure he was on the right track. Hoover took only two days to respond to Block's editorial draft, and took the liberty of totally re-writing the piece. In an accompanying letter to Block, Hoover stated:

> I do not think the question of my future is of any impor-
> tance or worth while, and continued discussion of it now, even
> in denial, beclouds the great problem before us and that is to
> get the Republican Party moving.[27]

Hoover changed the focus of the editorial to concentrate on a forthcoming meeting of 100 distinguished Republicans, whose duty it would
be to formulate a declaration of convictions and affirmative principles for
the Republican Party. In a bit of campaigning for those he felt would be
the most trustworthy and productive members, he named nine Governors, several Senators, and such leaders as Robert Moses and Robert A.
Taft as strong candidates to serve on the committee. Hoover quotes himself in the re-writing of Block's editorial:

> If the Republican Party has not learned the lesson that it
> must produce principles and programs besides being just
> against something, and joyriding on mistakes, it has not read
> history. You do not long hold the goal and devotion of men
> and women without definite purpose and principle. The Whig
> Party tried all that.

Although, in effect, a public relations release for how Hoover viewed
the future of the Party, the editorial was accepted by Block and he published it in some, but not all of his newspapers.

Not all of Block's readers believed that his editorials *were* always entirely fair. In the midst of controversy he was an authentic partisan, often
a firm adherent, almost a rabid militant, to the causes of the Republican
Party, a backer of campaigns and factions – whether frivolous or sound –
that he believed in, and in those instances he was capable of exhibiting
blind, prejudiced and sometimes unreasoning allegiance. Block was also
proud of what he was writing, and he would not allow his ideas to slip
into the background. William Jennings Bryan had argued that writers
should lift the cloak of anonymity, that editorial articles should be signed
by their writers, and that they, not only their newspapers, should stand up
for what they write.[28] Block certainly was not alone in signing his editorials. His colleagues Arthur Brisbane and William Randolph Hearst always signed *their* editorials; Block felt he could do no less. For years
Block's editorials appeared on page one of virtually all of his papers,

signed with his bold, self-assured hand: **Paul Block**. Neither a coward nor a miser, if he felt particularly impassioned by one of his position statements, he would also purchase space elsewhere for that particular editorial, sometimes even on the front page of other newspapers, such as the *New York Herald-Tribune*, *New York Sun*, and even in the venerable gray lady, *The New York Times*; also, just so that the ideas expressed wouldn't be missed, Block sent proofed galleys or typed courtesy copies to all of the people he mentioned, positively or negatively, in his editorials.

•••

The *Toledo Blade*, under Block's ownership and his direction as publisher, continued to prosper. By the late 1930s, circulation had skyrocketed to over 150,000 copies daily, and in a comparison with ten other leading newspapers such as the *Washington Star*, *Chicago Daily News*, *New York Sun* and *Cleveland Press*, the analysis showed that the *Blade* was far ahead of the other dailies in publishing nationally-known columnists, features and comic strips.[29]

Block continued to spend more time in Toledo, looking after what he considered his flagship paper. He usually stayed in a suite at the Commodore Perry Hotel, which had a special bed (with a super-soft mattress) that was pulled out and set up for him each time he visited the city. Because he had such difficulty sleeping at night, he insisted that he could sleep only in his specially-chosen bed, and before long every hotel in the dozens of cities in which he had business also had special "Paul Block beds" just for him whenever he was visiting that particular hotel.[30]

When he couldn't sleep, he read, and his favorite light reading at night was invariably detective and mystery stories, especially those of the genre that may be called pulp fiction. When he was in New York, every Friday he waited eagerly for the new edition of *True Detective Mysteries* to appear, and on Wednesdays he would send the office boy to the newsstands for his 10¢ copy of *Detective Fiction Weekly* so that he could read the next installment of such stories as "The Girl in the Desk," or "Behind the Green Lights," the adventures of "Happy" Houlihan and his police dog. He particularly liked the stories of Erle Stanley Gardner and Milo Ray Phillips.

On occasion, he became so impatient to know for example, how Inspector Neale could escape death at the hands of fiendish gangster Monk

Kelly, he would send someone down to *True Detective*'s offices on lower Broadway to try to obtain a galley proof of the story or an advance copy of the issue that contained the next installment. Since that procedure was often unsuccessful, Block pointed out to the magazine's circulation director that since he was placing full-page advertising (for such clients as Listerine mouth wash, and International Correspondence Schools) in their publications, he just *had* to have an advance copy delivered to his office hot off the press, a day or two earlier than it appeared on the newsstands. With the copy dutifully delivered each week by the publisher, Block would then sequester himself in his office, or take the magazine home with him for bedtime reading and lose himself in the next thrilling, cliff-hanging chapter of his favorite story.

Within a year after purchasing the *Toledo Blade*, Block had re-organized his business so that it was divided into three holding companies. The P.G.S. Corporation consisted of a corporation that held all the shares of stock that Block had acquired through his association with Hearst. Over the years, when Block sold or re-sold various papers to Hearst, part of the sale arrangement always included a sizeable amount of stock apportioned to Block, and so although he was not a majority stockholder in any of Hearst's papers, he built up a sizeable portfolio, which earned considerable profits.

The Paul Corporation held stock for Block's Consolidated Publishers, Inc., which in turn were the owners of record of the *Duluth Herald*, the *Toledo Blade* and the *Newark Star-Eagle*, in addition to Paul Block & Associates, the special advertising representative firm that started it all. Block personally held the stock in the Newark Bears, the *Brooklyn Standard Union*, the *Duluth News-Tribune*, and the *Toledo Times*.[31] He needed these numerous corporations because each newspaper was incorporated in the state where it was published, and state laws varied as to acquisitions, mortgages on properties owned, debentures and fair trade. Also, if one of the papers as a separate corporation failed and went bankrupt, for example, the rest of Block's newspapers or other holdings could not be assessed to make up any deficits.

Block really enjoyed his role as publisher, and he loved just being in the newsroom and talking to reporters and editors, press agents, publicity seekers, columnists, politicians and police officers. When it was a slow news day, he would wander down to the advertising or circulation department, and have just as much diversion talking numbers and business.

He was always amused with the adventures of one of the most colorful characters on the *Blade*, photojournalist Clarence Bailey, who was quite quiet in personality and somber in appearance, but who always seemed to find himself in some odd predicament. Once when he was using one of the old flashpowder cameras, Bailey took a picture of a prize cat that was to appear in The Peach. The flash so frightened the animal that it leaped high in the air, and when it landed it was dead, either from a heart attack or a broken neck. The owner was heartbroken and the *Blade* had to pay several hundred dollars in damages because it was a very special show cat.

At another time Bailey was assigned to take photographs of a new furniture line at a downtown store. When he was finished, he found it was past the store's closing time, and everyone had gone home. Since all of the doors were locked, he called the city desk of the *Blade*, and asked for help. They couldn't locate the owners of the store and so Bailey settled down on the largest, most comfortable sofa in the store until the workers returned in the morning to awake him. Block rocked with laughter when he heard of the incident.

Pittsburgh Post-Gazette

The somewhat labyrinthine story of how Paul Block became involved in the *Pittsburgh Post-Gazette* in 1927 was at that time unparalleled in American newspaper publishing history. It also reveals how the deep personal and business relationship of Paul Block and William Randolph Hearst came to maturity.

Both Block and Hearst, independently, had long been interested in entering the Pittsburgh newspaper market. The soot-covered city, with the rolled-up sleeves, hardened muscles and untiring energy of its workers, was at that time the second most populous city in the second most populous state in the country. It was known as the dynamic workshop of the world, the nation's industrial capital, especially in relation to the manufacture of iron and the mining of its coal reserves, growing up as it did around the steel mills of Andrew Carnegie. Pittsburgh was a city where fortunes had been made by men with commercial vision and inventiveness: Westinghouse, Knox, Schwab, Heinz and Mellon dominated the financial skyline. In terms of newspapers, it was the fifth largest market in the United States, with a total of some 84,000,000 lines of advertising in its eight publications: two morning newspapers, three on Sundays, and three evening papers.[32]

When Block began to consider Pittsburgh as a possible venue for another newspaper, his national chain of papers was already growing. He was thoroughly involved in the *Newark Star-Eagle*, the *Toledo Blade*, the *Duluth Herald* and his other Pennsylvania newspaper, the *Lancaster New Era*. He wanted to expand his interests, however. In March of 1927, Col. Frank Knox approached Block to talk about the possibility of entering the Pittsburgh newspaper field. Knox was a former publisher from New Hampshire, who had been hired by Hearst for his *Boston American*, and in a matter of months had become Hearst's new advisory executive. Knox had been a Rough Rider and fought with Theodore Roosevelt in the Spanish-American War (ironically, the war that Hearst was partially responsible for creating), and he was known as being almost maniacally efficient, blunt to the point of rudeness, and filled with a strong resolve in accomplishing anything that he set out to do. Block and Knox were the exact same age, had known each other for years from political and publishing conventions, and each respected and admired the other. Furthermore, Judge Elbert Gary (the city of Gary, Indiana was named after him), chairman of the board of the United States Steel Corporation and a bosom friend of Hearst's, was also trying to help Block and Hearst enter the Pittsburgh market, and talked to them about the possibilities of access. Block was more than attentive to Knox's and Gary's advice and proposals.

For Block, in addition to running the complicated and demanding business of a great metropolitan newspaper, there would be a tradition to uphold. The *Pittsburgh Gazette* (which underwent several reincarnations of its name), the forebear of the *Gazette-Times*, was founded in 1786 as the first newspaper west of the Allegheny Mountains. When such papers as *The New York Times*, the *Herald*, and the *Sun* were new, the *Gazette* was mature and reflected the life and times of the nation. In its fifth issue, the *Gazette* directed attention to the faults of the Articles of Confederation, which bound the states in a loose alliance, and demanded a correction to remedy the state of affairs which had left the people west of the Alleghanies – Pittsburghers – distressed by high taxes and the lack of sound money.[33] In 1787 it not only announced the framing of the Constitution of the United States, it published a copy of the actual document; it reported the deaths of Benjamin Franklin and George Washington; it upheld the Louisiana Purchase from Napoleon; in 1807 it published the news of the first steam boat, invented by Robert Fulton; it announced the advent of the first American railroad (in 1831); it reported in 1845 the tragedy of the Great Pittsburgh Fire, which also damaged the *Gazette's* own printing equipment; it was one of the chief spokesmen of anti-slavery forces in the North; it abetted Abraham Lincoln's election by organizing the Republican Party in Allegheny County; it published stories that discussed the discovery of gold in California, the assassination of Lincoln, World War I, and the Armistice; it opposed President Wilson's diplomacy, and after the war blamed him for the Senate's rejection of the Versailles Treaty.

If Paul Block took control of this leading and distinguished newspaper, he would be in charge of not just a commercial enterprise but a lineal descendant of a newspaper that chronicled the entire history of the United States, as well as the energetic city of Pittsburgh. As with the *Toledo Blade*, more than virtually any other of the papers he would own, Block's Pittsburgh venture would become a part of publishing and journalism history, and he would be its helmsman.

Knox, on behalf of Hearst, had been spending time in Pittsburgh attempting to discern the possibilities of his employer's entry into the newspaper field. What he discovered was that Pittsburgh was an over-newspapered city despite partially successful attempts at consolidation and buy-outs just four years previously. The population of 675,000 just could not support, either in advertising or in circulation, as many papers as were being published. Knox also learned through George E. Schroeder, owner of a piano company and a business entrepreneur, that Arthur E. Braun and George C. Moore, the trustees of the T.H. Given estate, owner of the *Pittsburgh Post* and the *Pittsburgh Sun*, were eager to sell their two publications, known affectionately in Pittsburgh as the "Braun papers." The Oliver family, one of the wealthiest in the city, owned the *Pittsburgh Gazette-Times* and the *Pittsburgh Chronicle-Telegraph* (those two papers were dubbed the "Oliver faction"); they too wanted to divest themselves of their properties. In addition to these locally-owned papers, in 1924 the Scripps-Howard chain had bought the *Pittsburgh Press*, a paper that Hearst had wanted to buy in 1921 but whose bid was refused by Oliver S. Hershman, its proprietor at that time. The era of privately-held chain newspapers, the owners of which had interests in other cities throughout the country, would soon take root in Pittsburgh as the first large city in the country so dominated completely by group publications. Arthur E. Braun, who was the president of the Farmer's Bank, issued a formal statement that justified his desire to sell his newspapers: "The tendency today is toward larger and stronger units in all industries. Cost of publishing has made the newspaper business turn toward consolidations. Present-day conditions require it. And in the hands of conscientious publishers, the unification of the newspaper field is a good thing for people as well as for the country."[34]

Hearst, using Frank Knox as his principal negotiator – he soon named him general manager of all of his newspapers, and in addition, publisher of the Chicago *Daily News* – suggested to Block that they enter an agreement to dominate the Pittsburgh newspaper market. Hearst knew that for monopolistic and personal reasons (people hated him, and he had often experienced refusals and rejections of his bids to acquire newspapers), he would not be able to buy all, or even most, of the newspapers in Pittsburgh, even though he could have afforded it and would have liked to have purchased them all. Braun had made it clear that he simply would not sell to Hearst. However, both Braun and Moore thought of Paul Block as "a man of human impulses, of high integrity and strong public spirit," and were perfectly willing to sell their newspapers to him.[35]

Secret meetings to discuss the Pittsburgh matter were held in Chicago throughout Decoration Day weekend in 1927, at the offices of Hearst's *Chicago American* and in Block's suite at the Drake Hotel. The Windy City was considered a reasonable halfway distance between Block's New York headquarters and Hearst's in California, and each man arrived in Chicago in his respective private Pullman car.

The two publishers devised a plan in which Block would buy the *Post* and the *Sun*, and Hearst the *Gazette-Times* and the *Chronicle-Telegraph*. As soon as the purchases were final, Block and Hearst would immediately trade one of their papers, each. Hearst would take over ownership of Block's *Sun* – meaning its title, subscription lists, equipment and personnel – and merge it with his *Chronicle-Telegraph*, forming a paper called the *Pittsburgh Sun-Telegraph*. Block would take, in return, Hearst's *Pittsburgh Gazette-Times*, and merge all of it with his *Post* into a paper called the *Pittsburgh Post-Gazette*. The result would leave Pittsburgh with just three papers where there had been eight: one morning paper (Block's *Pittsburgh Post-Gazette*), two evening papers (Hearst's *Pittsburgh Sun-Telegraph* and Scripps-Howard's *Pittsburgh Press*), and their two respective Sunday editions.

There was one enormous difficulty, however, in the proposed Block-Hearst design: Block did not have the cash reserve, nor could he borrow the large amount of money he needed to acquire both papers. The asking price for the *Post* and the *Sun* was close to $6 million for both newspapers; Block was temporarily cash poor since he had just purchased the controlling interest in the *Toledo Blade*.

In a clandestine verbal arrangement, Hearst agreed to secretly give Block all of the money needed for the purchase of the *Post* and *Sun*. Block would then purchase the papers under his own name, operate them (or their new entity) as Publisher, and sometime in the future have the right to pay Hearst (should he want to sell and Block want to buy) the entire price that would be estimated as fair value at that time to secure total ownership. When he arrived back in New York, Block had a Letter of Agreement drawn up that confirmed what had been consented to in Chicago, and then mailed it to Hearst for his signature.[36] Not covered in the Agreement but understood between them was that Block would receive a salary as Publisher, some stock that he would personally own, and the agreement that his company, Paul Block and Associates, would have a fixed-term arrangement to represent national advertising for the *Pittsburgh Post-Gazette*. Hearst also promised to dismiss the special representation firm, E. M. Burke, Inc., which handled the national advertising of the *Chronicle-Telegraph*, and replace it with Paul Block and Associates for the new entity, the *Pittsburgh Sun-Telegraph*. With everything in place, Hearst and Block and their representatives began negotiations to buy all four newspapers; it took close to two months to come to terms with the sellers.

The discussions and bargaining meetings were kept secret, and even the editors, reporters and staff people of the newspapers involved were uninformed of their pending fate. A leak occurred that transactions *were* taking place but none of the major participants would confirm, deny or even discuss any details as to who was buying from whom, which papers were involved, and when, if ever, the purchase, if any, would be made.

On Saturday, July 30, the *Gazette-Times* published a bold-faced, eight-column headline that proclaimed: **HEARST FAVORS MELLON FOR PRESIDENT**. The story consisted of an interview of Hearst by reporter Robert M. Ginter. Astute observers saw the importance of the story as a veiled announcement of Hearst's impending entrance into the city of Pittsburgh. Political analysts interpreted it a bit differently: they understood the blaring headline and front-page story as a sign of Hearst's ingratiation with the political machine of the city. He was saying in effect that although he usually supported progressive and liberal programs, he had no resistance to backing an archconservative such as Andrew W. Mellon, especially since Mellon was a native son. *The New York Times* speculated that "It was understood that Mellon interests are actually behind the deal," and that Hearst's advocacy of Mellon was "part of the program

laid down in the change of ownership."[37]   Mellon was a staunch Republican who urged upon Congress schedules of taxation that rested easily
upon the wealthy and big business: Hearst privately criticized him, but to
help his business in Pittsburgh, he fawned and groveled before Mellon
and his followers.

On Monday, August 1, 1927, at *exactly* 3:03 PM (a reporter, aware of
the historical significance of the moment, noted the time) Paul Block
signed the papers that made him the owner of the *Post* and the *Sun*; this
signation was followed by one of Hearst's representatives who signed for
him, taking ownership of the *Gazette-Times* and the *Chronicle-Telegraph*.
The actual amount of the purchase price was not announced, but insiders
and the trade press estimated that the four newspapers were bought for
approximately $10 million dollars.[38]   Minutes after all the parties shook
hands, Block and Hearst's representative signed additional papers, each
relinquishing or trading his one paper for the other. The rumor that Hearst
was the sole purchaser of the four papers, and that Block was standing in
for him, was "emphatically denied" by Block and by Col. Knox.[39] "As a
personal friend of Mr. Block's," said Col. Knox, "I went to him for Mr.
Hearst and interested him in the deal as it was ultimately carried out,"
implying, but not stating, that Hearst did not advance the money to Block.
Block also issued a statement at that time:

> In taking over the *Pittsburgh Morning Gazette-Times* and
> the *Pittsburgh Morning Post* and by consolidating them into
> one morning daily newspaper I am pleased to have some-
> thing to do with the correcting of the newspaper situation in
> Pittsburgh. Everyone acquainted with Pittsburgh has known
> it was overcrowded with newspapers. Not so long ago when
> the *Morning Dispatch* and *Evening Leader* were still in the
> field, Pittsburgh boasted of three morning papers and four
> evening papers and four Sunday papers... [The consolida-
> tion] is economically sound not only for the people of Pitts-
> burgh but for the advertisers as well.[40]

Braun and Moore made it clear that they were not – at least they *thought*
they were not – selling to Hearst: "Effective today the proprietorship of
this paper [the *Gazette-Times*] passes from the present owners to Paul
Block. Mr. Block has also bought the *Pittsburgh Sun*."

Judge Gary lived to see his friends Hearst and Block as publishers in
Pittsburgh...but just barely. He died two weeks after they commenced

publishing.

As soon as the consolidation was made public, rumors began to spread that the Curtis Publishing Company, owners of the *Saturday Evening Post,* the *Ladies Home Journal,* and the *Public Ledger* in Philadelphia – and other periodicals and newspapers – was going to start a new paper in the Iron City to compete with the Hearst-Block consortia. A further report had the Pulitzers interested in launching a new newspaper. Local Pittsburgh merchants, who felt that their advertising messages were being diluted by too many newspapers as it were, were happy about the consolidation and were not enthusiastic about the possibilities of yet *another* Pittsburgh newspaper to divert customers' attentions. Whether the retailers' attitudes ever reached or influenced any of the reported newspaper entrepreneurs is not known, but after Block and Hearst established their businesses in the city, Pittsburgh had to wait more than 50 years for a new daily newspaper to be launched.[41]

Block's first issue of the *Post-Gazette* was published on August 2, 1927, and he issued the following statement in that issue: "It will be our ambition to have the *Pittsburgh Post-Gazette* be a newspaper of which everyone may be proud. Its policies will be independent and the newspaper will be of such high character as to insure its welcome in every home." Since the consolidation took place almost overnight, Block let it be known in all seriousness that it might take a few days before "the new *Post-Gazette* will be as nearly perfect a newspaper" as it was his ambition to publish.[42] The most difficult part of the consolidation for Block was the decision as to which jobs would be absorbed by the combined paper, and which would have to be eliminated. Within two weeks after taking control and setting up the new entity of the *Pittsburgh Post-Gazette*, Block gave the orders to terminate some 300 jobs. The only area that survived any pruning was the editorial department, which numbered only about 40 editors, reporters, copy-editors and staff assistants: most of the news had been traditionally garnered from the wires of the Tri-State News Bureau.

Block immediately began to operate as though the *Pittsburgh Post-Gazette* was a *new* newspaper, which in a way it was, and he wanted it to reflect who *he* was. Unhesitatingly, he changed the look and the bearing of the paper, especially the front page, giving it a more lively (or "peppy" as he described it) appearance than the recently-defunct *Pittsburgh Gazette-Times.* Three days after he took control, Block trumpeted his theater companion Charles Lindbergh's visit to Pittsburgh with an 8-column headline, **LINDBERGH ARRIVES TODAY – GREAT RECEPTION**

PLANNED, together with a huge, two-column, extreme close-up photograph of "Plucky Lindbergh," as the newspaper called him, based on the name of a popular song in his honor. Sharing the lead article was a story of another of Block's friends, President Calvin Coolidge, who had just made his famous, and shocking, statement: "I do not choose to run." [43] One of the early big stories in the paper was a sad one for the city of Pittsburgh: the mighty Babe Ruth did *not* strike out. He hit three home runs on October 8th to help the New York Yankees defeat the Pittsburgh Pirates and sweep the World Series.[44] Bad news, as Block knew, also sells newspapers. By early October, the *Pittsburgh Post-Gazette*, at 234,238 net paid copies daily, achieved the largest circulation ever obtained by a Pittsburgh newspaper.[45]

The layout for the new *Pittsburgh Post-Gazette* was devised through discussions and long, labored letters between Hearst and Block, as was the layout for the new *Pittsburgh Sun-Telegraph*.[46] The idea was that Hearst would dramatize his *Sun-Telegraph*, as he did with his other 25 newspapers: heavy black headlines, startlingly big type, splashes of color, box scores on the front page prominently displayed along with general news, out-of-the-ordinary picture layout, stories that raked the dregs of human existence. In deliberate contrast, to avoid competition, Block's *Post-Gazette* would be comparatively conservative, dignified but sprightly, appealing to a more up-scale morning readership. He jokingly chided Hearst by telling him that two or three people had already mentioned that the *Pittsburgh Post-Gazette* was a fine paper, and so much needed, because of the "two terrible yellow newspapers" that were now dominating the evening field.

Hearst questioned Block's use of the two-column photograph on page one (even though it was a photograph of Lindbergh) as being too competitive with the appearance of the *Sun-Telegraph*. He wanted the *Pittsburgh Post-Gazette* to have a relatively conservative and sober look and not to be compared to his more-than-sensational *Sun-Telegraph*. The *Sun-Telegraph* was to be the champion of the masses, as Hearst saw it, and the *Post-Gazette* would be the friend of the elite. Block responded dutifully: "I have suggested cutting out the double-column illustration at least five times during the week unless, of course, something of great importance occurs."[47]

Ideally, Block wanted the *Pittsburgh Post-Gazette* to lead Pennsylvania's, or at least most of Pittsburgh's "thinking citizens," as he put it, into an Independent Republican party, so that it would be strong enough to elect candidates not dominated by machine bosses.

Block told Hearst that he realized that in the first few days and weeks, the *Post-Gazette* was not running "a real conservative" front-page, but he was somehow fearful of making it look too moderate. Sending Hearst tear-sheets of the front pages of a week's issues of the *Post-Gazette*, Block accompanied them with a letter that said, in part, that Hearst's own circulation director from the *Boston American* was in Pittsburgh for a week or so and gave his opinion that the *Post-Gazette* "would never sell or get any circulation looking as cold as it does." Block was using his own judgement in trying to shape the paper in the way that he believed it should be presented, always aware however that he had to answer to Hearst. As he wrote to Hearst: "The above will give you an idea of why I have not made it look as conservative as even you might have had in mind. However, this does not mean I am not willing to change it if you think it best."[48] The appearance, approach and contents of the *Pittsburgh Post-Gazette* became an ongoing colloquy that Hearst and Block continued for the next ten years, whether at San Simeon or Palm Beach, New York or Pittsburgh itself.

In addition to the paper's make-up and layout, Block immediately instigated other radical changes in the *Post-Gazette* operation: he brought Oliver J. Keller, a former Army officer and his editor of the *Lancaster New Era*, to Pittsburgh to take over the paper; he had raised the price of the paper from two cents to three (although considered by some observers as highly risky, circulation actually increased with the price hike since the *Post-Gazette* had become the only morning paper in town and had a command readership); and he elevated the advertising rates.

He ordered newsprint paper from Finland, which enabled the *Post-Gazette* to complete its daily run 20 to 30 minutes earlier because there was less breakage than usually occurred with domestic newsprint paper. It also cost less than domestic newsprint. That one strategy not only saved in both cost and overtime, but because the grade of the paper was better, it prevented the ink pans on the printing presses from accumulating small scraps of newsprint and paper lint which would often damage or blur the type or photographs.

He also began a tradition that up to that time no Pittsburgh newspaper ever dared to attempt: he insisted that large local advertisers sign contracts for the purchase of a certain number of lines, or pages of advertising, every year. If the advertiser used the amount of advertising agreed upon, he was charged at a lower rate. If he used less than that amount, he would be "short rated," or charged a higher rate. If the advertiser used more than the contract called for, there was a provision for paying an even lower rate.[49] Block realized that he was taking a risk by doing this because it also trapped him into a particular price per line which could not be altered for the term of the contract, but the advantage was that his advertising salesmen did not have to "chase" – as he put it – for ad copy or insertion orders every day or week. The advertising income was, therefore, predictable, and could be relied upon. Within two weeks as Publisher, Block's sales force secured 60 local contracts and more were being lined up daily. After the announcement of his advertising rate increase, his salesmen also secured 120 contracts for national advertising, most of it to start running that September. The *Post-Gazette* was becoming one of the most successful and largest morning dailies in the country.

A month later his circulation jumped to 227,000, and then soon after to over 300,000. The outgrowth of these staggering numbers was that the *Pittsburgh Post-Gazette* was beginning to carry more advertising than any other morning paper in the history of publishing in the city. The *Post-Gazette* was doing so well, William Block, Sr. recalls of his father's paper, that when the salesmen from Paul Block and Associates came to Pittsburgh they had no need to go to the *Post-Gazette*, and ironically spent more time at Hearst's *Sun-Telegraph* offices.[50]

Within the first month of publication, the *Post-Gazette* began to run all of its comic strips on one page, and Hearst did not like the system. Of all American publishers, Hearst was primarily responsible for cartoons and comic strips becoming one of the most popular forms of entertainment in the country; they turned out to be one of the most effective circulation builders that any newspaper could print. He was extremely clear as to what kinds of comics should appear, what position in the paper they should occupy, and how much should be paid to the cartoonists or their syndicates. He wanted Block to share his enthusiasm for comics as a sound business investment, and suggested that Block insert something for everybody, a potpourri of sophisticated strips and slapstick cartoons directed to the men, women, and possibly children who would read them. Hearst asked Block by telegram if he would run the comics distributed throughout the *Post-Gazette*, instead of clustering them on one page, and advised that Block study the *Chicago Tribune* as a model. Block canvassed his editors, and some of his business people, and mostly everyone believed that having all the comics on one page was a superior solution because it gave the reader who wanted comics a central place to find them: a funny page. The busy reader or one who was disinterested in comics, though, would not be annoyed by them when reading a business or news page. In order to appease Hearst, however, and also because his comic page was filled, Block ordered his editors to insert two new comic strips – "The Gumps" and "Moon Mullins" – to be distributed somewhere within the paper, and *not* on the comics page.[51] Eventually Block also bought the extremely popular "Terry and the Pirates" comic strip to be inserted in the *Post-Gazette*.

Block was conflicted; he wanted to promote the *Pittsburgh Post-Gazette* as the largest circulation of any newspaper in the city, yet he didn't want to hurt Hearst's *Sun-Telegraph*, which was just what might happen if an advertiser, dazzled by Block's figures, decided to drop out of the evening paper in favor of the morning. In what might be described as a form of business schizophrenia, he delayed publicizing or announcing his burgeoning figures, although shrewd advertisers did not have to be told; they began to notice that their business was increasing markedly every time they bought space in the *Pittsburgh Post-Gazette*.[52]

Block had certain difficulties, however, securing local advertising for the *Post-Gazette*. The argument used by the local merchants was that by the time readers found and responded to a retail ad in the morning paper, they were already at work and too busy to shop. The same ad placed in an evening paper, however – the retailers held – started the cash registers ringing up sales that very next morning because people had the opportunity to discuss the possible purchase while in their homes.

The counter-argument, that an ad placed in a morning paper motivated customers for *two* days, was simply not accepted by the advertisers. Block was delighted to secure retailer Edgar Kaufman's full-page ad every day in the back page of the final news section, but the store was also placing *multiple* ad pages in the evening and Sunday papers, proving that its management thought that the evening buy was more profitable and advantageous.[53]

The staff of the *Sun-Telegraph* was also aware that the *Post-Gazette's* circulation and national advertising was outstripping theirs. That led to a somewhat embarrassing event. During the first weeks that Block was in Pittsburgh, he stayed at the William Penn Hotel, attempting to get his new newspaper in order. He had brought his Circulation Manager of the *Toledo Blade,* Frank Newell, to Pittsburgh for several weeks to consult with the Circulation Department of the *Post-Gazette,* to help it run more efficiently. One evening, in a social setting, Newell was talking with some other newspaper people from Hearst's *Sun-Telegraph.* He mentioned that he worked for the *Toledo Blade.* Newell was promptly offered the job of Circulation Manager of Hearst's paper. Block was incensed when he heard about it, informing Hearst that his people obviously did not know that Block was *also* the owner of the *Blade,* and therefore felt free to make a corporate raid on him. Hearst immediately informed his people at the *Sun-Telegraph* of the error, and they desisted in attempting to recruit Newell.

In the first few months of taking control of the *Post-Gazette,* Block spent more time in Pittsburgh than he did in his hometown of New York; but he was also frequently in Toledo, Lancaster, Duluth and Newark, looking after his newspapers in those cities. In New York, he often left the running of the office and his special representation business to his assistant Dan Nicoll, and to his brother, Max Block.

As much as Hearst had wanted entry into Pittsburgh, and to dominate the market with his newspapers, he rarely visited the city itself. Communication between Block and Hearst, therefore, was for the most part by telephone, telegrams, and long letters. Both men yearned for personal face-to-face meetings, but with Hearst's 26 newspapers and his 12 magazines, and Block's nine newspapers, the *Pictorial Review*, and the many other papers that he was representing, it was difficult for them to find themselves in the same city at the same time. Eventually, Block would be in simultaneous control as president and publisher of ten papers, "a considerable chain of important newspapers," according to journalism historian Frank Luther Mott, and struggling to keep all of his properties in balance.[54] Block placed relatively discreet institutional advertisements in trade publications to help increase sales, and so that the publishing world would know who was in charge. They looked like this:

> Pittsburgh Post-Gazette
> Toledo Blade
> Milwaukee Sentinel
> Newark Star-Eagle
> Wisconsin News
> Brooklyn Standard Union
> Toledo Times
> Duluth Herald
> Duluth News-Tribune
>
> ***Paul Block***
> President and Publisher

Through their secretaries and their assistants, Hearst and Block kept
one another apprised of their respective schedules, and whenever it looked
as though they were both going to be in New York, where both had offices and homes, they would arrange to meet.

Hearst was coming to New York at the end of September, just weeks
after Block began his role as publisher of the *Pittsburgh Post-Gazette*, so
Block arranged for second-row tickets for Hearst and Marion Davies and
himself and Dina for "Jimmy Walker Night" at the Ziegfeld Follies of
1927. The Mayor, as guest of honor, would sit with them, and Irving
Berlin composed a song especially in Walker's honor:

> Who told Broadway now to be gay?
> Who gets his picture taken three times a day?
> Jimmy!
> We're glad to show,
> That we all know,
> That Jimmy's doing fine.
> Can't you hear those old New Yorkers hollering:
> Gimmie – gimmie – gimmie Jimmy for mine!

Although it was a social evening, and Block was happy to spend it with
his old nighttime friends, he informed Hearst that he was more pleased
because it would enable them to meet in order to discuss their new business arrangement with the *Pittsburgh Post-Gazette*. He had specific concerns that he put into a letter so that when they met, Hearst could be
prepared. The questions show how careful and solicitous Block was toward Hearst, and how he was searching for parameters of control. Block
was more than capable of acting on his own as the publisher of the *Pittsburgh Post-Gazette* – he already had over a decade of experience publishing the *Newark Star-Eagle* – but because of the strange financial arrangement he had with Hearst, he did not want to exceed his jurisdiction,
especially with a man so famous for running all of his enterprises with
the proverbial iron hand. Some of the questions on Block's agenda were:

- Shall I try to get more circulation, even though the figure
  should beat out the *Sun-Telegraph*?
- Shall I think more of circulation, than of profits?
- Or shall I consider both?
- Is the paper as it looks now about the way you would ad-
  vise making it up, or do you still feel it needs many changes?

- Am I to discuss problems with various men of your organization who have called on me and to whom I have tried
  to be extremely courteous, or am I to use my best judgment in everything, just as I do for my other newspapers?[55]

After the performance, Hearst invited the Blocks back to his home on
Riverside Drive; Mayor Walker declined the invitation, citing another
engagement. The social embarrassment of the very-married Hearst and
his friend Marion Davies, stepping out in public for the evening together,
was difficult for everyone to handle. Wherever Hearst went, he was followed by news photographers and reporters, and only recently a picture
of Hearst and his wife had been splashed all over the New York papers as
they were entering a costume ball at the Ritz (Millicent was dressed as a
Southern belle; Hearst wore white tie and tails). Somehow Hearst managed to keep photos of himself and Marion out of the press. It was common knowledge, however, that Marion Davies was Hearst's mistress, and
there were some unspoken, although clearly delineated, places that they
did not go as a couple. When not at San Simeon, Marion lived in her own
multi-million dollar brick and marble town house, which Hearst had bought
her, also on Riverside Drive, not far from his own apartment. Often he
lunched with Marion at her house and had dinner with his wife at their
own home. As long as he remained married to Millicent Willson Hearst,
however, Hearst could never permit Marion entry into his home in New
York, nor could she even be mentioned there; the night of the Ziegfeld
Follies with the Blocks was no exception. Disconcertingly, therefore,
Hearst and the Blocks first dropped off Marion at her house and then
went to Hearst's for a nightcap.

Famous for being the largest and most luxurious apartment in New
York City, perhaps in the world, Hearst's residence consisted of the five
top floors of the Clarendon apartment house at 137 Riverside Drive. He
had bought the building and evicted whole floors of tenants so that he
could construct his castle in the city, complete with a penthouse that he
had built on the roof, and a small bridge to an adjoining building so that
he or his special guests could exit secretly when the need arose. The
baronial living room looked like a precursor to the movie set of the film
Citizen Kane, dramatically filled with ancient armor, medieval tapestries,
and priceless *objets d'art*, reminiscent of what could be found in a ducal
castle of the House of Savoy. The thirty-five foot high windows, presented a sweeping view of the Hudson River, and the *mise en scene* spoke

of majesty and monarchy, of unbelievable wealth and decadent excess. A private elevator whisked the threesome to Hearst's main floor. Block had been at the Clarendon a number of times before at parties, with hundreds of other guests, but when the butler escorted him to the dramatic Great Room, he was a bit intimidated, though pleased that he was there to talk to Hearst privately. He had finally arrived at what seemed to be the realm of publishing and financial power. Millicent and Dina (who felt a bit uncomfortable that she had just furtively spent the evening with the two covert lovebirds) sequestered themselves in a drawing room over a midnight high tea, while Hearst and Block – alone – talked business. They smoked cigars and each drank a bottle of bock beer, salvaged from the kitchen, since the wine cellar – the largest in New York City – located on the twelfth floor, was locked. Inexplicably, neither Hearst nor the servants on duty had the key. Hearst was known to have taken an axe to the locks of the wine rooms on some past occasions, but in this case, Hearst and Block wanted to get right down to business and he avoided the dramatic demolition of his wine cabinets.

Hearst's answers to all of Block's questions were not simple, although they were sympathetic. He was intensely interested in the conclusions and recommendations that Block derived from his six-week Pittsburgh experience.[56] He also did not want to bring to bear his power over Block and thereby discourage him, and so most of the decisions, he said, would have to be Block's. *However,* he went on emphatically, there were some things he would like to see changed or addressed. Therein began a dialogue between the two, similar to hundreds of others that would occur periodically for well over ten years, with Hearst as mentor and superior, and Block as volunteer acolyte and subordinate partner, but publisher in fact and in deed. Block truly welcomed Hearst's input into his operation, and informed him of his cooperation as such: "I want to say that any suggestions or requests which you make are, naturally, very welcome to me; in the first place, because you have the right and, secondly, because you have the ability – and I mean the latter most sincerely."[57] Hearst realized the extent of his own pedantry, and sincerely wanted Block's responsive counterbalance. After a round of expounding, he joked: "This concludes the lecture on journalism from Professor Hearst for today; and the Professor hopes you will tell him a few things to offset the ideas he is unloading on you."[58]

Generally, Hearst was determined to sensationalize all of the newspapers under his control, but in the case of Block's *Pittsburgh Post-Gazette,* it did not serve his interest to do so. He would be competing against himself should Block follow all of Hearst's tested and age-old blends of published yellow: palliatives of sin, sex and violence combined with trumped-up concerns for the common man. "I know you will realize, Mr. Block, that I am not saying this at all because your politics differ from mine," he formally informed Block. "As a matter of fact, there is considerable advantage in having the politics of the *Post-Gazette* differ from that of the *Sun-Telegraph*."[59]

Even more than expressing his political agenda – he had long given up the belief that what the country needed was *him* – Hearst was inexorably interested in making, or at least not losing, money. His general advice to Block was to publish the *Pittsburgh Post-Gazette* as a relatively conservative but lively paper, in direct opposition to his *Pittsburgh Sun-Telegraph*. He proposed to Block: "I believe, without qualification, that the *Post-Gazette* should remain a conservative paper; but it must be of course an interesting conservative newspaper, and I think a powerful one."[60] Hearst went on to say that while the newspaper should be conservative in its news handling, it should not be "heavy."[61] Hearst pointed out that he did not mean that the *Post-Gazette* should be partisan toward the politically conservative movement, or become, in effect, a party organ. To try to rationalize his position and justify his stance to Block, Hearst used as a comparison his vigorously Democratic *New York American*, which according to Hearst was exclusively Democratic because it *wasn't* the only paper in town. The rationalization made no sense, however, to Block because there were still three papers in Pittsburgh, and it was logical and it made editorial and readership sense for each one of them to be partisan should they so choose. In any event, if Block could make a financial success of the *Pittsburgh Post-Gazette*, whatever its political persuasion, that is all that seemed to interest Hearst.

The following suggestions by Hearst were culled, not only from records of that initial meeting about the *Pittsburgh Post-Gazette*, but from other correspondence that Hearst and Block had during their joint working relationship in the Pittsburgh venture. In essence, Hearst counseled Block not to change the typography of the *Pittsburgh Post-Gazette,* or certainly not to make any radical transformations: "You would better see what you can do with the present general style of typography on the *Post-Gazette*, modifying it moderately as you progress, and never in the direction of the typography of the Hearst papers."[62] However, he added, "we could get more life with the same typography."[63] He talked of condensing the size of the paper to make it more easily read, adding more photos ("I don't think the pictures in the paper are interesting; they are almost all uniformly commonplace."[64]) accompanied by better-written captions, a comics page that pleased the reader ("not necessarily the editor"[65]), more financial news, better contributors to the sports pages, greater coverage of movies, and the inclusion of a feature called "March of Events" that appeared in many of Hearst's papers. He did not ask, but told Block that: "There will be no change in the fundamental character of the paper, but we hope to get better and briefer news, and more variety in consequence, and more interest and entertainment."[66]

The autumn of 1927 was unseasonably cold in Pittsburgh, and the winter of 1927-1928 was a brutal one, so retail stores sales were down because people were staying home and not shopping as much. As a result, the manufacturers that supplied those outlets also experienced a precipitous drop in income. In order to make up their losses, many retail stores in Pittsburgh just advertised less.[67] Block was worried about the drop in income in all of his newspapers, and as his special representation business also declined, it was difficult for him to cope. Hearst bluntly criticized Block's failure to prevent the hemorrhaging of money by the *Post-Gazette*. Since Block was already distressed about the problem, Hearst's comments only added to Block's frayed emotional state. But he was careful not to show his worry. Block diligently maintained an optimistic appearance outwardly, even when that was somewhat at odds with the real conditions. Thus he wrote in March of 1928: "But every sign seems to point to a revival of business this Spring, and already, the business in many industries is not only improving but breaking records."[68]

To Block, having a confident attitude toward the nation's economic future was almost every citizen's patriotic duty, and he believed that the love of one's country was the best preventive of financial ruin. In addition to his loyalist views as expressed in his editorials, he attempted to show in every way he could that he was proud to be an American. On Memorial Day in 1929, Block was in Pittsburgh and attended the parade that marched up the Boulevard of the Allies. He was touched by seeing not only veterans of World War I, but also those of the Spanish-American War and a small contingent of the Civil War as well, who hobbled nobly to the cheers of thousands. "[They] all serve to remind us that this nation has not lacked courage and character in times of crisis," he wrote. "And that is why America is the great country that it is."[69]

On Labor Day, 1929, the *Post-Gazette* joined with the Pittsburgh Aviation Industries Corporation to co-sponsor an airplane race from Pittsburgh to Cleveland for women aviatrix (as they were called then). The race was organized by Louise Thaden, a resident of Pittsburgh who had just won, to great public ovation, a cross-country air derby from Santa Monica, California to Cleveland, Ohio. Not only did readers delight in the story, but it helped to promote the fledgling realm of aviation itself. Block had a double purpose in sponsoring the event. He thought it would build circulation, and he wanted Pittsburgh to look upon air travel more favorably. Block had been hammering in his editorials that there was need for a large, municipal airport, and for the city to recognize the importance of air travel not only for travelers, but as a source of business. He thought that Pittsburgh could become a manufacturing center for airplanes, propellers, and other airplane-related equipment and necessities. Perhaps as a result of his lobbying for aviation at that time, two new plants opened in the city for airplane manufacture, other commercial projects began being planned, and an airmail route was inaugurated from Pittsburgh to St. Louis, and then to Washington, D.C.

Block used his sponsored air race as a catalyst for a 36-page special aviation edition of the *Post-Gazette*, which not only produced a sizable advertising income from airplane manufacturers, but helped to support the campaign for the airport which was eventually constructed.[70] The newspaper was becoming nicely profitable, and Block was becoming well-regarded in Pittsburgh. Eventually he would even incorporate his beloved Peach section into the *Post-Gazette*, asking his readers to give the new department of the paper a chance: "Anything that is new either makes an immediately favorable impression or a poor one," he wrote. "We urge our readers to follow this section for at least a week. We are confident if they do this they will like it."[71] He was extremely proud of the new Radio Department on the last page of the *Peach*, which made it easier for readers to find the program listings that they sought without having to search all over the paper for the information.

Then the stock market crashed. As the resulting Depression spread nationwide, and consumers cut back on their purchasing, less advertising was inserted in newspapers all over the country. Some papers struggled to survive. Block's *Pittsburgh Post-Gazette* had been in a sound financial condition, but it too suffered. In order to try to promote business in the *Post-Gazette* and to do something for the city of Pittsburgh, Block looked for opportunities to sponsor or participate in events. On Thanksgiving Day weekend, 1930, he sponsored a benefit performance at the

Stanley Theater for the city's unemployed. Stars such as Fred Stone, Charles Dillingham and Phil Baker performed, and there were acts from the Ripple Company and Shubert's "Artists and Models" review, all of whom – together with the musicians and the stagehands – donated their time and services. Block, dressed in a tuxedo, opened the evening by addressing the audience from the stage:

> There are many calls upon theater people to aid worthy causes, and their response is always so sincere and so gener- ous that the public would be ungrateful in the extreme if it did not do everything possible to show its appreciation. The fine array of talent that has volunteered for the benefit to- night assures one of the best shows of this character that Pitts- burgh has ever seen. Every dollar paid to admission will be turned over to help the unemployed, and every seat in this big theater is filled.
>
> The whole-hearted response to the appeal on every side is most heartening and inspiring. What a fine thing it is to pro- vide in this way some share of cheer and comfort for thou- sands who might otherwise find the Thanksgiving season bleak and sad! [72]

A few weeks later, Block pointed out in the *Post-Gazette* that there had been a slight upsurge in Pittsburgh business approaching that Christmas season, and this added to his advertising sales. McCreery's stores had hired more workers than they had in 1929, and also announced that they would give three percent of their sales from the receipts of the Friday and Saturday following Thanksgiving Day to a voluntary fund for the unem- ployed. [73] For a few months, it looked as though the worst was over. As soon as the mini-spurt of holiday shopping had ceased, however, busi- ness at the *Post-Gazette* began to look bleak again.

In addition to economic concerns, the end of 1930 also made clear to Block how complicated his relationship with Hearst was. Block carried a weight of concern on his mind: how could he do what he believed was right for the *Pittsburgh Post-Gazette*? He wanted to advance the paper in all ways and make money for it and himself, but what was he to do when he and Hearst disagreed? Block was distracted and restless and walked a wire-thin line when dealing with Hearst, but often he would have to speak out even if it meant compromising his situation. One such time was in December of 1930, when Arthur Brisbane, America's most famous editorial writer, the man who had made Hearst and himself millions, criticized the *Post-Gazette* in an editorial that appeared in the *Pittsburgh Sun-Telegraph*. Block felt that this displayed a certain disloyalty on Brisbane's part, since in effect they both worked for Hearst.

In what seemed to be a study in pirouette politics for both papers, Brisbane had written a front-page editorial criticizing the *Post-Gazette's* advocacy of John M. Hemphill, the liberal Democratic candidate (primarily for his stand against Prohibition) for the gubernatorial race in Pennsylvania. Hemphill was ultimately defeated by a narrow margin by the Republican candidate, the conservationist Gifford Pinchot – a *former* Governor of Pennsylvania – and a vigorous prohibitionist. Brisbane called Block's support of Hemphill a "circulation mistake." Block was affronted by Brisbane's observation. He felt he had to stand up for his newspaper, and in a matter of days, he was back with his own front-page editorial, which stated in part:

> You use the phrase "circulation mistake." It occasions some surprise because it is not our impression that the great list of newspapers, the William Randolph Hearst publications, with which you are so prominently associated, permit their editorial policies to be dictated by the circulation department. Certainly the *Post-Gazette* does not. But for your information, the *Post-Gazette's* circulation exceeds by almost 50,000 that of the next Pittsburgh daily paper, and the last official report of the three papers showed that the gap was widening as compared with the previous six months average. If that is a mistake, we hope to make more of them.
>
> As for the election itself, Mr. Pinchot was opposed by the *Post-Gazette* not because of any antagonism to him as an individual, but because of honest differences of opinion on the major issues involved, and because of his continued attacks against business interests at a time when cooperation with business would have been more desirable. [74]

Hearst never commented on the Brisbane-Block debate, and just allowed the two men, as rivals of a sort for his own involvement with them, to have their say against each other.

At another time, the two men got into a verbal argument over Judaism. Brisbane, a Christian, nevertheless pontificated that he knew more about the Jewish religion than Block. Although no Talmudic scholar, Block claimed that he did not ostentatiously display his knowledge of his own religion but that in any case, he certainly knew more by tradition, if not through formal learning, than Brisbane. The debate degenerated into each man asking the other such questions as what is the difference between the Midrach and the Torah, or challenging one another to name the tribes of Israel. No one won.

In 1931, the Retail Merchants' Association of Pittsburgh, consisting of the eleven leading stores in the city, all smarting from the general lack of business that they were experiencing, attempted to intimidate the *Post-Gazette* with the threat that if the newspaper did not lower its rates, they would move all of their advertising over to the *Sun-Telegraph*.[75] Although Hearst would have been delighted if he saw his revenue increase – and he was already realizing an increase in circulation over his rival *Pittsburgh Press* – it would have been a Pyrrhic victory, a triumph at too heavy the price, should the *Sun-Telegraph* rise in advertising lineage at the expense of Hearst-Block's *Post-Gazette*. Block succumbed to the pressure and lowered the rates, but did he make his decision because of Hearst's insistence, or was it his own business judgment?

It seemed that the only gratifying moment for Block in Pittsburgh during 1931 was when his friend Florenz Ziegfeld came to town with his Follies company that summer, arriving in a special nine-car train. The previous year, Ziegfeld had suffered his greatest theatrical loss in the theater, in his production of Rodgers' and Hart's musical *Simple Simon*, starring Ed Wynn.[76] Traditionally, Ziegfeld used Atlantic City as the venue for his out-of-town tryouts before heading back to the Great White Way, but when Block suggested that Ziegfeld try Pittsburgh as a place to open his season, the great showman jumped at the chance for something new.

Ziegfeld had opened a smaller show in Pittsburgh the year before, and liked both the critical response and the ticket sales. When Block promised him extensive publicity in the *Post-Gazette*, it sealed the plan. Eighty Ziegfeld Girls entertained, along with singers Helen Morgan and Harry Richman, and the comedian Jack Pearl. Block was also impressed with a dancer who used the single name "Mayfair" – a new Ziegfeld discovery – who people acclaimed as the hit of the show. In his publicity for Ziegfeld's Pittsburgh Follies, Block (perhaps thinking of Marion Davies) touted the exceptional qualities of the Girls: "There are girls from every state in the union who some day will be married to American millionaires and English noblemen or become famous moving picture stars, because all these things happen regularly to Ziegfeld Girls."[77] Despite the lack of money in Pittsburgh, ticket sales for the Ziegfeld Follies of 1931 were more than brisk. The show played to capacity sell-out crowds every night during its run.

Presidential Politics:
Calvin Coolidge, Herbert Hoover, Al Smith

Almost since the beginning of this nation as a democratic republic, Presidents and candidates for the office often established strong relationships with newspapers, editors and publishers. Thomas Jefferson encouraged the publishers of the *National Intelligencer*, and made many statements favorable to the press.[78] Abraham Lincoln once walked into the office of the *Chicago Tribune* and took out a subscription because he liked the new editorial change in the paper.[79] William McKinley held the first reception for newspapermen in the White House, and he loved to hold forth for quotation. Theodore Roosevelt, William Howard Taft, Woodrow Wilson and Warren G. Harding were partial to giving press conferences, formal or informal, depending on their schedules, their need to answer critics, and their pressures to announce or lobby for their causes.[80] As much as the press wanted access to the presidency for news, features, editorials and analysis, it followed that the White House needed the press to explain and rationalize its projects and policies. In effect, coverage in newspapers often influenced how the business of government was conducted. Following tradition, Paul Block, as the publisher of many newspapers, was given entry to the White House and other important echelons of government, and was even courted by the highest office holder of the land. What is intriguing to learn is just how very close Block did become to several American Presidents.

As noted previously, his relationship with Warren G. Harding was at least cordial, even intimate by Block's appraisal, but his connection with Calvin Coolidge went well beyond just a politically expedient and friendly rapport. They first met in 1919 when Coolidge was running for the Governorship of Massachusetts on the Republican ticket, and Block was representing the advertising of the *Worcester Telegram*. The main issue of the campaign revolved around the Boston police strike on September 9th of that year, when a crime wave spread across the city. Stores were looted, people shot and killed, and martial law was eventually enforced. Focusing on whether a governmental body had the right to put the city at risk, Coolidge's platform held that there should not be a right to strike against the public safety by anybody, anytime, anywhere.[81] Block resoundingly agreed, and this informed how he approached Coolidge's advertising campaign.

Although newspapers and some magazines – the only true mass media at that time – presented news stories about Coolidge's appeal for law and order, it was with a relentless advertising campaign that he successfully trumpeted his message and confronted his opponents. Block helped conceive a series of small but effective ads that addressed the Democratic opposition, and inserted them in the *Worcester Telegram* and other newspapers. The Democrats straddled the issue of the police strike, and ran on a ticket of class prejudice that they claimed the Republicans had against unionism; this strategy, it was believed, would garner the majority of votes from the state's industrial centers. As it developed, the voters of Massachusetts were so frightened and horrified by what had happened when there were no police in the city of Boston, that they opted for Coolidge as the law and order candidate, no matter what his party.

Coolidge's most effective advertisement, with the help of Block, showed cutaways or tearsheets of several New England papers; each contained photos and stories from their front pages, describing the carnage as the result of the police strike. A large headline stated:

REMEMBER SEPTEMBER the 9TH
Don't Let It Happen Again!
FOR LAW AND ORDER, VOTE FOR
CALVIN COOLIDGE[82]

The ad campaign worked and Coolidge was duly elected as Governor. As a result, he personally acknowledged Block's help in guiding him into office, and would never forget what he considered a favor. The two men began a series of letters of cordiality, exchange of Christmas cards, and personal visits that would continue for years, a record of which can be found in the Coolidge collection of the Forbes Library in Northampton, Massachusetts, and also in the National Archives in Washington. Elected Vice-President of the United States under Harding the following year, Coolidge then succeeded as President in 1923 as a result of Harding's mysterious death. He proved to be highly conservative in his economic policies, and had the full backing of Block in all of his newspapers.[83] A man of few words, Coolidge won the hearts of the American public with his wry wit, his calm and silent manner, and his uninhibited announcement that he took afternoon naps. He firmly believed that no newspaper could misquote his silence, and he operated with that philosophy for the six years that he was President. When a visitor to the White House told him that she had a bet that she could make him say more than two words, he exclaimed, "You lose!" The image of his legendary personality as "Silent Cal" continued to grow.

The six-year Presidency of Coolidge spanned times of unprecedented prosperity between the brief depression that followed World War I and the decade-long depression that arrived in 1930. These were also the years of the greatest prosperity for Paul Block, and he believed that part of his continued success was as a direct result of Coolidge's policies. Block was ebullient. With control or ownership of more than a dozen newspapers during that time, and the money that was pouring in from his involvement with *Pictorial Review's* advertising, and the accelerating income he was accumulating from his special representation firm, he had every reason to believe that the key to the buoyant economy had its roots behind the doors of 1600 Pennsylvania Avenue. "Prosperity is a fact," wrote Block. "Wages were never so high and labor so generally employed as at the present time."[84] Coolidge's statement, "The business of America is business," heartened Block. By 1925, advertisers were spending $1 billion a year in American media, and more than just a small amount of that money was going directly to Block.

Invitations from the White House came frequently, addressed to Paul and Dina Block, and the couple became accustomed to traveling to Washington. Often the Blocks merely dined with the President and his lovely wife Grace, usually on simple country fare, but on several occasions they were also their overnight guests. Before Block became the owner of the *Toledo Blade*, the paper had been editorially critical of Coolidge, suggesting that his ties with international bankers would negatively influence benefits that should rightfully go to the average citizen. But when Coolidge, in his opening message to Congress (the first of these ever to be broadcast over the radio) announced a tax cut, declared the death of the League of Nations, recommended that businesses should run with as little governmental regulation as possible, and insisted that Russia not be recognized until it paid back its debts, ("They hired the money, didn't they?" quipped the succinct Coolidge) the *Blade* praised his actions and pronouncements.[85]

If politics make strange bedfellows, as the editor of the *Hartford Courant,* Charles Dudley Warner, once pronounced, so do the vagaries of business and government, and it would be difficult to find two personalities so dissimilar but so strangely complementary than Coolidge and Block:

Coolidge, the Protestant Anglo-Saxon son of a farmer from the Green Mountains of Vermont; was unruffled and taciturn, a simple man who was a graduate of Amherst and an attorney. Block, son of a ragpicker, a Jewish immigrant with Eastern European roots, was an excitable, voluble, and mainly self-educated intense, businessman. Their commonality seemed to arise from a mutual respect of each other's power – Coolidge's within the government, Block's within newspaper publishing – and unlike many people of authority and influence they relied on and respected each other's deepest convictions. Block once wrote that the qualities of mind and heart that he most admired in Calvin Coolidge were "his kindliness, his courtesy, his modesty and his courage."[86] What Coolidge most admired in Block was the directness of his manner, tempered with a true warmth and genuineness. Both men also recognized that they needed each other for political and social gain.

Block had supported Coolidge with editorials, endorsements and news coverage in the *Newark Star-Eagle*, the *Brooklyn Standard-Union*, the *Duluth Herald*, the *Memphis News-Scimitar*, the *Lancaster New Era*, the *Pittsburgh Post-Gazette*, and the *Toledo Blade*. He ardently continued to back the President. Some of the many signed editorials in which Block ratified Coolidge's policies and decisions concerned such things as aid to hurricane victims in Puerto Rico,[87] his call for the nation to "get down to business,"[88] and his unusual and highly political appointment – since Coolidge was a Vermonter – of a Southerner (C. Bascom Slemp) to the post of Presidential Secretary, in the days before the job carried the title of Chief of Staff.[89] After Coolidge saw that editorial, he wrote to Block: "I want to tell you how appreciative I am of your generous attitude. You have been very good in all these matters, and I am quite sure you will have no occasion to regret your generosity."[90] Although it appeared that Block, as a friend, was accepting Coolidge's appointment of Slemp merely as an amicable gesture, it was actually more expedient and self-serving. Block's endorsement of Slemp, who was the son of a Confederate veteran and a member of the "Lilly White" – as it was known – faction of the Republican Party, had more to do with gaining Republican delegates from the South in the next national convention, and solidifying Block's business and political connections with the people of Memphis through his *Memphis News-Scimitar*, than it did with blindly following Coolidge's influence.

One of the more controversial aspects of Coolidge's Presidency was his support of the high protective tariff on European nations. Coolidge believed that the tariff greatly aided American business. Block published several editorials in which he stated that not only would a reduction of the country's tariff be disastrous to American industry, but it would retard European economic recovery.[91] "Europe can have all the free trade she desires," Block wrote. "We in America understand the source of our prosperity. The source of our healthy, happy industrial conditions is the protective tariff."[92]

Four months after Coolidge moved into the White House, Block sent the President and Grace Coolidge a small Christmas gift. Bestowing Christmas and birthday remembrances became a tradition he would maintain every year thereafter, with such presents as a mantelpiece clock, an unusual picture frame, or a basket of fruit, candies and flowers. Often the gifts were hand-delivered from the stores at which they were purchased in New York, such as Saks & Company or B. Altman's. Each favor was always acknowledged by a gracious note of appreciation by the President or his wife. On the wall in Block's office was mounted an autographed photograph of President Coolidge inscribed affectionately to Block.

In 1924, during what was referred to as a bitter campaign for the Presidency against John W. Davis, a personal tragedy befell Coolidge. His oldest son Calvin, Jr., began to suffer from what began as a mere blister on his foot, acquired while playing tennis on the White House courts. His foot became inflamed, and he died quite suddenly of a staphylococcus infection that led to blood poisoning. Biographies and accounts of that time indicate that the Coolidges were devastated. They felt diminished, stripped of hope, and permeated with a feeling of unnaturalness, as all parents who have had children who have died usually do. Block's heart was broken also since he was extremely fond of the boy and thought that his son Paul Block, Jr. and Cal, Jr. had a great deal in common: they both had an interest in things mechanical. Coolidge's son John remembered how his usually taciturn father reacted to the death: "Though father was tenderhearted, he rarely showed his feelings. But when they were taking my brother's casket from the White House after the services, my father broke down and wept momentarily. Calvin was my father's favorite. It hurt him terribly."[93] Coolidge would write a few years later about the agony he felt at the death of his son, and how the spark of leadership immediately and resoundingly left him as a result: "When he went, the power and glory of the Presidency went with him."[94]

Block reached out to Coolidge in every way that he could by sending him letters of condolence, visiting him at the White House, mentioning

the tragedy in an editorial ("He [Coolidge] quietly bore the sorrows..."[95])
and even sharing a poem with the President that Block had written about
someone close to him, possibly his father – John Block – who had died
shortly before that. Block felt that the catharsis of writing the poem had
consoled him slightly and he asked Coolidge if he might share it with
him, noting however that "...in your heart and in the heart of your brave
wife, there is a pain that will never leave, because of your recent great
loss."

> Why is it so quiet here?
> Ask me not I pray –
> Why, you answer with a tear?
> He has gone away –
>
> Gone, why,where, I want to know
> Ask me not I pray –
> Tell me, will he soon return?
>
> He has gone to stay.
>
> Mean you that we'll never see him?
> Not unless in dream.
> And his voice, when will we hear?
> When we cross the stream –
> When the Angels come from High
> Did this make him weep?
> No, he smiled and said good-bye
>
> And then he went to sleep.
>
> But though he's gone, his lot is bright
> And he does not need your tear,
> At his left are Angels, and on his right
>
> The Lord who brought him here.[96]

President and Mrs. Coolidge were touched by Block's heartfelt gesture, and they thanked the Blocks personally. They made it clear to Block
that they would always be in his debt. More invitations went out to Block
and Dina to come to the White House. From that time on, a true friendship was solidified, and as a result any favor that either man asked the
other, was instantly and emphatically granted. Coolidge kept inviting

Block to various events, from baseball games to formal dinners, and any time that Block was in Washington, Coolidge dropped all order of governmental business to see him.

It was through Block's long-term and genuinely sincere friendship with Coolidge, and his relentless campaigning for him in the 1924 election, ("Nearly every newspaper in the country is endorsing your policies today, so it shouldn't be strange if my newspapers speak kindly of them," Block wrote to Coolidge[97]) that William Randolph Hearst also became a supporter of the President. Block continually championed Coolidge by publishing special editions of his newspapers. For example, once each week during the 1924 campaign, Block ordered extra-large print runs that "conscientiously point out the importance of re-electing you and a Republican Congress," as he wrote his friend in the White House.[98] Since Hearst either owned or controlled some of Block's newspapers, he became resoundingly aware of Block's deep friendship and countenance of Coolidge.

After listening to Block talk personally about Coolidge, and reading Block's supportive editorials, Hearst began to establish a personal and positive understanding of the President. Within short order, Hearst also began to be invited to the White House, for visits with Coolidge. The relationship between the two was noted, with considerable surprise. An editorial in the *New Republic* commented on Hearst's and Coolidge's relationship:

> The friendship between Hearst and Coolidge was so inexplicable as to be one of the most significant and remarkable phenomena of the period. That Mr. Hearst, whose journalistic talons have been deeply sunk in the back of every national administration, regardless of party, since he became a figure in the publishing world, should turn his twenty-odd newspapers into almost pro-Administration organs, and have the brilliant Brisbane regularly and frequently anoint and glorify the President, instead of assailing him with his customary ferocity, is an interesting and amazing thing.[99]

In the spring of 1927, less than a year after he bought the *Toledo Blade*, Block constructed a new building for the newspaper, a three-story structure with Moorish overtones, and he outfitted it with the finest and most modern printing and typesetting equipment in America, perhaps in the world. He made a request of Coolidge that the President start the presses by pushing a button, the publishing equivalent of christening a ship. Coolidge was not asked to travel to Toledo: the button was to be placed in the Oval Office, and would connect the electricity to the Toledo plant and start the presses rolling. Although Coolidge detested anything that savored of the spectacular, he graciously acquiesced to his friend's request. So on May 1, 1927, at the exact agreed-upon moment, and with Block and his staff of 350 and a group of well-wishers waiting in Toledo, the President touched a special golden key that had been installed in the White House by Western Union. The giant printing presses began to roar and a new era in the publication of the *Toledo Blade* commenced.

"I am glad to hear of the progress made by this influential journal since you have taken hold of it," wrote Coolidge to Block.[100]   Block's friend Governor Alfred E. Smith also wished him luck in his new plant: "I know the excellent as well as influential standing of the *Blade* in its territory, and knowing you as I do, I am sure it will continue to have the kind of direction which a newspaper should have and which the people of the community deserve."[101]   It seemed as though half of the city of Toledo turned out for the opening ceremonies, including celebrities from many different walks of life. Babe Ruth attended, and as the Great Bambino – who would go on to hit 60 home runs that summer – stood on editor Grove Patterson's balcony, overlooking Superior Street, he tossed down autographed souvenir baseballs to the cheering crowd below. That evening, the building was illuminated on all sides by dozens of 1000-watt flood-lights. Drenched in light, the white building stood out in bold relief against the darkness. Toledo had itself a new center of attention, and the *Blade's* new quarters helped to raise civic pride.

Shortly before the opening of the new building, Block had another favor to ask of Coolidge. Twenty carrier boys, ranging in age from 12 to 16 years, the top deliverers in numbers of copies of the *Toledo Blade,* were being given a weekend in Washington, D.C. by the newspaper as a bonus gift for their hard work. Block asked the President if he would meet with the boys for a few minutes: "It would be an event in their lives which they would never forget," he wrote.[102]   Not only did Coolidge agree, but he suggested that they pose for a photograph. Coolidge spent time with the boys and each was given a group photograph with the President of the United States.

Coolidge liked being around young people, perhaps because of the loss of his son, and so he was particularly happy when Block, with Dina, brought his son Billy to the White House to meet the President. Coolidge

had had correspondence with Billy's older brother, Paul Block, Jr. because of a poem that the teenager had written (taking after his father)
about Charles Lindbergh's flight across the Atlantic. He had sent the
poem to the President and received a swift reply: Coolidge wrote that he
enjoyed the poem, and said that he thought that the boy had talent. Now
it was 12-year-old Billy's turn to interact with the President. Block especially wanted Billy to meet him, because it was the closing months of his
administration and Coolidge had made it clear that he was not going to
run again.

The Block family arrived at the White House in the morning, and after
introductions and pleasantries, and a service of tea, Coolidge and Block
began discussing the probable Herbert Hoover-Alfred E. Smith race for
the Presidency. In short order, Coolidge invited the Blocks to stay for
lunch. Billy, however, had made a date to dine with Johnny McLean, the
son of Ned McLean, owner of the *Washington Post*. "I'm sorry, Mr. President, I can't stay for lunch," said Billy, with all the importance and hubris
that a 12-year-old can muster. "I already have a luncheon appointment."
The silent President nodded and smiled. Block thought that the tableau
was hilarious. Later he said, almost proudly, who else but his son would
have the nerve to turn down an opportunity to have lunch with the President of the United States? Over 70 years later, Billy – now the revered
and self-effacing publisher, William Block, Sr. – would ruefully shake
his head at the memory of his own childhood audacity.[103]

As the economic boom and expanding economy continued, Coolidge
really did nothing to slow down the process, despite warnings that if checks
and balances were not instigated, and effective steps not taken to harness
the exploding stock market, a depression could follow. Despite the noised-
about possible financial collapse, Coolidge continued to make reassuring
and self-justifying statements about the economy and the state of affairs
of the nation. "It will be observed," said Coolidge later, "that all these
causes of depression, with the exception of the early speculation, had
their origin outside of the United States, where they were entirely beyond
the control of our Government."[104] Coolidge's enthusiasm so excited
Wall Street that it inspired an even larger volume of trading. Paul Block
agreed with most of what Coolidge was saying, and in his editorials in the
Toledo Blade and his other newspapers, he wrote that the country, if it
just calculated things correctly and had the right optimistic attitude, would
experience a future of even greater prosperity. His editorials were infused with assurances, and with recommendations for *laissez-faire*:

- We hear attacks on the extravagance of the age. We should hear more of the larger and larger number of people who are making wise and useful use of their money.[105]
- Speaking of Wall Street speculation, Chief Justice Taft recently said: "There seems to be enough money to lose. That is encouraging." It is encouraging, not because there is such widely distributed prosperity and because so little is lost foolishly, but compared with the money that is put to good purpose.[106]
- In the administration of public affairs, in industry, and in general business the nation has never been in a more fortunate position. The same situation is true in regard to our foreign relations.[107]
- The greater earnings of our people, an economic phenomenon which has been beneficial to all industry, has done more than enable them to spend more and to keep factories producing things which the earnings of our people buy. These greater earnings...have enabled us not only to have automobiles, radios, electric refrigerators, good clothes and good homes but also to have more and better schools and more widespread education throughout the land.[108]

Block, who was hopeful about his and the country's economic future, had wanted his friend Coolidge to run again in 1928 but understood the President's personal reluctance to do so. When Coolidge's cabinet member Herbert Hoover, the multimillionaire Secretary of Commerce, was nominated by the Republicans, however, Block was unsure about his candidacy. The Democrats had chosen Alfred E. Smith to run, and Block was better connected to Smith. His career as four-time Governor of New York State was continually covered by Block's New York area newspapers throughout the years that Block was publisher of the *Newark Star-Eagle*, the *New York Evening Mail* and the *Brooklyn Standard Union* (the latter toward the end of Smith's Governorship), and Block had had personal contact with Smith ever since he had been elected Sheriff of New York City in 1915. The two men had had many connections after that, and Block both admired and respected Smith's numerous reforms as Governor, as well as his rough and tumble city-boy personality, and his quickness to engage in open debate with anyone. Smith was an Irish Catholic who knew enough Yiddish to capture the attention and fire the imaginations of New York's large Jewish population. Up from poverty as was

Block, Smith, with his hoarse, raucous, New York-accented voice, was adored by the voters of the city, and even by people in some other urban parts of the country.[109] They were empathetic to his all-too-human traits: he had a rheumatic foot, he often made flamboyant and uninhibited use of a cuspidor, and was a master of deliberately uncouth English, with the habitual misuse of the word "radio," pronouncing the "a" as in "radish." His personality as the quintessential New Yorker captured the affection and the support of voters. In addition to all of that, Block's friend Jimmy Walker had been the hand-picked choice for Mayor by Governor Alfred E. Smith, and the connections between Smith and Block were greatly intertwined as a result of the Smith-Walker association.

The problem with Smith's candidacy, however, as far as Block was concerned, was that he was of the wrong party. Block had difficulty identifying with a candidate in a party not his own, despite his association with Walker, who of course was a Democrat. This reluctance was combined with Block's belief that the Democrats were closely organized from the neighborhood up and were therefore more prone to petty graft in the wards and throughout the county and state machines. The Republicans, Block believed, who were organized from big business *down*, were less tempted by local bribes or corruption, and since Block was becoming a part of big business himself, he felt that the GOP was the Party that best served his interests.

Block also had other complications with backing Smith. Hearst and Smith were engaged in one of the most embittered vendettas in politics at that time as a result of old wounds that started back in 1907, when Smith backed Big Tom Foley for Sheriff and Hearst opposed him in the *New York Journal*. Over the years Hearst continually attacked Smith for what he described as his "weakness" in municipal affairs. When Smith won the nomination for Governor of New York in 1918, Hearst ordered his reporters to attack Smith on any issue that could be found, bogus, or not.[110] Smith's abject refusal to allow Hearst to run as Senator with him on the same ticket during his 1922 campaign for Governor, cemented their mutual hatred, which would remain for the rest of their lives.[111] Since Block was becoming more and more involved with Hearst in handling the advertising for his many newspapers, he believed it was essential that he continue a friendly, working relationship with him. Although Hearst would never overtly force Block to follow a particular political line, or back a candidate he didn't believe in, there was certainly implicit pressure for Block to endorse Hearst's preference. Block had to yield to Hearst's influence and not express overt admiration or sponsorship of Smith.

In an editorial of campaign rhetoric (which was not written by Block), the *Toledo Blade* criticized Hoover's stand on the 18th Amendment's prohibition of the sale of alcohol, but nevertheless endorsed him. Hoover was elected President by the largest majority since George Washington, in an atmosphere of euphoria and a belief that the economic prosperity would continue for the foreseeable future. Block had been impressed with the new President ever since Hoover had headed up food and relief bureaus in Europe during World War I, and he had cooperated with him by giving coverage to Hoover's projects in *Pictorial Review*. In 1925, Block had attended a meeting of the Associated Advertising Clubs at which Hoover spoke; he had elevated the importance and significance of advertising, and put it into historical perspective. Block was vitalized by the talk. Hoover said, in part:

> So great has been this advancement in fact that while advertising at one time may have been looked upon as a nuisance and as an intrusion for the beguiling of the credulous only, it has now come to take a place as commercial news and as an economical method of salesmanship. Its first step in progress was when the medium, recognizing its responsibility to the readers, exercised censorship over extravagant, distasteful and misleading copy. This gave more credibility to truthful advertisements themselves...but the milestone which will mark the passage from a trade to a profession is the establishment of group ethics.[112]

Hoover believed that advertising aroused people to action, overcoming the lethargy of the old law of supply and demand, and that as a result of advertising, cottage industries were transformed into mass production factories employing millions of people. Writing about another of Hoover's speeches in which he stated that advertising "helped reduce prices and raise wages, enabling the millions employed in industry to buy the things they desire," Block observed: "In this brief paragraph is recorded the industrial history of the United States for the past fifty years and a prophecy for generations to come."[113]

Block publicly endorsed Hoover for all of the reasons cited, but he also had conflicting hopes that Smith might become the victor. Smith was the first Catholic ever to be nominated for the Presidency of the United States by either party, and therefore as an underdog, a friend, and a highly-effective Governor, he appealed to Block. To help Smith, Block had secretly opened a bank account in his son Billy's name, and deposited a little over $2,000 in it, a fairly large sum in those days. In order to help Smith's campaign without attaching his own name to it, Block withdrew all the money, had a cashier's check made out for the balance, and had the boy deliver the check to Smith's campaign headquarters. The 13-year-old Billy, pencil-thin, dressed in a dark suit, spiffed up with a white shirt and a handkerchief neatly folded in his breast pocket, made the grown-up presentation of the money to John Raskob, the chairman of Smith's finance committee. Also present to accept the money in Smith's behalf was the candidate for Lieutenant Governor, Herbert Lehman, and Mayor Jimmy Walker, who was the campaign chief of his mentor Al Smith.[114] Smith did not forget Billy's (or Paul Block's) largesse. Shortly after his defeat, Smith – upon Billy's request – wrote a brief article for the young boy, to appear in *The Hotchkiss Record,* his high school newspaper.[115]

The Downfall of Mayor Jimmy Walker

Jimmy Walker's successful first term led to a second in 1929. Much of Tammany Hall had changed by then. The death of Charles Murphy left New York's Democratic organization without an effective leader and Alfred E. Smith was focused on the Governor's race for New York.[116] Walker found himself alone, in terms of political guidance. His penchant for high living, always legendary, became even more marked with no political mentor to keep him in check. The Mayor was still loved by the citizens of New York City, but people were beginning to question his behavior when reports of extravagant nights routinely made the front pages. In three short years, America had gone from hedonistic to hard-bitten.

Nobody accused Walker of corruption, but ominous signs were in the offing regarding Tammany Hall. Strange tales relating to mob connections circulated and reporters, formerly so friendly to Gentleman Jim, ushered in the first of many critical attacks. Paul Block suffered along with his friend. The *Brooklyn Standard-Union* wasn't faring well, and many of his friends and relatives felt that his intransigence, first in wanting to buy the paper, and then in refusing to sell his interest in it, would ruin him financially. Block had closed his joint account with the Mayor in August of 1929, before the market crashed, but under advice from his broker Sailing Baruch he didn't do the same with his personal and some of his corporate money. Sailing Baruch had told Block that his brother Bernard, one of America's great businessmen and statesmen, was remaining in the market, and Block followed Sailing's advice. Later, he learned that Sailing had lied in order to protect himself against losing Block's account. Bernard Baruch *had* divested himself of his stock just in time, and became even more wealthy. Block, thus suffered heavy financial losses. He chose to keep them his secret. While many people were keening with distress over their losses in the stock market, both Block and Walker, each carrying his own burden, kept up their social whirl around town.

Unbeknownst to the two men, the small ripples of discontent that began in early 1929 were growing to large waves of accusation. That year, Walker raised his annual salary to $40,000, but refused to consider equal raises for other government positions. Some feel this provoked the beginning of formal investigations into how the City of New York was run, but others point to the unsolved murder of gambler Arnold Rothstein as the catalyst.

The unsolved murder dogged Walker's second term. Rumors of Tammany's mob connections, instead of being whispered quietly, were being reported openly by the New York Bar Association. Business executive Nathan Strauss, who had been a reporter for the *New York World* and the editor of *Puck* and the *Literary Digest*, was extremely outspoken about what was happening at City Hall: "The Walker administration marks a new low in incompetence and a new high in racketeering." Strauss's indignation may have been self-serving since he was considering a bid for the mayoralty of New York City himself. As a Jew, he thought he might not stand a chance of being elected since Herbert Lehman, the Lieutenant Governor, who was also Jewish, was going to run for Governor, and Lehman began to believe that the public might not tolerate two men of a minority group in such government offices.

Even when Strauss denounced Walker, in the strange and inconsistent realm that is politics, he visited Block, of whom he was fond, to ask his advice and to determine whether the publisher thought he had any chance at the mayoralty. Although Strauss was in effect after Walker's job, Block was already instinctively predicting the demise of his closest friend. He advised Strauss to run for the office.[117]

Members of the Bar Association asked Governor Franklin D. Roosevelt to probe charges of corruption in the appointment of city magistrates, but Roosevelt pointed out he did not have the power to remove magistrates. Roosevelt turned to the appellate division of the first judicial department to investigate the courts. This was the start of the most widespread probe

of the city since Boss Tweed's death.[118]   The appellate division chose a
former judge, Samuel Seabury, as the man to lead the investigation.

Seabury was by all accounts a fair and impartial judge; he was said to
be a 20th century man with 18th century manners. But he had two intense
political predilections: he hated Tammany Hall, and he really wanted
Fiorello LaGuardia to become Mayor of the City of New York. His dislike of Jimmy Walker, although not unduly manifested during the investigations, would later bring forth charges of bias in the investigation.
Seabury was a life-long Democrat, and an extremely rich lawyer, who
had stepped down from his position as Supreme Court Judge to run for
governor on a pro-Wilson Democratic ticket in 1916. But the denizens of
Tammany blockaded his campaign.[119]   Seabury never forgave or forgot
that New York's Democratic organization had eclipsed his political career. Eventually he would open three separate but obviously linked investigations in the city of New York: an investigation of the magistrate's
courts; an inquiry into the competency of District Attorney Thomas Crain;
and an examination into the entire city government.

The Tammany Hall organization, likened to an octopus with its ten-
tacles wrapped around the center of New York City's administration, had,
since the death of its leader Charles Murphy in 1914, become increasingly corrupt. When Seabury exposed the breadth and depth of the graft
running through the organization, most of New York's voters gasped in
horror. Judgeships had been purchased for $10,000 or $50,000, depending on the type of judgeship requested. [120]   Tammany relatives were put
on city payrolls, franchises were granted to friends, cops took bribes,
criminals and gamblers arrested in raids were told they could escape conviction if they joined the Democratic Party. [121]   Of the 514 persons arrested in gambling raids over a two year period, only five were held for
the court of special sessions.[122] Seabury laid bare the financial irregularities of Tammany Hall with his irrefutable paper trails. One by one,
Tammany leaders were called to the stand to explain how, on their municipal salaries, they managed to accrue savings that on average were ten
times their paid wage. They never had a satisfactory answer.

Seabury was pleased with his dramatic exposé thus far, but he wanted
more. Despite cries from Tammany Hall that he was a motivated politician seeking revenge, he expected Governor Roosevelt to approve a full-
scale inquiry into the city at large. Seabury wanted to strike at the heart
of Tammany Hall, and the heart was the Honorable James J. Walker. Governor Roosevelt was in a difficult spot: a Democratic judge wanted him

to instigate legal proceedings against a Tammany Hall-controlled New York City government, thereby effectively splitting the Democratic Party, of which Roosevelt was a member. The Republicans, who dominated the state (with the exception of New York City), made an attempt in 1930 to push the investigation through the state legislature. The Republicans withdrew, conferred, and returned intent on pushing the investigation through, which they did successfully. Governor Roosevelt instantly vetoed it. With charges of personal bias and partisanship already resounding in the halls of Tammany, Roosevelt wasn't going to approve a Republican-sponsored investigation. Seabury did not take issue with Governor Roosevelt's decision.

Seabury ordered his team to search every piece of financial paper that dealt with Mayor Walker's personal finances. The team discovered inadequacies, discrepancies and irregularities, but didn't have an illegal connection between the Tammany graft system and James Walker. It appeared the Mayor was aware of the nepotism, patronage and illegal payments, but didn't partake of any of it himself.

For months Seabury's team sifted through mountains of financial evidence they subpoenaed from Walker's banks, brokerage houses, and friends. Without specific evidence of corruption, Seabury knew he hadn't a chance of taking down Jimmy Walker, who was arguably still the most popular man in New York City. Somewhat dejected, the team began double-checking their work.

James T. Ellis, an accountant, had been assigned to search the records of the Chase National Bank. The rummaging was fruitless until one of the bank's tellers quietly told Ellis that Seabury's subpoena to the bank had one crucial omission: it didn't *require* the bank to show Letters of Credit. Ellis ran to Seabury with the news, and a new subpoena was issued asking for copies of the Letters of Credit. When Ellis tried to present the new search request, the Vice-President of Chase Bank, an ardent Walker supporter, refused to meet with him. Seabury threatened to have the bank closed, and only then did the Vice-President turn over what he had been so reluctant to reveal. It was a Letter of Credit from the Equitable Coach Company for $10,000, made out to and signed for by Walker. Startled, Seabury stared at the document. He realized that it was the proof he had been searching for, perhaps what he needed to destroy Tammany, and with it, the redoubtable Mayor Walker.

Throughout this examination the Mayor remained surprisingly cavalier, actually traveling abroad during the early part of the investigation.

Paul Block continued to see Walker socially, but effects of the Depression and his *personal* depression had made life much less effervescent for him. As a self-made man, it was excruciating for Block to watch the accumulated wealth from his years of hard work slowly dissipate. He kept his spirits up for Walker, though, and as true friends he and Dina offered their full support to the Mayor, even going so far as announcing their willingness to appear as character witnesses.[123] As the New Year arrived, Block was dismayed to learn that he was being accused of supplying Walker with money in exchange for favors. Aghast, he realized that his innocent brokerage account, opened after his talk with his son Billy, was the reason for his subpoena. As the inexorable Seabury bore on through the Tammany tangle around Walker, even Jimmy Walker lost his usual insouciance.

Walker and Block prepared to face the enemy together. Both had been called to testify in the same week, Walker on March 24th and 25th, Paul Block the 27th. Block attended the proceedings even when not on the stand, and was often cheered up by his friend Jimmy Walker's attitude, spirit, and even by his natty appearance. Walker, who was clearly Seabury's primary target in the probe, saw no reason to tone down his almost dandyish outfits. The first morning of the hearing, decked out in blue, with a pinky ring to match, and wearing a Panama hat, he drove up to the courthouse at a quarter to eleven. As the huge crowd gathered outside cheered, whistled, and shouted encouragement to him, the smiling Mayor clasped his hands overhead as if he were going into the ring for a championship fight.

Once inside, the crowd vociferously voiced its support for Walker, interrupting the proceedings frequently with yells of "Commie Red," references to Seabury and to their belief that Walker was being railroaded by him. Walker was an astute politician and a skilled attorney, and he was fully aware, when he mounted the witness chair, that he was fighting for his political life. Seabury questioned him exhaustively, asking first about the Equitable Coach Company, and challenging the Mayor's assertion that he had sponsored their bid for no other reason other than the company appeared sound.

Walker started to answer, then turned and faced the audience, speaking more to them than he was to Seabury, and sprinkling his replies with certain flashes of lightning. The Mayor countered that Seabury had no right to question the workings of an executive's mind or ask why he reaches his conclusions, just as no one has the right to question why the President of the United States vetoes a bill. To Seabury's increasing frustration, Walker played to the crowd, varying his answers from wisecracks to acidic retorts. Since the transaction involving the Equitable Coach Franchise was complex and concerned complicated financial data, the courtroom audience found the details hard to follow; but they understood, laughed at, and loved the Mayor's funny, sometimes brilliant responses.

Those fortunate enough to gain a seat in the courtroom were charmed by the Mayor's sway. Those who relied on the newspapers received quite a different story. As the graft exposé continued, the *Brooklyn Daily Eagle*, Block's rival, called Mayor Walker *"A $1 A Minute Man,"* since they had followed Walker through one complete work day, claiming he came in at 2PM and left at 6PM.[124] But the majority of the public still loved him; even as Walker exited the courthouse on his last day of testimony, a group of women actually tossed red roses at his feet.[125] He beamed. They sighed.

Paul Block, in the midst of all this drama, did not fare as well as his good friend Walker. Of course he hadn't Walker's dramatic personality – not many people did – and he didn't have the heart or the passion to work the crowds, but there were other reasons why he felt miserable. Block discovered it is never easy to be the friend of a celebrity, especially when the celebrity is embroiled in a scandal. As papers scrambled to make sensational news out of the story, Paul Block was painted as a sycophantic hanger-on, a rather silly patsy who Walker touched for a spot of cash when things were tight. Block became even more anxious over the thought of having to discuss how he formulated the idea of the brokerage account for Walker. He loathed the idea of exposing his children to the public eye, or of revealing such an intimate, simple story to the vicious cynics of the courtroom. As his turn to testify approached, Block grew ever more irritable and discomfited. Finally, on the 27th, Seabury asked Paul Block to take the stand. Seabury opened his interrogation with the customary offer of immunity. Following is a lengthy, although truncated, transcript of Block's testimony:

> SEABURY: "Mr. Block, as you probably heard me say in addressing others who have been called to the stand it has been our practice to tender such witnesses a waiver of immunity. No implication arises from the fact that I may do it. May I tender you such a waiver and ask whether you will sign it?"

BLOCK: " Yes, sir" (Witness signs waiver)

SEABURY: "Did you on February 10, 1927, open a joint account with Sailing W. Baruch Company, known as the P.B and J.J.W Joint Account?"

BLOCK: "I did."

SEABURY: "And was the P.B. yourself?"

BLOCK: "Yes, sir."

SEABURY: "And was the J.J.W. Mayor Walker?"

BLOCK: "Yes, sir."

SEABURY: "Had you any conversation with Mayor Walker prior to that time as to the account being opened?"

BLOCK: "Yes, sir."

SEABURY: "Now will you give us, as nearly as you can, the substance of the conversation?"

BLOCK: "I recall I said to the Mayor, "Jimmy, I'm going to try and make a little money for you. I am going to open a joint account for us and see if I can make a little money for you."

SEABURY: "Now, what did the Mayor say to you?"

BLOCK: "As I recall he said, 'Oh, you oughtn't to do that Paul,' and I said 'Yes, I am going to do it.' Something like that was said between us."

Seabury and his committee continue to question Paul about dates and conversations, to which Paul responds that his brother Max, who handles his accounts, would know better than he. Discussion on whether Paul's brother needs to be called.

SEABURY: "Now you recall that up to August 26, 1927 you had not received anything from that account?"

BLOCK: "No, I do not recall."

SEABURY: "Well now, in your conversation with the Mayor as to the circumstances under which the account was to be opened, there was never any agreement, was there, that if the account should result in a loss, Mayor Walker would pay a proportion of that loss?"

BLOCK: "There never was a discussion of that, but may I say...if there had been a loss in that account I would not have allowed him to stand it."

SEABURY: "You would have taken it?"

BLOCK: "I would have transferred the account to my personal account and I would not have allowed him to stand it, but there was no loss."

SEABURY: "You do not remember that he drew out some $102,500 from that account before you had received any thing from it?"

BLOCK: "I never knew this, no sir."

Seabury discusses with Block briefly technical questions about the account, to which Block replies he doesn't know, but his brother does.

SEABURY: "Each of you (Block and the Mayor) receiving approximately $246,000?"

BLOCK: "Yes"

SEABURY: "Will you be good enough to tell the Committee in your own way why you made this donation to the Mayor of the City of New York?"

BLOCK: "I shall be glad to. Of course, it wasn't a donation, as it turned out."

SEABURY: "Wasn't it a donation?"

BLOCK: "No, sir. It was a joint account."

SEABURY: "Mr. Block, isn't this true – You opened the account. (Paul Block assents) Mr. Walker never put a cent into it. (Block assents) The account realized a profit. (Block agrees again) That profit was almost a half a million dollars – you divided that equally between yourself and the Mayor. (Block assents). And if it hadn't been that you determined to give one half of that amount to Mayor Walker the whole would have been your own property?"

BLOCK: "It couldn't be after I told him it was a joint account."

SEABURY: "If you hadn't told him that he should have half interest in that account the whole would have been your property."

BLOCK: "I am convinced I never would have opened that account. I had an account down there in my name and I had one there in my name with Mrs. Block. I feel quite certain –

SEABURY: "I am not talking about her accounts."

BLOCK: "I never would have opened it. ..."

There follows a general discussion over whether Block gave or donated the money to Walker. Block tries to interject that he does similar things for others, but is cut off by Seabury.

After some wrangling, Steingut, a Democratic lawyer for Walker, objects to Seabury's asking why Block chose to give the money to Walker rather than another charity. Steingut objects, but Block is willing to answer.

BLOCK: "The Mayor had moved up to the – well I am not sure whether he had moved there yet – to the Ritz. The Mayor and I were very intimate friends for a great many years. He was my friend Jimmy Walker, not the Mayor of New York to me. I knew him for years before he was the Mayor. I suddenly got it in mind that I would like to make a little money for him."

Seabury questions Block more closely on how he got the idea of making money for Walker. Block reluctantly but cooperatively relates the story about Billy on that Sunday afternoon. Seabury launches into a string of questions designed to show that Walker drew heavily from the account throughout the two years. He asks Block if he brought Walker cash or a check, or both?

BLOCK: "We will say we had a luncheon and there was some remark, probably by me, that "Did you see what happened in the market yesterday?", meaning it had gone way up, and the Mayor said, not each time but this has happened, "Gee, that is great. I wonder if I can get some money," and I would always say "Certainly, how much do you need or want?" and he would mention the sum and I would either telephone to my brother, or to the broker and say "Will you send a check up to the Mayor?"."

Seabury interjects to reveal that Walker never repaid the money he took and that Block would have had to refill the account from a personal account, which was done in the approximate amount of $102,000. Block continues relating that he would often have the checks sent to City Hall or the Ritz, and sometimes he just kept the checks until the next time he saw the Mayor.

SEABURY: "My question was whether or not you had these checks reduced to cash and having the cash, you delivered the cash?"
BLOCK: "When the check would come, as a rule the Mayor

would say, "Could I have this cashed?" and then I would say "Certainly" and I would tell my brother to have it cashed; or he might tell that to me before the check even came, and he would say "Would you send me the cash?" ... In other words, we paid it to the Mayor exactly as he wanted it."

Seabury spends a long time ascertaining specific amounts of cash and how often deliveries were made.

SEABURY: "Did he tell you on any occasion that when he got the cash he was going to deposit the cash in his safe, in his home?"

BLOCK: "Never, no. I never heard those things."

SEABURY: "You understood, did you not, that when he asked for a check, he asked for it because he needed the proceeds of it at that time?"

BLOCK: "Well, I would say he *wanted* the proceeds at that time."

SEABURY: "You did not understand that he wanted it to deposit in his safe, in his home?"

BLOCK: "No, I never heard that."

Seabury asks Block if he would be able to identify checks and so forth from the account. Block insists that he cannot identify them with any degree of accuracy. Seabury offers to go over them with him, but Block is adamant that he cannot remember.

SEABURY: "I think that is all, Mr. Block."

BLOCK: "May I make a statement?"

SEABURY: "I am most happy to have you make any statement you want, Mr. Block."

BLOCK: "I never expected to make any such money for the Mayor. I thought if I could make $30,000 or $25,000 or $40,000 or possibly $50,000, that would be a marvelous thing to do. It turned out I couldn't make that little. The boom went and the stocks went up, and in the first nine months, I think, or ten months, it amounted to $220,000 for each of us. I don't mean I couldn't have stopped it, but I saw no reason for stopping it."

SEABURY: "And even this profit you speak of so deprecatingly, of $20,000, $30,000 or $40,000, would still have been quite a respectable profit?"

BLOCK: "I would have thought it a very large profit, be
cause in most of these – if I may say this – in these joint
accounts that I sent you a list, which joint accounts, of
course you know have nothing to do with any officials,
just friends or intimate friends of mine in business, and
people who worked for me and worked for some of my
newspapers, why the amount I would make for them I
would consider big if it was $2,000.

SEABURY: "And those are the dozens of others that you had
in mind a few moments ago?" (referring to earlier testimony).

BLOCK: "Yes, sir, those are the dozens of others."

SEABURY: "You didn't mean to give this committee the idea
that there were dozens of others for whom you opened joint
accounts with the understanding that if there was a loss
they should not contribute, but you should bear the whole
loss, and out of which profits to any such sum as half a
million dollars would accrue?"

BLOCK: "No understanding, but in nearly every one of these
cases, except in two or three, which were with men who
had much more money than I, I never would have allowed
them to stand the loss, if there had been a loss."

SEABURY: "As I understand it, none of these other accounts
have been of any public official other than this account for
the Mayor of the City of New York?"

BLOCK: "Positively, but this of course I did for my friend
Jimmy Walker, rather than for the Mayor of New York –
but he happened to be the Mayor."

SEABURY: "You want to make it clear, as I understand it,
that it was in his personal and individual capacity and not
in his official capacity that these moneys were conferred
upon him?"

BLOCK: "Positively, sir, positively."

*Seabury and others ask a few more questions and prepare
to terminate Mr. Block's testimony when Mr. Block asks if he
might again clarify a previous misconception held forth by
Seabury's questioning. Block has trouble forming his words,
saying it is a bit immodest of him to make this statement, but
it refers to Seabury's questions about why he chose Walker as
the recipient of his largesse.*

SEABURY: "Why was it that among all the persons and institutions in this city you made a donation to the Mayor of
the City? I think the question went something like that."

BLOCK: "I dislike to make this statement, again I say, because it is not modest, but as long as that question came up
I want you to know that in 1930, which is long after all this
happened, I gave $300,000 to charities and institutions—

Interruptions from the Chairman and Mr. Steingut.

BLOCK: "– and my books will show that. I hope you are not
– I know no one will question it. I regret to have to make
this publicly. I dislike it."

*There follows some more questioning by other members of
the committee, all along the same lines as Seabury's, asking
whether Block provided cash for Jimmy Walker. Block answers as many as he can, but admits to being tired and ill,
having had influenza for three days. Seabury hastens to finish, and, after a brief discussion in which it is decided Max
Block needn't come to the stand, Paul Block is excused at
3:25 PM on March 27, 1932.*

Paul Block breathed in relief, perspiring and looking weak as he stepped
down from the chair. He was satisfied overall with his testimony and was
content to have been given a moment to clear his name and Walker's
regarding the joint brokerage account. Awaiting the newspapers with
trepidation, Block anxiously hoped his story wouldn't be taken out of
context, especially his mentioning his son, William. *The New York Times'*
lead headline read: "HERRICK CONTRADICTS MAYOR ON STOCK;
SEABURY LINKS WALKER-SHERWOOD CASH; BLOCK'S SON,
10, 'INSPIRED' $246,000 GIFT."[126] This did not bode well for Block or
his family. As the investigation wore on, the ridicule worsened. *The New
York Herald Tribune* featured a poem purportedly written by a young boy
begging for help for his father:

> "...My pap's proud and poor and shy:
> He wouldn't ask for stock.
> I hope my story makes you cry.
> Oh, Mr., Mr. Block!"[127]

A statement after the poem said:

> "We are one who believed the conversation between Mr.
> Paul Block and his son Billy took place almost exactly as Mr.
> Block reported it on the witness stand. Still, we wonder
> whether Billy had ever appealed to his father on behalf of
> someone whose salaries were under $25,000 a year, automo-
> bile included."[128]

Will Rogers wrote an editorial to *The New York Times,* a dry, humorous statement saying "No boy ever pitied *him* when he was [honorary] Mayor of Los Angeles."[129] Paul Block, distraught at the embarrassment, wrote a letter of apology to his son, William, who was at school at Hotchkiss, in Connecticut.

> "...I want to tell you again how badly I feel that I am re-
> sponsible for getting you so much publicity, but you, who
> know that the story told is true, will surely be patient with me
> and you have certainly proven this up to date.
>
>   Affectionately,
>   Dad"[130]

Still more muckraking came from the newspapers when Paul Block was accused of seeking a city contract from Walker in exchange for the generous $246,000 "donation" he gave him. Senator Hastings pointed out that Block had invested $140,000 in a small tile company, the Beyer Corporation. This occurred about nine months after he opened the joint account with Walker, but Seabury had neglected to raise this issue during questioning. The gentleman in charge of the tile company sent a bid to the New York Board of Transportation without Block's knowledge. Upon learning of the submission and fearing it would cause embarrassment to the Mayor should he find out, Block immediately withdrew his financial backing from the project.[131] Although Block never made any money from the tile business and had indeed relinquished all connection to it several years before, his already damaged reputation suffered even more in the hands of the reporters.

Block was greatly disheartened by the investigation and the ensuing publicity that resulted. He felt maligned by many of the papers, especially *The New York Times*. Also, he resented Seabury's refusal to allow him to discuss plainly the confusion surrounding the Beyer Corporation. Eventually he wrote a letter of protest to Seabury himself, in which he stated: "If there was any doubt in your mind as to this [Block's innocence regarding the Beyer Corp.] you should have questioned me while I was on the stand rather than publicly make me the victim of unjust inferences unsupported by fact. I am surprised at this action on your part. In view of these facts, justice should prompt you to amend your statement to Governor Roosevelt in so far as this inference to me applies."[132]

Seabury did not amend his report. Block continued to fight against the treatment he received from the newspapers. Having built up everything he had from scratch, he wasn't about to allow unsubstantiated statements to forever tie ignominy to his family name. He wrote to *The New York Times*, berating them for publishing his words about his charity donations without clarifying the question that prompted his answer. "The answer was rather an immodest one. I disliked making it, but thought I ought to as long as Judge Seabury put that particular question to me. My only reason for calling this to your attention is because someone, I think, made an error in the handling of this particular part of the story. *The Times* was pretty hard on me, but I am not complaining. All those on *The Times* who know me must know that the joint account I had with the Mayor was just something that I did for a man who had been my friend for 18 years, and that, of course, I have never received anything in return nor would I have accepted anything."[133] Paul Block, being a newspaper man, was fully aware that future generations reading about Mayor Walker would draw their information from these articles. He was determined that the papers provide an accurate account of the situation. In this, he failed; the papers did not recount their erroneous implications, and Block never succeeded in clarifying the majority of the insinuations against him. The Seabury investigation stayed with the family for decades: in 1957, Billy Block, now known as William Block, Sr., sent a letter of protest to Roy W. Howard of Scripps-Howard Newspapers, contesting an article written by a Scripps paper that alluded to the graft of New York City and included his father's name.[134]

The indignities heaped upon Paul Block and his family weren't the only things preying on his mind. The country was in a deep economic depression, he himself was encountering not inconsiderable financial difficulty, and he was forced to witness the inevitable destruction of a very dear friend. Block almost couldn't stand up to the pressures. Speaking of the trial in Albany, his son William later wrote: "He was terribly nervous. By 1932 father was not a very well man. I don't know whether he'd burned himself out or what was wrong. He was terribly intense. He was not sleeping well. He had what he said were pains in his legs. He was very neurotic. He was not in good shape when we went to the hearing."[135]

To Block's horror, the investigation didn't end with Seabury. Seabury referred it to Governor Roosevelt, not as a formal charge "but for your [Roosevelt's] information so that you may determine what is to be done."[136] With reluctance, Roosevelt opened another hearing, over which he himself was to preside. To the utter dismay of Walker and Block, the whole debacle was to be lived through again. The hearings were held again, as before, with Roosevelt in charge. They officially started on August 11, 1932 with Walker taking the stand. [144] Roosevelt made clear that under Section 122 of the New York City Charter, the Mayor of New York City could be removed by the Governor of New York State. The one thing about the Walker case that confounded Walker's supporters, Paul included, was that Walker was not allowed to address his accusers or cross-examine witnesses. Seabury, and later Roosevelt, maintained that they were acting under a procedure for investigations, not trials, and therefore no cross-examinations were necessary. Walker was under severe and relentless attack. To be unable to counter-attack struck his team as unjust and they took the argument to the Supreme Court. Supreme Court Justice Staley ruled that Governor Roosevelt could not be removed because he is immune from interference by judicial process. But in a memorandum attached to his decision, the Justice held that the Governor should have summoned witnesses whose evidence Seabury had used and allowed the Mayor to cross-examine them.

A rumor had reached Block that Roosevelt – for ethical, legal and political reasons (the latter being the most essential and imperative) – was not going to convict or dismiss Walker, and this made Block feel somewhat more temporarily agreeable toward the Governor. Roosevelt, ensconced in the Governor's mansion in Albany, surrounded by his aides and Justice Felix Frankfurter, mused: "What if I give the little mayor hell and then let him off?"[137]

Walker had read William Randolph Hearst's signed editorial only days before, which suggested that under the existing injustice he should "resign and submit his case at the next election to the final and all-powerful court of public opinion."[138] He had also seen Block's editorial/news story of September 1, 1932, "Court Criticizes Roosevelt in Walker Case Procedure," in which Block reported Supreme Court Justice Ellis J. Staley's criticism that FDR had not given the Mayor a fair trial.[139] Although Block's piece was forceful and convincing, it was too late. Walker had telephoned Block early that evening and discussed his alternatives. By this time, Walker was tired of the constant harangue of defending himself. He took stock of his situation, spoke with his friends and especially to Paul Block, and tried to think clearly. He felt certain that Roosevelt would remove him. Exhausted, humiliated and financially broken, Walker turned to his old mentor Alfred E. Smith, who said: "Jim, you're through. You must resign for the good of the Party."[140]

Block immediately began working on another editorial concerning the Walker affair, which was to be inserted in his papers the next day. Roosevelt never had to decide whether to remove Walker: at 10:20 PM that evening – the Mayor's normal working or partying time – he called an unexpected press conference at City Hall in New York City. Ill, pale, angry and shaking, he became the first (but not the last) Mayor of New York City ever to resign the office. Walker simply could not take any more. "I hereby resign as the Mayor of the City of New York, said resignation to take effect immediately," Walker said tersely to the throng of newspapermen. He then slammed his door on the reporters.[141]

The next day, Block's statement about Walker was dignified but irate: "The great majority will applaud him for choosing a course which was necessitated by the impossibility not only of combating charges pressed by men with thwarted political ambitions, but also of overcoming a verdict that looked as if had been signed, sealed, and delivered, even before the trial had started."[142]

Jimmy Walker resigned as Mayor of New York on September 1, 1932. A few weeks later he left for Europe, where he lived for a few years with his new wife, Betty Compton. Walker always felt that if he had run again for Mayor after resigning, the people would have re-elected him, and that may have been an accurate assumption. In 1932, people were angry with Tammany Hall, and they punished Walker as a result. But by 1935 they had forgotten all about it, preferring to think only of "Gentleman Jim" and the good time he gave them early in his career. Calls went across the seas for him to return, newspapers began to carry bits of news about his antics. As Walker felt the renewed affection of New Yorkers, some of the bitterness of the trial lessened, and his spirits began to raise slightly. Paul

Block also recovered, but slowly. The years apart were difficult for both men, and when Jimmy Walker finally returned to New York in 1935, they had both saddened and aged considerably.

Chapter 10
The Burdens of Depression

The new President, Herbert Hoover, together with his Secretary of the Treasury, the Pittsburgh financier Andrew W. Mellon (at that time one of the world's richest men), would not publicly recognize or validate the nature or causes of the economic disaster that the country was experiencing. After mass demonstrations around the country protesting unemployment, Hoover, in a speech in March of 1930, predicted that the worst effect of the stock market depression on employment would be over in perhaps sixty days. Five months later, *The New York Times* published photographs of people on breadlines, in soup kitchens and selling apples, indicating that such activities had become a common sight all over the country. Although Paul Block continued to maintain deeply cordial relations with Hoover, he was concerned with the country's economic future, and therefore spoke out in his front-page editorials about the difficulties, as he understood them. The outgrowth of the Depression hastened a 25-percent closure of the nation's banks, which had devastating ramifications and threw millions out of work. Block quickly saw that Hoover's policies were not confronting the problem. It is a testament to Hoover's sense of graciousness and friendship that despite Block's criticisms of his procedures, the President still sought and curried his respect and favor.

Block was critical of Hoover's Wickersham Commission report on whether the Volstead Act which created Prohibition should be repealed, and although the findings and conclusions of the group were somewhat ambiguous, Hoover sharply differed with his own appointees in considering any revision of the Act, even in the distant future. As a result, Block seemed at first to give up hope of Hoover's success altogether in his first year in the White House, and lambasted the President in an editorial "Another Commission, Out of Commission," asking Congress to override him. In concluding his polemic, Block wrote:

O, America, where is thy leader?[1]

Block also felt that the passage of the Smoot-Hawley Tariff Act would
worsen conditions, as it called for closing off foreign commerce and markets, and he begged Hoover to repeal it: "We can no longer think in terms
of the United States alone," Block wrote convincingly. "We must think
in terms of the world."[2] Hoover's response to the possible repeal of Smoot-
Hawley was a dark prediction that would haunt him for years to come:

> Grass will grow in the streets of a hundred cities, a thousand
> towns; the weeds will overrun the fields of a million farms.[3]

One might wonder why Block and Hoover continued their close relationship, as they did for many years, despite their great differences of
opinion. In many ways, Block's friendship with Coolidge seemed to be
deeper than the fabric of his rapport with Hoover, but Hoover never was
a politician in the truest American definition of the word and his reaching
out to Paul Block was really the hallmark of his character: he was honest
and forthright and believed that Block was, too. Before his Presidency,
Hoover had been admired as a great humanitarian as a result of orches-
trating aid to the Belgian people after World War I, but he never quite
caught the public fancy; although he was the President of the United States
he was somewhat shy, and always properly dignified. Block shared both
of those characteristics.

Only a few months after Block's scathing editorial concerning Smoot-
Hawley, he and Dina were overnight guests of Herbert Hoover and his
wife Lou at the White House, his attack apparently forgiven by the President.[4] In a letter to her son Billy, written on White House stationery,
Dina Block mentioned that they had a "lovely visit" and found it all "interesting," (and also that she was sharpening up her backgammon game
in Washington, and was eager to play Billy upon her return home).[5]

Block endorsed Hoover for the 1932 election. Although his personal
and corporate financial condition was worsening almost daily, as was the
nation's, Block believed that the experienced Hoover was better than the
relatively untried Roosevelt; equally important, Block had a place in his
heart for "the poor little orphan boy," as he once described President
Hoover. In an editorial that appeared in all of his newspapers, Block
made a comment, the substance of which was also carried by news services and other newspapers all over the country. In essence, he held:

Who can say that any man could have done better than President Hoover? The crisis has now passed. The country's economic condition is improving but it still needs serious attention. The task is not for a practitioner who has several untried remedies. It is a job for one who has been in attendance, who knows best what is needed to bring recovery in the shortest possible period. President Hoover should be re-elected so he can continue helping in the business revival which now is on the rise.[6]

•••

Although he was a Republican, Block attended the 1932 Democratic convention in Chicago. As a newspaperman, he felt he should be part of one of this country's most important political processes, gathering material as an observer for one of his future editorials. He also knew personally three of the four candidates for nomination, Franklin D. Roosevelt, Alfred E. Smith, and John Nance Garner, Speaker of the House, and he felt that if he were present in Chicago, he might gain an exclusive interview of the winner for publication. He had not met the other candidate, Newton B. Baker, Woodrow Wilson's Secretary of War, but knew of him as a highly regarded statesman.

Block also attended the Convention because his old partner on the *New York Evening Mail*, Henry L. Stoddard, urged him to go. Stoddard had a lifetime of attending Republican, Democratic and Progressive conventions and he had been involved on every level over the years as delegate, journalist, go-between, and dealmaker. In the convention hall itself, Block and Stoddard did not sit in the press section but in a flag-bedecked box, where they felt they could better gauge the intensity of the delegates, and the temper of the packed galleries, which were more in tune with the excitement of battle, and where they could better observe the inevitable demonstrations and bandwagon parades, and be closer to the spirited and colorful eulogists. But in the boxes there was also a certain refinement and this appealed to Block: those seated there were mostly backers and distinguished guests, publishers and business executives, and he had an opportunity to talk with some of the people with whom he did business in the past.

Block was intensely interested in this convention because his friend Hearst, who was a Democrat, was thoroughly involved in possibly picking the candidate himself, and Block wanted to monitor and be witness to Hearst's potential king-making efforts. As it developed, Hearst *did* manipulate the Chicago Convention of 1932, but he never left his San Simeon castle in California to do it: all of his maneuvers were performed over the telephone, and through telegrams and other written or spoken missives.

Despising Alfred E. Smith because of the old political snub inflicted upon him, and fearing and disillusioned by Roosevelt and Baker as internationalists, Hearst, an absolute isolationist, wanted another candidate: John Nance Garner, the silver-haired, red-complected Texan, who had been in Congress with him in 1907, was Hearst's preference to win the nomination. It was said that Hearst had "discovered" Garner, and in the weeks before the Convention he ran a score of pro-Garner editorials and feature stories in all of his papers. Hearst vowed to swing all of California's votes to Garner.[7]

During the entire Chicago convention, as bartering for delegates took place in proverbial smoke-filled rooms, in darkened corridors and in the backrooms of restaurants, Hearst was giving instructions by telephone to Paul Block and to Joseph Willicombe, Hearst's alter ego employee, as to what he wanted.

Roosevelt sent a go-between to ask Hearst to meet with him, so that he could convince the publisher that his internationalist sentiments were on the wane: after all, he contended, he had repudiated the League of Nations months before. Joseph P. Kennedy also appealed to Hearst by telephone to at least meet with Roosevelt. Hearst refused. Since Block had become a Roosevelt detractor, *he* was not going to try to convince Hearst to back FDR. Actually, Block was secretly hoping that Garner would be nominated, because he felt Garner could not win the election, and then his friend Hoover would remain in the White House.

On the first three ballots, Roosevelt could not achieve the two-thirds majority of votes needed, and it appeared that he would soon be defeated, his chances of being President slipping into memory. Garner realized that he, too, was unlikely to emerge as the winner. A compromise candidate was being noised about.

Hearst called Block at his hotel and discussed the standing of the votes, the mood of the delegates, the psychology of the nominees, the rumors of the spectators and the politics of the moment. The fourth ballot was approaching and there was belief that Roosevelt would slip in the tally...and then be finished. Garner's chances seemed to be slim. That meant that unless Hearst could affect the outcome, the convention would choose either Smith or Baker. Not at all pleased with how the voting was developing, Hearst decided that for his purposes even Roosevelt would be preferable to either of those two. And although Garner was Hearst's first choice, he knew that Garner was amenable to the vice-presidential slot. Running as vice-president, Garner would bring with him the considerable number of electoral votes from Texas. If nothing else, it was believed that Garner's promise of votes was enough for Roosevelt to put him on the ticket.

Hearst told Block that he would accept a call from either Roosevelt or one of his representatives.

James A. Farley, Roosevelt's campaign manager, telephoned Hearst and said that Roosevelt asked him to say the following: "If you don't take me, you'll get Smith or Baker."[8]

Block asked Stoddard to visit him in his suite at the Ambassador, and he could hardly contain himself when the older man arrived. As Stoddard related in his political memoir, *It Cost To Be President*:

> Two hours later, Paul Block, the well-known publisher, and I sat in his room for a good-night exchange of opinion. He then said that he had been talking over the telephone with "W. R." and that a deal had been arranged by which the 69 Texas and California delegates, after complimenting Garner on two or three ballots, would swing to Roosevelt. He added that Garner would then go on the ticket as Vice-President."[9]

Whether it was Block or Willicombe who informed the California State Chairman, William G. McAdoo, of Hearst's reversal, is not known, but McAdoo's announcement when he took to the platform and discussed why the Western states had changed their vote, has gone down in history:

> California came here to nominate a President; she did not come here to deadlock the convention or to engage in another disastrous contest like that of 1924. California casts 44 votes for Franklin D. Roosevelt![10]

After the nomination the somewhat-trivial question came up as to the correct pronunciation of Roosevelt's name. He was not that well-known outside of his home state, so in case non-New Yorkers might stumble over how to address him, newspapers published a guide: it was to be pronounced "Rose-velt," in two syllables, to conform to the Dutch origin of the name where a double "oo" is pronounced as a single long "o."[11]

Thus Franklin D. Roosevelt was nominated, a man Hearst didn't really want to become President, and a man Block had grown to scorn, and yet both Hearst and Block were strangely involved in helping him to become President of the United States.

Perhaps as a result of his involvement at the Democratic Convention, Block became even more irritable over even the *possibility* of Roosevelt defeating Hoover. He continually complained about Roosevelt's campaign speeches prior to Election Day, stating that he felt that they contained nothing but generalities...and more generalities. "Nothing constructive is ever offered," Block wrote. "Are we to follow vague and intangible promises which are impossible to fulfill?"[12] He urged Roosevelt to commit himself on the issues, especially the Prohibition question, and the cost of local, state and national government.[13]

It is difficult in retrospect to understand or agree with Block's stated position about what he considered a reanimation of the economy, especially since 1932 has often been described by economists such as John Maynard Keynes as the "cruelest year" of the Depression, a sort of Dark Ages of the American economy.[14] Although the *Toledo Blade* itself wasn't faring all that badly, with an infusion of some new national automobile advertising (among others, ads appeared for Chrysler Straight Eights, the new Chevrolet Six, and the $995, banjo-framed Graham), most of Block's other newspapers were in deep financial trouble, and his advertising representation business was suffering because the amount of space being bought in newspapers all throughout the country was falling precipitously. From 1929 to 1933, the income from newspaper advertising dropped 40% nationally: Block's own newspapers, and those that he represented, were also caught in this decline. His backing of Hoover, and his redundant editorials on what he kept saying was the ebullience of the economy, might well have been a combination of blind fidelity, fanciful thinking, and pure political partisanship. He was clearly procrastinating about the inevitable.

Nevertheless, Block suffered. His public optimism about the future of the country did not match his private despair. Plagued with worry about the fate of his various companies and his personal empire, he began to defer making decisions, and spent more and more time away from the office on trips, ostensibly for business but in actuality more as journeys into avoidance. When back East, he generally stayed in bed for long times, literally with the covers pulled over his head, ensconced in his

Park Avenue apartment or his home in Greenwich. For years an insomniac, by the spring of 1932, his condition had worsened so that instead of finally falling off to sleep by three or four in the morning, as he usually did, he was now awake until dawn or even until the early morning every day. As he finally fell off and slept through the day, his business associates could not reach him for crucial decisions until he arose in the late afternoon, or sometimes in the early evenings. Even then, he complained that he was not rested. He began to exhibit many of the elements that today might be classified as clinical depression, or what was then called a nervous breakdown; in addition to his sleep disorder, a severe hypochondria seized him, he had a loss of energy, a feeling of inappropriate guilt over the predicament of his businesses, a difficulty in making even trivial decisions, and certain physical symptoms such as frequent stomach aches.

Because of the downturn of business, Block's companies began experiencing a serious cash shortage. His creditors started hounding him for payment: he owed money to paper companies, stockholders, noteholders, banks and other financial institutions, and there were some personal loans as well. Whispers of his newspapers being forced into bankruptcy, or a legally incited foreclosure of all of his businesses, began to reach him, and instead of confronting the situation with a reliance on his financial managers and advisers, at first he simply ignored the problem. One company suggested to Block that they move one of their own accountants into Block's financial department to assure themselves that they received their share of payments, and in order to do this they wanted to have their accountant counter-sign all of Block's checks.[15] Block felt that it would be acceptable to him if an accountant came in periodically to check the books of his corporations, but to have someone ensconced permanently with, in effect, budgetary co-control, would be too cumbersome and humiliating. He asked Max Steuer, his attorney, to see if he could avoid such an intrusion. The persuasive Steuer convinced the executives of the company to postpone placing their own financial man into Block's organization for the time being.

Whenever a creditor became too demanding, Block asked one of his friends – such as Bernard Baruch, William Randolph Hearst or Albert Lasker – to write to, or telephone, the creditor and tell him of Block's good will, and imply that payment would eventually be made. Hearst wrote the following letter to Max Steuer, so that it could be used as a general letter of reference should any creditors need evidence of Block's sincere intentions:

> I will be very glad if occasion offers to testify to the excep-
> tional abilities of Mr. Block as a journalist and also to the
> essential value of the properties he controls. The sincerity of
> my attitude is proven by the fact that I solicit, secure, and
> follow Mr. Block's advice on many business matters and that
> I place a large part of my advertising in his hands...[16]

The cynical Steuer felt that Block was wasting his time in convincing his friends to vouch for him. The combined force of influence of these letters on whether a creditor would call up the loan, according to Steuer, was worthless and had "as much weight as last year's snow," he posited to Block. "A thousand messages from the President of the United States would not be of the slightest avail," Steuer continued emphatically. [17] Block was ashamed to see his creditors and was fearful when speaking to them.

Affronted that people whom he considered friends were pressing him for money he owed them, Block told Steuer that it would be a point of honor to him – if the circumstances were in reverse, and people owed *him* money – never to call up a loan of a friend. Block told Steuer to tell his creditors to look at his past record of payment. As he explained it, he always *had* paid off his debts, and he would now...he just needed a little more time to weather the meager receipt of income he was experiencing. Steuer explained to Block what he considered to be the preposterousness of his strategy: "A historical narrative of what you paid off interests no-body because that is in the past. What creditors want to know in these days – and indeed, they have always wanted to know – is what have you now got with which to meet your obligations? What are your assets and your liabilities? Only in that way can a solution of the problem be arrived at. The circumstance that *you* [personally] would not press a debtor is not the yardstick by which to measure *other* people's attitudes."[18]

Block's liabilities in the summer of 1932 were nearing 2 million dollars, and so he had Steuer ask his major creditors if they were willing, or could agree, to wait until 1934 for repayment. Before doing this, however, Steuer talked to Block like a Dutch Uncle and begged him to get his affairs and his life in order. It is hard for an empty bag to stand upright, counseled Steuer, *but that does not mean that it is impossible.* Although they both had offices in Manhattan, and often met for dinner and talked on the telephone, Steuer felt he had to express his most salient arguments in writing; he felt that such formality might prod and intimidate Block into action. In a letter marked "Personal and Confidential," Steuer bluntly reiterated what he had been saying to Block for months:

> I wish that you would make up your mind to be well. I do not personally consider that you are physically ill. This thing requires your personal energetic attention. Your failing to give it is injuring you very seriously. You should be at your office and not talk about being sick. I do not mean by that that I do not appreciate that you do not feel one hundred percent, but I do believe that if you would just buckle up and fight and go back to your office, and attend to business and see people face to face, and have an accurate statement of your affairs on your desk, so that you yourself will understand what your real position is, there is a very good chance of you coming out of this alright. It cannot be done by the telephone messages [and letters] of friends and well-wishers, nor by substitutes. I beg of you to make up your mind that nobody is going to consider friendship in this situation...Nobody is your enemy. Nobody is unduly harsh. When you come and ask for a two years' postponement, the most natural thing in the world is to have that somebody ask why, and what will be the result at the end of the two years...Let's tell them [the creditors] what can be done, and then do it. I have the utmost confidence that you will be left in charge and that everything will work out all right, provided you will follow the suggestions I have tried to convey.[19]

As it developed, his creditors realized that if they forced Block out of business, they would receive only a token of what was owed them – if anything at all – and they all took the gamble that the economy would turn around. Block, although still complaining of his health and inability to sleep, began going to the office, and showed true courage in not only acknowledging his fears, but also conquering them. Steuer's reasoned and dynamic approach to a common sense solution served as Block's catalyst. Block immediately had a business plan devised, a spreadsheet of assets and liabilities drawn up, and a schedule of small payments implemented to be made to the most insistent creditors. He reasoned that if he could reduce some of his indebtedness, his creditors would be less likely to complain, whereas if he allowed his larger debts to remain, those creditors would turn into actual enemies.

Neither the economy nor Block's assets turned around immediately, but with the election of Franklin Delano Roosevelt in 1932, and the implementation of his radical policies, the anticipated hope of the economy began to build, and the patience of Block's creditors was rewarded.

Pittsburgh Post-Gazette Revisited

"The *Pittsburgh Post-Gazette* does not seem to be doing very well," wrote Hearst to Block in the spring of 1933. He asked Block if he would allow him to send one, or even two of his newspaper executives to "oversee" the operation of the paper. Block politely refused the request, but agreed to meet Hearst's representative; he wanted the meeting in New York, however, not Pittsburgh. "Please don't think it is only my pride I am thinking about," he wrote to Hearst, but pointed out that virtually the whole city of Pittsburgh – bankers, advertisers, suppliers, readers – believed that *he*, not Hearst the silent backer, was the owner of the *Post-Gazette*, and having a Hearst executive officially stationed at the office "might be embarrassing to me."[20] He would carefully listen to the delegate's suggestions, he told Hearst. Block also offered some balm for Hearst's consternation. He held that the national advertising of Hearst's *New York American,* which Block handled as special representative, although down in lineage (as was virtually every other newspaper in the country), was not faring all that badly. The *American* had lost a little over 5,000 lines in the month of April, he informed Hearst; bad enough, but compared to *The New York Times*, which had lost over 100,000 lines, and the *Herald Tribune,* which had lost more than 57,000 lines during that same period, the *American* was doing well.[21] Block also offered to journey to any one of Hearst's other 25 newspapers which might be "sick;" he hoped that he might use his expertise to help one of the ailing papers, as he had done with Hearst's *Baltimore American.*[22] Such an assignment would temper Hearst's disapproval of the *Post-Gazette's* decline, Block believed, and would strengthen his rapport with his old friend.

Concerned that Hearst might feel that the *Pittsburgh Post-Gazette* was facing an uncertain future, Block had numerous meetings and telephone calls with the older man, in which he tried to convince Hearst not to panic. Block pointed out that in the previous six years, more than 3 million dollars had been taken out of the business as pure profit, over and above all costs, expenses and salaries that were reimbursed, placing the paper in the forefront of six-day daily newspapers in the United States. He recognized, and wanted Hearst to understand, that the financial difficulties that the *Post-Gazette* experienced were a result of both the depressed economy and also the bind in which the paper had become ensnared. The other newspapers in Pittsburgh had reduced their local advertising rates and Block was forced to follow their policy in order to compete, giving him scant income from his retail space sales. And yes, it was true that national advertising was down in the pages of the *Post-Gazette*, but he pointed out that such was the case in morning papers everywhere, and the *Post-Gazette* was not an exception. "Even your strong morning papers in San Francisco and Los Angeles," he submitted to Hearst, "will show you what terrific losses there have been in national advertising and how much greater they have been in these papers, as in virtually all morning newspapers, compared with good evening papers."[23]

Block's main purpose of sharing his opinions was to make his "claim," as he wrote to Hearst, "that the situation in Pittsburgh is not a strange picture and is hardly any different from the pictures shown in other cities, and personally, I feel confident that if the steel and coal industry were to improve, that our paper would be back to where it was at one time."[24]

The evening papers in Pittsburgh were capturing the advertising for lower-priced items, typically because the demographic income of readers of evening papers was lower than that of readers of morning papers. Advertising for such things as automobiles, higher-priced appliances, financial services and other so-called luxury advertising, previously the province of the morning papers in Pittsburgh, was drying up, or at least greatly diminishing. Block believed and reiterated that when the business improved throughout the country, so would the economy in Pittsburgh, and then the paper would be back to being financially successful. He was realistic, however, and warned Hearst that such advancement in the city's economy might "not come for a long, long time," and if Hearst wanted to make changes in the content or appearance of the paper, Block – although somewhat skeptical – would honor those requests. He further advised Hearst, however, that if he made the *Pittsburgh Post-Gazette* more like the *Pittsburgh Sun-Telegraph* – a solution Block believed that Hearst was beginning to toy with – it might cost either one or the other newspaper some advertising, and possibly reduce the *Sun-Telegraph*'s circulation. He asked for sixty days to turn the *Post-Gazette* around, making a few of the changes that Hearst had wanted, and if there was no improvement in advertising and/or circulation after that, he would then do exclusively whatever Hearst demanded.[25] Hearst listened, absorbed what Block contended, and allowed him to do what he wanted. Subsequently business at the *Post-Gazette* began to recover, but slowly.

In order to elevate the *Post-Gazette*'s capital position, Block immediately concentrated on bolstering the editorial content of the paper, making sure that the editors had enough financial support to adequately cover the news, publishing well-known and entertaining columnists, and instituting features that appealed to reader interest. His thinking was based on sound publishing principles: issue a well-researched, factually reported and superbly written newspaper, with articles and news stories that are meaningful to the readership, and circulation will inevitably rise. As the numbers ascend, because the newspaper becomes a necessity or certainly a habit for the readers, advertisers will be drawn to the paper and revenue will assuredly increase: a well-respected paper will automatically attract advertisers. The editorial product would eventually build circulation through more robust newsstand sales and more subscriptions. Advertising income would then also rise, intertwined as it would be with the rising number of readers. The strategy was a strong business move.

As a start, Block approved and encouraged the use of a number of wire services, such as the Associated Press, the United Press, the Consolidated Press, the Chicago Tribune Service, the New York World Service, the Universal Service, and for Block, the plum of all wires, *The New York Times* Service. "It is with considerable pride that I am able to announce that we have arranged for a special wire," Block wrote two months after he commenced publishing the *Post-Gazette*, "giving us the complete *New York Times* service."[26] A flood of copy began to come through the teletype machines, which were kept busy 24-hours a day with the country's and world's news and pictures, and eventually the well-edited stories and photo spreads found their way on to the pages of the *Pittsburgh Post-Gazette*. Although the wire services were expensive, the *Post-Gazette* quickly became known as simply the best and most reliable newspaper in Pittsburgh because of its comprehensive national and international news coverage. The *Pittsburgh Post-Gazette* was availing itself of more wire service reports than any other paper in the country.[27]

Block also drew upon his experience with *Pictorial Review,* and published in the *Post-Gazette* a complete novel (in serial form) by Martha Ostenso, this one called *The Changing Bride*.[28]

Under Block's watch and through his instruction and direction, the *Pittsburgh Post-Gazette* assumed more of the mantle of community leadership than it ever had before in its history, and it established a reputation as a guardian of the public good. On a local level, Block published strong, personally-signed editorials and news exposés about the proliferation of slot machines in the Pittsburgh area; his paper criticized the Pittsburgh taxi strike;[29] condemned the exorbitant freight rates that affected the Pennsylvania coal industry; campaigned for safer conditions for iron and steel workers; called for more stringent penalty for habitual criminals;[30] demanded higher salaries for Pittsburgh police and firemen;[31] broke the story of the Pittsburgh Department of Supplies scandal which led to the conviction of Mayor Charles Kline; and warned the public of the impending danger of politicians becoming involved in, and possibly taking control of the public schools.[32] He outlined the ridiculousness of Pennsylvania's "Blue Laws" which would not permit such recreations as baseball games or concerts on Sundays, and he asked for their repeal.[33] "There is no reason why those who work during the week," he argued cogently, "should not be given the privilege of pleasant, healthy entertainment." Pennsylvania at that time was the only state represented in the major leagues which prohibited baseball on Sundays.[34]

Not all of his editorials assumed the mantle of a crusade. He commended Howard Heinz for what he did for Pittsburgh as its largest employer;[35] often talked glowingly of the Carnegie Institute; lauded the Ohio Waterway as "one of America's greatest public improvements;"[36] boosted the Pittsburgh Pirates baseball team;[37] and mourned the death of two Pittsburgh policemen killed in the line of duty.[38]

Through Block's signed editorials, the readership of the *Post-Gazette* began to be introduced to certain national and international issues that were significant to him...and also to them. The editorials mostly confronted the bleak economic picture and continued to beg for the repeal of the Volstead Act (which finally occurred on December 5, 1933). Throughout much of 1932 he wrote editorials that criticized Franklin Delano Roosevelt as, at worst, a "dangerous radical, and a political experimentalist"[39] and at best, "a pleasant, smiling cheerful Governor...but many doubt that he would be the forceful, aggressive, capable President that this country needs."[40] But after FDR took office on March 4, 1933, Block counseled patience for the new President and gave his allegiance to the country's new leader.

In the realm of international affairs, Block wanted to distance himself from the pro-German blot on his and Hearst's escutcheon, and he therefore editorialized about the Lausanne Conference and Germany's failure to have the moral stigma removed of being "officially" responsible for

World War I;[41] called for an arms reduction not only for Germany, but for "all of the citizens of the world" to help the global economic situation;[42] decried the rise of Hitlerism; and suggested an international embargo on German products and money in order to keep the Nazi dictator in check.[43]

In mid-March of 1936, Pittsburgh suffered the worst flood in its history; houses were swept away, electric power was suspended, and 20 feet of water in some streets in the downtown district made rowboats and skiffs the only means of transportation. The *Post-Gazette's* offices were flooded, but Block was determined to continue publishing. With a skeleton crew, the editors moved their makeshift operation to another newspaper, the *New Castle News*, and using its printing presses they managed to publish an attenuated edition of the *Post-Gazette*, minus many departments and most features. Due to the lack of engraving facilities, the *Post-Gazette* could not publish a host of late photos of the flood itself, but using yet another company to make the plates, in a matter of days the full coverage of the flood appeared, in words *and* pictures.

Block made sure that all of the workers of the *Post-Gazette* who would have regularly been employed during the flood period received full salary for the days missed. "Whether or not they have all been able to do their usual jobs is not important; there is no question of their eagerness to do everything in their power to assist in this emergency, and to assure Pittsburgh of consistent and accurate newspaper service no matter what the difficulties of the moment may be."[44]

In a short while, with the help of the National Guard, the city began to reclaim itself, the waters receded, relief workers helped the victims, curfews were lifted and the *Pittsburgh Post-Gazette* started publishing from its own plant once again.

Clare Boothe Luce

At that time, in 1934, Block learned that Bernard Baruch's close friend, Clare Boothe, managing editor of the famed *Vanity Fair,* was leaving her post and might be available to write for both his and the Hearst papers. Blond, brilliant and beautiful, Boothe seemed to be on a first-name basis with members of all of New York and international society, some of whom were friends of Paul Block's – Jimmy Walker and Cole Porter, Al Smith and Will Rogers – as well as many of the world's chieftains, such as Winston Churchill and Cornelius Vanderbilt. She was a minor member of Roosevelt's "Brain Trust."

Block contracted her for three 750-word columns a week, on subjects of her own choosing, but with the understanding that they should concentrate on the comings and goings of the social set, a sort of international Elsa Maxwell approach, and avoid a political slant since the *Post-Gazette* and his other papers were already filled to the margins with political commentary. Block named the column himself: "This World of Ours." He advertised it in the *Post-Gazette* and his other papers with exuberance: "No one in New York's aristocracy can write more knowingly or entertainingly of society. Her articles will be full of humorous, human appeal, as well as piquant revelations of modern smart life."

Boothe's first column, sub-titled, "Amazon at Night," displayed that she was a writer of substance, not given to frothy tidbits of gossip, a woman on the verge of liberation but who was conflicted. She gave an account of a midnight walk she took on Broadway:

> Now I was on Broadway, walking very fast toward the bright lights of Times Square, my chin buried in my furs, purse pressed close under my arms...A woman who has not four walls about her when she is alone at night, feels deserted or incomplete or ashamed, or brazen, or....inexplicably uneasy. At any rate she feels odd. This goes to show you, that the independence of my sex, when I can be shaken by such a silly and trivial notion, is something that does not go quite to the bone."[45]

Boothe toured Europe and mailed or wired her columns back to Block, some 61 of them over several months, but although her writing was excellent (with the exception of her spelling, and her occasional careless clichés: Block had to assign his top copyeditor to correct every one of her columns), the work was not to his liking. She had a wide range of interests, an ear for dialogue and a sense of the dramatic, but the pieces began to take on a *belles lettres* flavor, a self-conscious sense of their own literary quality. When she began writing about the *sturm und drang* of the Old World's destiny, with a political slant that the United States should arrest the cancerous growth of fascism, Block – who, like Hearst, was at that time leaning more toward isolationism – decided to cancel the column. The next year Boothe married Henry Luce, founder of Time, Inc., and she went on to become a diplomat. Some twenty years later, when she was U.S. Ambassador to Italy, she told William Block: "Your father was the only one who ever fired me, and moreover, he did it so nicely that I didn't realize I was being fired."[46]

FDR: From Apprehension to Appreciation

Paul Block's early feelings about Franklin D. Roosevelt were complex, as were the President's toward him. He was more than an enthusiastic campaigner for Roosevelt's race for Governor in 1928 – Block's editorials could be said to have actually guided Roosevelt into office and were the catalyst to his political success – but in 1932 he was agonizing over Roosevelt's treatment of his closest friend, Jimmy Walker. As related previously, barely eight weeks before FDR's landslide victory over the humbled Hoover, Mayor Jimmy Walker was mercilessly questioned by then-Governor Roosevelt in long, drawn-out sessions, as a follow-up to the Seabury trial. Roosevelt had not removed the Mayor from office as it was within his power to do so.

Barely two months after Walker's resignation, Block was still incensed, and hurt; he felt that Walker's downfall was obviously all Roosevelt's fault. Nonetheless, within 48 hours of FDR's election, Block sent him the following telegram:

> YOUR OVERWHELMING VICTORY PROVES THAT
> THE AMERICAN PUBLIC DESIRE YOU TO SERVE IN
> THE HIGHEST OFFICE THEY COULD TENDER YOU
> PERIOD I JOIN WITH THEM IN MY SUPPORT AND
> BEST WISHES FOR A SUCCESSFUL AND HAPPY AD-
> MINISTRATION
>
> PAUL BLOCK[47]

And on the very same day, eight of Block's newspapers published a rousing editorial of his advocacy for the new leader of the United States:

> We congratulate President-elect Roosevelt on his victory.
> Let us all join together in wishing him a successful adminis-
> tration. He is to be the head of our nation, and when he be-
> gins his term of office, we must stand behind him and sup-
> port him in every well-directed effort to help the country.[48]

Roosevelt, who may have been surprised by Block's gesture of encouragement, especially since he had been publicly vilified by the publisher for most of the previous year, nevertheless graciously responded to the telegram and editorial with a letter that acknowledged Block's "support and congratulations on our sweeping Democratic victory."[49]

Was Block behaving like a member of what the British call "the loyal opposition"? It appears to have been somewhat more than that. He seems to have felt his political affiliations or beliefs could be modified, like an entirely transferable commodity, tossing from side to side as during a sleepless night to find the most comfortable spot or position. His very political essence, his involvement and allegiances, his detractions and censoriousness, all seemed (as they do, perhaps, for most people) to be directly tied to his feelings about the safety of the economy, his and his family's own personal welfare, and his social commitment *at the moment* to the politician in question. Invitations to dine or to be an overnight or weekend guest at the White House, or to sit with the President at a baseball game, all of which made news and were invariably covered in the press of the nation, were great moments of prestige for Block, his family and his associates, as was – more importantly – his continually being asked his opinions and advice by the highest office-holder in the land. This might explain why he backed Roosevelt one moment, and Hoover the next, and then back and forth once again; contributed money to Al Smith's campaign and publicly supported Hoover *simultaneously*; called for an end to selecting a candidate on religious grounds and ended up denouncing Smith as a religious bigot; dined with the arch-conservative Calvin Coolidge in the dignity of the family quarters of the White House one night, and supped in a smoky speakeasy with the hedonistic liberal Jimmy Walker the next.

It might be argued that Block's political fluctuations were caused by his attempt to objectify his role as a newspaperman who tried to be open and fair to all candidates. But that explanation is refuted by his frequently partisan editorials, some of which were so pungent they might be called diatribes, for or against any specific government official or policy. It seems, rather, that Paul Block was a political expedient and a mutable factionalist, perhaps not quite as chameleon-like as his associate William Randolph Hearst, but entirely capable of metamorphosing his beliefs at any given moment.

Although Block was his own man politically (he backed Alfred E. Smith at a time when Smith and Hearst despised each other, for example) there was undoubtedly some Hearstian influence on Block's political sensibilities. As Hearst's political whims seemed to change on an almost daily basis, so did Block's, although not always in the same direction. It is difficult to estimate the extent of Hearst's effect and affect upon Block, but since Block admired and highly respected Hearst, a certain amount of partisan sway was present. Also, Hearst was basically Block's financial backer (and in the case of Block's special representative business, Hearst was his employer) so Block made every attempt to maintain their relationship on cordial and allegiant terms in all areas: social, financial and political. As a result, during the years many of Hearst's political constructs and persuasions found political affirmation in Block's news and editorial columns. For example, Hearst was certainly pro-German during World War I; he wanted to run with Alfred E. Smith on the Democratic ticket (and was denied); he and his political henchmen secured the nomination of Franklin D. Roosevelt for the Presidency (to avoid Smith's victory), and then became disillusioned with Roosevelt. Turning against him, the two became lifelong enemies. In these areas, there are certainly parallels to Block's actions. However, Block wanted to appear independent of Hearst's influence. In an editorial that appeared in 1931, he had it both ways. Block wrote, in part:

> We do not always agree with the policies of William Randolph Hearst and we do not expect him always to agree with ours.
> But recently, Mr. Hearst spoke over the radio on the causes and cure for the present business depression, and although people may differ on some of his viewpoints, no one will disagree with him in his statement about the Government's loss of income from the impossible and unenforceable Volstead Law.[50]

Just weeks before Roosevelt's inauguration, Block was invited to Washington to appear before the Senate Finance Committee to offer his solutions to the economic crisis, which had created a near panic that was gripping the country. Since he had written dozens of editorials and delivered a number of speeches about the economy over the years, he was thought of by members of the Senate and by Sen. Reed Smoot, Chairman of the Committee, to be a citizen who had something important to say about the future of the country. Before going to Washington, Block discussed his testimony by telephone with former President Herbert Hoover, financier Bernard Baruch, and Block's *Toledo Blade* editor Grove Patterson. Block started off by saying that a great deal of study had been given on how to get out of the Depression; what the country needed was prompt and constructive action. He offered the Committee ten proposals that he felt might have possible positive effects on the economy. In essence, he recommended:

1. Cooperation between the President-elect and Congress in devising the most effective measures to meet the country's imperative needs.
2. Appointment of a coalition cabinet comprising both Democrats and Republicans to assure the fullest measure of public confidence, although Block said he feared that the two-party system would prevent such an arrangement.
3. Reduction of war debts or trade concessions for a fixed percentage for each million dollars that a debtor nation spent in the United States, with a possible further reduction for decrease in armaments by that country.
4. Balancing the budget by levying a small manufacturers' sales tax, and reducing non-service-connected disability payments to those veterans who did not serve overseas or who were not injured in actual service of the World War. All of this would be designed to cut the cost of government.
5. Remaining on the gold standard to ensure sound currency and integrity of contracts so as not to lose confidence in the American dollar, and establishing agreements with nations that were off the gold standard so that all countries would be on a nearly-equal basis in international trade.
6. Repeal of the Eighteenth Amendment, because of the large excise tax this would bring to the treasury, which would possibly result in the reduction of present day taxes, including the manufacturers' sales tax. Repeal of the Amendment would, according to Block, also have a great effect on the morale of the citizenship.
7. Large-scale public works programs with preference for unemployed veterans, to provide a way for a general revival of business and to expand the credit of the country.
8. Moratoriums on farm mortgages and reduced interest rates, although a plan must be found to help the farmers.
9. Higher prices for farm products, without resort to federal subsidies.
10. Readjustment of tariff schedules, with a consideration of raising tariffs on the products of countries that use depreciated currency.[51]

In concluding his advice, Block said: "I would like to add just this word. These are desperate and discouraging days. Mere talk and more talk will not help. Only action, prompt action – *today* and not tomorrow – will meet the situation."[52]

Later, Block expanded and reiterated upon some of his proposals in one of his many editorials in the *Pittsburgh Post-Gazette* and his other papers, in which he asked for a way to be found to limit farm production, and set minimum harvests; he suggested that interest charges be reduced and re-valuations placed on farms, as well as for small home owners, so the sanctity of the home could be preserved; he urged that the President *promptly* start the large public works program that he was promising so that the millions of unemployed could finally get back to work.[53]

Normally, Roosevelt would have formally acknowledged in writing Block's appearance at the U.S. Senate, as well as thanking him for his editorials of support, but he was on a fishing trip off Jacksonville, Florida, on Vincent Astor's yacht. The very next day after Block testified, and two hours after Roosevelt returned from his fishing trip, the President rode in an open-air limousine through downtown Miami. A would-be assassin, wild-eyed Giuseppe Zangara, standing 15-feet from the motor-cade, aimed and fired his gun directly at Roosevelt. An alert, amazingly courageous woman by-stander struggled with Zangara, which caused his shots to miss Roosevelt by inches; but Mayor Anton J. Cermak of Chicago, riding with him, was hit and eventually died from his injury. Four others were seriously wounded.[54]

Block was relieved, as was the nation, that the President-elect was not injured in the shooting, and when two weeks later Roosevelt gave his first inaugural address, a bold, reassuring speech that gave hope to millions, ("Let me first assert my firm belief that the only thing we have to fear is fear itself – nameless, unreasoning, unjustified terror which paralyzes needed efforts to convert retreat into advance.") Block was gratified, thrilled and inspired. After Roosevelt called a special session of Congress a week later where he demanded the re-opening of sound banks, re-organization of other banks, and the control of the currency by bringing all banking institutions under the domain of the Federal Reserve system, Block became optimistic about the economy for the first time in years. He wrote: "The new administration has made a fine start. It deserves support from all of us...the future looks very bright but we must all help to make this a reality by our actions in showing confidence in our country."[55]

Astonishingly, Block seemed to approve of what seemed to be the autocratic, some said dictatorial, style that the President-elect had been
displaying before he even got into office. Block was not the only citizen
so inclined. Since the country seemed to be coming apart, various magazines and at least one Senator were seriously encouraging a dictatorship:
in addition to the drastic unemployment with millions out of work, and
the symbolic although very pragmatic soup lines, thousands of people
had stood on the Capital steps chanting, "Feed the hungry, tax the rich!"
The possibilities of revolution were being noised about. People were
hoarding gold. There was serious doubt whether the federal payroll could
even be met in the very month that Roosevelt was to be inaugurated.[56]
Others decried the augmentation of Presidential power, but Block and
most businessmen – in fact most of the country – realized that Roosevelt's
actions were the only way to obtain a speedy resolution to the economic
emergency that was having such a deleterious effect on both the nation's
psyche and its pocketbook.

Early in the year, Block saw the newly-released film *Gabriel Over the
White House* ("The picture that will make 1933 famous!" blared the advertisements), starring Walter Huston and Franchot Tone, and then referred to it in one of his editorials as an allegory that should be taken
seriously. In the film, a newly-elected President turns out to be a crooked
politician but after being in an auto accident he re-appraises his life, fires
his entire Cabinet, finds a way to adjourn Congress because of its inac-
tion, and he becomes a somewhat-benevolent dictator. He organizes those
without jobs into an army of workers, thus solving the unemployment
dilemma; he has all of the major gangsters in the country executed, eradi-
cating the crime problem; and by a display of the might of the nation's
armed forces, he frightens the debtor foreign nations into paying off their
indebtedness.

Coming at such a difficult time in the history of the nation's economy,
the film was seen not just as an analogy, but as the personification of a
New Deal fantasy. Block pointed out that the cinematic character of the
President in *Gabriel Over the White House* "makes himself dictator, but
in such a manner that things are accomplished for the good of the people."
Block went on to imply that although America did not want a dictator, to
bring the country back to where people can make a living and find some
happiness, dictatorial methods might be necessary.[57]

In a matter of months, tyrant or not, Roosevelt did more to democratize
the nation's financial and credit structure than any other President in the

history of the country. Although Block's worries were far from over, he felt that the economy was about to revivify, and the *Pittsburgh Post-Gazette* and some of his other papers were showing some progress. The circulation of the *Toledo Blade* began to increase almost immediately under Roosevelt's presidency and rose by 14,000 during the New Deal's first two years.[58] Block wrote to Roosevelt barely two weeks after he took office:

> As an Independent Republican newspaper man, but, first of all, as an American, may I take this occasion to express my gratitude, and pride at what you have accomplished for our citizenship in the short time that you have served in your honored position. Knowing my American history pretty well, I cannot recall of an instance where so much was accomplished in so short a time by any other President. I congratulate you and I wish you continued good health and success in your efforts for our country.[59]

In an interview that he gave to *Editor & Publisher* a week later, Block said: "Although I did not support President Roosevelt for election, I am wholeheartedly in favor of every step he has taken up to date and believe that if Congress will continue to cooperate with him, most of our major problems will soon be rectified."[60] Block's sentiments were in accord with many other publishers of the day in what seemed to be a groundswell of phenomenal unity of newspaper support during the national crisis. Such newspapermen as Paul Patterson of the *Baltimore Sun*, Fred Fuller Shedd of the *Philadelphia Bulletin*, Elzey Roberts of the *St. Louis Star and Times*, Arthur J. Sinnott of the *Newark Evening News*, and William Allen White of the *Emporia Gazette*, many of whom had been staunch supporters of Hoover – also showed their approval of Roosevelt's strategies.[61]

Paralleling Block's thorough involvement in politics, which included everything from meetings at the White House to attending political conventions, and from conducting an extensive correspondence with Governors, Senators, Congressmen and Presidents, to campaigning for reforms in his editorials, Block had almost ten businesses to run and he did everything he could to increase their revenue during those bleak times. Raising the circulation of his papers with solid and influential reporting was one tactic Block used. He was particularly proud of the work done by Ray Sprigle, an investigative reporter on the *Pittsburgh Post-Gazette*. A burly Pennsylvania Dutchman who sported a Stetson hat and smoked a corn-cob pipe, Sprigle marched to his own drummer, from the kinds of assignments he would accept to the unique way he went about gathering the information for the stories, and the way he wrote them.

Circulation advanced somewhat at the *Post-Gazette* when Sprigle, disguised as a miner – complete with hard-hat, overalls and grimy face and hands – wrote a dispassionate but beautifully-written series on the inner workings, dynamics and tensions of a nearby mining strike. The impact and the handling of the stories as they appeared was so powerful that remarkably, strikers and mine-owners alike commented favorably on them. Sprigle's reporting career would eventually lead the *Post-Gazette* to its first Pulitzer Prize for a story he would do in the future.[62]

•••

On Monday evening, July 24, 1933, Dina and Paul Block, with their sons Billy and Paul, Jr., sat in their large and gracious living room at Friendship in Greenwich, Connecticut and listened to a radio broadcast on their Atwater-Kent. What they heard was President Roosevelt's explication of the National Recovery Act (NRA); he spoke in a simple, conversational tone without any hint of conventional political rhetoric or oratory. Block was transfixed as he heard Roosevelt discuss the NRA as "experimental" but necessary in a nation-wide cooperative effort to restore purchasing power. Roosevelt affirmed that it would raise wages and make jobs, it would promote production and increase prices so that working people could make a living and farmers and manufacturers could realize a fair profit. Talking of the NRA's future, Roosevelt said: "The people of this country can guarantee its success." Block was so impressed by the content, sincerity and reasonableness of the talk that he telephoned Western Union just before 10 PM and sent the following telegram to Washington:

> HON FRANKLIN D. ROOSEVELT
> THE WHITE HOUSE   WASH DC
>
> YOUR SPEECH TONIGHT WAS THE MOST HUMAN I
> HAVE EVER LISTENED TO STOP I COMMEND YOU
> SIR AND CONGRATULATE THE COUNTRY
>
> PAUL BLOCK[63]

Block could hardly wait to begin working on his editorial concerning Roosevelt's talk, and started it the next day at his office on Madison Avenue; the piece ran in all of his papers 24 hours later. Block reiterated the essence of Roosevelt's speech and outlined all of the advantages of the program. He ended by stating that if the program worked it would mean a stabilization of business and constant wages for everybody; his rallying cry was: "Let's go to it."[64]

As Roosevelt raised the public's confidence, and the economy looked as though it might improve, only the most stubborn remained skeptical. Block did not. After Hugh Johnson, the perennially-rumpled, outspoken and impulsive NRA administrator – newly-named by Roosevelt – promised three million, then four million, and finally *six* million new jobs by Labor Day, Block believed that the Roosevelt administration had found the golden key to unlock the gates of prosperity so long shut for him and the rest of the country. The stock market was up, and some factories began re-hiring their laid-off workers. After Block divested himself of his publishing millstone – *The Brooklyn Standard-Union* – some of his other newspapers were, if not prospering, at least showing signs of gain.

FDR's first summer as President – 1933 – was the hottest on record. But despite the sweltering heat, the President's Re-employment Agreement was inaugurated in late August, and Block embraced it for as many of his newspapers as possible; he even emblazoned the poster of the symbol of the NRA – a blue rampant eagle upon a red background scroll, proclaiming, "We Do Our Part" – on the walls of his newsrooms, printing plants and business offices.

It's been thought by a number of Block observers that his eventual rupture with Roosevelt was as a result of the grudge that he had developed because of Roosevelt's treatment of Mayor Jimmy Walker. There is no question that Block was disenchanted by Roosevelt during the Seabury trials that forced Walker's abdication, and that Block wholeheartedly campaigned against Roosevelt in 1932, but clearly as soon as FDR was elected Block accepted and endorsed not only the man but his policies. He particularly praised and honored Roosevelt's ability to raise the country's confidence in itself.

Roosevelt reciprocated. As with Coolidge and Hoover, Block was a frequent guest in the White House during the new Roosevelt administration, and the two men continued their correspondence that had started when the 46-year-old Roosevelt was running for Governor and Block had supported him. In the first two years of FDR's Presidency, Block averaged approximately one editorial every few weeks that were, for the most part, highly positive of virtually everything that Roosevelt was doing to steer the country back on to its feet. Block was ecstatic, of course, when the Volstead Act was repealed, and although he immodestly took a certain amount of credit – through his tireless anti-Prohibition editorials over the years – for the success of bringing liquor back to the American public and the re-opening of saloons, he acknowledged Roosevelt's contribution. Block also championed the President's public work's programs, his reorganization of the banks, his request of businessmen to raise wages, and his plan of re-payment for lost bank deposits: "We, every one of us, know that in the whole country there does not live a better American than our President Franklin D. Roosevelt, and that not only does he desire to bring the nation out of the Depression, but to assist every citizen, insofar as he is able, to earn a better livelihood...we reiterate our faith in President Roosevelt's Americanism."[65]

Chapter 11
Influencing National & International Politics

Assessing the Status of Europe

Block's faith in FDR was short-lived. Starting in the summer of 1934, Block stopped his boosterism of Roosevelt and changed the way he characterized the President. Years later, Governor Herbert Lehman recalled that Block had been such a great supporter of the 1928 Roosevelt-Lehman administration in New York, that he simply did not know why Block suddenly turned against Roosevelt in the mid-'30s.[1] We do know that Block strongly believed that while promises may get you friends, it is performance that keeps them, and he began to believe that there had been a lack of meaningful accomplishment on Roosevelt's part. This began to erode his opinion of FDR. No longer did Block hold that Roosevelt was the great leader who, with the American people, had a rendezvous with destiny. Block took issue with the Wagner Bill for giving government too much regulation over the affairs of private citizens;[2] he called for Congress to limit the power of the President;[3] he charged that Roosevelt had not fulfilled his campaign promises;[4] he was wary of Roosevelt's move to massive rearmament and aid to the British; and finally, in September of 1935, Block came close to calling the President a liar when FDR, in one of his "fireside chats" on the radio, said that the economic situation was getting better. Block claimed that there were at that time close to 10 million unemployed, virtually the same number who were out of work in 1933; essentially, he continued, *nothing* had really been accomplished by the Roosevelt Administration in putting people back to work.[5] When pressed, Block conceded that the NRA did away with child labor, promoted minimum wage standards, and improved working conditions in industry.[6] What Block may not have understood was that previously-hungry people had more to eat, there were less homeless because of the various relief programs that Roosevelt had instigated, and that *per capita*, there were less people out of work because the population had increased by several million since Roosevelt took office. Nonetheless, the economic catastrophe that was the Depression was overwhelming – and not just in the United States.

In the early 1930s, the Depression had spread to much of the world. Economic hardships had combined with political instability, to create what seemed like the rumblings of war. During the summer of 1934, Paul Block steamed to Europe on the *Majestic* with his wife and two sons. It was primarily a business trip, combined with some research he wanted to do on some journalistic pieces concerning the situation in Europe; Block spent much of the time there utilizing the skills he'd developed when he was a reporter years before, and writing feature articles on his findings, which were published in all of his newspapers. As he later explained, "In my desire to study at first hand, the economic and political conditions existing today in the important countries of Europe, I made it a point to interview not only men in government and business, but working people of all classes."[7]

He had planned his key meetings way in advance, using some influential people, including Cardinal Hayes of New York, as intermediaries. Since Block was a fairly large contributor to the Catholic Church in New York, church officials were happy to exert their influence in arranging contacts. The highlights of the trip were supposed to be an interview with Adolf Hitler in Germany, with Chancellor Engelbert Dollfuss of Austria, and finally with Benito Mussolini in Italy. Circumstances in Europe changed some of his plans.

The Blocks landed in England first, and Block spoke to Members of Parliament, to businessmen, and to workers. He was impressed that the "gloom of three years ago" was gone, and pointed out that Big Ben, the most famous clock in the world, was being brightened up again with a new coat of gilt, a symbol, he said, of British recovery.[8] Indeed, in 1931 Britain had been on the verge of bankruptcy. As a reaction to that crisis, Parliamentary elections late that year had voted in a coalition, primarily a Conservative government which was much to Block's liking. His article of July 27th applauded the healthier economy and better living conditions; he even delighted in the apparent growth of the theater and film industry, and gave credit for much of these to such governmental actions as tax reductions, lowered bank rates, and other "drastic measures which

the National Government took to balance the budget" – such as reducing
the amount paid to the thousands of unemployed people. Block acknowledged that there were some pessimistic people in London who were concerned that the gains were only superficial (as indeed they proved to be),
and that there would be chaos to come, but he concluded that conditions
in England were better than in the U.S., and the country had a "new spirit
of hope."

Filled with that promise, the Blocks crossed the Channel and visited
France. It was Block's first time in the City of Light since July of 1914,
when he sat in a restaurant in an atmosphere of tense expectation. The
refrain of "worried whispers," as he described it then, was pervasive: "Is
it war?"[9] The ironic repetition of the events of twenty years before did
not escape him. Now Paris was again permeated with the same sense of
foreboding.

The Blocks stayed at the Hotel Ritz on the Place Vendôme, and in addition to taking his family sightseeing, Block ate in as many of the fine
French restaurants as time would allow. The rich French food began to
tell on Block's constitution, although he never refused just one more
Roquefort canapé or vanilla-whipped cream cake, or extra spoonful of
velouté sauce atop a sizable order of his chicken croquettes. Back in the
hotel one night, after a day of over-indulgence, he had so much indiges-
tion that he writhed in pain as Dina kept calling room service for glasses
of Bicarbonate of Soda. The next morning they argued over Block's intemperance. "O.K., I'll never do it again," Block reassured her. "I don't
believe you," Dina replied. "Give it to me in writing." And so Block
pulled a piece of hotel stationery out of the desk drawer, and penned the
following note:

Hotel Ritz   *Adresse*
Place Vendôme   *Télégraphique*
Paris   *Ritzotel – Paris*

*I, Paul Block, promise to do exactly what
I am told, by my wife Dina Block regarding
any diet, health, etc.*

                              Gladly
                              Paul –

The report Block filed from Paris a few days later was far from exult-
ant. "When I arrived at Paris from London," he wrote, "I seemed to be
transported from a clear sky of hope to a fog of gloom. Having listened
to many bright prophecies in England, it gave me a jolt to hear French
people say 'We have never been so despondent in France since the War,
and darker days are ahead.'"[10] Prices throughout France were so high
that tourism, one of the country's principal sources of income, was virtually nonexistent. He reported on the strain and "sadness" he saw throughout Paris, not only because of the Depression but because the French
were already deeply concerned that there would be another war in Europe. The week before, Austrian Nazis had murdered their Chancellor,
Englebert Dollfuss, in his office, shooting him and refusing to allow him
medical assistance or, ultimately, a priest, until he bled to death four hours
later. Dollfuss' murder was clearly traced to Hitler sympathizers. With
the more efficient aeroplane, Germany was then only five hours flying
time from Paris, and its citizens were frightened.

Nonetheless, Block's optimism won out. He convinced himself that
although France was suffering because of its serious economic problems,
which he detailed in the report, the country was not as bad off as others.
Why, then, was there such "sadness"? "Being a temperamental people,"
he reasoned, "they act, look and feel, pessimistic." He found, however,
reason for some good cheer:

> Now the French are feeling the depression and they are
> disheartened. How they can come out of it, without the pur-
> chasing power of other countries, especially for their luxury
> goods for which France is famous, is a question hard to an-
> swer at the moment.
> One thing, however, should not be forgotten. The French
> people have always been thrifty and the majority still have
> money. The farmers and their folks which comprise nearly
> half of the entire population can produce all they need to eat
> on their own patch of land and it is these farmers (or peasants
> as they are called) who give strength to the Republic of France
> and are a barrier against Socialism.[11]

Finally, Block referred to the Nazi regime as a clear threat to all of
Europe.[12] But even here, his comment is surprisingly sanguine: "Should
the Hitler government in Germany fall and be replaced by a less fanatical
regime which most Frenchmen believe will occur," as apparently did Block

himself, "sad faces will turn to smiles and with it more faith in the future and possibly better times."

Block had the prudence to have his wife and sons avoid Germany, never forgetting that he and they were Jewish. He was fully aware of Hitler's danger, and had already written editorials condemning the German government for attempting to destroy "religions and races, the stifling of free states and a free press"[13] although it is surprising that Block did not write at that time more specifically against the horrific acts that Hitler's regime had already committed against Jews. How Block, as a Jew, was given any kind of free access in Germany is a mystery. It is even more surprising that he received the government's cooperation, especially in his request to meet Hitler. Berlin was already engaged in planting the seeds of the Holocaust: Jews were being humiliated and beaten on the streets. Nazi party members were legally forbidden to shop in Jewish stores, and many products were stamped *Rein deutsches Erzeugnis* (pure German goods). Cameras and radios were forbidden to be owned by Jews. Hotels and boarding houses were not permitted to rent to Jews. Jewish-owned banks, such as the Dresdner Bank and Bleichröder's, were simply confiscated by Hitler. Since the Catholic Church helped Block to gain entry into Germany with appropriate introductions, it is possible that the German officials assumed he was Catholic also. Considering the ruthlessness of Goebbel's intelligence corps, however, Block was putting himself at risk entering Germany in 1934.

Dina and the boys drove to the south of France, and met Block later in Rome. Meanwhile, he traveled alone to Berlin for his scheduled meeting with Hitler. Germany was tense. On June 30th, just before the Blocks landed in England, Hitler had ordered a brutal "cleansing action" against some of the top people of one of his elite military groups, the SA, which was supposedly about to revolt against him. On that "night of the long knives," Hitler approved the murder of what has been estimated at between 150 and 200 people. Instigated because of political rivalry, the murders extended far beyond the leadership of the SA, and culminated with the execution of Captain Ernst Roëhm, Hitler's right-hand man. Hitler saw the crushing of the SA leadership as a demonstration to people inside and outside Germany that those who opposed his regime would pay with their lives.

For all that foreign observers were repulsed with the barbarism, many seem to have interpreted it as merely an internal affair. They still thought that in diplomatic matters, Hitler would behave as a relatively respon-

sible statesman.[14]   But the strongest force holding Hitler in check had
been Germany's ailing President, Paul von Hindenburg. Though he had
given Hitler the position of Chancellor, he retained major power for himself, including control of the army.

Block arrived in Berlin in the morning, and Hitler came to the city,
from Berchtesgaden in the Bavarian Alps, that night. Block was told by
Hitler's staff, however, that von Hindenburg was critically ill and that
Hitler could not remain in Berlin because he had to rush to Neudeck to
the President's estate in East Prussia, to discuss the succession. Block's
arranged interview of Hitler was therefore cancelled. The article that he
eventually wrote about Germany was thus based on conversations he had
with businessmen, shopkeepers, clerks and workers, and with some friends
who knew people in government. As in the rest of his journey, he also
reported on what he saw and experienced in the city. And he made several predictions of Germany's probable future.

Block noted the large proportion of uniformed men in the streets, "almost more solders and police than ordinary citizens," yet pointed out that
there was surprisingly little "Heil Hitler" salutes, and that he found that
many people were willing to speak frankly to him. The people looked
"haunted and scared," Block wrote, but he pointed out that Berlin was
still a beautiful city. He walked along the spectacular and historic *Unter
den Linden*, the boulevard that Napoleon had marched down in 1806 when
he conquered the city, and found it almost deserted.

Block stayed at the Adlon, one of the great hotels of the world, and
known as the best address in Berlin: *1 Unter den Linden*, at the corner of
Wilhelm Strasse. Its opulence epitomized Berlin and semiotically proclaimed that Germany was prosperous...at least for some. Under Hitler,
the section of the city where Block stayed had become an unofficial government quarter, *Das Regierungsviertel*, and he could see from the window of his suite such buildings as the Reich's Propaganda Ministry, and
the Ministry of Justice. Ironically, weeks before, the wealthy Jews who
lived on the streets near the Adlon, such as *Leipziger Strasse* and *Behren
Strasse*, had been forced to move, and Block found himself staying in
what was declared a *Judenfrei* zone.

Two years before, Block had seen the film *Grand Hotel,* based on Vicki
Baum's play *Menschem im Hotel*, and the film's setting was, if not based
on the Adlon, at least inspired by it. It was there that Greta Garbo, as the
character Grusinskaya, wearing sunglasses and swathed in chinchilla,
strode across the hotel lobby toward the elevators, her brow furrowed,

wanting to be alone.

Traditionally, the Adlon was where foreign dignitaries, heads of state, debutantes and rich industrialists dined, danced and dealt. Hitler was in and out of the hotel often. The German magazine *Innendekoration* called the Adlon a symbolic building which "outshone all others not only in Berlin or in Germany, but even in New York, Paris and London."[15]

One night while dining alone in the huge Rheingold at the Adlon – with its nave of a *faux* medieval cathedral – Block requested the orchestra to play some old German *völkisch*, folk songs that his mother, Mary Block, used to sing to him and his brothers and sisters when they were children. He asked the orchestra leader specifically if he knew *Roslein auf der Heide,* a romantic ballad. When the music began to play, Block noticed that many of his fellow diners began to silently cry. "I am sure the sentiment expressed through those tears," he wrote, "were not only for this old melody, but also for the old Germany, the Germany before Hitler."[16]

Still fluent in German, Block found it easy to communicate. "I have talked with government officials and taxi-drivers, with clerks and waiters, with business men and electricians. I found at least 60 percent were not of the Nazi party and a number of them seemed proud of it." One man he interviewed showed Block his pay stub. A relatively high-paid worker, his salary was 165 marks, 50 pfennigs per month; deducted from this was 21 marks for taxes, leaving him the equivalence of $60 American dollars a month, hardly enough to feed and clothe a family, let alone to see to their proper nourishment.[17] Block attributed what he perceived as an anti-Nazi feeling among some Germans to their bitterness because of Nazi assassinations of Catholic leaders and priests, and because of the very serious economic hardships in the country. He gave examples of low salaries, high prices, and higher taxes which, he felt, only naturally created disillusionment with the Hindenburg regime. Sadly, he wrote that of all of the hundreds of people he observed while he was in Berlin, he only saw two laughing.

"What surprised me, however, was also to find so many officials who are not of the Nazi party. Many of them spoke well of Hitler, but were bitter against the crowd which surrounds him, especially Goering and Goebbels."[18] To support this, Block told of a story that had been related to him by a friend who was very intimate with the former crown prince. "The crown prince claims to admire Hitler very much, but said that in some respects Hitler reminds him of his father, the former Kaiser, namely, that he is surrounded by men who do not tell him the truth." In Berlin, as in Paris, he proclaimed the city "sad."

As a publisher, Block was amazed and disheartened at what had happened with many German newspapers. Berlin had been known as the *Zeitungstadt*, the newspaper city, but by the time Block arrived in Germany the great Jewish publishers, Rudolf Mosse and Jacob Ullstein, had been virtually forced out of business. Their *Vossische Zeitung*, which had been published since 1703, making it one of the longest continually-published newspapers in the world, became Nazi property, and was "Arayanized" just a few months before Block arrived in Berlin. By law – the *Reichsschrigftellergersetz* – no Jewish journalist could work on any newspaper. No newspaper was permitted to accept advertisements for products or services sold, distributed or manufactured by Jews. Obituaries, birth or marriage notices of Jews were banned in all newspapers. Theodor Wolff, the distinguished Jewish editor of the *Berliner Tageblatt*, one of the city's most popular papers, was removed from his job.

Block wrote: "I visited the famous Herren Club, which is now called the German Club. It is here that the real conservatives meet regularly and where the plans for the downfall of Hitler may still be arranged." Block then predicted that:

> The death of Hindenburg will no doubt strengthen Hitler's power at first, but will probably prove his undoing in the end. The Conservative people, though they are scared and pale at the moment, will eventually show their true feelings, especially if some leader arises who has the courage to fight Hitler …
>
> It is the consensus of opinion that this new leader will be a military man and that with the fall of Hitler there will be a military dictatorship for a period and then a limited monarchy with the Crown Prince or one of his sons as the titular head.
>
> There may be much bloodshed before this occurs, but that a change is on the way, seems as certain as death. The German people are awakening, and before long they will trample on the assassins and atheists who at the moment are in control.[19]

The day after Block wrote that piece, von Hindenburg died. Adolf Hitler assumed von Hindenburg's position as President, also retaining his own role as Chancellor. In effect, he was now functioning as Kaiser, President and Parliament, both legislator and executive, and commander in chief of the army as well.

Block continued his journey by train, heading southeast, and reaching Vienna a few days later. What he found there was a city under martial law. He stayed at the almost-empty Bristol Hotel, one the city's finest, where there seemed to be more managers and clerks in frock coats, and more porters and page-boys, than there were guests. As he unpacked in his room, he saw from his balcony a huge crowd gathering in front of the Opera House. A military band began playing the Austrian National Anthem, and people slowly bared their heads. It was not a holiday or special occasion, Block discovered later, simply a daily routine of national obeisance promulgated more out of fear than chauvinism or pride. The city, even more than Berlin, took on the atmosphere of an armed camp.

He made a tour of the famous Viennese coffee houses, but where there had been literally thousands of them, many with sidewalk cafes, there were now only hundreds. He could find none that had music. The Viennese still sipped their coffee, "but the laughter and the smiles are gone," as Block described it.[20] The Café Central, where Lenin and Trotsky plotted the October Russian Revolution, and the great Wilhelm Steinitz played chess, was still there but practically empty.[21]

Within a few days, Block was given a private audience by Austria's new Chancellor, Kurt von Schuschnigg. They met in the same rooms of the Ballhaus in which the former Chancellor Dollfuss had been assassinated. Since Austria was under martial law, the building and street around it were protected by a regiment of heavily armed soldiers. As Block entered the building, there was a soldier, with steel helmet, rifle and sabre, on nearly every other step of the staircase. Block found the new Chancellor, who had been the Minister of Education, to be a highly educated and cultured man who "spoke very frankly." Schuschnigg explained the need for martial law and for a prohibition against political parties "...because of the necessity of having all factions working together in harmony and patriotism for all Austria,"[22] and assured that new elections would be held in October or November. Block wrote that "The new Chancellor Schuschnigg is a man of the finest character, intellectual and just." Yet again, Block found the population to be demoralized.

Aware that Austria's survival was in great peril, Block nonetheless found loyalists who had faith in the future and talked of a time of peace after the Nazis were "eliminated." He realized that Austria's prospects were largely dependent on outside forces. "As I see it," he wrote, "the future of Austria depends on the Great Powers. That England, Italy and France desire to keep it an independent State, of this there is very little doubt, but any false step by Hitler may make of Austria a battleground such as Serbia was in 1914." [23]

Heading south, Block rejoined his family in Rome: Italy was to be the last visit of this trip, and for him the high point. "I had the honored privilege of a visit with the great Mussolini today," he wrote on August 12th. "I think it was the most interesting interview I ever had." Block's son William remembers his father telling the family about the interview, and said that Block "was very much impressed" by Mussolini, though throughout the time he was alone with the dictator, he kept feeling that he was "being watched from hidden observation points." [24]

Block was not alone in being impressed by the physically powerful, charismatic leader, who despite his dictatorial methods still retained respect among many foreign countries. Mussolini's rigid government effected some efficiencies in Italy, and until he took aggressive moves against other countries in 1935, a surprising number of people admired him. Some of these were people close to Paul Block. New York's Mayor Jimmy Walker visited Italy in 1927, to see the Pope – and Mussolini. Grove Patterson, editor of the *Toledo Blade*, met with the dictator in 1932, and reported afterwards that Mussolini had interviewed *him*. And Hearst, too, had visited Mussolini and later declared: "He is a marvelous man. It is astonishing how he takes care of every detail of his job." [25]

Benito Mussolini had named himself *Il Duce*, or leader, of the National Fascist Party, and Italy's Parliament had granted him full control in 1922. His usurpation of power had been an inspiration for the then-fledgling Nazi Party in Germany, where Hitler was proclaimed "Germany's Mussolini." [26] Yet the two dictators had very different goals, at first. Once a newspaperman, Mussolini had been the editor of *Avanti*, the paper of the Milan Socialist Party prior to the first World War. But as a Fascist, he and his black-shirted members fiercely rejected Communism, and adhered to radical right principles that glorified the state and subordinated individuals to state authority. Declaring religion "indispensable," *Il Duce* reached an accord with the Vatican in 1931. In 1933 he signed a non-aggression pact with the U.S.S.R., and called FDR a dictator. But he had not yet declared Italy as an ally of Germany. Indeed, Mussolini and Hitler had never even met until 1934, in Venice, just two months before Block's trip.

Up until that summer of 1934, Mussolini had been considered a "reasonable" leader. The bombastic outbursts of temper came later, as did his invasions of Africa. During his first decade in power, it appears in retrospect that *Il Duce* was attempting to prevent the war that he saw as inevitable. Balancing politics precariously, he tried to side with the United States, Great Britain and France, which had been Italy's allies during WWI, while supporting some of the countries that he felt had been treated unfairly by the Peace Treaties. Though Germany had warred against Italy, it was now suffering the huge burden of reparations payments, made even more difficult by the Depression. Mussolini warned numerous times that unless the Treaty of Versailles (1919) was modified, there would be "not only revolution in Germany but war in Europe."[27] Europe's leaders finally agreed that the debt was too high to be feasible, and recommended at the Lausanne Conference to reduce Germany's payments. However, the pact could not be made final until the United States agreed to it. Paul Block wrote an editorial in July of 1932, urging that the administration support the European recommendations. He said of Germany that: "Debts are sacred obligations, but if past obligations interfere with the present and future peace and prosperity of the world, then we believe America will not wish to stand out alone."[28]

In 1933 Mussolini proposed that the United States, Great Britain, France and Germany have a Four Power Pact. His theory was that the four could carry out "peaceful revision," with Italy and Great Britain acting as mediators between France and Germany. This might have placated Germany, and would doubtless have helped Italy as well. With a somewhat revived Germany, it would have been easier for Italy to gain some of the concessions from France that Mussolini had been seeking. But the assassination of Austrian Chancellor Dollfuss made Mussolini lose all compassion for Germany's legitimate complaints. Hitler's ambitions were unquenchable. Mussolini changed his stance, and advocated a firm stand against Germany's growing aggression. He maintained a position of protective caution against Hitler for the next two years.

Mussolini's headquarters were in the *Palazzo Venezia* in Rome. A magnificent building, *Il Duce* had selected a particularly grandiose room for meeting – and impressing and intimidating – his guests. Its vast ceiling was supported by marble columns, its floor decorated with elaborate tile work, and at the far end was an immense fireplace large enough to hold two dozen men standing up. As Block was shown into this enormous room, which he estimated to be about 100 feet long and half as wide, the size of an auditorium, he saw only two pieces of furniture in the far, far corner: a small flat-topped desk, which held a lamp, and a seven foot candelabra. And behind it, the room's only chair, in which sat Italy's leader. Like other visitors, Block was forced to walk what must have felt like an interminable distance across the room, as Mussolini rose and stood waiting. During the interview, he continued to stand, sometimes leaning against the wall, while Block stood near his desk.

Many of the photographs Block had seen of the dictator showed *Il Duce* in his characteristic pose, dressed in the black shirt and gray uniform of the Fascist Militia, with his hands on his hips, his legs apart, his overly-large jaw and barrel chest thrust aggressively forward. He appeared to be a big, powerful man. As Block came close, he saw to his amazement that Mussolini was only of medium height – 5-foot-six-inches tall, Block's own height. Mussolini was dressed in a white linen suit, instead of his usual military uniform, and Block, to his own surprise, found him to be a "gentle, smiling, courteous host, but with a personality which would be difficult to match." They conversed in English. Aware that Block had been travelling across Europe, Mussolini asked many questions about the economic conditions in the countries Block had visited, and asked what conditions were like in the United States. When Block reported that he had found conditions in England to be far better than elsewhere, even better than in the U.S., Mussolini asked how Block accounted for that. Block praised the election that had brought the British Conservative Party into power, and then suggested that the mental attitude of the British people, inspired by their faith and confidence in their new government, was largely responsible for promoting a revival in business. That was one of Block's chief beliefs. Lack of such confidence led, he felt, to the sadness he had seen in France, Germany and Austria, and which he greatly feared at home. Mussolini agreed.

The two discussed many subjects, and Block reported that "I cannot remember when I have had the privilege of talking so openly and frankly to a person of his rank. Certainly not with most of our executives in Washington." They spoke of Mussolini's experiences as an editor and publisher "and his courageous efforts in fighting, through his newspaper, brainless and dishonest politicians." Ultimately that gave Block the opening to ask, as diplomatically as possible, what he knew to be a potentially insulting question.

> I told him that he certainly must know of the great loyalty
> and devotion his countrymen have for him. I told him, if I
> recognized this in the cities and villages which I had visited,

surely he must know these facts better than I. He smiled and thanked me. I then said, 'Why not therefore give to your people the thing that is most precious to all civilization, the thing that will bring you the applause of the whole world – a free press?' Mussolini smiled and said slowly: 'Mr. Block, we have a free press, but, when an editor writes something that we feel would hurt our people, then we call his attention to it.'

It was my turn to smile, having learned that [in Italy] the newspaper writer's attention to a story is usually called even before it is written and so I said, 'Well, Your Excellency, let us trust that in the very near future, newspapers in your country will be permitted to publish news and editorial expressions, to which the editors' attention will not be called, either before or after the story has appeared.'

We shook hands as heartily as if we had been old friends and I withdrew, leaving behind me a man whom I consider the greatest personality of the present century.[29]

Block's article went on to praise the improvements in Italy – the new roads, bridges, electric power houses, railroad stations, and trains that now ran on regular schedules. He found numerous factors that were better than they had been before World War I. For Block, one of the most significant features was that although Italy was affected by the Depression that had spread around the world,

> ...people seem quite willing to accept the bitter with the sweet because of their great faith in Il Duce. Talk to them, and they will admit that their salaries are low and their taxes high; that they eat meat only once or twice a week, living on spaghetti, noodles and vegetables... They will tell you they are certain that when Mussolini has finished his work, they will be the richest people in the world! By this they mean the happiest, and from appearances one would imagine that the majority have reached that goal already....
>
> ...Il Duce has done many things, some good, some questionable, but one thing is sure, he has imbued the citizens of Italy with faith and loyalty toward their homeland.[30]

At the end of this, the last article written during his European trip, Block summarized his attitude toward Mussolini and Hitler, with some rather strange commentary on the FDR administration. Reflecting on the "happiness" he saw among Italian people, he was reminded of "the mental change which came to the great majority of the American people right after Franklin Roosevelt was elected President. The only difference is that many of our citizens have lost faith in our administration, whereas the Italian people are stronger for Mussolini today than ever before."[31] Block reassured his readers that despite Mussolini's accomplishments, "I am no more a fascist today than I was before I came to Italy," and speculated that while a dictatorship might have been necessary in Italy after the war, "this does not mean any kind of dictatorship was or is necessary in the United States." He concluded:

> After observing the conditions in the various countries I have just visited, I am convinced more than ever, that what we need in the United States is "progressive conservatism" and not communism, Hitlerism, Fascism or "theorism," such as we are to a degree receiving today at the hands of the young experimenters who hold authoritative positions in our administration at Washington.[32]

Block was clearly disillusioned with Roosevelt. When he returned to New York at the end of August, on the *Conte de Savoia*, several reporters interviewed him about the conditions he had found in Europe. His first comment was sarcastic: "I was happy to note this morning that the Statue of Liberty was still here. I was afraid the New Dealers might have torn it down and when I saw it still standing I uttered a prayer of thanks."[33]

Paul Block was certainly a loyal American. He seems, though, to have been at least somewhat naïve in his interpretation of international political issues. He recognized Hitler as a despot, but felt that the German people would themselves defeat him politically. As early as the spring of 1933, he had written: "Sooner or later, when they [the German people] find that millions upon millions of people all over the world will no longer buy goods made in Germany, they will rise and crush this poisonous regime which is trying to make a barbaric people out of the cultured German nation."[34] A year later he still hadn't really changed his mind about the future of Germany.

He admired Mussolini, who just a few weeks after Block met him went on to warn Italians to prepare for war, and began to colonize Albania; early the next year, *Il Duce* began invading Ethiopia and other African countries. Hitler, hoping the world would be distracted by these events in Africa, supported Mussolini's invasions, and the two dictators drafted a treaty of alliance in the fall of 1936.

One of Block's greatest oversights, though, was his likening of some of Franklin D. Roosevelt's New Deal policies to Adolf Hitler's views. When Henry Wallace, FDR's Secretary of Agriculture, proposed an Agricultural Adjustment Act that would give his department the power to tell farmers – who were being given benefit payments for crop reduction – what crops they could plant, and set up a licensing system for all food producers, distributors and handlers, Block was incensed.

> Anyone who believes in freedom for individuals in their personal and business affairs must oppose such extraordinary restraints upon the liberty of our people. Those who have adopted the extreme views of the communists or the Hitlerites, may favor such restrictions upon American initiative, but liberty-loving Americans are not yet ready to believe that the broad program of economic recovery sponsored by the President, and so loyally supported by the great masses of our people, call for any such communistic interference by the government in the affairs of private citizens.[35]

In Block's passion for *laissez faire* policy, he rejected any Federal control over American business, and interpreted any restriction as an encroachment of freedom.

FDR's Revelation to Block

Strangely, even while Block was criticizing Roosevelt, and millions of his readers were being exposed to his negative views of the President, the two men still continued if not a rapport, at least a friendly personal truce. Block's request for a private luncheon at the White House with the President was usually granted within a week of the call, and their conversations took on a free-form style touching upon all of the areas that interested either man.[36] Roosevelt was extremely charming, cordial and sympathetic toward Block, listening with rapt attention for a few minutes and then breaking in with a series of questions, which became progressively sharper and more astute as he went on. Since Roosevelt was crippled and his mobility was circumscribed, every visitor to him became an informant of the world "outside," and Block fulfilled that role each time they met. Whenever Block was in Washington, usually staying at the Carlton Hotel, he would often stop off at the White House and see Roosevelt, sometimes only for a few minutes, and then they would simply concentrate on just one issue or an exchange of friendly gossip.[37] Roosevelt thought of starting his own newspaper when he retired, one that contained no advertisements or editorials – only news – and he liked to talk to Block about the dynamics and possibilities of the newspaper publishing business.[38]

At one meeting, Block asked the President if he would give American business a respite for six months, without all of the bureaucratic entanglements, government regulations, and bills that Congress was threatening. In effect, Block was asking Roosevelt to give American business a brief moratorium on further reform, and especially on levying more taxes. Block went on to say that the laws and measures being planned by FDR's Administration were more concerned with establishing long-term reform than immediate recovery. Roosevelt's "second" New Deal, as outlined in his annual message to Congress in January of 1935, was enormously popular with the workers and the average citizen. His major goals were security of livelihood through the better use of national resources; security against unemployment, old age, illness and dependency; and slum clearance and better housing. The chief beneficiaries of Roosevelt's plans were labor and the smaller farmers.[39] Block pointed out that the President was not doing enough for business. "Why not give Industry a period of six months in which to make good?" he asked. Roosevelt listened but was not willing to concede the very fabric of the political philosophy of his Presidency. Reform, and help for the little man, was what the New Deal was all about.

A few weeks later, Block published an open letter to Roosevelt, making the same points that he had made at their meeting, and ending with the following plea: "We have had over five years of Depression now. Many experiments have been undertaken, but not this one, to let Industry alone for a few months. Will you try it out, Mr. President?"[40] Roosevelt never responded.

Their relationship continued, however. They were scheduled to have a private luncheon on May 29, 1935. But although it had been confirmed, after Block read *The New York Times* on the morning of the 27th, he thought the appointment with the President would have to be cancelled. The Supreme Court had just delivered a major set-back to Roosevelt's New Deal, ruling unanimously in *Schechter Poultry Corp. v. United States* that the President's National Recovery Act of 1933 was unconstitutional, holding that Congress had given virtually "unfettered powers" to the NRA, and that this was "utterly inconsistent" with their jurisdiction and power.[41]

Block, feeling that Roosevelt might be embarrassed or uncomfortable to meet him under the circumstances, immediately called Marvin McIntyre, one of the President's secretaries, to determine whether FDR wanted to cancel the impending lunch, or postpone it for a later date. After checking with the President, McIntyre called Block and told him that on the contrary, the President looked forward to having the luncheon and also wanted to discuss the controversial Supreme Court ruling with him.[42] Roosevelt had been taken by surprise by the Supreme Court dictum; it appeared that he had no alternative plans ready.

Just weeks before Block's luncheon with the President, William Randolph Hearst had written Edmond D. Coblentz, his veteran editor of the *New York American*, to formally solidify his opposition to Roosevelt: "I think we will have to settle down to a consistent policy of opposition to this Administration." Hearst was infuriated by the Roosevelt experimentalists because they demanded that decentralizing and re-distributing the wealth was a necessity.[43] Block was equally irked by the Administration's policy of exhausting the proprietary and supervisory class in order to support what he considered to be a dependent class. Although, during the preparation of this book, no documentation could be found in either the Hearst or Block archives, or anywhere else, that would prove that Hearst applied pressure, intimidation or influence on Block relative to the New Deal, it would seem likely that Hearst could have sent a letter to Block at the *Pittsburgh Post-Gazette*, (similar to the letter he sent to Coblentz), dictating an anti-Roosevelt policy. That Block and Hearst reached a consensus respectively on their own on the evils of Franklin Delano Roosevelt, also seems likely. Both men feared the social consequences of the New Deal: a diminution of their power as business leaders, with more control going to the working class.

For his May luncheon with Block, Roosevelt decided to dine *al fresco* since the weather was mild. The table was already set with hot and cold dishes when Block was escorted to the White House porch exactly at noon on that Wednesday. Within a few minutes, President Roosevelt arrived, wheeled in his specially-made chair. Block stood, they shook hands, greeted each other, and moved to the table. After the waiters had poured the wine and served the food, they left, quietly closing the French doors behind them. The two men were alone, and began to talk.[44] Block went right to the issue at hand, a discussion of the story that was headlines on the front pages of every newspaper in the country, including all of his: the Supreme Court ruling on the illegality of the NRA. Roosevelt told Block that he was very "displeased" at the ruling but that he did not intend to abandon the principles of the NRA, even if it had to be organizationally disbanded.[45] As the afternoon went on, Block saw that Roosevelt's displeasure could be better described as dismay, perhaps even outrage. Elaborating further, Roosevelt stated that he had reached the limit of his tolerence with the Supreme Court, a group of nine men who were all over 60 years old and generally conservative, including four who Roosevelt described as "Tories." He had come to regard the Court as a cabal, or a clique, thwarting the will of the people.[46] The whole judicial system had to be overhauled, he said angrily. "What are you going to do, Mr. President?" asked Block.

Roosevelt then revealed a possible solution to how he might confront his dilemma. As Block listened, amazed, the President related an analogy: When William Gladstone, the liberal 19th-century Chancellor of the Exchequer and Prime Minister of England, was anxious to have the House of Lords pass the Irish land act, he was at first vote defeated. He went to King Edward VII and discussed the matter with him, and the King reluctantly agreed to limit the veto power of the House of Lords by naming two hundred new members of the peerage, all hand picked and politically obliged to vote as they were directed.[47]

Another version of the Block luncheon and the House of Lords story was related by a biographer of Roosevelt, Frank Friedel. He claimed that Roosevelt told Block not of Gladstone, but of Lord Asquith. In that version Asquith had forced the balking House of Lords to pass a health and unemployment insurance program in 1911 by threatening to create a sufficient number of peers to carry the measure.[48] Whatever the true construct of the story, Roosevelt made what turned out to be an imprudent and ill-judged commentary about what he might do with the Supreme Court to Paul Block, a growing enemy.

Roosevelt looked at Block with a cunning grin, cigarette holder clenched between his teeth, as he intimated that he might have to follow Gladstone's example, but that in any event, he would have to wait until the next year's nominations and elections were over before he could act. Block knew what Roosevelt was driving at, and he could barely believe what he had heard: Roosevelt wanted the Judicial branch of government to be made subservient to the Executive branch. In effect he was calling not for a judicial readjustment, but an enlargement of his own powers, a move to establish the sovereignty of the Presidency. Block felt that Roosevelt should not have been surprised by the Supreme Court ruling, citing the opinions of leading lawyers that the Blue Eagle would eventually be ruled out on Constitutional grounds. Many employers had already begun to violate the National Labor Relations Act, which indicated how confident they were that the Supreme Court would invalidate much of the NRA. The fact that the nine Justices were unanimous in their decision also proved how clear cut the issue was, Block pointed out.[49] What he was thinking but did not say to Roosevelt was that the Supreme Court reversal might prove auspicious for the Republicans in the coming 1936 elections.

One wonders why Roosevelt chose Paul Block to be among the first people in the nation that he would tell of his secret plan to "pack" the Supreme Court, knowing that Block would evince a strong conservative objection to any such measure. Also, the press-astute Roosevelt would not have been confused into thinking that the luncheon was "off the record" unless he had established those parameters at the outset. Roosevelt would, or should have known that Block, as a newspaper man, would assuredly publicize the essence of the President's comments, knowing as he did that what Roosevelt had said to him was front-page news.

Before Block had a chance to decide what to do about the news, however, the very next day Roosevelt told a similar story to those assembled at the Newspaper Men's Conference. Although Block was invited to the Conference, other business matters took him from Washington, and he only heard, secondhand, that Roosevelt had alluded to the Gladstone story, but was much more vague than he had been with Block about his possible re-adjustment of the judiciary.[50] Perhaps because his meaning had been so obscure, at first nothing appeared in any newspaper concerning Roosevelt's planned manipulations.

Summer in London, 1935: The Wager

During that summer, Block went to Europe again with Dina and 21-year-old Billy, who had been attending Yale as a history major. Though Billy had studied the European situation, and father and son read newspapers daily to keep up with the changing circumstances, they were all taken aback by the reality of what they saw around them. Europe seemed to be exploding: Greece was under military rule; Austrian freedom was conceded by Hitler under a pact he signed with Chancellor Kurt von Schusnigg; Spain was engaged in a civil war; Paris had many injured as police battled rightists; England was preparing for war and a mass manufacture of gas masks was taking place.

In England, the Blocks were guests of the "Imp of Fleet Street," Lord

Beaverbrook, who was becoming a close friend of Paul Block. Block met with the British publisher in Beaverbrook's mammoth suite at the Hyde Park Hotel, and the family was invited to his country home, Cherkely Court, in Leatherhead, a short drive from London in the lush English countryside known as North Downs. Cherkely was a huge, antiquated mansion, a magnificent estate somewhat on par with the royal family's Sandringham Castle, to which it was compared. The grounds were lush and awe-inspiring, with a winding driveway and to the great pride of Beaverbrook, every kind of tree grown in England studding the property. Cherkely had a private screening room, and so many other amenities that Beaverbrook spent most of his time there, rather than in London. He would go weeks without visiting his own newspaper office.

As a widowed host, Beaverbrook was known for holding some of the most scintillating and exquisite dinner parties in the United Kingdom. Winston Churchill and other members of Parliament would often sup at Beaverbrook's table, partially to gain electoral support from the press lord but mainly for his hospitality.

One particular dinner party given by Beaverbrook was especially memorable for the Blocks. The guest list included, among others, Viscount Castleross, one of the most popular columnists in London at that time; George Creel, the American journalist/editor who was a member of the national Advisory Board of Roosevelt's WPA, and who was on a fact-finding mission to England; and H.G. Wells, the novelist and journalist noted for his prescient science-fiction novels. At the very time that the Blocks met Wells, his film *Things to Come,* for which he wrote the screenplay based on his novel *The Shape of Things to Come* (1933), was being screened all over London. The film was a strange combination of Wellsian pessimism (he predicted that there would be a World War II which would last 30 years) versus a utopian view of how science can triumph over the dark forces of evil. It was the most ambitious science fiction film since *Metropolis* and the greatest sound film of that genre made to that date.[51]

Beaverbrook and Wells had known each other for years. In the early 1920s, Wells wrote a five-part series for Beaverbrook in his *Sunday Express*, describing a visit he had made to the relatively-new Soviet Union. Circulation increased by 80,000 as a result and Beaverbrook was forever thankful.[52] Wells also included a Beaverbrookian character, not quite as colorful as the real Beaverbrook, in a number of his novels such as *Men Like Gods.*[53]

William Block remembers that when Wells arrived at Cherkely, he told everyone that because of a dental problem he was having, he could not have any alcohol, probably because of the pain-killing drug he was taking. When a tray of martinis was served, however, the short, portly, small-footed man announced in a high-pitched voice that he would take one after all. "We thought you weren't drinking," someone said. "I'm not," replied Wells. "I just want to look at it." And William Block said he placed the glass on a table near him, and looked at it longingly throughout the evening.[54]

Beaverbrook was addicted to making grand pronouncements, and one that he would make that evening concerned his opinion – wrongful as it turned out to be – that there would be no outright war in Europe because England, France, Russia and Poland would align against Germany, and Hitler would be afraid to march against the weight of those countries.

Eventually, the discussion came around to American politics. Wells held forth. He had interviewed Roosevelt at the White House in 1934, and although the President spoke with frankness to him, he did not tell Wells anything other than what was popular knowledge about the New Deal or the true political situation in the United States. Wells described Roosevelt as a revolutionary character, and in an article that he wrote for *Liberty Magazine* soon after his talk in Washington, Wells predicted that Roosevelt would be overthrown. Now, two years later, he was shifting his opinion: Roosevelt, according to Wells, could bring about a revolution in American thought without necessarily provoking a revolutionary crisis.[55]

Speculation rang out as to whether Roosevelt would be elected to a second term. When Wells asked the others to predict the outcome of the election, Creel, a member of Roosevelt's administration, said he believed that Roosevelt would take 42 states and lose only six. Block, of course, disagreed. Alf Landon would be the next President, he contended; Roosevelt would be defeated. Wells said he was willing to take a wager that Roosevelt would win – $100, if anyone dared accept. Block said immediately, "I'll take it." Then Viscount Castleross spoke up: "Not so fast, Mr. Block. I'd like a piece of that." Block chuckled and said, "Wait a minute, gentlemen. I'm not a bookie!" The always-facile-with-words-Wells turned and gibed: "Not a bookie, Mr. Block, a philanthropist."[56]

Revealing Roosevelt's Plans

That summer, Block took Friendship on a tour of the mid-Western and far-Western states, almost as though he was running for office himself, and talked to as many people as he could find "in all the political and economic conditions of the nation." The trip was a mirror image duplicate of another journey he had made around the country in the late spring of 1934. Talking to businessmen, editors, farmers, factory workers, railroad men and others, Block explored the differences that one year had made in the public's perception of the Administration. He revealed what he had learned in a radio address:

> At that time [1934] I found a strong undercurrent of distrust and skepticism among businessmen toward the Administration's effort to spend our way to prosperity! The working people, however, were still hopeful that the New Deal experiments might succeed. As far as the farmers, most of them seemed satisfied, especially those who had benefited materially from AAA subsidies.
>
> I have [now] found a striking change in sentiment. Not only is business stronger than ever against the New Deal but workers in both industry and agriculture, who were previously either satisfied or "on the fence," are definitely turning against it! And it is most interesting to note how very clear-visioned these workers are on existing problems today and for the future.
>
> The President is weaker today than at any time since his election. Of this there is not a question of doubt.[57]

Ten weeks went by before Block made any public allusion to his private meeting with Roosevelt, and the President's implication that he might make attempts to pack the Supreme Court. On August 11th, Block's friend Herbert Hoover made a statement in Chicago to the effect that the nation had a right to know whether the Administration was contemplating any changes in the Constitution.[58] Block followed Hoover's statement with a brief editorial that, without revealing everything he knew, simply asked a question: "Not only Mr. Hoover but all our citizens have a right to ask what changes the President proposes to have made in the Constitution and if it is true that he plans to "pack" the Supreme Court as he recently, but privately, intimated."[59]

A few weeks later, Block published a fairly long editorial on the U.S. Constitution, asking Americans not to take for granted the privileges that are offered by the Bill of Rights. He eloquently wrote: "Only one who has lived for awhile in the whispering fear that permeates the cities, the towns, the villages – the very homes – in Germany, Russia, Italy, and some other nations across the seas, can understand the tragedy that lies in the death of freedom. It is as though the candle of man's spirit has been extinguished. It is as though the light of his eyes has gone out."[60] To emphasize his point, Block published the Constitution in full in the *Post-Gazette* and several of his other papers.

When it became clear that Roosevelt would be re-nominated and possibly re-elected for a second term, Block decided to do everything he could to stop him, even to the point of writing Roosevelt, and trying to convince him that another term would not be to his advantage: "I have wondered more than once why men accept such heavy burdens and responsibilities and are willing to continue them for so many added years, via a re-election."[61]

Then, in what developed to be one of the most scathing attacks ever conducted against the New Deal, Block spoke before a group of 150 lawyers and judges, and the Mayor of Toledo, at a Bar Association dinner at the Commodore Perry Hotel on December 3, 1935. Frank S. Lewis, who was an officer in the Toledo Bar Association, and the attorney who had been so instrumental in the *Toledo Blade* Talmadge-Buggie affair, introduced Block as a "personal acquaintance and friend" who had shown constant concern over the welfare and affairs of the city. Making allusion to the importance and quality of newspapers to the civic life of Toledo, Lewis then turned the lectern over to Block.[62]

Block referred to the city of Toledo for just a moment, stating that he had just celebrated his 28th anniversary of association with the *Toledo Blade*, and that it was this alliance with the newspaper that brought him into touch with the life of the city. Continuing, Block realized that the assembled crowd would be more interested in what he had to say about the national scene rather than the vagaries of local politics. He led up to it smoothly:

> If there ever was an invitation which I should have refused it is the one that your committee was good enough to send to me, asking me to dine with you and to say a few words to you. I certainly have looked forward to dining with you, but to speak to a body of orators such as most attorneys are, is really out of order...but now that I am here, I am wondering what I can say that may be of interest to you...I suppose the most important subject under discussion today is the coming election...[63]

Block then inveighed against Roosevelt, and attempted to show how the New Deal was putting the country in peril. He made several major points:

- As a boy, I had been brought up to have the greatest respect for the President of the United States. In those days I never felt it was right to criticize the head of our nation and these ideals grew up with me and I suppose in later years I kept my peace when inwardly I felt that even a President can be wrong. But I can't sit aside any longer. I want to shout from the housetops. I want everyone to learn what I have been learning and to see what is going on as I have seen it.
- Today it just seems impossible not to find fault with most of the actions of the New Dealers. The things that they do are so fantastic and also so tragic that it just seems out of order to sit by and let them carry on.
- Most of it would seem humorous if it weren't tragic and most of it we might excuse as unfortunate, if it was not leading us to socialism and even communism.
- I say to you that our President is surrounded by men just as dangerous and just as anxious to overthrow our democratic form of government as were the Mussolinis, the Hitlers and the Stalins who overthrew their form of government.
- It is no longer a matter of reform versus recovery, but state socialism versus American traditions and institutions.
- We must write and speak, yes, shout out and clearly explain to all who will listen, what these dangers are, so that the Frankfurter boys, the Tugwells, and the rest of the radical socialists and communists will be eliminated from public life.
- Everybody who makes any money is now working eight months out of the year for the government, and who is able to do this indefinitely?
- Ask any housewife and she will tell you how much more it costs her today to run her house. Every article of food is from 10 percent to 60 percent higher than it was a year ago.
- Mr. Roosevelt *can* be defeated.

The audience that Block was addressing was known to be split down the middle politically, half Republicans, half Democrats, and so the applause was sporadic and inconsistent after any given statement. A consensus of laughter did occur, however, when Block talked of the Administration's fiscal irresponsibility, citing specific projects in which the government was squandering some of the citizens' tax money. Among the examples were $208,000 for a survey to determine the character of certain peculiar aromas in New York City; $12,000 to repair leaks in abandoned artesian wells in New Mexico; $500,000 for instruction in general housework in St. Louis. Although he did not put a dollar figure on it, Block said one of the most ridiculous expenditures that had been made was for a study to search worthless birth and death records in the state of Michigan. "This last enterprise," Block continued, "unwittingly repaid the public for the large sum expended with the information that Mae West had a husband." Applause was strongest when he told the group: "What can and must be done is to rid ourselves of the insanity that hovers within the Administration."

Block interrupted his own speech by asking the dozen or so members of the press who were present whether they would put down their pencils since what he was about to say was "in confidence." It seemed in an instant that the entire audience grew markedly more attentive in anticipation of what he was going to divulge. "This is not for publication," he stage-whispered conspiratorially, and he then went on to relate in detail the meeting he had with the President in May, Roosevelt's comments about the Supreme Court, his allusion to how Gladstone "packed" the House of Lords, and FDR's implication that he would do the same with the Court. Most of the audience was both astounded and numbed by the revelation.

Back on the record, Block concluded his speech by dramatically holding up a copy of the full-page editorial that he had inserted in *The New York Times,* seven years before in 1928, that backed Roosevelt in his campaign for Governor of New York State. Ruefully, Block said: "I know of course that others did more than I did, but if by chance my editorials and my work helped to make him Governor, which position, of course, is responsible for making him President, then I shall ask our Heavenly Father to forgive me this great error."[64] This last statement made headlines around the country.

Remarkably, the press honored Block's plea for confidentiality, and although his speech was covered widely in the nation's press, and by the wire services, not a word was published then about Roosevelt and the Supreme Court. The next day, however, at least one member of the audience wrote to Roosevelt, giving an almost word-for-word account of Block's confidential story.[65] Roosevelt was furious when he heard about what he considered to be Block's indiscreet remarks, and in a matter of days he had Stephen T. Early, the Press Secretary to the President, look into the matter. Early wrote to Block and asked whether it was true that Block had given an account, as they had learned, of the "private conversation and luncheon," and, if so, whether the details as given to them were accurate. Block responded, in part:

> I did not, at any time, understand that the story told to me by the President was a confidential one...I am sorry if the President feels that I quoted from a confidential story. It is not my custom to do this and I wish to repeat again that I at no time, understood this story (which is not quoted correctly in your letter) to be confidential.[66]

Thereafter, the correspondence was dropped, the issue temporarily shelved until 1937, and Paul Block became intensely *persona non grata* in Roosevelt's White House.

Backing Alf Landon Against Roosevelt

A few days after his tirade in Toledo, and after attending to some necessary *Toledo Blade* business, Block boarded "Friendship," his private railroad car, for a trip to Topeka, Kansas, to meet the Governor of the State, Alfred M. Landon. He stopped off first in Chicago to join two colleagues, who were also traveling by train. William Randolph Hearst was riding in a specially-leased Pullman, along with his famed columnist and editor Arthur Brisbane. Cissy Patterson, the editor of the *Washington Herald*, arrived in her own private car, "Ranger." The three cars were then attached to the Santa Fe Limited, which pulled them to Topeka. The powerful group of newspaper publishers had agreed to travel together to give themselves the opportunity to talk politics. They were headed to Topeka to try to determine whether they should support what was beginning to look like Landon's 1936 run against Roosevelt for the Presidency of the United States.

Landon had been twice-elected Governor of Kansas. A lawyer and a businessman, he had been associated with the progressive faction of the Republican party for close to 25 years. Although he and Block both attended the famed Bull Moose party's Chicago convention in 1912, they had never met. Landon had been elected in 1932 to his first term as

Governor despite the Democratic sweep of that year, and did even better in the non-presidential year of 1934, becoming the sole Republican gubernatorial incumbent in the nation to be re-elected. This phenomenal political feat made Landon a leading contender to challenge Roosevelt in 1936.[67]

"Alf" (as he was known to everybody) Landon invited the four millionaire publishers to lunch at the plain wood-framed Governor's Mansion, and the cordial Landon put himself on display. He introduced his wife and two children, and rode his two-year-old son around the living room on his shoulders. Then he and his guests sat down to lunch and an exchange of ideas. Dubbed both "The Kansas Lincoln" and "The Kansas Coolidge," Landon did actually split logs like Honest Abe, but he was tight with money, and as Block discovered, wasn't similar to Coolidge in any other way. Less reticent in conversation, he was much more impassioned than Coolidge, more out-going, homespun and friendly.[68] "Genuine" is a word that Block used to describe the made-in-middle-America Landon. "Blandly ineffectual" and "guileless and lacking in color," however, were other observations that were being made across the country.

Hearst's views of the incumbent President had been made public for more than two years, and that autumn he had attacked Roosevelt's "foreign, fascist ideas of personal dictation."[69] Hearst came to think of Landon as an able and direct man whose old shoe quality might galvanize the country against the glib and urbane aristocrat that was Franklin D. Roosevelt. "I think he's marvelous," he said. "Landon can be nominated and elected." When asked her opinion, Mrs. Patterson simply said, "Mr. Landon is simply grand."[70]

After Block's Toledo Bar Association speech, he had committed himself to prevent Roosevelt's re-election at any cost, so he welcomed the opportunity of meeting a significant and vital candidate who might have possible chances against the Democratic ticket. Block believed Landon to be still committed to the liberal Republicanism that was espoused by Theodore Roosevelt, to whom Landon had pledged his loyalty and service in 1912.[71] During the luncheon, the group reached an agreement that a more prudently-fiscal government had to be established, and that people of property of "at least one mule," as Landon put it so charmingly, should think of a coalition ticket, or anything else that could work to fight the growing inflation. Block told Landon of his luncheon with Roosevelt and the Gladstone allusion; Landon would later use this information to futilely smoke out Roosevelt's intentions toward the Supreme Court.[72]

Although the four publishers were captivated by the rugged Kansan, he made no promises regarding his future actions or policies. As they talked, Block and Hearst were covertly comparing Landon to Col. Franklin Knox, Hearst's own publishing executive, the man who was partially responsible for engineering the Block-Hearst publishing consortia in Pittsburgh. Knox was also entering the race as a Republican candidate. In a poll conducted in the spring of 1935 by the Republican party leaders, Knox was ahead of Landon as the preferred presidential nominee.[73] Hoover also let Block know that he felt that Knox, even though he had never held political office, was the more electable candidate over Landon. Somewhat later, Hoover changed his mind about Landon, claiming that "You can't beat somebody with nobody," and correctly predicted Landon's nomination.[74]

Despite his affection and respect for Knox, Block came away from his meeting with Landon believing him to be a person of "great intellectual and physical vigor," a plain, simple, natural man, and one who deserved to be President.[75] To Block, Landon was ideal: he was progressive, had balanced the state's budget, was a fiscal conservative, and his personal fortune had been made from oil. Shortly after Block and company left Topeka, an unidentified friend of Landon's asked State officials to send the Governor instructions for entering his name in Ohio's primaries in May. Since he had Hearst, Patterson, Brisbane and Block in his pocket, Landon felt he had enough support to run.

Six months later at the Republican convention in Cleveland, Landon would win the nomination unanimously, and Franklin Knox would be chosen as his vice-presidential running mate. Block wrote of the ticket: "Both men believe in the American governmental system and the Constitution. They are standing on a fine, liberal, workable platform that will be fulfilled and not scrapped as was the Democratic one in 1932. Landon and Knox go forth in a holy crusade for the preservation of the American form of government, American principles, and the rights, privileges and liberties of the American people."[76]

Over the next four months, Block continually editorialized in favor of the Landon-Knox ticket; he went on the radio (WOR and the Mutual Broadcasting System[77]) in an attempt to damage the New Deal and recognize and salute the Republican team; he gave interviews to the trade press and other newspapers; he began a new series in his own papers, "Paragraphs by the Publisher," which were largely attacks on Roosevelt and the New Dealers; and he made sure that photos and stories of Landon and his family were continually inserted into the *Pittsburgh Post-Gazette*, the *Toledo Blade,* and his other newspapers as well. As someone said, if the Landons were not being accepted as "America's Best-Loved Family," they certainly were being *shown* as "America's Best-Photographed Family," mainly due to the promotional efforts of Paul Block and his cohort William Randolph Hearst.

Block worked fervently to win his $100 wager with H.G. Wells, but he was quite certain about the outcome; he seriously believed that Landon would walk away with the election.

As Block had been described by some writers over the years as Hearst's puppet, so was Landon referred to by pro-New Dealers as his marionette, manipulated from above by the invisible strings of the publisher. They pointed to the assignments that Hearst had given to Damon Runyon and Adela Rogers St. Johns – two of America's most gifted and famous writers – to pen positive Landon articles for his magazines, *Cosmopolitan* and *Good Housekeeping* respectively, as proof that Landon was "selling out" to Hearst in order to get the publicity that he needed in order to get elected. In addition, it was noted that *all* of Hearst's papers, as did Block's, carried a disproportionate amount of Landon-related feature articles, compared to other editorial material that was published. Hearst's enormous financial resources, and his reputation for acquisition – paintings, sculpture, castles, newspapers, people – made anyone or any group associated with him suspect of being "bought." In actuality, most of Landon's policies were formed and expressed before he even met Hearst, just as most of Block's knowledge of newspaper publishing was gained before he became Hearst's business associate.

Block's continuing support of the Republican campaign of 1936 became less of an elucidation of the strengths of Landon and more a continuing hypercriticism of Roosevelt and the New Deal. Just weeks before the election Block attempted to inflict as much injury as he could on the Administration with the following litany of aversion:

- The Roosevelt administration stands for wasteful government.
- The Roosevelt administration stands for unconstitutional government.
- The Roosevelt administration stands for the high cost of living.
- The Roosevelt administration stands for big business

against little business.
- The Roosevelt administration stands for neglect of the Civil Service.
- The Roosevelt administration stands for class struggle.
- The Roosevelt administration stands for unsound money.
- The Roosevelt administration stands for the invasion of private rights.
- The Roosevelt administration stands for the invasion and usurpation of the states.[78]

As though Roosevelt were directly answering Block, two nights before the election, at a massive rally in Madison Square Garden, the President delivered a scathing peroration that brought the audience to a standing ovation:

> Never before in all of our history have the forces been so united against one candidate as they stand today. They are unanimous in their hatred for me...and I *welcome* their hatred.
>
> I should like to have it said of my first administration that in it, the forces of selfishness and of lust for power met their match.
>
> I should like to have it said of my *second* administration that in it, those forces met their master.[79]

Almost up to the last minute of the election, Block continued to allude to the fear that Roosevelt, if re-elected, might "plan to pack the Supreme Court in order to attempt to dictate to industry, thereby hindering employment."[80]

The Literary Digest polled two-and-a-half million people to ask who they would vote for, and published the outcome a few days before the actual vote, predicting who would win the election on the following Tuesday. As did many newspaper publishers across the country, Block gave widespread publicity to the poll. It predicted that Roosevelt would raise only 40% of the popular vote, whereas Landon would gain 54.4%; on the basis of electoral votes, the tally further indicated that Landon's lead would be even more decisive, giving him 370 votes to Roosevelt's 161.[81] Considered along with the Gallup Poll to be one of the most accurate and reliable forecasters, *The Literary Digest* had a 99% correct prediction in 1932; and in 1928 it accurately forecast the first break-up in the solid

Democratic South since the Civil War. In 1920 and 1924, it also correctly predicted the outcome of those elections. The figures animated and inspired Block into thinking that Landon would actually win.

The results of the actual election, therefore, came as an overpowering shock. Block looked at the vote tallies with stunned disbelief: Roosevelt had won the biggest political victory since James Monroe's in 1820, gaining 523 electoral votes, as opposed to 2 (Maine and Vermont) for Landon. The election ended Maine's reputation as the national political bellwether, and it occasioned James A. Farley, Roosevelt's campaign manager, to coin a new phrase: "As Maine goes, so does Vermont." The publishers of *The Literary Digest* announced that the magazine would have to change its polling methods because it may not have reached a representative cross-section of the population, missing the "lower strata." Because of the egregious polling error and the resultant breech of credibility among its readers, the magazine went out of business.

Block was depressed at the thought of another term of office for Roosevelt, and for a short while seemed to give up the fight against him. He chose not to sign his lead editorial in the *Toledo Blade* and the *Pittsburgh-Post Gazette* on the day after the election. Recognizing the victory as Roosevelt's personal triumph because of his "winning personality, his charm of manner and his eloquence," and giving the "dictator" his due by pledging the support of the Block papers, nonetheless the editorial warned its readers not to be taken in by the resonances of the results: "Regardless of the outcome, we can't believe that the result of yesterday's election is to be construed as an endorsement of the New Deal in its entirety."[82]

For several months Block's editorial pen, usually dipped in New Deal avarice, was strangely dry and immobile. The circulation figures of his newspapers were dropping and he was involved in righting them. The Depression continued to take a devastating toll on business. Both of Block's sons, who would eventually go to work for their father, wondered in retrospect, years later, whether the drop in the circulation of the *Pittsburgh Post-Gazette* had been partially caused by their father's continuous attack on an Administration in which the newspaper's readers wanted to believe. Paul Block, Jr. wrote to *his* own son John Robinson Block, giving him some background on Block's feud with Roosevelt:

> This will give you some idea of the depth of feeling against
> FDR, and may have had something to do with the decline of

the *Post-Gazette* in the '30s. Normally, it doesn't hurt to have readers angry at the editorial policy, but if you continue it year in and year out for a decade against an administration that the people come to believe is taking care of them, then the rule may not hold."[83]

And William Block, Sr. wrote in his memoirs:

> There was a consistent barrage of propaganda run in the *Post-Gazette* and *Blade,* against Roosevelt and against Wallace, the Secretary of Agriculture, and not just on the editorial pages. Because of the propaganda, Pittsburgh steelworkers, who were strongly for Roosevelt, started a boycott of the *Post-Gazette*. It hurt the *Post-Gazette* circulation at the time.[84]

Despite his financial entanglements and pressures, Block jumped to the cause as soon as he believed Roosevelt was beginning to overextend his authority. Roosevelt, emboldened by his victory at the polls, recommended that six new jurors be added to the Supreme Court, and Block responded immediately: "It is obvious that his [Roosevelt's] purpose is to appoint men who in one way or another have shown their preference for his political philosophy."[85] He added: "Take away the absolute independence of the judicial branch, and you weaken the very foundations of the American system of government and open the road to dictatorship."[86]

Block continued to bring the public's attention to the forefront of Roosevelt's Supreme Court maneuvers. In May of 1937, he wrote that if Roosevelt continued to insist on his own way, placing himself and his will above the well-being of the whole nation, it would be at great peril to the national good.

That summer, Roosevelt was dealt a severe blow – and Block received a windfall reward – as the Senate, by a vote of 70 to 20, effectively killed the President's plan for the expansion of members. The Senate voted to allow the justices to retire at age 70, *if they so desired*; Roosevelt's proposal to force *mandatory* retirement at 70 was defeated. It's been said that Roosevelt was depressed for weeks over the Senate's ruling; Block, on the other hand, was jubilant. In the next few months, Block's newspaper life would improve considerably.

Block Buys *Post-Gazette* from Debt-Ridden Hearst

At the same time that Block's financial situation began to improve somewhat, fiscal misfortune started to insert itself in the life of William Randolph Hearst. Over the years, he had overbought and overspent, and never kept his attention directed to the dynamics of the bottom line of any of his properties. All of Hearst's holdings, his works of art, the three castles, the newspapers and magazines were suffering under loans, mortgages, debentures, calls for stock, and other obligations to the 28 banks with which he did business. He had invested $50,000,000 in New York real estate alone, and the high amount of interest he was paying was punishing. It was estimated that he had invested another $50,000,000 in art, much of it overpriced. His insurance and taxes were said humorously to be as high as the national budgets of small countries. Hearst's total debt in 1937 was better than $126,000,000; his financial advisors insisted that there was only one way to stave off bankruptcy, and that was to divest himself of as many businesses as he could, and to liquidate or consolidate others…and, of course, to stop buying art.

Hearst began to dismantle his newspaper empire. His flagship newspaper, the *New York American*, was combined with his *New York Journal* to become the *New York Journal-American*. He simply went out of business with the *Rochester Journal* and *Sunday American,* and he ceased operations with the *Pictorial Review* (which he had purchased from William Ahnelt several years after Block left the company). Hearst was forced to borrow $1,000,000 from Cissy Patterson after he sold her the *Washington Herald*, and he even had to take a loan from his mistress, Marion Davies, who sold some of the jewels that he had continually given her as gifts for over 25 years, to come up with another $1,000,000.[87] He then sold most of his radio stations.

In the summer of 1937, Hearst approached Block to determine whether Block wanted to buy the *Pittsburgh Post-Gazette*, which had just celebrated its sesquicentennial anniversary. After ten years of operating the *Pittsburgh Post-Gazette* as publisher, Block wanted nothing better than to be the true owner, and their original agreement had been that if Hearst ever wanted to sell, Block would be given the first option to buy. Having recently emerged from the difficulties with the *Duluth News-Tribune* and the *Milwaukee Sentinel*, and even though business was slack and he was relatively cash poor, Block believed he might be able to manage the purchase price of the *Pittsburgh Post-Gazette*. Hearst was desperate for money, and was willing to take much less than he might have at other, more flush times in his life. Block produced a relatively small amount of cash of his own, floated sundry bonds, and transferred money from some of his other newspapers in order to meet the cost of the *Post-Gazette*. After the negotiations were completed, the final price of "considerably more than $2,500,000"[88] was agreed upon; it was thought at the time that the paper would have been worth perhaps twice that much if it had been sold at another time to another buyer. No publicity was given to the negotiations – everything was discussed, agreed upon and signed in secret – since to the world, Block, not Hearst, had been the owner of the *Pittsburgh Post-Gazette* all along. When the sale was consummated, Block made a brief statement to the press that Hearst had "retained a considerable amount of stock in the *Post-Gazette*"[89] when Block bought it in 1927, which was, of course true. His statement, however, never clarified that it was Hearst's money that enabled Block to buy the paper in the first place, and so the *Post-Gazette* had been his paper in name only, he being the operative publisher notwithstanding. No additional public comments were made by either party. Both Hearst and Block wanted their version of the story to remain that way.

That summer, Block traveled to the Allegheny Mountains to the tiny town of Loretto, Pennsylvania, about 75 miles from Pittsburgh, to receive an Honorary Doctorate in Literature at the College of St. Francis's commencement exercises. Delivering the commencement address, the now-Dr. Block once again used the opportunity of a public forum to condemn and attack Roosevelt and his administration:

> I have no thought that Mr. Roosevelt wishes to become a dictator. He is a God-fearing, patriotic American. But, intentionally or not, the machinery is being pieced together which will give him or any successor the same powers that foreign dictators have. The process has been described in cold blood by the Italian historian Malaparte, who shows how democracies have been overthrown without violence, merely by turning the instruments of democracy against itself. The use of parliaments, the use of constitutions, the use of controlled courts are all tools ready at hand for any would-be dictator. I say to you young gentlemen that the fate of our country lies in your hands, to do with what you will.[90]

In a matter of weeks, perhaps inspired by his new status with the *Post-Gazette*, and his new academic title, Block would emerge as a fearless publisher, and be thrust into the national limelight to an even greater extent than he had ever been before.

Chapter 12

Winning a Pulitzer and Confronting FDR

Unearthing a Truth About
Justice Hugo Black

Although the manly contest of poker was the game of choice of Herbert Bayard Swope, former editor of *The World* – then defunct – he was easily tempted by Paul Block into a series of bridge games during the last weekend of August 1937. The two men had come to Saratoga Springs to have a rousing time, and after the races were over for the day, they would often play rubbers of bridge with financier Robert Lehman and whoever else was available that Block and Swope knew; between them they seemed to know everybody who was also vacationing in Saratoga. Swope was then President of the New York State Racing Commission.

Block and Swope had many connections aside from their interest in gambling and Block's unsuccessful attempt to buy *The World* in 1930. They had several friends in common: among others, Irving Berlin, Bernard Baruch, Al Smith, Harry F. Guggenheim, and especially Florenz Ziegfeld, for whom Swope had acted as press agent for a short time. Their only point of difference was over Jimmy Walker: Swope always disparaged the former Mayor; Block championed him. As Jews, Block and Swope belonged to the Criterion Club in New York, and they often dined together at Jack and Charlie's famed "21 Club."

One particular hot summer night in Saratoga proved to be auspicious for Block as the two men played game after game far into the morning. The six-foot-one-inch, red-headed and red-faced Swope was a non-stop conversationalist, and what he liked to talk about more than just about anything else was politics. At that moment, he was particularly volatile about a forthcoming appointment to the Supreme Court. It had been reported that upon the voluntary retirement of Associate Justice Willis Van Devanter when he reached the age of 80, Roosevelt had sent the name of ex-Senator Hugo L. Black, a courtly Alabamian, to the Senate for confirmation as Van Devanter's successor.

Swope began to expound on what he considered to be the corruption of that possible appointment. He reminded Block of a 21-part series that appeared in *The World* in the early 1920s, which had also been syndicated in other papers throughout the country. It was an expose of the Ku Klux Klan that described the hooded bigots to be not just a small band of fanatical white supremacists, but a movement of national power that had great political rule not only over the South but other parts of the country, as well. The KKK took its name from the vigilantes that terrorized the South's blacks during the Reconstruction era after the Civil War; by 1921, the night riders counted more than 500,000 members and broadened their agenda of hate to include Catholics, Jews and other minority or alien groups. *The World's* circulation had seen a gain of 60,000 readers after the first week the series ran, and the paper was awarded a Pulitzer prize for its fearless coverage.

Then Swope said something shocking. He wondered if Block had known that Hugo Black was a member of the Klan; indeed, had been *their* candidate for the Senate in 1926. *The World* had implied that Black was a member of the Klan but the government had never done anything about it. Now, 14 years later, what if a newspaper were to do an unmasking (in every sense of the word) of the Supreme Court nominee? The problem was that although just about everyone in Alabama either knew or suspected that Black had been a member of the Klan, no one could actually prove it. Swope was disgruntled that no journalists or newspapers were going after the story.

Block, although taken aback, knew a news story when he heard one. He was on his feet in minutes, heading to his hotel room to call the *Pittsburgh Post-Gazette*. Block was furious with Roosevelt. Now all of his editorializing and pronouncements over the past two years – starting with that luncheon at the White House – seemed to be proving his theme was right, and he was justified in trumpeting to the nation that Roosevelt's intentions toward the Supreme Court *were* dishonorable. Hugo L. Black had served in the Senate for 10 years as a populist-progressive, and a staunch supporter of the New Deal. Roosevelt's attempt at manipulating Black on to the Supreme Court bench seemed to be the President's surreptitious way of packing the Court, after all. If the information about

Black's nefarious membership could be proven true, Paul Block would have an opportunity to implicate Roosevelt for what the President had done, and perhaps even block the confirmation of Black to the Court. "Hugo Black won't have to buy a new robe," quipped Swope to the quickly-exiting Block. "He can have his white one dyed black."[1]

It was midnight when Block called the city desk at the *Pittsburgh Post-Gazette.* He spoke to the night editor, Joe Shuman, expounded on the story, and put it into context. Block told Shuman to drop anything and everything he was doing, and call Ray Sprigle at home – he lived on a 103-acre farm in Moon Township, where he raised chickens when he wasn't working on stories – and make sure he was on the next plane to Birmingham, "to get a story on Black's membership in the Klan."[2] Furthermore, Block told Shuman, Sprigle should spare no expense in gaining the story; if information had to be paid for, or sources demanded money, Sprigle should comply.[3]

Sprigle was the paper's most incisive investigative reporter, a man who always returned with a dynamic and compelling story. Shuman woke the reporter, explained what Block wanted him to do, and four hours later Sprigle *was* in the air heading toward Alabama. Sprigle was a Republican and as much of a critic of Roosevelt as Block, so the assignment took on a special resonance for him.

On the same day that Sprigle initiated his Alabama investigation, Hugo Black's appointment was confirmed by the Senate, with a vote of 63 to 16, and so there was little that could be done to dislodge the lifetime appointment; but if Sprigle could prove that Black had been a registered member of the Klan, it would help to discredit Roosevelt, and perhaps any future appointments, at any level, that he might make. It might also forever tarnish any Court rulings that Black would hand down. For three days, Sprigle peered into files, probed townspeople, asked questions about Black, met with ex-Klansmen, examined documents and records and thoroughly explored the workings of the Klan in Birmingham. He could not find a record of Hugo Black's membership until he met Jim Esdale, a disbarred lawyer and former Grand Dragon of the Knights of the Ku Klux Klan. As was his style when he was working on an important story, Sprigle temporarily ingratiated himself into people's lives. He did the same with Esdale.

Jim Esdale was not prone to be friendly toward Hugo Black. When he was disbarred, Esdale had hoped that Black would come to his aid, but that never happened; nor did Black ever re-pay any Klan members with jobs or patronage for helping him gain his Senate seat. Sprigle met Esdale at the latter's home on the outskirts of Birmingham, and as Esdale chewed tobacco, the smoke from Sprigle's gargantuan corn-cob pipe created a blue haze that settled over the living room like a cloud. They talked for hours. Most of their conversation did not revolve around Black, but about farming and general down home matters.

When Esdale discovered that Sprigle was a chicken farmer, he plied the reporter with questions because he was about to set his son up with a flock of Leghorns, and neither he nor his son really knew much about the science of raising chickens. Leghorns were perfect as egg-layers, said Sprigle, but not good for eating. White Wyandotte chickens were the perfect birds to raise since they were delicious to eat, were large birds with plenty of meat on them, and they were also prolific layers.

Because Sprigle was so sage about chickens and so free with his advice, and because Esdale had begun to like him and had years ago grown disenchanted by Black, the next day he decided to help the reporter in his quest for a story. In his office, Esdale opened his old iron safe, and allowed Sprigle to go through a cache of several boxes of documents it contained. Examining the records, Sprigle discovered that Black had, indeed, been a dues-paying member of the Klan from 1923 to 1925, and that the "invisible empire" – as Klansmen liked to call themselves – hand-picked Black when he was an obscure local prosecutor and an aspiring politician, and propelled him, with financing and campaigning, into the United States Senate. Black had formally resigned from the Klan when he was running for his Senatorial seat, but 14 months later he was inducted back into the KKK as a life member, delivering a speech at his induction ceremony that promised that he would forever uphold the principles of the Klan.[4]

Although Sprigle had gathered all he needed to make a story, Paul Block wanted more, and since the confirmation had already been ratified, the time element was no longer a factor. Sprigle spent weeks in Birmingham gathering even more evidence for his eventual exegesis. "He was secure in his job for life, whatever we turned up on him," said Sprigle regretfully about Hugo Black, but he still searched for further damning evidence.[5] William F. Mylander, a reporter for the *Post-Gazette's* Washington bureau, had unearthed a speech by Black early in his Senatorial career in which he said, "Show me the kinds of steps a man made in the sand five years ago, and I'll show you the steps he is likely to make in the same sand five years hence." This particularly revealing and consequently damaging quote would eventually be used in the Sprigle story.

The first article of the Sprigle series on the Hugo Black scandal ran on the front page of the *Pittsburgh Post-Gazette* on September 13, 1937. Written in flamboyant and graphic prose, supported by an enormous amount of documentary evidence, the series was also syndicated to other papers around the country. Block chose to run the series simultaneously in the *Toledo Blade*, and introduced it with a front-page editorial that said: "When Senator Hugo L. Black's name was first presented for the Supreme Court bench, it was stated in the Senate and published in many newspapers that he had been elected as a Klan candidate...The *Blade* has dug them [the facts] out and will present them in a striking series of six articles."[6]

Sprigle mapped out the details of Black's membership in the Klan, reported on stenographic records of meetings he had attended, reproduced replicas of letters that he had written to the Klan. "I realize," Justice Black wrote to the Klan upon receiving life membership, "that I was elected by men who believe in the principles that I have sought to advocate and which are the principles of this organization."[7] Sprigle described various Klan ceremonies in which Black participated, and gave a history of his ascendancy to the Senate through the help of the Invisible Empire. The series produced so much interest and was so well-received by readers, that it was thought that it would threaten Black's assumption of his duties on the bench, and might force his resignation.

During the appearance of the *Pittsburgh Post-Gazette* articles by Sprigle, Justice Black was in London, refusing to talk to reporters or make any statement about his involvement with the Klan. His comment to a reporter at that time was highly criticized: "I don't see you. I don't know you. And I don't answer you."[8] America was in an uproar over what was going to be done about him. Paul Block was proud of the articles, for which he had served as catalyst. When Hugo Black's ship docked at Norfolk, Virginia at dawn on September 29th, 75 photographers and reporters (including Ray Sprigle) were on hand to question him. They were escorted on board and lined up around his cabin door. Eventually, he emerged. Questions about the Sprigle stories were bellowed out to him but he implied that he really didn't know about them; in any event, he would not give a statement about his future with the Supreme Court. The *Post-Gazette's* Mylander walked up to him, held out Sprigle's articles that had appeared 18 days before and said, "Mr. Justice, here are copies of the newspapers carrying six articles in which we are all interested.

Would you care to look them over?" Black tensed his lips tightly. "Who
are you?" he said angrily. "Mylander of the Paul Block newspapers,"
was the response. Black paused for a second or two, and then replied
sarcastically: "Suppose you take them back to Mr. Block." He then closed
the door of his cabin and that was the end of the non-interview, non-
statement.[9]

In addition to running the Sprigle articles, Block personally editorialized about the controversial appointment, rhetorically asking what would
have happened if Hugo Black had been on the Supreme Court during the
hearing concerning the recent Scottsboro Case where a group of nine
young blacks were being railroaded to either their deaths or 75 to 99
years in prison, allegedly for raping two white women in Alabama: "The
Supreme Court intervened," wrote Block, "and set aside the verdict of
the State, holding that the trial had not been fair because blacks had been
barred from serving on the jury." [Additionally, one of the women re-
canted her testimony]. Would a Klansman have taken the same stand for
equal civil rights?"[10]   Block also wrote that Roosevelt was trying to replace "conservatism and liberalism with radicalism," and that his naming
of Black struck "at the very root of the whole American system of government."[11]

In the midst of the *Pittsburgh Post-Gazette*–Hugo L. Black debate, Paul
Block filed the only libel suit he ever brought to court, and the first lawsuit in the history of the Republic concerning a Supreme Court nomination. Just days after the last of the Sprigle series appeared, on September
25th the *Nation* published an article titled "Who Exposed Black?" by
Robert S. Allen, taking issue not with the authenticity of the contents of
Sprigle's work, but the intent and the identity of who authored them.
According to Allen, the true hero of the *Post-Gazette* series was a man by
the name of Frank Prince, a former reporter of the *New York Journal*, and
an "undercover public relations advisor of the University of Pittsburgh,"
who had recently opened a detective agency in New York City, and who
was hired, according to Allen, by Hearst, Block, and the North Atlantic
Newspaper Alliance, all in a conspiracy to discredit the favored Roosevelt
choice, neo-liberal Hugo L. Black. Moreover, Allen had accused Paul
Block and the *Pittsburgh Post-Gazette* of trying to bring Black down in a
further attempt to attack labor leader John L. Lewis. Actually, Paul Block
thought of Lewis as someone who *was* attempting to hurt business and
industry no matter what the cost. The connection between Hugo Black
and Lewis was entirely tenuous. (The only linking seemed to be that Black,

as Senator, was once pressured by Lewis to vote for a bill that created a commission to allocate and control production; and to help his chances in the next election, Black *did* vote for it.)

Block was sitting on the Sprigle articles as potentially the first Pulitzer Prize that he would have ever won for any of his papers; he was incensed at the piece in the *Nation* for that reason alone. But the political and moral implication of Allen's polemic also enraged him. He gave a copy of the *Nation* to his attorney Max Steuer, and told him to sue. Steuer first wrote to the *Nation* demanding a retraction ("This whole matter is a figment of the imagination," he stated), and pointing out that Prince was entirely unknown to Block. When he received no reply, Steuer had the *Post-Gazette* publish the letter, and the *Post-Gazette*'s editor, Oliver J. Keller also went at the *Nation,* sending them a proof copy of Steuer's letter and a protest of his own, talking of the "entirely false statements" contained in the Allen piece. Subsequent inquiries of the University of Pittsburgh indicated that neither the Chancellor nor the Publicity Director had ever heard of the mysterious Frank Prince.

The libel suit dragged on for several years. All the while, during 1937 and 1938, Block, Sprigle and the staff of the *Pittsburgh Post-Gazette* awaited the results of that year's Pulitzer Prizes. It's been suggested that the real reason that the suit never went to trial was that Block did not want to give a deposition that would reveal his financial arrangement with Hearst (overlooking the fact that by 1938 there was no such arrangement), and also because Max Steuer's legal fee would have been $25,000 – a more than hefty price in those days – if the case went to court, and Block was trying to save that amount of money.

Roosevelt claimed that he had no idea that Hugo Black had been in the Ku Klux Klan, and he felt that the new Justice had to confront the *Pittsburgh Post-Gazette* articles with some sort of a statement in order to overcome the stigma that was undermining Black's reputation. There was an unprecedented amount of mail coming to the White House demanding an explanation. Black decided to make a speech on radio, and he and an old law associate, Crampton Harris of Birmingham, worked together in preparing it.

All three radio networks and 318 stations carried Black's speech. Supposedly, no other broadcast in history, with the exception of King Edward VIII's abdication in 1936, had as many listeners, an audience estimated at 40 million.[12] Block and Dina listened from Friendship, in Connecticut. H. L. Mencken astonishingly referred to the speech as one of the classics of American rhetoric, on a par with the Gettysburg Address.

In part, Hugo Black complained that the "planned and concerted campaign against" him was "calculated to spread racial and religious hatred," although he never explained how this was being done. He admitted to joining the Klan, later resigning and never joining again. He never explained his motives for joining in the first place, nor did he denounce the Klan. He did say: "Before becoming a senator I dropped the Klan. I have had nothing whatever to do with it since that time. I abandoned it. I completely discontinued any association with the organization. I never resumed it and never expect to do so." In a somewhat imperious manner he closed by saying that when his statement was over, the discussion of the matter was closed.[13]   And so it was. Why the public was silent after that is not known, but as soon as Black took his seat on the bench, the furor subsided. A brief, benign hearing was held by the Judiciary Committee, but the matter was soon abandoned. Three days after the radio broadcast, the now-politically correct Mr. Justice Black would hire a Jewish law clerk, a Catholic secretary and a black messenger. Black would serve on the Supreme Court bench for 37 years, and ironically end up being one of the most liberal Justices in American history. Ray Sprigle did win the Pulitzer Prize for the *Pittsburgh Post-Gazette* the following year, for "a distinguished example of a reporter's work," according to the selection committee. In 1939, the *Nation* published an apology, and Block formally dropped the case.

Although Block felt vindicated and justified in what he had accomplished in forcing Black to admit the stain on his reputation, he never again mentioned in public the infamy of the Supreme Court nomination of Hugo L. Black by Franklin D. Roosevelt.

FDR Refuses to Start the Presses

Toward the end of 1937, Block was making arrangements to construct and open a new, 65,000 square foot building of steel and stone for the *Pittsburgh Post-Gazette*, and he selected an impressive site: the proud corners of the Boulevard of the Allies and Grant Streets, relatively near the spot where the Monongahela, Allegheny and Ohio rivers converge. It was a gamble. Although he could not afford the $1,500,000 plant at the height of the Depression, he felt it was the only way to grow, and if he didn't take the chance, it was possible that the *Post-Gazette* would slip even further back. With the opening of the new plant, Block would be employing more people than the *Post-Gazette* ever had in its history.

Equipped with a giant battery of high-speed presses, it would be capable of printing more copies faster than it ever had before. Block stated that the building, with all new printing, typesetting and mailing equipment, and with mechanical and technical refinements in every department, would be one of the finest newspaper plants in the country.

As he did for the opening of his new plant for the *Toledo Blade* a decade before, Block wanted to have a gala ceremony for the *Post-Gazette's* new home. At the *Blade* inaugural, President Calvin Coolidge had pressed a button that activated the presses in the new plant; Block wondered who he could get to do the same thing for the *Post-Gazette*. The attendant national publicity had been great when Coolidge cooperated with the *Toledo Blade* launching; Block wanted that same coverage with the *Post-Gazette*, and he also wanted to honor the plant and its employees.

After discussion with his colleagues and some of his New York friends, everyone came to the conclusion that to have anyone else *other* than the President of the United States to start the presses rolling would be a disappointment, and almost an insult to the paper. It was also felt that not asking Roosevelt to participate in the paper's inaugural would be considered an affront to him. Block was incredulous at the suggestion. How could *he*, of all people, ask the President to do *anything* for him? He had criticized, accused, and offended Roosevelt in every public forum that he could find for the previous six years; he had informed the nation about Roosevelt's plan to pack the Supreme Court; he had held him up to ridicule for his appointment of Hugo Black; Roosevelt and Block had severed all communication and correspondence. Block's people persisted, however. What did he have to lose by asking? It was suggested that perhaps such a gesture might also relax the tension between him and the President.

Walking the fine line between self-confidence and conceit, prompted by those around him, Block finally wrote to Col. Marvin H. McIntyre, Secretary to the President, and asked if President Roosevelt would be "gracious enough" to press a button in the White House "which will start our machinery going."[14]   The tentative date for the completion of the building was February 15, 1938. Words such as "brazen," "audacious" and "shameless" come to mind when thinking of Block's request of Roosevelt, and one wonders whether through some trick of the mind, or psychological pressure, he came to believe that he had the *right* to make such a solicitation.

To add some justification to his request, Block included in his letter a reprint of a positive FDR editorial, "Roosevelt Deserves Credit for Meetings With Business Men,"[15] that had appeared in all of his newspapers two weeks before, to indicate to the President that he was not exclusively an Administration-hater, and that he was capable of commending FDR when he accomplished important things. And for good measure, Block also enclosed a reprint of a news photo that had appeared in the *Pittsburgh Post-Gazette* showing a painting of Roosevelt, *The New Dawn*, by Howard Chandler Christy, reproduced to publicize the President's fight on infantile paralysis.[16] Block had made attempts to be impartial. Even during the controversial and heated campaign of 1936, where Block did everything he could do to depose Roosevelt, he'd insisted that the *Post-Gazette* present both sides of the issues – Republican *and* Democratic – via a regular feature, the substance of which was provided by the parties themselves. In effect, Block gave each political party equal space: they provided the copy, which was unedited by the *Post-Gazette's* staff.[17]

Block's letter produced a minor political uproar in the White House, and although seemingly a trivial matter to an outside observer, Roosevelt and his staff took the whole situation quite seriously. McIntyre went to Stephen T. Early, Roosevelt's Press Secretary, to see whether he thought Block's idea should be accommodated and whether they should approach the President with the proposal. Early's response was succinct: "He [Roosevelt] should do it."[18] However, when McIntyre then went to Roosevelt, the President said to send a letter declining the request. He gave no reason to McIntyre for his decision. On January 28, 1937, McIntyre lied to Block that although "there wasn't a rule against it," Stephen Early had been declining a great many similar requests, and "quite frankly," they felt it would be embarrassing to make an exception in Block's case.[19]

The matter was not closed in the White House, however. Even though the refusal had been sent, Early thought the President was making a mistake. His reasoning was that the President had pressed buttons for various newspaper plants and other occasions before and so the precedent had been established. Equally important, however, were the political ramifications. It was Early who first rebuked Block for his revelation of the court packing luncheon; but as a former member of the press, Early knew how important newspapers could be. Early wanted to re-build the relationship between Roosevelt and Block and he thought that this little gesture could be the catalyst. Block was a relatively powerful newspaper publisher, Early contended, and he told the President that such an act "will do no damage and might be very helpful" in winning Paul Block's support. Aside from that, Early believed that Block "could be far worse than he has been," and that if the button-pushing event could be arranged, it should be. Roosevelt was having none of it. He could neither forgive, nor forget the dozens, if not hundreds of digs, jabs and barbs that Block had inflicted upon him ("President Still Seeks to Pack the Supreme Court;" "President Roosevelt Dodges Governor Landon's Challenge;" "End Labor War – Curb Dictatorship – Restore Democracy"). He was also becoming piqued over how his own staff, namely "Mac" and "Steve" as the President called them, was countering his wishes; he scrawled in bold, black ink on the bottom of a memo about Block's request: [20]

NO!
That is final
__FDR__

Hardly a "yes" man, Early simply could not accept the President's intransigence; he continued to hold that Roosevelt was making a political error. He wrote to McIntyre: "I still think the President should press the button; despite the past, I believe it will help the future."[21]   What Early apparently did not know about his President was that although Roosevelt was known for his loyalties, he also could be quite capable of maintaining a long-term grudge.

Block did not know, of course, of the contretemps that he had caused in the White House, and he was under the assumption (from McIntyre's refusal letter to him of January 18, 1938) that Roosevelt had not even been apprised of his request. Not to be denied by an underling, Block wrote McIntyre a three-page single-spaced letter from his home (he had been ill for about a month with influenza), citing all of the reasons why Roosevelt should participate in the inauguration of the new *Post-Gazette* building. Using all his salesmanship ability, Block attempted to convince McIntyre that the President would be pleased "to do this for the men and women of the *Post-Gazette* family." Block also mentioned that he had told two of Roosevelt's best friends, who also happened to be close friends of his, that he was going to ask the President to "start the new plant off," and that if now the President didn't start the presses rolling, Block would be in "a rather embarrassing position."

The strangest part of Block's letter came as a postscript: "I have supported many of the President's measures and all of his social measures and no one has higher regard for the President than I have, except that I do not agree with some of his policies because I fear they are harmful to the country."[22] If the usually-diplomatic Block felt that this last sentence would impress the President with its honesty, then his reasoning was bordering on if not absurdity, then naïveté at best.

Neither McIntyre nor Early had the temerity to approach Roosevelt with any further arguments in favor of Paul Block. Just as Block had closed the door on Roosevelt in his newspapers and in his speeches, Roosevelt was now closing the door on Block.

The *Pittsburgh Post-Gazette* inauguration ceremony had been postponed until March 9th, mainly because Block was still in bed with the flu, and some finishing touches had to be completed on the building. A day before the ceremony he and Dina rode in his private railroad car to Pittsburgh and settled in for the evening at the William Penn Hotel. He was still half-expecting Roosevelt to agree. Just so there would be no misunderstanding, however, McIntyre wired Block: "REGRET DELAY REPLYING YOUR LETTER. ALSO REGRET COULD NOT ARRANGE ACCEDE TO YOUR REQUEST."[23]

At the gala, dignitaries and business leaders from the city and the state attended, and Block himself pushed the button that started the presses. He said, quite poetically, to the assembled crowd: "Today the rhythmic roar and rumbling roll of giant presses moving at amazing speed, sound a thrilling note in Pittsburgh's progress as they record a milestone in the history of the *Post-Gazette*. We are justly proud of this new home of ours – a home in which our co-workers will have more light, more space, more comfort, and we trust, more happiness."[24] At the reception afterward, he read a number of telegrams and letters that he had received from Senators, Governors and Congressmen, all wishing him good luck with the new printing plant; the messages included, ironically, one from the Vice President of the United States, John Nance Garner. Block made a few statements saying that through the construction of the great plant, the *Post-Gazette* was showing its faith in the city of Pittsburgh, and that the paper would now be able to render an even higher standard of service to the city and the whole tri-state area.

As Block mingled in the crowd, he let it be known how hurt he was that he had not received a wire of best wishes from Roosevelt. Talking of the President, Block shook his head and said to one of the partygoers, "If I would have gotten just two or three words – 'Congratulations on your new building' – or something about my courage in undertaking new construction these days, or something of that order"...and then his voice trailed off.[25]

Depression and War: the Close of the Thirties

It wasn't easy to maintain courage as the economy continued to worsen. Block's businesses in 1938 were having difficulties. His special representative business was doing poorly since advertising was down across the country; he was left with only 16 papers to service. Of the newspapers he owned, he was struggling with the *Newark Star-Eagle* and would have to sell it the following year. His papers in Duluth and Milwaukee had been sold the year before. His only remaining newspapers were the *Toledo Blade*, the *Toledo Times* and the *Pittsburgh Post-Gazette*, and none of the three were making great amounts of money.

By the late 1930s, despite Roosevelt's reforms and the best efforts of the federal government and American industry, the soup kitchen had become part of the American landscape; adult scavengers going through garbage cans for food were a common sight in cities across the country. In February of 1938, over 100,000 workers protested layoffs in Detroit. A study released in July of that year stated that the South had 21% of the nation's population, yet earned only 9% of the national income: the annual wage throughout the Southern states was $865. The unemployment figure nationally was reaching 10 million.

The only minor balm for Block's businesses was the country's adoption of the Revenue Act of 1938, which reduced corporate income taxes in the hope that it would stimulate the economy. Roosevelt refused to sign the bill, but it became the law anyway. The only surcease of difficulty for average workers, however, was trying to forget their troubles: radio, music, fiction and movies were engaged in a golden age of frivolity, and the broadcasts of *Fibber McGee and Molly, Gangbusters,* and *Amos n'Andy* competed with the on-screen talents of the matinee idols Fred Astaire, Greta Garbo, Clark Gable and little Shirley Temple.

All of the editorials, save three, that appeared in Block's papers throughout 1938 were about the economy in one way or the other, but a vital spark, a *raison d'être* that had been his trademark, seemed to go out of him. He was not fighting for or against the issues of the day as forcefully as he had in the past, nor did he seem all that eager to communicate his views on the problems (and occasionally the strengths) of the country.

Depressingly, *Time* magazine's Man of the Year was Adolf Hitler. In 1939, Block changed his direction a bit, and although he continued to criticize the administration's handling of the economy, he now also condemned their foreign policy as far as Hitler and the war in Europe were concerned.

In late September of 1939, Lord Beaverbrook came to New York enroute to Canada, and Paul Block asked if he could interview him about the war for the *Post-Gazette* and his other newspapers. At that time, Beaverbrook was one of the chief statesmen in the United Kingdom. Beaverbrook acceded, but with one important caveat: he didn't want Block to mention his name. The resulting interview/editorial, by-lined by Block, suggested that although he was not revealing the name of his source, he thought "most of our readers will be interested in a general idea, at least, of his views."[26] Beaverbrook predicted that England would win the war in Europe, although he believed that there would be many dark days before a final victory would be achieved. He pointed out that since the Allies would fight largely on the defensive Western Front, they would starve Germany out economically and physically. He asserted that neither Russia nor Italy really wanted to fight for Germany; and that he did not expect aid or manpower from the United States. "He felt the greatest assistance America could give," Block wrote, "would be encouragement to England and France for the principles for which they were fighting." In conclusion, Beaverbrook said that he could not see how anyone could accept any promises or agreements by Hitler (such as a predicted peace offering that was being rumored) after the way such pledges had been broken during the previous year. Block was ambivalent about United States military intervention in behalf of England; at that moment in time he, like Hearst, was more inclined toward isolationism.

The Dispiriting Sale of the *Newark Star-Eagle*

By the fall of 1939, Block was struggling to keep his papers going. The effort was wearing; it seemed that his life was just one long process of getting tired. Unlike young people, who may feel tired at the *end* of an action or a venture, Block seemed tired all the time, even at the beginning of a new speculation. He felt drained from all of the years he had struggled, in charge of thousands of employees and responsible for millions of dollars in all of his businesses. The constant traveling, and the very idea of acquiring yet another newspaper made him weary. Despite the fact that a number of his newspapers were still making money during the dispirited years of the Depression, Block, by no longer trying – perhaps the only true failure in life – was almost admitting to a certain default of aspiration, a collapse or breakdown of his lifelong will to succeed.

In November of 1939, after almost a quarter of a century of publishing the *Newark Star-Eagle*, Block, exhausted and dispirited, decided to sell the paper's name, good will and circulation list to S. I. Newhouse, publisher of the rival paper, the *Newark Ledger*. He issued a frank, sincere and lengthy statement that was published in the *Star-Eagle* on Friday, Nov. 17, 1939, announcing that the paper would be shut down the very next day. In brief, here are extracts from Block's rationale:

> Right up to a very few days ago I interviewed, at the request of our executives, some men who they thought had shown an interest [in buying the paper]. I offered it to these backers (but only for my executives) for a sum less than one-half of a standing offer I had for the property. Unfortunately, after many weeks of effort, nothing came of it...
>
> ...And so I repeat my regret that the *Star-Eagle* cannot continue, and the still greater regret that this may mean the loss of jobs for so many fine men and women.
>
> I am in hopes that with one less newspaper in the field, the improvement which will come to the other papers will be so substantial that many of the former *Star-Eagle* employees will be engaged by them.
>
> The *Star-Eagle's* weak financial condition will not stand in the way of all released employees receiving dismissal pay. I shall personally see to this.
>
> Paul Block

The Newhouse people tried to accommodate and hire as many of Block's workers as possible into what was now a new entity called the *Newark Star-Ledger*. Dan Nicoll's son-in-law, who had been managing editor of the *Star-Eagle*, was made features editor of the new *Star-Ledger*, and some photographers, sports writers, and circulation personnel of Block's were hired by Newhouse. Hale Williamson, the editor of the *Star-Eagle's* Peach section, joined the editorial department of the *Toledo Blade*. A minor pyrrhic victory for Block occurred when Newhouse asked him to become national advertising manager for the *Star-Ledger*. Up until that time, Newhouse handled its own national advertising for the *Star-Ledger*, the *Long Island Daily Press*, and several of its other papers. Block's representation added prestige and dollars to the Newhouse company, and the relationship lasted for years.

Despite his lowering spirits, Paul Block continued to fight his way through the hustling, competitive newspaper business. He was increasingly tired, but he kept trying to elevate his life by conscious endeavor. The bittersweet and brief experience of wanting to buy *The World,* however illusory the attempt, still rankled him. Before he could sink deeper into a perpetual state of irritability, however, he found himself engaged in yet another battle with Franklin D. Roosevelt, and this one somehow energized him.

The Guru Letters

The scene at the White House one July evening in 1940 was particularly surrealistic. The President of the United States and his advisors were engaged in discussions of the soul, reincarnation and spiritual truth, and the name of Paul Block dominated the conversation. What occurred that night, in such an out of the ordinary tableau, is now a part of political history.

Just a few days before, at the Democratic convention in Chicago, Franklin D. Roosevelt had been nominated for President for an unprecedented third term – which many were opposed to simply on principle – and Henry A. Wallace, his former Secretary of Agriculture, was nominated for Vice-President; when Wallace's name was presented, there was an eddy of boos and catcalls from the delegates. Roosevelt reacted with rage and made it clear that he would not accept either James Farley or James F. Byrnes as his running mate. If Wallace, a personal friend of the President's and his chosen heir for the Presidency, was not nominated, Roosevelt would withdraw from running himself, he said; he even wrote a note to that effect and had it delivered to the Convention. He was withdrawing his name if the delegates would not nominate Wallace. They finally accepted Wallace just so they could have Roosevelt.[27]

Wallace was a militant New Dealer, and as an Iowan his potential for gaining the farm vote was enormous. The public thought of him, however, as a turncoat Republican and a Rooseveltian puppet. Without question, he was the darling of the liberals and the *bête noire* of the conservatives, and according to some, something of a mystic and a hopeless dreamer. "Hail-fellow-well-met" he was not. Block began to discern great possibilities in bringing down Wallace, and by possible reflection, Roosevelt too. If he could discredit Wallace, Block believed, he might be able to turn the tide of the impending election.

On that hot July night in Washington, Roosevelt sat in the West Wing in the Fish Room (later re-named the Map Room by John F. Kennedy), so-called because of his aquarium of tropical specimens and various mounted sailfish and other trophies from his frequent fishing trips. Tensely, he mixed and stirred a pitcher of martinis as he awaited his first guest. This was no social occasion, however. Roosevelt had called a secret, emergency meeting of some of his top advisors. Paul Block, Roosevelt's perennial *agent provocateur,* was again causing possible future discomfort for the Administration, but this time Roosevelt had no easy solutions. If Block was not stopped, he could prevent Roosevelt and Wallace's election; and Wendell Willkie, the Republican candidate and Block's choice, could become the next President of the United States.

Block's impending attack on Roosevelt and Wallace was not only because he sought their defeat, but because he believed that Willkie would make a great President, likening him to Abraham Lincoln, Grover Cleveland and Theodore Roosevelt for the straightforward, and unselfish way that he, and they, attacked various national problems. Willkie was a highly successful businessman, and not just a career politician, so Block could relate to him. "In politics," Block wrote, "Mr. Willkie is apparently an absolute independent. He refuses to praise one party and damn the other. What he is interested in is bringing about recovery, as quickly and as soundly as it can be done, without regard to party labels or class distinctions. The New Deal is reactionary and not liberal, Mr. Willkie says, because it has concentrated power in the hands of the government."[28]

At the White House that evening, Roosevelt's military aide and appointments secretary, Edwin "Pa" Watson, arrived first and began a light-hearted banter which on most occasions cheered the President, but on that particular evening would not distract him. Harry Hopkins, Roosevelt's Secretary of Commerce and his most trusted advisor and confidante, came next, even though he was not feeling well; he was carrying a "top secret" portfolio with information on Paul Block. Stephen T. Early, the White House press secretary, made an appearance, as did Senator Robert F. Wagner; Robert H. Jackson, the Attorney General; and finally the pince-nezed Bernard Baruch, Roosevelt's and Wallace's friend, counselor and "go-between" for the President.[29] The group did not represent Roosevelt's "Brain Trust" in its entirety, but they were all men that he had confidence in, and he knew that no word would leave that room unless he agreed to it.

The purpose of the unusual meeting was to discuss a packet of photostatic copies of letters that had come into the possession of Harry Hopkins, and which compromised Wallace as a member of a secret cult. Hopkins prided himself in having "spies" in every newspaper office in the country, and one of his people at the *Pittsburgh Post-Gazette* had secured copies of the letters, which were going to be used for a series of stories in that paper, written by Ray Sprigle.[30] Hopkins had heard that Block was prepared to go to press not only in the *Post-Gazette*, but in his other papers as well, perhaps within days. Paul Block had bought the letters in behalf of the Republican National Committee, and he and Roy Howard, president of the Scripps-Howard newspaper chain (who, like Block, had first supported Roosevelt and then turned into an ardent detractor), were going to publish the letters in their own newspapers, and then release them, free of charge, to every daily newspaper in the country.[31] The rumor was that Block had paid $10,000 for the letters. Hopkins even had a few copies of Sprigle's drafts, ostensibly given to him by the *Post-Gazette* spy.[32] In addition to showing the letters to Roosevelt, Hopkins had copies sent by courier to Wallace, who was on the campaign trail.

Attorney General Jackson related afterwards that at the White House meeting the letters were thought "to be very damaging," and that Block's "power as a promoter of publicity was considerable and there was real anxiety about what to do about it."[33] Hopkins was particularly upset over the import of the letters and took the purported Paul Block threat with great seriousness.[34]

The cache of letters was voluminous, well over a hundred, and Hopkins summarized to the assembled group the contents of those specific letters that were most damaging to Wallace. The letters were written clandestinely over a period of years, 1933-1934 for the most part, to a man named Nicholas Roerich, a White Russian mystic and internationally-known painter and poet of spiritual themes, who Wallace addressed as "Dear Guru" or "Dear Master," and to Roerich's wife Helena, for whom Wallace used the code name "Zenda." Some of Roerich's followers believed him to be God. Most of the letters seemed to be in Wallace's handwriting, and they were verified to be so by handwriting experts later on.

Roosevelt was entirely familiar with Roerich, and had given him his wholehearted approval when Wallace, during the drought and dust storms of 1934, chose Roerich to lead an expedition to the Orient to look for certain drought-resistant grasses and plants which were believed to grow in Outer Mongolia and Tibet; the expedition was comprised of plant scientists from the Department of Agriculture. A sensational news story appeared at that time stating that Roerich was really searching for Shangri-la; another claimed he was looking for the site of the second coming of Jesus Christ. Although the expedition was not successful (because of conflicts with Roerich and the scientists; and also because the Soviet government was claiming that Roerich was making political speeches in Mongolia), Wallace and Roosevelt nevertheless continued their interest in Roerich and his philosophy. When Wallace terminated the expedition, however, it was Roosevelt who asked Wallace why he couldn't have been more patient with the old man.

In 1935, Block had described Wallace as "taking a bite from the Communist apple," and hoped that Roosevelt would throw him out of his Cabinet (along with several others of the "Brain Trust"), quoting the familiar line from *The Mikado*: "They'll none of them be missed, they'll none of them be missed."[35] As much as he had grown to despise Roosevelt, Block thought that Wallace as Vice-President was not only irrational, but preposterous.

Wallace's involvement in the occult went beyond Roerichism. He studied Buddhism, the cabala, numerology, the mystical dances of the American Indian, and the philosophy of the medieval aesthetes; his interest in agrarian genetics and astronomy, hardly branches of the occult, were certainly experimental and singular for the day. He had an abiding curiosity of all religions and religious customs and systems, as did the Episcopalian Roosevelt, and although it was never publicized, their interest in the cabala and religious exaltation is what drew the two men together.

Roerich had created a symbol, the Banner of Peace (three red spheres within a circle), which represented an anti-war project that also attempted to gain promises that in case of war no cultural treasures would be destroyed. Twenty-two nations, with Wallace lobbying for their cooperation, signed what became known as the Roerich Pact, and Roerich was nominated for, but did not win, the Nobel Prize. Pope Pius XI and King Albert of Belgium were enthusiastic supporters of the Roerich pact. Roosevelt signed for the United States in a formal ceremony at the White House. In the 1930s, a museum was created in New York City which contains Asian art treasures and hundreds of Roerich's art works (including the libretto he had written and sketches for the costumes and scenery he designed for the first performance of Stravinsky's *Sacre du Printemps*); the museum remains there, open, today. Wallace continually visited it, sometimes ignoring his cabinet responsibilities.[36]

A tall, thin, aesthetic looking man with a gray Fu Manchu moustache and beard, Roerich dressed in oriental clothing, had a shaved head and assumed the aura and luminosity of a benign holy man. Herbert Hoover had received Roerich in the White House in 1929. Block himself had, coincidentally, sat only a few seats away from Roerich in 1928 when both had attended the New York gala performance of *Die Fledermaus,* presented by the Moscow troupe *La Chauve-Souris.* But Roosevelt had a longstanding acquaintanceship with the "guru." They had met when Roosevelt was Governor of New York State, and he talked of Roerich affectionately.[37] Some of Roerich's followers had visited Roosevelt quite frequently at his home at Hyde Park, and at 1600 Pennsylvania Avenue. A painting of Roerich's, *Himalaya,* hung in the White House. One art critic said of him that, "Like Moussorgsky, Rimsky-Korsakoff and Dostoyevsky, he is one of the towering geniuses of Russian history."[38]

What none of the men in the Fish Room knew that evening was that it had been Roosevelt who had introduced Roerich to Wallace, because of Roosevelt's mother's interest in theosophical and spiritual matters, and Roosevelt's own curiosity and intense interest in central Asia.[39] Roosevelt made no mention that evening in the White House of his own connection to Roerich. In the Franklin D. Roosevelt Library at Hyde Park, New York, there are eight letters from Helena Roerich to Roosevelt, all concerning spiritual and mystical matters, and all implying that Roosevelt either initiated the correspondence or answered Madame Roerich's inquiries.

Now, though, a relationship with Roerich could hurt the election campaign, and the new Block-induced dilemma was at hand: would Block publish the Wallace letters and articles about them, and if so, what would be the consequences? To illustrate what Roosevelt and his advisors were considering that night, here is a sample of a typical letter from the collection that began to be known as the "Guru Letters," and which Block intended to publish:

> Dear Guru,   12 March 1933
>
> I have been thinking of you holding the casket – the sacred most precious casket. And I have thought of the New Country going forth to meet the seven stars under the sign of the three stars. And I have thought of the admonition "Await the Stone."

> We await the Stone and we welcome you again to this glo-
> rious land of destiny, clouded though it may be with strange
> fumbling fears. Who shall hold up the compelling vision to
> those who wander in darkness? In answer to this question we
> again welcome you to drive out fear. We think of the People
> of Northern Shambhalla (sic) and the hastening feet of the
> successor of the Buddha and the Lightning flashes and the
> breaking of the New Day.
>   And so I await your convenience prepared to do what I am
> here to do.
>   May Peace, Joy and Fire attend you as always.
>
> G
>
> In the great haste of this strange maelstrom which is
> Washington.[40]

"G" was the initial of Wallace's cultic name, Galahad, given to him by
Helena Roerich. Occasionally Wallace would also use the name Parsifal
(both of Arthurian legend) in writing to Roerich. Although extremely
adulatory and cabalistic in tone, this particular letter was innocent enough,
and a number of other letters seem to be seeking nothing more than spiritual guidance. Roosevelt and his Fish Room advisors, however, felt that
if published by Block, these letters were exactly the sort of thing that
would label Wallace a certified crackpot. They made his personality and
mental state appear to be unsound.

Perhaps to head off any further inquiry directed toward himself, and to
alleviate the tension in the room, Roosevelt turned to the Attorney General and asked: "Hell, Bob, you've got the FBI. Can't you find Henry in
bed with this woman? Can't you turn this into a romance – this writing of
letters? Everybody would understand *that*, but nobody would understand
the writing of this kind of letters without any romance in it."[41] What
Roosevelt was saying was that the American people might understand a
love affair, but they would never forgive one of their leaders being involved in the supernatural. At another point, completely changing the
mood of the meeting, the angered Roosevelt refused to speculate as to
whether Wallace could or should be eliminated from the Democratic ticket
altogether before Block struck.[42] Roosevelt would not tolerate any discussion of dumping Wallace.

Other letters by Wallace were not only mystical but undiplomatic, and

were models of indiscretion, written as they were by a government official. Almost all of them are in a special Roerichian code: Roosevelt is
called "The Flaming One," "The Wavering One" and "The Mediocre One,"
and even "The Great One." Cordell Hull (who would go on to win the
Nobel Peace Prize five years later) is referred to as "The Sour One;"
Winston Churchill as "The Roaring Lion;" the country of Russia as "The
Tiger;" the British as "The Monkeys." Wallace talked about how he cured
himself of headaches at formal Senatorial and state dinners by passing a
Tibetan amulet over his forehead, and he discussed with Roerich the
significance of certain religious symbols such as the Christian cross, the
Mongolian lama's reliquary, and the American Indian medicine man's
charms and rattles.[43]   The letters talked of Roosevelt's appeasement of
the Russians, the immediacy of war, and the intrigues of American government and politics. What in some ways would have been the most
damaging to the campaign was a negative discussion of the deterioration
of Roosevelt's mental and physical condition.[44]

Baruch suggested an injunction against Block's publication of the letters; the problem with that approach, countered the President, was that
even if the suit prevented the publication of the *actual* letters, it would
insure a great amount of publicity about them, and then curiosity would
be added to the damage because a sense of mystery would be established.[45]
Hopkins, who kept referring to the circumstances of the letters as "tragic,"
suggested expedients of retaliation against Block that sounded as if they
would make excellent sample chapters for a spy novel, and the solutions
were equally and totally unrealistic.[46]   Someone else suggested that an
attempt could be made to buy the letters back from Block, but everyone
who was present who knew Block well – Roosevelt, Baruch, Early –
thought that there was no chance of him agreeing to that ploy.

Roosevelt saw the chance of his re-election crumbling. He had to establish a plan to fight Block. Before they ended their meeting that night,
the President and his advisors decided on three pieces of action against
Block. First, they would send a contingent of officials to meet with
Wallace, who was already on the campaign trail, and instruct and tutor
him as to how to the handle the press if and when the story broke. Second, all of the available people from the Democratic Party and from the
White House who were involved in publicity, and who could be spared,
would be sent to New York City (where Paul Block lived) to try to head
the story off, or failing that, to try to minimize and control the damage as
best as possible. Third, the Attorney General was instructed to meet with

Lurleen Wallace, the candidate's wife, to see that she did not make any "unfortunate responses" should she be interviewed by a reporter from the Block newspapers, or anyone else.[47]   With the Fish Room meeting over, everyone went to work to try to stop or minimize Block's potential attack.

If Block elected to publish the content of the letters, Roosevelt had a retaliatory strategy, he confided the next day to an assistant of his, Lowell Mellett (the former editor of the *Washington News*). The Democrats could counterattack by spreading gossip and planting stories about a certain woman friend of Wendell Willkie's, Irita Van Doren, literary editor of *The New York Herald-Tribune*, who happened not to be his wife. "Awful nice gal," clucked the President. "But nevertheless, there is the *fact...*" [that she is his mistress]. And if that wasn't enough to make Willkie look bad, there was always the story that the Democratic Party had discovered that Willkie refused to pay for the upkeep of his mother's cemetery plot.[48] Somehow, perhaps through Bernard Baruch who was a friend of both Block *and* Roosevelt, the alternative tactic plan by the Presidential staff got back to Block. Since Willkie had been trying to set up a meeting with him, Block went to meet the candidate and he determined that the two rumors, about Willkie's mother and about his mistress, were true. Willkie, perhaps because he was afraid of the Democratic retaliation, or because of ethical reasons, we do not now know, asked Block not to publish the Guru Letters.

Block called for a meeting of some of the Republican Party leaders and Willkie supporters at his comfortable apartment in the Waldorf Towers Hotel to discuss the Guru Letters. His neighbor, who lived in the same building – Herbert Hoover – was there, as was Joseph Martin, Republican minority leader of the House, and then Republican National Chairman, and a contingent of Republican Party strategists. Block informed the group that his reporter Ray Sprigle had just returned from the West where, to no avail, he attempted to interview Henry Wallace. Getting wind of Sprigle's trip (perhaps tipped by Harry Hopkins's spy in the *Pittsburgh Post-Gazette*) the Democrats sent an emissary to Wallace to thoroughly school him in handling the Pulitzer Prize-winning reporter. When Sprigle arrived, Wallace was calm and laughing and suggested that the letters had been around for years, and that people had been trying to sell them, also for years, all to no avail. He was equipped with a drafted statement that had just a touch of campaign rhetoric, possibly written by White House attorneys, and he read it aloud to Sprigle. It said, in part:

> The documents in question have been hawked around for many years, at times to private individuals, at other times to publishers. Your publisher [Paul Block] must know the story of the disgruntled discharged employee, a tax evader, who dares not re-enter this land, from which all this stems. The American public is of age. It will interpret as political bankruptcy any such publication, since your first proposed article, as drafted, is not only libelous and outrageous in its departure from the truth, but clearly is designed to raise in the midst of our citizenry minority religious suspicions and hatreds."[49]

They were forgeries, Wallace claimed as an aside, and he could prove it. He wouldn't say anything more, and never did.[50] His intransigence in discussing the matter may well have prevented him from running for President in 1948.

Someone else at Block's meeting said that he heard that a United Press reporter tried to interview Wallace about the "Guru Letters" and was handed a statement, perhaps the same one he read to Sprigle, to the effect that he would sue anyone for libel who published them.[51] Block told the group that he was sure that if he published the correspondence, the Democrats would be back with recriminations concerning Willkie's personal life, and that in any event innocent people might be hurt by their publication. It was felt that aside from the immorality of it, it was bad politics. Joseph Martin later revealed in a masterpiece of revisionist thinking: "I didn't know anything about this fellow, 'Guru.' Maybe he had a great many more followers than any of us realized. Why back away from their votes? Everything considered, therefore, I decided that the Republicans would not use those letters. That put an end to the matter."[52] In conclusion, neither Roosevelt nor Block blinked, nor did they rush to engage. The shadow of the letters hung over the Democrats all through the campaign and it wasn't until Wednesday morning, November 6th, 1940, when Roosevelt knew he had won a third term in office, that he finally began to stop worrying about the threat of Block's "Guru Letters."

The Final Years, and a Shift From Isolationism

The possibilities and promise that the "Guru Letters" held for him gave Block a temporary renewal of hope, and he seemed to regain his fire when columnist Dorothy Thompson delivered her salvo from Paris that the two-party system should be dropped and that Roosevelt be automatically elected for a third term because of the gravity of the war in Europe. "Miss Thompson seems to have lost her perspective," Block shot back, countering the radical thoughts that she had expressed in her nationwide column. Mentioning that her suggestion encouraged a form of dictatorship, he concluded: "There is less excuse than ever before for us to turn aside from the American way which has stood the test of time for a century and a half and, we confidently trust, will endure for a long time to come."[53]

After he abandoned the idea of using the Guru Letters against Wallace, and Roosevelt succeeded in winning his third term, Block immediately fell back into what was becoming a familiar morass of despondency. He was disturbed over the fact that Hearst's empire had shrunk to half its size, and that Brisbane had died. Some of the people that he had worked with at the *Toledo Blade* since 1908 had also died recently, and that too depressed him.

All during the late 1930s, Paul Block's health was not good. Family members complained that most of what he was experiencing was hypochondriacal; that he was suffering from extreme depression and overwork which centered on imaginary physical ailments. Initially, there may have been some truth to those observations, but as the French philosopher, E.M. Cioran has pointed out, imaginary pains are by far the most real we suffer; they are the true agony since we feel a constant need for them, and are forced to invent them because there is simply no way of doing without them. If at first some of the aches and pains that Block was suffering *were* produced by his psychological or existential pressure, they were no less distressing or anguishing than if he had had a "real" breakage or damage to his body.

He worried and tormented himself constantly, not only about the draining strength of his businesses, which was a real and present strain on him, but at what others might consider trifles: whether Billy was getting enough sleep; how Paul was doing in his scientific education; whether a particular employee liked him or not; whether Dina truly forgave him of a minor blunder of forgetfulness; whether the birthday gift that he gave a friend was sufficient enough token; whether to venture out on a frigid day. His melancholy thoughts burgeoned into a litany of woe. He was often indisposed and frequently could not really say what was bothering him.

Block began spending more time in his apartment in the Waldorf Astoria Towers, not because he didn't love Friendship in Greenwich, but because he wanted to be near his doctors, who he had begun to frequent much more regularly. His pains – in his stomach, his back and his legs – came frequently; no one could claim anymore that they were psychosomatic. He had almost daily injections of morphine, but none of his doctors, Dr. J. Ralph Jacobi, Dr. Theodore Lucas, or Dr. William Harris could find the specific cause of his agony. Block referred to it as rheumatism, but it proved to be much more devastating than that.

In April of 1941, he wrote two editorials, both concerning aid to England. The first, which was arguably the single most important opinion piece he ever wrote in his life, announced that he had changed his mind about sending aid to England and maintaining an isolationist position. Reversing the opinion he had expressed in a March editorial, Block now wrote that the United States must not withhold assistance. "America must prove its determination to keep democracy alive. We must deliver goods to Britain ourselves, in spite of the risk of being pulled into war."[54] Block's polemic represented the first newspaper in the country that supported the view that we had to become England's ally.

Beaverbrook was grateful and overwhelmed by Block's change of position as stated in his editorial, and responded with an important letter of thanks:

> May 30, 1941
>
> …The copy of the *Pittsburgh Post-Gazette* which you sent to me is the most moving example of the help you give to our cause.
>
> Once more, you show yourself as a leader of the vanguard of our supporters. And the debt of gratitude owed to you by the people of Britain is deep indeed. They look to the United States in gratitude for what you have done already, and in confident expectation.
>
> They realize that, like themselves, your nation moves slowly at the start. But they are certain that when the full tide of your production begins to flow, the victory of freedom will be in sight.
>
> Max (Beaverbrook)

The second editorial by Block commended his friend Franklin Knox (who despite the fact that he was in the "wrong" party, had been named by Roosevelt as Secretary of the Navy) for backing up his editorial position on England. At a meeting of the American Newspaper Publishers

Association in New York (it was held, ironically, in the Waldorf, ten floors below Block's apartment), which Block attended with nearly one thousand other publishers, Knox acknowledged Block's editorial that had appeared eight days previously, and stated that the war was "plainly *our* war" and that we had to do everything necessary to assure an English victory. Block pointed out that Knox's statement "was in perfect accord with our editorial" and that he was glad "that this Government has come to agree with the position we took."[55] They were the last position statements that Block would ever write, and it is not a rush to judgment to conclude that it is possible that his ideas about support for England helped precipitate America's direct involvement in World War II.

Soon after Knox's speech, Dina and Block took a transcontinental trip to California to be the guests of William Randolph Hearst at San Simeon. They were accompanied by Dr. Lucas, now in constant attendance, who apparently had given up his practice to do nothing but to treat Paul Block exclusively. Family members believed that Block was paying the doctor an exorbitant amount of money, and that because he could have painkilling injections on demand, Block was almost becoming addicted. He certainly became increasingly dependent on the shots. Dina became incensed that Dr. Lucas seemed to be living off the money that Block was paying him, and distressed that he was always with them, taking a guest room at Friendship for weeks on end, sleeping in their private railroad car when he traveled with them, and only leaving the suite at the Waldorf to go home to his own apartment to sleep at night.

Despite his pain, Block's respite at San Simeon was a good time for him, and he spent several weeks at the castle with his old friend. Both men were night owls and they would spend hours sitting on the verandah as the sky grew black, listening to the crashing sea and discussing all manner of things – the state of the world, the newspaper business, government and politics – especially Block's opinion on aid to England: Hearst remained an isolationist but recognized that war was "More than a probability. In fact, it may be set down as a certainty."[56] They also discussed the forthcoming film *Citizen Kane,* a *cinema à clef* of Hearst's life, directed by Orson Welles. Hearst had covertly seen a copy of the film shortly before Block arrived, and before it was released, and he was enraged. He was doing as much as he could to have the film suppressed but it was due to open in a matter of weeks.[57] One wonders if Block was worried about whether he would appear as a character in the film, since he had introduced Marion Davies to Hearst.

Hearst seemed to take up where Block was leaving off: he had recently commenced writing a daily column for his papers, since he never could find a suitable replacement for Arthur Brisbane.[58]   Titled "In the News," Hearst wrote the column in longhand, sometimes using a large, green crayon, and Block was amazed that Hearst could write a complete, ready-to-publish editorial in the space of about an hour.   Occasionally Hearst would discuss with Block what he was going to write, since the pieces were often autobiographical, and he would reminisce with Block as a way of jogging his own memory. Hearst was close to 80; Block was 66, although for some unexplained reason he admitted only to being 63. Both men had between them well over 100 years in the newspaper business. Both of them had strong memories of Park Row, the Ziegfeld Follies, World War I, politics, and journalism.

While at San Simeon, Block developed an infection on his lip; it was an ugly abscess, first thought to be a cold sore by Dr. Lucas, but when Block failed to develop a cold, and when the sore grew larger and darker, the doctor believed it to be something much more serious. As a result of his appearance, Block became extremely self-conscious. It was thought that the vacation should be cut short and Block should return home in case further, more extensive treatment might be needed.

Enroute back to New York, Block stopped in Toledo to do a few days' work for the *Blade,* and also to see Billy. Talking of his father's lip sore, William Block remembered: "I never saw anything like that on anyone, or certainly not on him."[59]   Block continued east, spent a day in Pittsburgh at the *Post-Gazette,* and then finally returned home and ensconced himself in the Waldorf Towers.

Billy was to be drafted in the Army, and he discussed with his brother Paul whether he should seek a postponement or not because it was obvious that Block was seriously ill. It was decided that he would go ahead and be drafted. What Billy didn't know was that his father wanted him near him, and afraid that the young man might object to any paternal interference, Block began making discreet inquiries as to how he could have his son transferred from Fort Hayes, Ohio to a base near New York City.

Without Billy's knowledge, Block wrote several letters to former President Herbert Hoover to see if he could intervene. Hoover was happy to help; he wrote, first, to the publisher of the *Army and Navy Journal* in Washington, D.C.   When that failed, he wrote to Lt. General Hugh A. Drum, the commanding officer of Governor's Island, off Manhattan, in

New York Bay, and he received a positive response.

Two months later, Billy was transferred to an intelligence department of the 1st Army Headquarters on Governor's Island, just a five-minute ferry ride from Manhattan. Since the country was not yet at war, Army personnel were permitted to live off base as long as they were present for muster by the time reveille sounded in the morning. As a result, Billy moved in with his parents at the Waldorf Towers, and went to Governor's Island every morning to serve in the Army. Block was so happy to have his son near him that he told Hoover, in thanking him for arranging it, that Billy's presence would probably get him well in the near future.[60]

Block's condition was finally diagnosed at the Cornell-NYU Medical Center: he had both pancreatic *and* liver cancer. It was inoperable, and chemotherapy and radiation therapy as possible cures had not yet been developed to any kind of stage that would have been of help. Block was given only a few weeks to live.

Block's last days were difficult for the family, and traumatic for Billy Block. A live-in nurse took an overly-proprietary interest in her patient – William Block thought in retrospect that she may have fallen in love with Block – and she would often lock the bedroom door and not allow anyone, including Dina, to enter. A sense of rivalry over Block's care began to develop between the two women, but Dina felt she couldn't dismiss the nurse because she was taking such good care of Block, and he was responding somewhat positively to her ministrations.

Soon, Block began to go in and out of consciousness, and lapsing into a semi-comatose state. When it looked as though he could die at any time, Billy petitioned for a 10-day furlough from the Army, was granted it, and stayed at home helping his mother as best he could. On June 22, 1941, Billy was in the living room at the Waldorf, reading the Sunday edition of *The New York Times,* which ran an 8-column, blaring headline on its front-page:

HITLER BEGINS WAR ON RUSSIA, WITH ARMIES
ON MARCH FROM ARCTIC TO THE BLACK SEA;
DAMASCUS FALLS; U.S. OUSTS ROME CONSULS

Dr. Jacobi emerged from the bedroom and gently announced to Billy and Dina that Paul Block had just died. If he had been conscious, Block probably would have wanted to know what newspaper his son was reading and what he thought of the situation.

•••

The funeral arrangements were difficult to make. Dina went into mourning and asked Billy to see to as many of the details as possible. Since he had little experience with funerals, he found it arduous and complex to make a selection for a casket. Judaic law forbids ostentation at a funeral, following the premise that simple burial rites enforce the principle of "democracy in death;" thus no family, however impoverished, would be ashamed of the simplicity of the coffin or the plainness of the shroud. Jewish burial is as expeditious as can be arranged. There is no "wake."

After conferring with the Rabbi of the Temple Emanuel-El, Dina's synagogue, it was arranged that Paul Block's funeral would be in two days. Paul, Jr. handled the task of notifying Block's friends, relatives and associates, calling them and sending telegrams all over the country, and choosing a contingent of honorary pallbearers. People responded immediately over the telephone or by wire within hours. Herbert Hoover wrote a note to Paul Block, Jr. and had it delivered to Block's suite:

> My Dear Paul
>
> I shall be very glad indeed to serve as you wish.
>
> Your father has been my loyal friend for a quarter of a century. I am deeply shocked at his passing and the loss to all of us. My loss must be much less than yours and your mother's.
>
> I wish to extend to you the deepest sympathy both of Mrs. Hoover and myself.
>
> Faithfully yours,
> Herbert Hoover[61]

At the appointed hour, the Temple filled with one of the largest-attended funeral services in its history; over 500 mourners came to pay their respects, as if Block were a head of state. In the front rows, in addition to Block's wife and children, his sisters and brothers and other

relatives, sat a phalanx of his friends and colleagues, almost a living biography of the man. To know the names of this last group, many of
whom were listed as honorary pallbearers, is to understand the history of
Paul Block. They included: Herbert Hoover, Jimmy Walker, Alfred E.
Smith, Bernard Baruch, Irving Berlin, Frank Knox, Bernard F. Gimbel,
Herbert Lehman, Lee Shubert, Henry L. Stoddard, and at one of the few
funerals that he ever attended in his life, William Randolph Hearst. Hearst
gave a formal, albeit heartfelt, statement to the press: "I am shocked and
grieved beyond measure to hear of the death of my good friend, Paul
Block. Journalism will feel the loss of a really great publisher, and the
country will miss one of its most valuable and valued citizens."[62] Spread
throughout the Temple were people from all walks of life who knew and
loved Paul Block: newspaper reporters, advertising men, porters and waiters who worked on his private railroad car, servants and groundskeepers
from his house and his apartment, doormen, fellow bridge players, policemen, and just plain friends. In an unusual gesture at a Jewish funeral
service, there was an arrangement of red roses atop the casket.

At 1 PM, the exact moment that the service began, his newspaper employees in Toledo and in Pittsburgh stopped preparing the presses and the
linotype machines, ceased typing or talking on the telephone, and a moment of silence for "P.B." was observed.

Dr. Samuel H. Goldenson officiated, with the organ prelude *Come, Sweet
Death* opening the service, and then Cantor Moshe Rudinow sang *The
Lord is My Shepherd*. Grove Patterson gave the eulogy, and he said later
that although he had spoken in public thousands of times, he was not
certain – because he was so emotionally distraught – that he would be
able to speak in behalf of his friend and colleague that afternoon. Patterson
had tears in his eyes when he said: "He suffered from the ravages of a
passion for perfection. He was not satisfied with anything less than the
best of which his associates were capable. Consequently he was a continuing and a durable inspiration that did not drive but led." Patterson
went on to say that Block showed great courage as a publisher, much
generosity as a public benefactor, and immense loyalty as a friend.

Block was entombed in a mausoleum at the Kensico Cemetery in
Westchester, not very far from his estate, Friendship. Dr. Goldenson led
the mourner's prayer of *Kaddish* (although it does not contain one reference to death) at the cemetery. Afterwards, friends and relatives returned
to Block's apartment where they were served, among other things, hard-
boiled eggs, said to be symbolic of the need for life to go on...among the

mourners.

Block's death made headlines in newspapers all over the country, and expressions of sympathy and floral tributes by the hundreds poured in for Dina and the family. Arthur Hays Sulzberger, publisher of *The New York Times,* wrote of Block's wide influence as a philanthropist; his old friend Alfred E. Smith talked of his unselfishness; Sen. Robert A. Taft reported that Block's death was a great shock to him; Lord Beaverbrook, who had moved up in British government to be next in rank to the Prime Minister, was devastated over his friend Paul Block's passing and wrote of his profound sorrow, and his affection and admiration for the American publisher. Paul Block, Jr. received a heartbreaking letter from E. Minemura, a Japanese servant who worked for the Block household for many years, and who had left the United States to return to his native country: "He was the most kind-hearted gentleman I ever had contact with during my long stay in your country. I will never forget how well your mother and father treated me when I was their household employee. I am sending you this humble condolence of mine for the loss of your beloved father, and I wish, from the bottom of my heart, for you to try to cheer your mother at this great loss, because she has only you and your brother left now." [63]

On the day after Block died, his favorite editorial cartoonist, Cy Hungerford, drew a touching sketch, which was published in the *Toledo Blade* and *Pittsburgh Post-Gazette*. It summed up how a great many people were feeling about Paul Block's death at the time. The picture shows the door open to Paul Block's office (his name is on the door), and the office is empty. A gentle light, or presence, is emanating from around Block's desk. The caption reads:

"Away, But His Spirit Lives"

Endnotes

In doing the research for this book, the author found numerous newspaper and magazine clippings, tear sheets, galley proofs and letters pertaining to Paul Block or his publications. They were in the archives and scrapbooks of newspapers, libraries, historical societies and corporations. Some were yellowed and brittle, virtually ready to turn into dust. Many had been marked with a date stamp, but without an indication of a page or section number. Some of the letters and memoranda were undated. Because the information contained in these cuttings and letters was valuable, they have been included as sources in the Endnotes, but in some cases without a specific page location of where they appeared in the original newspaper or magazine, and in some cases with only an approximation of the date they were written.

These documents were found in the files and morgues of Blade Communications, Inc., the Block family archive, the Brooklyn Public Library's archive of the *Brooklyn Eagle* (with stories from the *Brooklyn Standard Union*), the *Toledo Blade*, the *Pittsburgh Post-Gazette*, the *Elmira Telegram*, the New York Historical Society, the Municipal Archives of New York, the Bancroft Library of the University of California at Berkeley, the *Newark Star-Eagle*, the Chemung County Historical Society, *Editor & Publisher*, and *Printer's Ink*, as well as the Presidential libraries of Warren G. Harding, Calvin Coolidge, Herbert Hoover and Franklin D. Roosevelt, the archive of Governor Alfred E. Smith, and the archive of Mayor James Walker.

Researchers who are interested in studying more about the life and career of Paul Block may consider going to microfilms of the newspaper and magazine sources indicated, looking up the dates noted, and searching for the correct page upon which the story appears.

Endnotes for Chapter One

1 Advertising herald, circa Nov.1870, Chemung County Historical Society.

2 Michelle L. Cotton, *Mark Twain's Elmira 1870-1910* (Elmira, NY: Chemung County Historical Society, 1985), pp. 4-5.

3 Samuel T. Williamson, *Imprint of a Publisher* (New York: Robert M. Mc Bride & Co., 1948), p. 47.

4 Chemung Historical Society, *Chemung County...its History* (Elmira,

New York: Chemung County Historical Society, 1961), p. 65; also Dr. Herbert A. Wesbey, Jr., "Intellectual Life of Elmira," *Chemung Historical Journal*, June 1997; p. 4642.

5 Chemung Historical Society, *Chemung County...its History,* p. 65.

6 Elmira Advertising Association, *Elmira Past and Present*; fact sheet, circa 1894.

7 Cotton, p. 12.

8 Kamphoefuer, Helbich and Sommerv *News From the Land of Freedom* (Ithaca, NY: Cornell University Press, 1991) p. 22.

9 Chemung County Historical Society, *German Heritage of the Chemung Valley, History* (Elmira, New York: Chemung County Historical Society, 1987), pp. 6-7.

10 Kamphoefuer, p. 51.

11 "Elmira – The Queen City," *Chemung Historical Journal*, June 1969, pp. 1837-1839.

12 Cotton, p. 40.

13 Cotton, p. 38.

14 *Williams Elmira City Directory; Hanford's Elmira City Directory*; and *Elmira City Directory*, 1882-1896.

15 Chemung Historical Society, *Chemung County...its History,* p. 46.

16 Elisabeth Carr Chapman, "The Homes, the People of Elmira's Eastside," *Chemung Historical Journal*, Dec. 1967, p. 1649.

17 Chapman, p. 1651.

18 Elmira city directories, 1882-1896.

19 Benjamin F. Levy, *The First Jewish Settlers in Elmira and Vicinity, 1848-1906,* a lecture at the Chemung County Historical Society, 4 Jan. 1934, p. 4.

20 Levy, p. 8.

21 Levy, p. 7.

22 Gerald Sorin, *A Time for Building: The Third Migration* (Baltimore: The Johns Hopkins University Press), 1992. p. 4

23 Levy, p. 25.

24 Chapman, p. 1652.

25 John Burnham, *The Ragpicker or Bound and Free* (New York: Mason Bros. Publishers, 1855), p. 1.

26 "Jewish Synagogues," *Elmira Past and Present*, Elmira Advertising Association,1894, and Levy, p. 24.

27 Cotton, p. 39.

28 Frank L. Mott, *A History of American Magazines 1865-1885* (Cam-

bridge: Harvard University Press, 1968), vol. 3 p. 691.

29 Ausburn Towner, *Our County and Its People: A History of the Valley and County of Chemung* (Elmira: D. Mason & Co., Publishers, 1892), p. 409.

30 Frank Luther Mott, *American Journalism* (New York: Macmillan, 1962), p. 507.

31 *The Elmira Telegram*, masthead guarantee, 1887.

32 *N.W. Ayer & Son's Newspaper Annual*, advertisement 1885, p. 754.

33 "Harry S. Brooks," *A Biographical Record of Chemung County* (Elmira, New York: S.J. Clarke Publishing Co., 1902), p. 68.

34 Mott, *American Journalism*, p. 507.

35 Frank Thayer, *Newspaper Management* (New York: D. Appleton and Co., 1926), p. 70.

36 James Melvin Lee, *History of American Journalism* (Boston: Houghton Mifflin Co., 1923), p. 380.

37 Alfred Mc Clung Lee, *The Daily Newspaper in America* (New York: Macmillan, 1937), p. 166.

38 Towner, p. 408.

39 Towner, pp. 406-409.

40 Susan B. Roberts, "Elmira – The Queen City" originally published in 1898, re-published in *The Sunday Telegram,* 7 Feb. 1909.

41 Mott, *American Journalism*, p. 584.

42 Samuel T. Williamson, *Imprint of a Publisher* (New York: Robert McBride & Co., 1948), p. 85.

43 *N.W. Ayer & Son's Newspaper Annual and Directory*, advertisement 1885, p. 55.

44 Sylvia G. Faisboff and Wendell Tripp, *A Bibliography of Newspapers in Fourteen New York Counties* (Albany: N.Y. State Historical Association ,1978), p. 85.

45 *Elmira Telegram*, 6 Jan. 1895, p. 2.

46 Eugene C. Harter, *Boilerplating America:The Hidden Newspaper* (Lanham, MD: University Press of America, 1995, pps. 17-57.

47 Joseph G. Herzberg, *Late City Edition* (New York: Henry Holt and Co., 1947), p. 213.

48 *Elmira Telegram*, 6 Jan. 1895, p. 4., and others.

49 *The Illustrated London News,* 23 Dec. 1854, p. 1.

50 *Elmira Daily Advertiser*, 5 Aug. 1889, p. 3.

51 Lee, p. 323.

52 Ralph Frasca, *The Rise and Fall of the Saturday Globe* (Cranbury,

NJ: Susquehanna University Press, 1992), p. 71.

53 *Elmira Daily Gazette*, 10 Feb. 1890, p. 7.

54 Towner, p. 408.

55 Eva C. Taylor and Frances B. Myers, "Once Upon a Time," *Chemung County Historical Journal*, Sept. 1962, p. 1025.

56 Charles Elkins Rogers, *Journalistic Vocations* (East Norwalk, CT: D. Appleton and Company, 1931), p. 198.

57 Frank Presbrey, *The History and Development of Advertising* (Garden City, NY: Doubleday, Doran and Co., 1929), p. 230.

58 Rogers, p. 199.

59 *Elmira Telegram,* 31 Aug. 1890, p. 9.

60 *Elmira Telegram*, 31 Aug. 1890.

61 Tom Byrne, "Cyclists Travel Area," *Chemung Historical Journal*, June 1997, p. 4638.

62 Harry S. Brooks to Paul Block, letter of 15 Aug. 1904, Blade Communications archive.

63 Harry S. Brooks to Paul Block, letter, 31 Oct. 1908, Blade Communications archive.

64 "Off For New York – Paul Block and 'Colonel,' the *Telegram* Mascot, Leave for the Metropolis," *Elmira Telegram*, 6 April 1890.

65 Caption under the promotional photograph of Paul Block and Colonel, circa 1887, Blade Communications archive.

66 *Elmira Telegram*, 21 Dec. 1890, p. 11.

67 *Elmira Telegram*, 23 Aug. 1891, p. 6.

68 John Robinson Block, interview of Dina Wallach Block, New York City, 21 Jan. 1977, Block family archive.

69 Harry S. Brooks to Paul Block, memorandum, 23 Aug. 1894.

70 T.D. Nostwich, ed., *Theodore Dreiser: Journalism*, Vol. One, (Philadelphia, University of Pennsylvania Press, 1988), preface.

71 *Elmira Telegram*, 25 Dec. 1890, p. 8.

72 *Elmira Telegram*, circa 1893.

73 John Robinson Block, interview of Dina Wallach Block.

74 *Elmira Telegram*, 10 Aug. 1889, p. 6.

75 *Elmira Telegram*, circa Jan. 1891, p. 5.

76 *Elmira Telegram,* 6 Jan. 1891, p. 5.

77 *Elmira Telegram*, 25 April 1891, p. 7.

78 *Elmira Telegram*, 18 March 1894, p. 9.

79 Harry S. Brooks, "Why Some Young Men Succeed," *Elmira Telegram,* circa 1915, editorial.

80 Harry S. Brooks, *Elmira Telegram*, circa 1920, unsigned editorial.

81 *Elmira Telegram*, 6 Jan. 1895, p. 9.

82 Lee, p. 356.

83 Charles F. Wingate, ed., *Views and Interviews on Journalism* (New York: F. B. Patterson, Co., 1875), p. 275.

84 *Elmira Telegram*, 5 June 1892, p. 4.

85 *Elmira Telegram,* 14 Jan. 1894, p. 5.

86 *Elmira Star-Gazette*, 14 July 1926, p. 8.

87 Towner, p. 409.

Endnotes for Chapter Two

1 Jensen, Oliver, ed., *The Nineties* (New York: *American Heritage Publishing Co.*, 1967), p. 10.

2 *The Life History of the United States, Reaching for Empire, 1890-1901* (New York: Time-Life Books, 1964), p. 65.

3 Edward Robb Ellis, *The Epic of New York City* (New York: Old Town Books, 1966), p. 459.

4 Eric Homberger, *The Historical Atlas of New York City* (New York: Henry Holt and Co., 1994), p. 99.

5 James Trager, *West of Fifth* (New York: Atheneum, 1987), p. 4.

6 *Toledo Blade*, 21 Oct. 1929, p. 8b.

7 Abraham Cahan, "The Russian Jew in America," *Atlantic Monthly*, July 1898, p. 32.

8 E. Idell Zeisloft, *The New Metropolis* (New York: Scribner's, 1899) p. 62.

9 "Metropolitan Home Delivery Methods," *Editor and Publisher*, 30 May 1925, p. 14.

10 *Newspaperdom,* Apr. 1893, p. 3.

11 Allen Churchill, *Park Row* (New York: Rinehart & Co., 1958), p. 18.

12 Joseph Howard, Jr., "Howard's Journalistic Observations," *New York Recorder*, June 1892, p. 44.

13 James Melvin Lee, *History of American Journalism* (Boston: Houghton Mifflin Co., 1923), p.262.

14 Lee, p. 37.

15 Sworn circulation statement, *The New York World*, 25 Sept. 1895, p. 1.

16 *Newspaperdom,* 16 Jan. 1896, p. 8.

17 Frank Luther Mott, *American Journalism* (New York: The Macmillan

Company, 1962), p. 499.

18 *N.W. Ayer & Sons Newspaper Annual and Directory, 1881 to 1900.*

19 *Printer's Ink,* 20 Sept. 1917, pp. 100-101.

20 *Newspaperdom,* 16 Jan. 1896, p. 8.

21 *Newspaperdom,* Apr. 1894, p. 456.

22 John K. Winkler, *W.R. Hearst: An American Phenomenon* (New York: Simon & Schuster, 1928), p. 99.

23 Lee, p. 373.

24 Michael Emery and Edwin Emery, *The Press in America,* 7th ed. (Englewood Cliffs, N.J.: Prentice Hall, 1992), p. 305.

25 Edmond D. Coblentz, ed., *Newsmen Speak* (Berkeley: University of California Press, 1954), p. 121.

26 *Editor & Publisher,* 4 Nov. 1916, p. 8.

27 John Robinson Block, interview of Dina Wallach Block, New York City, 21 Jan. 1977, Block family archive.

28 *Editor & Publisher,* 7 Sept. 1918, p. 13.

29 Roger Butterfield, "Pictures in the Papers," *American Heritage,* June 1962, p. 48.

30 *New York World,* 25 Sept. 1895, p. 16.

31 Ben Procter, *William Randolph Hearst: The Early Years, 1863-1910* (Oxford and New York: Oxford University Press, 1998), pp. 80-82.

32 Marcus M. Wilkerson, *Public Opinion and the Spanish-American War: A Study in War Propaganda* (Baton Rouge: Louisiana State University Press, 1932).

33 Soon Jim Kim, *An Anatomy of the Hearst Press Campaign to Fortify an American Isthmian Canal,* Ph.D. dissertation, University of Maryland, 1982, p. 89.

34 Mott, p. 539.

35 *Printer's Ink,* 1 Jan. 1920, p. 142.

36 Michael Schudson, *Discovering the News* (New York: Basic Books, 1978), p. 19.

37 *Newspaperdom,* 2 Feb. 1896, p. 11.

38 *Printer's Ink,* 24 June 1915, p. 155.

39 *N.W. Ayer & Son's Newspaper Annual,* 1894, p. 1312.

40 *Newspaperdom,* 2 Apr. 1896, p. 7.

41 *Fowler's Publicity* (New York: Publicity Publishing Company, 1897), p. 971.

42 E. T. Gundlach, *Facts and Fetishes in Advertising* (New York: Consolidated Book Publishers, Inc., 1931), p. 22.

43 *Newspaperdom,* Mar. 1893, p. 16.

44 *Printer's Ink,* 18 Mar. 1915, p. 37.

45 *Printer's Ink,* 24 June 1915, p. 86.

46 *Printer's Ink,* 24 June 1915, pp. 155-156.

47 *Editor & Publisher,* 15 Mar. 1924, p. 11.

48 *Printer's Ink,* 16 June 1919, pp. 17-20.

49 *Printer's Ink,* 24 June 1915, p. 154.

50 "'Good Old Days' Were 'Pretty Bad' says Halsted," *Editor & Publisher,* 10 Dec. 1946.

51 *Newspaperdom,* 19 Dec. 1895, p. 496.

52 *N.W. Ayer & Son's Newspaper Annual and Directory,* 1899, pp. 1404-1405.

53 *N.W. Ayer & Son's Newspaper Annual and Directory,* 1896, p. 1320.

54 Ralph Frasca, *The Rise and Fall of the Saturday Globe* (Cranbury, N.J.: Susquehanna University Press, 1992), p. 40.

55 *N.W. Ayer & Son's Newspaper Annual,* 1896, p. 1320.

56 Herman G. Halsted to Dina Block, letter of 13 July 1941, Block family archive.

57 *The New York Times,* 3 Nov. 1900.

58 Amy Janello and Breenan Jones, *The American Magazine* (New York: Harry M. Abrams, 1991), p. 196.

59 Gerald J. Baldasty, "The Media and the National Economy," quoting Hower, *A History of Macy's,* in *The Significance of the Media,* ed. James D. Startt and William David Sloan, (Northport, AL.: Vision Press, 1994), p. 177.

60 "Where National Advertising Needs Help," *Printer's Ink,* 3 July 1919, p. 36.

61 *Editor & Publisher,* 4 Nov. 1916, p. 32.

62 *N.W. Ayer & Sons Newspaper Annual and Directory,* 1898, p. 1376.

63 Homberger, p. 174.

64 *Printer's Ink,* 25 Aug. 1897, p. 42.

65 Irving Fang, *A History of Mass Communication* (New York: Focal Press, 1997), p. 63.

66 *Elmira Telegram,* 7 May 1893, p. 8.

67 William Block, Jr., ed., *Memoirs of William Block* (Toledo: Blade Communications, 1990), p. 4.

68 *Printer's Ink,* 13 Apr. 1916, p. 33.

69 Dan Rather, ed., *Our Times: America at the Birth of the Twentieth Century,* based on 1926 study by Mark Sullivan (New York: Scribner,

1996), p. 230.

70 Daniel Pope, *The Making of Modern Advertising* (New York: Basic Books, 1983), p. 194.

71 Pope, p. 194.

72 *Newspaperdom,* 26 Sept. 1895.

73 Samuel Hopkins Adams, "The Great American Fraud," *Collier's,* 13 Jan. 1906, pp. 18-20.

74 *Printer's Ink,* 1903.

75 Adams, pp. 18-20.

76 *Collier's Magazine,* 4 Nov. 1905.

77 Samuel Hopkins Adams, "The Patent Medicine Conspiracy Against the Freedom of the Press," *Collier's,* 4 Nov. 1905.

78 Adams, "The Patent Medicine Conspiracy."

79 *Printer's Ink,* 8 Feb. 1912.

80 John Robinson Block, interview of Dina Wallach Block, 21 Jan. 1977.

81 Henry F. Pringle, *Theodore Roosevelt: A Biography* (New York: Harcourt, Brace & Co., 1956), pp.132-150.

82 *Toledo Blade,* 6 Mar. 1930, p. 106.

83 Pringle, pp. 132-150.

84 Bill Harris, *The History of New York City* (New York: Portland House, 1989), pp. 134-135.

85 Chris McNickle, *To Be Mayor of New York* (New York: Columbia University Press, 1993), p. 13.

86 Clifton Daniel, ed., *Chronicle of America* (New York: D.K. Publishing, Inc., 1997), p. 528.

87 From the *Toledo Blade* archive.

88 From the *Toledo Blade* archive.

89 From the *Toledo Blade* archive.

Endnotes for Chapter Three

1 James Trager, *West of Fifth* (New York: Atheneum, 1987), p. 143.

2 William Block, Jr., ed., *Memoirs of William Block* (Toledo, Ohio: Blade Communications, Inc. 1990), p. 4.

3 *National Encyclopedia of American Biography* (New York: James T. White & Co., 1953), Vol. 38, p. 448.

4 Henry L. Stoddard, *As I Knew Them* (New York: Harper & Bros., 1927), p. 2.

5 *The New York Times,* 14 Dec. 1947.

6 *Printer's Ink*, 18 Dec. 1919, p. 115.

7 *Printer's Ink*, 11 Sept. 1919, pp. 174-175.

8 *Printer's Ink*, 25 Nov. 1920.

9 Laura Longley Babb, ed., *Keeping Posted* (New York: Universe Books, 1977), p. vi.

10 *Washington Post*, 14 Oct. 1901.

11 *Editor & Publisher,* 13 Feb. 1926, p. 8.

12 Thomas Harrison Baker, *The Memphis Commercial Appeal* (Louisiana State University Press, 1971), pp. 209-210.

13 John Robinson Block, interview of Dina Wallach Block, New York City, 21 Jan. 1977, Block family archive.

14 Will Irwin, ed, *The American Newspaper* (Ames, Iowa: Iowa State University Press, 1969), p. 50.

15 *Printer's Ink*, March 4, 1920, p. 83.

16 Herman Halsted, letter to Dina Block, 13 July 1941, Block family archives.

17 *Editor & Publisher*, 29 Aug. 1903, p. 5.

18 *Saturday Evening Post*, 30 June 1928.

19 *Printer's Ink,* 1 May 1913, pp. 12-13.

20 *Printer's Ink*, 1 April 1920, p. 91.

21 Alfred McClung Lee, *The Daily Newspaper in America* (New York: The Macmillan Company, 1947), p. 119.

22 *Advertisers News,* circa 1902, p. 21.

23 *Editor & Publisher*, 29 Aug. 1903, p. 10.

24 William Block, Sr., letter to the author, 25 Feb. 1999.

25 Paul Goldberger, *The Skyscraper* (New York: Alfred A. Knopf, 1982), p. 38.

26 Rebecca Zurier, Robert W. Snyder, Virginia M. Mecklenberg, *Metropolitan Lives* (New York: W. W. Norton, 1989), p. 87.

27 Richard Zacks, *An Underground Education* (New York: Doubleday, 1997), p. 310.

28 *The Fourth Estate*, 24 Feb. 1906, p. 5.

29 John Gunther, *Taken at the Flood* (New York: Harper & Brother, 1960), pp. 83-84.

30 *National Census of 1900*, Vol. 166, ED 756, sheet 14, line 30.

31 Roger Butterfield, "Pictures in the Papers" (New York: American Heritage, June 1962), pp. 32-55.

32 *Elmira Star Gazette*, Aug. 7, 1997, p. 1.

33 Patricia Frantz Kery, *Great Magazine Covers of the World* (New

York: Abbeville Press, 1982), p. 241.

34 Amy Janello and Brennon Jones, *The American Magazine* (New York: Harry M. Abrams, 1991), p. 25.

35 Mary Ellen Zuckerman, *History of Popular Women's Magazines in the U.S.* (Westport, CT: Greenwood Press, 1988), p. 18.

36 *Pictorial Review*, Sept. 1906.

37 *Pictorial Review*, Nov. 1904.

38 *Pictorial Review*, Sept. 1906.

39 *Pictorial Review*, Sept. 1906.

40 *Pictorial Review*, Aug. 1906.

41 *Pictorial Review*, Nov. 1904.

42 *Pictorial Review*, Nov. 1904.

43 *Printer's Ink*, March 1915.

44 R.W.B. Lewis, *Edith Wharton* (New York: Harper & Row, 1975), p. 456.

45 *Pictorial Review,* Aug. 1925.

46 *Pictorial Review 25th Anniversary Issue 1899-1924*, 1924.

47 Address to Members of Associated Industries of America, 1910.

48 *Pictorial Review*, advertisements, 1912-1913.

49 Zuckerman p. 35.

50 *Printer's Ink*, Sept. 1914.

51 Zuckerman, p. 39.

52 Zuckerman, p. 80.

53 *Printer's Ink*, Dec. 1915.

54 Paul Block contribution lists, Blade Communications, Inc. archive.

55 *The New York Times*, 6 Oct. 1949, p. 31.

56 *Memoirs of William Block,* p. 2.

57 *Printer's Ink*, July 1917.

58 *Printer's Ink*, Dec. 1917.

59 *Printer's Ink*, advertisement, 1917.

60 *Printer's Ink*, May, 1918.

61 *Printer's Ink*, May 1919.

62 *Printer's Ink*, July 1920.

63 *Pictorial Review*, August 1923.

64 *William Ahnelt,* letter to Paul Block, circa 1924, Block family archive.

65 *William Block, Sr., letter to the author*, 24 Feb. 1999.

66 *William Block, Sr.*, letter *to the author*, 24 Feb. 1999.

67 John Robinson Block, interview of Dina Wallach Block, 1977.

68 Dina Block, letter to Mrs. William Ahnelt, circa 1943. Block family

archive.

Endnotes for Chapter Four

1 Frank Luther Mott, *American Journalism, A History: 1690-1960* (New York: Macmillan Group, 1962).

2 James Melvin Lee, *History of American Journalism* (Boston and New York: Houghton Mifflin Company, 1923).

3 *N.W. Ayer & Son's Newspaper Annual and Supplement*, 1901, p. 640.

4 *Printer's Ink*, 6 Apr. 1911, p. 46.

5 *Printer's Ink*, 19 Aug. 1920, p. 109.

6 *Printer's Ink*, 19 Aug. 1920, p. 109.

7 *Printer's Ink*, 19 Aug. 1920, p. 109.

8 *Editor & Publisher*, 13 July 1918.

9 *Editor & Publisher*, 13 Nov. 1920.

10 *Editor & Publisher*, 11 Nov. 1920.

11 *New York Evening Mail*, circa 1917.

12 *Editor & Publisher*, 27 Nov. 1920.

13 *Editor & Publisher*, 13 July 1918.

14 *Editor & Publisher*, 2 June 1917.

15 Alfred McClung Lee, *The Daily Newspaper in America: The Evolution of a Social Instrument* (New York: Macmillan Group, 1947)

16 *Editor & Publisher*, 14 Dec. 1918.

17 *Editor & Publisher*, 14 Dec. 1918.

18 *Editor & Publisher*, 14 Dec. 1918.

19 *Editor & Publisher*, 14 Dec. 1918.

20 *Editor & Publisher*, 14 Dec. 1918.

21 Piers Brendon, *The Life and Death of the Press Barons* (New York: Atheneum, 1983), p. 144.

22 Brendon, p. 144.

23 Brendon, p. 144.

24 *Editor & Publisher*, 13 July 1918.

25 *Editor & Publisher*, 13 Nov. 1920.

26 *Editor & Publisher*, 20 Nov. 1920.

27 *Editor & Publisher*, 27 Nov. 1920.

28 William Block, Sr., letter to author, 11 Jan. 2000.

29 Stephen Bates, *If No News, Send Rumors* (New York: St. Martin's Press, 1989), p. 232.

30 William Block Sr., letter to author, 24 Feb. 1999.

31 Leo E. McGiven, *The News* (New York: News Syndicate Co., 1969),

p. 33.

32 McGiven, p. 47.

33 William Block, Jr., ed., *Memoirs of William Block* (Toledo, Ohio: Blade Communications, 1990).

34 *Editor & Publisher*, 3 Feb. 1917, p. 9.

35 *N.W. Ayer & Son's Newspaper Annual and Directory*, 1916, p. 604.

36 *Editor & Publisher*, 13 Feb. 1926.

37 *Editor & Publisher*, 2 Apr. 1932, p. 14.

38 *N.W. Ayer & Son's Newspaper Annual and Directory*, 1910, p. 1280.

39 *N.W. Ayer & Son's Newspaper Annual and Directory*, 1916, pp. 604-605.

40 *Newark Eagle*, 18 Jan. 1916, p. 2.

41 *Printer's Ink*, 27 Jan. 1916, p. 73.

42 *Newark Eagle*, 29 Jan. 1916, p. 2.

43 *The Newark Eagle and the Newark Star*, 29 Jan. 1916, p. 1.

44 *The Newark Eagle and the Newark Star*, 29 Jan. 1916, p. 1.

45 Ferdinand Lundberg, *Imperial Hearst* (New York: Equinox Cooperative Press, 1936), p. 330.

46 *N.W. Ayer & Son's Newspaper Annual and Directory*, 1919, p. 604.

47 *N.W. Ayer & Son's Newspaper Annual and Directory,* 1919, p. 604.

48 *Newark Star-Eagle*, 12 Jan. 1923, p. 1.

49 *Newark Star-Eagle*, 25 Jan. 1923, p. 1.

50 *Newark Star-Eagle*, 25 Jan. 1923, p. 1.

51 "The Star-Eagle Magazine" of the *Newark-Star Eagle*, 2 Feb. 1923, p. 1.

52 *Newark Star-Eagle*, 8 June 1923, p. 9.

53 *Newark Star-Eagle*, 8 June 1923, p. 9.

54 *Newark Star-Eagle*, 4 June 1923, p. 11.

55 *Newark Star-Eagle,* 5 Nov. 1925, p. 11.

56 Patrolman's Benevolent Association, Proclamation to Paul Block, 7 March 1927, Blade Communications Inc. archive.

57 *Newark Star-Eagle*, 5 April 1923.

58 *Newark Star-Eagle*, 29 Aug. 1923

59 *Newark Star-Eagle*, 7 Dec. 1923.

60 *Newark Star-Eagle*, 8 Feb. 1923, p. 1.

61 *Newark Star-Eagle,* 12 Oct. 1923, p. 17.

62 William W. Lutz, *The News of Detroit* (Boston: Little, Brown & Co., 1973), p. 18.

63 *The Detroit Journal*, 12 Feb. 1917.

64 *The Detroit Journal*, 19 Feb. 1917.

65 *Printer's Ink*, 23 Dec. 1920, p. 115.

66 Grove Patterson, *I Like People* (Boston: Little, Brown & Co., 1954), p. 113.

67 *Editor & Publisher*, 29 July 1922, p. 7.

68 *Editor & Publisher*, 29 July 1922, p. 7.

69 *Detroit Journal*, 21 July 1922, p. 1.

70 *Editor & Publisher*, 29 July 1922, p. 7.

71 *The New York Times*, 28 Feb. 1921, p. 17.

72 *Editor & Publisher*, 5 Mar. 1921, p. 28.

73 *Memphis News-Scimitar*, 30 July 1923.

74 *Memphis News-Scimitar*, 12 Jan. 1921.

75 *Memphis News-Scimitar*, 23 Aug. 1921.

76 *Memphis News-Scimitar*, 18 Jan. 1921.

77 *Memphis News-Scimitar*, 19 Sep. 1921.

78 *Memphis News-Scimitar*, 5 June 1923.

79 *Memphis News-Scimitar*, 10 June 1923.

80 *Memphis News-Scimitar*, 13 Jan. 1921.

81 *Memphis News-Scimitar*, 27 Jan. 1921.

82 Ann Meeks, "Scimitar Alley," *The Commercial Appeal*, 29 Apr. 1993, p. E2.

83 Paul Block to Pres. Calvin Coolidge, letter of 22 Dec. 1923, Block family archive.

84 Pres. Calvin Coolidge to Paul Block, letter of 27 Dec. 1923, Block family archive.

85 *Memphis News-Scimitar*, 29 Apr. 1921.

86 *Memphis News-Scimitar*, 21 Jan. 1921.

87 *Memphis News-Scimitar*, 21 Apr. 1922.

88 *Memphis News-Scimitar*, 25 Apr. 1922.

89 *Memphis News-Scimitar*, 25 Apr. 1922.

90 *Memphis News-Scimitar*, 25 Apr. 1922.

91 *Memphis News-Scimitar*, 19 Feb. 1923.

92 *Memphis News-Scimitar*, 13 June 1921.

93 *Memphis News-Scimitar*, 15 Feb. 1921.

94 *Memphis News-Scimitar*, 17 Jan. 1921.

95 Perre Magness, "Pause to recall heroism of Tom Lee," *Memphis Commercial Appeal*, 4 May 1989.

96 Perre Magness, "Pause to recall heroism of Tom Lee," 4 May 1989.

97 William Block, Sr., to Angus McEachran, editor of *The Commercial*

Appeal, letter of 23 May 1997.

98 Thomas H. Baker, *The Memphis Commercial Appeal* (Baton Rouge: Louisiana State University Press, 1971), p. 267.

99 *Editor & Publisher*, 19 Feb. 1927.

100 Alfred McClung Lee, *The Daily Newspaper in America* (New York: Macmillan Company, 1937) p. 214.

101 Lee, p. 214.

Endnotes for Chapter Five

1 Dorshka Raphaelson, comment to the author, New York, Nov. 1997.

2 Lorraine Glennon, ed., *Our Times* (Atlanta: Turner Publishing, 1995), p. 215.

3 Paul Block contribution lists, 1915-1935, Block family archive.

4 Paul Block contribution lists, 1915-1935, Block family archive.

5 Eddie Cantor, letter to Paul Block, circa 1939, Block family archive.

6 *The New York Times*, 10 Apr. 1922.

7 *The New York Times*, 21 Jan. 1928, p. 2.

8 Paul Block contribution lists, Block family archive.

9 Captain George Fried, letter to Paul Block, circa Feb. 1928, Block family archive.

10 Stone Mountain Conference Monumental Association of Atlanta, Georgia, letter to Paul Block, 2 April 1928, Block family archive.

11 Paul Block to Evelyn Wagner, Office of the Mayor, New York City, letters of 6 Oct. 1927; 21 Aug. 1928; 6 Feb. 1929; 8 Feb. 1929; 22 Apr. 1929.

12 *Editor & Publisher*, 14 Jan. 1928, p. 16.

13 Richard Welch, "Glamorous Jimmy Walker: The Night Mayor of New York City," *Vanity Fair*, April 1932, p. 33.

14 William Block, Jr., ed., *Memoirs of William Block* (Toledo, Ohio: 1990) p. 23.

15 Paul Block, letter to Mayor James Walker, circa 1926, Municipal Archive of New York.

16 Mayor James Walker, letter to Paul Block, circa 1926. Municipal Archive of New York.

17 *The New York Times,* 19 July 1927.

18 *Brooklyn Standard-Union*, April 1929.

19 Richard Welch, p. 35.

20 William Block, Jr., p. 23.

21 Governor Franklin D. Roosevelt, letter to Paul Block, 8 Oct. 1931.

Franklin D. Roosevelt archive, Hyde Park, N.Y.

22 Paul Block contribution lists, Block family archive.

23 William Block, Jr., p. 22.

24 William Block, Jr., p. 22.

25 William Block, Jr., p. 23.

26 Richard Welch, p. 35.

27 *The New York Times*, 28 Nov. 1927, p. 25.

28 Block newspapers, 18 May 1928.

29 *The New York Times*, 17 Mar. 1929, p. 30.

30 Decree bestowing on Paul Block the title of Knight, as a Cavalier of the Order of the Crown of Italy, signed by His Majesty Vittorio Emmanuel III, the King of Italy, October 12, 1928. Block family archive.

31 Admiral Richard Byrd to Paul Block, letters circa 1928, Block family archive.

32 Admiral Richard Byrd to Paul Block Jr., letter of 3 May 1928.

33 *The New York Times*, 20 Aug. 1929.

34 *Duluth Herald*, 1 Jan. 1923.

35 *Editor & Publisher*, 1 Jan. 1921, p. 6.

36 *Editor & Publisher*, 1 Jan. 1921, p. 6.

37 *Duluth Herald*, 1 Jan. 1923.

38 "History of the Duluth News-Tribune," circa 1989; Block family archive.

39 *Duluth Herald*, 3 Jan. 1923, p. 10.

40 Alfred McClung Lee, *The Daily Newspaper in America* (New York: The Macmillan Co., 1947), p. 421.

41 *The Duluth News-Tribune,* 19 June 1929, p. 4.

42 Paul Block to C. Bascom Slemp, letter of 29 Sept. 1924, Calvin Coolidge archive.

43 Pres. Calvin Coolidge to Paul Block, letter of 7 Oct. 1924.

44 Dina Block to Paul Block, Jr., postcard dated 7 Aug. 1935, Block family archive.

45 *Duluth News-Tribune*, 19 Aug. 1929, p. 1.

46 Randolph Carter, *The World of Flo Ziegfeld* (New York: Praeger Publishers, 1974), pp. 149-150.

47 *Editor & Publisher*, 7 Dec. 1929, p. 2.

48 "History of the Duluth News-Tribune," circa 1989, Block family archive.

49 R. D. Handy to David Lawrence, letter of 30 Aug. 1932; letter from Paul Block to David Lawrence, 19 Sept. 1932.

50 *Duluth News-Tribune*, 27 May 1929, p. 1.

51 *Duluth News-Tribune*, 1 Jan. 1933, p. 7.

52 Agreement between The Herald Company, The Paul Corporation and Northwest Publications, Inc.; 26 June 1936, p. 3.

53 Agreement between The Herald Company, The Paul Corporation and Northwest Publications, Inc.; 26 June 1936, p. 29.

54 Agreement between The Herald Company, The Paul Corporation and Northwest Publications, Inc.; 26 June 1936, pp. 29-30.

55 Paul Block and Associates, letter signed by Max Block, to Northwest Publications, Inc., July, 1936, Blade Communications, Inc. archive.

Endnotes for Chapter Six

1 *Collier's World Atlas and Gazetteer*: (New York: P.F. Collier & Son Corp., 1935 ed.), p. 251.

2 *Editor & Publisher*, 24 Feb. 1923, p. 36.

3 *Editor & Publisher*, 24 Feb. 1923, p. 36.

4 *Lancaster New Era*, 12 Mar. 1923, p. 1.

5 William Block, Sr., interview by the author, Pittsburgh, Pa., Sept. 4, 1997.

6 Paul Block, deposition given in State of Ohio, Lucas County Court of Common Pleas, re. Wright vs. Buggie, 7 Sept. 1927, pp. 88-89.

7 *Editor & Publisher*, 13 Feb. 1926, p. 8.

8 Statement of the Cost of the Stock of the Newark Star Publishing Company, circa 1926, Blade Communications, Inc. archive.

9 *The New York Times,* 7 Feb. 1926.

10 Paul Block, letter to Pres. Calvin Coolidge, 1 Feb. 1926, Blade Communications, Inc. archive.

11 Paul Block, letter to President Calvin Coolidge, 13 Feb. 13, 1926, Forbes Library, Northampton, Mass.

12 *Editor & Publisher,* 22 May 1926 p. 51.

13 John M. Harrison, *The Blade of Toledo: The First 150 Years* (Toledo, Ohio: Toledo Blade Co., 1985), p. 213.

14 Ferdinand Lundberg, *America's 60 Families* (New York: The Citadel Press, 1939), p. 49.

15 Lundberg, p. 50.

16 *Elmira Star Gazette*, 7 Aug. 1997.

17 Pullman "Friendship" floor plan, circa 1928, Block family archive.

18 Charlton Ogburn, *Railroads: The Great American Adventure* (Washington D.C.: National Geographic Society, 1977).

19 The Pullman Co., letter to Paul Block, 1929, Block family archive.

20 Friendship train log, circa 1929-1932, Block family archive.

21 President Calvin Coolidge, letter to Paul Block, 1 March 1926, Forbes Library, Northampton, Mass.

22 The Pullman Co., letter to Paul Block, 1929, Block family archive.

23 Ogburn, p. 134.

24 Friendship train log, circa 1929-1932, Block family archive.

25 William Block, Sr., interview by the author, July 1997.

26 Mortgage deed between Paul Block and Tillie S. Jaretzki, May 1926, Blade Communications, Inc. archive.

27 R. I. Dunigan of Paul Block and Associates, letter to Albert Lasker, 10 Oct. 1941, Blade Communications, Inc. archive.

28 R. I. Dunigan of Paul Block and Associates, letter to Albert Lasker, 10 Oct. 1941, Blade Communications, Inc. archive.

29 John Robinson Block, interview of Dina Wallach Block, New York City, 21 Jan. 1977, Block family archive.

30 William Block, Sr., interview by the author, July 1997.

31 George Walsh, *Gentleman Jimmy Walker* (New York: Praeger Publishers, 1974), p. 194.

32 Donald Day, *Will Rogers* (New York: David McKay Co. 1962), pp. 240-241.

33 Day, p. 358.

34 *Hotchkiss School Newspaper*, 22 June 1929.

35 *The New York Times*, 2 May 1930.

36 Peter Liveright, interview by the author, Spring 1998.

37 Peter Liveright, interview by the author, Spring 1998.

38 William Block, Sr., interview by the author, July 1997.

39 Clifton Daniel, ed., *The Chronicle of America* (New York: D.K. Publishing Inc., 1997), p. 654.

40 *Editor & Publisher*, 3 Nov. 1934, p. 8.

41 *Editor & Publisher*, 3 Nov. 1934, p. 14.

42 Paul Block, letter to William Block, 1 Nov. 1934, Block family archive.

43 Paul Block, letter to William Block, 1 Nov. 1934, Block family archive.

44 Paul Block, letter to Paul Block, Jr., 5 Nov. 1934. Block family archive.

45 *Editor and Publisher*, 10 Sept. 1927, p. 12.

46 William Block Jr., ed., *Memoirs of William Block* (Toledo, Ohio:

Blade Communications, Inc., 1990), p. 20.

47 *Newark Star-Eagle*, 12 Nov. 1926.

48 *The New York Times*, 8 Sept. 1927.

49 *Dictionary of American Biography* (New York: Scribner, 1974 ed.), p. 436.

50 *Dictionary of American Biography* (New York: Scribner, 1974 ed.), p. 436.

51 *The New York Times*, 10 Jan. 1928, p. 35.

52 Bruce Chadwick, *Baseball's Hometown Teams* (New York: Abbeville Press, 1941), p. 120.

53 *The New York Times,* 29 Apr. 1928, p. 18.

54 Chadwick, p. 86.

55 Henry W. Thomas, *Walter Johnson, Baseball's Big Train* (Arlington, VA.: Phenom Press, 1995), p. 309.

56 Thomas, pp. 302-309.,

57 William Block, Jr., ed., *Memoirs of William Block*, pp. 20-21.

58 *The Newark Star-Eagle,* 12 Nov. 1931.

59 *The Newark Star-Eagle,* 29 Nov. 1931.

60 *The Newark Star-Eagle,* 13 Nov. 1931, p. 1.

61 *The Newark Star-Eagle*, 12 Nov. 1931.

Endnotes for Chapter Seven

1   Based on various reports from a private detective, "H.A.F." and "Operative No. 11" to Paul Block, throughout August, 1927; Blade Communications archive.

2   John M. Harrison, *The Blade of Toledo: The First 150 Years* (Toledo: Toledo Blade Company, 1985), p. 214.

3   William Block, Sr., letter to the author, 11 Jan. 2000.

4   *Toledo Blade*, 24 Oct. 1936.

5   William Block, Sr., interview by the author, 27 July 1997.

6   Harry R. Illman, *Unholy Toledo* (San Francisco: Polemic Press, 1985), p. vi.

7   *Toledo Blade*, 26 Dec. 1893.

8   *Toledo Blade*, 24 Oct. 1936.

9   *Toledo Blade*, 24 Oct. 1936.

10   *Toledo Blade*, 14 Feb. 1848.

11   Grove Patterson, *I Like People* (Boston: Little, Brown & Co., 1948), p. 103.

12 *N.W. Ayer & Son's Guide to Periodicals*, 1897, p. 657.

13 C. S. Van Tassel, article on the history of the *Toledo Blade*. *Toledo Blade*, 24 Oct. 1936.

14 Harrison, p. 94.

15 William Block, Sr., letter to the author, 11 Jan., 2000.

16 *Toledo Blade*, 24 Oct. 1936.

17 Patterson, p. 128.

18 *Toledo Blade*, 3 Apr. 1922.

19 Patterson, p. 86.

20 Patterson, p. 86.

21 Grove Patterson, "The Shield of Democracy," address at the Association of National Advertisers, 24 Oct. 1940.

22 Jack Lessenberry, "Remembering Grove Patterson," *Toledo Blade*, 8 Nov. 1981.

23 Jack Lessenberry, "Remembering Grove Patterson," *Toledo Blade*, 8 Nov. 1981.

24 Jack Lessenberry, "Remembering Grove Patterson," *Toledo Blade*, 8 Nov. 1981.

25 *Pittsburgh Post-Gazette*, 9 Oct. 1937.

26 Advertising booklet published by the *Toledo Blade*, circa 1939.

27 *Toledo Blade*, 31 Dec. 1926.

28 *Route List & Directory of the Toledo Blade*, 1929, Blade Communications, Inc. archive.

29 *Toledo Blade*, 3 July 1928.

30 *Toledo Blade*, 31 July 1928.

31 George Seldes, *Lords of the Press* (New York: Blue Ribbon Books, 1941), p. 65 ff; Ferdinand Lundberg, *Imperial Hearst* (New York: Equinox Cooperative Press, 1936), p. 180 ff.

32 George Walsh, *Gentleman Jimmy Walker* (New York: Praeger Publishers, 1974) p. 90.

33 Patterson, *I Like People*, p. 125 ff.

34 Edmond D. Coblentz, ed., *Newsmen Speak* (Berkeley: University of California Press, 1954), pp. 22-23.

35 Paul Block, letter to Grove Patterson, 19 Dec. 1935, *Toledo Blade* archive.

36 *Twenty Years...and What they Have Meant in Newspaper Development*; a pamphlet, circa 1945, published by the *Toledo Blade*. *Toledo Blade* archive.

37 *Toledo Blade,* 3 Feb. 1936.

38 William Block, Sr., letter to the author, 11 Jan., 2000.

39 William Block, Sr., Chairman of the *Pittsburgh Post-Gazette*, letter to William Block, Jr., President of Blade Communications, Inc., 4 Aug. 1997.

40 Historical Financial Data: The Toledo Blade Company, 1922-1941, Blade Communications, Inc. archive.

41 *Toledo Blade*, 1 Feb. 1936.

42 *Toledo Blade*, 3 Feb. 1986.

43 *Toledo Blade*, 11 Apr. 1936.

44 Paul Block, letter to Grove Patterson, 2 Jan. 1940, Blade Communications, Inc., archive.

45 *Toledo Blade*, 30 June 1985.

46 Press release issued by the *Toledo Blade*, circa 1938, *Toledo Blade* archive.

47 Paul Block, deposition given at Lucas County Court of Common Pleas, 7 Sept. 1927.

48 *Toledo, Ohio and the Toledo Blade*: commemorative pamphlet, 1936, Blade Communications, Inc. archive.

49 Paper samples from the *Toledo Blade* archives, 4 Mar. 1940.

50 John Grigsby, former reporter of the *Toledo Blade;* interview by the author, 14 Aug. 1997.

51 *Columbus Evening Dispatch*, 26 Feb. 1940; The *Des Moines Register*, 23 Jan. 1940. *Toledo Blade* archive.

52 Paul Block, letter to Florence E. Cottrell, 23 Feb. 1940, *Toledo Blade* archive.

53 Paul Block, letter to Grove Patterson, 2 Jan. 1940, *Toledo Blade* archive.

54 Paul Block, letter to Florance E. Cottrell, 15 Jan. 1940 (dictated 13 Jan. 1940), *Toledo Blade* archive.

55 Daniel Nicoll, memorandum to William Block, 14 May 1940, *Toledo Blade* archive.

56 Paul Block, letter to Dan Nicoll, 20 May 1940, *Toledo Blade* archive.

57 Dan Nicoll, letter to Paul Block, 3 Feb. 1940, *Toledo Blade* archive.

58 Grove Patterson, letter to Paul Block, 21 Feb. 1940, *Toledo Blade* archive.

59 Paul Block, letter to Lou Schwab, 26 Nov. 1940, *Toledo Blade* archive.

60 Paul Block, letter to Grove Patterson, 23 Feb. 1940, *Toledo Blade* archive.

61 Paul Block, letter to Lou Schwab, 26 Nov. 1940, *Toledo Blade*

archive.

62 John E. Drewry, ed., *Post Biographies of Famous Journalists* (Athens, GA.: University of Georgia Press, 1942), p. 347.

63 Frank Luther Mott, *American Journalism, A History: 1690-1960* (New York: The Macmillan Company, 1962), p. 722.

64 Lundberg, p. 234.

65 Katharine Graham, *Personal History* (New York: Alfred A. Knopf, 1997), p. 55.

66 John Tebbel, *An American Dynasty* (New York: Doubleday & Co., 1947), p. 310.

67 *The New York Times*, 14 June 1927.

68 Donald Day, *Will Rogers* (New York: David McKay, Co., 1962), p. 210.

69 William Block Jr., ed., *Memoirs of William Block* (Toledo: Blade Communications, Inc., 1990), p. 23.

70 A. Scott Berg, *Lindbergh* (New York: G. P. Putnam's Sons, 1998), p. 159.

71 Charles Chaplin, *My Autobiography* (New York: Plume Books, 1992), p. 304.

72 Mott, *American Journalism*, p. 157.

73 Kenneth T. Jackson, ed., *The Encyclopedia of New York City* (New Haven: Yale University Press, 1995), page 811.

74 *The New York Times,* 5 May 1927.

75 Mott, *American Journalism*, p. 157.

76 *Editor & Publisher*, 4 Aug. 1927.

77 Paul Block, letter to Alfred E. Smith, 23 March 1927, George Groves Collection, Franklin D. Roosevelt Library, Hyde Park, N.Y.

78 *Editor & Publisher*, 4 Aug. 1927.

79 *Brooklyn Standard-Union*—Clippings, 1928-1932.

80 *Brooklyn Standard-Union*—Clippings, 1928-32.

81 *Brooklyn Eagle*, circa 1928.

82 *Brooklyn Standard-Union,* 1 Feb. 1929.

83 *Brooklyn Standard-Union*, 12 Jan. 1932.

84 William Block, Jr., ed., *Memoirs*, p. 32.

85 *Brooklyn Standard-Union*, 1 Nov. 1928.

86 *The New York Times*, 5 Nov. 1928.

87 Louis Howe, letter to Paul Block, 27 March 1933, Franklin D. Roosevelt Library, Hyde Park, N.Y.

88 *Brooklyn Standard-Union*, circa 1930.

89 McShane & Matthews, *Across America—Brooklyn Swaggers* (New York: Associated Press, 1958).

90 Mayor James J. Walker of New York, letter to Paul Block, circa 1930, New York Municipal Archive.

91 *Standard-Union* Clips – 1928-1932.

92 *Standard-Union* Clips – 1928-1932.

93 *Brooklyn Standard-Union,* 10 Aug. 1929.

94 President Herbert Hoover, letter to Paul Block, 23 Aug. 1929, Block family archive.

95 *Brooklyn Standard-Union*, 17 Jan. 1931.

96 Governor Franklin D. Roosevelt, letter to Paul Block, 3 Jan. 1931, Blade Communications, Inc. archive.

97 *Editor & Publisher*, 12 Mar. 1932.

98 *Editor & Publisher*, 12 Mar. 1932.

99 *The New York Times,* 1932.

100 *Elmira Star Gazette*, 7 Aug. 1997.

101 McShane & Matthews, *Across America*.

Endnotes for Chapter Eight

1 Cabell Phillips, *The New York Times Chronicle of American Life: From the Crash to the Blitz, 1929-1939* (New York: The Macmillan Company, 1969), p. 30.

2 *The Nation*, 25 Sept. 1937.

3 *Toledo Blade,* 15 Nov. 1929, p. 1.

4 Alfred McClung Lee, *The Daily Newspaper in America. The Evolution of a Social Instrument* (New York: The Macmillan Company, 1947), p. 628.

5 Michael Hanson, letter to Max Block, 2 Oct. 1929, Blade Communications, Inc. archive.

6 *The Milwaukee Journal*, 25 June 1924.

7 *The Milwaukee Journal*, 25 June 1924.

8 Paul Block to W.R. Hearst, Letter of Agreement, 10 June 1927, Blade Communications, Inc. archive.

9 Paul Block, letter to William Randolph Hearst, 31 July 1929, Blade Communications, Inc. archive.

10 Robert W. Wells, *The Milwaukee Journal* (Milwaukee, Wisc., 1981), p. 214.

11 Dan Nicoll, letter to Paul Block, Jr., 14 Aug. 1948, Blade Communications, Inc. archive.

12 *The Milwaukee Sentinel*, 1 Oct. 1929, p. 1.

13 *The Milwaukee Sentinel*, 9 Oct. 1929, p.1.

14 *The Milwaukee Sentinel*, 12 Oct. 1929, p.1.

15 Gov. Franklin D. Roosevelt, letter to Paul Block, 29 Sept. 1929, Franklin D. Roosevelt Library, Hyde Park, N.Y.

16 Gov. Franklin D. Roosevelt, letter to Paul Block, 29 Oct. 1929.

17 *Editor & Publisher*, 26 Oct. 1929, p. 50.

18 William Block Jr., ed., *Memoirs of William Block* (Toledo: Blade Communications, 1990), p. 46.

19 Letter from Paul Block to William Randolph Hearst, 28 Dec. 1933, Blade Communications, Inc. archive.

20 Letter from Paul Block to William Randolph Hearst, 16 Feb. 1938, Blade Communications, Inc. archive.

21 William Randolph Hearst letter to Paul Block, 8 Aug. 1933, Bancroft Library, University of California at Berkeley.

22 Paul Block, from a synopsis of letters to William Randolph Hearst, circa 1927-1936, Blade Communications, Inc. archive.

23 Geoffrey Konta, letter to Paul Block, quoting William Randolph Hearst's telegram that was a confirmation of telephone call from Konta to Block, 3 Feb. 1930, Bancroft Library, University of California at Berkeley.

24 Geoffrey Konta, letter to Paul Block, quoting William Randolph Hearst's telegram that was a confirmation of telephone call from Konta to Block, 25 Jan. 1930, Bancroft Library, University of California at Berkeley.

25 Paul Block, letter to William Randolph Hearst, 1 Aug. 1933, Bancroft Library, University of California at Berkeley.

26 Michael Emery and Edwin Emery, *The Press and America* (New York: Prentice Hall, 1992), p. 512.

27 William Block, Sr., letter to the author, 11 Jan. 2000.

28 Robert W. Wells, *The Milwaukee Journal*, 1981, p. 425.

29 Letter from Paul Block to William Randolph Hearst, c/o *The Los Angeles Examiner*, 28 July 1933, Blade Communications, Inc. archive.

30 Paul Block, letter to William Randolph Hearst, 1 Aug. 1933, Bancroft Library, University of California at Berkeley.

31 United Press International, wire copy, 13 Sept. 1937.

32 United Press International, wire copy, 13 Sept. 1937.

33 *Editor & Publisher*, 18 Nov. 1939, p. 7.

34 *Editor & Publisher*, 12 Dec. 1931, p. 8.

35 John K. Winkler, *W.R. Hearst: An American Phenomenon* (New York: Simon & Schuster, 1928), p. 22.

36 *The New York Times*, 12 Feb. 1931, p. 23.

37 *Los Angeles Times*, 16 Feb. 1931.

38 Ferdinand Lundberg, *Imperial Hearst* (New York: Equinox Press, 1936) p. 199.

39 *Los Angeles Express*, 16 Feb. 1931, p. 1.

40 Leo C. Roster, report in "The Washington Correspondents," *Social Science Research Council*, circa 1936, Washington, D.C.

41 Roster.

42 *The New York Times Chronicle of American Life, from the Crash to the Blitz, 1929-1939* (New York: The Macmillan Company,1969), p. 62.

43 *Los Angeles Express*, 14 Feb. 1931, p. 22.

44 *Los Angeles Express*, 16 Feb. 1931, p. 2.

45 *Los Angeles Express*, 16 Feb. 1931, p. 2.

46 *Los Angeles Express*, 16 Feb. 1931, p. 2.

47 *Los Angeles Express*, 16 Feb. 1931, p. 2.

48 *Los Angeles Express*, 16 Feb. 1931, p. 1.

49 *Los Angeles Express*, 17 Sept. 1931; p. 2.

50 *The New York Times*, 25 Feb. 1931.

51 James Barrett, ed., *The End of the "World,"* (New York: Harper & Row, 1931), p. 3.

52 *The Fourth Estate*, January 1924.

53 *The Saturday Review of Literature*, March 1931.

54 Jonathan Daniels, *They Will Be Heard* (New York: McGraw Hill, 1965), p. 279.

55 *The New York Times*, 27 Feb. 1931, p. 2.

56 *The New York Times*, 25 Feb. 1931.

57 *The New York Times*, 25 Feb. 1931.

58 Barrett, ed., *The End*, p. 112.

59 *The New York Times*, 25 Feb. 1931.

60 *The New York Times*, 25 Feb. 1931.

61 Barrett, ed., *The End*, p. 64.

62 Barrett, ed., *The End*, pp. 81-82.

63 *Editor & Publisher*, 28 Feb. 1931.

64 Barrett, ed., *The End* p. 78.

65 Barrett, ed., *The End* p. 82.

66 James Wyman Barrett, *Joseph Pulitzer and His World* (New York: Vanguard Press, 1941), p. 433.

67 Barrett, *Joseph Pulitzer*, p. 433.
68 *The New York Times*, 8 Apr. 1931.
69 Barrett, *Joseph Pulitzer*, p. 433.
70 *Los Angeles Express*, 1 June 1931, p. 2.
71 *Los Angeles Express*, 21 July 1931, p. 24.
72 *Los Angeles Express*, 3 Aug. 1931, p. 8.
73 *Los Angeles Express*, 17 Aug. 1931, p. 4.
74 *Los Angeles Express*, 2 June 1931, p. 3.
75 *Editor & Publisher*, 14 Feb. 1931, p. 6.
76 *Los Angeles Express*, 18 May 1931, p. 1.
77 *Los Angeles Express*, 3 Mar. 1931, p. 1.
78 *Los Angeles Express*, 6 July 1931, p. 3.
79 *Los Angeles Express*, 4 May 1931, p. 1.
80 *Pittsburgh Post-Gazette,* 18 July 1931.
81 *Editor & Publisher*, 12 Dec. 1931, p. 8.
82 *Editor & Publisher*, 12 Dec. 1931, p. 8.
83 *Editor & Publisher*, 18 Nov. 1939.

Endnotes for Chapter Nine

1 *Editor & Publisher*, 30 Aug. 1930, p. 34.
2 *Toledo Blade*, circa Oct. 1930.
3 *Editor & Publisher*, 1 Nov. 1930, p. 15.
4 John M. Harrison, *The Blade of Toledo: The First 150 Years* (Toledo: Toledo Blade Co., 1985), p. 226.
5 Grove Patterson, *I Like People* (Boston: Little, Brown & Co., 1954), p. 132.
6 Grove Patterson, "The Man We Call 'P.B.,'" *Toledo Blade*, 28 Mar. 1927.
7 *Editor & Publisher*, 27 Jan. 1934, p. XIII.
8 Herman W. Liebert, interview by John Robinson Block, 14 April 1977.
9 Herman W. Liebert, interview by John Robinson Block, 14 April 1977.
10 Paul Block, editorial, "The Hitler Speech," *Toledo Blade*, 18 May 1933.
11 Paul Block, editorial, "A Manufacturer's Sales Tax," *Toledo Blade,* 25 May 1933.
12 Paul Block, editorial, "Business with Russia," *Toledo Blade*, 5 June 1933.
13 Paul Block, editorial, "For a Three-Cent Coin," *Toledo Blade*, 9 Apr. 1934.

14 Paul Block, editorial, "Eliminate the Washington 'Dream Walkers,'"
Toledo Blade, 24 Apr. 1934.

15 Paul Block, editorial, "Hauptmann Breaks Under Examination,"
Toledo Blade, 26 Jan. 1935.

16 Paul Block, editorial, "Cross-Examination Withers Hauptmann,"
Toledo Blade, 28 Jan. 1935.

17 Morton Sontheimer, *Newspaperman* (New York: Whittlesly House,
1941), p. 197.

18 Harrison, *The Blade,* p. 213.

19 *Toledo Blade*, 17 Oct. 1928.

20 *Toledo Blade*, 24 Nov. 1928.

21 *Toledo Blade*, 5 Apr. 1929.

22 *Toledo Blade*, 6 Nov. 1930.

23 *Toledo Blade*, 17 June 1932.

24 Liebert interview, 1977.

25 Letter from Paul Block to Calvin Coolidge, 13 Feb. 1926. Forbes
Library, Northampton, Mass.

26 Paul Block, Jr., letter to Paul Block, circa April 1936, Blade Communications, Inc. archive.

27 Herbert Hoover, letter to Paul Block, 28 Nov. 1937.

28 James Melvin Lee, *History of American Journalism* (Boston:
Houghton Mifflin Co., 1923), p. 448.

29 *Toledo Ohio and the Toledo Blade*, promotion booklet, 1939.

30 Harrison, *The Blade*, p. 218.

31 Summary chart of Paul Block's holdings, compiled in 1939, *Toledo
Blade* archive.

32 *Editor & Publisher*, 6 Aug. 1927, p. 1.

33 *Pittsburgh Post-Gazette,* 26 Oct. 1936.

34 *Pittsburgh Post-Gazette,* 26 Oct. 1936.

35 *Pittsburgh Post-Gazette*, 2 Aug. 1927.

36 Paul Block and William Randolph Hearst, Letter of Agreement, 10
June 1927, Bancroft Library, University of California.

37 *The New York Times*, 2 Aug. 1927, p. 23.

38 *Editor & Publisher*, 6 Aug. 1927, p. 1.

39 *Editor & Publisher*, 6 Aug. 1927, p. 1.

40 *Editor & Publisher*, 6 Aug. 1927, p. 1.

41 *Pittsburgh Post-Gazette*, 2 Aug. 1927.

42 *Pittsburgh Post-Gazette*, 2 Aug. 1927.

43 *Pittsburgh Post-Gazette*, 4 Aug. 1927.

44 *Pittsburgh Post-Gazette*, 8 Oct. 1927, p.1.

45 *Pittsburgh Post-Gazette*, 5 Oct. 1927.

46 Paul Block, letter to William Randolph Hearst, 20 Aug. 1927, Bancroft Library, University of California.

47 Paul Block, letter to William Randolph Hearst, 20 Aug. 1927.

48 Paul Block, letter to William Randolph Hearst, 20 Aug. 1927.

49 William Block, Sr., letter to the author, 11 Jan. 2000.

50 William Block, Jr., ed., *Memoirs of William Block* (Toledo: Blade Communications, Inc., 1990), p. 36.

51 Paul Block, letter to William Randolph Hearst, 16 Sept. 1927, Blade Communications, Inc. archive.

52 Paul Block, letter to William Randolph Hearst, 16 Sept. 1927,

53 William Block, Sr., letter to the author.

54 Frank Luther Mott, *American Journalism, A History: 1690-1960* (New York: The Macmillan Company, 1962), p. 650.

55 Paul Block, letter to William Randolph Hearst, Sept. 16, 1927, Block family archive.

56 Geoffrey Konta, letter to Paul Block, 13 Oct. 1927, Bancroft Library, University of California.

57 Paul Block, letter to William Randolph Hearst, 13 April 1933, Blade Communications, Inc. archive.

58 William Randolph Hearst, letter to Paul Block, 23 May 1933, Blade Communications, Inc. archive.

59 William Randolph Hearst, letter to Paul Block, 23 May 1933.

60 William Randolph Hearst, letter to Paul Block, 23 May 1933.

61 William Randolph Hearst, letter to Paul Block, 23 May 1933.

62 William Randolph Hearst, letter to Fred Eldridge, copy to Paul Block, 15 April 1933, Blade Communications, Inc. archive.

63 William Randolph Hearst, letter to Paul Block, 15 April 1933, Blade Communications, Inc. archive.

64 William Randolph Hearst, letter to Paul Block, 15 April 1933.

65 William Randolph Hearst, letter to Paul Block, 15 April 1933.

66 William Randolph Hearst, letter to Paul Block, 15 April 1933.

67 *Pittsburgh Post-Gazette*, 14 Mar. 1928.

68 *Pittsburgh Post-Gazette*, 14 Mar. 1928.

69 *Pittsburgh Post-Gazette,* 30 May 1929.

70 *Pittsburgh Post-Gazette,* 30 May 1929.

71 *Pittsburgh Post-Gazette*, 16 Sept. 1940.

72 *Pittsburgh Post-Gazette*, 28 Nov. 1930.

73 *Pittsburgh Post-Gazette*, 21 Nov. 1930.

74 *Pittsburgh Post-Gazette*, 13 Dec. 1930.

75 Alfred McClung Lee, *The Daily Newspaper in America: The Evolution of a Social Instument* (New York: The Macmillan Company, 1947), p. 372.

76 Randolph Carter, *The World of Flo Ziegfeld* (New York: Praeger Publishers, 1974), p. 150.

77 *Pittsburgh Post-Gazette*, 13 June 1931.

78 John Tebbel, *An American Dynasty* (New York: Doubleday & Co., 1947), p. 18.

79 Tebbel, p. 18.

80 Michael Emery and Edwin Emery, *The Press and America* (New York: Prentice-Hall, 1992) p. 210.

81 *Editor & Publisher*, 20 Nov. 1919, pp. 8-10.

82 *Editor & Publisher*, 20 Nov. 1919, pp. 8-10.

83 *The Memphis News-Scimitar*, 5 May 1925.

84 *Toledo Blade*, 26 Oct. 1926.

85 Harrison, *The Blade*, p. 200.

86 *Toledo Blade,* 1 Jan. 1933.

87 *Toledo Blade*, 19 Sept. 1928.

88 *The Memphis News-Scimitar*, 5 May 1925.

89 *The Memphis News-Scimitar*, 26 Aug. 1923.

90 Calvin Coolidge, letter to Paul Block, 20 Dec. 1923, Forbes Library, Northampton, Mass.

91 *Toledo Blade*, 26 Oct. 1926.

92 *Toledo Blade*, 27 Oct. 1926.

93 *The New York Times,* 4 June 2000.

94 Calvin Coolidge, article in *Cosmopolitan*, March 1929.

95 *Toledo Blade*, 11 Mar. 1929.

96 Paul Block, letter (with poem) to President Calvin Coolidge, 6 Oct. 1924; Forbes Library, Northampton, Mass.

97 Paul Block, letter to President Calvin Coolidge, 11 May 1925, Forbes Library, Northampton, Mass.

98 Paul Block, letter to President Calvin Coolidge, 14 May 1924, Forbes Library, Northampton, Mass.

99 John K. Winkler, *William Randolph Hearst* (New York: Hastings House, 1955), p. 222.

100 President Calvin Coolidge, letter to Paul Block, 7 April 1927, *Toledo Blade* archive.

101 *Toledo Blade*, 2 May 1927.

102 Paul Block, letter to Everett Sanders, secretary to the President, 6 April 1927, Block family archive.

103 William Block, Sr., interview by the author, July 1997.

104 Starkey Flythe, Jr., ed., *The American Story* (Philadelphia: Curtis Publishing Co. 1975), p. 272.

105 *Toledo Blade,* 17 Sept. 1928.

106 *Toledo Blade,* 17 Sept. 1928.

107 *Toledo Blade*, 29 Nov. 1928.

108 *Toledo Blade*, 17 May 1929.

109 Norman Hapgood and Henry Moscowitz, *Up From City Streets* (New York: Grosset & Dunlap, 1927), p. 74.

110 Alfred Connable and Edward Silverfarb, *Tigers of Tammany* (New York: Holt, Rinehart, Winston, 1967), p. 264.

111 Winkler, *William Randolph Hearst*, pp. 207-208.

112 Herbert Hoover, "Truth in Advertising Work is Achieving a Notable Success," speech given circa 1925 to The Associated Advertising Clubs annual meeting; found in "Prosperity and Thrift: The Coolidge Era and Consumer Economy, 1921-1929," Calvin Coolidge Papers., Library of Congress.

113 *Toledo Blade,* 4 Apr. 1930.

114 William Block, Jr., ed., *Memoirs*, pp. 27-28.

115 Alfred E. Smith, letter to William Block, 18 Jan. 1932, Block family archive.

116 Richard Welch, "Glamorus Jimmy Walker: the Night Mayor of New York City," *Vanity Fair*, April 1932, p. 35.

117 *The Reminiscences of Nathan Strauss, 1950*, Columbia University Oral History Project, copyright by the Trustees of Columbia University, 1975.

118 Edward Robb Ellis, *The Epic of New York City* (New York: Old Town Books, 1966), p. 542.

119 Herbert Mitang, "The Downfall of Jimmy Walker: Judge Seabury Cleans Up New York," *The Atlantic Monthly*, October 1962, p. 98.

120 Ellis. p. 541.

121 Ellis. p. 540.

122 Ellis. p. 541.

123 *The New York Times* , circa 1932.

124 *Brooklyn Daily Eagle*, 15 May 1932.

125 Mitang, p. 107.

126 *The New York Times*, 28 March 1932.

127 *New York Herald Tribune*. June, 1932.

128 *New York Herald Tribune*. June, 1932.

129 *The New York Times*, 29 May 1932.

130 Paul Block, letter to William Block, Jr., 1 June 1932. Block family archive.

131 Louis Gribetz and Joseph Kaye. *Jimmie Walker, The Story of a Personality* (New York: Dial Press, 1932).

132 Gribetz and Kaye, p. 329.

133 Paul Block, letter to Louis Wiley, 7 July 1932, Block family archive.

134 William Block, Sr., letter to Roy W. Howard, 28 June 1957, Block family archive.

135 Block, Jr., ed., *Memoirs*, p. 23.

136 Mitang, p. 108.

137 Frank Friedel, *Franklin D. Roosevelt: A Rendezvous with Destiny* (Boston: Little Brown and Company, 1990), p. 76.

138 *Toledo Blade*, 2 Sept. 1932.

139 *Pittsburgh Post-Gazette* and *Toledo Blade*, 1 Sept. 1932.

140 *Pittsburgh Post-Gazette* and *Toledo Blade*, 1 Sept. 1932.

141 Jay Maeder, ed., *Big Town, Big Time* (New York: Daily News Books, 1999), p. 68.

142 *Toledo Blade*, 2 Sept. 1932.

Endnotes for Chapter Ten

1 *Toledo Blade,* 22 Jan. 1931.

2 *Toledo Blade,* 9 June 1930.

3 Cabell Phillips, *The New York Times Chronicle of American Life: From the Crash to the Blitz, 1929-1939* (New York: Macmillan, 1969), p. 75.

4 *The New York Times,* 30 Sept. 1931.

5 Dina Block to William Block, letter of 29 Sept. 1931, Block family archive.

6 *The New York Times*, quote of Paul Block, 12 Oct. 1932.

7 *The New York Times*, 2 July 1932; p. 1.

8 Henry L. Stoddard, *It Costs To Be President* (New York: Harper & Brothers, 1938), p. 316.

9 Stoddard, p. 316.

10 Paul F. Boller, Jr., *Presidential Campaigns* (New York: Oxford University Press, 1985), p. 233.

11 *The New York Times*, 2 July 1932.

12 *Pittsburgh Post-Gazette*, 4 April 1932.

13 *Pittsburgh Post-Gazette*, 21 April 1932.

14 Barrington Boardman, *From Harding to Hiroshima* (New York: Red Dembner Books, 1988), p. 136.

15 Max D. Steuer to Paul Block, letter of 6 April 1932, Blade Communications archive.

16 William Randolph Hearst to Max D. Steuer, letter of 15 May 1932, Bancroft Library, University of California.

17 Max D. Steuer to Paul Block, letter of 16 May 1932, Blade Communications archive, Toledo, Ohio.

18 Max Steuer to Paul Block, 16 May 1932.

19 Max Steuer to Paul Block, 16 May 1932.

20 Paul Block to William Randolph Hearst, letter of 19 April 1933, Blade Communications archive.

21 Paul Block to William Randolph Hearst, letter of 11 May 1933, Blade Communications archive.

22 Paul Block to William Randolph Hearst, 11 May 1933.

23 Paul Block to William Randolph Hearst, letter of 19 April 1933; Blade Communications archive.

24 Paul Block to William Randolph Hearst, 19 April 1933, Bancroft Library, University of California.

25 Paul Block to William Randolph Hearst, 19 April 1933, Bancroft Library, University of California.

26 *Pittsburgh Post-Gazette*, 31 Oct. 1927.

27 J. Cutler Andrews, *Pittsburgh's Post-Gazette* (Boston: Chapman & Grimes, 1936) p. 296.

28 *Pittsburgh Post-Gazette*, 2 March 1933.

29 *Pittsburgh Post-Gazette*, 22 Jan. 1930.

30 *Pittsburgh Post-Gazette*, 8 Jan. 1929.

31 *Pittsburgh Post-Gazette*, 9 Dec. 1928.

32 Andrews, pps. 297-298.

33 *Pittsburgh Post-Gazette*, 1 Feb. 1929.

34 *Pittsburgh Post-Gazette*, 2 Nov. 1935.

35 *Pittsburgh Post-Gazette*, 11 Oct. 1928.

36 *Pittsburgh Post-Gazette*, 17 Oct. 1929.

37 *Pittsburgh Post-Gazette*, 22 Aug. 1929.

38 *Pittsburgh Post-Gazette*, 22 Dec. 1928.

39 *Pittsburgh Post-Gazette*, 26 Oct. 1932.

40 *Pittsburgh Post-Gazette*, June 29, 1932.

41 *Pittsburgh Post-Gazette* and *Toledo Blade*, 11 July 1932.

42 *Pittsburgh Post-Gazette* and *Toledo Blade*, 27 July 1931.

43 *Pittsburgh Post-Gazette* and *Toledo Blade*, 28 April 1933.

44 *Pittsburgh Post-Gazette,* 19 March 1936.

45 *Pittsburgh Post-Gazette*, 1 June1934.

46 *Pittsburgh Post-Gazette*, clipping, circa spring 1954.

47 Paul Block to Hon. Franklin D. Roosevelt, Western Union telegram, 9 Nov. 1932. The Franklin D. Roosevelt Library, Hyde Park, New York.

48 *Toledo Blade*, 9 Nov. 1932.

49 Governor Franklin D. Roosevelt to Paul Block, letter of 19 Nov. 1932.The Franklin D. Roosevelt Library, Hyde Park, New York.

50 *Pittsburgh Post-Gazette,* 10 June 1931.

51 *Toledo Blade*, 14 Feb. 1936.

52 *Toledo Blade*, 14 Feb. 1936.

53 *Pittsburgh Post-Gazette* and *Toledo Blade*, 3 March 1933.

54 *The New York Times*, 16 Feb. 1933.

55 *Pittsburgh Post-Gazette* and *Toledo Blade*, 10 March 1933.

56 Barrington Boardman, *From Harding to Hiroshima,* (New York: Red Dembner Books, 1988), p. 151.

57 *Toledo Blade*, 3 March 1933.

58 Roger H. Hall, *Paul Block: The Self-Made Man and the New Deal*, Master's Thesis, College of Bowling Green, 1989, p. 64.

59 Paul Block to Franklin D. Roosevelt, letter of 18 March 1933; Franklin D. Roosevelt Library, Hyde Park, New York.

60 *Editor & Publisher*, 25 March 1933, p. 6.

61 *Editor & Publisher*, p. 6.

62 J. Cutler Andrews, p. 298.

63 Paul Block to Franklin D. Roosevelt, telegram of 24 July 1933; Franklin D. Roosevelt Library, Hyde Park, New York.

64 *Toledo Blade,* 26 July 1933.

65 Block Newspapers, 13 April 1934.

Endnotes for Chapter Eleven

1 Herbert H. Lehman, reminiscences, 1961, Columbia University Oral History Project, p. 500.

2 *Toledo Blade*, 5 June 1934.

3 *Toledo Blade*, 12 Sept. 1934.

4 *Pittsburgh Post-Gazette*, 20 Aug. 1935.

5 *Toledo Blade*, 7 Sept. 1935.

6 Paul Block, speech to the Toledo Bar Association, 3 Dec. 1935.

7 Paul Block, *A Study of Conditions in Europe*, the Block newspapers (Toledo: Toledo Blade, 1934), preface.

8 *Pittsburgh Post-Gazette*, 9 Aug. 1934.

9 *Pittsburgh Post-Gazette,* 13 Aug. 1934.

10 *Pittsburgh Post-Gazette,* 13 Aug. 1934, pp 7-8.

11 *Pittsburgh Post-Gazette,* 13 Aug. 1934.

12 *Pittsburgh Post-Gazette,* 13 Aug. 1934, p. 9.

13 *Toledo Blade*, 8 July 1934.

14 Ian Kershaw, *Hitler: 1889-1936 Hubris.* (New York: W.W. Norton & Company, Inc., 1998), p. 522.

15 Alexandra Richie, *Faust's Metropolis: A History of Berlin* (New York: Carrol & Graf, 1998), p. 215.

16 *Pittsburgh Post-Gazette*, 17 Aug. 1934.

17 *Pittsburgh Post-Gazette*, 17 Aug. 1934.

18 Paul Block, *A Study*, p. 12.

19 Paul Block, *A Study*, p. 12.

20 *Pittsburgh Post-Gazette*, 21 Aug. 1934.

21 Paul Block, *A Study*, p. 14.

22 Paul Block, *A Study*, p. 13.

23 Paul Block, *A Study*, p. 14.

24 William Block, Jr., ed., *Memoirs of William Block* (Toledo: Blade Communications Inc., 1990), p. 39.

25 W.A. Swanberg, *Citizen Hearst* (New York: Scribners, 1961), p. 430.

26 Kershaw, p. 180.

27 Christopher Hibbert, *Il Duce: The Life of Benito Mussolini* (Boston: Little, Brown and Co., 1962), p. 67.

28 *Toledo Blade*, 11 July 1932.

29 Paul Block, *A Study*, p. 16.

30 Paul Block, *A Study*, p. 18.

31 Paul Block, *A Study*, p. 17.

32 Paul Block, *A Study*, p. 19.

33 John M. Harrison, *The Blade of Toledo: The First 150 Years* (Toledo: Toledo Blade Co., 1985), p. 248.

34 *Pittsburgh Post-Gazette,* 28 April 1933.

35 *Toledo Blade*, 5 June 1934.

36 Paul Block and M.H. McIntyre, Assistant to the President, exchange

of telegrams, 22 May-24 May 1935, Franklin D. Roosevelt Library, Hyde Park, New York.

37 Paul Block, letter to Louis Howe, Secretary to the President, 12 April 1934; Franklin D. Roosevelt Library, Hyde Park, New York.

38 Frank Freidel, *Franklin D. Roosevelt: A Rendezvous with Destiny* (Boston: Little, Brown and Co., 1990), p. 599.

39 Richard B. Morris, ed., *Encyclopedia of American History* (New York: Harper & Row, 1982), p. 413.

40 Block Newspapers, 11 June 1935, *Toledo Blade* archive.

41 Arthur M. Schlesinger, Jr., ed., *The Almanac of American History* (New York: Barnes & Noble Books, 1993), p. 472.

42 Eva Epstein Shaw, letter to Franklin D. Roosevelt, 4 Dec. 1935, Franklin D. Roosevelt Library, Hyde Park, New York.

43 John K. Winkler, *William Randolph Hearst* (New York: Hastings House, 1955), p. 262.

44 Epstein Shaw, letter of 4 Dec. 1935.

45 Epstein Shaw, 4 Dec. 1935.

46 Schlesinger, Jr., p. 472.

47 Epstein Shaw, 4 Dec. 1935.

48 Friedel, p. 194.

49 *Toledo Blade*, 8 May 1935.

50 Paul Block, letter to Stephen T. Early, 18 Dec. 1935, Franklin D. Roosevelt Library, Hyde Park, New York.

51 Douglas Menville and R. Reginald, *Things to Come* (New York: Times Books, 1977), p. 62.

52 Tom Driberg, *Beaverbrook: A Study in Power and Frustration* (London: Weidenfeld and Nicholson, 1956), p. 144.

53 David C. Smith, *H.G. Wells: Desperately Mortal* (New Haven: Yale University Press, 1986), p. 282.

54 William Block, Jr., ed., *Memoirs*, p. 43.

55 Lovat Dickson, *H.G. Wells: His Turbulent Life and Times* (New York: Atheneum, 1969), p. 299.

56 William Block, Jr., ed., *Memoirs*, p. 43.

57 Paul Block, radio address, NBC Network, 19 Aug. 1935.

58 *Toledo Blade*, 13 Aug. 1935.

59 *Toledo Blade*, 13 Aug. 1935.

60 *Pittsburgh Post-Gazette*, 16 Sept. 1935.

61 Paul Block, letter to President Franklin D. Roosevelt, 7 Feb. 1936, Block family archive.

62 *Toledo Blade,* 4 Dec. 1935.

63 *Toledo Blade,* 4 Dec. 1935.

64 *Toledo Blade,* 4 Dec. 1935.

65 Epstein Shaw, letter of 4 Dec. 1935.

66 Paul Block, letter to Stephen Early, 18 Dec. 1935; Franklin D. Roosevelt Library, Hyde Park, New York.

67 Charles Van Doren, ed., *Webster's American Biographies* (Chicago: G. & C. Merriam Co., 1974), pp. 603-604.

68 Donald R. McCoy, *Landon of Kansas* (Lincoln: University of Nebraska Press,1966), p. 223.

69 *The New York Times,* 30 Sept. 1935.

70 *Newsweek,* 21 Dec. 1935.

71 *Toledo Blade,* 15 June 1936.

72 Friedel, p. 206.

73 McCoy, p. 220.

74 *Pittsburgh Post-Gazette,* 3 June 1936.

75 *Pittsburgh Post-Gazette,* 3 June 1936.

76 *Toledo Blade,* 25 June 1936.

77 Paul Block, radio broadcast over WOR and affiliated stations of the Mutual Broadcasting System, 3 July 1936.

78 *Toledo Blade,* 4 Aug. 1936.

79 *The New York Times,* 2 Nov. 1936.

80 *Pittsburgh Post-Gazette,* 19 Oct. 1936.

81 *Toledo Blade,* 31 Oct. 1936.

82 Block newspapers, 4 Nov. 1936.

83 Paul Block, Jr., letter to John Robinson Block, 12 Dec. 1977; also appears in Blade communication brochures, Block family archive.

84 William Block Jr., ed., *Memoirs,* p. 45.

85 Block newspapers, 8 Feb. 1937.

86 Block newspapers, 8 Feb. 1937.

87 Swanberg, p. 483-490.

88 *Editor & Publisher,* 18 Sept. 1937, p. 7.

89 *Editor & Publisher,* 18 Sept. 1937, p. 7.

90 *Toledo Blade,* 9 June 1937.

Endnotes for Chapter Twelve

1 Roger K. Newman, *Hugo Black* (New York: Pantheon Books, 1994), p. 246.

2 Sally Kalson, "Chickens Had Role in Sprigle's Pulitzer," *Pittsburgh*

Post-Gazette, 16 Sept. 1986.

3 Newman, p. 248.

4 Newman, p. 248.

5 Newman, p. 248.

6 *Toledo Blade*, 11 Sept. 1937.

7 *Pittsburgh Post-Gazette*, 30 Sept. 1937.

8 *Pittsburgh Post-Gazette*, 30 Sept. 1937.

9 Newman, p. 255.

10 *Pittsburgh Post-Gazette*, 13 Sept. 1937.

11 *Toledo Blade*, 19 May 1937.

12 Newman, p. 258.

13 *The New York Times*, 2 Oct. 1937, p. 1.

14 Paul Block, letter to Col. Marvin H. McIntyre, 14 Jan. 1938, Franklin D. Roosevelt Library, Hyde Park, New York.

15 Block Newspapers, 30 Dec. 1937.

16 *Pittsburgh Post-Gazette*, circa December 1937; Franklin D. Roosevelt Library, Hyde Park, New York

17 *Pittsburgh Post-Gazette*, 2 Sept. 1940.

18 M.H. McIntyre, memo to Stephen Early, January 18, 1938; Franklin D. Roosevelt Library, Hyde Park, New York.

19 Letter from M.H. McIntyre to Paul Block, 28 Jan. 1938, Franklin D. Roosevelt Library, Hyde Park, New York.

20 Stephen Early, memorandum to M.H. McIntyre, 29 Jan. 1938; FDR's notations, circa late February, 1938; Franklin D. Roosevelt Library, Hyde Park, New York.

21 M.H. McIntyre, memorandum to Stephen Early. 4 March 1938, Franklin D. Roosevelt Library, Hyde Park, New York.

22 Paul Block, letter to Marvin H. McIntyre, 1 March 1938, Franklin D. Roosevelt Library, Hyde Park, New York.

23 M.H. Mc Intyre to Paul Block, official government business telegram, 8 March 1938, Franklin D. Roosevelt Library, Hyde Park, New York.

24 *Pittsburgh Post-Gazette*, 7 March 1938.

25 Judge M.A. Musmanno, memorandum to M.H. Mc Intyre, 9 March 1938, Franklin D. Roosevelt Library, Hyde Park, New York.

26 *Pittsburgh Post-Gazette*, 6 Oct. 1939.

27 Sol Barzman, *Madmen & Genuises* (Chicago: Follett Publishing Company, 1974), pp. 230-231.

28 *Toledo Blade*, 3 April 1940.

29 R.H. Jackson, reminiscences, 1952; transcript pages 864-875; Columbia University Oral History Project.

30 Dwight MacDonald, *Henry Wallace: The Man and the Myth* (New York: The Vanguard Press, 1948), pp. 116-121.

31 Dwight MacDonald, pp. 116-121.

32 John C. Culver and John Hyde, *American Dreamer: A Life of Henry A. Wallace* (New York: W.W. Norton, 2000), p. 240.

33 Jackson, p. 867.

34 MacDonald, p. 123.

35 *Pittsburgh Post-Gazette*, 27 Feb. 1935.

36 Torbjorn Sirevåg, *The Dilemma of the American Left in the Cold War Years: The Case of Henry A. Wallace* (Oslo: Americana Norvegica 4, 1973) p. 418.

37 Torbjorn Sirevåg, p. 419.

38 Ivan Norodny, quoted in *Nicholas Roerich* by Garabed Paelian (Sedona, Ariz.: Aquarian Educational Group, 1974), p. 38.

39 Henry Wallace, reminiscences, 1949, Columbia University Oral History Project.

40 Henry A. Wallace, letter to Nicholas Roerich, 12 March 1933, Samuel I. Rosenman Collection; Franklin D. Roosevelt Library, Hyde Park, New York.

41 Jackson, p. 870.

42 Norman D. Markowitz, *The Rise and Fall of the People's Century: Henry A. Wallace and American Liberalism, 1941-1948* (New York: The Free Press, 1970), p. 339.

43 MacDonald, p. 122.

44 Jackson, p. 868.

45 Jackson, p. 868.

46 MacDonald, p. 121.

47 MacDonald, p. 869.

48 Harrison, p. 253.

49 *Des Moines Register*, 4 April 1948.

50 MacDonald, pp. 123-124.

51 Frederick W. Henshaw, reminiscences, 1953, Columbia University Oral History Project; p. 161.

52 Joseph Martin, *My First Fifty Years in Politics* (New York: McGraw-Hill, 1960), p. 117.

53 *Toledo Blade,* 16 May 1940

54 Block newspapers, 16 April 1941.

55 Block newspapers, 26 April 1941.

56 W.A. Swanberg, *Citizen Hearst* (New York: Scribners, 1961), p. 494.

57 Frank Brady, *Citizen Welles* (New York: Scribners, 1989), pp. 286-287.

58 John W. Winkler, *William Randolph Hearst* (New York: Hastings House, 1955), p. 279.

59 William Block, Sr., interview by the author, 4 Sept. 1997.

60 Paul Block, letter to Herbert Hoover, 21 April 1941.

61 Herbert Hoover, letter to Paul Block, Jr., 22 June 1941, Herbert Hoover Presidential Library.

62 *Toledo Blade,* 23 June 1941.

63 E. Minemura, letter to Paul Block, Jr., 4 Aug. 1941; Blade Communications archive.

Bibliography

There are no previous biographies of Paul Block, and he apparently was loathe to give interviews, because there are very few discussions of his life and career extant in the public and trade press. The microfilms of the newspapers that he published, such as the *Toledo Blade*, the *Pittsburgh Post-Gazette*, the *Newark Star-Eagle*, and the *Brooklyn Standard-Union* – and others – were of enormous help in analyzing not only Block's editorials, but the makeup of his newspapers, their political philosophies, and the kinds of articles, advertisements, and news stories that he published.

Block family archives and the records of Blade Communications, Inc. were consulted, as well as other library collections as noted in the Acknowledgments. Oral history interviews, contemporary accounts, diaries, business reports, memoirs and court transcripts were also studied.

Adams, James Truslow. *The Epic of America*. Boston: Little, Brown and Co., 1932.

Albens, Josef. *Interaction of Color*. New Haven: Yale University Press, 1963.

Allen, Frederick Lewis. *Since Yesterday*. New York: Perennial Library, 1972.

Allen, Irving Lewis. *The City in Slang*. Oxford and New York: Oxford University Press, 1993.

Alsop, Joseph. *FDR*. New York: The Viking Press, 1982.

Andrews, J. Cutler. *Pittsburgh's Post-Gazette*. Boston: Chapman & Grimes, 1936.

Asinof, Eliot. *1919, America's Loss of Innocence*. New York: Donald I. Fine, Inc., 1990.

Babb, Laura Longley, ed. *Keeping Posted*. New York: Universe Books, 1977.

Baker, Paul R. *Stanny: The Gilded Life of Stanford White*. New York: Free Press, 1989.

Baker, Thomas Harrison. *The Memphis Commercial Appeal*. Baton Rouge: Louisiana State University Press, 1971.

Barrett, James., ed. *The End of the "World."* New York: Harper & Row, 1931.

Baruch, Bernard. *Baruch: The Public Years*. New York: Holt, Rinehart and Winston, 1960.

Barzman, Sol. *Madmen & Geniuses*. Chicago: Follett Publishing Co., 1974.

Bates, Stephen. *If No News, Send Rumors*. New York: St. Martin's Press, 1989.

Beard, Charles A. and Mary R. Beard. *New Basic History of The United States*. New York: Doubleday, 1968.

Beaverbrook, Lord. *Don't Trust to Luck*. London: London Express Newspapers, Ltd. 1948.

Beer, Thomas. *The Mauve Decade*. New York: Carroll and Graf Publishers, 1926.

Berger, Meyer. *The Story of The New York Times*. New York: Simon & Schuster, 1951.

A Biographical Record of Chemung County, New York. S.J. Clarke Publishing Co., 1902.

Birmingham, Stephen. *The Rest of Us*. London: Macdonald, 1984.

Block Jr., William, ed. *Memoirs of William Block*. Toledo: Blade Communications, 1990.

Block, Marc. *The Historian's Craft*. New York: Alfred A. Knopf, Inc., 1964.

Block, Paul. *A Study of Conditions in Europe*. Toledo: Toledo Blade, 1934.

Boardman, Barrington. *From Harding to Hiroshima*. New York: Red Dembner Books, 1988.

Boller, Paul F. Jr. *Presidential Campaigns*. Oxford and New York: Oxford University Press, 1984.

Boorstin, Daniel J. *The Americans: The Democratic Experience*. New York: Random House, 1973.

Boylan, James. *The World and the 20's*. New York: The Dial Press, 1973.

Brady, Frank. *Citizen Welles*. New York: Scribners, 1989.

Brendon, Piers. *The Life and Death of the Press Barons*. New York: Atheneum, 1983.

Brooks, John. *Telephone*. New York: Harper & Row, 1975.

Brubaker, John H. III. *The Steinmans of Lancaster*. Lancaster: New Era Publishing Co., 1992.

Burnham, John. *The Ragpicker or Bound and Free*. New York: Mason Bros. Publishers, 1855.

Butterfield, Roger. *The American Past*. New York: Simon & Schuster,

1947.

Byron, Joseph. *New York Life at the Turn of the Century.* New York: Dover Books, 1985.

Carter, Randolph. *The World of Flo Ziegfeld.* New York: Praeger Publishers, 1974.

Chancellor, John and Walter R. Means. *The News Business.* New York: A Mentor Book, 1983.

Chiasson, Lloyd, Jr. *Three Centuries of American Media.* Englewood, CO: Morton Publishing Co., 1999.

Churchill, Allen. *Park Row.* New York: Rinehart & Co., 1958.

Coblentz, Edmond D., ed. *Newsmen Speak.* Berkeley: University of California Press, 1954.

Cochran, Thomas C. and William Miller. *The Age of Enterprise.* New York: Harper & Row, 1961.

Coit, Margarel L. *Mr. Baruch.* Boston: Houghton Mifflin Co., 1957.

Connable, Alfred and Edward Silverfarb. *Tigers of Tammany.* New York: Holt, Rinehart, Winston, 1967.

Cotton, Michelle L. *Mark Twain's Elmira 1870-1910.* Elmira, NY: The Chemung County Historical Society, 1985.

Couch, Jim F. and William F. Shughart II. *The Political Economy of the New Deal.* London: Edward Elgar, 1998.

Culver, John C. and John Hyde. *American Dreamer: A Life of Henry A. Wallace.* New York: W.W. Norton, 2000.

Dallek, Robert. *Hail to the Chief.* New York: Hyperion, 1996.

Damon-Moore, Helen. *Magazines for the Millions.* Albany: State University of New York Press, 1994.

Daniel, Clifton. *Chronicle of America.* New York: D.K. Publishing, Inc. 1997.

Daniels, Jonathan. *They Will Be Heard.* New York: McGraw Hill, 1965.

Davies, Marion. *The Times We Had.* New York: Bobbs Merrill, 1975.

Davis, Kenneth S. *FDR – The New York Years.* New York: Random House, 1985.

Day, Donald. *Will Rogers.* New York: David McKay Co., Inc., 1962.

Dickson, Lovat. *H.G. Wells: His Turbulent Life and Times.* New York: Atheneum, 1969.

Douglas, Ann. *Terrible Honesty.* New York: Farrar, Straus and Giroux, 1995.

Drewry, John E., ed. *Post Biographies of Famous Journalists.* Athens, GA: University of Georgia Press, 1942.

Driberg, Tom. *Beaverbrook: A Study in Power and Frustration.* London: Weidenfeld and Nicholson, 1956.

Ellis, Edward Robb. *The Epic of New York City.* New York: Old Town Books, 1966.

Emery, Michael and Edwin Emery. *The Press in America.* 7th ed. New York: Prentice Hall, 1992.

Faber, Doris. *Printer's Devil to Publisher.* Hensonville, New York: Black Dome Press, 1996.

This Fabulous Century 1870-1900. New York:Time-Life Books.

Faisboff, Sylvia G. and Wendell Tripp. *A Bibliography of Newspapers in Fourteen New York Counties.* Albany: N.Y. State Historical Association, 1978.

Fang, Irving. *A History of Mass Communication.* New York: Focal Press, 1997.

Fedler, Fred. *Lessons from the Past.* Prospect Heights, IL: Waveland Press, Inc., 2000.

Ferrell, Robert H., ed. *The Twentieth Century – An Almanac.* New York: World Almanac Publications, 1984.

Ferris, Paul. *The House of Northcliffe.* New York: World Publishing, 1972.

Flythe, Jr. Starkey., ed. *The American Story.* Philadelphia: Curtis Publishing Co. 1975.

Fowler, Gene. *Beau James.* New York: Viking Books, 1949.

Frasca, Ralph. *The Rise and Fall of the Saturday Globe.* Cranbury, NJ: Susquehanna University Press, 1992.

Friedel, Frank. *Franklin D. Roosevelt: A Rendezvous with Destiny.* Boston: Little Brown and Co., 1990.

Garraty, John A. *The Nature of Biography.* New York: Vintage Books, 1957.

Gatewood, North., ed. *Fifty Years in Pictures.* New York: Doubleday & Co., 1979.

Gelderman, Carol. *All the President's Words.* New York: Walker & Co., 1997.

Glennon, Lorraine, ed. *Our Times.* Atlanta: Turner Publishing, 1995.

Goldberger, Paul. *The Skyscraper.* New York: Alfred A. Knopf, 1982.

Grafton, John. *New York in the Nineteenth Century.* New York: Dover, 1980.

Graham, Katherine. *Personal History.* New York: Alfred A. Knopf, 1997.

Gramling, Oliver. *AP – The Story of News.* New York: Farrar & Rinehart,

Inc., 1940.

Green, Abel and Joe Laurie Jr. *Show Biz*. New York: Henry Holt and Co., 1951.

Greenbaum, Masha. *The Jews of Lithuania*. Hewlett, NY: Gefan, 1995.

Gribetz, Louis and Joseph Kaye. *James Walker, The Story of a Personality*. New York: Dial Press, 1932.

Grun, Bernard. *The Timetables of History*. New York: Simon & Schuster, 1991.

Guiles, Fred Laurence. *Marion Davies*. New York: McGraw Hill Book Co., 1972.

Gundlach, E. T. *Facts and Fetishes in Advertising*. New York: Consolidated Book Publishers, Inc., 1931.

Gunther, John. *Taken at the Flood*. New York: Harper & Bros., 1960.

Hale, William Harlan. *Horace Greeley*. New York: Harper & Bros., 1950.

Hammack, David C. *Power and Society*. New York: Columbia University Press, 1987.

Hapgood, Norman and Henry Moscowitz. *Up From City Streets*. New York: Grosset & Dunlap, 1927.

Harris, Bill. *The History of New York City*. New York: Portland House, 1989.

Harrison, John M. *The Blade of Toledo: The First 150 Years*. Toledo: Toledo Blade Company, 1985.

Harter, Eugene C. *Boilerplating America:The Hidden Newspaper*. Lanham, MD: University Press of America, 1995.

Hernon, Peter and Terry Ganey. *Under the Influence*. New York: Simon & Schuster, 1991.

Herzberg, Joseph G. *Late City Edition*. New York: Henry Holt and Co., 1947.

Herzstein, Robert E. *Henry R. Luce*. New York: Scribner's, 1994.

Hibbert, Christopher. *Il Duce: The Life of Benito Mussolini*. Boston: Little, Brown and Co., 1962.

Hinshaw, David. *Herbert Hoover: American Quaker*. New York: Farrar Straus & Co., 1950.

Hoffman, Eva. *Shtetl*. New York: Houghton Mifflin, 1997.

Homberger, Eric. *The Historical Atlas of New York City*. New York: Henry Holt and Co., 1994.

Hoover, Edgar M. and Raymond Vernon. *Anatomy of a Metropolis*. Cambridge, MA: Harvard University Press, 1959.

Howe, Irving and Kenneth Libo. *How We Lived*. New York: Richard Marek Publishers, 1979.

Hutchens, John K. and George Oppenheimer. *The Best in the World*. New York: Viking, 1973.

Ickes, Harold L. *Freedom of the Press Today*. New York: Vanguard Press, 1941.

Illman, Harry R. *Unholy Toledo*. San Francisco: Polemic Press Publication, 1985.

Irwin, Will, ed. *The American Newspaper*. Ames, Iowa State University Press, 1969.

Jackson, Kenneth T., ed. *The Encyclopedia of New York City*. New Haven: Yale University Press, 1995.

Jacobs, Maurice and Leo M. Glassman. *Biographical Encyclopedia of American Jews*. New York: 1935.

Janello, Amy and Breenan Jones. *The American Magazine*. New York: Harry M. Abrams, 1991.

Jenkins, Simon. *Newspapers: The Power and the Money*. London: Faber and Faber, 1979.

Jennings, Peter and Todd Brewster. *The Century*. New York: Doubleday, 1998.

Jensen, Amy La Follette. *The White House*. New York: McGraw Hill, 1965.

Jensen, Oliver, ed. *The Nineties*. New York: American Heritage Publishing Co., 1967.

Johnson, Walter. *1600 Pennsylvania Avenue*. Boston: Little, Brown & Co., 1960.

Kamphoefuer, Helbich and Sommer. *News From the Land of Freedom*. Ithaca, NY: Cornell University Press, 1991.

Kendall, Paul Murray. *The Art of Biography*. London: George Allen & Unwin Ltd., 1965.

Kershaw, Ian. *Hitler: 1889-1936 Hubris*. New York: W.W. Norton & Company, Inc., 1998.

Kery, Patricia Frantz. *Great Magazine Covers of the World*. New York: Abbeville Press, 1982.

Keylin, Arleen, ed. *If Elected...* New York: Arno Press, 1976.

Keylin, Arleen, ed. *The Depression Years*. New York: Arno Press, 1976.

Kirkpatrick, Ivone. *Mussolini*. New York: Hawthorne Books, 1964.

Kiseloff, Jeff. *You Must Remember This*. New York: Harcourt Brace Jovanovich, 1989.

Kluger, Richard. *The Paper.* New York: Alfred A. Knopf, 1986.

Kolowrat, Ernest. *Hotchkiss.* Salisbury, CT: New Amsterdam, 1992.

Kraut, Alan M. *The Huddled Masses: The Immigrant in American Society, 1880 – 1921.* Harlan Davidson, Inc., 1982.

Kurth, Peter. *American Casandra.* Boston: Little, Brown & Co., 1990.

Le Brun, George P. *It's Time to Tell.* New York: Morrow, 1962.

Leach, William. *Land of Desire.* New York: Vintage Books, 1993.

Lee, Alfred McClung. *The Daily Newspaper in America. The Evolution of a Social Instrument.* New York: The MacMillan Group, 1947.

Lee, James Melvin. *History of American Journalism.* Boston: Houghton Mifflin Co., 1923.

Lewis, Alfred Allan. *Man of the World.* New York: Bobbs-Merrill, 1978.

Lewis, R.W.B. *Edith Wharton.* New York: Harper & Row, 1975.

The Life History of the United States, Reaching for Empire, 1890-1901. New York: Time-Life Books, 1964.

Lindley, William R. *Twentieth Century American Newspapers.* Manhattan, KS: Sunflower University Press, 1993.

Lipphard, William B. *Fifty Years an Editor.* Valley Forge, PA: The Judson Press, 1963.

Lockwood, Charles. *Manhattan Moves Uptown.* Boston: Houghton Mifflin Co., 1976.

Lomask, Milton. *The Biographer's Craft.* New York: Harper & Row, 1986.

Lord, Walter. *The Good Years.* New York: Harper & Brothers, 1960.

Lowenthal, Marvin. *A World Passed By.* New York: Harper & Bros., 1933.

Lown, Bella. *Memories of My Life.* New York: Pangloss Press, 1991.

Lundberg, Ferdinand. *America's 60 Families.* New York: The Citadel Press, 1939.

Lundberg, Ferdinand. *Imperial Hearst.* New York: Equinox Cooperative Press, 1936.

Lutz, William W. *The News of Detroit.* Boston: Little, Brown and Co., 1973.

Lynch, Denis Tilden. *The Wild Seventies.* New York: D. Appleton – Century Co., Inc., 1941.

MacAdams, William. *Ben Hecht.* New York: Scribner's, 1990.

MacDonald, Dwight. *Henry Wallace: The Man and the Myth.* New York: The Vanguard Press, 1948.

Madsen, Axel. *Gloria and Joe.* New York: Arbor House, 1988.

Maeder, Jay, ed. *Big Town, Big Time.* New York: Daily News Books, 1999.

Mann, Arthur. *The Progressive Era.* New York: Holt, Rinehart & Winston, 1975.

Margolis, Max L. and Alexander Marx. *A History of the Jewish People.* New York: The Jewish Publication Society of America, 1927.

Markowitz, Norman D. *The Rise and Fall of the People's Century: Henry A. Wallace and American Liberalism, 1941-1948.* New York: The Free Press, 1970.

Marqusee, Mike and Bill Harris. *New York.* New York: Barnes & Noble, 1985.

Martin, Joseph. *My First Fifty Years in Politics.* New York: McGraw-Hill, 1960.

Maurois, André. *Aspects of Biography.* New York: Frederick Ungar Publishing Co., 1966.

McCoy, Donald R. *Landon of Kansas.* Lincoln: University of Nebraska Press,1966.

McGiven, Leo E. *The News.* New York: News Syndicate Co., 1969.

McNickle, Chris. *To Be Mayor of New York.* New York: Columbia University Press, 1993.

McShane & Matthews. *Across America—Brooklyn Swaggers.* New York: Associated Press, 1958.

Meeker, Richard H. *Newspaperman.* New York: Ticknor & Fields, 1983.

Menville, Douglas and R. Reginald. *Things to Come.* New York: Times Books, 1977.

Milton, Joyce. *The Yellow Kids.* New York: Harper & Row, 1989.

Mitang, Herbert. *Once Upon a Time in New York.* New York: The Free Press, 2000.

Moquin, Wayne. *Makers of America – Natives and Aliens – 1891-1903.* Chicago: Encyclopedia Britannica Educational Corp., 1971.

Morris, Kenneth, Marc Robinson and Richard Krall. *American Dreams.* New York: Harry N. Abrams, 1990.

Morris, Lloyd. *Incredible New York.* New York: Random House, 1951.

Morrison, Samuel Eliot. *Oxford History of the American People.* New York: Oxford University Press, 1965.

Mott, Frank L. *A History of American Magazines.* Cambridge: Harvard University Press, 1930-1957.

Mott, Frank Luther. *American Journalism, A History: 1690-1960.* New York: MacMillan, 1962.

Mowry, George E. *The Era of Theodore Roosevelt.* New York: Harper & Row, 1958.

Nevill, Ralph. *The World of Fashion: 1837-1922.* London: Methuen & Co. Ltd., 1923.

Newman, Roger K. *Hugo Black.* New York: Pantheon Books, 1994.

New York: A Collection from Harper's Magazine. New York: W.H. Smith Publishers, 1991.

Nostwich, T.D., ed. *Theodore Dreiser: Journalism, Vol. One.* Philadelphia: University of Pennsylvania Press, 1988.

O'Connor, Richard. *The Scandalous Mr. Bennett.* New York: Doubleday & Co., 1962.

Ogburn, Charlton. *Railroads.* Washington, D.C.: National Geographic Society, 1977.

Oppel, Frank. *Gaslight New York Revisited.* Secaucus, NJ: Castle Books, 1989.

Oppel, Frank. *Tales of Gaslight New York.* Secaucus, NJ: Book Sales, Inc., 1985.

Paelian, Garabed. *Nicholas Roerich.* Sedona, Arizona: Aquarian Educational Group, 1974.

Patterson, Grove. *I Like People.* Boston: Little, Brown & Co., 1954.

Phillips, Cabell. *The New York Times Chronicle of American Life: From the Crash to the Blitz, 1929-1939.* New York: Macmillan, 1969.

Pope, Daniel. *The Making of Modern Advertising.* New York: Basic Books, 1983.

Presbrey, Frank. *The History and Development of Advertising.* Garden City, NY: Doubleday, Doran and Co., 1929.

Pringle, Henry F. *Theodore Roosevelt: A Biography.* New York: Harcourt, Brace & Co., 1931, 1956.

Procter, Ben. *William Randolph Hearst: The Early Years, 1863-1910.* Oxford and New York: Oxford University Press, 1998.

Rather, Dan, ed. *Our Times.* New York: Scribner, 1996.

Richie, Alexandra. *Faust's Metropolis: A History of Berlin.* New York: Carroll & Graf, 1998.

Riordon, William L. *Plunkitt of Tammany Hall.* New York: E.P. Dutton, 1963.

Robinson, Judith. *The Hearsts.* Newark: University of Delaware Press, 1991.

Robinson, Ray. *American Original: A Life of Will Rogers.* Oxford and New York: Oxford University Press, 1996.

Rogers, Charles Elkins. *Journalistic Vocations.* East Norwalk: D. Appleton and Company, 1931.

Rogers, Daniel T. *The Work Ethic in Industrial America, 1850-1920.* Chicago: University of Chicago Press, 1978.

Roskolenko, Harry. *The Time That Was Then.* New York: The Dial Press, 1971.

Roster, Leo C. *The Washington Correspondents.* Washington, D.C.: Social Science Research Council, circa 1936.

Salwen, Peter. *Upper West Side Story.* New York: Abbeville Press, 1989.

Sanders, Marian K. *Dorothy Thompson.* New York: Avon Books, 1974.

Schlesinger Jr., Arthur M. *The Age of Roosevelt: The Coming of the New Deal.* Boston: Houghton Mifflin Co., 1959.

Schlesinger Jr., Arthur M. *The Age of Roosevelt: The Crisis of the Old Order.* Boston: Houghton Mifflin Co., 1957.

Schlesinger Jr., Arthur M., ed. *The Almanac of American History.* New York: Barnes & Noble Books, 1993.

Schroeder, Joseph J., Jr. *The Wonderful World of Ladies' Fashion.* Chicago: Follett Publishing Co., 1971.

Schudson, Michael. *Discovering the News.* New York: Basic Books, 1978.

Seldes, George. *Lords of the Press.* New York: Blue Ribbon Books, 1941.

Shannon, David A. *Between the Wars: America, 1919-1941.* Boston: Houghton Mifflin Co., 1979.

Shepard, Richard F. *The Paper's Papers.* New York: Times Books, 1996.

Shirer, William L. *20ᵗʰ Century Journey.* New York: Simon & Schuster, 1974.

Smith, David C. *H.G. Wells: Desperately Mortal.* New Haven: Yale University Press, 1986.

Sobol, Louis. *The Longest Street.* New York: Crown Publishers, 1968.

Sontheimer, Morton. *Newspaperman.* New York: Whittlesly House, 1941.

Sorin, Gerald. *A Time for Building: The Third Migration.* Baltimore: The Johns Hopkins University Press, 1992.

Startt, James D. and William David Sloan. *The Significance of the Media.* Northport, AL: Vision Press, 1994.

Steele, Ronald. *Walter Lippmann and the American Century.* New York: Vintage Books, 1981.

Stephens, Mitchell. *A History of News.* New York: Penguin Books,

1988.

Stewart, Kenneth and John Tebbel. *Makers of Modern Journalism.* New York: Prentice-Hall, 1952.

Stoddard, Henry L. *As I Knew Them.* New York: Harper & Bros., 1927.

Stoddard, Henry L. *It Costs to Be President.* New York: Harper & Bros., 1938.

Sullivan, Mark. *Our Times, Volume V.* New York: Charles Scribner's Sons, 1933.

Sullivan, Mark. *Our Times.* Edited by Dan Rather. New York: Scribners, 1996.

Sulzberger, Arthur Ochs. *Page One.* New York: Times Books, 1986.

Swanberg, W.A. *Citizen Hearst.* New York: Scribners, 1961.

Talese, Gay. *The Kingdom and the Power.* New York: World Publishing Co., 1969.

Tebbel, John. *An American Dynasty.* New York: Doubleday & Co., 1947.

Tebbel, John. *The Media in America.* New York: Thomas Y. Crowell Inc., 1973.

Thayer, Frank. *Newspaper Management.* New York: D. Appleton and Co., 1926.

Thayer, William Roscoe. *The Art of Biography.* New York: Charles Scribner's Sons, 1920.

Thomas, Henry W. *Walter Johnson, Baseball's Big Train.* Arlington, VA: Phenom Press, 1995.

Toland, John. *Adolf Hitler.* New York: Doubleday, 1976.

Towner, Ausburn. *Our County and Its People: A History of the Valley and County of Chemung.* Elmira: D. Mason & Co. Publishers, 1892.

Trager, James. *West of Fifth.* New York: Atheneum, 1987.

Traxel, David. *1898.* New York, Alfred A. Knopf, 1998.

Tuchman, Barbara W. *Practicing History.* New York: Ballantine Books, 1981.

Tuchman, Barbara. *The Proud Tower.* New York: Macmillan, 1966.

Turner, Hy B. *When Giants Ruled.* New York: Fordham University Press, 1999.

Van Doren, Charles., ed. *Webster's American Biographies.* Chicago: G. & C. Merriam Co., 1974.

Vanden Heuvel, Jan. *Untapped Sources.* New York: Gannett Foundation Media Center, 1991.

Waldrop, A. Gayle. *Editor and Editorial Writer.* New York: Rinehart & Co., 1948.

Wallace, Henry A. *The Price of Vision.* Boston: Houghton Mifflin Co., 1973.

Walsh, George. *Gentleman Jimmy Walker.* New York: Praeger Publishers, 1974.

Weisberger, Bernard. *The American Heritage History of the American People.* New York: American Heritage Publishing Co., 1971.

Wells, Robert W. *The Milwaukee Journal.* Milwaukee: The Milwaukee Journal, 1981.

Wharton, Edith. *A Backward Glance.* New York: Charles Scribner's Sons, 1933-1934.

Wilbur, Ray Lyman and Arthur Mastick Hyde. *The Hoover Policies.* New York: Charles Scribner's Sons, 1937.

Wilkerson, Marcus M. *Public Opinion and the Spanish-American War: A Study in War Propaganda.* Baton Rouge: Louisiana State University Press, 1932.

Willensky, Elliot. *When Brooklyn Was the World. 1920-1957.* New York: Harmony Books, 1986.

Williams, Harold A. *The Baltimore Sun: 1837-1947.* Baltimore: The Johns Hopkins University Press, 1987.

Williamson, Samuel T. *Imprint of a Publisher.* New York: Robert M. Mc Bride & Co., 1948.

Wilson, Edmund. *The American Earthquake.* New York: Da Capo Press, 1996.

Wines, Robin W. *The Historian as Detective.* New York: Harper & Row Publishers, 1969.

Wingate, Charles F., ed. *Views and Interviews on Journalism.* New York: F.B. Patterson, Co. 1875.

Winkler, John K. *W.R. Hearst: An American Phenomenon.* New York: Simon & Schuster, 1928.

Winkler, John K. *William Randolph Hearst.* New York: Hastings House, 1955.

Zacks, Richard. *An Underground Education.* New York: Doubleday, 1997.

Zeisloft, E. Idell. *The New Metropolis.* New York: Scribner's, 1899.

Ziff, Larzer. *The American 1890.* New York: The Viking Press, 1966.

Zinsser, William, ed. *Extraordinary Lives.* New York: Book of the Month Club Inc., 1986.

Zlotnick, Joan. *Portrait of an American City.* Millwood, NY: Kennikat Press, 1982.

Zuckerman, Mary Ellen. *History of Popular Women's Magazines in the U.S.* Westport, CT: Greenwood Press, 1988.

Zurier, Rebecca, Robert W. Snyder and Virginia M. Mecklenberg. *"Metropolitan Lives."* New York: W. W. Norton, 1989.

Index

About the Author

Dr. Frank Brady is Chairman of the Communications, Journalism and Media Studies Department of St. John's University in New York. He is the author of ten books, including several biographies of contemporary figures: Aristotle Onassis, the shipping tycoon; Bobby Fischer, the chess player; and Orson Welles, the film director.

Dr. Brady has been the editor and publisher of a number of national magazines, and has written over 200 published articles.

Aside from writing and teaching, Dr. Brady's most avid passion is competing in tournament chess.

Above: Paul Block's first newspaper job was as "Master" of "Colonel," the St. Bernard mascot of the *Elmira Telegram* in upstate New York. The 10-year-old Block shows off his ward in 1885, standing in front of the *Telegram*'s office.

Left: Dina and Paul Block in 1910, three years after their marriage, in front of the large seaside house they rented for the summer in Deal, New Jersey.

The young Paul Block was a dynamic newspaper advertising representative before he became a publisher. A feature article about Block and some of his early associates (pictured above) appeared in a 1906 issue of *The Fourth Estate*, a magazine about newspaper publishing.

Left: John Block, Paul's father, had the appearance and bearing of a college professor. In 1922, shortly before his death, he poses with Block's sister, Mollie.

Below: Block loved to travel by car, train or boat. Here, at sea in 1924, squinting from the sun, he sits with Paul, Jr., while little Billy sits in Dina's lap.

Above: Among Paul Block's happiest times was when he was at a baseball game. During the 1927 World Series, he shakes the hand of Pittsburgh Pirates' manager Donie Brown. Standing between them is Block's friend, Mayor Jimmy Walker. Pittsburgh was shut out by the indomitable Yankees, who won the series 4-0.

Above: At another game during the 1927 World Series, Block (at right) attended with three of his friends: (from left) Florenz Ziegfeld, Irving Berlin and Sailing Baruch, all part of New York City's Jewish inner circle.

Block was close – politically and socially – with several Presidents, but none more than Calvin Coolidge (at right), with whom he is seen here on the White House lawn in 1926.

Above: Block was pensive at the hearing of his friend Jimmy Walker in 1932. Seated on the witness stand, Block fended off implications that there were financial improprieties between himself and the Mayor. Walker ultimately resigned as Mayor of New York City.

Above: In front of the home of Governor Alfred Landon (center) of Kansas in 1936. Block (right) and William Randolph Hearst (left) did everything possible, albeit unsuccessfully, to get Landon elected as President. Much to Block's rue, Landon received only eight electoral votes to Roosevelt's 523, in the greatest landslide in Presidential election history.

Above: In 1936, Block attended a business dinner with Grove Patterson, the distinguished editor of the *Toledo Blade*. The two men were more than just compatible colleagues: they were close friends.

Below: Dina Block was Paul's constant companion and helpmate. She ran their huge estate in Connecticut, traveled with him, and tried to help him in his businesses wherever possible. Here, in 1936, they attend a publishing dinner.

A typical portrait, probably taken in the mid-1930s, of the jaunty – and impeccably dressed – Paul Block. Despite the pressures of the Depression, he exudes
confidence and self-reliance.